Celebrating Women's History

A Women's History Month
resource book

Celebrating Women's History

A Women's History Month
resource book

Mary Ellen Snodgrass, *editor*

Foreword *by*
Mary Ruthsdotter, *projects director,*
National Women's History Project

National Women's
History Project

GALE
An ITP Information/Reference Group Company

Changing the Way the World Learns

NEW YORK • LONDON • BONN • BOSTON • DETROIT
MADRID • MELBOURNE • MEXICO CITY • PARIS
SINGAPORE • TOKYO • TORONTO • WASHINGTON
ALBANY NY • BELMONT CA • CINCINNATI OH

Mary Ellen Snodgrass, *Editor*

Gale Research staff

Kelle S. Sisung, *Developmental Editor;* Peg Bessette, *Acquisitions Editor;* Lawrence W. Baker, *Managing Editor;* with thanks to Jolen Marya Gedridge, Camille Killens, Andrea Kovacs, Jessica Proctor, and Allison McNeill

Mary Beth Trimper, *Production Director;* Evi Seoud, *Assistant Production Manager;* Shanna Philpott Heilveil, *Production Assistant*

Cynthia Baldwin, *Production Design Manager;* Michelle DiMercurio, *Cover and Page Designer*

Benita L. Spight, *Manager, Data Entry Services;* Gwendolyn S. Tucker, *Data Entry Coordinator;* Frances L. Monroe, *Data Entry Associate*

Library of Congress Cataloging-in-Publication Data

Celebrating women's history : a Women's History Month resource book /
     Mary Ellen Snodgrass, editor.
               p.   cm.
          Includes bibliographical references and index.
          ISBN 0-7876-0605-7 (acid-free paper)
          1. Women—History—Study and teaching—Activity programs.
     2. Women's History Month—Handbooks, manuals, etc.   I. Snodgrass,
     Mary Ellen.
     HQ1122.C45 1995
     305.4'09—dc20   95-43315
                                                                        CIP

10 9 8 7 6 5 4 3 2 1

Now turn on one wing, higher, even higher,
Back and forth, to right and left,
Until you eventually rest on the wind—
While you concentrate on a task more wonderful still—
Your feathers are outlining the mystic alphabet!
My heart rises and my spirit is lifted
As I travel this path I have chosen long ago . . .

The Voyage of Bran

Table *of contents*

Contents

Government

Health

History

Humor

Interdisciplinary Activities

Journalism

Contents

Music

Religion

Science

Social Science

Speech and Debate

Sports

Writing

Women's *history: reclaiming the past; revisioning the future*

By Mary Ruthsdotter, Projects Director,
National Women's History Project

Test your women's history I.Q.!

1. 16 million women won the right to vote through an amendment to the U.S. Constitution. Did this happen in 1795, 1848, or 1920?

2. The global movement to stop the indiscriminate use of pesticides and herbicides was launched by her book. Can you name this scientist/author? Extra points for the title of that 1962 best-seller.

3. Whose daring refusal to move to the back of a segregated bus sparked the Civil Rights Movement of the 1950s and '60s?

4. Which Latina has repeatedly been the leading money winner in the Ladies Professional Golf Association?

5. Who was the only member of Congress to vote against U.S. entry into both World War I and World War II?

6. Where and when was the world's first conference held to discuss women's rights?

7. Which activist spoke out bravely for Native Americans' rights nationwide and before Congressional committees in the 1880s?

8. With her creative business sense, she became the first black woman millionaire in the United States. Who was she?

9. The first Asian American woman elected to Congress won her seat in 1964. Who was she, and for how long did she serve?

10. Which dancer revolutionized the art in the early 1900s with her progressive ideas?

How do you think you did? You can check yourself against the answers found on p. xvi. Most Americans find their "Women's History I.Q." amazingly low. The reason is simple: The traditional focus of classroom history lessons has been on the major political, economic, and military events of the past and the leaders who were directly associated with them. This narrow concept of history has excluded nearly all the important contributions made by women, kept from these public-arena activities by social custom or law.

But a strong wind of change is blowing. The multiplicity of National Women's History Month celebrations that are held each March are helping remedy the situation, bringing women and their remarkable accomplishments the acclaim they merit. People across the country have enjoyed programs ranging from costumed children staging performances to photo displays on battleships and in local banks. Contingents dressed as historic women have joined hometown parades, Girl Scout troops have conducted oral history projects with senior center participants, and theaters have staged women's history film festivals.

With the ideas outlined in *Celebrating Women's History: A Women's History Month Resource Book* users will be able to join in the reformation that is afoot. *Celebrating Women's History* introduces notable women, the organizations they founded, and events of women's history to a variety of audiences through an assortment of memorable activities. Activity participants are invited to explore the lives of women of diverse cultures (like the Inuit), organize art expositions lauding the traditional views of woman at work, and to create walks of fame and databases of women's firsts in the arts, sports, and science. The possibilities are, literally, endless.

Celebrating Women's History Month on a national scale provides an impetus for a year-round exploration of the simple question, "What have women done?" It quickly becomes apparent that women have made major contributions in business, the arts, politics, social service, science, to *all* areas of human life.

When we begin to explore this new world, we start to see our nation's past in a new, stronger light. As if through a wide-angle lens, more comes into view. As if more focused, the details that were missing become clear. And, as we discover how much has previously been obscured from our view, our expanded perspective encourages us to ask new questions and make new judgements; it allows us to see ourselves and our connection to historic processes differently. Because we see the past with new eyes, we see new possibilities in the present, and an enriched vision for the future.

As we discover this expanded view of women's history, we encounter countless women whose names we cannot know: the hundreds of thousands of native women who resisted European settlement of their lands and did whatever they could to help their people survive; the African women kidnapped and brought to this land as slaves, who not only survived, but instilled both hope and the spirit of survival in future generations; the millions of women who left their homelands and often their families for the hopeful possibility of a new life in America; Mexican women who suddenly found themselves living in a foreign country when the land they had settled changed hands after the Mexican American War; and Asian women immigrants, some imported as slaves, some as picture brides, others following husbands seeking a dream of a better life. Their individual stories may be lost to us today, but the drama of their collective lives continues to impact our own, however indirectly.

In this new world of women's history, we also meet up with impressive individuals whose names and deeds have been recorded for the part they played in shaping their communities and the ideas of their day:

- Anne Hutchinson (1591–1643) was a respected member of Plymouth Colony, Massachusetts, but her audacity as a woman to conduct religious discussions became unacceptable to male church leaders. Hutchinson was tried for heresy and banished to the wilderness. The religious freedom she advocated later became a cornerstone of civil rights in the United States.

- Sacajawea (ca. 1786–1812), a young Shoshoni, captured by the Hidatsa, sold to a French Canadian, and hired by the Lewis and Clark expedition. Multilingual and a skilled survivalist, her presence proved essential for the progress, health, and safety of the party as they explored the Louisiana Purchase.

- Susan B. Anthony (1820–1906) and Elizabeth Cady Stanton (1815–1902) were prominent leaders of the 72-year movement to win the right to vote for women. The combination of Anthony's sharp political instincts with Stanton's forceful writing made them a formidable team for 50 years.

- Harriet Tubman (1820–1913) escaped slavery, then courageously returned to the South nineteen times, leading over 300 others along treacherous paths to freedom. During the Civil War, she served as a spy and scout for the Union Army. Later, Tubman supported suffrage for women and blacks.

- Eleanor Roosevelt (1884–1962) traveled the country using her position as America's First Lady to promote reforms benefiting women, minorities, and the poor. As a United States delegate to the newly formed United Nations, she became known as "The First Lady of the World" for her international humanitarian work.

- Frances Perkins (1880–1965) was the first woman appointed to the Cabinet of a U.S. president. As secretary of labor, Perkins was instrumental in designing New Deal legislation for reforms such as unemployment insurance, Social Security, and the minimum wage.

- Maria Martinez (1887–1980) rediscovered the ancient Tewa Indian techniques of firing polychrome and "black on black" pottery. Sharing her skills with others in her tribe, the Tewa of New Mexico achieved prosperity and international fame through their beautiful ceramics.

- Chien-Shiung Wu (b. 1912), a research physicist at Columbia University, disproved a fundamental law of physics, the conservation of parity. Her revolutionary finding, coupled with her reputation for accuracy in her laboratory work, earned Wu numerous international awards and the reputation of "queen of nuclear physics."

Ignorance of the lives and accomplishments of women like these leaves an unmistakable impression that women as a whole haven't done much of value. When female heroes cannot be named or mental images of women's contributions cannot be formed, that false impression is confirmed. But knowing just some of the great stories, having even a few genuine women heroes to recall, can change this situation. Girls and women need these positive role models to help gain a sense of pride and to locate their place in the world, to direct their own lives and help live them in ways that best suit them as individuals; boys and men need to know about the real lives of real women, not just the media-presented images that all too often portray passive, helpless victims. It's impossible to say precisely what changes a human life, but it's clear that knowing about the lives of others both like and unlike ourselves is a major part of altering prejudices and sometimes a source of strength and inspiration.

An introduction to women's history embodied in a text such as *Celebrating Women's History* can serve a number of purposes. The discovery that women have a proud history and a rich legacy of accomplishment can inspire a girl or woman to expect more from herself, or to accept the challenge of new responsibilities. Simultaneously, it can help reduce negative impressions some people, male and female alike, may carry of women's worth and capabilities. Finally, it can underscore the appeal that is, indeed, resounding: That it is time for all people who are committed to a more accurate telling of the United States' story to widen the scope, to routinely insist upon the inclusion of that entire category of lives and events too often overlooked—the stories of multicultural women's history.

The National Women's History Project (NWHP) is a nonprofit organization established in 1980 to promote a widespread public recognition of women's diverse lives and accomplishments. Members of the staff originated the first celebrations of National Women's History Week as a local activity in northern California, and continue to spearhead the organizing of what has become National Women's History Month.

With a staff of thirteen, the NWHP serves as a clearinghouse for women's history curriculum and program resources. They provide information, referrals, and technical assistance to educators, historians, community organizers, workplace activists, librarians, parents, and unaffiliated individuals on a year-round basis. They maintain a strong research library and extensive files on historical and contemporary women and a wide range of history topics, along with reference lists of women's history performers, state specific resources, women's history films, posters, and organizations.

To build upon the momentum created by celebrations of women's history across the country, the NWHP established a nationwide participant organization in 1982, the Women's History Network. The NWHP also publishes Network News, *a quarterly, 8-page newsletter of the latest projects, events, ideas, and resources for retrieving and promoting women's history. In addition, a semi-annual membership directory details the Network's initiatives to facilitate networking and organizing efforts.*

To bring multicultural women's history information to people wherever they live or work, the NWHP operates a mail-order Women's History Resource Service. On a regular basis, staff members review all new women's history materials as they are published or produced, selecting for their catalogs only the best sources; those which are multicultural, interesting to read, and historically accurate. They also produce curriculum units, planning guides, posters and display sets, and topical videos.

NWHP staff serve as national gender equity consultants, women's history lecturers, and consultants for the development of elementary and secondary classroom materials. In addition to providing in-service training sessions for schools nationwide, each summer they conduct a four-day intensive training session in California for K–12 educators and equity specialist from around the world.

Quiz Answers:

1) 1920, after an exhaustive, 72-year campaign. 2) Rachel Carson, *Silent Spring*. 3) Rosa Parks, in Montgomery, Alabama, 1955. 4) Nancy Lopez, the youngest woman ever named to the LGPA Hall of Fame. 5) Jeannette Rankin of Montana, the first woman elected to the House of Representatives. 6) Seneca Falls, New York, in July 1848. 7) Sarah Winnemucca, a Paiute, later the tribal chief. 8) Madam C. J. Walker made her fortune in the early 1900s with her line of cosmetics for black women. 9) Patsy Mink of Hawaii served six terms (1964–1976 in the House of Representatives, and was re-elected in 1991. 10) Isadora Duncan, who performed barefoot in free-flowing costumes.

Preface

Composing a celebration of women's history was not a burden for me. I decided long ago that my membership in the world's sisterhood is a proud membership overflowing with opportunity, pride, and support. Having observed my grandmother, a home health care provider, and my mother, a hosiery worker, I recognized in childhood that accepting full membership in humankind demands commitment, self-worth, and a large portion of the grunt work, the pushing and shoving that reactivates the stalled wheels of progress. Such oneness in service produces the good kind of fatigue and the warm-hearted fellowship with sisters who pass along generous handfuls of love and humor. From my Southern upbringing, I knew early in my teens that Scarlett O'Hara is more than a fictional character: she embodies the strength that women have always displayed in social upheaval—from Vietnam's chaos to the shantytowns of Johannesburg, from the Great Wall of China to the streets of Bosnia. The Scarletts of history have exercised the spiritual brawn that defies hunger, menace, and the soul-starving despair that follows massive loss and dismaying future. Of such women history was made. My role in the thanks department was simple—to nail up the historical markers, shine the gold stars that deck their struggle, and gather around the upcoming generation of both genders for a gladsome, universal cheer.

While I rummaged about in boxes of books, articles, clippings, films, recordings, speeches, and other data, my main problem lay in choosing the best, those most likely to be passed over, and the ones whose willingness, pluck, and spirit of adventure spurred them to the dark corners of discovery armed with the feeblest of lights. To Sister Kenny, Sally Ride, Elizabeth Blackwell, Aung Sang Su Kyi, Sarah Winnemucca, Myrlie Evers, the women who crossed the prairie in freighted conestogas, and the myriad unnamed foremothers who have tended home, field, garden, and loom, I stand in awe of their collective courage and persistence. As I listed and researched, one of the least familiar of these historical figures came into focus like a new planet forming at the end of a telescope. Far in the distance, I grouped details about Auguste-Charlotte Bartholdi. I didn't recall her name from any reading or history course, but her face stood in my memory as boldly as the profiles on Mount Rushmore, as clearly defined as the bas-relief on a Lincoln head penny. From many sources, I restructured her biography—a French model working for a sculptor during a twenty-year international effort to honor American democracy.

Crowned with light rather than jewels, the statue of Charlotte Bartholdi, intent on illuminating the path of freedom seekers, steps over broken chains. As I put together the strong aquiline nose, gallant posture and uplifted torch, I recognized her—the Statue of Liberty—from a different perspective. After Emma Lazarus completed the identifying process for the "Mother of exiles," I grasped America's gratitude for the official speaker of welcome:

> Give me your tired, your poor,
> Your huddled masses yearning to breathe free,
> Send these, the homeless, tempest-tost to me,
> I lift my lamp beside the golden door!

No longer a composite symbol, she was real, is real—somebody's mother, somebody's model, and the world's emblem of liberty.

Like my late-blooming acquaintance with Charlotte Bartholdi, the public's opportunity to grow in appreciation of a two-gender history caps years of intense pressure by civic leaders, educators, and historians to forge an inclusive past. The 300 exercises in *Celebrating Women's History* offer a range of similar Aha! experiences. Whether classroom activities, church projects, neighborhood festivals, club or Scout presentations, or personal readings and handicrafts, the tasks proposed in each entry provide new vistas on women in action, women making a difference with their lives. By visualizing female cattle drovers, Olympic medalists, explorers of microbiology, rulers of ancient states, translators and writers, creators of computer languages, climbers of mountains, navigators of rivers, or fulfillers of dreams, the missing gender in history rounds out the picture. The shaded spots that once lauded no woman on the battlefield, none in decision-making roles, none in religious hierarchy now shine in the light.

Acquiring this fuller sense of the past challenges people of all ages and backgrounds to retrace known paths. This time, the story of improved health will pay homage to Dr. Elizabeth Delany, Clara Barton, Dr. May Chinn, Florence Nightingale, and Mother Clara Hale; a reexamination of world monuments will picture Mumtaz, Sheba, and Maya Lin; and an arts festival will honor Anna Moses, Barbra Streisand, Sappho, Marian Anderson, Zoe Caldwell, Buffy Sainte-Marie, Isabel Allende, and Kiri Te Kanawa. In all disciplines, studies of women's place in housing, finance, conservation, entertainment, religion, government, philosophy, and civil rights will answer the questions that have muddied outdated histories: What have women done? Did they take part in anything important? Did they accomplish anything of worth? A united chorus of voices will be ready with the answer—You bet!

Content

Celebrating Women's History contains 300 activity suggestions organized into 29 chapters covering a variety of interests: Arts and Crafts, Business and Labor, Cinema, Dance, Design, Drama, Education, Fashion, Food and Cooking, Foreign Language, Geography, Government, Health, History, Humor, Interdisciplinary Activities, Journalism, Language, Law and Civil Rights, Library Research, Literature, Mathematics and Computers, Music, Religion, Science, Social Science, Speech and Debate, Sports, and Writing. Activities range from games and contests to bulletin boards, instructional programs, and individual study. Each activity includes a descriptive heading, the name of the originator if the item came from an outside source, a key to the intended age/grade level or audience, a concise description of the activity, a detailed procedure, suggested budget amount, and sources. Also included are alternative applications that will allow users to adapt the activities to suit a variety of situations.

To assist the reader in locating items most appropriate to a particular group, *Celebrating Women's History* includes four indexes: the first listing activities in alphabetical order; the second organized by age/grade level; the third arranged by budget, with costs ranging from under $25 to more than $100; and finally, the general key word index. To further help the user in his or her endeavors, a bibliography appendix is included that lists key books, CD-ROMs, and films and videos, as well as a general resource appendix with information on contacting archives, associations, centers and groups, electronic packagers, multimedia suppliers, museums, music distributors, newsletters, online sources, periodicals, publishers, and video distributors that focus on women and women's history.

Acknowledgments

I thank the following for their help in compiling *Celebrating Women's History:* Billy King, State Library, Raleigh, North Carolina; Gary Carey, writer and editor, Lincoln, Nebraska; my sister Frances Hilton, Chapter One Books, Hickory, North Carolina; Laura Kelleher, Elbert Ivey Library, Hickory, North Carolina; Burl McCuiston, Lenoir-Rhyne College Library, Hickory, North Carolina; Wanda Rozzelle, Catawba County Library, Newton, North Carolina; Jeanne Wells, rare book researcher, Portland, Oregon. Many thanks to Mary Ruthsdotter and the staff at the National Women's History Project for all their efforts; they proved especially helpful by adding their expert voices throughout the project.

A thank you must go to acquisitions editor Peg Bessette, copy editor Pam Shelton, and kudos to art director Michelle DiMercurio for her truly inspired cover and page design. A final and very special thank you to my secretary, Andrea Pittman, who collates, staples, researches, files, and performs all the other claptrap of office work without complaint.

The editor and Gale Research welcome comments and suggestions for this and future editions of *Celebrating Women's History.* Please contact:

Editor, *Celebrating Women's History*
Gale Research
835 Penobscot Bldg.
Detroit, MI 48226
Telephone: (313) 961-2242
Toll-free: (800) 347-GALE
Fax: (313) 961-6741

M.E.S.
December, 7, 1995

Arts *and* crafts

Art *laboratory*

Age/Grade Level or Audience: Elementary, middle school, or high school art class activity; art museum workshop focus; children's museum art contest or library project; poster or side-walk art competition; cooperative community mural.

Description: Study the styles of famous female artists.

Procedure: Have participants review and discuss the styles of famous female artists. Ask open-ended questions:

- What is unique about this artist's view of reality? What materials go into this type of creative project? What skills does this artist utilize?

- What does this work demonstrate about the time in which it was created?

- How has the artist captured a complex interplay of shapes, colors, and contrasts? Is there an obvious attempt at balance or contrast?

Have students choose among these women for inspiration and challenge:

- Bridget Riley (op)

- Marie Laurençin, Rosa Bonheur (oil)

- Natalya Goncharova, Frida Kahlo, Lois Mailou Jones (folk art)

- Gwen John (portraits)

- Frances Hodgkins (watercolor)

- Jennifer Bartlett, Mary Cassatt (impressionism)

- Paula Modersohn-Becker (post-impressionism)

- Helen Frankenthaler (expressionism)

- Louise Bourgeois, Nancy Graves, Barbara Hepworth, Käthe Kollwitz, Kate Millet, Louise Nevelson, Germaine Richier (sculpture)

- Sonia Delaunay, Ines de La Fressange, Claire McCardell, Jean Muir (theatrical costuming)

- Katherine Hamnett, Edith Head (fashion)

- Beatrix Potter, Neysa McMein (illustration)

- Dale Messick, Barbara Brandon (cartooning)

Budget: $$

Sources:

Bailey, Brooke. *The Remarkable Lives of 100 Women Artists.* Bob Adams, Inc., 1994.

Hay, Susannah. *The Women's Heritage Scrapbook.* Caillech Press, 1992.

Hunzeker, Patricia. "In Search of Indonesian Ikat." *Handwoven,* September/October 1994, 56–58.

LaDuke, Betty. *Women Artists: Multi-Cultural Visions.* The Red Sea Press, 1992.

Latino Art and Culture in the United States. Crystal, 1995. (Multimedia)

Linnea in Monet's Garden. Crystal, 1995. (Video)

Martin, Jean, gen. ed. *Who's Who of Women in the Twentieth Century.* Crescent Books, 1995.

Microsoft Art Gallery. Crystal, 1995. (CD-ROM)

Notable Women Artists. Knowledge Unlimited, 1995. (Posters)

Alternative Applications: Maintain a showcase at a library, museum, or civic center for the display of local art pertaining to the lives of women and girls. Concentrate on domestic and utilitarian as well as professional and aesthetic poses and studies. Mark each with a placard naming artist, title, date, and location or setting. Enhance the collection during a centennial or founder's day celebration with antique photography, sketches, or portraits from early times.

A day *in the life* of an *Inuit woman*

Age/Grade Level or Audience: Elementary, middle school, or high school human cultures study; home-school activity; children's museum or library project; scout or 4-H display; county fair booth; poster contest.

Description: Use art to express a day in the life of an Inuit woman.

Procedure: After oral readings and display of pictures, filmstrips, posters, artifacts, maps, or videos about Eskimo or Inuit life in the upper Northern Hemisphere, create a frieze, individual posters, or pages in a scrapbook depicting a day in the life of an Inuit woman. Stress the traditional division of labor between men and women and the value of an obedient, hard-working wife to a prosperous family. Begin the study by listing and defining these and other vocabulary words:

a-gu-tuk	blubber	innie	pauluk
ajagak	bola	i'noGo tied	qamutit
amouti	cache	kammik	qarmat
atigi	cat's cradle	kuspuck	qasgiq
aungaak	char	labret	qulliq
ayahaaq	dance house	mukluk	seal oil lamp
baleen	ear pull	nallaqtaq	shaman
bilberry	giviak	nuglutang	tundra
blanket toss	husky	parka	umiak

Read stories about the native lifestyle from the woman's point of view. Ask students to name ways that Inuit women would spend an ordinary day in summer, fall, winter, or spring. Discuss the role women have played in rearing families, providing for their needs, and sharing their play.

Before beginning the frieze or artwork, have participants sketch various poses of female villagers performing important tasks. Use these examples as models:

- chanting or singing traditional songs, poems, and prayers at a drum dance
- collecting fish from a stone weir or trap
- sorting soft down, fur, feathers, or moss to fill pillows or line boots and mittens
- consulting a **shaman** to cure family members of bad dreams, infertility, sickness, or injuries
- cutting dried skins with an **ulu** to make parkas, **mukluks,** mittens, and **amoutis**
- cutting sod for a **qarmat,** a temporary house built on a rocky ledge
- drying **bilberries** for use in winter meals
- drying wet laundry or skins for use in kayaks or **umiaks**
- lashing a tarp over a **qamutit,** a long sled mounted on runners glazed with icy mud
- making amulets—such as an **i'noGo tied** or **aungaak**—to protect children from harm
- making ceremonial masks and painting them with **inua** or spirit pictures
- melting snow for household water
- packing a small load on a dog saddle and lashing it into place with thongs
- pounding blubber to extract fuel oil for lamps, ointment, lubricants, and cooking
- preparing a summer house out of snow walls and a skin roof
- repairing tents and dog harness for sleds
- sealing blocks of snow into an igloo
- sewing a **housewife**—an embroidered bag for carrying personal items—as a gift for a bride, newcomer, or visitor
- sewing and embroidering **kuspucks** from cotton muslin or canvas for summer wear
- smoking char to store for winter meals
- supervising children sliding down an igloo roof or playing ear pull, cat's cradle, or blanket toss
- teaching small children to play **ajagak,** a ring toss game that challenges the player to catch on a pin a pierced disk of bone or wood, or demonstrating **ayahaaq,** a similar game requiring the player to catch a bone on a sharpened stick, or **nuglutang,** a disk game played with a circlet suspended from the ceiling.

Ask volunteers to explain the method of each task and its purpose. For instance, ask why weatherproofing igloos and mukluks is important for the family's survival on the tundra or snowy plains or why telling or acting out favorite stories is a good use of time during severe winter storms.

Budget: $$

Sources:

Balikci, Asen. *The Netsilik Eskimo.* Natural History Press, 1970.

Fitzhugh, William W., and Susan A. Kaplan. *Inua: Spirit World of the Bering Sea Eskimo.* Smithsonian Institution Traveling Exhibition Service, 1983.

George, Jean Craighead. *Julie of the Wolves.* Harper & Row, 1972.

Hahn, Elizabeth. *The Inuit*. Rourke, 1990.

Newton, Shirlee P. *The Inuits*. Franklin Watts, 1993.

Oman, Lela Kiana. *The Epic of Qayaq*. Carleton University Press, 1995.

Patterson, Lotsee, and Mary Ellen Snodgrass. *Indian Terms of the Americas*. Libraries Unlimited, 1994.

Yue, Charlotte, and David Yue. *Igloo*. Houghton Mifflin, 1988.

Alternative Applications: Organize a parents' night program or window display of Eskimo women and their traditional functions as wife, mother, and villager. Begin with a map of areas where Eskimos live and a list of animals and plants they depend on for food, clothing, tools, transportation, weapons, and shelter, especially moss, bilberries, ptarmigan eggs, seal, whale, caribou, char, and snow hare. Have participants set up model clay figures, spool dolls, shapes made from pipe cleaners, flexible dolls, masks, string toys, or stick puppets dressed in scraps of hide, felt, or cloth and place them in a sandbox or shadow box or on a display or window shelf. Accompany each scene or group of figures with a card explaining the purpose of the woman's activities or cooperative efforts, as with the skinning of fish or seals, the curing of hides for use in clothing or making kayaks and umiaks; also cooking, sewing, smoothing the inner surface of an igloo, smoking fish or meat, or training daughters in ritual dance or worship, tattooing, singing, or making baleen earrings.

For a large group, allow students to select other tribes to demonstrate the female members' duties. Consider a variety:

Abenaki	Comanche	Kwakiutl	Salish
Aleut	Cree	Mahican	Sauk
Algonquin	Creek	Mandan	Seminole
Anasazi	Crow	Maya	Shawnee
Apache	Dakota	Micmac	Shoshone
Arapaho	Delaware	Mohawk	Sioux
Arawak	Dorset	Navajo	Taino
Assiniboin	Fox	Nez Percé	Timucua
Athapascan	Haida	Nootka	Tlingit
Aztec	Hidatsa	Olmec	Toltec
Catawba	Hopi	Paiute	Ute
Cherokee	Huron	Pawnee	Washoe
Cheyenne	Inca	Pima	Winnebago
Chickasaw	Iroquois	Pomo	Yahi
Chippewa	Kiowa	Potawatomi	Yuma
Choctaw	Kutenai	Pueblo	Zuñi

Edna *Hibel*

Age/Grade Level or Audience: Elementary, middle school, or high school art class lecture; home-school art activity; art museum or library display or research project; cooperative community mural; public lecture.

Description: Present posters or slides of the work of a lesser-known female artist.

Procedure: Outline the life and work of Edna Hibel. Include these facts about her career:

- Edna Hibel has been busy with art since fourth grade. A native of Allston, Massachusetts, she began serious study in art at age twelve by joining an adult anatomy class.

- George Michael, a Greek portraitist, saw Edna's work the next year and offered her free lessons. With his encouragement, she expanded into new media and gained artistic focus. Four years later, she entered the Boston Museum School of Fine Arts and also began selling her work.

- In her early twenties, Edna studied fresco and watercolors under Eliot O'Hara. With funds from the Ruth Sturtevant Fellowship, she traveled to Mexico in 1939. Extreme dysentery kept her housebound, but her mother solved her need to study Mexican lifestyles by bringing people to pose for Edna.

- During her adult career, Edna opened a gallery in Rockport, Massachusetts. She sold "Mexican Beggar," "My Grandmother," "Greek Dancers," "Two Brothers," "Africa," "Veronique and Child," and "Recorder," just some of her most striking works in watercolors, oil, gesso, charcoal, silk painting, pencil, ceramics, porcelain, bone china, crystal relief, and fresco.

- Critics have begun to appreciate the versatility and mastery of Edna Hibel, who travels widely, always keeps an eye on new methods and models, and never loses her zest for art. Today her work is highly prized by collectors and museums.

Budget: $$$

Sources:

Cossi, Olga. *Edna Hibel: Her Life and Art*. Discovery Enterprises, 1994.

Fuentes, Carlos. Introduction to *The Diary of Frida Kahlo*. Abrams Books, 1995.

Alternative Applications: Discuss Edna Hibel's comments about her life as an artist:

"What a blessing it has been to be an artist. It is such a thrill to see my ideas take shape, grow, and mature as I search for beauty and meaning in the colors, lines, forms, and their dynamics. How else could I ever express my deepest feelings about humanity. . . ." (Cossi, p. 2).

Ask participants to write a personal application of this statement to their lives and to the work of other female artists; for example, Frida Kahlo, Rosa Bonheur, Mary Cassatt, and Georgia O'Keeffe. Encourage them to discuss why beauty and challenge are important to the search for meaning and contentment. Conclude with a reading of participants' expressions about their life's work.

Flag *women*

Age/Grade Level or Audience: Preschool or elementary world history or art activity; mother's day out program; library reading circle focus; home-school art project; history club contest; children's museum poster or sidewalk art contest; cooperative community mural.

Description: Organize a study of women of the world through art.

Procedure: Have participants draw or mold from clay or papier-mâché a woman in typical or folkloric dress of a chosen country; for example, parka and snow goggles for northern Canada,

5

ao dai tunic and black silk pants with clogs and conical straw hat for Vietnam, suit and blouse for the United States, camisa and gathered skirt with squash-blossom hairdo for Native Americans of the Southwest, and muu-muu or sarong and thong sandals for Indonesia. Encourage some groups to draw clusters of infants, young girls, women, and matrons depicting a variety of locations, jobs, poses, and social levels. Instruct participants to place a national flag in each drawing.

Budget: $$

Sources:

Bradfield, Nancy. *Historical Costumes of England.* Barnes & Noble, 1971.

Feininger, Andreas. *New York in the Forties.* Dover Books, 1994.

Gorsline, Douglas. *What People Wore.* Dover Books, 1994.

Moxley, Susan. *Play with Papier-Mâché.* Lerner Group, 1996.

Müller, Claudia. *The Costume Timeline: 5000 Years of Fashion History.* Thames & Hudson, 1992.

Paterek, Josephine. *Encyclopedia of American Indian Costume.* ABC-Clio, 1994.

Thomson, John. *Victorian London Street Life in Historic Photographs.* Dover Books, 1994.

Ventura, Pietro. *Clothing: Garments, Styles, and Uses.* Houghton Mifflin, 1993.

Alternative Applications: Arrange a display of world flags on a library counter, school showcase, classroom table, or civic center bulletin board. Have groups select a flag and create a hand puppet, mask, paper-bag puppet, or doll outfit to illustrate folkloric or typical dress of the country; for example, a peasant frock with gathered neck and ornate apron and boots worn by a Polish woman dancing a polka or a sealskin amouti, leggings, boots, and snow goggles for an Inuit girl on her sled.

Georgia O'Keeffe and the creative process

Originator: Gary Carey, writer and editor, Lincoln, Nebraska.

Age/Grade Level or Audience: Elementary, middle school, or high school art study; home-school art project; children's museum or library presentation; scout or 4-H display; street fair booth; poster or sidewalk art contest; cooperative community mural.

Description: Present a study of creative expression by examining the life and works of Georgia O'Keeffe.

Procedure: Discuss the interest in found art in the work of Georgia O'Keeffe. Comment on her life in the American Southwest, the influences of other artists and photographers, her immersion in nature and the contrast of earth tones and sky, and her application of found objects to simple landscapes. Have participants imitate Georgia O'Keeffe's method and styles by expressing their own viewpoint on nature and creating a photographic study, drawing, mural, sculpture, jewelry, sketch, mosaic, or painting featuring earth tones and natural shapes in their own area; for example, oak trees, brooks, sheer cliffs, pebbly beaches, cacti, ponds, skylines, or lakes. Discuss the importance of light as a source of inspiration and control.

Budget: $$$

Sources:

Ball, A. Jacqueline, and Catherine Conant. *Georgia O'Keeffe in New Mexico: A Guide.* Blackbirch, 1994.

Eldredge, Charles C. *Georgia O'Keeffe: American and Modern.* Yale University Press, 1993.

Georgia O'Keeffe. Crystal, 1995. (Video)

Lynes, Barbara B. *Georgia O'Keeffe.* Rizzoli, 1993.

Shuman, B. *Georgia O'Keeffe.* Rourke, 1993.

Alternative Applications: Present slides or prints or show a video about Georgia O'Keeffe's way of studying nature and creating art from her impressions. Ask participants to bring to class simple objects—stones, geodes, seed pods, pine cones, fruits, vegetables, leaves, limbs, eggs, or bird's nests—to use as models. Discuss how O'Keeffe utilized bold colors and *chiaroscuro* to make the work stand out from the background. Have participants create their own O'Keeffe-style drawings on paper in acrylics, colored pencil, chalk, charcoal, or watercolor.

Happy *birthday!*

Age/Grade Level or Audience: Preschool or elementary school art activity; mother's day out focus; English-as-a-second-language or library reading circle project; home-school art focus; children's museum or library display; elementary school poster or sidewalk art contest.

Description: Teach lettering and counting by creating a women's history month calendar.

Procedure: Present participants with an oversized calendar made of twelve large squares drawn on one long mural or a chalkboard, or a series of a dozen butcher-paper or tagboard sheets. Have volunteers copy or stencil the names or abbreviations for the appropriate months at the top of each section. Have adult aides or volunteers determine the birthdays of famous women by, for example, gleaning them from newspapers and magazines or from dictionaries, biographies, reference works, and databases. Assign each participant a person with a different birthday. Beside the person's name, have the presenter draw a representative symbol. Make room on the calendar for multiple names on a single date. Use these multicultural examples as models:

January 23	zoologist Dian Fossey	gorilla
February 4	activist Rosa Parks	bus
March 16	conductor Sarah Caldwell	baton
April 23	composer Penina Moïse	G clef
May 31	physicist Chien-Shiung Wu	calipers
June 30	singer Lena Horne	microphone
July 18	author Jessamyn West	pen and ink
August 16	dancer Suzanna Farrell	ballet shoes
September 10	Chief Alice Davis	Seminole dress
October 8	chemist Mary Pennington	test tube
November 18	Chief Wilma Mankiller	Cherokee insignia
December 28	planter Elizabeth Lucas Pinckney	indigo

Budget: $$

Sources:

Buckingham, Sandra. *Stencil It!* Firefly Books, 1995.

Bulloch, Ivan. *Play with Models.* Lerner Group, 1996.

"Celebrate Women." Windsor, Calif.: National Women's History Project. (Poster of Birthdays)

Clark, Judith Freeman. *Almanac of American Women in the Twentieth Century.* Prentice Hall, 1987.

Great American Women. Knowledge Unlimited. (Posters)

Hughes, Phyllis. *Indian Children Paper Dolls.* Red Crane, 1990.

"Women Who Dare." Windsor, Calif.: National Women's History Project, 1995. (Calendar)

Zyromski, Page. "Wycinanki." *Cobblestone,* June 1995, 24–25.

Alternative Applications: Assign elementary students a study of computer sorting by placing birth dates, careers, and names in separate columns in a database program. Demonstrate how a computer realigns data by whatever information it receives. Create separate versions of the birth dates of famous women: chronologically by date, alphabetically by name, and alphabetically by career, with names under each topic also alphabetized. Print out copies in large point size to use as a wall chart, hall decoration, banner, or table runner for a women's history covered-dish dinner. Appoint a committee to decorate the finished print-outs with symbols, flowers, calligraphy, stenciling, cartoons, or caricatures.

Just *for you*

Age/Grade Level or Audience: All-ages community art contest or cooperative community mural; elementary, middle school, or high school art project; art museum or mother's day out activity; home-school history lesson.

Description: Organize an art expo entitled "A Woman I Wish I Had Known."

Procedure: Invite the public to honor a notable woman with an entry or display at a civic art expo. Follow the examples below:

- acrylic art depicting the training of astronaut Christa McAuliffe
- puppet depicting the stage antics of actress Nell Gwyn
- basket recognizing the work of weaver Datsolali
- batik pareu recognizing Princess Sirikit of Siam
- coil-pot trophy to swimmer Gertrude Ederle
- collage featuring the many contributions of Eleanor Roosevelt
- earrings from the ceremonial jewelry of Catherine the Great of Russia
- indigo quilt recognizing Ayano Chiba's skill with color and piecework
- mask picturing Theodora, empress of Byzantium
- medal championing the speeches of suffragist Lucy Stone
- mosaic highlighting the life of Queen Esther
- origami animals championing the primatological studies of Dian Fossey

- pen-and-ink sketch of a tableau in Queen Isabella's life

- photo of an invention by Sarah Knight

- poster art featuring the costumes and roles of Sarah Bernhardt

- shadow box featuring the writings of Beatrix Potter

- smocked or embroidered apron characterizing poet Hildegarde of Bingen

- tile honoring Sister Kenny, creator of a treatment for polio

- tissue art displaying the vibrant colors of Renaissance artist Elisabetta Sirani

Using standards of 50% creativity, 10% proportion, 25% artisanship, and 15% accuracy, offer awards suitable to three levels: children, teens, and adults. Display works along with brief note-card histories in this form:

<u>Name:</u>	Ntozake Shange
<u>Occupation:</u>	Poet, playwright, performer
<u>Personal history:</u>	Born October 18, 1948, in Trenton, New Jersey
<u>Achievements:</u>	Author of *for colored girls who have considered suicide/when the rainbow is enuf* (1976); *Mother Courage and Her Children* (1979); *I Live in Music* (1994); *Sassafrass, Cypress & Indigo* (1982); *Liliane* (1994)
<u>Honors:</u>	Obie (1977, 1979); *Los Angeles Times* Book Award (1981); Taos World Poetry Heavyweight Champion (1992, 1993, 1994)

Budget: $$$$$

Sources:

Buckingham, Sandra. *Stencil It!* Firefly Books, 1995.

Bulloch, Ivan. *Play with Models.* Lerner Group, 1996.

Clay: Functional Pottery. Crystal, 1995. (Video)

"Female Mail." *On the Issues,* spring 1995, 7.

Hughes, Phyllis. *Indian Children Paper Dolls.* Red Crane, 1990.

Masks and Face Coverings. Crystal, 1995. (Video or filmstrip and audiocassette)

Moxley, Susan. *Play with Papier-Mâché.* Lerner Group, 1996.

"1994 in Review: The Good News." *Ms.,* January/February 1995, 46–53.

Pollock, Junco sato. "Out of the Blue." *Piecework,* September/October 1994, 38–43.

Siegel, Arlene. *Sculpture Classroom.* Crystal, 1995. (Video)

Vance, Donna Williams. "Ntozake Shange Finds the Poetry in Sisterhood." *USA Today,* December 6, 1994, 5D.

Wright, Mary. "In Search of Cornish Guernsey and Knit-Frocks." *Piecework,* September/October 1994, 70–75.

Alternative Applications: Assign participants a segment of a painted community mural. Establish a parade or fiesta theme with individual entries stressing the achievements of notable women in politics, foods, science, technology, the arts, entertainment, and history. Choose from these and other women:

- actor Emma Thompson

- Catawba Indian organizer Wanda George Warren

- choreographer Jeraldyne Blundsen

- columnist Ellen Goodman

- diplomat Raisa Gorbachev

- economist Heidi Hartmann

- educator Janine Pease-Windy Boy

- energy secretary Hazel O'Leary

- environmentalist Rachel Carson

- journalist Barbara Walters

- leader Catherine Tekakwitha

- poet Audre Lorde

- singer Leontyne Price

Local *cyclorama*

Age/Grade Level or Audience: Preschool, elementary, or middle school art class project; home-school interdisciplinary study; children's museum or library display; scout or 4-H history project; county fair craft exhibit or booth; woman's club poster or sidewalk art contest; interscholastic art expo.

Description: Organize a review of local women's history by creating an around-the-room cyclorama.

Procedure: Have participants create an artistic representation of the history of local women. Appoint volunteers to study resource materials, and complete a list of facts and events to cover. Adapt the cartoon format of the Bayeaux Tapestry as a model. Sketch the proportions of the cyclorama and fill in simple captions, giving names, accomplishments, and dates. Use a single method; for example, oil on canvas or pencil on butcher paper. Or combine a variety of techniques, including stained glass, needlework, watercolor portraiture, acrylic mapping, papier-mâché masks, and mural art. Arrange to preserve the finished women's history in a local museum or the genealogy room of the public library.

Budget: $$$$$

Sources:

Buckingham, Sandra. *Stencil It!* Firefly Books, 1995.

Davis, Ki. *Collage Techniques.* Crystal, 1995. (Filmstrips)

Gillard, Glenys. *Tapestry Is Easy.* Seven Hills Books, 1994.

Masks and Face Coverings. Crystal, 1995. (Video or filmstrip and audiocassette)

Moxley, Susan. *Play with Papier-Mâché.* Lerner Group, 1996.

Alternative Applications: Compose a local women's history on a computer or word processor. Using a desktop publishing program, illustrate entries with clip art, maps, genealogies, stick figures, photos, sound clips, movie stills, newspaper clippings, and drawings. Present the published monograph as a table favor for a Women's History Month banquet or distribute monographs at a tent market in a park or at city hall.

Miss *Liberty*

Age/Grade Level or Audience: Elementary, middle school, or high school mechanical drawing or outlining lesson; home-school art project; children's museum or library activity; scout or 4-H display; county fair booth; parade float entry; civic club program; women's study focus.

Description: Present a detailed study of the artistry and history of the Statue of Liberty and its growth into a national monument.

Procedure: Divide the study of "Miss Liberty" into three parts: how the work was designed and constructed, why the French made the statue and also constructed a smaller model for display on the Seine River in Paris, and what the statue means to Americans, immigrants, and visitors to the United States. Follow this topic outline as a springboard to understanding and discussion:

I. The French and the Statue of Liberty

  A. Beginnings

   1. Conception of sculptor Edouard-René Leboulaye in 1865

   2. Site surveyed in 1871 for use as a lighthouse lit with kerosene

   3. Clay model using the sculptor's mother, Auguste-Charlotte Bartholdi, completed in 1875, in Paris

     a. Plaster-covered, full-sized models constructed in Paris

     b. Final segments begun in 1884

   4. Officially named "Liberty Enlightening the World"

  B. Construction

   1. Frederic Auguste Bartholdi, supervising sculptor

   2. Alexandre Gustave Eiffel, designer of 90-ton inner pylon

   3. 142 steps to the torch

   4. Segments joined to pylon

  C. Cost

   1. A joint French-American effort established in 1875

   2. French donations of $400,000

   3. Display of the torch and right hand at the Centennial Exposition in 1876 to raise funds for completed statue

   4. Joseph Pulitzer's effort to raise American funds for the pedestal begun in *The World,* March 1885

     a. $100,000 in funds from 121,000 donors

     b. By April 1886, $300,000 in U.S. donations provided—enough to build the pedestal

  D. Shipping

   1. Loaded in 214 crates

   2. Shipped on the *Isère*

   3. Arrival on September 17, 1885

   4. Dedication held on October 28, 1886

II. Location and design

A. Location

1. Bedloe's island, a twelve-acre island in the Atlantic Ocean on Upper New York Bay, off the coast of the borough of Manhattan and east of Jersey City, New Jersey

2. Ten-pointed, star-shaped structure at the base formed Fort Wood, built 1806–1811

3. A segment of the Statue of Liberty National Monument

4. An adjunct to the Ellis Island complex

5. Site renamed Liberty Island in 1956

6. Accessible by 15-minute ferry ride from Battery Park

B. Shape

1. Pose copied from the Colossus of Rhodes, one of the Seven Wonders of the World

2. Robed female with broken chain at her feet

3. Hand-held torch containing sixteen electric lights

4. Seven-pointed crown and observation deck accommodating twenty people

5. Law tablet inscribed "July IV, MDCCLXXVI"

6. Built in *repoussé* style, i. e., hammered against the inner walls of a mold

C. Materials

1. 154-foot steel, granite, and concrete pedestal designed by Richard Morris Hunt in 1881

2. Concrete colonnade below the upper balcony

3. 151-foot statue made of 204 tons of 3/32-inch thick copper

4. Riveted with unthreaded bolts to steel ribs to withstand strong winds and changes in temperature

D. Upkeep and refurbishment

1. Major remodeling in the 1980s costing $30 million

2. Scaffolding of the torch to upgrade and repair inner deterioration

a. Windowless torch supplanting earlier slotted frame

b. Viewing platform rebuilt

c. Emergency elevator added

d. Iron ribs reconstructed using steel

3. Exterior remodeling

a. Copper coating cleaned

b. Rivets replaced

c. Stains and rust removed

4. Establishment of a private Ellis Island Foundation

a. $160 million raised

b. Complex enhanced to honor immigrants

III. Miss Liberty, Symbol to the World

    A. Attraction

        1. Two million visitors annually

        2. Museum honoring immigrants added in the pedestal

        3. A glass elevator or a climb of 189 stairs to the top of the pedestal

        4. View of New York Harbor

        5. 2 1/2-hour tour

    B. Celebrations

        1. Formal presentation to the U.S. Ambassador to France July 4, 1884, in Paris

        2. American reception with parade and flotilla on October 28, 1886

        3. President Grover Cleveland and his cabinet officiating

        4. Rededication on July 4, 1986

        5. Centennial celebration on October 28, 1986

    C. Symbolism

        1. Expression of freedom

        2. Depiction of tyranny crushed at Liberty's feet

        3. Memorial to American-French alliance during the Revolutionary War

        4. Symbolic welcome to immigrants from 1890–1920

        5. Emblem of strength on government-issued war bonds during both world wars

        6. Named a national monument in 1924

        7. Part of the National Park Service trust since 1933

    D. The French Miss Liberty

        1. Donated in 1885 by Americans living in Paris

        2. Built on the Seine River, a picturesque spot frequented by tourists

        3. A standard stop on the Bateau Mouche tour of the Seine

Have groups draft or sketch detailed studies of the figure, head, hand, torch, crown, tablet, base, and island. Make detailed notation of the statue's actual measurements.

Budget: $$

Sources:

Bossert, Jill. *Liberty: A Centennial History of the Statue of Liberty in Post Cards.* Madison Square, 1986.

Dillon, Wilton S., and Neil G. Kotler, eds. *The Statue of Liberty Revisited: The Making of a Universal Symbol.* Smithsonian Institution, 1993.

Gabriele. *Statue of Liberty and Ellis Island.* Penny Lane Publications, 1986.

Holland, F. Ross. *Idealists, Scoundrels, and the Lady: An Insider's View of the Statue of Liberty—Ellis Island Project.* University of Illinois Press, 1993.

Maestro, Betsy. *The Story of the Statue of Liberty.* W. W. Morrow, 1989.

Alternative Applications: Lead a discussion of "The New Colossus," a sonnet written by Emma Lazarus, New York philanthropist and poet, in 1883 and engraved on Miss Liberty's pediment in 1903.

> Not like the brazen giant of Greek fame,
> With conquering limbs astride from land to land;
> Here at our sea-washed, sunset gates shall stand
> A mighty woman with a torch, whose flame
> Is the imprisoned lightning, and her name
> Mother of Exiles. From her beacon-hand
> Glows world-wide welcome; her mild eyes command
> The air-bridged harbor that twin cities frame.
> "Keep ancient lands, your storied pomp!" cries she
> With silent lips. "Give me your tired, your poor,
> Your huddled masses yearning to breathe free,
> Send these, the homeless, tempest-tost to me.
> I lift my lamp beside the golden door!

Ask participants the following open-ended questions:

- Does Miss Liberty appear defensive about the pomp of ancient lands?

- What kind of figure was the old colossus?

- Why did Bartholdi choose a female colossus?

- How was Bartholdi influenced by Marianne, the female symbol of liberty popular during the French Revolution?

- How would you recast the figure today to give an updated example of American interest in homeless or tyrannized people?

- How has America responded to the Irish, Haitians, Cubans, Asian boat people, Bosnians, Kurds, Jews, Russians, and other influxes of refugees?

- Why have later waves of immigrants referred to the Statue of Liberty as "Mother of Exiles?"

- Why would Americans want a Mother of Exiles at their major port city?

- What does the lamp symbolize?

Modern *women at work*

Age/Grade Level or Audience: Elementary, middle school, or high school art series; retirement home or home-school art project; children's museum or library activity; scout or 4-H workshop.

Description: Sponsor an art display featuring current views of women at work.

Procedure: Organize an art project, contest, or workshop in which participants concentrate on creating images of women at work. Include manual, intellectual, and machine labor. Feature farmlands, gardens, boats, offices, airports, playing fields, studios, courts, schools, home kitchens, and other workplaces. Consider the following possibilities:

- Caribbean women cutting and binding sugar cane

- Dutch farm women milking cows and goats

- female lawyers questioning clients

- female roadside produce sellers unpacking crates in Cuba

- Israeli women conducting military exercises at a kibbutz

- migrant women planting tobacco in South Carolina

- missionaries and nuns holding pre-school classes in India

- Moroccan women dyeing yarn

- Sicilian women knitting sweaters

- Sri Lankan women tufting rugs

- Vietnamese women irrigating a field with pedal power

- women herding and shearing sheep in New Zealand

Suggest these as artistic media: clay, linoleum blocks, watercolors, oils, pastels, charcoal, banners, mosaic tiles, woodcuts, sidewalk chalk drawings, wood carving, embroidery, stenciling, calligraphy, origami, or found objects.

Budget: $$$$

Sources:

Buckingham, Sandra. *Stencil It!* Firefly Books, 1995.

Bulloch, Ivan. *Play with Models.* Lerner Group, 1996.

Felman, Jill Lynn. "Judy Chicago's Holocaust Project." *Lilith,* summer 1994, 15–16.

Hughes, Phyllis. *Indian Children Paper Dolls.* Red Crane, 1990.

Oehler, Rosemarie. "Witness to the Harvest." *World Vision Partners,* winter 1994–1995, 2–7.

Roth, Joan. "Thru a Feminist Lens: Joan Roth Photographs a World of Jewish Women." *Lilith,* summer 1994, 17–22.

Zyromski, Page. "Wycinanki." *Cobblestone,* June 1995, 24–25.

Alternative Applications: Sponsor a photography workshop. Teach the qualities of figure-ground, chiaroscuro, focus, contrast, and balance. Set the theme of "Women at Work" in the context of local women professionals, shopkeepers, grocers, artisans, factory workers, servants, drivers, housekeepers, child care providers, migrants, herders, fishers, and day laborers. Exhibit completed and matted work in a city hall, school gym, mall, or open-air festival.

Mother's *Day*

Age/Grade Level or Audience: Preschool or elementary art lesson; mother's day out program; library reading circle; home-school art project; children's museum or library series; women's club art contest; cooperative community Mother's Day festival.

Description: Organize an interactive study of Mother's Day.

Procedure: Introduce the various facts behind the origin of Mother's Day:

- Following the bloody Franco-Prussian War, pacifist and suffragist Julia Ward Howe appealed to women on a global scale to set aside a day for celebrating peace.

Beginning in 1872, Howe's Mother's Day was celebrated for several years in and around Boston, Massachusetts. It eventually disappeared from public notice before World War I.

- Anna "Mother" Jarvis worked tirelessly during the Civil War to organize women's brigades in support of the many wounded and dying soldiers, regardless of the side on which they fought. In 1878, during a Sunday school lesson, she issued the hope that "someone, sometime, will found a memorial mother's day. There are many days for men, but none for mothers."

- Sparked by her mother's plea, Jarvis's daughter Anna began a campaign. In 1905, following her mother's death, the younger Anna wrote streams of letters to men of prominence such as President William Taft and former President Theodore Roosevelt, asking that an official Mother's Day be adopted.

- By 1907 a Mother's Day service was instituted on the second Sunday of May at the West Virgina church where Anna Jarvis had taught.

- The custom spread, and soon churches in over 45 states, as well as Puerto Rico, Hawaii, Mexico, and Canada, were celebrating Mother's Day. The governor of West Virginia officially proclaimed Mother's Day in 1912; Pennsylvania adopted the practice in 1913. In 1914, a Congressional resolution, signed by Woodrow Wilson, formally recognized Mother's Day as a national event.

Supply participants with alternative media to create the following mementos of Mother's Day:

- finger paintings of mothers who also work as nurses, ambulance drivers, dentists, or doctors

- banner featuring white and red carnations or roses, symbols of Mother's Day

- flag depicting a famous mother; for example, Rose Kennedy, mother of John, Bobby, and Ted Kennedy

- hand puppet characterizing a famous mother; for example, Sacajawea and her son Pompey on his cradleboard

- shadow box showing a view of a cabin, hogan, pueblo, tepee, igloo, cave, apartment, trailer, or other type of home and illustrating the daily chores performed by a mother for her children

- collage of mothers and children from around the world in folkloric dress

- book marks with "Mother's Day" in calligraphy

- tray markers proclaiming "Happy Mother's Day" for a retirement home or center for the handicapped

- papier-mâché crown and regal jewelry to honor mothers or grandmothers on Mother's Day

Budget: $$$

Sources:

Buckingham, Sandra. *Stencil It!* Firefly Books, 1995.

Gore, Wilma W. *Mother's Day.* Enslow Publications, 1993.

Hatch, Jane M, ed. *The American Book of Days.* H. W. Wilson, 1978.

McGraw, Sheila. *Dolls Kids Can Make.* Firefly Books, 1995.

———. *Papier-Mâché for Kids.* Firefly Books, 1995.

Schauffler, Robert H. and Susan T. Rice. *Mother's Day: Its History, Origin, Celebration, Spirit, and Significance as Related in Prose and Verse.* Omnigraphics, 1990.

Alternative Applications: Have participants work together in one or more groups to compose a poem suitable for a Mother's Day card. Assign a 2–3 member committee to determine the tone and style of the poem. Allow participants to work privately on their own versions; then come together to share lines, ideas, and images to create a draft of the poem. Write the draft on a chalkboard, or photocopy and participate as a group in editing and upgrading. Select an appropriate photo, drawing, sketch, tissue art collage, or other motif to accompany the poem; for example, Scotch plaid, braided edge, tulips and iris design, a photo of a mother reading a bedtime story, or a drawing of a mother showing her children the machinery at her workstation.

The *primitive art of* Grandma Moses

Age/Grade Level or Audience: Preschool, elementary, or middle school art lesson; homeschool biography study; children's museum or library series; essay contest.

Description: Organize an art study or exposition of the works of Grandma Moses.

Procedure: Summarize for participants the artistic methods and subjects found in the prolific work of artist Anna Mary Robertson Moses, better known as Grandma Moses. Provide art books, prints, note and greeting cards, filmstrips, slides, and other examples of her New England portraits of bucolic nineteenth-century life. Concentrate on the best of her 1,000 canvases:

"Applebutter Making"	"Bringing in the Maple Sugar"
"Catching the Thanksgiving Turkey"	"The First Skating"
"Haying Time"	"The Night Before Christmas"
"Over the River to Grandma's House"	"The Quilting Bee"

Distribute butcher paper, note pads, glass panes, wood shingles, cardboard, and other materials on which students can practice primitive art using colored markers, chalk, crayon, tempera, acrylics, or oil paints. Discuss the types of character action, seasonal indicators, farm work, church activities, and community involvement that might be depicted on each person's original "Grandma Moses"-style art work. Hold a contest for the most original use of simple lines, shapes, and the vibrant use of color that accompanies primitive style. Award winners books and prints of Grandma Moses' works.

Budget: $$$

Sources:

Armstrong, William H. *Barefoot in the Grass: The Story of Grandma Moses.* Doubleday, 1971.

Biracree, Tom. *Grandma Moses.* Chelsea House, 1989.

Kallir, Otto. *Grandma Moses.* New American Library, 1975.

Kallis, Jane. *Grandma Moses: The Artist behind the Myth.* Clarkson N. Potter, 1982.

O'Neall, Zibby. *Grandma Moses.* Puffin Books, 1994.

Alternative Applications: Discuss with students the way in which widowhood and advancing age allowed Anna Mary Moses to transform herself into Grandma Moses, an artist appreciated around the world even in her own lifetime. Note the following passages in her life:

1860	Anna Mary Robertson is born near Greenwich, New York, on September 7.
1872	Anna Mary works as a hired farm laborer.

1887	She marries Thomas Salmon Moses, a farmer, and settles near Staunton, Virginia.
1905	The Moses family and their five surviving children move to Eagle Bridge, New York.
1927	Anna Mary is widowed and lives for a time with son Hugh Moses.
1935	She gives up sewing because of arthritis in her hands.
1936	She moves to the home of her daughter, Winona Fisher, in Hoosick Falls, where she begins painting on canvas, glass, and boards.
1938	Louis J. Caldor discovers her work in a local drugstore and offers her a contract.
1940–61	Her primitive art appeals to middle America and demand for her work grows.
1952	Grandma Moses publishes *My Life's History* (Harper & Brothers, 1958).
1960	New York State Governor Nelson Rockefeller proclaims September 7 as "Grandma Moses Day." Later that year, she suffers pneumonia.
1961	Grandma Moses dies on December 13.
1962	A posthumous illustrated copy of Clement Moore's "The Night Before Christmas" features her work.

Discuss the concept of compensation, which encouraged Anna Mary Robertson to use her interests and talents for the creation of beauty and history, a reflection on the lifestyle and outlook of her youth.

Quilted *memories*

Originator: Gary Carey, writer and editor, Lincoln, Nebraska.

Age/Grade Level or Audience: Any-age crafts activity; retirement home program; library display; home-school art project; history club presentation; children's museum or civic preservation project.

Description: Create a quilt commemorating local women.

Procedure: Have participants design and create a memory quilt or wall hanging. Choose events or women in local history; for example, the achievements of the first midwife, a successful female entrepreneur, or the most notable educator in the county. Consider significant movements and events:

Chisholm Trail	Mariel Boatlift
civil rights marches	polio camp
Civil War hospital	Trail of Tears
Donner Pass tragedy	well-baby clinic
girls' college	women's clinic
Gold Rush	women's museum
Long Walk	World War II victory garden

Display at a civic center, museum, courthouse, library, or school. Or, auction the completed work for a worthy cause, such as scholarships for homeless girls or a battered women's shelter.

Budget: $$

Sources:

Granick, Eve Wheatcroft. *The Amish Quilt*. Good Books, n.d.

Irwin, John Rice. *A People and Their Quilts*. Schiffer, 1984.

Laury, Jean Ray. *Ho for California: Pioneer Women and Their Quilts*. E. P. Dutton, 1990.

Pellman, Rachel Thomas. *Tips for Quilters*. Good Books, n.d.

Simms, Ami. *Creating Scrapbook Quilts*. Mallery Press, 1993.

Alternative Applications: Assist beginning quilters in making small, colorful items employing a theme of local women's history out of a variety of fabrics, felt, ribbon, and knit scraps. Make pot holders, dresser scarves, pillow shams, doorknob covers, draft protectors, Christmas ornaments, place mats, table runners, or coasters incorporating shapes of pottery, profiles of heroines, wheels to honor explorers and travelers, trees to commemorate gardeners and landscapers, and windows to denote architectural designs. Embroider the name of each honoree on the item.

Snapshots *tell the story*

Age/Grade Level or Audience: Elementary, middle school, or high school art project; photography lab activity; home-school study; children's museum or library presentation; scout or 4-H introduction to photography; county fair booth; civic club contest.

Description: Sponsor a display featuring the steps contained in a single act of historical "woman's work."

Procedure: Organize a photography project, contest, or workshop. Study the work of such famous photographers as Tina Modotti, Annette Messager, or Consuelo Kanaga and the comments by art historian Sarah M. Lowe. Have participants snap individual poses of a multi-step process. For example, use friends to act out the role of early laundresses. Begin with a basket of clothes by a stream. Continue with these posed shots:

- sorting clothing
- soaking the most soiled garments
- gently lathering and rinsing light fabrics
- soaking briefly in a bucket of herbal rinse-water
- rinsing in flowing stream
- wringing and spreading wash over bushes or temporary clotheslines
- pounding soaked clothes between rocks
- hanging remaining laundry to dry
- folding dry laundry and packing in a basket or hamper

Create a similar still-photo scenario with shot sequences depicting baking yeast bread, freshening mattresses and pillows, ironing starched garments, churning butter, canning pickles, planting and digging potatoes, winnowing and grinding grain, sewing a hem, weaving wool thread, cultivating and harvesting corn, feeding a baby, making buckskin moccasins, cleaning fish, or polishing shoes. Use no modern gadgetry. Rely on primitive methods from early times.

Budget: $$$$

Sources:

Conkelton, Sheryl, and Carol S. Eliel. *Annette Messager*. Abrams Books, 1995.

Lowe, Sarah M. *Tina Modotti: Photographs*. Abrams Books, 1995.

Oehler, Rosemarie. "Witness to the Harvest." *World Vision Partners,* winter 1994–1995, 2–7.

Zurkowsky, Herb. "Frozen on Film." *Montreal Gazette,* June 5, 1995, 8D.

Alternative Applications: Create a photo album of women in your area performing these and other rigorous, heavy, or repetitive chores:

answering a switchboard	baking sourdough bread
canning peaches	assembling window displays
hanging draperies	packing boxes
shopping for groceries	stocking shelves
typing	waiting on tables
washing an infant	weeding flower beds

Order your pictures in the most demonstrative arrangement to give your subject dignity and worth. Make no comment. Let the pictures speak for themselves.

What *are women made of?*

Age/Grade Level or Audience: Elementary or middle school art project; home-school or art museum workshop; children's craft contest or summer library handwork; women's club competition; cooperative community crafts tutorial.

Description: Study the crafts of women living during the Victorian era.

Procedure: Invite local craft experts to form a volunteer consortium. Divide participants into groups for training in crafts typically performed by women of the Victorian era, such as candlewicking, quilting, and appliqué. Include these activities:

- Collect and dry rose blossoms, mint, lavender, nasturtiums, and strawflowers for potpourri. Blend with drops of fragrant oil and sew into sachets or pour into bowls for air freshener.

- Make a tool for spool knitting by hammering four small finishing nails around the inner edge of a wooden spool end or hollow dowel. Loosely loop thin cotton yarn around each nail in a clockwise pattern. Continue around a second time by drawing the free end of the yarn lightly against the next nail and lifting the loop below it over the yarn and the top of the nail. Continue around the four nails as the spool knitting drops out the bottom of the spool. When rope reaches the desired length, tie off ends. To make a belt or curtain tie, apply tassels to ends of knitted cord and decorate with a button or sea shell.

- Make lacy Christmas ornaments or doilies by tatting or crocheting with delicate cotton yarn. Spray with starch to add body to finished craft items.

- Paint china platters, flower vases, and urns with views of wildflowers and birds.

- Position models before a lighted screen and snip their silhouettes out of black paper. Paste to matting or scalloped doily. Frame or attach to a suncatcher.

- Press wildflowers and garden blossoms between blotting paper and put between the pages of heavy books for several days. Tint dried plants with watercolors and arrange on note paper, mat board, coasters, place mats, or wall hangings. Glue in position and spray with a light varnish, if appropriate.

- Weave lengths of ribbon into a square. Press and sew edges into place. Sew two squares together and stuff with acrylic for a pillow or pin cushion.

Budget: $$$$$

Sources:

Hiney, Mary J. *Victorian Ribbon and Lacecraft Designs*. Sterling, 1993.

Johnson, Ceci. *Quick and Easy Ways with Ribbon*. Chilton, 1993.

Lierman, Deonna, and Andy Rector, eds. *An Ark Full of Crafts: For a Boatload of Fun*. Standard Publications, 1993.

Marsh, Tracy, ed. *Victorian Crafts*. Trafalgar, 1993.

Mayne, Maggie M. *Floral Stencils for Interior Design*. HarperCollins, 1993.

137 Crafts for Kids. Meredith Books, 1995.

Alternative Applications: Study a list of acceptable hobbies for young Victorian women. Add drawings of girls in aprons, smocks, and pinafores intently working at a craft. Note that interest in nature or physical education was generally not allowed because young ladies were disgraced by sweating in public. Even croquet and badminton were considered to be rather daring at first because female participants sometimes became too involved in the competition.

Woman *as sculptor*

Age/Grade Level or Audience: Elementary, middle school, or high school art lesson; lecture series; art museum workshop; museum or library display; civic exhibit.

Description: Study the sculpture of women artists.

Procedure: Design a book display outlining the creative efforts of female sculptors: fountains, museum pieces, bas-relief, monuments, and architectural ornament. Highlight these works:

- Augusta Savage's *Lift Every Voice and Sing*

- Barbara Hepworth's *Mother and Child* and *Sea Form*

- Camille Claudel's mythic characters

- Edmonia Lewis's *Death of Cleopatra* and *Henry Wadsworth Longfellow*

- Elisabet Ney's portrait busts

- Faith Ringgold's *The Family of Woman*

- Harriet Hosmer's *Zenobia*

- Judy Chicago's *The Dinner Party*

- Louise Nevelson's found objects

- Magdalena Abakanowicz's wood sculpture

- Maya Lin's Vietnam Memorial

- Miriam Schapiro's collage

Summarize commentary from numerous sources on the work of women artists working in bronze, marble, clay, papier-mâché, welded iron, wood, mixed media, and found objects.

Budget: $$

Sources:

Camille Claudel. Critics Choice, n.d. (Video)

Goddard, Peter. "Density in Flight." *Montreal Gazette,* June 3, 1995, 6H.

Hay, Susannah. *The Women's Heritage Scrapbook.* Caillech Press, 1992.

Martin, Jean, gen. ed. *Who's Who of Women in the Twentieth Century.* Crescent Books, 1995.

Naylor, Colin, ed. *Contemporary Artists.* St. James Press, 1995.

Alternative Applications: Have participants of high school age or above screen the movie *Camille Claudel* (Cannon Films, 1988), which received Oscar nominations for Isabelle Adjani's starring role and for best foreign film. Provide a biographical overview of Claudel's study with mentor Auguste Rodin, the physical labor involved in her work, the failed love relationship between Claudel and Rodin, Rodin's intimidation, and Claudel's mental collapse. Conclude with a panel discussion of the frustrations and pressures experienced by women who seek their own path in artistic expression and the rewards that often come to creative people long after their death.

Women *in art*

Age/Grade Level or Audience: Adult art appreciation research topic; art museum workshop; museum or library display; civic symposium; travel column or local arts newsletter feature.

Description: Lead a symposium discussing the standard poses in art.

Procedure: Present a slide program or collection of art prints, lithographs, photographs of sculpture and bas relief, and posters of the world's most famous female models. Note the following patterns:

- disdainful rulers (*Nefertiti; Queen Victoria*)
- idlers (*Le Dejeuner sur l'Herbe; The Clothed Maja*)
- mythic women (*The Statue of Liberty; Venus de Milo; Winged Victory of Samothrace; Blind Justice; Sacajawea*)
- pure women (*Rest on the Flight into Egypt; Pietà; The White Girl; The Family of Woman; The Betrothal;* Degas's ballerinas)
- teasing or alluring women (*The Gypsy; Mona Lisa; The Naked Maja; Jane Avril Dansant*)
- toiling women (*The Gleaners; Hagar in the Wilderness*)
- the Virgin Mary (*The Madonna of the Rocks; The Black Madonna; The Flight into Egypt; The Annunciation*)
- women in distress or under attack (*The Rape of the Sabine Women; Pietà; Leda and the Swan; The Weeping Woman; Ophelia; Guernica*)

Contrast the work of notable female artists that naturalizes the poses of mother and child, meals, rituals, work scenes, or women in outdoor settings. Begin with this list:

Camille Billops

Rosa Bonheur

Selma Hortese Burke

Ralba Carriera

Mary Cassatt

Elizabeth Catlett

Barbara Chase-Riboud

Jane A. Davis

Edna Hibel

Clementine Hunter

Lois Mailou Jones

Frida Kahlo

Edmonia Lewis

Berthe Morisot

Alice Neel

Mattie Lou O'Kelley

Lyubov Popova

Augusta Savage

Budget: $$

Sources:

At the Louvre with the Masters. Crystal, 1995. (Video)

Bailey, Brooke. *The Remarkable Lives of 100 Women Artists.* Bob Adams, Inc., 1994.

Gustafson, Fred. *The Black Madonna.* Sigo Press, 1991.

Hay, Susannah. *The Women's Heritage Scrapbook.* Caillech Press, 1992.

Latino Art and Culture in the United States. Crystal, 1995. (Multimedia)

Linnea in Monet's Garden. Crystal 1995. (Video)

Microsoft Art Gallery. Crystal, 1995. (CD-ROM)

Notable Women Artists. Knowledge Unlimited, 1995. (Posters)

Women in Art. Fawcett, 1991.

Alternative Applications: In a formal lecture, slide presentation, or chalk talk, summarize the conventions that developed around the Virgin Mary in painting, sculpture, and bas-relief. Note that she is usually portrayed as pale, slender, dark-haired, and usually much younger than her husband. She is often depicted as she nestles with or gazes down at her child. In other poses, her eyes and attention are fixed at the crucified Christ, at an angel, upward, or inward. Her gestures are simple, composed, or filled with awe; her actions are limited. Her clothing tends to be a shapeless white tunic gathered in empire style and draped with a blue cape or stole to conceal hair, hips, and breasts. The colors blue and white symbolize purity and loyalty or consecration. Symbolic additions often include a lily, rose, halo, sacred heart, or aura to imply virginity and piety.

Business *and labor*

Barbie, *girl in a million*

Age/Grade Level or Audience: Middle school or high school discussion; women's studies series; business or adolescent psychology research topic; Business and Professional Women's League presentation; newspaper column.

Description: Discuss the Barbie doll phenomenon.

Procedure: Lead a panel discussion of doll history, from eye-shutting baby dolls, drink-and-wet dolls, and walking and talking dolls to the invention of Barbie in 1959, a multi-million dollar business spawned by Ruth Handler and marketed by Mattel. Consider the following debate of feminist and parental concerns:

- carefree, irresponsible attitude; air of sophistication or self-absorption in fashion, hairstyles, possessions, and appearance
- breast-centered, figure-enhancing fashions, poses engineered to give maximum exposure to Barbie's buxom figure in advertising photos
- influence of an idealistically proportioned doll body on girls' eating disorders, particularly bulimia and anorexia nervosa
- affect of a statuesque, white-skinned role model on a broad range of girls and boys from various ethnic backgrounds, genetic makeups, and physiques
- materialistic values encouraged by Barbie accessories, Ken and other doll companions, bloated wardrobes and paraphernalia, and high-pressure advertising

Determine how a focus on Barbie has influenced over three decades of young girls and what values and expectations the doll instills in children concerning body shape, skin color, and suitable activities for girls and women.

Budget: $

Sources:

Healy, Michelle. "Brain behind Barbie." *USA Today,* March 9, 1994, 5D.

Jensen, Particia. *Barbie Show Time!* Western Publications, 1992.

Slate, Barbara. *Barbie.* Marvel Entertainment, 1992.

Theriault, Florence, ed. *Barbie: A Value Guide and Description of the Barbie Doll.* Gold Horse, 1994.

————. *Barbie Rarities.* Gold Horse, 1992.

Alternative Applications: Compose an essay, PTA handout, or editorial commenting on the formation of a strong positive self-image in girls. Describe the types of toys that encourage healthy concerns and behaviors. Include a list of children's animated feature films that promote the "Barbie doll stereotype"; for example, *Pocahontas, Snow White, Aladdin,* and *Cinderella.*

Factory *girls*

Age/Grade Level or Audience: High school or college history or business class or club presentation; union or small business association lecture series; Business and Professional Women's League forum; newspaper column or newsletter; investment club or women's studies seminar; civic clubs, Chamber of Commerce or merchants' association history display.

Description: Present a bulletin-board display on the nineteenth-century American factory system and women workers.

Procedure: Stress the influence of patriarchy on the factory system, which looked to women—usually single, uneducated, rural, and poor—for cheap, malleable labor. Along with drawings of machinery, bobbins, water wheels, yarn, and hands threading machines, include the following data:

- Francis Cabot Lowell studied English looms in 1811 and returned to Waltham, Massachusetts, to harness his own version to the current of the Charles River. With cheap power, he believed he could profitably clean fibers, pick and card, weave, print, and ship finished cloth from his Lowell Manufacturing Company.

- After his death, other entrepreneurs attempted the same alliance of free power and onsite completion of the cloth-making process. To keep costs low, recruiters hired rural women and children (who would work cheaper than men and make fewer demands on management) and transported them by wagons, called "slavers," to their factories.

- The lure of the Lowell factories was ready cash, averaging $3.50 per week. After paying half of their earnings back to the company for board in company-owned housing and food from the company store, workers sent the rest to their families or saved for a dowry. However, a fall in prices forced mill owners to adapt to the market slide by cutting piece rates and wages, firing experienced laborers, and hiring immigrants, who worked cheaper than the Lowell women.

- The workers liked living near the sea and being in a more cosmopolitan atmosphere than their farm backgrounds had provided. Their private lives were closely monitored and attendance at the local Episcopal church was obligatory.

- The workweek encompassed thirteen hours per day Monday through Friday and eight hours on Saturday for a total of 73 hours. Inside the mill, the atmosphere was stifling, with steam, machine oil, and kerosene lamp fumes. Windows were often bricked shut to eliminate distractions. Workers frequently lost fingers or hanks of hair in open machine works and succumbed to brown lung disease from inhaling cotton fibers.

- Memorable feminists from this milieu include abolitionist Harriet Hanson Robinson, union organizer Sarah Bagley, and poet Lucy Larcom, all of whom share unpleasant vignettes of life at the Lowell mills.

Budget: $$

Sources:

Bader, Bonnie. *East Side Story*. Kaleidoscope Press, 1993.

Coherty, Jonathan L., ed. *Women at Work: 153 Photographs by Lewis W. Hine*. Dove Publications, 1987.

Cornish, Mary, and Lynn Spink. *Organizing Unions*. Second Story Press, 1995.

Dublin, Thomas, ed. *Farm to Factory: Women's Letters, 1830–1860*. Columbia University Press, 1993.

Goldin, Barbara Diamond. *Fire! The Beginnings of the Labor Movement*. Viking, 1992.

Jensen, Joan M., ed. *With These Hands*. Feminist Press, 1995.

Kent, Zachary. *The Story of the Triangle Factory Fire*. Children's Press, 1989.

Kessler-Harris, Alice. *Women Have Always Worked: A Historical Overview*. Feminist Press, 1995.

King, Lydia. *Factory Women in Taiwan*. Morningside, 1994.

Larcom, Lucy. *A New England Girlhood*. Corner House, 1995.

Michelson, Maureen R., ed. *Women and Work: In Their Own Words*. NewSage Press, 1995.

Plight and Progress: The Papers of Gertrude Tuckwell, Trade Unionist. Research Publications, 1995. (Microfilm)

Selden, Bernice. *The Mill Girls*. Atheneum, 1983.

Stern, Madeleine B. *We the Women: Career Firsts of Nineteenth-Century America*. University of Nebraska Press, 1995.

Weisman, JoAnne B. *The Lowell Mill Girls: Life in the Factory*. Discovery Enterprises, 1991.

Weisz, Pam. "Workers' Rites of Passage." *Humanities*, September/October 1994, 13–17.

What You Take for Granted. Women Make Movies, Inc., 1994. (Video)

Alternative Applications: Present differing views on these labor issues as they relate to women and families:

- affirmative action
- closed shops
- downsizing
- environment
- health insurance and HMO's
- lockouts
- mill villages
- OSHA
- "riffing"
- scabs
- sexual harassment
- Triangle Shirtwaist Factory fire
- unionism
- Worker's Compensation

Screen *Norma Rae*, *The Dollmaker*, *Matewan*, or *Silkwood* and discuss managerial tactics that reflect the quandary of the Lowell factory women and other workers trapped by limited opportunities or intimidation within a patriarchal or exploitative system. Suggest ways that women can join together in efforts to defeat manipulative, opportunistic employers and entrepreneurs interested in profits at any cost.

Fire *in the Triangle shirtwaist factory*

Age/Grade Level or Audience: Elementary library reading circle or vocabulary presentation; elementary lesson in phonetics; middle school study of labor history; read-aloud prompt for English-as-a-second-language discussion.

Description: Read aloud a short history of the Triangle Shirtwaist Factory fire and develop a glossary of significant labor terms.

Procedure: Present an oral reading of Bonnie Bader's *East Side Story*. Have participants take notes as they listen and ask questions about difficult words or phrases. Write these terms on the chalkboard. Divide participants into small groups to create a pronunciation key for the book. Place on the chalkboard or a wall chart the h-base pronunciation system to help participants write phonetic spellings of unfamiliar terms. Use the following sounds:

a as in lamb	[lam]	ih as in lip	[lihp]
ah as in lock	[lahk]	oh as in loaf	[lohf]
aw as in laud	[lawd]	oo as in lose	[looz]
ay as in lace	[lays]	ow as in loud	[lowd]
ee as in leak	[leek]	uh as in lump	[luhmp]
eh as in left	[lehft]	y as in light	[lyt]

Have participants concentrate on these terms from the book:

boarder	jurors	shirtwaist
bureau	league	sponsor
Catholic	manslaughter	strike
challah	memorial	strikebreaker
commission	organizers	supervisor
demonstrator	peddler	sweatshop
guarantee	promote	tenement
herring	pushcart	union
immigrant	reform	verdict
inspection	saloon	Yiddish

Have students complete each entry with an original illustrative sentence that refers to the work of female cutters and sewers at the Triangle Shirtwaist Factory. Follow this model: Many of the seamers had to whisper to their associates in *Yiddish* because not all women workers understood directions in English.

Budget: $

Sources:

Bader, Bonnie. *East Side Story*. Kaleidoscope Press, 1993.

Dublin, Thomas, ed. *Farm to Factory: Women's Letters, 1830–1860*. Columbia University Press, 1981.

Goldin, Barbara Diamond. *Fire! The Beginnings of the Labor Movement*. Viking, 1992.

Kent, Zachary. *The Story of the Triangle Factory Fire*. Children's Press, 1989.

O'Sullivan, Judith, and Rosemary Gallick. *Workers and Allies: Female Participation in the American Trade Union Movement, 1824–1976*. Smithsonian Institution Press, 1975.

Railroad Women. Women Make Movies, Inc., 1994. (Video)

Selden, Bernice. *The Mill Girls*. Atheneum, 1983.

Trade Secrets: Blue Collar Women Speak Out. Women Make Movies, Inc., 1994. (Video)

Weisman, JoAnne B. *The Lowell Mill Girls: Life in the Factory*. Discovery Enterprises, 1991.

Women of Steel. Women Make Movies, Inc., 1994. (Video)

Alternative Applications: Have readers of Bonnie Bader's *East Side Story* draw a Venn diagram, which is composed of two interlinking circles. Ask volunteers to list in the left circle the concerns of laborers and in the far right the aims of managers. Place in the overlapping section any terms that affect both laborers and managers. Use the following diagram as a beginning:

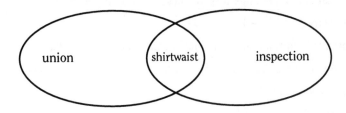

Get a job; make a career

Age/Grade Level or Audience: Middle school, high school or college career fair; Business and Professional Women's League or YWCA newsletter; small business association seminar; newspaper column or newsletter; women's studies forum; educational radio or television presentation; civic club, Chamber of Commerce, or merchants' association career day.

Description: Organize a forum where speakers and presenters can encourage women in the professions, business, or the arts.

Procedure: Hold career day during Women's History Month. Invite successful local women to speak on the following topics:

- bookkeeping, tax accounting, investment advice
- desktop publishing and advertising
- floral arranging, horticulture, and lawn care
- home-centered businesses in freelance writing, editing, and art
- law and law enforcement
- medicine, medical technology, home health care
- pet grooming, training, and boarding
- photography, graphic arts, design, and portraiture
- sewing, upholstery, draperies, or tailoring

Present students or potential employees with such significant information as the state of the job market, local training centers, approximate cost of education and of setting up in business, partnerships and franchises, investment opportunities, Keogh plans, investment clubs, and other methods of assuring income and health care for home and family.

Feature a particularly successful story, preferably one that local people can readily identify with. For example, distribute handouts naming these women:

- Paula Cholmondeley, president of Miraflex Products
- Gun Denharat's Hanna Andersson Corporation
- Freda Ehmann, founder of Ehmann Olive Products
- Ann M. Fudge, president of Maxwell House Coffee

- Ruth Handler, creator of Nearly Me
- Michele J. Hooper, president of Caremark International
- Brenda J. Lauderbak, President of Wholesale Group footwear
- publisher Mary Ann Liebert
- Irene Natividad, founder and principal of Natividad and Associates
- Francis Preston, president and C.E.O. of the Broadcast Music Association
- financier Muriel Siebert
- Bonnie Tempesta, owner of La Tempesta Bakery
- Julia Tuttle, Miami land developer

Highlight the accomplishments of these Women of Enterprise Award winners:

- Judi Bliss, publisher of Mindplay institute
- Gail Davis, owner of K.D.Y. Enterprise
- contracter Olga Mapula, owner of The Communications Group
- Barbara Robinson, founder of Star Associates training institute
- Paula Washow, president of Alpha Omega Security

Also, describe the success of one newcomer in business, for example, Betty Carrington-Griffin:

In 1988, Betty Carrington-Griffin moved to Perry, Oklahoma, and began a couturier business from her home. To augment domestic sewing, she hired workers and specialized in imported African fabrics. She produces home fashion shows featuring a professional model and offers a 25% commission to the hostess who displays her goods. Betty likes owning her own business because she makes her own schedule and her work involves constant contact with fabrics, boutiques, design students and clients, mail order business, and new challenges, including Hollywood, where she made Kente-print garments for *The Lion King*. To boost business, she hosts a Black History Month and numerous bridal fashion shows and highlights original garments designed by her team of workers.

Budget: $$$

Sources:

Adler, Jerry. "The Rise of the Overclass." *Newsweek*, July 31, 1995, 32–46.
"African Fabrics Marketer." *Vocational Biographies Inc.*, 1995.
Bamford, Janet. "The Working Woman 50." *Working Women*, May 1995, 37–61.
Career Discovery Encyclopedia. Rosen, 1993.
Careers Discovery Library. Rourke, 1995.
Careers: Professional Pursuits. Rosen, 1995. (Video series)
Edwards, Loraine, and Midge Stocker, eds. *The Woman-Centered Economy: Ideals, Reality, and the Space in Between.* Third Side Press, 1995.
Encyclopedia of Careers and Vocational Guidance. Rosen, 1993. (CD-ROM)
Fisher, Anne B. "When Will Women Get to the Top?" *Fortune*, September 21, 1992, 44–56.
Green, Lisa. "Businesswomen Overcame the Odds." *USA Today*, June 23, 1995, 3B.
Kasindorf, Jeanie Russell. "Martha, Inc." *Working Woman*, June 1995, 26–31, 66, 68–69.
Norment, Lynn. "50 Years of Progress in Corporate America." *Ebony*, April 1995, 99–114B.
Paul, Marla. "What Do You Want to Be When You Grow Up?" *Chicago Tribune*, June 25, 1995, Sect. 6, 1.
Rubenstein, Carie. "Lifelines of the Rich and Famous." *Money*, fall 1988, 132–134.

Also, reference librarians, vocational biographies, business magazines and trade papers, including *Forbes, INC, Business World, W, U.S. News and World Report, Wall Street Journal, Barrons,* and online sources such as Newsbank, Silver Platter, and the Internet.

Alternative Applications: Present capsule biographies of women who have attained their goals in a particular field. For example, for a meeting of girls and women interested in law, have members of the local bar association discuss the success of these attorneys:

- American Airlines chief legal officer Anne McNamara
- American Corporate Counsel Association chair Sara Holtz
- American Express legal counsel Louise M. Parent
- American Online legal counsel Ellen Kirsch
- Black Entertainment Television chief legal officer Debra Lee
- corporate attorney Hilary Rodham Clinton
- counsel for Aetna Life and Casualty Zoë Baird
- Federal Home Loan Mortgage legal counsel Maud Mater
- Halston Borghese attorney Lisa Whitney
- law professor Anita Hill
- Los Angeles public defender Marcia Clark
- Supreme Court judge Ruth Bader Ginsburg

Allow time for one-on-one counseling, panel discussions, short presentations on special interests, videos, demonstrations, and presentations on the possibilities of blending law with public service, politics, accounting, the military, or journalism.

Hi-ho! *Come to our fair*

Age/Grade Level or Audience: Community farmer's market; growers' association consortium; small business association project; newspaper column, open forum, or educational radio or television presentation; civic clubs, Chambers of Commerce, or merchants' association fair.

Description: Organize a co-op or seasonal farmer's market to showcase the contributions of local farm women and to highlight the value of female settlers and entrepreneurs to the area.

Procedure: At a vacant parking lot, fairgrounds, field, school, church, abandoned warehouse, or public gathering spot, set up a regular farmer's market or direct-to-consumer co-op one day per week to market these products and services:

- baked and canned goods, pickles, relish
- Christmas greenery, dried arrangements, craft items
- clothing, linens, and other woven wares
- dairy items, including cheese, dips, spreads, eggs, and cream
- fruit, vegetables, nuts, spices, herbs
- house plants, seed packets, seedlings, shrubbery

31

- jewelry

- jams and jellies, honey and molasses

- live animals and pets

- potpourri, fragrances, candles

- pottery

Consider anything made, produced, harvested, raised, decorated, and sold by women. In addition to direct sales, advertise these services:

- advertising, free-lance writing and editing

- antiques and antiquing

- cleaning, decorating, or catering

- cosmetics, hair and nail care

- custom decorative painting, needlework

- handwriting classes and custom calligraphy

- interior design services

- landscaping and pond construction

- lessons in swimming, golf, tennis, tai chi, karate, ta kwon do or other self defense, and dance instruction

- massage, yoga, or Lamaze classes

- photography, portraiture, and art lessons

- pick-your-own gardens, tree farms, orchards, and vineyards

- tutoring, summer classes, and specialized care for the handicapped or elderly

Distribute brochures at libraries, schools, visitors' bureaus, hotels, area magazines, and highway rest stops. Display banners and posters along with advertisements for farms, ranches, and home businesses. Provide the following:

- elected board of directors and manager

- set day and time limit

- alternatives for bad weather

- access to change and other banking services

- road signs and markers

- covered trestle tables, tarps, or sheds

- scales and free containers in a variety of sizes

- free samples, for example, chunks of melon or cups of hot cider

- attractive and clean facilities, including restrooms and water fountains

- parking and shuttle service for the elderly and handicapped

- refreshments including fruit juice, hot pastries, popcorn, fruit, or light snacks

- follow-up articles in local media to announce success, offer new services, or extend hours

As a commemoration of community history, create a pamphlet or monograph detailing the contributions of women and their families who settled the area and established farms, industries, wineries, orchards, herds, and other small businesses. Use as models Eliza Tibbetts, planter of the first navel orange trees in the New World; Freda Ehmann, founder of the California olive industry; and Julia Tuttle, Florida crop developer. Include a map of the area with arrows pointing to pick-your-own gardens, places of interest, museums, guided walking tours, pueblos, reservations, communes, missions, and other historical sites. List hours, entrance fees, access for the handicapped and small children, gift shops, and entertainment, particularly covered picnic tables, amusement parks, outdoor dramas, and dining facilities featuring live performances.

Budget: $$$$

Sources:

Griffin, Lynne, and Kelly McCann. *The Book of Women: 300 Notable Women History Passed By*. Bob Adams, 1992.

Katzenstein, Herbert. *Direct Marketing*. C. E. Merrill, 1986.

The Livelong Day: Working in the World. Rosen, 1992.

Minding My Own Business. Landmark Media, Inc., 1993. (Series of six videos)

A Web Not a Ladder. Landmark Media, Inc., 1994. (Video)

Contact county agents, U.S. Small Business Administration, local health department, state department of agriculture, Home Demonstration Club, 4-H, Girl Scouts, church women's leagues, League of Women Voters, sororities, genealogical societies, history clubs, and Friends of the Library.

Alternative Applications: Create a business fair to showcase local female entrepreneurs. Distribute business cards, forms for advance orders or specialty items, monogramming service, recipes, brief county histories, songs featuring local people and their accomplishments, and religious services or hymns conducted by women. Decorate wall space with posters naming women in the community who pioneered such offerings as herbal medicine, midwifery, dame schools, needlecrafts, cosmetology, innkeeping, cafés, catering, and home nurse care. Invite a school or community college art class to make display sketches of historic homes, slave quarters, spring houses, tobacco barns, sheepcotes, pueblos, fisheries, and potting sheds.

The *language of business*

Age/Grade Level or Audience: Middle school or high school language or vocabulary study; women's study seminar; business or journalism research topic; Business and Professional Women's League presentation; newspaper column.

Description: Focus a discussion group on terms traditionally applied in the business world, along with those that have recently evolved, and their subsequent effect on women in the workplace.

Procedure: Divide participants into groups to study the implications of words as applied to men and women in the business world. Consider these terms and their applications to jobs and advancement:

assertiveness	leadership	restructuring
balance of power	mommy track	role model

empowerment	networking	team player
facilitator	old boy network	tunnel vision
flex time	open-minded	values-negative
gender neutral	p.c.	wage gap
glass ceiling	performance review	want-it-all
holistic	power base	wanna-be manager
househusband	reinventing business	

Define jingoism as it applies to the business world. Explain how catchphrases can deflate efforts to equalize opportunities for all. Further, explore what terms have historically been considered acceptable in the workplace, and which terms would never have been used in the past (e.g., househusband). Conclude with a debate on affirmative action and its affect on both women and minorities.

Budget: $

Sources:

Aburdene, Patricia, and John Naisbitt. *Megatrends for Women*. Random House, 1992.

Maggio, Rosalie. *The Dictionary of Bias-Free Usage: A Guide to Nondiscriminatory Language*. Oryx, 1991.

Mills, Jane. *Womanwords*. Macmillan, 1989.

Alternative Applications: Search newspapers and magazines, letters, cartoons, radio advertisements, film clips, TV newscasts, and business journals and form a hit list of pictures, phrases, and words that have become outmoded due to the greater equality of men and women within the workplace. Discuss the continued usage of terms such as Workmen's Compensation, chairman, man's work, pink-collar ghetto, steno pool, and waitress. Create a bulletin board or scrapbook or hold a symposium suggesting ways that women can be drawn into a bias-free, gender-neutral marketplace as investors, workers, buyers, consumers, managers, partners, and owners.

Mad *and sad about ads*

Age/Grade Level or Audience: Elementary, middle school, or high school journalism or creative writing activity; college marketing class focus; Friends of the Library project; media feature; civic club or women's club symposium; Chamber of Commerce display.

Description: Conduct a workshop on the evolution of the portrayal of women in advertising.

Procedure: Organize a study of women in the advertising of decades past. Select a representative sample of magazines with general appeal: *Life, Look, Reader's Digest, McCall's, Ladies Home Journal, Post, People, Time, U.S. News and World Report, Fortune, Forbes,* and *Newsweek.* Have participants begin in the current year and complete the following exercises:

- Count the total number of full-page ads in one issue.

- Compute the percentage of full-page ads featuring women.

- List poses under a variety of headings—doing housework, caring for children, cooking, relaxing, shopping, performing a traditionally "male-only" craft or skill, sharing work with a mate, competing in sports, working at a "pink-collar" job, working in a professional capacity, being awarded for achievements, or serving as an adornment to a male escort.

Have participants perform the same study on an issue from the same month and day exactly ten years ago. Continue this study as far back as you have issues and time to study them. Appoint a spokesperson from each group to comment on stereotypes, portrayal of women as housewives with little comprehension of problem-solving techniques, and the relegation of women of color to roles as menials, caregivers, maids, or cooks. Ask participants to draw conclusions about the picture of developing empowerment of women as portrayed in the media.

Budget: $$

Sources:

"The Divas of Madison Avenue." *USA Today,* June 12, 1995, 3B.

Gross, Michael. *Model.* W. W. Morrow, 1996.

Myers, Jack. *Adbashing: Surviving the Attacks on Advertising.* American Media, 1993.

Roman, Kenneth, and Jane Masas. *The New How to Advertise.* St. Martin, 1992.

Weir, Walter. *How to Create Interest-evoking, Sales-inducing, Non-irritating Advertising.* Haworth, 1992.

Wells, Melanie. "Ad Breakthrough." *USA Today,* June 12, 1995, 1B.

Wright, John S., and John Mertes. *Advertising's Role in Society.* Books on Demand, 1994.

Alternative Applications: Have participants study some of publishing's most long-lived symbols of women in text, audio, or video advertisements or on the labels of products they represent. Stress the most recognizable figures:

Aunt Jemima (syrup)	Ivory girl (soap)
Betty Crocker (baking)	Mabel (beer)
Breck girl (shampoo)	Mrs. Paul (frozen foods)
Campbell Kids (soup)	Sara Lee (desserts)
Coppertone girl (suntan lotion)	St. Pauli Girl (beer)

Comment on advertisers' alterations in the dress, behavior, features, cultural orientation, age, and race of such female symbols over the years. Also, name and describe efforts to sell personal items, particularly deodorants, depilatories, razors, palliatives for menstrual cramps and PMS, sanitary pads and tampons, douche solutions, vaginal creams and sprays, condoms, women's laxatives, incontinence supplies, and other products aimed primarily at a female audience.

Wagons *west:* the *rush for gold*

Age/Grade Level or Audience: Elementary, middle school, or high school history/art activity; school or community art presentation; after-school activity; women's studies consortium; local women's history celebration.

Description: Sponsor a wall mural featuring women's roles in the settlement of the West.

Procedure: Organize a local contest or competition in which groups prepare a mural, multi-panel cartoon, mosaic, life-size shadow box, or diorama of women's roles in the settlement of the west, particularly during the gold rush years. Depict peripheral historical data on the telegraph and railroad, stage and wagon mail and parcel delivery, entertainment, health care, inns and restaurants, agriculture and farming, and the creation of permanent settlements. Consider the following dramatic scenarios as models:

- In the 1850s and 1860s, Plains and Coastal Indian families as well as Mexican families were dispossessed by prospectors. Tribes such as the Sioux, Arapaho, and Cheyenne were ousted from their land because their villages lay in the path of the Bozeman Trail, which led to gold fields in Montana. Theodora Kroeber's biography of the Indian Ishi reports that his adopted cousin disappeared while in flight from white frontiersmen and that his mother and grandmother died while in hiding.

- In 1849 female café managers, laundresses, barbers, boardinghouse mistresses, and innkeepers offered amenities to people hurrying to take advantage of the gold rush at Sutter's Mill, at the juncture of the Sacramento and American rivers. Eliza Jane Forest, posing as Mountain Charley, ran a saloon in Nevadaville. Charlie Parkhurst, also a woman in man's clothing, concealed her sex for several decades while driving stages for Wells Fargo. Because gambling and drinking offered an outlet for male energies and frustrations, women set up gambling parlors or worked as blackjack and faro dealers and supervised game of rondo, chuck-a-luck, three-card monte, and wheel of fortune. Churches and towns sponsored socials, spelling bees, corn shuckings, hymn fests, picnics, athletic contests, fiestas, rodeos, and dances.

- Western cities as cosmopolitan as San Francisco suffered a lack of teachers, cooks, laundresses, and nurses, who could consequently command a high wage for their work. In 1847 the city's population was 70% male. Diarist Sarah Royce commented that a homely woman could feel like a belle in a land where women were scarce. The unfavorable balance of sexes caused fights or shootings that often ended in serious injury or death. A harsh social backlash awaited men who married Indian women. Derided and excluded from local camaraderie, these men were known as "squaw men."

- Elizabeth Gunn traveled by ship from the East Coast around the South American horn and north to California in 1851, completing a grueling sea journey. Mary Jane Megquier made a similar journey from New York to Panama, where gold-rush inflation boosted prices for food and other necessities. Megquier's report estimates that 2,000 Americans inhabited Panama, a popular stopover en route to California. In letters to her daughter, she described the passage north from Panama to Acapulco, San Blas, San Diego, and Monterey.

- In her journal, Sarah Royce describes stocking a covered wagon, herding domestic animals, and following a copy of John Fremont's *Travels* as a trail guide from Salt Lake City to the "Golden Gate," a nickname for California. Along the way, her party became confused at the Humboldt River. Fellow traveller H. B. Scharmann noted that following a supper of a single cup of tea or coffee, his wife wept in despair as their wagon maneuvered along the trail in the dark.

- Margaret Frank commented that the dust that rose from the hard, crusty soil caused people to seek cover for their eyes and protection for breathing by tying handkerchiefs over their faces and wearing goggles. In a similar eyewitness account, Lucy Cook wrote in 1852 that a party of men stopped to dig a grave for a woman not yet dead of cholera.

- Before reaching the Truckee River in 1849, Sallie Hester attributed the death of oxen to fatigue, heat, and thirst. That same year, Margaret Haun reported assisting at the burial of a mother and infant whom fellow pioneers buried in unmarked cairns alongside the trail.

- In 1850 Margaret Fink quailed at trails lined with carcasses of dray animals, jettisoned bedding, clothes, and household articles as well as tools, firearms, and harnesses. Some families were forced to abandon all their possessions and make the journey on foot.

- A suggested tally of foods for the journey included 125 pounds of pork, 80 pounds of rice, 125 pounds of flour, ¼ bushel of onions, ½ bushel of beans, jugs of vinegar, crocks of pickles, and parcels of dried apples and peaches. In rainy weather, women often cooked under the wagon on a limited fire or served cold suppers.

- One 1849 diary entry depicted women and young girls near starvation, some eating grass to survive and dosing their families with brandy as the only source of painkiller.

- In an overview of camp life, Louise Clappe concluded that, in 1852, labor-intensive mining required a person to stir constantly with a hoe to wash gold from the slurry pouring through a sluice box. Other jobs, like dynamiting hillsides, ferrying loads of rocks for dumping, and making trips to town for assays, resulted in untimely deaths due to accident, injury, robbers, and claim-jumpers, leaving many women and children stranded.

- City women worked equally long, arduous jobs baking, ironing, and heating water for public baths and laundries. One nameless California letter-writer reported in 1849 that she had no time for socializing because her boardinghouse demanded all her energy, even though boarders provided their own plates and utensils and supplied her with foodstuffs to cook for them. Her boarders, equally overworked, cared more about gold than friendships or courtesy.

- Augusta Tabor, who managed a chain of three general stores during the Nevada silver strikes of the 1850s and 1860s, helped her husband Horace by taking her turn at the sluice box. She used a magnet to separate iron bits from ore. The Tabors earned millions by bankrolling prospectors in exchange for a portion of the profits.

- In Nevada City in 1850, hotel owner Luzena Stanley Wilson set up a trestle table from boards and stakes driven into the soil. On it she served twenty miners her first night in business. Because they cheerfully paid a dollar each, she named her hotel El Dorado.

Budget: $$$$

Sources:

Emert, Phyllis Raybin, ed. *All That Glitters: The Men and Women of the Gold and Silver Rushes.* Discovery Enterprises Ltd., 1995.

Kroeber, Theodore. *Ishi, Last of His Tribe.* Bantam, 1964.

Levenson, Dorothy. *Homesteaders and Indians.* Franklin Watts, 1971.

———. *Women of the West.* Franklin Watts, 1973.

Levy, Joann. *They Saw the Elephant.* Archon Books, 1990.

Miller, Brandon Marie. *Buffalo Gals: Women of the Old West.* Lerner Group, 1996.

Prairie Cabin: A Norwegian Pioneer Woman's Story. Instructional Video, 1991. (Video)

Rosebud Yellow Robe. *An Album of the American Indian.* Franklin Watts, 1971.

Sarah Plain and Tall. Critics Choice, n.d. (Video)

Schlissel, Lillian. *Women's Diaries of the Westward Journey.* Schocken, 1992.

Skylark. Critics Choice, n.d. (Video)

Stratton, Joanna L. *Pioneer Women: Voices from the Kansas Frontier.* Simon & Schuster, 1981.

Women of the West. Knowledge Unlimited, 1995. (Video)

Alternative Applications: Change the format of this exercise to a puppet show featuring felt or broadcloth hand puppets, bag puppets attached to wooden dowels, shadow actors behind a screen, or jointed dolls. Provide these and other backdrops:

assay office	conestoga wagon	Oregon Trail
boardinghouse	courthouse	Rocky Mountains
Boot Hill	depot	rodeo
Bozeman Trail	dugout	San Francisco
cabin	gallows	school
café	gambling hall	sod hut
camp	Indian reservation	stagecoach
Carson City	laundry	Sutter's Mill
cemetery	livery stable	trading post
church	mission	waystation

Stress any combination of locations central to the history of the gold rush era. Have participants study a variety of sources about the settlement of the West:

chronicles	filmstrips	photos
church documents	folklore	pulp fiction
costumes	histories	sketches
cowboy lore	legends	songs
diaries	letters	verse
editorials	maps	videos
epitaphs	microfilm	wanted posters

Emphasize the role of girls and women of all races and social levels. Characterize their share of the glory, work, risk, and profit.

What's *your pleasure—Miss, Mrs., or Ms.?*

Age/Grade Level or Audience: Middle school or high school language or business study; business or journalism research topic; Business and Professional Women's League or American University Women letter-writing presentation; newspaper column.

Description: Discuss the significance of terms, honorifics, and abbreviations attached to women's names.

Procedure: Present a chalkboard display or overhead projection of the terms usually applied to women's names. Include professional, religious, and military titles as well as marital status and plural forms, both as whole words and in abbreviated form:

Adm.	Judge	Mrs.
Attorney General	Ll.D.	M.S.
Atty.	Lt.	Ms.
Bishop	Lt. Col.	Ph.D.
B.S.	Lt., J.g.	Pres. Pro Tem.
Capt.	M.A.	Prof.
C.E.O.	Madam	Pvt.
Chair	mademoiselle	Rep.
Chairwoman	Maj.	Rev.
Chief Justice	Maj. Gen.	R.N.
Col.	M.B.A.	Sec.
Com.	M.D.	señora
Congresswoman	mesdames	Sgt.
D.D.	mesdamoiselles	Sir or Madam
doña	M.F.A.	Sister
Dr.	Miss	Sr.
D.V.M.	Mlle.	Supt.
Ed.-in-chief	Mmes.	Treas.
Gen.	M.P.	V.P.

Comment on the value of a term like Ms., which avoids the question of marital status in a business situation where such information is unnecessary. Have students create a wall of honor using some of the following people for starters: Sen. Carol Moseley-Braun, Sister Kenny, Rev. Mary Beth Turner, Dr. Joycelyn Elders, Ms. Sandra Cisneros, Col. Margarethe Cammermayer, Adm. Grace Hopper, Atty. Hillary Clinton, and Marcia Gillespie, ed.-in-chief. In addition, have groups of students design posters illustrating the appropriateness of gender-neutral terms.

Budget: $

Sources:

Maggio, Rosalie. *The Dictionary of Bias-Free Usage: A Guide to Nondiscriminatory Language.* Oryx, 1991.

———. *How to Say It.* Prentice Hall, 1990.

Mills, Jane. *Womanwords.* Macmillan, 1989.

Snodgrass, Mary Ellen. *Letter Writing.* Media Materials Publishing, 1991.

Alternative Applications: Choose partners and assume the identities of notable women, e. g., Florence Nightingale, R.N.; Madame Chiang; Mlle. Camille Claudel; Pres. Elizabeth Dole; Justice Sandra Day O'Connor; and Laurie N. Rozakis, Ph.D. Organize an exercise in writing

39

or typing business and social letters, invitations, and announcements to each other, including envelopes. Have each reply use the appropriate address for women of scholarly, military, or civil rank.

Women's *unions:*
e pluribus unum

Age/Grade Level or Audience: High school civics or history lesson; college history research topic; Women's History Month presentation on labor history; Business and Professional Women's League or League of Women Voters presentation.

Description: Compose a time line illustrating women's roles in union activity.

Procedure: Create a chronology of American women's push for equal pay and better working conditions. Include these data:

- On **December 5, 1791,** Alexander Hamilton, Secretary of the Treasury, lauded women and children for their contributions to American manufacturing.

- The first organized women's labor protest occurred in **1824** in Pawtucket, Rhode Island, and was sparked by longer hours and reduced piecework pay in a local weaving mill. The activism of these textiles workers, most of whom were women and children, spread to Baltimore, Maryland; Paterson, New Jersey; Dover, New Hampshire; Lynn, Massachusetts; and Philadelphia and Manayunk, Pennsylvania.

- The leaders of a Massachusetts shoebinders' strike of **1833** were members of the Female Society of Lynn, Massachusetts.

- In **October 1836,** textile workers in Lowell, Massachusetts, issued a prepared statement rejecting the "yoke of avarice."

- With the assistance of Elizabeth Cady Stanton, Lucretia Mott, and Elizabeth Oakes Smith, an integrated union called the Female Labor Reform Association formed in **1845** to fight both slavery and the exploitation of female workers. The cry for equality in labor brought Helen Keller, Susan B. Anthony, Mother Mary Harri Jones, Louisa May Alcott, and Charlotte Perkins Gilman into the controversy. Abraham Lincoln added his voice in support of the movement in **1860.**

- By **1861,** the obvious need for female laborers was made clear at the United States Arsenal in Watertown, Massachusetts, where women filled much-needed cartridges.

- The first national women's trade union, the Daughters of St. Crispin, united in **1869** in Lynn, Massachusetts.

- In **1886,** Leonora O'Reilly, aided by Josephine Shaw Lowell, Arria Huntington, and Mrs. Robert Abbé, founded the Working Women's Society.

- Crusader journalism exposed sweatshop conditions in "The Female Slaves of New York—Sweaters and Their Victims," in **1888.**

- In **1889,** Jane Addams and Ellen Gates Starr opened Hull House as a community aid and educational center for women.

- Professing to "guard the home," the National Women's Trade Union League was founded in **1903.**

- In **1909,** 20,000 immigrant seamstresses working in New York City revolted against management.

- Militant support from Emma Goldman, Elizabeth Gurley Flynn, Mother Jones, and Lucy Gonzalez Parsons was countered by charges of communism levied against such feminist union organizers of the International Workers of the World (IWW) in **1905.** Female strikers for the IWW collected money in Ohio, struck hops farms in California, and pressured factory managers in Pittsburgh, Pennsylvania, and Ludlow, Colorado. The peak of anger was reached after the Triangle Shirtwaist Company fire **March 25, 1911,** where locked doors condemned seamstresses to death from fire, smoke inhalation, and fatal leaps from the roof and windows. The backlash from management across the nation spawned acts of arson, murder, and vigilante beatings, killing Fannie Sellens in Brackenridge, Pennsylvania, and Ella May Wiggins, in Gastonia, North Carolina.

Budget: $

Sources:

Bader, Bonnie. *East Side Story*. Kaleidoscope Press, 1993.

Dublin, Thomas, ed. *Farm to Factory: Women's Letters, 1830–1860*. Columbia University Press, 1981.

Foner, Philip S. Women and the American Labor Movement. The Free Press, 1982.

Goldin, Barbara Diamond. *Fire! The Beginnings of the Labor Movement*. Viking, 1992.

Hooks, Janet M. *Women's Occupations through Seven Decades*. U.S. Government Printing Office, 1947.

O'Sullivan, Judith, and Rosemary Gallick. *Workers and Allies: Female Participation in the American Trade Union Movement, 1824–1976*. Smithsonian Institution Press, 1975.

Schneider, Dorothy, and Carl F. Schneider. *Women in the Workplace*. ABC-Clio, 1993.

Selden, Bernice. *The Mill Girls*. Atheneum, 1983.

Weatherford, Doris. *American Women's History*. Prentice Hall, 1994.

Weisman, JoAnne B. *The Lowell Mill Girls: Life in the Factory*. Discovery Enterprises, 1991.

Alternative Applications: Make a collage of political cartoons, photographs, and such slogans as "Molly M'Guire Men." Stress themes and scenes of militancy, armed intervention, racial unity among female workers, female degradation, child labor, class war, and solidarity among textile and mine workers. Inscribe a border with these names of prominent union leaders: Catherine De Rorre, Emma Tenaynca, Josephine Hulett, Selma Borchardt, Dolores Huerta, Elizabeth Hoeppel, Elizabeth Koontz, Lucy Parsons, Mary Moultrie, Mother Jones, Emma Goldman, and Olga Madar.

Cinema

Eleanor and *The Lion in Winter*

Age/Grade Level or Audience: High school or college history, French, or drama class; improvisation exercise; term paper topic; cinema or historical society round table; women's studies seminar; newspaper film column.

Description: Discuss the historical accuracy of *The Lion in Winter* from the perspective of Eleanor of Aquitaine.

Procedure: Read and summarize the details of the life of Eleanor of Aquitaine (1122–1204), wife of King Louis VII of France and later of King Henry II of England, one of the most powerful women in history. List these details:

- duchess of Aquitaine—a large, powerful region in southwestern France—and countess of Poitiers—center of learning, art, and courtly sophistication and wit

- queen of France (1137–1152) until divorced by Louis Capet for failing to produce a male heir

- married Henry Plantagenet and became Queen of England with properties reaching from Scotland to Spain

- shocked the populace by joining the Second Crusade at age 25 and traveling with troops of men and monks

- mother of Marie, Alix, Henry, King Richard the Lion-hearted, Geoffrey, King John, Matilda, Joanna, and Eleanor of Castile

- lost Henry to his mistress, Rosamond Clifford

- connived with sons Henry and Richard in 1173 to try and spark an English rebellion against King Henry

- spent years in an English prison at Henry's insistence until his death in 1189

- mourned her favorite son, Richard, one of history's most ardent warriors, who died while king of England in 1199

Contrast the truth of Eleanor's life with the implications of the triple Academy Award-winning film, which depicts the warring family late in Henry's reign, shortly after young Henry's death. In the cinema version, the king must choose to pass the throne to Richard the Lion-hearted, Geoffrey, or John Lackland. Comment on the role of Alis and of Philip II. Conclude with the actual events that led to John's crowning and the signing of the Magna Carta.

Budget: $$

Sources:

Kaplan, Zoe. *Eleanor of Aquitaine.* Chelsea House, 1987.

Kelley, Amy. *Eleanor of Aquitaine and the Four Kings.* Harvard University Press, 1950.

Konigsburg, E. L. *A Proud Taste for Scarlet and Miniver.* Atheneum, 1973.

The Lion in Winter. Avco/Embassy-Haworth, 1968. (Video)

Meade, Marian. *Eleanor of Aquitaine: A Biography.* E. P. Dutton, 1980.

Owen, D. D. *Eleanor of Aquitaine, Queen and Legend.* Blackwell Publications, 1993.

Alternative Applications: Analyze the film depiction of Queen Eleanor's ability to deflect evil intentions in others by manipulation, wit, grace, skill, and charm even though she spends most of her time shut away in one of Henry's castles. Note that Eleanor is bilingual and keeps abreast of world events that impact England and France, especially the conniving of disloyal churchmen. Explain why her role in *The Lion in Winter* earned Katharine Hepburn an Oscar. How does John Barry complement Eleanor's film persona with music suited to scenes that she dominates?

Film *biographies*

Age/Grade Level or Audience: Middle school or high school literature or mass media study; term paper topic; cinema society series; civic or history club presentation; women's studies research topic; newspaper film column.

Description: Study the life of a female writer or performer as presented on film.

Procedure: Present one or a series of cinematic or made-for-television films detailing the life of a writer. Choose from these:

- *The Barretts of Wimpole Street* (1934, 1956)
- *The Bell Jar* (1979)
- *Born Free* (1966)
- *Cheaper by the Dozen* (1950)
- *Camille Claudel* (1989)
- *Cross Creek* (1983)
- *The Diary of Anne Frank* (1959)
- *Farewell to Manzanar* (1976)
- *Gypsy* (1962)
- *Heart like a Wheel* (1983)
- *Helen Keller* (1984)
- *I Know Why the Caged Bird Sings* (1979)
- *Impromptu* (1991)
- *The Miracle Worker* (1962)
- *Our Hearts Were Young and Gay* (1944)
- *Out of Africa* (1985)
- *Out on a Limb* (1987)
- *Simone de Beauvoir* (1982)

- *The Sound of Music* (1965)
- *Three Came Home* (1950)
- *Zora* (1990)

Present a fact sheet to accompany the program, detailing, for example, the escape of Agnes Newton Keith, who was interned in Borneo during the Japanese attack on Malaysia in 1941; describing Maria Augusta's decision to accept a marriage proposal and become the Baroness von Trapp; or accounting for Maya's move from Stamps, Arkansas, to her mother's house in St. Louis in *I Know Why the Caged Bird Sings*.

Budget: $$$

Sources:

"Maria Augusta Trapp." *Current Biography.* H. W. Wilson, 1968.
McDougal, Stuart Y. *Made into Movies: From Literature to Film.* Harcourt Brace, 1985.
Stones, Barbara. *America Goes to the Movies.* National Association of Theatre Owners, 1993.
Walker, John, ed. *Halliwell's Film Guide.* HarperPerennial, 1995.
Refer to the appendix for listings of film and video rental services.

Alternative Applications: Select one writer whose biography appears on film, for example:

Joy Adamson	Emily Kimbrough
Maya Angelou	Gypsy Rose Lee
Elizabeth Barrett Browning	Joy Davidman Lewison
Ernestine Gilbreth Carey	Shirley MacLaine
Isak Dinesen	Dorothy Parker
Anne Frank	Sylvia Plath
Jeanne Wakatsuki Houston	Marjorie Kinnan Rawlings
Zora Neale Hurston	Eleanor Roosevelt
Agnes Newton Keith	George Sand
Helen Keller	Cornelia Otis Skinner

Contrast the implications of the film with other points of view from literary and film criticism, interviews, biography, autobiography, history, letters, journals, or diaries. Present an oral contrast of sources and commentaries. From which source do you get the most realistic picture of the subject? What questions remain about character or motivation?

Filming *The Kitchen God's Wife*

Age/Grade Level or Audience: Middle school or high school drama or creative writing class or drama assignment; school or community reading theater screenwriting activity; women's studies course discussion topic; civic or neighborhood celebration of Women's History Month; women's club writing contest.

Description: Create dramatic scenes as part of a movie or version of Amy Tan's *The Kitchen God's Wife*.

Procedure: The filming of *The Joy Luck Club* has proved that Amy Tan's books make worthy cinema stories. Have participants work in groups to select costumes, makeup, music, lighting, setting, sound effects, and props to accompany a filming of following scenes from *The Kitchen God's Wife,* Tan's second novel. Provide butcher paper, tagboard, or a storyboard on which to set up scenes. Consider these events in which female characters carry the preponderance of the action:

- In Shanghai during the early summer of 1925, Lu elopes with Winnie's mother, leaving Winnie in the hands of jealous wives. Because Winnie is a concubine's child, she is sent east by ferry to live with disgruntled relatives on Tsungming Island.

- Twelve years later, the Chinese government hires Claire Chennault to train pilots during the war against Japanese aggressors. Meanwhile, Winnie buys an elaborate trousseau and housewares before marrying Wen Fu.

- In need of moral support after Wen Fu turns out to be an abusive psychopath, Winnie becomes friends with Helen, who soon marries Jiaguo, Wen Fu's superior officer.

- By the end of the summer 1937, pilots' wives are no longer safe in the east and leave Hangchow by boat for Yangchow. In November 1937, Japanese troops overrun Nanking; Helen rescues Winnie from a riot.

- After the Japanese bomb Pearl Harbor on December 7, 1941, Winnie meets Jimmy Louie. Enraged that she is escaping his control, Wen Fu rapes Winnie, then pretends to agree to a divorce but demands custody of one-year-old Danru.

- After Japan's surrender, Wen Fu and his family return to Shanghai in September 1945 to take control of the house and diminished fortunes of Winnie's invalid father, Jiang, a ruined textiles magnate.

- For plotting to escape from an abusive husband, Winnie is arrested in 1947; in early 1948, she faces a court trial, is humiliated by the press, and goes to jail.

- On May 10, 1949, Wen Fu signs divorce papers in front of witnesses at the telegraph office; four days later he rapes Winnie. She holds him at gunpoint and forces him to sign another set of divorce papers. The next day, she escapes on one of the last flights from communist China and joins Jimmy Louie in Fresno, California. Nine months later, Pearl Louie is born.

- On Christmas Day 1989, Helen divulges that Wen Fu is dead of heart disease. Winnie tells her daughter Pearl the terrible secret that has always troubled her—that Wen Fu may have sired Pearl.

Budget: $$

Sources:

"Amy Tan." *Current Biography.* H. W. Wilson, 1992.

"Amy Tan" (interview). *Arizona Republic* (Phoenix), October 5, 1993.

Baker, John F. "Fresh Voices, New Audiences." *Publishers Weekly,* August 9, 1993, 32–34.

Bannister, Linda. "Three Women Revise: What Morrison, Oates, and Tan Can Teach Our Students about Revision." March 31–April 3, 1993, ERIC.

Bernikow, Louise. "Book Review." *Cosmopolitan,* June 1991, 36.

Chatfield-Taylor, Joan. "Cosmo Talks to Amy Tan: Dazzling New Literary Light." *Cosmopolitan,* November 1989, 178.

Chua, C. L. Review of *The Kitchen God's Wife.* In *Magill's Literary Annual.* Salem Press, 1992.

Dew, Robb Forman. "Pangs of an Abandoned Child" *New York Times Book Review,* June 16, 1991, sec 7, p. 9, col. 1.

Dixler, Elsa. "Our Holiday Lists." *Nation,* December 30, 1991, 851–52.

Erdrich, Louise. "What Writers Are Reading." *Ms.,* July/August 1991, 82–83.

"A Fiery Mother-Daughter Relationship." *USA Today,* October 5, 1993, D12.

Hughes, Kathryn. "Sweet-Sour." *New Statesman & Society,* July 12, 1991, 37–38.

Iyer, Pico. "The Second Triumph of Amy Tan." *Time,* June 3, 1991, 67.

Joy Luck Club. Critics Choice, n.d. (Video)

Masterplots II: Women's Literature Series. Salem Press, 1995.

Ong, Caroline. "Re-writing the Old Wives' Tales." *Times Literary Supplement,* July 5, 1991, 20.

Rowland, Penelope. "American Woman." *Mother Jones,* July/August 1989, 10.

Shapiro, Laura. "From China, with Love." *Newsweek,* June 24, 1991, 63–64.

Somogyi, Barbara, and David Stanton. "Interview with Amy Tan." In *Poets & Writers,* September–October 1991, 24.

Tan, Amy. "Excerpt of 'Kitchen God's Wife.' " *McCall's,* July 1991, 115.

Young, Pamela. "Mother with a Past: The Family Album Inspires a Gifted Writer." *Maclean's,* July 15, 1991, 47.

Zia, Helen. "A Chinese Banquet of Secrets." *Ms.,* November/December 1991, 76–77.

Zinsser, John. "Audio Reviews—*The Kitchen God's Wife* Written and Read by Amy Tan." *Publishers Weekly,* June 7, 1991, 44.

Alternative Applications: Organize a film study of refugee and wartime scenarios in *Farewell to Manzanar, Julia, Plenty, A Town Like Alice, Except for Me and Thee, Gone with the Wind, Sophie's Choice, Playing for Time,* and *The Joy Luck Club.* Appoint a panel to summarize women's or girls' views of war and to enumerate their struggles against cold, panic, flight, disease, injury, unpredictable transportation, rumor, crowded housing, rationed supplies, tenuous leadership, hostile invaders, political upheaval, questionable loyalties, and clogged escape routes.

Meryl's *movies*

Age/Grade Level or Audience: Women's History Month seminar; cinema or historical society film festival; women's studies class round table; newspaper or magazine feature; television film critics series.

Description: Discuss the diverse roles in movies featuring actress Meryl Streep.

Procedure: Lead a discussion of the numerous female personae played by Meryl Streep in these films:

A Cry in the Dark	*Kramer vs. Kramer*
Death Becomes Her	*Manhattan*
The Deer Hunter	*Out of Africa*
The French Lieutenant's Woman	*The River Wild*
The House of the Spirits	*Silkwood*
Julia	*Sophie's Choice*

Contrast the parts that call for her to play a refugee from Nazi Germany, the clairvoyant wife of a patriarchal Latin politician, an actress playing a mentally unbalanced schemer, a coffee planter, and a survivalist on a treacherous canoe trip. Delineate the characters' relationships

47

with husbands, lovers, children, parents, and strangers. Determine Meryl Streep's strengths as an actor in serious drama, romance, historical fiction, and comedy.

Budget: $$

Sources:

Actors and Actresses. Vol. 3 of *International Dictionary of Films and Filmmakers.* St. James Press, 1992.

Maychick, Diana. *Meryl Streep.* St. Martin's Press, 1985.

Rebichon, Michel. "Meryl Streep : L'Appel du Large." *Studio,* Février 1995, 74–77.

Stones, Barbara. *America Goes to the Movies.* National Association of Theatre Owners, 1993.

Walker, John, ed. *Halliwell's Film Guide.* HarperPerennial, 1995.

Alternative Applications: Summarize the career of Meryl Streep. Cite examples of empathy in her characterizations of women, as with Karen Blixen's acceptance of her white friend's Somali mistress, Mrs. Kramer's decision to fight for custody of her son, Clara Trueba's kind-hearted gesture of washing the body of her deceased sister-in-law, and Sophie's mental torment over giving up her little girl to Nazi killers. Determine which roles have placed the most demand on Streep's ability to create verisimilitude amid suffering, frustration, doubt, loss, and indecision.

Movie *melodies*

Age/Grade Level or Audience: Quiz for adult movie fans; table favor for a Women's History Month banquet; cinema or historical society newsletter; women's studies class handout; newspaper film column.

Description: Identify the movie, song, and person to whom the song is dedicated or the person described.

Procedure: Fill in the missing element in each list of three categories—song title, character, movie. For example, the song "Anastasia" describes the character and movie of the same name. The rest of these are not so easy:

1. "My Own True Love"/ _____ /Gone with the Wind

2. " _____ "/Elsa the lion/*Born Free*

3. "Bess, You Is My Woman Now"/Bess/ _____

4. "Moon River"/ _____ /Breakfast at Tiffany's

5. "Chim Chim Cheree"/ _____ /Mary Poppins

6. "In the Garden"/Edna Spalding/ _____

7. "Pardon Goddess of the Night"/Hero/ _____ /

8. "I'm Gonna Wash That Man Right Out of My Hair"/ _____ /South Pacific

9. "I Will Follow Him"/ _____ /Sister Act

10. "I Don't Want to Play in Your Yard"/Louise Bryant/ _____

11. "Papa, Can You Hear Me?"/ _____ /Yentl

12. "_____" /Etta Place/*Butch Cassidy and the Sundance Kid*

13. "Shall We Dance?"/_____ /*The King and I*

14. "The Rain in Spain"/_____ /*My Fair Lady*

15. "Don't Rain on My Parade"/_____ /*Funny Girl*

16. "We Need a Little Christmas"/Mame/_____

17. "_____"/Sleeping Beauty/*Sleeping Beauty*

18. "It's Just a Little Bitty Piss-Ant Country Place"/_____ /*The Best Little Whorehouse in Texas*

19. "_____"/Dorothy/*The Wizard of Oz*

20. "Bibbidy-Bobbidy-Boo"/_____ /*Cinderella*

ANSWERS:

1. Scarlet O'Hara
2. "Born Free"
3. *Porgy and Bess*
4. Holly Golightly
5. Mary Poppins
6. *Places in the Heart*
7. *Much Ado about Nothing*
8. Nellie Forbush
9. Delores Van Cartier
10. Reds

11. Yentl
12. "Raindrops Keep Falling on My Head"
13. Anna Leonowens
14. Eliza Doolittle
15. Fanny Brice
16. *Mame*
17. "Someday My Prince Will Come"
18. Miss Mona
19. "Somewhere Over the Rainbow"
20. Fairy Godmother

Budget: $$

Sources:

Jacobs, Dick, and Harriet Jacobs. *Who Wrote That Song?* Writers Digest Books, 1994.

McDougal, Stuart Y. *Made into Movies: From Literature to Film.* Harcourt Brace, 1985.

Stones, Barbara. *America Goes to the Movies.* National Association of Theatre Owners, 1993.

Towers, Deidre, ed. *Dance Film and Video Guide.* Princeton, 1991.

Walker, John, ed. *Halliwell's Film Guide.* HarperPerennial, 1995.

Alternative Applications: Vary the game of movie songs by giving participants a chance to name the female character and actress after hearing a recording or a piano rendition of the song connected with her. Use these for starters:

- "The Sound of Music"—Maria von Trapp (Julie Andrews)

- "Hello Dolly"—Dolly (Carol Channing)

- "The Way We Were"—Katie (Barbra Streisand)

- "What'll I Do?"—Daisy Buchanan (Mia Farrow)

- "My Wishing Doll"—Jerusha Bromley Hale (Julie Andrews)

- "The Rain in Spain"—Eliza Doolittle (Audrey Hepburn)

Ruth *Prawer Jhabvala*

Age/Grade Level or Audience: High school or college literature discussion or term-paper topic; cinema society round table; women's studies seminar; newspaper film column.

Description: Contrast the novel and film versions of *Heat and Dust* as a representation of the feminist art of Ruth Prawer Jhabvala, novelist, screenwriter, and film collaborator with James Ivory and Ismail Merchant.

Procedure: After a study of the novel *Heat and Dust,* screen the film version. Have participants consider significant themes in Jhabvala's study of the women of India. Include these questions:

- Why is Olivia Rivers unprepared for life in colonial India as the wife of a British official and as a memsahib?

- What does the title suggest about physical discomfort and its effect on human behavior?

- What limitations on Indian women contrast Olivia's apparent freedom of movement, reliance on servants, education, and source of money for amusements?

- What does Olivia fail to understand about Indian philosophy, sexism, and culture?

- Why does Olivia immerse herself in a foreign lifestyle and give up her marriage and native land?

- What does piano music symbolize in each scene? What irony arises from the discordant sound of the Nawab's unused piano?

- After her move to the hill country, how is Olivia changed by her experiences and by solitude?

- In what way is Douglas Rivers an unsuitable husband for Olivia? How does she fail him as wife? Why does she turn to Harry for guidance?

- What powerful, sustaining characters offer Olivia support and understanding, particularly Maji, the wise woman and midwife?

- How does Olivia's enjoyment of picnics, visits, and dinners contrast the seclusion of the Nawab's mother and other palace women in typical Indian purdah?

- How does Olivia become alienated, powerless, manipulated, and victimized?

- Describe the unidentified speaker's attempt to understand Olivia as a woman of her time and as a romantic figure.

- Explain why Olivia yields to the Nawab, who is reputed to be a dacoit chieftain.

- How does a pregnancy jeopardize both Olivia's marriage to Douglas and her affair with the Nawab?

- Why is abortion a risky solution to Olivia's social and romantic dilemma?

- Why does Olivia withdraw from life and live in seclusion? What are her other options? What does her alter ego learn about her own life after tracing Olivia's last years in the mountains?

Budget: $$

Sources:

Gooneratne, Yasmine. *Silence, Exile, and Cunning; The Fiction of Ruth Prawer Jhabvala.* Orient Longman, 1983.

Jhabvala, Ruth Prawer. *Heat and Dust.* Simon & Schuster, 1975.

Rabinowitz, Dorothy. "Heat and Dust." *Saturday Review,* April 3, 1976, 30.

Sondhi, S. "Dowry Deaths in India." *Ms.,* January 1983, 22.

Sucher, Laurie. *The Fiction of Ruth Prawer Jhabvala.* St. Martin's Press, 1989.

Alternative Applications: Study a series of Jhabvala's screenplays, including these:

Bombay Talkie (1971)	*Madame Sousatzka* (1988)
The Bostonians (1983)	*Mr. and Mrs. Bridge* (1990)
The Europeans (1979)	*Quartet* (1981)
Heat and Dust (1983)	*A Room with a View* (1986)
Howard's End (1992)	*Roseland* (1977)
Jefferson in Paris (1995)	*Shakespeare Wallah* (1965)

Lead participants in a discussion of prevalent feminist themes and female character types, especially the strong, nurturing earth-mother and the vapid, unhappy socialite. Comment on Jhabvala's absorption in the blended themes of duplicity and self-deception. Lead a panel in ascertaining Jhabvala's impact on American movies, particularly those centered on social class, warped or conflicting values, feminism, and failed social roles.

Screen *women*

Age/Grade Level or Audience: Adult Women's History Month seminar; cinema or historical society discussion group; women's studies class research topic; newspaper or magazine film column.

Description: Discuss the believability and/or accuracy of female roles in movies.

Procedure: Organize a film series and lead a post-screening discussion of the following titles and topics. Discuss the contribution of actors to the believability of the role; for example, the terror and insecurity of Shirley Boothe, who plays the discarded wife in *Come Back Little Sheba.* Consider the female roles in these films:

The Grapes of Wrath	Ma Joad's ability to hold a family together during the depression
Murder on the Orient Express	a group of women participate in a group revenge killing
Life with Father	a wily wife outsmarts a patriarchal husband and a wily girlfriend gets her way
Sommersby	a farm wife tries to defend her lover from hanging for killing a returning Civil War veteran
The Music Box	an adoring daughter discovers that her father is a war criminal
I Remember Mama	a wise mother serves as a role model for her maturing daughter
Out of Africa	a female homesteader tries to succeed in Kenya during World War I
Lorenzo's Oil	a grieving mother defies medical opinion to rescue her son from a terminal disease

The Trip to Bountiful	an aging mother-in-law attempts to escape the constant criticism of her son's wife
Stanley and Iris	a widow assists an illiterate man to learn to read
Terms of Endearment	an overbearing mother copes with her daughter's failed marriage and death
Nuts	a prostitute defends herself against a confrontation with her abusive stepfather
The Wind and the Lion	an American woman learns to admire her Arabic kidnapper
The World According to Garp	an evolving feminist raises her fatherless son, writes a book, opens a women's clinic, and becomes a cult hero
Rambling Rose	an incest victim attempts to support herself and cope with her appeal to men
A Passage to India	an English girl faces both her failed engagement and her false accusation of rape against an Indian physician
Medicine Man	a young female lab assistant comes to terms with the purpose of science and the meaning of service to humanity

Budget: $$

Sources:

Kuhn, Annette. *Women in Film*. Fawcett, 1991.

Stones, Barbara. *America Goes to the Movies*. National Association of Theatre Owners, 1993.

Walker, John, ed. *Halliwell's Film Guide*. HarperPerennial, 1995.

Warner Brothers Screen Plays: Women's Films. Research Publications, 1995. (Microfilm)

Alternative Applications: After a screening of a film with strong female characters, organize a round table discussion of society's response to assertive women. Use these titles as possible starting points:

Absence of Malice	*Hustle*
Agnes of God	*Impromptu*
The Big Easy	*Like Water for Chocolate*
Class Action	*The Lion in Winter*
Cleopatra	*Little Women*
Dances with Wolves	*Queen*
Driving Miss Daisy	*The Remains of the Day*
East of Eden	*Shining Through*
Eat Drink Man Woman	*Steaming*
A Few Good Men	*Suddenly Last Summer*
The Glass Menagerie	*The Taming of the Shrew*
Hawaii	*Tender Is the Night*
Howard's End	*Thelma and Louise*

Taping *a day in a castle*

Age/Grade Level or Audience: Elementary or middle school drama or creative writing laboratory; school or community children's reading theater presentation; teacher education course project; civic or neighborhood celebration of Women's History Month; women's club photography contest.

Description: Videotape dramatic scenes that demonstrate the life of a woman and her daughters and female servants in a medieval castle.

Procedure: Make a tape of "A Day in a Castle," featuring reality rather than a fantasy Camelot. Depict one day's schedule in the lives of women in a castle involved in holiday preparations, the arrival of guests, winter weather, plague, or enemy invasion. Present the following scenes:

- chambermaid pulling down wall hangings and tapestries for dusting, beating, repair, and airing
- scullery maid scrubbing pots and kettles with handfuls of sand
- dairymaid straining buckets of milk and setting pans of cream to chill and separate in the buttery
- housemaid sweeping out old straw and gnawed bones and spreading fragrant straw and clover from the granary over the greatroom floor
- maid's daughter filling oil lamps, wiping the bases, and trimming the wicks before returning them to wall sconces
- grandmother storing honey, preserving beeswax, and curing healing bee pollen, herbs, roots, and plants in bunches by hanging them upside down in a drying shed
- pastry cook grinding pepper, coarse sea salt, and dried herb leaves and seeds with a mortar and pestle
- kitchen maid turning a roasting calf on a spit and baking meat pastries in a brick oven
- kitchen mistress instructing a tinker on which pots and skillets need mending
- harper or lute player tuning her instrument and practicing a scale in a sunny room
- young girl curtseying and dancing to the harper's music and pretending to take part in a morris dance
- children learning to wind yarn into balls after it has been dyed, shrunk, and dried
- mother setting up a stretching frame to hold a tapestry depicting her family's crest or coat of arms
- governess reading aloud a French *lai* by Marie de France or playing backgammon, checkers, cards, or chess with children
- older woman sorting needles and beginning to knit mittens and a matching wimple or snood
- a female relative or visitor playing solitaire by the fireside of a warm bower while the chambermaid pours buckets of hot water for her mistress's shampoo
- visiting nun rendering fat and green herbs to make a salve to cure chilblains

Form groups to act out each scenario. Make simple costumes from found objects such as cardboard, scarves, sheets, and aprons. Tape the final performance in a smooth interplay of women and girls going about their daily tasks while the men are away in the fields, traveling, or working in the courtyard below.

Budget: $$

Sources:

Cooper, J. *Castles*. Rourke, 1991.

Gee, Robyn. *Living in Castle Times*. Osborne Publishing, 1982.

James, Alan. *Castles and Mansions*. Lerner, 1989.

Macauley, David. *Castle*. Houghton Mifflin, 1982.

————. *Castle*. (Video)

Maynard, Christopher. *Castles*. Kingfisher, 1993.

Unstead, R. J. *See Inside a Castle*. Grisewood & Dempsey, 1986.

Alternative Applications: Organize a pantomime of varied castle chores, such as frying meat on a spider or tapping a cider barrel. Have students number their papers to correspond to each performance. Award a prize to the participant who correctly guesses the most number of activities and the tools used to complete them. Use this quiz as a model:

Match tool with chore by placing the correct letter in the blank.

_____	1. making yarn	A. sconce
_____	2. roasting meat	B. bellows
_____	3. replacing wall candles	C. spindle
_____	4. blending salve	D. trencher
_____	5. lighting the fire	E. spit
_____	6. embroidering a crest	F. cupping kit
_____	7. soaking cloth	G. mortar and pestle
_____	8. treating a swollen limb	H. stretcher
_____	9. removing baking from the oven	I. fulling tub
_____	10. serving meat slices	J. paddle

ANSWERS:

1. C	6. H
2. E	7. I
3. A	8. F
4. G	9. J
5. B	10. D

World *women in film*

Age/Grade Level or Audience: High school or college literature or mass media study; term paper topic; cinema society series; civic club, history club, or women's studies round table; newspaper film column.

Description: Organize an international film festival centering on women's lives around the world.

Procedure: Present a regularly scheduled series of free or low-cost film or video screenings, each to be followed by brief commentary and audience response. Consider these possibilities:

The Apple Game (Czechoslovakia)

Babette's Feast (France/Scandinavia)

Daughters of the Dust (United States/African-American women)

Dust (Belgium)

El Norte (Latina)

Erendira (Latina)

The Family Game (Japan)

Farewell to Manzanar (United States/Japanese-American women)

Fool's Fire (United States)

The Girl (Hungary)

Good Riddance (Canada)

Heat and Dust (India)

The Hiding Place (Holland)

Hour of the Star (Brazil)

Hyenas (Senegal)

Indochine (France/Vietnam)

Jean de Florette (France)

Joan of the Angels (Poland)

Karakyuki-San (Japan)

The Killer (Hong Kong)

La Vie de Boheme (France)

Like Water for Chocolate (Mexico)

Little Women (United States)

Little Vera (Russia)

Manon of the Spring (France)

The Match Factory Girl (Finland)

Maxine Hong Kingston: Talking Story (Japanese-American)

Mi Vida Loca (U. S. Latina)

Moscow Does Not Believe in Tears (Russia)

Narayama Bushi-Ko (Japan)

Sadako and the Thousand Paper Cranes (Japan)

Sa-I-Gu (Korea)

Sarafina (South Africa)

Shadow over Tibet: Stories in Exile (Tibet)

Song of the Exile (Hong Kong)

The Sound of Music (Austria)

Sugarbaby (Germany)

Thérèse (France)

A Town like Alice (England/Malaysia/Australia)

Wedding in Galilee (Israel)

Budget: $$$

Sources:

Blumenthal, Eileen, and Julie Taymor. *Julie Taymor: Playing with Fire*. Abrams Books, 1995.
Kuhn, Annette. *Women in Film*. Fawcett, 1991.
Stones, Barbara. *America Goes to the Movies*. National Association of Theatre Owners, 1993.
Walker, John, ed. *Halliwell's Film Guide*. HarperPerennial, 1995.
Warner Brothers Screen Plays: Women's Films. Research Publications, 1995. (Microfilm)
Refer to the appendix for listings of film and video rental services.

Alternative Applications: Make a film library or museum card file of works set in foreign locales that present intense studies of women's lives, for example, the part played by Youki Kudoh in *Picture Bride* or by Meryl Streep in *The House of the Spirits*. Create a code to indicate whether the main themes center on escapism, family, work, profession, religion, politics, creativity, or feminism.

Dance

Anna *Pavlova, danseuse*

Age/Grade Level or Audience: Elementary, middle school, and high school humanities or arts study; women's club program; dance or library group presentation; newspaper feature; women's history newsletter, bulletin board, brochure, or time line.

Description: Detail the life and stage career of Anna Pavlova for incorporation in notes.

Procedure: Present pictures, drawings, and descriptions of Anna Pavlova, one of Russia's prima ballerinas. Flesh out the following data with more research into her biography and create a succinct set of program notes:

- beginning study and initial interest at age ten followed by her debut at the Imperial Ballet School in St. Petersburg, Russia
- first solo performance at the Marinsky Theater in 1899; study with Enrico Cecchetti in 1905; and appearance with Nijinsky in 1909
- American debut in 1910 in *Coppélia;* greatest roles: *Giselle, Cléopâtre, Pavillon d'Armide, Les Sylphides*
- home in London and marriage to Victor Dandré
- tours with *The Magic Flute, Amarilla, Fairy Doll, Invitation to the Dance* at height of prestige, about 1915
- most evocative costumes: *Sleeping Beauty, Giselle, The Gavotte, Rondino, Bacchanale, Dragonfly*
- acting debut as lead in *The Dumb Girl of Portici* in 1916
- media acclaim and strength of performances
- conclusion of her career
- altruism toward European orphans of World War I

Comment on Anna Pavlova's lasting fame and the legends that surround her remarkable roles in *Giselle* and *Swan Lake.*

Budget: $

Sources:

Dandre, Victor E. *Anna Pavlova in Art and Life.* Ayer, 1994.

Franks, A. H., ed. *Pavlova: A Collection of Memoirs.* Da Capo, 1981.

Magriel, Paul, ed. *Pavlova.* Henry Holt & Co., 1947.

Miguel, Parmenia. *The Ballerinas: Famous Dancers from the Court of Louis XIV to Pavlova.* Da Capo, 1980.

Oliveroff, Andre. *Flight of the Swan: A Memory of Anna Pavlova.* Da Capo, 1979.

Alternative Applications: Have participants isolate the physical and emotional qualities in Anna Pavlova that enhanced her training and enabled her to remain productive on stage over a longer period than most prima ballerinas enjoy. Discuss the solo and partnered movements for which she was famous. Contrast her to Margot Fonteyn, Gelsey Kirkland, Tanaquil Leclerq, Martha Graham, Alicia Alonso, Makarova, Judith Jamison, or Isadora Duncan. Conclude the study of Anna Pavlova's contribution to dance with chalk or watercolor sketches of her most popular costumes.

Dancers

Age/Grade Level or Audience: Women's studies database or research topic; arts council project; dance group performance; newsletter or bulletin board feature or brochure; Friends of the Library project.

Description: Establish a centralized database of films, photos, videos, literature, and demonstrations on women's contributions to dance.

Procedure: Introduce participants to the most famous female dancers and their contributions to freedom of movement, style, costume, performance, and choreography. Include the most significant works of these women:

- Altynai Asylmuratova, prima ballerina in the Kirov's *Firebird*

- Josephine Baker, exotic black dancer who sought appreciation among European audiences eager for her *Revue Nègre*

- Francesca Corkle, offbeat star of the Joffrey Ballet Company who starred in *Remembrances*

- Agnes de Mille, choreographer of popular works like *Rodeo, Oklahoma, Carousel,* and *Brigadoon,* as well as the somber *Fall River Legend* (1952), the depiction of Lizzie Borden's killing of her parents

- Isadora Duncan, free-spirited choreographer, stage performer, and trainer of young dancers, whom she directed to such diverse music as "Le Marseillaise" and "The Blue Danube Waltz"

- Katherine Dunham, student of West Indian rhythms and producer of *Shango, Nostalgia, Blues, Flaming Youth,* and *Ragtime*

- Annabelle Gamson, avant-garde performer of the Dance Theater Workshop

- Martha Graham, teacher and choreographer of intense, emotional modern dance, particularly *Primitive Mysteries, Clytemnestra, Diversion of Angels,* and *Canticles for Innocent Comedians*

- Cynthia Gregory, prima ballerina of numerous companies, beginning with the Santa Monica Civic Ballet; also, star in *Raymonda,* which Rudolf Nureyev choreographed for her

- Judith Jameson, whose *Cry* introduced the fight for civil rights into the American dance theater

- Shirley MacLaine, Broadway hoofer and actor in *Pajama Game, Gypsy in My Soul, Can-Can, Irma La Douce,* and *The Turning Point*

- Anna Pavlova, the darling of the Russian stage in *Giselle, Swan Lake,* and other classic roles along with the more exotic *Autumn Bacchanale* and *Oriental Impressions*

- South African native Juliet Prowse, dazzlingly athletic highstepper in *Can-Can* and *Bolero*

- Ginger Rogers, partner of Fred Astaire in a lengthy film career including *Flying down to Rio, Stage Door,* and *Kitty Foyle,* which won Rogers an Academy Award in 1940

- Anna Sokolow, student of Martha Graham and Juilliard choreographer who produced *Lyric Suite, Rooms,* and *Camino Real*

- Ruth St. Denis, romanticist whose turn from Eurocentric dance to Asian costumes and steps transformed choreography and influenced choreographers Martha Graham and Doris Humphrey

- Maria Tallchief, prima ballerina for whom George Balanchine choreographed *Firebird;* director of lyric opera for the Ballet of Chicago

Budget: $$$$$

Sources:

The Astaire and Rogers Collection. Pacific Arts Publishing, n.d. (Video)

Bentley, Toni. *Costumes by Karinska.* Abrams Books, 1995.

Bland, Alexander. *A History of Ballet and Dance in the Western World.* Praeger, 1976.

"Body Language." *Ms.,* January/February 1995, 74–78.

Dalva, Nancy "Twyla Tharp at American Ballet Theater." *Ink,* spring 1995, 2–5.

Duffy, Martha. "The Kirov Loses Focus." *Time,* July 10, 1995, 60.

———. "Point Perfect." *Time,* February 13, 1995, 72–74.

Griffin, Lynne, and Kelly McCann. *The Book of Women: 300 Notable Women History Passed By.* Bob Adams, 1992.

Halpern, Alice. *The Technique of Martha Graham.* Morgan Press, 1994.

Hay, Susannah. *The Women's Heritage Scrapbook.* Caillech Press, 1992.

Isadora Duncan: Movement from the Soul. Direct Cinema Ltd., 1989. (Video)

Kendall, Elizabeth. "Drop, Rise, Breathe." *Dance Ink,* July 3–August 31, 1995, 27–28.

Martha Graham: An American Original in Performance. N.p., n.d. (Video)

Martin, Jean, gen. ed. *Who's Who of Women in the Twentieth Century.* Crescent Books, 1995.

"Milestones." *Time,* May 8, 1995, 41.

O'Connor, Barbara. *Barefoot Dancer: The Story of Isadora Duncan.* Lerner Books, 1994.

On the Move: The Central Ballet of China. Direct Cinema Ltd., n.d. (Video)

Reflections of a Dancer: Alexandra Danilova. Direct Cinema Ltd., n.d. (Video)

Alternative Applications: Have participants search for reviews, still shots, videos, and movies of a variety of dancers, including these:

Alicia Alonso	Paloma Herrera	Ginger Rogers
Pina Bausch	Rachel Kaplan	Quita Rivera
Violetta Boft	Ruby Keeler	Ruth St. Denis
Darcey Bussell	Gelsey Kirkland	Lynn Seymour
Marge Champion	Tanaqui Leclerq	Antoinette Sibley
Cyd Charisse	Liz Lerman	Maria Tallchief
Peggy Choy	Lydia Lopokova	Marjorie Tallchief

Evelyn Cisneros	Shirley MacLaine	Shirley Temple
Janet Collins	Natalia Makarova	Twyla Tharp
Jane Comfott	Alicia Markova	Galina Ulanova
Blondell Cummings	Bebe Miller	Ninette Valois
Suzanne Farrell	Juliet Prowse	Violette Verdy
Carla Fracci	Marie Rambert	Miranda Weese
Cynthia Gregory	Jennifer Ringer	Esther Williams

Note which dancers excelled in varied movie and stage styles (tap, point, modern, gymnastic, avant-garde, ballroom, chorus line, staged solo, folkloric) and which evolved their own troupes and schools.

Dancers *on canvas*

Age/Grade Level or Audience: Elementary, middle school, and high school humanities or art study; women's studies research topic; dance club program; library or museum group seminar; newspaper feature; art history newsletter, bulletin board, or brochure.

Description: Explore the world of dance as detailed by Edgar Degas, painter of dancers.

Procedure: Present slides, pictures, drawings, prints, and descriptions of Degas's study of dancers. Have participants study the change in Degas and his art as he lost more of his vision and focused his delight in the gauzy beauty of young ballerinas, their garments, and the grace of their form and movements, even while tying on toe shoes and rearranging their tutus. Lead a discussion of the following questions:

- What casual poses does Degas capture?

- What qualities do his dancers share; for example, age, concentration, and absorption in their work.

- How does his study fit the definition of impressionism more than realism?

- What aspects of a ballerina's career does he exclude; for instance, partnering, leaps, and corps de ballet?

Budget: $$$

Sources:

Broude, Norma. *Edgar Degas*. Rizzoli International, 1993.

Degas. Chronicle Books, 1993.

Loyrette, Henry. *Degas*. Abrams Books, 1993.

Melmoth, Sebastian. *Degas*. Book Sales, Inc., 1993.

Valery, Paul. *Degas, Danse, Dessin*. Schoenhof, 1994.

Alternative Applications: Have participants prepare individual papers on Degas's study of the dancer. Read aloud contrasting conclusions about Degas's style, appeal, and the relationship between the subjects of his middle period with those of his earlier and later works. Note the stress on color, pose, complexion, rounded limbs, hair, and light rather than line or architectural structure. How does Degas divorce his figures from the background? Why do they appear ethereal and gauzy?

Dancing *to movie music*

Age/Grade Level or Audience: Kindergarten or preschool activity; children's PTA performance; women's studies photography bulletin board; children's dance club or dance class project.

Description: Organize a group of preschool girls to choreograph dances set to Walt Disney movie sound tracks.

Procedure: Introduce participants to the sound tracks of *Beauty and the Beast, Cinderella, Sleeping Beauty, Pinocchio, Fantasia, The Lion King,* and *Pocahontas.* Have individuals create solo dances or groups choreograph scenes for a female *corps de ballet.* Encourage dancers to study the age, size, and actions of the main female characters or to select leading male figures to pantomime; for example, Pinocchio, Doc, the wizard, the lioness, or the Prince in *Cinderella.* Suggest events that require careful study, for example, Pocahontas's initial reaction to Captain John Smith, the lion cub's relationship with his friends, the stepmother's trick that puts her stepdaughter to sleep, and Beauty's quandary over how to love a hideous beast. Have participants describe, perform, or draw the movements they prefer for each scene.

Budget: $

Sources:

Abrams, Robert E. *Treasure of Disney Animation Art.* Abbeville Press, 1992.

Beauty and the Beast. Walt Disney Productions, 1991. (Audiocassette)

Bentley, Toni. *Costumes by Karinska.* Abrams Books, 1995.

Fisher, Maxine. *The Walt Disney Story.* Franklin Watts, 1988.

Medearis, Angela Shelf. *Dancing with the Indians.* Holiday House, 1991.

Pocahontas. Walt Disney Productions, 1995. (Audiocassette)

Alternative Applications: Conclude a session of watching or listening to movie music from Walt Disney's animated movies with a sketching lesson. Have participants create appropriate costumes, shoes, and headpieces for Pocahontas, Cinderella, Sleeping Beauty, the Fairy Godmother, the Wicked Stepmother, and Beauty as well as the lioness, ugly stepsisters, and other minor female figures. Discuss how the colors will blend with the background and what fabrics the costumer would choose to create a specific effect.

Esther *Williams*

Age/Grade Level or Audience: Middle school and high school humanities or arts class; cinema or women's club program; dance or library group study; newspaper feature; women's history newsletter, bulletin board, brochure, or time line.

Description: Compose a brief sketch of the unusual dance career of Esther Williams.

Procedure: Present pictures, drawings, film clips, and descriptions of Esther Williams's combination of dance and swimming. Include these facts about her career:

- A model and champion swimmer at age fifteen, Esther Williams, dubbed "Hollywood's Mermaid," lucked into a ready-made role with little competition, but never made the break from waterscapes and silly flirtations into serious drama.

- Hired by Billy Rose in the early 1940s to star in *Aquacade* at the San Francisco World's Fair, eighteen-year-old Williams combined a wholesome athleticism with the Bette Grable-brand pinup beauty popular with soldiers during World War II.

- In 1942 she appeared in *Andy Hardy Steps Out.* Two years later, she evolved the unusual melding of swimming and dance in MGM's *Bathing Beauty,* a Latin-beat musical starring an overload of male talent—Red Skelton, Basil Rathbone, Keenan Wynn, and Xavier Cugat.

- Into her thirties, Williams continued as a non-actor in fourteen water-bound movies, the best of which are *Ziegfeld Follies* (1946), *On an Island with You* (1948), *Neptune's Daughter* (1949), *Take Me Out to the Ballgame* (1949), *Duchess of Idaho* (1950), and *Million Dollar Mermaid* (1952). Her leading men ran the gamut from Victor Mature, Frank Sinatra, Gene Kelly, and Van Johnson to the sexy Latin Ricardo Montalban and Tarzanesque Johnny Weissmuller.

- Her final American film, *Jupiter's Darling* (1955), incorporated her stereotypical part as an eyelash-batting cutie in the mythic role of a divine child and Hannibal's love, a part designed by Hermes Pan for the film co-starring Howard Keel, Marge and Gower Champion, and George Sanders. The underwater high jinks opposite Greek male statues and stock shots of classic poses rounded out her career.

- Ultimately a business woman, Williams left swimming and movies, married Fernando Lamas, and established a line of swimming pools bearing her name.

Budget: $$$

Sources:

Katz, Ephraim. *The Film Encyclopedia.* Perigee Books, 1979.

Kendall, Elizabeth. "Esther Williams." *Dance Ink,* July 3–August 31, 1995, 2–5.

Strait, Raymond, and Leif Henir. *Queen of Shadows: The Unsuspected Life of Sonja Henie.* Madison Books, 1990.

Walker, John, ed. *Halliwell's Film Guide.* HarperPerennial, 1995.

Alternative Applications: Have participants define the exotic blend of dance and sport that comprises water ballet. Comment on the place of water ballet among the fine arts and as a legitimate entry in Olympic water sports. Lead a panel discussion of what makes a successful blend; for example, the psyche of World War II veterans and films featuring the girl-next-door beauty and grace of Esther Williams. Explain why Esther Williams epitomized escapism and buoyancy with her graceful combinations of swimming strokes and dance poses. Summarize the styles of swimsuits and costumes that complement her films. Contrast Williams's athletics-to-acting career with that of Norwegian Olympic skater Sonja Henie.

Heroines

Age/Grade Level or Audience: Elementary or junior high dance or drama presentation; physical education activity; PTA performance.

Description: Create dances honoring heroines.

Procedure: Have participants choreograph solo dances, pantomimes, or vignettes honoring famous women. Include Anne Frank, Esther Hautzig, Jahan Sadat, Amelia Earhart, Marie Curie, Helene Schweitzer, Louisa May Alcott, Golda Meir, Indira Gandhi, Chiang Ching, Nellie

Bly, Mary Renault, Emmeline Pankhurst, Margaret Fuller, Susan La Flesche Picotte, Helen Keller, Clara Barton, Florence Nightingale, and Rigoberto Menchu. Present dances or scenes set to stirring music and performed on stage or as shadow forms behind a screen.

Budget: $$$

Sources:

Fortier, Margaret, ed. *Women's History: Celebrating Women's History Month.* Cowles, 1995.

Hay, Susannah. *The Women's Heritage Scrapbook.* Caillech Press, 1992.

Heroines: Remarkable and Inspiring Women. Crescent, 1995.

James, Edwart T., and Janet W. James. *Notable American Women, A Biographical Dictionary.* Belknap Press, 1973.

Nobel Prize Winners. H. W. Wilson, 1995.

Alternative Applications: Organize a dramatic procession of heroines in costume. Have participants of all ages dance and pantomime the roles of famous women from various walks of life. Choose Joan of Arc, Harriet Tubman, Eleanor Roosevelt, Grace Hopper, Jacqueline Kennedy Onassis, Pat Schroeder, Molly Yard, Susan B. Anthony, Pearl Buck, Nadine Gordimer, Aung San Suu Kyi, Barbara McClintock, Toni Morrison, Julia Morgan, Catherine the Great, Empress Theodora, and other women of courage.

May *dance*

Age/Grade Level or Audience: Children's PTA performance; kindergarten or preschool activity; physical education workshop; women's club newsletter or bulletin board feature; children's dance club or dance class project.

Description: Present a formal May Day.

Procedure: Revive May Day customs by grouping girls for May Day activities. Assign one group to decorate a playground pole with real or paper flowers, ivy, colored stickers, tinsel, crepe paper, and other pastel-colored ornamentation. Have another group fill May baskets with paper flowers or live wildflowers and greenery. Ask a volunteer to set the May Queen doll in a small chair and decorate both to match the Maypole. Instruct dancers in winding ribbons in and out around the Maypole, dancing measured steps to a sprightly flute or recorder melody, and paying respects to the May Queen, whom they elect and place on a flower-decked throne in the center of activities.

Budget: $$$

Sources:

Hatch, Jane M, ed. *The American Book of Days.* H. W. Wilson, 1978.

Pierre, Sharon. *Making Holiday Folk Toys and Figures.* Sterling, 1987.

Warren, Jean, and Elizabeth S. McKinnon. *Small World Celebrations: Multi-Cultural Holidays to Celebrate with Young Children.* Warren Publishing House, 1988.

Alternative Applications: Have students photograph spring flowers and create a May Day bulletin board to accompany the Maypole dance, a May picnic, and other outdoor festivities. Tack flower pictures around a calligraphic poster detailing the importance of the Roman goddess Floralia to May festivities, which date to the time of Maia, a pagan spring goddess. Have participants pantomime the myth of Proserpina, whose abduction causes her mother, Ceres, goddess of growing things, to halt the growth of plants and flowers during the dark winter months that Proserpina spends in the Underworld with her abductor/husband, Hades. Print letters showing how Maia became the word May: **Maia → May.**

Raid *on the* Can-Can

Age/Grade Level or Audience: Dance club presentation; dance research topic; cinema club program; newsletter or bulletin board feature or brochure; Angels of the Theater project; women's studies activity.

Description: Present a panel discussion of the can-can.

Procedure: Discuss the phenomenon of the can-can. Include multiple topics: its popularity, style, costume, dancers and promoters, scandal, and variations. Note these facts:

- In 1830, the French can-can, a bubbly, rhythmic line-dance deriving its name from the French for *duck* and performed in rapid 2/4 time, aroused interest in Parisian clubs for its introduction of high kicks and frontal views of a mass of petticoats, wispy lingerie, high heels, garters, and fishnet hose. Punctuated by the blasts of police whistles, the dance evolved into a rowdy stage show expressing an energetic enthusiasm and flirtation.

- As a showstopper in revues, stage shows, and music hall fare, the can-can became a focal point of European theatrical entertainment for the remainder of the nineteenth century and was featured in one of Paris's tourist havens, Le Moulin Rouge, where it was often paired with performances of its opposite, the sadistic *apache danse*. Imitators like the Nelson girls of Berlin, American television's June Taylor Dancers, and the Rockettes of Radio City Music Hall in New York City developed the aspect of precision kicks by hiring dancers who fit a pre-conceived height, weight, and skills profile.

- Painter Henri de Toulouse-Lautrec popularized exaggerated, garishly bright Montmartre dance-hall scenes in his paintings and art nouveau posters and lithographs that feature can-can dancers whom he knew well: Valentin le Désossé, Chocolate, May Belfort, La Goulue, Yvette Guilbert, and his favorite model, Jane Avril. His sympathy for the desolate career of the Parisian dance-hall girl and prostitute brought into focus the gritty reality behind the exuberant, rowdy careers of entertainers, courtesans, and B-girls.

Budget: $$

Sources:

Ash, Russell. *Toulouse-Lautrec: The Complete Posters*. Trafalgar, 1992.

Kuhn, Annette. *Women in Film*. Fawcett, 1991.

Stones, Barbara. *America Goes to the Movies*. National Association of Theatre Owners, 1993.

Towers, Deidre, ed. *Dance Film and Video Guide*. Princeton, 1991.

Walker, John, ed. *Halliwell's Film Guide*. HarperPerennial, 1995.

Warner Brothers Screen Plays: Women's Films. Research Publications, 1995. (Microfilm)

Alternative Applications: Screen the 1960 film *Can-Can*, starring Shirley MacLaine, Juliet Prowse, Frank Sinatra, Maurice Chevalier, and Louis Jourdan. Discuss the attempt to present women's dance history with touches of song, humor, and professionalism. Note the importance of Cole Porter's music—"C'Est Magnifique," "I Love Paris," and "Just One of Those Things"— and the underlying theme that women must be protected and rescued. How does the screen version of the can-can portray the lives of women who make their living as dancers and cabaret entertainers?

Rainbow *dancers*

Age/Grade Level or Audience: Children's PTA performance; kindergarten or preschool activity; women's studies newsletter or bulletin board feature; children's dance club or physical education project.

Description: Teach girls dances of women from other cultures.

Procedure: Introduce participants to a variety of women's dances. Name the occasion and demonstrate the steps. For example, read aloud Angela Shelf Medearis's *Dancing with the Indians* and ask volunteers to illustrate how the dance is performed. Discuss these details:

- Dancers wear shells on wrists and ankles to produce a jingling sound. Sometimes the participants are called jingle dancers. What other wrist and ankle jewelry would make a similar sound? From what materials could you make a dancer's wrist and ankle noisemakers?

- Dancers deck themselves from head to toe in satin ribbons of all colors. Why do they dance around a fire? What does the fire do to the swirling colors of the ribbons? How could you make a similar decoration and dance around a lamp to produce bright colors?

- Dancers perform in moccasins that make gentle sounds. Why do Indian dancers prefer moccasins? What are moccasins made of? How could you make a similar pair of shoes or substitute a soft shoe from home?

- Dancers move, dip, bow, and twirl to the music. Why do they make these motions? How do these steps cause their shells to jingle and their ribbons to float in the air? What music or musical instrument would you choose for a similar dance?

- How does the women's part of the program differ from the men's rattlesnake dance and the concluding stomp dance? Why do women produce a characteristic dance by themselves?

Ask a parallel set of questions about other women's dances, including the hula, handkerchief dance, can-can, chorus line, belly dance, highland fling, girl's puberty rite dance, and Maypole dance. Have participants name the country of origin, colors, clothing, jewelry, hats and headpieces, shoes, decoration, music, and steps that typify these dances. Post a map for students to point to the country of origin. For example, the can-can developed in Paris, France; the hula comes from Polynesia; and the highland fling developed in Scotland.

Budget: $$

Sources:

Bentley, Toni. *Costumes by Karinska*. Abrams Books, 1995.

Martin, Jean, gen. ed. *Who's Who of Women in the Twentieth Century*. Crescent Books, 1995.

Medearis, Angela Shelf. *Dancing with the Indians*. Holiday House, 1991.

Pierre, Sharon. *Making Holiday Folk Toys and Figures*. Sterling, 1987.

Warren, Jean, and Elizabeth S. McKinnon. *Small World Celebrations: Multi-Cultural Holidays to Celebrate with Young Children.* Warren Publishing House, 1988.

Alternative Applications: Form small groups to make up women's dances to celebrate festive seasons and holidays. Think up ways to honor women's roles during these special occasions:

All Saint's Day	Cinco de Mayo	Purim
anniversary	Flag Day	Ramadan
Arbor Day	Halloween	Sadie Hawkins Day
Bar Mitzvah	Kwanzaa	St. Patrick's Day
Bas Mitzvah	Lady Day	Simchat
Bastille Day	Lent	Torah
birthday	Mardi Gras	Thanksgiving
Black History Month	Michaelmas	Twelfth Night
Canada Day	Native American Day	Whitsuntide
Chinese New Year	New Year's Day	Women's History Month

Sisters

Age/Grade Level or Audience: Women's club program; dance research topic; subject for a newsletter, bulletin board, brochure, or column; women's studies seminar; arts council display.

Description: Contrast the development and careers of Maria and Marjorie Tallchief.

Procedure: Introduce a comparison of the lives and talents of Maria Tallchief and her younger sister Marjorie. Note the following facts about them:

• Of Osage parentage and the granddaughters of a chief, Maria, born in Fairfax, Oklahoma, in 1925, and Marjorie, born two years later in Denver, Colorado, studied in California under Bronislava Nijinska. Maria moved on to classes with Ernest Belcher and George Balanchine, who became her first husband. (She later married Henry Paschen.) She was known for her high arch and toes of equal length, which could easily accommodate toe shoes. Marjorie studied with David Licine in California; she earned fame for her lithe frame and beauty.

• The sisters' careers moved rapidly in different directions. Maria joined the School of American Ballet and danced at age fifteen in *Chopin Concerto.* In the Ballet Russe de Monte-Carlo, she starred as Coquette in *Night Shadow* and in *Sylvia,* both starring roles created by her husband, George Balanchine. Marjorie danced with the Ballet Theatre in *Graduation Ball* and appeared as Queen of the Wilis in *Giselle* and as Medusa in *Undertow.*

• Maria Tallchief won acclaim for her strength and grace in classic roles in *Caracole, Scotch Symphony,* and *The Nutcracker Suite* rather than the lighter, more avant-garde dance style showcased by her appearances in *Orpheus, Serenade, Gaité Parisienne, Miss Julie, Don Quixote, Flower Festival at Genzano,* and *The Firebird.*

- Marjorie, also slim and vivacious, had her stage successes with the de Cuevas troupe, which she joined at age twenty. Ten years later, when she moved to the Paris Opera, her style elicited raves for its fluidity and lyricism. One of Marjorie's most exotic roles was opposite her husband, dancer-choreographer George Skibine, in *Le Prince du Désert* and *Romeo and Juliette*. She starred in a broad range of works: *Concerto, Idylle, Annabel Lee, Graduation Ball, Camille, Le Prisonnier du Caucase,* and *L'Oiseau de Feu.*

- Maria received the Capezio Dance Award in 1965 for discipline, style, and individuality and the best lyrical team award at the Théâtre des Champs-Elysées. Marjorie won a plum position as première danseuse étoile with the Paris Opéra Ballet in 1955.

- Marjorie and Maria retired in 1966. Maria settled in Chicago; Marjorie moved to New York to be near her children.

Budget: $$

Sources:

Berss, Marcia. "The Zhen-uine Article." *Forbes,* June 5, 1995, 104–105.

Bland, Alexander. *A History of Ballet and Dance in the Western World.* Praeger Publishers, 1976.

Cumming, Doug. "Shaping Young Minds." *Atlanta Journal and Constitution,* July 9, 1995, 1G, 6G.

Erdrich, Heidi. *Maria Tallchief.* Raintree, 1992.

Terry, Walter. *On Point!: The Story of Dancing and Dancers on Toes.* Dodd, Mead, 1962.

———. Foreword to *American Dance Portfolio.* Dodd, Mead, 1964.

Alternative Applications: Use the lives of the Tallchief sisters as a springboard to the study of other famous sisters, for example:

- activists Christabel and Sylvia Pankhurst

- actors Olivia de Havilland and Joan Fontaine, Jennifer and Meg Tilly, Patricia and Roseanna Arquette, Daryl and Paige Hannah, Michelle and Dee Dee Pfeiffer, Jean and Maureen Stapleton, Vanessa and Lynn Redgrave, Zsa Zsa and Eva Gabor

- columnists Ann Landers and Abigail Van Buren

- composers Nadia and Lily Boulanger and Patty, Mildred, and Jessica Hill, who wrote "Happy Birthday to You"

- editors Jackie Kennedy Onassis and Lee Radziwill

- educators Joyce Oatman and Florence Alexander

- entrepreneurs Gail, Jane, Susan, Elaine, Teresa, and Leighlonn Zhen

- inventors Beatrice and Mildred Kenner and Teresa and Mary Thompson

- ruling family Queen Elizabeth II and Princess Margaret Rose and Trung Trac and Trung Nhi of first-century Vietnam

- singers and entertainers Gypsy Rose Lee and June Havoc, Lorna Luft and Liza Minelli, the Lennon sisters, and the Andrews sisters

- social activists and writers Edith and Grace Abbott

- writers Anne, Charlotte, and Emily Brontë, and Vanessa Bell and Virginia Woolf

Twyla *Tharp*

Age/Grade Level or Audience: Dance club presentation; dance group study; newsletter or bulletin board feature or brochure; Friends of the Library project; women's studies activity.

Description: Characterize Twyla Tharp as a multi-talented leader of the dance community.

Procedure: Introduce participants to the multi-faceted career of dancer and choreographer Twyla Tharp. Comment on Tharp's quirky style and her use of modern rhythms, instruments, lighting, and stagecraft. Apply definitions of modern art, street rhythms, gymnastics, improvisation, and relaxed format to Tharp's most significant presentations. Contrast her style with that of Martha Graham, Ruth St. Denis, Judith Jameson, Maria and Marjorie Tallchief, Katherine Dunham, Margot Fonteyn, Jacqueline Baker, and Isadora Duncan. Append a chronology of Tharp's creations and the critical response to each.

Budget: $$

Sources:

Dalva, Nancy. "Twyla Tharp at American Ballet Theater." *Ink,* spring 1995, 2–5.

Martin, Jean, gen. ed. *Who's Who of Women in the Twentieth Century.* Crescent Books, 1995.

Nathan, Jean. "The Art of Seduction." *Ink,* spring 1995, 9–13.

Tharp, Twyla. *Push Comes to Shove.* Bantam Books, 1992.

Alternative Applications: Contrast Tharp's brash daring of choreography and dance-step combinations with the sensuous dance photos of Isabel Muñoz. What unusual pairings does Muñoz make of legs, torsos, and the body's rhythmic response to music? How does Muñoz utilize light and texture to enhance her poses and convey the sense of movement? Describe her ability to "dismember" dancers by focusing light and lens on hands, midriffs, arms, thighs, jaw, back, and musculature.

Design

Architects *and designers*

Age/Grade Level or Audience: Middle school or high school history or art project; college art, engineering, or design focus; women's history lecture; library or museum display; civic or women's club program; media feature or column; narrated city walking tour.

Description: Present an overview of the impact of female architects and designers on buildings and interiors.

Procedure: Describe or illustrate with models, slides, or photographs the work of Maya Ying Lin creator of the Vietnam memorial. Lead a discussion of her meaningful breaks with past sculpture; for example, Lin's use of a bunker-type setting, monochromatic stone and etched names, and personal reaction of veterans, survivors, friends, family, politicians, critics, and artists. Justify the appointment of a non-white female designer. Contrast Lin's vision with that of the designers of the Lincoln Memorial, Capitol Dome, Gettysburg Monument, Tomb of the Unknown Soldier, and the tribute to the Korean War. Assess the vision and skill demonstrated by Lin in both the Civil Rights Memorial in Montgomery, Alabama, and the Wexner Center at Ohio University.

Budget: $

Sources:

Adams, Brooks. "Hidden Heroines: Passionate Perspectives." *Harper's Bazaar,* April 1988, 102–110.

Bailey, Brooke. *The Remarkable Lives of 100 Women Artists.* Bob Adams, 1994.

Barna, Joel Warren. "Women in Architecture." *Texas Monthly,* January 1990, 45–47.

Bolz, Diane M. "The Graphic Arts' Pioneering Women." *Smithsonian,* May 1995, 36.

Coleman, Jonathan. "First She Looks Inward. Architect Maya Lin." *Time,* November 6, 1989, 90–93.

Crowe, Sylvia. *Garden Design.* Garden Art Press, 1995.

Danto, Arthur C. "Art: The Vietnam Veterans Memorial." *Nation,* August 31, 1985, 153–56.

De Witt-Koenig, Carolyn. "Women in Architecture: Is the Future Finally Here?" *Architectural Record,* July 1988, 35.

Diamonstein, Barbaralee. "Architecture on a Human Scale." *Ms.,* October 1986, 53, 88.

Edith Henderson's Home Landscape Companion. Peachtree, 1995.

Felman, Jyl Lynn. "Judy Chicago's Holocaust Project." *Lilith,* summer 1994, 15–16.

"Hearst's Home Was Her Castle." *Vogue,* June 1988, 86.

Hess, Elizabeth. "A Tale of Two Memorials." *Art in America,* April 1983, 120–27.

Hollander, Anne. "Grès Matter." *Dance Ink,* July 3–August 31, 1995, 24–25.

Kirschenbaum, Jill. "The Symmetry of Maya Ying Lin." *Ms.,* September–October 1990, 20–22.

Kramer, Carol. "The Wall: Monument to a Nation's Sacrifice." *McCall's,* June 1988, 42–43.

Lin, Maya Ying. "Beauty and the Bank: The Skyscraper Is Reborn in Hong Kong." *New Republic,* December 23, 1985, 25–29.

Lorenz, Clare. *Women in Architecture: A Contemporary Perspective.* Rizzoli, 1990.

Malone, Mary. *Maya Lin, Architect and Artist.* Enslow, 1995.

Musleah, Rachel. "Two Historic Lattingtown Mansions to Be Opened for Rare Tour." *New York Times,* November 13, 1994, L29.

Russell, Beverly. "Breaking into the Erector Set." *Savvy Woman,* March 1989, 76–81.

———. "Design for Living." *New Statesman and Society,* August 18, 1991, 33.

———. *Women of Design.* Rizzoli, 1992.

Sorkin, Michael. "What Happens When a Woman Designs a War Monument?" *Vogue,* May 1983, 120–21.

Swerdlow, Joel L. "To Heal a Nation." *National Geographic,* May 1985, 555–74.

Tauber, Peter. "Monument Maker." *New York Times Magazine,* February 24, 1991, 48.

Thurman, Christa C. Mayer, ed. *Lissy Funk: A Retrospective.* Art Institute of Chicago, 1988.

Tobias, Tobi. "Mirror Mirror." *Dance Ink,* July 3–August 31, 1995, 23.

"Top Women Architects." *Ebony,* August 1995, 54–58.

"Unsung Woman Architect." *Colonial Homes,* February 1991, 34–37.

Wade, Marcia Jo. "No Exceptions." *Horizon,* May 1988, 33–36.

Alternative Applications: Discuss the creative works of these women designers, architects, landscapers, and town planners. Note the locations of their most significant creations and the way they reflect a time, place, style, or mindset:

Natalye Appel	Janet Kaplan
Pamela Babey	Laurette M. LeGendre-Purse
Gretchen Bellinger	Ivenue Love-Stanley
Sara Holmes Boutelle	Phyllis Martin-Vegue
Donna D. Carter	Cheryl L. McAfee
Judy Chicago	Elizabeth McClintock
Clodagh	Heather McKinney
Alex Barnes Donaphin	Julia Monk
Donna Criner de Jongh	Julia Morgan
Elsie de Wolfe	Mother Joseph
Rosina Emmet	Sylvia Owen
Ellen Thayer Fisher	Elizabeth Plater-Zyberk
Lee Foster-Crowder	Michaele Pride-Wells
Mary Edna Fraser	Ethel Reed
Sarah E. Fuller	Hermine E. Ricketts
Val Glitsch	Theodate Pope Riddle
Eileen Gray	Remedios Varo
Beverly K. Hannah	Alice Trythall Washburn
Lizabeth B. Humphrey	Roberta Washington
Gertrude Jekyll	Sarah Winchester

Comment on unusual details, materials, retrospective techniques, and pragmatic structures in their works; for example:

- Alexa Barnes Donaphin's work on Harlem's North General Hospital

- Beverly K. Hannah's restoration of the Hartford Memorial Baptist Church in Detroit

- Cheryl L. McAfee's work on the Olympic Stadium in Atlanta

- colonial homes in Connecticut designed by Alice Trythall Washburn in the 1920s

- Donna Criner de Jongh's design of the Camille Olivia Hanks Cosby Academic Center at Spelman College

- Donna D. Carter's design of the Austin Texas Fire Station #17

- Eileen Gray's Tempe A Pailla, satellite mirror, and lacquered lotus table

- Elizabeth Scott's Shakespeare Memorial Theatre at Stratford-on-Avon

- Elsie de Wolfe's interior designs

- Gertrude Jekyll's landscapes

- the Hearst Estate in San Simeon, California, designed by Julia Morgan

- Ivenue Love-Stanley's work on Atlanta's Olympic Aquatic Center

- Judy Chicago's *The Dinner Party*

- Laurette M. LeGendre-Purse's design of the Mount Vernon Neighborhood Health Center in Mount Vernon, New York

- Lockjaw Ridge in Lattingtown, New York, a structure designed by America's first female major architect, Theodate Pope Riddle

- Paine Webber building in Boston, designed by Joan Goody

- Phyllis R. Miller Elementary School by Hermine E. Ricketts

- reconstructions by Michaele Pride-Wells

- Roberta Washington's renovation of the Sara P. Huntington House in Manhattan

Make a map locating their finished designs. Note their debts to classical architecture and foreign influence.

Chesswomen

Age/Grade Level or Audience: Elementary after-school or scout carving project; art class activity; chess club contest; home-school art or logic assignment; children's museum cooperative workshop.

Description: Design a Women's History Month chess set.

Procedure: Draw a chess board featuring red and white squares and blue borders. Make chesswomen out of carved soapstone or pine, baked clay, papiér-mâché, dowels, stacked rocks, or other found objects. Label each figure on the pedestal with the name of a founding mother. Consider these names:

- Susan B. Anthony and Sojourner Truth (kings)

- Lucretia Mott and Sarah Winnemucca (queens)

- Lucy Stone, Dorothy Day, Harriet Tubman, and Carrie Chapman Catt (4 bishops)

- Gloria Steinem, Dolores Huerta, Billie Jean King, Patsy Mink (4 knights)

- Kathleen Battle, Marian Anderson, Sarah Caldwell, Wilma Mankiller (4 rooks)

- Toni Morrison, Amy Tan, Abigail Adams, Juliette Low, Barbra Streisand, Pat Schroeder, Madeleine Kunin, Clara Barton, Queen Victoria, Mary Decker, Margaret Fuller, Geraldine Ferraro, Barbara Jordan, Ellen Goodman, Coretta Scott King, Rosa Parks (16 pawns)

Have participants study the rules of chess and learn together to play the game. Hold chess matches with school clubs or challengers from other areas. Place the chess set on display annually during Women's History Month.

Budget: $$$

Sources:

Bradfield, Nancy. *Historical Costumes of England.* Barnes & Noble, 1971.

Feininger, Andreas. *New York in the Forties.* Dover Books, 1994.

Functional Pottery. Crystal, 1995. (Video)

Gorsline, Douglas. *What People Wore.* Dover Books, 1994.

McGraw, Sheila. *Dolls Kids Can Make.* Firefly Books, 1995.

————. *Papiér-Mâché for Kids.* Firefly Books, 1995.

Müller, Claudia. *The Costume Timeline: 5000 Years of Fashion History.* Thames & Hudson, 1992.

Paterek, Josephine. *Encyclopedia of American Indian Costume.* ABC-Clio, 1994.

Alternative Applications: Alter other popular board games by incorporating women from history into the playing pieces. Consider these game pieces and boards:

backgammon pieces	mah jongg
checkers	Monopoly board
Clue	Parcheesi
goh	playing cards
I Ching	tarot cards

A diorama of *Uncle Tom's Cabin*

Age/Grade Level or Audience: Film club, after-school or scout shadowbox; history or art class, homebound or disabled children's cooperative activity; home-school arts research; children's museum or library display.

Description: Organize a series of set designs to accompany a reading of Harriet Beecher Stowe's *Uncle Tom's Cabin.*

Procedure: Have participants create a series of sketches, a diorama, shadowboxes, a frieze or mural, or a set of acrylic drawings on cloth to accompany major scenes in *Uncle Tom's Cabin.*

Begin by selecting the most moving, evocative portraits of slave life and emphasize the author's selection of details. Follow these models:

- a backdrop for the February day when slave dealers bargain with Mr. Shelby for the purchase of Uncle Tom, Jim Crow, and Eliza, Jim's mother

- Uncle Tom's cabin, which stands near Mr. Shelby's home and features climbing roses, a garden, and slaves participating in worship

- sunset at the Ohio River, where Eliza struggles to cross on ice while carrying Harry so that both can be free in the North

- the boat bound for New Orleans on the Mississippi River as Haley moves a coffle of chained slaves on board and adds Lucy and her child

- the Quaker home of Simeon and Rachel Halliday, where Eliza and Harry wait for news of George, then flee together toward the Canadian border

- Miss Ophelia's room, where she attempts to wash, trim, dress, and educate Topsy

- the deathbed of Little Eva, where St. Clare begins studying the Bible and ponders his guilt in keeping slaves

- Legree's foul, musty sitting-room, the site of Cassy's vengeance over the super-stitious overseer

Include other meaningful scenarios; for example Mr. Shelby's dining room, an inn near the Ohio River, a tumble-down shed, the auction market, a New Orleans street, and Uncle Tom's gravesite. Stress the contrast between opulence and squalor, warmth and discomfort, cramped quarters and the outdoors.

Budget: $$$

Sources:

Ashton, Jean. *Harriet Beecher Stowe: A Reference Guide*. G. K. Hall, 1978.

Bentley, Toni. *Costumes by Karinska*. Abrams Books, 1995

Gorsline, Douglas. *What People Wore*. Dover Books, 1994.

Gossett, Thomas F. *Uncle Tom's Cabin and American Culture*. SMU Press, 1985.

Jakoubek, Robert. *Harriet Beecher Stowe*. Chelsea House, 1989.

Moers, Ellen. *Harriet Beecher Stowe and American Literature*. Stowe-Daye, 1978.

Müller, Claudia. *The Costume Timeline: 5000 Years of Fashion History*. Thames & Hudson, 1992.

Reynolds, Moira D. *Uncle Tom's Cabin and Mid-Nineteenth-Century United States Pen and Conscience*. McFarland & Co., 1985.

Stowe, Harriet Beecher. *Uncle Tom's Cabin*. Harper & Row, 1965.

Sundquist, Eric, ed. *New Essays on Uncle Tom's Cabin*. Cambridge University Press, 1987.

Alternative Applications: Have participants select other historic works by female authors or biographies of real women and work in small groups designing sets for a library or museum display, including dolls, murals, or paper figures to illustrate the number and placement of characters. Consider these works:

- Amy Tan's *The Kitchen God's Wife*

- Jeanne Wakatsuki Houston and James Houston's *Farewell to Manzanar*

- Joy Adamson's *Born Free*

- Lorraine Hansberry's *To Be Young, Gifted, and Black*

- Margaret Landon's *Anna and the King of Siam*

- Maya Angelou's *I Know Why the Caged Bird Sings*

- the book of Esther

- the diary of Queen Victoria

- Laura Ingalls Wilder's *Little House* series

- Mildred Taylor's *Roll of Thunder, Hear My Cry*

- Yoko Kawashima Watkins's *So Far from the Bamboo Grove*

- Zlata Filipovic's *Zlata's Diary*

For *love of Mumtaz*

Age/Grade Level or Audience: Middle school or high school history or art project; women's history lecture or slide presentation; library or museum display; civic or women's club program; media feature or column.

Description: Describe the purpose and design of the Taj Mahal, named for Mumtaz Mahal (Chosen of the Palace).

Procedure: Illustrate with original models and drawings, book illustrations, slides, or photographs the Taj Mahal, designed by Shah Jahan, a Moghul emperor (fl. 1628–1658). Jehan wanted a lasting tribute to his wife Mumtaz, formally known as the Arjunand Banu Begum, who became the Shah's favorite wife in 1612. She died in Burhanpur during childbirth with her fourteenth pregnancy. Present a tourist map locating the domed tomb located at the center of symmetrical reflecting pools, gardens, and turrets, across the Jumna River from the Shah's palace in Agra, India. Cite its inception in 1631 and completion in 1648. Comment on the white marble and red sandstone that comprise the facade. Discuss the selection of advisers from Persia and other parts of Asia and the employment of 20,000 workers to perform meticulous drawings, calligraphy, masonry, inlaying, and artisanry in a 40,000-rupee monument to the Shah's consort. Discuss the place of the Taj Mahal in Islamic and Asian architecture.

Budget: $

Sources:

Begley, W. E., and Z. A. Desei, eds. *The Taj Mahal; The Illumined Tomb*. University of Washington Press, 1990.

Nath, R. *The Tajmahal and Its Incarnation*. Asia Book Corporation, 1985.

Oak, P. H. *Tajmahal: The True Story*. Ghosh, 1989.

Alternative Applications: Have members of a study team draft copies of the Taj Mahal's embellishments:

alabaster screens	domes	parapets
arches	fantasy motifs	passages from the Koran
borders	floral patterns	pinnacles
burial vault	minerets	towers
cenotaphs	mosque	walkways

Explain why Shah Jahan did not complete his plans for a corresponding mausoleum for himself. Conclude by reproducing the Taj Mahal in perspective on a desktop graphics program.

Honoring *Quaker women*

Age/Grade Level or Audience: Middle school or high school history or writing project; college art or design class group presentation; women's history lecture; library or museum newsletter topic; civic or women's club program; media feature or column.

Description: Design an informative booklet with locational markers and maps to honor notable Quaker women.

Procedure: Design a brochure or booklet detailing the efforts of famous Quaker women to help end slavery, secure women's right to vote, and secure civil liberties. Illustrate with pen-and-ink drawings, sketched portraits, or clip art; include a map showing significant sites. Distribute booklets to elementary schools, scout troops, or through local libraries. Name these people and their influence on history:

- Anne Austin and Mary Fisher, the first American Quakers, were deported back to England shortly after their arrival in 1656. Other Quaker females who preached and set up relief centers for the poor in Maryland and the Massachusetts Bay Colony were flogged, placed in stocks, or hanged.

- Mary Dyer, the first female Quaker martyr in the New World, was sent to the gallows in Boston.

- In 1766, Quaker healer Margaret Hill Morris opened a practice in Philadelphia.

- Jemima Wilkinson, who called herself "Publick Universal Friend" began an itinerant ministry and relief mission among blacks and native Americans in the late 1780s throughout Rhode Island and Connecticut.

- For over two decades during her husband's role as Quaker founder of Pennsylvania, Guglielma Springett Penn served as a visiting nurse.

- Hanna, William Penn's second wife, managed the colony of Pennsylvania during troubled times resulting from her husband's stroke in 1712.

- In 1830, Abby Kelly Foster, one of the first open abolitionists, served as an organizer and officer of the Lynn, Massachusetts Female Anti-Slavery Society.

- Prudence Crandall of Canterbury, Connecticut, opened the first girls school in 1831 and fought community disapproval for allowing a black student to attend classes.

- Elizabeth Blackwell began private medical studies in 1845 and became the first American female doctor. In 1856, her sister, Emily Blackwell, helped her establish the New York Infirmary for Women and Children as a clinic and nurse/midwife training center.

- In the 1860s many unnamed Quaker station-masters on the Underground Railroad and nurses offered their aid to slaves and soldiers.

- Mary Ann Shadd Cary opened a training academy for black children in Canada, a scant distance from Detroit, Michigan.

- Charity Rodman Rotch's estate underwrote a school for orphans in Massillon, Ohio, in the mid-1820s.

- Lucretia Mott founded the Philadelphia Female Anti-Slavery Society in 1838. The society profited from the conversion of Sarah and Angelina Grimké, daughters of a slave owner who set a precedent for women by speaking before groups of both sexes. Sarah published *Letters on the Equality of the Sexes,* a work that made public the strong sympathy women felt for slaves since, under the law, both women and blacks worked and survived at the whim of men.

- With co-organizer Elizabeth Cady Stanton, Lucretia Mott convened the first Women's Rights Convention in Seneca Falls, New York, in 1848.

- Susan B. Anthony (born Adams, Massachusetts), one of the most controversial Quaker feminists, sought division of property and child support for divorced women and their children in 1860.

- Jane Addams (born Cedarville, Illinois), suffragist and social worker, became America's first female winner of the Nobel Peace Prize in 1931; fifteen years later, educator and pacifist Emily Balch (born Jamaica Plain, Massachusetts) won a Nobel Peace Prize for her devotion to unions, international peace efforts, and education.

- From 1953–1964, Mary Steichen Calderone served as the medical director of Planned Parenthood, then founded the Sex Information and Educational Council of the United States (SIECUS).

Budget: $$

Sources:

Axelrod, Dr. Alan, and Charles Phillips. *What Every American Should Know about American History.* Bob Adams, 1992.

Clark, Judith Freeman. *American Women in the Twentieth Century.* Prentice Hall, 1987.

Clement, J., ed. *Famous Deeds of American Women.* Corner House, 1975.

Dennis, Denise. *Black History for Beginners.* Highsmith, 1992.

Fantham, Elaine, et al. *Women in the Classical World.* Oxford University Press, 1994.

Gentz, William H., gen. ed. *The Dictionary of Bible and Religion.* Abingdon Press, 1986.

Great Lives from History: American Women Series. Salem Press, 1995.

Griffin, Lynne, and Kelly McCann. *The Book of Women: 300 Notable Women History Passed By.* Bob Adams, 1992.

Harrison, Cynthia, ed. *Women in National Politics.* University Publications of America, 1995.

Sochen, June. *Herstory: A Woman's View of American History.* Alfred Publishing, 1974.

Weatherford, Doris. *American Women's History.* Prentice Hall, 1994.

Alternative Applications: Supply a religion class, Women's History Month lecture hall, library, or museum with a time line or database of events in the history of the Society of Friends, or Quakers, whose women made a strong stand against slavery, human misery, unfair taxation, ignorance, and disenfranchisement. Use this list as a beginning:

- George Fox (1624–1691) founded the "Inner Light," "Children of Light," or "Publishers of Truth" movement in 1650, which caused Puritan authorities to jail thousands for dissent and blasphemy. Quakers, named because they "trembled at the word of the Lord," fled persecution, imprisonment, and restrictive laws in the British Isles and Northern Europe and reestablished their mystical reform activities in the Caribbean and the American colonies.

- Men and women sat apart during worship, but both sexes claimed the title of "minister" and addressed communal meetings on social and religious concerns.

- Fox accompanied missionaries to North America and the Caribbean from 1671–1673 and returned to the mission field in 1677. His wife, Margaret Fell Fox, was imprisoned three times for her ardent faith and for leading a contingent of Quaker women in silent worship in defiance of the Church of England, a political and social act of rebellion that she continued until her death in 1702.

- The Quakers put up a strong front of pacifism in the face of mob attacks, and continued refusing military service and the use of "his lordship" or "saint" as titles. They defied the Pope, oaths of fealty, and ministry, synod, and liturgical restraints, including tithing, baptism, and a reliance on the Bible alone as the only source of divine guidance. Their devotion to "plainness" led them to use formal pronouns (thee, thou, thy, thine, thyself, thyselves) and to avoid pagan names for days of the weeks and months of the year, which they called "third day" or "tenth month."

- In 1682, William and Guglielma Penn established Rhode Island as a haven for Quakers, who set an example of tolerance through their friendship with Native Americans.

- In the early and mid-nineteenth century, the group's work against racism toward black slaves and Native Americans earned them the suspicion and hatred of both white supremacists and plantation owners, who hired patrollers and bounty hunters to locate Quaker stations on the Underground Railroad. Their additional pressures to reform prisons and provide relief for refugees, the insane, and the homeless lodged Quakers among liberals and radicals.

- Bryn Mawr, a Quaker women's college, initiated classes in 1885. President Martha Carey Thomas served the school as educator and dean from 1894–1921, taking as her motto, "In intellect there is no sex."

- During World War I, pacifists took a non-violent role in military hospitals, rehabilitation centers, supply centers, and front-line support. During the Korean War, Quakers established relief services for refugees. Throughout World War II and the Vietnam War era, Quakers followed their consciences and either registered for the draft as pacifists or refused complicity with war.

- The twentieth century produced strong Quaker action on behalf of migrant workers, the homeless, and families of miners. Two eminent activists of the 1920s and 1903s were the Quaker sisters Edith and Grace Abbott, who published works on industry, prison, immigrants, and social services.

- In 1947, the Quakers won the Nobel Peace Prize for their philanthropic work dating before the American Revolution.

In *the garden*

Age/Grade Level or Audience: Middle school or high school history or art project; garden or travel club tour; photography class focus; college art, landscaping, or design class; women's history lecture; library or museum display; civic or women's club program; media feature or column; narrated walking tour.

Description: Organize a series of lectures on women's contributions to landscaping and gardening.

Procedure: Study surrounding areas for examples of unusual arboretums, garden nooks, lawns, orchards, herb gardens, vegetable farms, mazes, and other examples of landscaping designed and carried out by women. Lead a symposium of experts and interested gardeners. Discuss the use of vegetables, annual flowers, and herbs in the design of homes, and why women choose growing things as an outlet for energy, love of color, and development or design. Mention fences and hedges, dry walls, knot gardens, streams, rock sculpture, downtown garden spots, topiaries, water gardens, aviaries, and xeroscapes. Comment on the efforts of Emily Dickinson, Gertrude Jeykll, Harriet Beecher Stowe, Sarah Orne Jewett, and Adelaide Alsop Robineau in creating spots of beauty. Describe the influence of women's gardens on artists, photographers, and art historians Frances and Mary Allen, Wallace Nutting, Gustav Stickley, Childe Hassam, Robert Vonnoh, John Leslie Breck, and May Brawley Hill.

Budget: $$$$

Sources:

Hill, May Brawley. *Grandmother's Garden: The Old-Fashioned American Garden, 1865–1915.* Abrams Books, 1995.

Musleah, Rachel. "Two Historic Lattingtown Mansions to Be Opened for Rare Tour." *New York Times,* November 13, 1994, L29.

Russell, Beverly. "Design for Living." *New Statesman and Society,* August 18, 1991, 33.

Sherr, Lynn, and Jurate Kazickas. *Susan B. Anthony Slept Here: A Guide to American Women's Landmarks.* Random House, 1994.

Alternative Applications: Using desktop publishing, create a traveler's brochure, map, and directory to gardens within driving distance of your area. Briefly classify each according to annual festivals, location, nearby restaurants or tea rooms, access to the handicapped, gift shops, and suitability for children. Designate stately homes and restoration projects, scenic drives, and historic importance; for example, the area around Louisa May Alcott's home in Concord, Edith Wharton's home in Lenox, Redstone School and the Wayside Inn on the Lexington Road in Sudbury, Sleepy Hollow Cemetery, and Walden Pond are all within easy driving distance in Western-Central Massachusetts.

A monument *to a stubborn woman*

Age/Grade Level or Audience: Elementary or middle school writing and art activity; after-school library project; Women's History Month contest; history club international study.

Description: Present a proposal for a living monument to Burmese dissident and freedom fighter Aung San Suu Kyi.

Procedure: Set up a contest for which entrants must present a written description, site preparation chart, and top, front, back, and side views of a monument honoring the heroic clash between Aung San Suu Kyi and her Myanmar captors. Emphasize these dramatic moments in the struggle:

- house arrest in July 1989 at her Rangoon lake residence on charges of spying into the crimes of a powerful junta that slew 3,000 student protesters

- Myanmar usurpers' overthrow of the government elected in the May 1990 election, which Suu Kyi's party, the National League for Democracy, won

- the murder of Aung San, Suu Kyi's father, and Suu Kyi's differences of opinion with Burma's State Law-and-Order Restoration Council, led by General Than Shwe

- an upsurge in national markets and alliances with other countries, all of which depend on a restored sense of free markets and stable government for Burma

• Suu Kyi's post-release rejoicing with well-wishers and her warnings that Burma still has much to achieve in order to retain autonomy and free itself from future power-brokers

Urge contest entrants to honor Suu Kyi's optimism, youthful features, welcoming gestures, respect for people's rights, realism, and hope for the nation's growth and prosperity.

Budget: $$$$

Sources:

Clifton, Tony. "She Is Not Alone." *Newsweek,* July 24, 1995, 44.

Martin, Jean, gen. ed. *Who's Who of Women in the Twentieth Century.* Crescent Books, 1995.

Spaeth, Anthony. "Setting Free 'The Lady.'" *Time,* July 24, 1995, 48.

Alternative Applications: Expand the contest to include other "stubborn ladies" to memorialize, for example, Rosa Parks, Hélène Schweitzer, Lillie Langtry, Vanessa Redgrave, Camille Claudel, Dolores Huerta, Queen Elizabeth I, and Sojourner Truth. Consider a variety of designs: a fountain, state park, skyline drive, tower, mall complex, or futuristic kindergarten.

Picturing *a home*

Age/Grade Level or Audience: Elementary, middle, or high school literature or art project; library or museum display; reading group project; after-school or scout activity.

Description: Design the exteriors and interiors of homes that are described in accounts written by women.

Procedure: After reading a fiction or non-fiction work by a woman in which living spaces are vividly depicted, have participants design the exteriors and interiors of the dwelling as accurately as possible, using details from the text. Discuss how different roles for women are reflected in different types of housing (a city apartment versus a pioneer cabin, for example) and the kinds of work typically required of women in these diverse settings. Consider these titles:

• Ann Petry's *The Street*

• Caroline Kirkland's *A New Home, Who'll Follow*

• Willa Cather's *My Antonia*

• Laura Ingalls Wilder's *Little House on the Prairie*

• Elizabeth Gaskell's *Cranford*

• Edith Wharton's *House of Mirth*

• George Eliot's *Middlemarch*

• Nadine Gordimer's *July's People*

• Harriet Jacobs's *Incidents in the Life of a Slave Girl*

Budget: $

Sources:

Cather, Willa. *My Antonia.* 1918. University of Nebraska Press, 1994.

Eliot, George. *Middlemarch: A Study of Provincal Life.* 1871–72. Oxford University Press, 1959.

Gaskell, Elizabeth. *Cranford.* 1853. Oxford University Press, 1977.

Gordimer, Nadine. *July's People.* Viking Press, 1981.

Jacobs, Harriet A. *Incidents in the Life of a Slave Girl.* Oxford University Press, 1988.

Kirkland, Caroline M. *A New Home, Who'll Follow? or, Glimpses of Western Life.* 1855. Rutgers Universtiy Press, 1990.

Petry, Ann Lane. *The Street.* 1946. Beacon Press, 1985.

Wharton, Edith. *The House of Mirth.* 1905. Penguin, 1985.

Wilder, Laura Ingalls. *Little House on the Prairie.* HarperCollins, 1975.

Alternative Applications: Read the biography of a woman from another century. Research the architecture of that time period, then act as though you are an architect and this woman is your client. Design sketches of the interior and exterior of a home for her. Keep in mind her personality, interests, and practical needs, in addition to the architecture of the period. Wouldn't Marie de Médicis want something different than Harriet Tubman?

Sketchers *ahoy!*

Age/Grade Level or Audience: Elementary children's library or museum project; children's art class focus; homebound or disabled children's activity; history class poster series; home-school art assignment; home demonstration or 4-H Columbus Day display.

Description: Create a display of the world's most important ships carrying a female name.

Procedure: Have students create a ship gallery featuring these historic models:

- *Annie Jane*
- Christopher Columbus's *Pinta, Niña,* and *Santa Maria*
- clippers *Ann McKim* and *Sea Witch*
- diesel-powered *Selandia*
- *Doña Paz*
- *Empress of Ireland*
- *Lady of the Lake*
- luxury liners *Queen Mary, Queen Eliabeth,* and *Queen Elizabeth II*
- *Pomona*
- *Princess Alice*
- *Princess Victoria*
- *Reina Regenta*
- steamboats *Mississippi Queen, Delta Queen* and *Charlotte Dundas*
- steamer *Caroline Brest*

Determine how each got its name. Explain why ships are traditionally referred to as "she" by recounting these cultural myths:

- Ship, from the Teutonic *schiff,* is derivative of the Old Norse *skop,* meaning "fate." It reflected the symbol of the goddess Frigga, whose name ultimately lent itself to the terms "frigging" and "frigate." Frigga was the goddess who ruled their ship-shaped burial mounds.

- These mounds eventually developed into the Norman temples, which were designed in the shape of a ship. The Norse death ship, called a *ludr,* defined as a boat, coffin, or cradle returned the dead back to the Mother-sea or the marine womb. This death vessel was always referred to in the feminine, which may account for the common practice of referring to ships as "she."

- In Egypt, Osiris, the God of Death, returned to life in the "morning boat" tended by a spirit called Matet, the equivalent of the Dawn-Mother.

- The Romans worshipped Isis as a ship goddess and revered the boat as a symbol of her womb. In the temples of Isis one finds the "bark of Isis" carved in stone.

Budget: $$

Sources:

Berenstain, Michael. *The Ship Book.* McKay, 1978.

Grady, Sean M. *Ships: Crossing the World's Oceans.* Lucent Books, 1992.

Kindersley, Dorling. *Ships and Boats.* Macmillan, 1992.

Mitchell, John C. *Great Lakes and Great Ships.* Suttons Bay Publications, 1991.

Valenzi, Kathleen, ed. *Historic Ships of America.* Howell Press, 1991.

Wilbur, C. Keith. *Tall Ships of the World.* Globe Pequot, 1986.

Alternative Applications: Have participants deliver an oral report from research into a single ship named for a woman; for example, the *Queen Elizabeth II.* Instruct the speaker to begin the report by drawing the model's shape on the chalkboard, overhead projector, or handouts and identify it as a merchant vessel, submarine, liner, tug, steamer, sternwheeler, or other type. Label these important parts:

after deck	galley	sail
anchor	halyard	sail lockers
bilge	hatch	par
bow	keel	starboard
bowspit	mast	staterooms
bulkhead	poop deck	stern
companionway	porthole	tiller
deadlights	pumps	wheelhouse
figurehead	punt	winch
forecastle	ratlines	yardarm

A thank-you *garden*

Age/Grade Level or Audience: Combined civic, school, and garden club venture.

Description: Create a memorial garden to honor a local woman.

Procedure: Solicit land or private funds to underwrite the creation of a nature walk, biking trail, campground, arboretum, conservatory, telescope, fountain, aviary, or city garden nook to commemorate the work of a famous local woman. For example:

- Carson Valley, Nevada, might choose to honor Washo basket-maker Datsolali, whose work in the 1890s fed her family while also breaking records for the amount paid a native crafter.

- Monroeville, Alabama, could pay homage to Harper Lee, bestselling author of *To Kill a Mockingbird,* a classic Southern novel.

Completed gardens should provide pleasant walks, overviews, a pond, or nature lore about local birds and plants. Landscapers should incorporate a plaque, portrait bust, or full-sized statue of the honoree as a focal point.

Budget: $$$$$

Sources:

Adams, Brooks. "Hidden Heroines: Passionate Perspectives." *Harper's Bazaar,* April 1988, 102–110.

Bailey, Brooke. *The Remarkable Lives of 100 Women Artists.* Bob Adams, 1994.

Edith Henderson's Home Landscape Companion. Peachtree, 1995.

Sherr, Lynn, and Jurate Kazickas. *Susan B. Anthony Slept Here: A Guide to American Women's Landmarks.* Random House, 1994.

Alternative Applications: Provide a local museum yard, park, arboretum, or town square with a functional marker commemorating a notable female figure from history, politics, sports, the arts, medicine, or invention. Choose a geodesic dome, planetarium, wind chime, light show, annual outdoor drama or tableau, or aquarium. A worthy candidate might be Eleanor Roosevelt, the spearhead of the human rights commission of the fledgling United Nations. Acknowledge her skill as negotiator and humanitarian at UN headquarters in New York or at her summer home in Hyde Park.

Women *in colonial times*

Age/Grade Level or Audience: Elementary or middle school history or art presentation; college alumni or historical society project; women's history or museum newsletter topic; civic or women's club program; media feature or column.

Description: Design a series of colonial historical displays that feature women in traditional scenes.

Procedure: Create a series of showcases, mannequins, models, or demonstrations of colonial women and their interests and activities. Include the following:

- teaching children to make shuck dolls, holiday garlands, embroidered samplers, pottery, or hornbooks

- churning milk, setting cream to curdle into cottage cheese, and shaping, pressing, and salting wheels of cheese

- collecting, straining, and cooking maple sap into syrup and cakes or cones of sugar

- chopping sorghum and cooking, skimming, cooling, and bottling molasses

- putting up apple butter and cider, salted meat and fish, leather breeches beans, and dried apples and peaches for winter

- operating a loom with home-dyed, homespun wool and linen yarns and sewing garments for a family

- trimming hair, treating and wrapping sprains and broken bones, and drying healing herbs

- preparing bed ticks and pillows from goose down

- making fragrant hand soap, sachets, and candles

- turning pine cones and greenery into home decorations

Preserve authentic gestures and costumes and realistic interiors of historic cottage or cabins. For example, set small clay figurines on a sand table and show them involved in such activities as ninepins, horseshoe pitching, or shovelboard. Post paragraphs to explain the significance of each.

Budget: $$$$

Sources:

The American Colonies. Knowledge Unlimited, 1995. (Video)

Axelrod, Dr. Alan, and Charles Phillips. *What Every American Should Know About American History.* Bob Adams, 1992.

Kalman, Bobbie. *Early Settler Life Series.* Crabtree, 1995.

———. *Historical Communities Series.* Crabtree, 1995.

Sochen, June. *Herstory: A Woman's View of American History.* Alfred Publishing, 1974.

Stenson, Elizabeth. *Early Settler Activity Guide.* Crabtree, 1993.

Weatherford, Doris. *American Women's History.* Prentice Hall, 1994.

Alternative Applications: Organize a colonial show-and-tell event. Have participants act out movements, then name the activity and the utensils necessary for each chore. For example:

- churn butter and turn it out into a pan to drain and pat into a solid cake with a paddle

- twist and shape loose wool, cotton, or flax fibers into thread on a spinning wheel or shape yarn into a skein on a weasel

- knead dough in a dough tray, then let rise and slide finish loaves into an oven with a bread paddle

- tie cords to a dowel, then dip wicks into melted paraffin or beeswax and herbs for scented candles and tapers

- knot or loop rag strips together, then weave on cord woof strands into a rag rug

- collect duck down and feathers, snip off sharp ends, then stuff into casings for dolls, draft catchers, pillows, bolsters, and mattresses

Drama

Crossing *The Bridge of San Luis Rey*

Age/Grade Level or Audience: High school literature or drama project; reading theater improvisation; college creative writing assignment.

Description: Retell Thornton Wilder's dramatic story from a female perspective.

Procedure: Select a female character to replace Brother Juniper, a Franciscan friar from Italy who narrates the original novella. Retell the story of the victims who died at noon on Friday, July 20, 1714, from the collapse of a willow bridge on the road from Lima to Cuzco, Peru. Have the speaker introduce the bridge setting, which the Incas wove around 1600 to shorten the distance over the Andes Mountains. Begin the exposition and rising action by introducing the main female characters, particularly the wayfarers who plunge to the valley below:

- Doña María, the Marquesa de Montemayor, who regrets her alienation from her haughty daughter and who bequeaths a wealth of letters, which become monuments of Spanish literature
- Doña Maria's daughter, Clara, who marries a nobleman, emigrates to Spain, and shuts her mother out of her life
- the Abbess Madre María del Pilar of the Convent of Santa María Rosa de las Rosas, who is in charge of placing orphans with foster parents
- Pepita, the foster daughter who dutifully follows Doña Maria on a daily jaunt through the streets
- Camila, the real name of Perichole, the dissolute actress whom Uncle Pio trains and adores

Conclude with a round table discussion of the book's focus on loss and grief. Give particular attention to the Abbess's advice to Clara:

"Love will have been enough; all those impulses of love return to the love that made them. Even memory is not necessary for love. There is a land of the living and a land of the dead and the bridge is love, the only survival, the only meaning."

Organize an improvisation of these interlinked lives and the effect of the accident that kills five people crossing the bridge.

Budget: $

Sources:

Dobyns, Henry F., and Paul L. Doughty. *Peru: A Cultural History.* Oxford University Press, 1976.

Goldstein, Malcolm. *The Art of Thornton Wilder.* University of Nebraska Press, 1965.

Markham, Clements R. *Cuzco: A Journey to the Ancient Capital of Peru;* and, *Lima: A Visit to the Capital and Provinces of Modern Peru.* Kraus Reprints, 1992.

Wakefield, Celia. *High Cities of the Andes.* Wide World Publishing/Tetra, 1988.

Wilder, Thornton. *The Bridge of San Luis Rey.* Avon, 1955.

Alternative Applications: Screen the black-and-white 1944 United Artists film version of *The Bridge of San Luis Rey,* starring Lynn Bari, Francis Lederer, Louis Calhern, and Donald Woods. Lead a discussion of the circumscribed lives of women in a Catholic milieu that draws the survivors to repeated efforts to confess and cleanse themselves of guilt. Comment on how the theme and focus would change if the movie were set in New Zealand, Pakistan, Iraq, Belarus, Bali, or Zaire.

Flora *Macdonald, patriot*

Age/Grade Level or Audience: High school or college drama or creative writing class or drama assignment; school or community reading theater presentation; women's studies course enactment; civic or neighborhood celebration of Women's History Month; history club program.

Description: Block scenes from an improvisation of the life of Flora Macdonald, Scottish heroine and patriot.

Procedure: Organize a practice session in improvisation by having students work in groups to present connecting scenes from the life of Flora MacDonald, the Scottish heroine who assisted Bonnie Prince Charlie, the doomed Catholic heir of James I, in his attempt to seize the English throne. Precede the dramatization with these facts:

- Born in 1722 in Milton, South Uist of the Outer Hebrides and nicknamed "the fair," Flora, the only daughter of Ranald Macdonald, was a farm girl who was reared by her mother and stepfather, Hugh Macdonald of Armadale. She later lived with her brother Angus in Milton. Her patrons, Laird Alexander and Lady Margaret Macdonald, educated her, provided Flora privileges suited to the aristocracy, and introduced her to their Jacobite politics.

- Utilizing her clan connections, Flora Macdonald supported the 24-year-old Scottish pretender to the throne, Charles Edward Stuart, a boyishly handsome would-be royal poetically called Bonnie Prince Charlie. In 1745, dramatically labeled "The Year of Charlie," the prince staged a failed rebellion later known as the Jacobite Uprising. From exile in Rome, he made a dash at the Isle of Eriskay on July 23. Blessed with good fortune against a host of British troops he proclaimed his reign and pushed on for Edinburgh, which he captured on September 17.

- On November 17, accompanied by pipers, Charlie entered Carlisle. By December, he had established several strongholds in England and returned to Scotland after Christmas, content that he would regain England's thrones for the Stuarts. The year 1746 began with victories for his Jacobite supporters, but on April 16 the Duke of Cumberland's army, whom loyal Scots termed "butchers," demonstrated its reputation for savagery. After an hour of fighting against double the manpower, Charlie acknowledged a crushing defeat at the Battle of Culloden Moor. The English bayoneted survivors and burned captured Scots and their families in a barn. The lost cause and its savage conclusions became a favorite subject of poets, painters, and balladeers.

- While vacationing on Benbecula Island on June 28, Macdonald encountered Charlie, who had fled Culloden unscathed and now moved freely among islanders despite a reward of $60,000 offered by the English for his capture. When Charlie was endangered by British search parties—including her own stepfather—Flora borrowed clothing from Lady Clanranald and disguised the prince as her spinning woman, Betty Burke. Brazenly, Flora underwent questioning in her stepfather's camp and obtained passports for herself and "Betty."

- Because the fords were watched by King's men, Flora Macdonald arranged to meet the prince after sunup at a shepherd's cottage. The plan nearly foundered when Tory guards stopped by the hut for fresh milk. The prince hid along the shore and flagged Macdonald from the crags. She supplied a linen frock, quilted petticoat, apron, and tan mantle and hid pistols in each pocket. In a rough gale, she accompanied the prince by eight-oared fishing boat toward the Isle of Skye, where guards fired on the wherry when its occupants failed to pull to for a routine search.

- The rowers made for Kilbride. Again, the prince hid in the rocks while Flora sought her patron's intervention. With the help of Lady Margaret Macdonald and her husband's grain buyer, the trio rescheduled the prince's crossing to the Isle of Ramsay. In female dress, the prince refused to mince along and strode with a manly gait while Flora Macdonald rode alongside on horseback. At a ford, he dismayed locals by lifting his skirts higher than proper for a serving woman and earned the name of that "odd Muckle trallup of a carline."

- Legend and eyewitness accounts credit the prince with a hearty appetite for the food and brandy provided by bold Scotswomen and the prince's host, Laird Malcolm Macleod. At Portree on Skye, the prince returned to men's clothing. His relationship with Flora was brief and businesslike. After a two-day stay, the prince bid her farewell, thanked her for her assistance, boarded the wherry, and sailed away into hiding to the south. He returned to France on September 20 aboard the *L'Heureux.*

- When the British learned of Flora Macdonald's treachery, they arrested her on November 8 and jailed her, first on the *Royal Sovereign* moored in the Thames River and a month later in the Tower of London, where traitors were usually beheaded and their heads displayed on pikes. Already a figure of romance and courage among Scots and English loyalists, she acquired pardon the next July, but remained at the home of Lady Primrose, an admiring Jacobite.

- Flora Macdonald sailed back to the Isle of Skye to a heroine's welcome. In January 1750, she married Allan (or Alex) Macdonald of Kingsburgh, father of her children (numbered between seven and ten by uncertain historians). At age 52, she immigrated to a tobacco plantation in Fayetteville, North Caroline, where her husband was imprisoned for aiding Tories during the American Revolution and Flora was wounded in the fighting.

- In her late fifties, Macdonald journeyed back to Scotland alone where her husband eventually rejoined her. She died March 5, 1790, in Kingsburgh and was buried at Kilmuir, Isle of Skye, under an epitaph by Dr. Samuel Johnson, who honored her courage and fidelity.

Add dash and color to the improvisation by imagining how Flora Macdonald would have convinced English soldiers that her traveling companions took no part in the rebellion. Round out the sketches by playing Scottish ballads and folksongs.

Budget: $$

Sources:

"Annie Laurie: Folksongs of the British Isles." Angel Records, Middlesex, England, 1993.

Douglas, Hugh. *Flora Macdonald: The Most Loyal Rebel*. Alan Sutton Publishing, 1993.

Erickson, Carolly. *Bonnie Prince Charlie*. Morrow, 1990.

Fletcher, Inglis. *Scotswoman*. Queen's House, 1976.

Maclean, J. P. *Flora MacDonald in America*. Scot Press, 1984.

MacTaggart, Ken. "The Young Pretender." *In Britain,* July 1995, 12–16.

McLaren, Moray. *Bonnie Prince Charlie*. Marboro Books, 1990.

"On the Prince's Trail." *Realm,* July/August 1995, 54–55.

Alternative Applications: Have groups work together on an outdoor drama lauding the legendary Flora Macdonald. Assign one group to dance scenes in which pipers accompany tartan-clad Highlanders dancing a victory celebration. Supply Macdonald with suitable lines of cheer and support for an unlikely succession of the Stuart pretender to the English throne. Offer a playbill featuring a time line of Flora Macdonald's life and the lyrics to the "Skye Boat Song," written by Robert Louis Stevenson:

Skye Boat Song

Loud the winds howl, loud the waves roar,
Thunder clouds rend the air;
Baffled our foes stand by the shore,
Follow they will not dare.

(refrain)

Speed bonnie boat like a bird on the wing.
Onward the sailor cry;
Carry the lad that's born to be king
Over the sea to Skye.

Thought the waves leap, soft shall ye sleep,
Oceans a royal bed.
Rocked in the deep, Flora will keep
Watch by your weary head.

Many's the lad fought on that day
Well the claymore could wield;
When the night came silently lay
Dead on Culloden's field.

Burned are our homes, exile and death
Scatter the loyal men;
Yet ére the sword cool in the sheath
Charlie will come again.

The Lady *on radio*

Age/Grade Level or Audience: Elementary or middle school drama or creative writing lesson; drama club project; school or community reading theater original presentation; women's studies course presentation; civic or neighborhood celebration of Women's History Month; woman's club follies or talent show.

Description: Create a female character in the style of early radio.

Procedure: Work within groups to script, rehearse, and present a female version of an early radio series. Use these as models:

Adventures of Harry Nile	*Falcon Show*	*Night Gallery*
Boston Blackie	*Family Theater*	*Sealed Book*
Cape Cod Mystery Theater	*Green Hornet*	*The Shadow*
Dark Fantasy	*Lone Ranger*	*The Whistler*
Dick Tracy	*Mercury Theater*	

Appoint a special team to provide a variety of sound effects either from tapes or CDs or using original methods; for example, walking across gravel or opening a creaky door. Begin and end scenes with mood music. Complete the verisimilitude with these advertisements from the period: Staley's Laundry Starch, Octagon Soap, Lydia Pinkham's Compound, and White Camelia Hair Dressing.

Budget: $

Sources:

MacDonald, J. Fred. *Don't Touch That Dial!* Nelson-Hall, 1979.

Mott, Robert L. *Radio Sound Effects: Who Did it, and How, in the Era of Live Broadcasting.* McFarland & Co., 1992

Sterling, Christopher H., et al., eds. *History of Broadcasting: Radio to Television.* Ayer, 1972.

Wireless Music and Audio Collection. Minnesota Public Radio, n.d.

Wolff, Howard, and Irwin Jacobson. *Radio: A Blast from the Past.* Sound Music Publications, 1988.

Alternative Applications: Work with a group to compose a radio script featuring a female heroine for an episode of *Star Trek, Dirty Harry,* or *Perry Mason.* For instance, replace Perry Mason in the courtroom with a female stand-in who solves the case with maximum courtroom drama, legal expertise, and logic.

Living *in the old west*

Age/Grade Level or Audience: Middle school or high school drama class or drama improvisation; school or community theater skits; after-school activity; teacher education model; civic or neighborhood celebration of Women's History Month.

Description: Present a tribute to women of the early American West.

Procedure: Organize original skits, pantomime, blackouts, one-act plays, puppet or shadow theater, or improvisations of scenes from women's lives in pioneer days. Feature these known figures:

Polly Bemis	Mary Fields	Cynthia Ann Parker
Bright Eyes	Mary Elizabeth Lease	Etta Place
Calamity Jane	Maconaqua	Nellie Tayloe Ross
Maria Chona	Biddy Mason	Sacajawea

Dame Shirley	Lola Montez	Belle Starr
Datsolali	Esther McQuigg Morris	Frances Willard
Diamond Lil	Carry Nation	Sarah Winnemucca
Diana Fletcher	Annie Oakley	Laura Ingalls Wilder

Consider these situations as models:

- Frances Willard, president of the Women's Christian Temperance Union, campaigns for woman's suffrage, public schools, better conditions for working women, and peace

- Datsolali violates Paiute laws against selling crafts and earns $10,000 for a basket done Washo style

- Nellie Tayloe Ross stands before the people of Wyoming and is sworn in as governor in 1925

- Maconagua, a Caucasian woman from Pennsylvania kidnapped by the Miami, insists on remaining with the tribe, rearing her two sons, and speaking the language of the Miami rather than English

- Mary Elizabeth Lease, the "Cyclone of Kansas," studies law and advises grangers to work together to fight off railroad land-grabs

- dressed in men's chaps and buckskins, Calamity Jane performs trick shooting with a rifle in a traveling wild-west show

- Cynthia Ann Parker, Caucasian wife of Chief Pete Nocona and mother of Comanche military leader Quanah Parker, supports guerrilla bands evading military orders to move their tribe to the Oklahoma reservation

- Belle Starr, wife of Cherokee Sam Starr, carries on a blood feud against the men who murdered Jim Reed, her first husband, and drove her away from their Texas home

- Maria Chona, Papago autobiographer and medicine women, leads anthropologist Ruth M. Underhill over Arizona Territory in the 1930s

- "Stagecoach" Mary Fields accepts a job as a stagecoach driver and mail deliverer and learns to harness a team of oxen for heavy hauling or dredging

- Bright Eyes, also called Susette La Flesche, Omaha writer and social worker, presses local politicians to support the Dawes Act, which allowed Indians to purchase land

- Esther McQuigg Morris, serves as justice of the peace in South Pass City, Wyoming, in 1870

- Carry Nation invades saloons and bars in Topeka, Kansas, and hacks barrels of beer and countertops with a hatchet before going to jail on behalf of the Women's Christian Temperance Union

- Sarah Winnemucca, Paiute interpreter and guide, writes textbooks for the children of her school near Humboldt Lake, Nevada

Add ordinary roles: sweetheart, wife, widow, hired girl, healer, heiress, coquette, land owner, ranch manager, squatter, mother, cook, nurse, midwife, *curandera,* actor, driver, saloonkeeper, teacher, religious leader, rider, painter, writer, potter, gardener, herder, fisher, hunter, or hiker. Play these parts:

- a New Mexican *curandera* traveling on muleback to a distant ranch to treat an outbreak of typhoid fever with dried wild cherry root, willow bark, and mint tea

- an indentured house servant whose main job is tending the fires under black kettles and shaving soap into the water to wash the weekly laundry, which she scrubs, wrings out, and dries on a pegged laundry stretcher before ironing each piece with a coal-stoked flatiron

- the manager of a restaurant serving meals to gold prospectors, stagecoach passengers, pony express riders, Indian agents, wranglers, *vaqueros,* or itinerant preachers

- a noted midwife who travels many miles to treat sickly infants and stressed mothers with massage, inhalant teas, and herbs gathered from the desert

- an Apache mother carrying a newborn in a cradleboard suspended from a tumpline about her forehead and leading a horse pulling a travois to a new home in Indian Territory, west of Fort Smith, Arkansas

- a Pawnee girl helping her family harvest camas roots, sweet grass, and wild turnips for food and as trade goods

- a storyteller for a Southwestern tribe who teaches children the value of living pueblo-style, where the winds cool the indoor air and the lofty rooms remain safe from animal and human predators

- a Quaker homesteader carrying a harmonium for the parlor of a log cabin on the Snake River and bringing song books to use in a frontier music school

- a seamstress sewing children's clothes, shirts, pinafores, dresses, jackets, sunbonnets, pantaloons, long underwear, bloomers, riding skirts, aprons, chaps, boots, handbags, saddlebags, shoes, and hats

- a public health nurse during an epidemic of scarlet fever, measles, diphtheria, or whooping cough

- a neighbor to a band of Navajo weavers who offers to teach local pioneer women their methods of making blankets in exchange for candles, tapers, and soap

- the eldest daughter of the commanding officer of Fort Kearney who must make appearances at socials, dance with soldiers, bake cookies, serve punch, and put on a strong show of enjoyment for the sake of her father's cavalry career

- an aged Indian woman carrying a bullboat from one side of rapids to another to pick huckleberries or bearberries or to catch fish in a stone weir, smoke them over a pine chip flame, and bury them in a cache for winter

- a widow of a farmer who died leaving herd animals to tend and sell, cows to milk, chickens to feed, vegetables to irrigate and harvest, and small children to rear far from a town, church, or school

- a small Oklahoma girl who carries a basket to the open prairie to collect buffalo chips to keep the family's sod hut warm during winter and to provide fuel for cooking and heating water

- a Shoshone basket-weaver who cuts willow withes, soaks them for weaving, and makes trays, sunshades, backrests, baskets, and toys for her family and as trade items

- a bartered bride from Philadelphia who joins husband and stepsons in cutting, transporting, and notching logs for a cabin to be roofed with sod until the family earns enough for finished lumber to build a permanent dwelling, barn, and fencing

Budget: $$

Sources:

Chona, Mary. *Papago Woman.* Holt, 1979.

Cole, Adelaide M. "Mary Draper Ingles: Pioneer Heroine." *Daughters of the American Revolution Magazine,* March 1991, 195–97.

Coolidge, Olivia. *Women's Rights: The Suffrage Movement in America.* E. P. Dutton, 1966.

Dances with Wolves. Critics Choice, n.d. (Video)

Dorothy Molter: Living in the Boundary Waters. Direct Cinema Ltd. n.d. (Video)

Emsden, Katherine. *Voices from the West: Life along the Trail.* Discovery Enterprises, 1992.

Her Own Words: Pioneer Women's Diaries. Instructional Video, 1986. (Video)

Levenson, Dorothy. *Homesteaders and Indians.* Franklin Watts, 1971.

———. *Women of the West.* Franklin Watts, 1973.

Levy, Jo Ann. *They Saw the Elephant: Women in the California Gold Rush.* University of Oklahoma Press, 1992.

Liza's Pioneer Diary. Direct Cinema Ltd., n.d. (Video)

Luchetti, Cathy. *Women of the West* Orion Books, 1982.

Marks, Paula Mitchell. "Our Frontier Weaving Heritage." *Handwoven,* September/October 1994, 72–76.

Miller, Brandon Marie. *Buffalo Gals: Women of the Old West.* Lerner Group, 1996.

Prairie Cabin: A Norwegian Pioneer Woman's Story. Instructional Video, 1991. (Video)

Reiter, Joan Swallow. *The Old West: The Women.* Time Life Books, 1978.

Rosebud Yellow Robe. *An Album of the American Indian.* Franklin Watts, 1971.

Sarah Plain and Tall. Critics Choice, n.d. (Video)

Schlissel, Lillian. *Women's Diaries of the Westward Journey.* Schocken, 1992.

Skylark. Critics Choice, n.d. (Video)

Stratton, Joanna L. *Pioneer Women: Voices from the Kansas Frontier.* Simon & Schuster, 1981.

Women of the West. Knowledge Unlimited, 1995. (Video)

Alternative Applications: Hold a city or neighborhood costume party for girls and women dressed as female characters from the Old West. Offer prizes for most original costume, best hairstyle, most original braids, and best square dancer. Set up backdrops depicting saloons, main street, a watering trough, ferry, jail, windmill, buckboard, frontier courtroom, one-room school, sod hut, bullboat, gallows, or log trading post. Photograph participants in traditional poses. Keep a scrapbook of festive events, including original barbecue recipes, roping, and bareback riding.

On the *job with May Chinn*

Age/Grade Level or Audience: Elementary or middle school drama or history pantomime; improvisational drama club; school or community reading theater presentation; teacher education course enactment; civic or neighborhood celebration of Women's History Month; history club program.

Description: Pantomime an average day in the busy schedule of Dr. May Chinn, one of the first African-American female doctors.

Procedure: Have groups study the life of Dr. May Chinn. Allow groups to select daily activities to pantomime, either in costume on stage or behind a screen as shadow figures. Use these as models:

- examining mothers and infants at her clinic in Harlem, New York, during the late 1920s
- working in Harlem Hospital as the only female doctor among disapproving males
- riding with ambulance crews on emergency calls at night and on holidays
- working for New York's Department of Public Health at public day care centers
- studying cervical cancer with Dr. George Papanicolaou, whose pap test helped end deaths from cervical cancer
- marching with other black professionals in the 1963 crusade for civil rights led by Dr. Martin Luther King, Jr.
- joining Dr. Elise Strang L'Espérance at the Strang Clinic network, where Dr. Chinn remained for nearly fifty years
- giving advice to slum dwellers who lack preventative medicine, inoculations, plumbing, heat, food, and education
- entering a tenement by kerosene lamp under police escort to treat wounds resulting from family violence or examining victims of a fistfight, stabbing, or shooting

Have participants discuss why it is worthwhile to relive Dr. Chinn's experiences or the experiences of any woman in history. Does the retelling make the experiences more memorable, or lead to a better understanding of the obstacles women have conquered?

Budget: $

Sources:

Abram, Ruth J., ed. *Send Us a Lady Physician: Women Doctors in America, 1835–1920*. W. W. Norton, 1985.

The Black Women Oral History Project. Vol. 2. Meckler/K. G. Saur, 1990.

Butts, Ellen R., and Joyce R. Schwartz. *May Chinn: The Best Medicine*. W. H. Freeman, 1995.

David, George. "A Healing Hand in Harlem." *New York Times*, April 22, 1979.

May Chinn Papers. Schomburg Center for Research in Black Culture, New York City.

Alternative Applications: Have participants make a list of the background music and sounds, historically accurate costumes, lighting, makeup, backdrops, and medical equipment needed for a movie or television miniseries on Dr. May Chinn and on her association with the Strang Clinics. Select an appropriate name for the movie; consider a slate of actors for the parts of Dr. May Chinn and Dr. Elise Strang and some descriptions of extras to play the roles of ambulance attendants and drivers, patients, victims, police officers, and bystanders.

On stage, *on screen*

Age/Grade Level or Audience: Middle school or high school drama film festival; school or community theater presentation, women's studies research database; newspaper feature series; open forum; civic or cinema club's celebration of Women's History Month.

Description: Present a tribute to a select group of female actors.

Procedure: Organize a community screening of films or videotapes of movies that feature themes, performances, concepts, language, music, and ideals of female writers, designers, directors, singers, or actors. Have a panel discuss the value of the woman's perspective in these examples:

- a selection of movies featuring Audrey Hepburn, including *Breakfast at Tiffany's, The Children's Hour, The Nun's Story, My Fair Lady,* and *Roman Holiday*

- Barbra Streisand's myriad characterizations in *Funny Girl, Funny Lady, Nuts, The Way We Were,* and *Yentl*

- Vanessa Redgrave's success in historical roles: *Agatha, Isadora, The Bostonians, Playing for Time, Three Sovereigns for Sister Sarah,* and *Young Catherine*

- Cher's rebellious roles in *Mask, Silkwood,* and *Moonstruck*

- *Daughters of the Dust,* filmed in the outer banks of South Carolina and Georgia and featuring the strong female community of dwindling Gullah villages

- dramatic poet Caroline Knox's "Wilma," from *Sleepers Wake*

- the movies of New Zealand filmmaker Jane Campion: *Sweetie, An Angel at My Table,* and *The Piano*

- Oprah Winfrey's flexibility as talk show host and as a featured performer in *The Color Purple* and *The Women of Brewster Place*

- women's roles as physical and spiritual nurturers in *Eat Drink Man Woman, Babette's Feast, Out of Africa, Grapes of Wrath, The House of the Spirits, Like Water for Chocolate,* and *The Joy Luck Club*

Budget: $$$$

Sources:

Acker, Ally. *Reel Women: Pioneers of the Cinema, 1896 to the Present.* Continuum Publishing Co., 1993.

Horn, Barbara Lee. *Ellen Stewart and La Mama: A Bio-Bibliography.* Greenwood Press, 1993.

Kaplan, E. Ann. *Women and Film: Both Sides of the Camera.* Routledge, 1983.

Knox, Carolina. *Sleepers Wake.* Timken, 1994.

Robinson, Alice M., Vera Mowry Roberts, and Milly S. Barranger. *Notable Women in the American Theatre.* Greenwood Press, 1989.

Severson, Molly, ed. *Performing Artists.* UXL, 1995.

Walker, John, ed. *Halliwell's Film Guide.* HarperPerennial, 1994.

Alternative Applications: Collect input from a class, community group, or movie club and present a film festival starring participants' favorite female film performers. Consider works by these stars:

Julie Andrews	Shirley MacLaine	Sissy Spacek
Bette Davis	Jeanne Moreau	Meryl Streep
Ruby Dee	Rita Moreno	Elizabeth Taylor
Sally Field	Esther Rolle	Shirley Temple
Katharine Hepburn	Winona Ryder	Cicely Tyson
Lena Horne	Simone Signoret	Sigourney Weaver

Accompany the program with a monograph or program listing performances, awards, television and stage appearances, and critical commentary.

Showstoppers *and femme fatales*

Age/Grade Level or Audience: Middle school or high school drama class or drama club practice; school or community theater improvisation; women's studies laboratory theater; local celebration of Women's History Month.

Description: Present skits depicting history's flamboyant and notorious women.

Procedure: Organize original skits, pantomime, blackouts, one-act plays, puppet theater, or improvisations of events in the lives of notorious female figures from history and legend. Incorporate into your drama media focus on these accused or suspected showstoppers and shady ladies:

- card sharks (Poker Alice Tubbs)
- con artists (Ellen Peck)
- cross dressers (Sarah Emma Edmonds, Murray Hall)
- crusading antifeminists (Maribel Morgan)
- crusading feminists (Bella Abzug, Sonia Johnson)
- eccentrics (Lillie Hitchcock Coit, Marlene Dietrich)
- exhibitionists (Frances Johnston, Lillian Russell, Lillie Langtry)
- female criminals (Bonnie Parker, Ma Barker, Anne Bonney)
- murderers (Lucrezia Borgia, Laura Fair)
- madames (Mag Woods, Julia Bulette, Ah Toy)
- mistresses (Nell Gwynn, Lola Montez)
- notorious entertainers (Sally Rand, Mae West)
- opportunists (Diamond Lil, Chiang Ch'ing)
- serial brides (Aimée Crocker, Elizabeth Taylor, Zsa Zsa Gabor)
- shockers (Isadora Duncan, Victoria Woodhull)
- shooters (Annie Oakley, Calamity Jane, Mattie Silks, Phoebe Pember)
- spies (Mata Hari, Sarah Emma Edmonds, Pauline Cushman)
- temptresses (Salome, Adah Menken, Cleopatra)
- wartime tormentors (Axis Sally, Tokyo Rose, Hanoi Hannah)
- wayward royalty (Messalina, Catherine the Great)

Budget: $$

Sources:

Levenson, Dorothy. *Women of the West.* Franklin Watts, 1973.

Miller, Brandon Marie. *Buffalo Gals: Women of the Old West.* Lerner Group, 1996.

Stephens, Autumn. *Wild Women.* Conari Press, 1992.

Alternative Applications: Use desktop publishing or pen and ink to produce wanted posters advertising the most notorious women in history; for example, spies Pauline Cushman or Mata Hari, poisoner Lucrezia Borgia, or propagandists Hanoi Hannah or Seoul City Sue. Describe each by height, build, coloring, and habits, name male partners or mates, using these as models

- Clyde Barrow and Bonnie Parker
- Etta Place, Butch Cassidy, and the Sundance Kid
- Livia and Augustus Caesar

Name the city or area where each is best known and the activities for which each is wanted: bank robbery, poisoning, car theft, treason, vote stealing, election rigging, conspiracy, treason, complicity with the enemy, kidnapping, spying, or unlawful flight.

To the *polls*

Age/Grade Level or Audience: Middle school or high school creative writing laboratory; school or community theater presentation; women's studies collaborative theater; newspaper feature series.

Description: Produce a video or a series of skits detailing women's fight for the right to vote.

Procedure: Organize small groups to act out confrontations, give readings, and role-play the initiatives of women toward full enfranchisement. Include these scenes:

- **March 11, 1776** Abigail Adams writes to her husband John Adams to provide women full representation in the new government.

- **July 19–20, 1848** Elizabeth Cady Stanton and Lucretia Mott initiate the world's first women's convention at Seneca Falls, New York, to press for their legal rights to the ballot. James Gordon Bennett reported in the *New York Herald* that Lucretia Mott would make a good U.S. president.

- **October 1850** Attendance is heavy at the National Woman's Rights Convention in Worcester, Massachusetts.

- **1851** Sojourner Truth addresses a suffragist convention in Akron, Ohio with her famous "Ain't I a Woman" speech.

- **January 1868** Elizabeth Cady Stanton, Parker Pillsbury, and Susan B. Anthony issue *The Revolution,* a pro-suffrage newspaper.

- **December 10, 1869** Wyoming's legislature gives women the right to vote in state elections.

- **Thanksgiving Day, 1872** Susan B. Anthony and her sister are arrested for registering to vote in the November 5 election. Their trial in June 19, 1873, in Canandaigua, New York, ends in a guilty verdict and a $100 fine, which Anthony refuses to pay.

- **1882** Congress appoints a committee to study women's demands. Four years later, supporters press for a vote, but legislators table the discussion.

- **February 25, 1887** The Senate rejects women's suffrage by a two to one vote.

96

. . . .
Celebrating *women's history*

- **1890** Crusaders for suffrage join efforts in the coordinated National American Woman Suffrage Association. Three years later, Carrie Chapman Catt, a former school principal and journalist, leads the battle in Colorado.

- **1900** Carrie Chapman Catt is elected president of the National American Woman Suffrage Association, which convenes in Washington, D.C.

- **1910** Inez Millholland Boissevain rides a white horse and carries a banner urging "Forward into Light." She dies six years later in Los Angeles while delivering a suffragist speech.

- **May 5, 1912** 10,000 women march down Fifth Avenue in New York City in a pro-suffrage demonstration.

- **March 4, 1913** A mob attacks suffrage paraders in Washington, D.C.

- **March 1913** Everett P. Wheeler opposes voting rights for women in a speech before the New York State Association. He declares that children will suffer from neglect if women become involved in politics.

- **February 14, 1916** Suffragists flood Congressional mailboxes with valentines reminding the legislators of women's rights to full representation.

- **1917** Alice Paul leads the National Women's Party. Quiet picketing at the White House leads to arrest, brutalization, verbal abuse, force-feeding of women on hunger strikes, and solitary confinement. On June 22, Lucy Burns and Katherine Morey are arrested for obstructing traffic. They carry banners with Woodrow Wilson's own words inscribed: "We will fight for the things we have always held nearest to our hearts, for democracy, for the right of those who submit to authority to have a voice in their own government."

- **January 10, 1918** Congress passes the Anthony Amendment; the Senate rejects it.

- **May 1919** Woodrow Wilson encourages Congress to pass the Anthony Amendment. After a 72-year struggle, the measure succeeds on **June 4, 1919.**

- **August 26, 1920** The ratified 19th Amendment is added to the U.S. Constitution.

- **February 15, 1921** Adelaide Johnson completes a statue honoring Susan B. Anthony, Lucretia Mott, and Elizabeth Cady Stanton. The work stands in the first floor crypt of the U.S. Capitol.

Include words and deeds by these women or create an honor roll on the playbill:

- Amidon, Beulah, poet
- Belmont, Mrs. O. H. P., philanthropist
- Blackwell, Alice Stone, journalist
- Brown, Rev. Olympia, Wisconsin state leader
- Clafflin, Rev. Adelaide, suffragist
- Day, Dorothy, social worker and editor
- Duniway, Abigail Scott, Pacific Northwest suffragist
- Gage, Matilda Joslyn, crusader
- Harrison, Ella, orator
- Howe, Julia Ward, songwriter
- James, Ada Lois, Wisconsin social reformer

- Johnson, Grace, temperance advocate

- Laidlaw, Harriet Burt, New York state leader

- Leslie, Mrs. Frank, philanthropist

- McCulloch, Catharine Waugh, Illinois state leader, lobbyist, and attorney

- Morris, Esther, Wyoming state leader

- Owens, Helen Brewster, organizer

- Park, Maud Wood, Massachusetts state leader

- Rankin, Jeannette, first U.S. congresswomen

- Roberts, Margaret, Idaho state leader

- Robinson, Harriet Hanson, mill worker

- Shaw, Rev. Anna Howard, suffragist

- Somerville, Nellie Nugent, Mississippi state leader and temperance worker

- Stone, Lucy, feminist, who married in 1855 and kept her maiden name

- Terrell, Mary Church, organizer, clubwoman

- Truth, Sojourner, evangelist and reformer

- Warren, Nina Otero, New Mexico legislator

- Wright, Martha, supporter and demonstrator

Budget: $$$$

Sources:

Flexner, Eleanor. *Century of Struggle.* Belknap Press, 1976.

Holland, Patricia G., and Ann D. Gordon, eds. *The Papers of Elizabeth Cady Stanton and Susan B. Anthony.* Scholarly Resources Inc., 1989. (Microfilm)

Meyers, Madeleine, ed. *Forward into Light: The Struggle for Woman's Suffrage.* Discovery Enterprises, 1994.

Scott, Anne Firor, ed. *Woman's Suffrage.* University Publications of America, 1994.

Van Voris, Jacqueline. *Carrie Chapman Catt, A Public Life.* Feminist Press, 1987.

Wheeler, Marjorie S., ed. *One Woman One Vote: Rediscovering the Woman Suffrage Movement.* NewSage Press, 1995.

Alternative Applications: Start a summer writing project by organizing volunteers to script a women's history play or outdoor drama, *To the Polls!,* to commemorate the events leading up to enfranchisement of female citizens. Study police uniforms, women's costumes, vehicles, and other details from the period to create an aura of accuracy.

Woman *as director*

Age/Grade Level or Audience: Middle school or high school drama class or drama lesson; school or community theater discussion; women's studies lecture; newspaper column or feature series; open forum; civic or neighborhood celebration of Women's History Month; monograph or playbill.

Description: Create extended definitions of major stage and movie terms using women-centered examples.

Procedure: Compile a list of major stage or movie terms. Using examples from films directed by women, define each term with detailed analysis of scenery, staging, character development, theme, symbol, props, music, lighting, and costume. Cover these important terms:

action	exposition	romance
allegory	falling action	round character
antagonist	flat character	set piece
aside	hero	soliloquy
catastrophe	incongruity	stagecraft
climax	ingenue	stereotype
comedy	leitmotif	symbol
complication	masque	tone
conclusion	melodrama	tragedy
conflict	motif	tragicomedy
crisis	obstacle	vignette
destiny	protagonist	villain
dramatic irony	resolution	

Refer to these movies directed by women:

- *Awakenings,* Penny Marshall
- *Children of a Lesser God,* Randa Haines
- *Daughters of the Dust,* Julie Dash
- *The Doctor,* Randa Haines
- *A League of Their Own,* Penny Marshall
- *Little Man Tate,* Jodie Foster
- *Paris Is Burning,* Jennie Livingston
- *The Prince of Tides,* Barbra Streisand
- *Rambling Rose,* Jennie Livingston
- *Session Man,* Laura Groppe
- *Stepkids,* Joan Micklin Silver
- *Swept Away. . .,* Lina Wertmüller
- *This Is My Life,* Nora Ephron
- *Triumph of the Will,* Leni Riefenstahl
- *Yentl,* Barbra Streisand

Collect the definitions in a single database for future reference, additions, and deletions. Leave the database open for group study and analysis.

Budget: $$

Sources:

Aburdene, Patricia, and John Naisbitt. *Megatrends for Women*. Villard, 1992.

Acker, Ally. *Reel Women: Pioneers of the Cinema, 1896 to the Present*. Continuum Publishing Co., 1993.

Kaplan, E. Ann. *Women and Film: Both Sides of the Camera*. Routledge, 1983.

Miller, Lynn Fieldman. *The Hand that Holds the Camera*. Garland Publishing, 1988.

Slide, Anthony. *Early Women Directors*. A. S. Barnes, 1977.

Walker, John, ed. *Halliwell's Film Guide*. HarperPerennial, 1994.

"Women Who Made the Movies." VCI Home Video, 1991. (Video)

Alternative Applications: Compose an essay comparing the female roles in two films made by female directors. Consider these parallel themes:

- the supernatural in *Daughters of the Dust* and *Big*

- prejudice in *Yentl* and *This Is My Life*

- physical handicap in *Children of a Lesser God* and *Awakenings*

- maturity in *Stepkids* and *Little Man Tate*

- vulnerability in *The Prince of Tides* and *Rambling Rose*

- female strengths in *Paris Is Burning* and *The Doctor*

Discuss variations on a single theme, as with the vulnerability of the psychiatrist and patient in *The Prince of Tides* and the vulnerability of Rose, her employers, and her wooers in *Rambling Rose*. Comment on the differences in tone and purpose between the two films.

Women *and theater*

Age/Grade Level or Audience: Middle school or high school drama class or drama club research topic; school or community theater program notes; women's studies poster series; newspaper column or open forum; civic or neighborhood arts celebration.

Description: Publish a group of articles on the role of women in theater.

Procedure: Select a topic relating to women's roles in theater history and write a brief overview to appear in a school paper, local column, tourist brochure, Women's History Month handout, poster, monograph, or program to be distributed in an entertainment complex, library, or museum.

Consider these topics:

- Anne Bracegirdle and seventeenth-century audiences

- children's drama or reading theater

- drama by female authors

- England's female legacy: Fiona Shaw, Vanessa Redgrave, and Joan Plowright

- Helen Hayes, America's First Lady of the Stage

- men playing women's parts in Elizabethan drama

- Nell Gwynn and the Restoration stage

- spicy lady's roles of the English Restoration stage
- women's work for the National Theater Project
- women who won an Oscar or Tony
- women's comedy in vaudeville

Budget: $$$

Sources:

Aburdene, Patricia, and John Naisbitt. *Megatrends for Women*. Villard, 1992.

Chinoy, Helen Krich, and Linda Walsh Jenkins, eds. *Women in American Theatre*. Theatre Communications Group, 1987.

Davis, Tracy, C. *Actresses As Working Women: Their Social Identity in Victorian England*. Routledge, 1992.

Dillon, Ann, and Cynthia Bix. *Theater: Contributions of Women*. Dillon Press, 1978.

Horn, Barbara Lee. *Ellen Stewart and La Mama: A Bio-Bibliography*. Greenwood Press, 1993.

Howe, Elizabeth. *The First English Actresses*. Cambridge University Press, 1992.

Robinson, Alice M., Vera Mowry Roberts, and Milly S. Barranger. *Notable Women in the American Theatre*. Greenwood Press, 1989.

Severson, Molly, ed. *Performing Artists*. UXL, 1995.

Alternative Applications: Collect essays by local theater buffs, teachers, literature specialists, journalists, drama critics, arts council members, actors, directors, stage managers, or drama historians. Create a scrapbook or monograph that stresses the role of women in the development of your area's community theater. Note unusual adaptations, particularly signing for the hearing impaired, dance theater, reader's workshops, amateur or unpublished one-act plays, improvisation, youth theater, pantomime, puppet shows, or laboratory theater.

Women *workers*

Age/Grade Level or Audience: Elementary or middle school history dramatization; union or small business association newsletter feature; Business and Professional Women's League program; women's studies forum; youth theater improvisation.

Description: Create a dramatic scenario in which servant women and girls from historical periods meet to discuss their work.

Procedure: Have participants work in groups to create a scenario set in an early-to-late eighteenth-century town in any country or island on the globe. Select a setting at a holiday gathering, town water hydrant or pump, weekly market, or commons where working women gathered to discuss matters relevant to their employment. Include several types of workers:

bondwomen	hired girl	chambermaid
nanny	cook	housekeeper
seamstress	indentured servant	slave
governess	laundress	wetnurse

Have participants discuss, in detail, their positions. Describe a typical day from morning to night. In what type of environment do they work? What is their pay? How content in their jobs are they? Are they treated kindly? Are they overworked? And what are their options in the workplace, or their opportunities for an education?

Budget: $$

Sources:

Kessler-Harris, Alice. *Women Have Always Worked: A Historical Overview.* Feminist Press, 1995.

Michelson, Maureen R., ed. *Women and Work: In Their Own Words.* NewSage Press, 1995.

Schneider, Dorothy and Carl J. Schneider. *Women in the Workplace.* ABC-Clio, 1993.

Weatherford, Doris, *American Women's History.* Prentice-Hall, 1994.

Alternative Applications: Compile a chart contrasting working conditions, expectations, education, and responsibilities of female workers. To begin the matrix, compare cook, governess, housekeeper, indentured servant, laundress, and wetnurse.

Education

Fairy *tales: Mirrors for womanhood*

Age/Grade Level or Audience: Teacher education class seminar; renewal credit workshop for language teachers; Women's History Month presentation or monograph.

Description: Conduct a seminar to study the impact of fairy tales on young readers.

Procedure: Invite student teachers, language arts teachers, guidance counselors, and librarians to a seminar on fairy tales that present a stereotyped or skewed vision of female worth. Discuss the following issues and themes in story or movie versions of these:

"Aladdin"	"Pocahontas"
"Alice in Wonderland"	"The Princess and the Frog"
"Beauty and the Beast"	"Rapunzel"
"Cinderella"	"The Red Shoes"
"Goldilocks and the Three Bears"	"Rose Red"
"The Little Match Girl"	"Sleeping Beauty"
"The Little Mermaid"	"Snow Queen"
"Little Red Riding Hood"	"Snow White"
"The Little Snow Girl"	"Thumbelina"
"Peter Pan"	"The Wizard of Oz"

Possible focuses of discussion include:

- action as an unwomanly behavior
- beauty as woman's most enduring trait
- belief that men rescue women and that women need rescuing and protecting
- helplessness as the perpetual state of women
- motherhood and home as the prime goals of women

Contrast Eurocentric lore with that of Native Americans, Africans, Asians, and Polynesians. Determine what concepts appear to be universal, especially the reverence for beauty, goodness, amiability, and virginity. Conclude with comments on the lasting effects of childhood lore on the self-concepts of girls. Appoint an *ad hoc* group to make a list of stories, videos, games, and CDs that teach young women empowerment and self-reliance.

Budget: $$$

Sources:

Andersen, Hans Christian. *Complete Hans Christian Andersen Fairy Tales*. Outlet Book Company, 1993.

Barchers, Suzanne. *Wise Women: Folk and Fairy Tales from around the World*. Libraries Unlimited, 1990.

Cinderella. Walt Disney Productions, 1984. (Video)

The Little Mermaid. Walt Disney Productions, 1989. (Video)

Phelps, Ethel J. *The Maid of the North*. Henry Holt & Company, 1982.

———. *Tatterhood and Other Tales*. Feminist Press at The City University of New York, 1978.

Pocahontas. Walt Disney Productions, 1995. (Video)

Red Riding Hood/Goldilocks. 1990. (Video)

Rumplestiltskin. 1982. (Video)

San José, Christine, and Debrah Santini. *Cinderella*. Boyds Mills Press, 1994.

Von Franz, Marie-Louise. *The Feminine in Fairy Tales*. Shambhala Publications, 1993.

Wray, Kit. *Rapunzel*. Boyds Mills Press, 1991.

———. *Snow White*. Boyds Mills Press, 1991.

Alternative Applications: Present an overview of the changing roles of girls and women in children's fantasy literature. Contrast early stereotypical fairy tales with more current children's literature that presents females as active, assertive, rational, multifaceted, talented, and self-reliant. Read aloud or view film or cartoon versions of these titles:

- Madeleine L'Engle's *A Wrinkle in Time*
- Natalie Babbitt's *Tuck Everlasting*
- Richard Adams's *Watership Down*
- Robert C. O'Brien's *Mrs. Frisbie and the Rats of NIMH*
- Robin McKinley's *Beauty*
- E. B. White's *Charlotte's Web*

Encourage local libraries to make book, CD, audiocassette, and video versions of these titles a focus of summer reading programs.

Grammar *as history teacher*

Age/Grade Level or Audience: Language education model; renewal credit workshop; elementary and middle school language or grammar class drill or individualized work packets; Women's History Month English-as-a-second-language research; GED or adult literacy training

Description: Teach a lesson on sentence variety that presents information about women in history.

Procedure: Present a handout modeling varied sentence structure as a method of alleviating sameness in writing and speaking. Identify grammatical structures that realign information for the sake of stress and appeal. Use this example as a beginning:

- Harriet Beecher Stowe published a book about slavery. She had no idea that her book would push the nation toward war. (two simple sentences)

- How can a novel influence the thinking of an entire nation? (rhetorical question)

- Stowe, <u>who was an ardent abolitionist,</u> pictured the damage that slavery did to black families. (nonrestrictive adjective clause)

- Uncle Tom, <u>a decent old family retainer,</u> represents Christian qualities. (appositive phrase)

- <u>Because she wants to flee with her husband to Canada,</u> Eliza attempts to cross the Ohio River on floating chunks of ice. (introductory adverb clause)

- <u>To make amends for injustice,</u> George Shelby returns home to free his slaves. (introductory infinitive)

- <u>As a defense of her abolitionism,</u> Stowe published *A Key to Uncle Tom's Cabin.* (introductory prepositional phrase)

- In 1852, Stowe earned world recognition from the publication of *Uncle Tom's Cabin;* four years later, she completed *Dred: A Tale of the Great Dismal Swamp,* a less successful book. (compound sentence)

- <u>Writing a humanitarian masterpiece</u> was Harriet Beecher Stowe's intent. (gerund phrase)

- <u>Perceiving the power of the printed word,</u> Stowe realized that her skill as a fiction writer had benefited the nation. (introductory participial phrase)

Budget: $

Sources:

Maggio, Rosalie. *The Dictionary of Bias-Free Usage: A Guide to Nondiscriminatory Language.* Oryx, 1991.

Mills, Jane. *Womanwords.* Macmillan, 1989.

O'Hare, Frank. *Sentence Combining.* National Council of Teachers of English, 1973.

Snodgrass, Mary Ellen. *The English Book.* Perma-Bound, 1991.

Alternative Applications: Divide students into groups to prepare flash cards on topics including usage, capitalization, punctuation, spelling, idioms, and levels of language. Incorporate women's history into each example. Place the cards in a display case or on a bulletin board as a double lesson in language and women's history.

Irene *Hunt—teacher and writer*

Age/Grade Level or Audience: Middle school or high school young-adult author's day; civic teacher appreciation presentation; civic club or book club presentation celebrating American Education Week.

Description: Describe the multifaceted career of Irene Hunt.

Procedure: Present a handout emphasizing the positive impetus of teaching as a preparation for other careers; for example, politics, real estate, business, management, library science, publishing, sales, and computer programming. As a model, list the stages in the career of Irene Hunt: teacher, college professor, supervisor, consultant, and author of young adult historical fiction.

- Born May 18, 1907, in rural Newton, Illinois, Irene Hunt grew up sharing oral stories with her father, Franklin Hunt, who encouraged her natural abilities as a storyteller.

- When her father died in 1914, she lived with her sister Beulah and her grandparents and studied her grandfather's ability to sing, fiddle, and act out biblical lore. His lively narratives from the Civil War made the firing on Fort Sumter and the Battle of Bull Run seem real.

- Hunt earned language and education degrees from the University of Illinois and the University of Minnesota and studied psychology in post-graduate work.

- She taught public school English and French in Oak Park, Illinois, from 1930–1945, then worked as an instructor in the psychology department of the University of South Dakota for four years before returning to public school in Cicero, Illinois, as a junior high history teacher.

- At 57, while working as a language arts consultant in North Riverside, Illinois, she set out to pursue her ambitions of making American history come alive with drama and historical fiction.

- She won a Newbery Medal for the semi-autobiographical *Up the Road Slowly* and was nominated for the Newbery Medal for *Across Five Aprils* (1964), a Civil War-era novel drawn from her grandfather's stories. Later titles include *Trail of Apple Blossoms* (1968), *No Promises in the Wind* (1970), *The Lottery Rose* (1976), *William* (1978), and *Claws of a Young Century* (1980). For her innovative writing, Hunt won the Charles W. Follett, American Notable Book, Friends of Literature, Lewis Carroll Shelf, Dorothy Canfield Fisher, and Clara Ingram Judson Memorial awards.

- Retired to St. Petersburg, Florida, she continued her career as teacher-turned-writer of historical fiction as a means of developing values and character in children. In published advice to aspiring writers, she encouraged them to study their own childhood memories, both trivial and significant.

Form a round table to discuss the tasks and talents that transfer from the classroom into other fields: organizing, illustrating, dramatizing, researching, authenticating, and narrating. Explain how Irene Hunt's positive experiences in the classroom and in educational supervision prepared her for the role of writer.

Budget: $

Sources:

Beem, Wendell Bruce. "Aunt Irene." *Horn Book,* June, 1970, 429–33.

DeMontreville, Doris, and Donna Hill, eds. *Third Book of Junior Authors.* H. W. Wilson, 1972.

Hunt, Irene. "Try to Remember. . . ." *Today's Education,* February, 1973, 43–44.

———. "Writing for Children." *The Writer,* March 1970, 17–20.

Alternative Applications: Have individuals study the influence of teaching careers on these writers of young adult fiction:

- Catherine Marshall *(Christy, Julie)*

- Cynthia Voigt *(Homecoming; Izzy, Willy Nilly; Dicey's Song; Wings of a Falcon)*

- Mildred Taylor *(Roll of Thunder, Hear My Cry; Let the Circle Be Unbroken; Song of the Trees)*

- Paula Danziger *(The Cat Ate My Gymsuit, Can You Sue Your Parents for Malpractice?, Amber Brown Is Not a Crayon)*

- Ursula LeGuin *(Earth-Sea Trilogy, The Lathe of Heaven, The Left Hand of Darkness)*

Have each participant report on the influence of teaching on the writer's style and point of view. Note scenes between teacher and student in each work and discuss innovative methods of influencing and counseling in the classroom setting.

Modeling *logic*

Age/Grade Level or Audience: Teacher education lesson model; renewal credit workshop for writing teachers; interdisciplinary logic exercise; Women's History Month English research; GED or adult literacy training program.

Description: Draw graphic lessons in logic featuring women's history as the subject.

Procedure: Present a handout modeling varied methods of grouping, webbing, diagramming, integrating, supporting, relating, prioritizing, or outlining ideas. Use these models as ways to teach students to think clearly:

- *least-to-greatest:* Draw a triangle. Place these ideas in priority order, ranging from least important to most important:

Effects of Frequent Pregnancies

* normal *

** nuisance **

* embarrassment *

***** discomfort *****

*** loss of time from job ***

**** drain on family finances ****

** too many parental responsibilities **

********* death of the mother *********

*********** family dysfunction ***********

************* family dissolution *************

************** threat to the planet **************

• *greatest-to-least:* Draw an inverted triangle. Place ideas in reverse-priority order, ranging from most important to least important:

Building Female Self-Esteem

*********** integrating all aspects of the self ***********

********* creating feelings of self-worth *********

*********** expressing oneself ***********

**** developing lasting relationships ****

****** changing bad habits ******

**** increasing friendships ****

****** feeling better ******

** looking better **

• *webbing:* Draw a focal point and attach ideas that relate to it. String together related ideas like these methods of studying women's history:

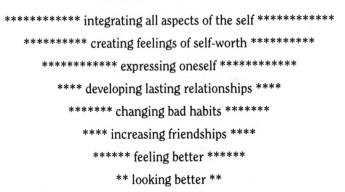

• *flow chart:* Present ideas horizontally, or vertically as one leads to the other. String together evolving concepts horizontally, like these:

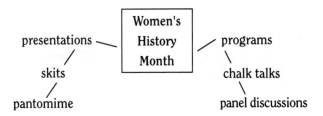

or vertically, like these:

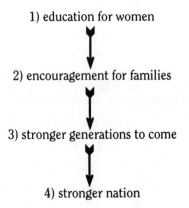

- *cause and effect matrix:* String related ideas chronologically as you lead to a valid conclusion. Move from one related topic to another in this style:

1) World War II requires women to work to replace to replace men **+** 2) women join

all phases of the military in non-combat roles **+** 3) women experience equality **+**

4) women return to peacetime roles and set new goals to achieve equality in opportunities,

pay, and advancement **=** RESULTS: Women's Rights Movement

- *main ideas table:* Support a tabletop with four legs. Use four supporting ideas to undergird or strengthen a major idea:

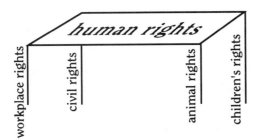

- *cycle diagram:* Draw a cycle of events that replicate themselves. Use topics that move the sequence of events in repeated revolutions:

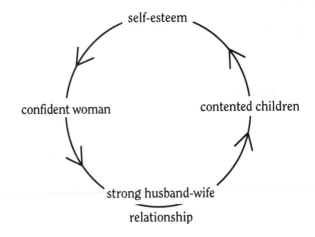

Present other sets of information. Have groups determine which logic method best displays the flow of ideas. Use these data as models:

- changes in the female outlook from childhood to old age
- effects of classroom experience on girls' choices of careers
- home training as a groundwork for stable adulthood
- problems of sexism that infiltrate all community levels

Budget: $

Sources:

Hester, Joseph P. *Building Bridges: Conflict Resolution.* New View Press, 1996.

———. *Teaching for Thinking.* Carolina Academic Press, 1994.

Hester, Joseph P., and Don R. Killian. *Cartoons for Thinking: Issues in Ethics and Values.* Trillium, 1984.

Johannessen, Larry R. *Designing and Sequencing Prewriting Activities.* ERIC Clearinghouse on Reading and Writing, 1982.

Proett, Jackie, and Kent Gill. *The Writing Process in Action.* National Council of Teachers of English, 1986.

Alternative Applications: Present participants with logic lessons to fit to suitable diagrams. Consider these statements:

- crime against women leads to decaying cities where people are afraid to work, dine, or shop after dark

- progressive deterioration of hormones and an unhealthy lifestyle lead to osteoporosis

- strong parental acceptance and approval produces women who respond well to the demands of home, family, and career

Use desktop publishing to create a monograph of logic diagrams. Place copies in public and college libraries.

Preparing *women* *for motherhood*

Age/Grade Level or Audience: Nursing mothers' or midwives' refresher lecture; women's clinic bulletin-board display; hospital parenthood course; women's health workshop; high school or college library reference list.

Description: Present the history of midwifery, the Lamaze Method, and La Leche League.

Procedure: Draw up a brief overview of the changes in attitudes toward motherhood in recent decades. Emphasize these points:

- Midwifery, supported briefly by the Sheppard-Towner act of 1920, then driven underground, resurged with feminist support in the late 1960s to give women more control over birthing procedures that doctors tended to treat most often as surgery. As state governments began to reassess the spiraling cost of hospital care, they relaxed opposition to midwives, who now practice privately, in women's clinics, and in hospitals. The American College of Nurse-Midwives, established in Washington, D.C., in 1955, offers coursework and certification in midwifery. In 1982, the Midwives Alliance of North America began a network of information and support groups to assist midwives in their work.

- Lamaze Movement, the dissemination of a technique that channels physical responses to birth into beneficial rhythms, began in France and was established in Detroit in 1958. Through lectures, film, and exercises, women and their coaches train for a mother-assisted, anesthetic-free delivery.

- La Leche League began in Chicago in the 1970s as a counter-movement to pornography and media depiction of breasts as sex objects. Followers denounced bottle feeding as cumbrous and unnatural and returned to breast feeding as a more healthful, convenient method of assuring balanced nutrition and disease-fighting antibodies in their infants.

Budget: $$

Sources:

Breastfeeding: A Problem-Solving Manual. Essential Medical Information Systems, 1991.

Brecher, Deborah, and Jill Lippitt, compilers. *The Women's Information Exchange National Directory.* Avon, 1994.

Lamaze Ready Reference Guide for Labor and Birth. Shapiro Kuba, 1990.

Midwife's Pregnancy and Childbirth Book: Having Your Baby Your Way. Henry Holt, 1990.

The PDR Family Guide to Women's Health and Prescription Drugs. Medical Economics, 1994.

Alternative Applications: Hold a mother's information fair. Distribute journals, brochures, and leaflets on sources of information geared to help mothers prepare for assisted birth, home delivery, or breast feeding. Inquire about videos, handouts, books, and instructors from these sources:

> *Birth Notes* (a quarterly magazine)
> Association for Childbirth at Home, International
> P.O. Box 430
> Glendale, CA 91205-1025
>
> La Leche League International, Inc.
> P.O. Box 1209
> Franklin Park, IL 60131
> 708-455-7730
> 800-LALECHE
> FAX: 708-455-0125
>
> *Midwifery Today* (a quarterly journal)
> P.O. Box 2672
> Eugene, OR 97402
> 503-344-7438

Prize *for the best*

Age/Grade Level or Audience: Middle school American Education Week bulletin board; media feature; civic club contest; education course presentation; local panel discussion.

Description: Sponsor a contest to reward outstanding female educators.

Procedure: In anticipation of Women's History Month, assemble a committee of adults, students, educators, administrators, PTA officials, librarians, family counselors, and textbook authors to reward your area's best female teacher. Provide an overview focussing on innovative professionalism. Use the example of the Ebon International Preparatory Academy.

Founder Florence Alexander, a registered nurse, and her sister, award-winning teacher Joyce Oatman, administer Ebon International Preparatory Academy, a predominately black boarding school for children from preschool to grade twelve in Monroe County, Georgia. The school's strengths include:

- balancing an Afro-centric curriculum with global concerns
- busing students from Atlanta area
- emphasizing computer skills
- fostering a progressive philosophy
- highlighting a spirit of challange
- providing up-to-date science labs
- stressing self-esteem rather than test scores

Set up criteria to enhance the educator selection process. Look for energy, vision, divergent thinking, quality education, respect for children, and love of classroom teaching.

Budget: $$$$$

Sources:

Black Americans of Achievement: Mary McLeod Bethune. Instructional Video, 1994. (Video)

Cumming, Doug. "Shaping Young Minds." *Atlanta Journal & Constitution,* July 9, 1995, 1G, 6G.

Edelman, Marion W. *The Measure of Our Success: A Letter to My Children and Yours.* Beacon Press, 1992.

Pica and Barnes. *Teaching Matters.* Heinle & Heinle, 1990.

Alternative Applications: Maintain a Women's History Month roster of effective female educators, classroom aids, librarians, coaches, counselors, and administrators in the local school system, including private schools, day care centers, colleges, and community colleges. Select a token as a reward: for example, an apple-shaped key chain with a citation about education by Mary McLeod Bethune, Madeline Huner, Marva Collins, Annie Sullivan, or Anna Leonowens.

Teachers *as winners*

Age/Grade Level or Audience: College career study; education course presentation; local panel discussion or religious study celebrating American Education Week; teacher renewal workshop.

Description: Present model lessons based on the methods of award-winning teachers.

Procedure: Study the classroom methods of these and other famous teachers:

- Anna Harriette Leonowens, Welsh tutor of Prince Chowfa Chulalongkorn, subsequent ruler of Siam
- Annie Sullivan, teacher of Helen Keller
- Barbara Scot, teacher in Nepal
- geneticist Francine Essien, 1994–1995 U.S. Professor of the Year
- Laura Ingalls Wilder, prairie schoolteacher

- Vivian Gussin Paley, winner of the MacArthur grant for 1995

- Marva Collins, creator of a ghetto academy for Chicago's disadvantaged black children

Create strategies, handouts, flannel and bulletin boards, audio and video cassettes, art projects, skits, board games, and other methods of presenting concepts to students. Choose a subject that depicts women's history or interests, for example:

- genetics and X-linked diseases

- radium and the work of Marie Curie

- Sheba, Queen of Ethiopia

- the chemistry of female hormones

- the rule of Catherine the Great of Russia

- the relationship between civil rights and women's rights

- beginning French for elementary grades, featuring *les femmes des bureaux et les femmes des fermes*

- Latin sentence structure featuring women's dress, i. e., *palla, tunica, stola*

- the 1990 census and women's place in industry and agriculture

- algebra problems that apply to the homemaker or mother of the family

Videotape lessons in progress to use as models for future teacher preparation courses and workshops. Provide a voice-over explaining the purpose of each segment of the lesson and methods of individualizing instruction.

Budget: $$$

Sources:

Gibson, William. *The Miracle Worker.* Knopf, 1957.

Griffin, Lynne, and Kelly McCann. *The Book of Women: 300 Notable Women History Passed By.* Bob Adams, 1992.

Hill, Marie Somers, and Joyce C. Ragland. *Women as Educational Leaders: Opening Windows, Pushing Ceilings.* Corwin, 1995.

John-Hall, Annette. "Learning, Teaching, Helping—They're in Her Genes." *Sacramento Bee,* April 3, 1994, C1, 5.

————. "Professor of the Year Preceded Her Students over Major Obstacles." *Detroit Free Press,* April 2, 1995, 4J.

Landon, Margaret. *Anna and the King of Siam.* HarperCollins, 1944.

Mahany, Barbara. "Mrs. Paley's Lessons." *Chicago Tribune Magazine,* June 25, 1995, sect. 10, 12–18, 28.

Pickerill, Martha. "Profiles of Four Occupations." *Careers and Colleges,* Spring 1995, 32–40.

Scot, Barbara J. *The Violet Shyness of Their Eyes.* Calyx Books, 1994.

St. Pierre, Suzanne. *Marva.* Carousel Film & Video, 1979. (Film)

Markowitz, Ruth Jacknow. *My Daughter, the Teacher: Jewish Teachers in the New York City Schools.* Rutgers University Press, 1993.

Perlmutter, Donna. "Yvonne Mounsey." *Dance Magazine,* August 1994, 42–43.

"Preparing for the 21st Century." *Ebony,* March 1995, 36–42.

Also, the Internet, America Online, and databases such as Silver Platter, Newsbank, and ERIC.

Alternative Applications: Assign members of a group the task of studying the life of a famous children's governess. Worthy examples are Dorothea Dix and Louisa May Alcott. Conduct a panel discussion or group session to discuss these topics:

- early influences on the governess's career

- preparation for a career in teaching

- pivotal moments in the governess's life

- successes and failures with students

- outlook for advancement and career satisfaction

Invite participants to present any evidence of uniqueness or innovation in the governesses, through readings, photos, art, or acting. Contrast the reality of a governess's position in the home with the literary versions, especially the title character in Charlotte Brontë's *Jane Eyre* or the governess in Henry James's *The Turn of the Screw*. Discuss how the governess's tasks and social rank differed from those of hired girl, charwoman, migrant worker, indentured servant, housekeeper, chambermaid, or slave.

Fashion

Dressed *for fashion, dressed for men*

Age/Grade Level or Audience: Middle school or high school biology or social history project; college history or sociology lecture; women's history symposium; library reading circle discussion; language or vocabulary study; home-school research series; civic or women's club program; children's museum or library display; media feature.

Description: Present a program that explores women's fashions throughout history or culturally acceptable alterations to the body that impair health.

Procedure: Describe worldwide fashion or cultural trends through the ages that have caused women inconvenience, pain, poor hygiene, impaired body function, and even endangerment to health and emotional well being out of a need to please society's dictates or cater to the tastes of future husbands or prospective in-laws. Ask a volunteer to demonstrate on a plastic model or sketch the trend. Use the following commentary on the labret as a model:

- The labret is a circle or disc of bone, shell, wood, stone, or glass worn on a thong through the underlip as a pendulum adorning the chin, often as a symbol of aristocratic birth or prestige. By pulling the lip down, the wearer exposes the bright pink inner tissue, thought attractive by the Haida and Tlingit of British Columbia. The Eskimo version of the labret forms a spool or oval plug that fits into an incision in the lip, which parents slit in a female child's mouth and gradually widen with larger labrets. The Bering Sea Eskimo uses an off-center plug labret for men and a beaded hook for women. The Aleut adorn only men with the lip disc.

Describe each object or procedure on this list and its purpose as well as its liabilities. Note that, even if given a choice, women usually submit if they want to be valued as chaste and obedient, or admired by family, tribe or community, or future mates. Discuss additional drastic body alterations as well as garb that hinders female freedom:

- brass collars
- breast augmentation
- depilatories
- electrolytic removal of facial or body hair
- false fingernails and toenails
- foot binding
- girdles and corsets
- high heels

- hobble skirts

- liposuction

- pierced ears, nose, nipples, or umbilicus (belly button)

- scarification

- tattooing

- uplift bra

- waist cinch

Budget: $

Sources:

Barber, Elizabeth Wayland. *Women's Work: The First 20,000 Years.* W. W. Norton, 1994.

Clark, Gillian. *Women in Late Antiquity: Pagan and Christian Lifestyles.* Oxford University Press, 1993.

Duffy, Martha. "A New Touch of Class." *Time,* April 17, 1995, 54–68.

Hansen, Joseph, Evelyn Reed, and Mary-Alice Waters. *Cosmetics, Fashions and the Exploitation of Women.* Pathfinder, 1995.

Müller, Claudia. *The Costume Timeline.* Thames & Hudson, 1992.

Paterek, Josephine. *Encyclopedia of American Indian Costume.* ABC-Clio, 1994.

Patterson, Lotsee, and Mary Ellen Snodgrass. *Indian Terms of the Americas.* Libraries Unlimited, 1994.

Summers, Barbara. *Skin Deep: The Story of Black Models in America and Abroad.* Amistad Press, 1995.

Tobias, Tobi. "In the Beginning We Are Seamless." *Dance Ink,* July 3–August 31, 1995, 23.

Yarwood, Doreen. *The Encyclopedia of World Costume.* Bonanza, 1986.

Alternative Applications: At the high school and college levels discuss the cultural, religious, and sexual reasons for the clitoridectomy, a form of female circumcision that removes the pleasure centers of the sex organs, sometimes as late as the victim's twelfth year. Note that practitioners often use a razor blade, piece of glass, or other crude, unsterilized tool to complete the ritual act, which some African and Islamic cultures consider an assurance of virginity. Compare the loss of labia or labia and clitoris to the more painful act of infibulation, a ritual pinning of the labia with thorn, skewer, or stitches that results in limited openings to the urethra and vagina, loss of clitoral stimulation, and thick scar tissue that must be slit or stretched before the first sexual contact and cut numerous times to allow multiple childbirths. Account for the religious and cultural taboos levied against women who refuse to endure these rites of passage: for example, banishment, public condemnation, humiliation, and embarrassment for the family.

Dressed *for success*

Age/Grade Level or Audience: K–4 school project; history database; library reading circle bulletin board; language or vocabulary study; home-school art project; children's museum or library research.

Description: Initiate an association game of female names with symbols of successful roles in society and places of importance in history.

Procedure: Present participants with a list of names of famous women. Have students match names to drawings or flannel board cutouts of garments, uniforms, equipment, or other items that distinguish them. Consider these pairings:

- 1995 West Point graduate Rebecca Elizabeth Marier—West Point uniform and diploma
- astronaut Sally Ride—flight suit, helmet, oxygen tanks
- humanitarian Audrey Hepburn—travel bag, UNICEF insignia, baby scale
- journalist Christian Amanpour—microphone, tape recorder, flak jacket
- nurse Clara Barton—nurse's uniform, bandages, medicine bottles
- physicist Marie Curie—chart of the elements, symbol for radium
- prime minister Benazir Bhutto—gavel, brief case, ceremonial crest
- rehabilitation nurse Sister Elizabeth Kenny—towels, lotion, crutches
- skater Kristi Yamaguchi—ice skates, skate skirt, Olympic medal
- sociologist Cherokee chief Wilma Mankiller—briefcase, reservation map, native insignia
- student Dorothy Counts—book bag, notebook paper, pencil
- swimmer Gertrude Ederle—swimsuit, goggles, and swim cap
- U.S. Secretary of the Department of Labor Ivey Baker Priest—account books, GNP charts, national seal
- U.S. soccer goalie Tisha Venturini—chest guard, knee pads, helmet

Have participants add other equipment or items of dress as they learn more about each person.

Budget: $$

Sources:

Anniversary Flier. American Civil Liberties Union, 1995.

Axelrod, Dr. Alan, and Charles Phillips. *What Every American Should Know about American History.* Bob Adams, 1992.

Clark, Gillian. *Women in Late Antiquity: Pagan and Christian Lifestyles.* Oxford University Press, 1993.

Clark, Judith Freeman. *An Almanac of American Women in the Twentieth Century.* Prentice Hall, 1987.

Clement, J., ed. *Famous Deeds of American Women.* Corner House, 1975.

Dennis, Denise. *Black History for Beginners.* Highsmith, 1992.

Great Lives from History: American Women Series. Salem Press, 1995.

Griffin, Lynne, and Kelly McCann. *The Book of Women: 300 Notable Women History Passed By.* Bob Adams, 1992.

Hampton, Henry, and Steve Fayer. *Voices of Freedom: An Oral History of the Civil Rights Movement from the 1950s through the 1980s.* Bantam Books, 1990.

Harris, Laurie Lanzen, ed. *Biography Today.* Omnigraphics, 1993.

Harrison, Cynthia, ed. *Women in National Politics.* University Publications of America, 1995.

Karlekar, Malavika. Introduction to *Changing Lives: Life Stories of Asian Pioneers in Women's Studies.* Feminist Press, 1995.

Lunardini, Christine A. *What Every American Should Known About Women's History.* Bob Adams, 1994.

Alternative Applications: Conclude a study of women in history by creating a game book of dot-to-dot puzzles, scrambled words, anagrams, seek-and-find puzzles, and mazes. Use a variety of topics: sports, medicine, inventions, entertainment, teaching, the military, building and design, scholarship, and leadership. Have students work in groups on each puzzle and present it to other groups to test its level of difficulty. With adult help, complete the grids, drawings, and word games on a desktop publishing program. Use the finished game book as a table favor, PTA or library handout, or hospital waiting room diversion. Trade games with other schools to add to the collection.

Dressing *up history*

Age/Grade Level or Audience: Elementary or middle school art activity; home-school cooperative project; children's museum or library display; county fair booth or city hall Women's History Month exhibit.

Description: Host a Women's History Month dress-up contest.

Procedure: Provide outlets for interest in historical figures by sponsoring a costume party. Set age limits according to the difficulty of these tasks:

- Dress a mannequin in the clothing of a particular period or select a portrait, photo, or description of a specific outfit worn by a famous person to copy. For example, choose the dress of Virginia Dare, the first European born on the North American continent; the Queen of Hawaii, whom Captain Cook met on his first visit to the Sandwich Islands; or Catherine the Great, Russia's powerful empress. Provide each mannequin with a card explaining period, style of dress, activities, and jewelry, flowers, or other adornment.

- Create a similar model by using a plastic doll. Stand the finished historical figure against a backdrop depicting a scene that comes to mind in stories of the person's life. For instance, place Belle Starr in Civil War times and costume; put Kristi Yamaguchi in an ice rink decorated with Olympic flags; or place Anna Leonowens in a nineteenth-century schoolroom in the palace of King Phra Maha Mangut, ruler of Siam.

- Make clay figures showing Arapaho women working together at a common task, such as skinning elk, drying salmon over a rack, guiding a sled over ice, cooking over a woodstove, plucking a wild fowl, or paddling a bullboat.

- Draw stick or cartoon figures of medical researchers looking into a microscope, treating a patient, entering data in a computer, or piloting a space capsule.

Budget: $$$

Sources:

First-Start Biographies. Troll Associates, 1995.

Kalman, Bobbie. *Early Settler Life Series.* Crabtree, 1995.

———. *Historical Communities Series.* Crabtree, 1995.

Point of View: An Overview of U. S. History. Scholastic, 1995. (Laserdisc)

Wisdom, Cynthia Newman. "Help History Come Alive with Mannequins." *Teaching K–8.* October 1994, 44–45.

Alternative Applications: Hold a shadow-box contest in which entrants celebrate women's history with a scene in which women take an active role in community or national life. Consider actress Helen Hayes performing in *Anastasia,* Shirley Chisholm organizing a national presidential campaign, Betsy Ross cutting and sewing stars on a flag, Maori women entering English classes taught by Anglican missionaries, or German women supporting their husbands in an attack on the fighting forces of Julius Caesar.

Fanny *Bishop, entrepreneur*

Age/Grade Level or Audience: Middle school or high school journalism or creative writing assignment; college marketing task; media miniseries; civic club or women's club project; Chamber of Commerce or Business and Professional Women's League display.

Description: Present a brief lecture on the business acumen of Pendleton Mills founder Fanny Kay Bishop.

Procedure: Introduce the concepts and family-oriented business practices of Pendleton Mills, one of America's leading manufacturers of woolen blankets and clothing. Include these data:

- Begun in 1890 under the management of Fanny Kay Bishop, who learned retailing and manufacturing from her father, Thomas Kay, an English weaver, Pendleton Mills is a conservatively managed, established business.

- To assure the company a long life, Fanny Bishop and her husband Clarence sent sons Morton, Clarence Jr., and Broughton to the Philadelphia Textile Institute to study the industry. With a $30,000 investment and matching funds from the town, the Bishops purchased their first mill in Pendleton, Oregon. They named the company after the community and have remained anchored on the west coast. From selling blankets to Indians (including one photographed around the shoulders of Nez Percé Chief Joseph), the company first specialized in ceremonial woollens, then applied its experience to clothing.

- Pendleton has produced a strong following among wool fanciers, whether lovers of logging shirts and tartan ties or wearers of matching skirts, slacks, and sweaters. The high-end cost of their product line places Pendleton beyond the discounters into a separate category reserved for people who prefer lasting, classic clothing over fashions dictated by fancies.

- Drawing on 2,000 employees, headquarters in Portland, Oregon, and thirteen mills spread as far east as Dorr, New Hampshire, the company sells in the neighborhood of $150 million annually, a steady figure despite the fact that Pendleton Mills disdains catalog sale (the chief method of its competitors L. L. Bean, J. Peterman, and Land's End) and rejects hiring out most of its work to sweatshops in Asia, Indonesia, or Mexico.

- Beginning with the purchase of untreated wool, Pendleton's buyers garner raw materials that require grading, sorting, cleaning, spinning, dyeing, and weaving before they reach a sewing machine. Of the finished product, 15% sells from Pendleton's own stores and affiliates.

- Since brother Clarence Bishop's death, managing brothers Mort Jr. and Broughton Bishop remain conservative, as do the other members of the family; John, Peter, Clarence Jr., Charles, and Morton III. The management team maintains a market niche among loyal users of their durable, dependable garments. Pendletonites write fan letters to the office, raving about the service of the company's quality woolens.

• The leader of the line is the outdoor shirt, which brings in 40% of company revenues. Relying on past successes, the company continues to pursue its original intent—to sell quality goods at a fair price. Opting for no cut-rate deals or under-the-counter methods, the Pendleton label maintains an enviable spot above Macy's, Bloomingdale's, The Gap, The Limited, and other teen-oriented retailers, relying more on clients like Lord & Taylor, Nordstrom, and Dillard, as well as specialty boutiques.

Budget: $

Sources:

Berman, Phyllis. "From Sheep to Shirt." *Forbes,* May 22, 1995, 162–64.

Block, Toddi Gutner. "Mother Knew Best." *Forbes,* July 3, 1995, 52–53.

Frances Steloff: Memoirs of a Bookseller. Direct Cinema Ltd., n.d. (Video)

Graham, Pauline, ed. *Mary Parker Follett: Prophet of Management.* Harvard Business School Press, 1995.

Lomax, Alfred L. *Later Woolen Mills in Oregon.* Binfords & Mort, 1974.

———. *Pioneer Woolen Mills in Oregon.* Binfords & Mort, 1941.

Machan, Dyan. "Sharing Victoria's Secrets." *Forbes,* June 5, 1995, 132–33.

Martin, Jean, gen. ed. *Who's Who of Women in the Twentieth Century.* Crescent Books, 1995.

Alternative Applications: Contrast business methods, materials, and outlook of other lines begun by women. Feature these entrepreneurs:

Madame Alexander, dolls	Donna Karan, fashion
Elizabeth Arden, cosmetics	Norma Kerr, food
Mary Kay Ash, cosmetics	Sherry Lansing, cinema
Laura Ashley, textiles	Estee Lauder, cosmetics
Lucille Ball, TV production	Mary Wells Laurence, advertising
Josephine Bay, financier, exporter	Jean Nidetch, diet
Olive Ann Beech, aircraft	Jacqueline Onassis, editing
Hazel Bishop, cosmetics	Mary Quant, fashion
Helen J. Boiardi, foods	Anita Roddick, fashion
Lane Bryant, fashion	Ida Rosenthal, fashion
Carmen Callil, publishing	Helena Rubinstein, cosmetics
Coco Chanel, fashion	Margaret Rudkin, foods
Joan Ganz Cooney, broadcasting	Elsa Schiaparelli, fashion
Debbie Fields, food	Dorothy Schiff, publishing
Eileen Ford, modeling agency	Margarete Steiff, toys
Katherine Graham, publishing	Frances Steloff, bookseller
Peggy Guggenheim, art	Martha Stewart, publishing
Phyllis Henning, publishing	Linda Wachner, cosmetics

Lisa Henson, entertainment

Claire Giannini Hoffman, financier

Margery Hurst, management

Madame Sarah Walker, hair care

Maggie Lena Walker, financier

Lila Wallace, publishing

Fashion, *beauty, and acumen*

Age/Grade Level or Audience: High school or college business fair; Business and Professional Women's League symposium; small business association open house; newspaper column or newsletter; investment club campaign focus; women's forum or educational radio or television presentation.

Description: Organize local agents or vendors for the wide array of products marketed, designed, and promoted by women to present a program on the vision and method of the successful female entrepreneur.

Procedure: Have a representative or vendor of a female-owned, female-created product express the vision and determination characteristic of the entrepreneur. Feature these giants of the industry:

Mary Kay Ash	Antonia Axson Johnson	Sharon Snyder
Gertrude Boyle	Donna Karan	Donna Steigerwaldt
Coco Chanel	Anne Klein	Martha Stewart
Josephine Chaus	Harriet Gerber Lewis	Ann Taylor
Maryjo Cohen	Loida N. Lewis	Elizabeth Taylor
Helen Copley	Liz Minyard	Joyce Raley Teel
Han Feng	Miuccia Prada	Susie Tompkins
Sondra Healy	Lynda Resnick	Lillian Vernon
Joan Helpern	Helena Rubinstein	Adrienne Vittadini
Marian Ilitch	Muriel Siebert	Diane Von Furstenberg

Punctuate commentary, slides, posters, sales brochures, sales and distribution figures, and product demonstrations with important facts about gains and losses, evaluating the market, setting up strategy, hiring a factory staff and sales force, developing a signature product such as the Prada backpack or Elizabeth Taylor's signature fragrance collection, and following through on customer needs and demands. Display the complete line of Mary Kay cosmetics for men and women and relate the following brief overview of her success:

- Married at age seventeen, Mary Kay Ash lacked the money for tuition and attended the University of Houston for only one year in her quest to earn a medical degree. A single parent she reared two sons and a daughter while working for the World Gift Company, a Dallas firm specializing in household items.

- In 1963, Ash left her post as national director and started her own cosmetic factory based on a single formula for a moisturizing lotion. Her second husband's death precipitated a crisis which Ash solved by naming her son Richard as company administrator and, eventually, one of the youngest presidents on the New York Stock Exchange.

121

- By the end of the first year, the Mary Kay Cosmetics Company moved to new offices to accommodate an in-house staff of 200 and over 100,000 field agents, who sold their products on the spot at parties or in private home consultations rather than by mail order. By the mid-1980s, the crew of Mary Kay beauty consultants doubled, partially from their own success and partially from Ash's continual expression of thanks and confidence expressed through buttons, pins, furs, jewelry, and, at the top of Mary Kay's gift list, monogrammed pink Cadillacs.

- A combination of pep talks, quality products, staff rewards, and the founder's hard work and poise pushed the Mary Kay Cosmetics label into Argentina, Australia, Puerto Rico, Guam, and Canada. She expanded the line with men's skin care products bearing the Mr. K label.

- Mary Kay has won the Horatio Alger Award (1978), the Cosmetic Career Woman of the Year (1979), Direct Selling Hall of Fame Award (1979), a profile on *60 Minutes* (1979), and the Golden Plate Award from the American Academy of Achievement (1980). In addition, she has been featured in *Business Week* and *Who's Who*.

- In 1985, Richard Rogers helped buy back company stock in a move to privatize. As a result of her successful challenge to Avon, Mary Kay Cosmetics has put Ash's worth over $320 million. In addition, she has published articles in *Working Woman* (December 1984) and *Cosmopolitan* (August 1985), and a biography, *Mary Kay: The Success Story of America's Most Dynamic Businesswoman* (Harper & Row, 1987). Additional awards include the National Sales Hall of Fame (1989) and the Kupfer Distinguished Executive Award (1993).

- Part of Ash's success derives from her sensitivity to women's issues, particularly the use of the Dreize test, which injures, blinds, or torments animals during testing. To end the working relationship between the cosmetics industry and animal cruelty, Ash has sponsored tissue testing at Johns Hopkins University. In addition, she has served as a director of the Wadley Institute of Molecular Medicine, has promoted breast screening for the American Cancer Society, and, in 1993, opened the Mary Kay Ash Cancer Research Laboratory in Dallas.

Budget: $$

Sources:

Anderson, John, and Valerie Wright. "Mary Kay Ash, Dallas, 1971." *Texas Monthly,* August 1989, 146–48.

Baldwin, Pat. "No Time to Quit." *Dallas Times Herald,* July 9, 1989.

Bamford, Janet. "The Working Woman 50." *Working Woman,* May 1995, 37–61.

Black Americans of Achievement: Madam C. J. Walker. Instructional Video, 1992. (Video)

Chan, Mei-Mei. "Mary Kay Ash." *Chicago Tribune,* July 18, 1986.

Chicago Tribune, February 15, 1991, F14.

Current Biography. H. W. Wilson, May 1995, 14–18.

"The Divas of Madison Avenue." *USA Today,* June 12, 1995, 3B.

Donovan, Jennifer Boeth. "Thanksgiving at Mary Kay's." *Woman's Day,* November 24, 1987, 185–88.

Duffy, Martha. "A New Touch of Class." *Time,* April 17, 1995, 54–68.

Kasindorf, Jeanie Russell. "Martha, Inc.," *Working Woman,* June 1995, 28–31, 66, 68–69.

Karp, Abby. "Optimism Reigns at Mary Kay." *Baltimore Sun,* April 13, 1987.

"The Mary Kay Guide to Beauty: Discovering Your Special Look." *Publishers Weekly,* August 19, 1983, 65–66.

Rotenier, Nancy. "Antistatus Backpacks, $450 a Copy." *Forbes,* June 19, 1995, 118–20.
Rubenstein, Carie. "Lifelines of the Rich and Famous." *Money,* fall 1988, 132–34.
Schupack, Deborah. "Biz Buzz." *Working Woman,* June 1995, 11–12.
Stuttaford, Genevieve. "Tender Power." *Publishers Weekly,* December 23, 1988, 72–73.

Also, audiocassette of Mary Kay (Recorded Books), business magazines and trade papers, and online sources such as Newsbank, Silver Platter, ProQuest, American Online, or Internet.

Alternative Applications: Center a career fair with a mall tree of products and services designed, promoted, or created by women. Place data-filled placards alongside these goods or pictures clipped from catalogs:

- animal feed from Kay Akey Creech's Carl S. Akey
- candies from Ellen Gordon's Tootsie Roll Industries
- car wax from Sondra Healy's Turtle Wax
- clothing by Josephien Chaus, Adrienne Vittadini, Anne Klein, Joan Helpern, Carole Little, Gertrude Boyle's Columbia Sportswear, or Donna Karan
- computer goods from Marta Weinstein's Logistix, Kavelle Bajaj's I-NET, Rachelle Friedman's J & R Music World, Patricia Gallup's PC Connection, and Pauline Lo Alker's NPI software
- eggs from Lois Rust's Rose Acre Farms
- electronics from Suzanne Millard's electrical equipment company
- fertilizer from Sharon Snyder's Cornbelt Chemical Company
- fish oil products from Celia Meilan's International Proteins
- flowers from Ruth M. Owades's Calyx and Corolla
- foundation garments from Linda Wachner's Warnaco and Donna Wolf Steigerwaldt's Jockey International
- fragrance by Estee Lauder, Jessica McClintock, or Elizabeth Taylor
- Franklin Mint collectibles from Lynda Resnick's Roll International
- fuel from Nanci Mackenzie's U.S. Gas Transportation
- groceries from Loida N. Lewis's Beatrice, Joyce Raley Teel's Raley's, and Liz Minyard and Gretchen Minyard Williams's Minyard Food Stores
- health-care services from Dian Graves Owen's Owen Healthcare
- Irma Elder's Ford dealership, which supplies cars to Hertz and Budget rentals
- jewelry from Aya Azrielant's Andin International
- kitchen appliances from Maryjo Cohen's National Presto
- magazines, books, and articles on Martha Stewart's designs, recipes, and gardening advice
- meat products from Annabelle Lundy Fetterman's Lundy Packing
- newspapers from Helen Copley's Copley Press
- oil products from Antonia Axson Johnson's Axel Johnson
- packaging from Ann McIlrath Drake's DSC Logistics
- plumbing fixtures from Harriet Gerber Lewis's Gerber Plumbing Fixtures

- skin-care products from Helena Rubinstein cosmetics or Elizabeth Arden's chain of salons or facials by Mary Kay

- stationery from Ebba Hoffman and Sharon Hoffman's Smead Manufacturing

- tires from Ann Gaither's J. H. Heafner Company

- toys by Pleasant Rowland's Pleasant Company

- travel information from Christel DeHaan's Resort Condominiums International

- videos from Oprah Winfrey's Harpo Entertainment Group and entertainment from Marcy Carsey's Carsey-Werner

- wholesale books and magazines from Barbara Levy Kipper's Charles

Fashion's *faces*

Age/Grade Level or Audience: Middle school or high school women's history bulletin board; college history or sociology research project; Business and Professional Women's League presentation; library reading circle project.

Description: Present a program on women who have made it to the top in fashion design and modeling.

Procedure: Display posters on female models and designers who have influenced the way women dress and view themselves. Combine photos with a brief introduction and discuss the product line or trend associated with each. For example compare the waif-look as exemplified by Twiggy in the 1960s and Kate Moss in the 1990s. Include these giants of the industry:

Karen Alexander	Bridget Hall	Suzy Parker
Nadja Auermann	Lauren Hutton	Mary Quant
Naomi Campbell	Iman	Isabella Rossellini
Coco Chanel	Irina	Claudia Schiffer
Pat Cleveland	Beverly Johnson	Brooke Shields
Anita Colby	Sheila Johnson	Jean Shrimpton
Cindy Crawford	Grace Jones	Barbara Summers
Linda Evangelista	Dorian Leigh	Dorothea Towles
Pat Evans	Elle MacPherson	Twiggy
Lisa Fonssagrives	Kate Moss	Amber Valetta

Budget: $$$

Sources:

Belafante, Ginia. "The Runway Girls Take Off." *Time*, April 17, 1995, 66–68.
Gross, Michael. *Model: The Ugly Business of Beautiful Women*. W. W. Morrow, 1995.
Levine, Joshua. "We Have Shares." *Forbes*, March 27, 1995, 75–78.
Summers, Barbara. *Skin Deep*. Amistad Press, 1995.

Alternative Applications: Discuss the use of female models in selling toys, lotion, dishwashing detergent, jewelry, hosiery, makeup, exercise equipment, and clothing. What types of products traditionally feature women in ads? How have ads changed over the past century, as women made their way out of the kitchens and into society? Discuss the short career span of a fashion model and the tendency of advertisers to reject signs of aging. Determine if the business has historically been as hard on males as females, and other trends of the industry.

Knitting *as history*

Age/Grade Level or Audience: Women's History Month newspaper feature; library or museum monograph; history club lecture; civic preservation project; high school or college history research topic.

Description: Summarize the role of knitting in history.

Procedure: Compose an essay on knitting in which you establish the relevance of the development of knitting to the Middle Ages, a time when the stirrup, moldboard plow, spinning wheel, and central heating changed the lifestyle of European communities. Mention these facts:

- Before knitting, clothing made of skins failed to protect the hands in outdoor work and encumbered the fingers during intricate motions; for example, threading a line through a fishhook, stringing a bow, tending herds, or harnessing draft animals.

- Knitting produced garments that could conform to the shape of the neck, foot, hand, and fingers, and users liked the stretch of the garment and the warmth wool trapped next to the skin, particularly when worn under metal helmets or armor. Because of knitting, people were able to go about their tasks in cold weather without losing body heat. The agony of chilblains and frostbite were reduced among people who worked outdoors.

- The demand for knitting put a new cottage industry to work to produce snoods, wimples, caps, sweaters, jerkins, leggings, mittens, scarves, and gloves. Breeders insisted on animals that grew the softest, most malleable fibers, particularly merino sheep and Andean alpacas. Merchants used these useful knitted woolens as trade items.

Comment on the practicality and utility of knitting, which is an example of women's industriousness that receives little comment in histories.

Budget: $$

Sources:

Barber, Elizabeth Wayland. *Women's Work: The First 20,000 Years.* W. W. Norton, 1994.

Clark, Gillian. *Women in Late Antiquity: Pagan and Christian Lifestyles.* Oxford University Press, 1993.

Macdonald, Anne L. *No Idle Hands: The Social History of American Knitting.* Ballantine, 1988.

Müller, Claudia. *The Costume Timeline.* Thames & Hudson, 1992.

Yarwood, Doreen. *The Encyclopedia of World Costume.* Bonanza, 1986.

Alternative Applications: Create a time line of a knitted garment, from the raising of sheep through shearing, picking out burs, washing, soaking in conditioning water, carding, spinning, dyeing, and producing a garment. Estimate how long the average woman would spend outfitting a family with knitted goods.

125

Paper *dolls*

Age/Grade Level or Audience: Elementary or middle school geography frieze; after-school or scout project; homebound or disabled children's scrapbook; mother's day out program; library reading circle handwork; language or vocabulary study; home-school costume research; children's museum or library project.

Description: Draw and dress female figures from history in natural poses—walking, sitting, conversing, driving.

Procedure: Have participants draw two-dimensional figures in a variety of racial, age, physical, social status, and cultural detail, involving their figures in exercise, work, cooking, gardening, relaxation, and travel. Supply each with appropriate dress, jewelry, body markings, and hair styles. Develop a variety of views: an elderly Native American from the pre-colonial era, a young pregnant Hispanic during the age of conquest, a fifteenth-century African American toddler, a mature Pacific Islander integrating European customs, a working-class Russian from the nineteenth century, or a teenage Caucasian from California in the 1970s. Glue figures to cardboard or tagboard and cut out. Using either colored markers on paper or bits of cloth, plastic, feathers, leather, glitter, ribbon, and lace, create appropriate costumes for many phases of female lives throughout history. Consider these possibilities:

- infant Shoshone—cradleboard, soft moccasins, pierced ears, woven **babiche** swaddling, moss diaper

- teenage Pacific islander—ceremonial lei, cormorant feather cape, thong sandals, Mother Hubbard, grass skirt, bare breasts, anklet

- ancient Egyptian queen—cobra-fronted headdress, sheer linen tunic, embroidered collar, kohl-darkened eyebrows and lids, knotted sash, gold loop earrings

- tenth-century Chinese aristocrat—gilded headdress, elevated sandals, thick socks, wide-sleeved robe in deep colors with lighter colors lining sleeves, braided sash, rice powder makeup

- young African-American from Harlem, New York, in the 1920s—short silk tunic with bugle beads, feather boa, bobbed hair, cigarette holder, Mary Jane shoes, white hose, bangle bracelets, and beaded cloche

- young Caucasian from California in the 1970s—tie-dyed shirt, bell-bottom jeans, peace symbol on a thong, multiple pierced earrings, waist-length straight hair, earth shoes, braided belt

- middle-aged Hispanic from Mexico City in the 1890s—embroidered ankle-length tunic, light underskirt, chignon decorated with a gardenia or hibiscus blossom, turquoise and silver bracelet and earrings, **huaraches**

- elderly French socialite of the 1860s—bodice with lace **fichu** or **tucker,** broad velvet skirt over full slip and pantelettes, reticule, black leather pumps, bonnet in contrasting color with full taffeta ties, locket

- young Inuit mother of the fourteenth century—sealskin leggings, **amouti** with inner strap for infant, snow goggles, mittens, **mukluks** with moss lining

Display the finished paper dolls on frames in a glass case or the ledge of a museum, classroom, city hall, or library. Include brief descriptions of styles, purpose, materials, and unusual methods of decoration; for example, tattooed skin, shell pendulums, abalone beading, quilling, ruching, monograms, pearls, crests, animal drawings, feathers, or claws. Have students append an alphabetized pronouncing gazetteer of such unusual terms as fichu, babiche, reticule, huaraches, chignon, tucker, amouti, stomacher, labret, lava-lava, pareu, and mukluk.

Budget: $$

Sources:

Barber, Elizabeth Wayland. *Women's Work: The First 20,000 Years.* W. W. Norton, 1994.

Bradfield, Nancy. *Historical Costumes of England.* Barnes & Noble, 1971.

Feininger, Andreas. *New York in the Forties.* Dover Books, 1994.

1500–1600 Colonial America. Knowledge Unlimited, n.d. (Video)

Gorsline, Douglas. *What People Wore.* Dover Books, 1994.

McGraw, Sheila. *Dolls Kids Can Make.* Firefly Books, 1995.

———. *Papiér-Mâché for Kids.* Firefly Books, 1995.

Müller, Claudia. *The Costume Timeline: 5000 Years of Fashion History.* Thames & Hudson, 1992.

Paterek, Josephine. *Encyclopedia of American Indian Costume.* ABC-Clio, 1994.

Thomson, John. *Victorian London Street Life in Historic Photographs.* Dover Books, 1994.

Alternative Applications: Create a handout sheet of hypothetical characters from history and have students match several items that would adorn or dress each. Use the following model:

_____ 1. teenage Pacific islander during the age of exploration

_____ 2. infant Shoshone in a Native American village of the 1750s

_____ 3. ancient Egyptian queen

_____ 4. 10th-century Chinese aristocrat

_____ 5. young African American from Harlem, New York, in the 1920s

_____ 6. young Caucasian from California in the 1970s

_____ 7. middle-aged Hispanic from Mexico City in the 1890s

_____ 8. elderly French socialite of the 1860s

_____ 9. young Inuit mother of the fourteenth century

a. amouti with strap for infant

b. anklet

c. beaded cloche

d. bell-bottom jeans

e. black leather pumps

f. bobbed hair

g. bonnet

h. broad velvet skirt

i. ceremonial lei

j. chignon

k. cigarette holder

l. cobra-fronted headdress

m. cormorant feather cape

n. corset

o. cradleboard

p. earth shoes

q. elevated sandals

r. embroidered ankle-length tunic

s. embroidered collar

t. feather boa

u. full slip

v. gardenia

w. gilded headdress

x. gold loop earrings

y. huaraches

z. knotted sash

aa. light underskirt

bb. locket

cc. Mary Jane shoes

dd. moss diaper

ee. Mother Hubbard

ff. mukluks with moss lining

gg. pantelettes

hh. peace symbol on a thong

ii. pierced ears

jj. rice powder makeup

kk. sash

ll. sealskin leggings

mm. sheer linen tunic

nn. short silk tunic with bugle beads

oo. snow goggles

pp. soft moccasins

qq. taffeta ties

rr. thick socks

ss. thong sandals

tt. tie-dyed shirt

uu. turquoise and silver bracelet

vv. turquoise and silver earrings

ww. waist-length straightened hair

xx. white hose

yy. wide-sleeved robe in deep colors with lighter colors lining sleeves

zz. woven babiche swaddling

ANSWERS:

1. b, i, m, ee, ss

2. o, dd, ii, pp, zz

3. l, s, x, z, mm

4. q, w, jj, kk, rr, yy

5. c, f, k, t, cc, nn, xx

6. d, p, hh, tt, ww

7. j, r, v, y, aa, uu, vv

8. e, g, h, u, bb, gg, qq

9. a, ff, ll, oo

Selling *to women*

Age/Grade Level or Audience: Advertising and marketing strategies seminar; commercial art class focus; newspaper column or open forum; educational radio or television series.

Description: Create a hall frieze, poster series, or display case of varied appeal to the female market from both contemporary society and the decade of the 1950s.

Procedure: Collect a variety of products and sales approaches from old and new magazines, television, billboards, brochures, labels, newspaper inserts, and other sources. Divide the advertising methods into categories such as these:

- <u>Snobbery</u> an attempt to step beyond the ordinary, to live above the standards of working-class people, or a boost in class or prestige through the acquisition of a certain garment, vehicle, piece of furniture, jewelry, magazines, or fad item. (Watch for words such as *world-class, exclusive, luxury, up-to-date,* and *pampered.*)

- Sadism a denunciation or devaluation of women through the negative depiction of male-female relations as victimizer and prey, often found in sexy clothes, leather goods, and perfume. (Notice terms such as *subdue, overpower, crawl, beg, tame,* and *whimper*.)

- Mom and Apple Pie comparison of current women to a fantasy era when women cared only for their homes, their kitchen, farmland, and depended on men to run their lives. This ploy frequently accompanies the creation of labor-saving foods that mimic something people once labored over; for example, pudding, cake, pie, or casseroles. (Look for words like *old-timey, nutritious, dependable,* and *American-style*.)

- Sensuality bare-limbed, sexy models who are abnormally thin and who tout a product that suggests weight-reducing properties, in particular, cigarettes, which marketers connect with the weight gain that smokers anticipate when they give up smoking. Other sensual products include makeup, jewelry, wigs, depilatories, and linens. (Be alert for references to swishy, slippery fabrics, whipped makeup bases, and fluid words such as *shantung, charmeuse,* and *quiana*.)

- Modernity speedy, easy products that allow women to escape home drudgery and enjoy driving, vacationing, hobbies, or time with families. These qualities often apply to vans, cleaning products, frozen meals, camping gear, and other outdoor necessities. (Watch for terms like *in minutes, drudgery, simple, one-step,* and *no-bake*.)

Budget: $$

Sources:

Aburdene, Patricia, and John Naisbitt. *Megatrends for Women.* Random House, 1992.

"Cyberbuzz: Master Networker Pauline Lo Alker." *Working Woman,* June 1995, 12.

Machan, Dyan. "Knowing Your Limits." *Forbes,* June 5, 1995, 128–30.

———. "Sharing Victoria's Secrets." *Forbes,* June 5, 1995, 132–33.

Ritchie, Karen. *Marketing to Generation X.* Lexington Books, 1995.

Rotenier, Nancy. "Antistatus Backpacks, $450 a Copy." *Forbes,* July 19, 1995, 118–20.

Still Killing Us Softly. Cambridge Documentary Films, 1987.

Also review magazines published from 1950–1959, including *Ladies Home Journal, Life, Look,* and others.

Alternative Applications: Make a video of a decade-to-decade view of women as the target of advertising campaigns. Note the entrance of important products or changes in packaging. Include frozen juice, Barbie and Ken dolls, hair spray, panty hose, cigarettes, microwave ovens, recycled paper goods, concentrated laundry detergent, non-polluting stain removers, frozen meals, health-conscious diet foods, and feminine hygiene products.

Food *and* cooking

Chef *Julia Child*

Age/Grade Level or Audience: Women's studies presentation; civic club program; media open forum; radio or television feature; women's club brochure; women's history museum handout.

Description: Describe in detail the contributions of Julia Child to American and world cuisine.

Procedure: Present a multimedia talk on the work of Julia Child, pioneer of television chefs, spokesperson for the American point of view on food preparation, and author of a variety of books on culinary method and style. Include film clips from "The French Chef," a bulletin board, handout, or overhead list of her achievements:

- Born Julia McWilliams in Pasadena, California, on August 15, 1912, she studied at a Montessori school and graduated from Smith College with a history major. She debated between two choices of careers: writing fiction or playing basketball.

- As an advertising copywriter for W. & J. Sloane, a noted furniture dealer, she wearied of cutlines and layouts on furniture and joined the Office of Strategic Services (OSS), forerunner of the CIA, serving first as a file clerk at the Washington office and then in the field bureau in Sri Lanka.

- In 1943, she met cartographer Paul Cushing Child, an experienced OSS agent ten years her senior and a lover of good food. They shared an assignment in China, where Paul taught Julia Asian cooking methods.

- After World War II, Julia enrolled at the Hillcliffe School of Cookery in Beverly Hills, California, and married Paul. At their Washington, D.C. flat, she cooked while Paul worked for the Foreign Service.

- In 1948, Paul transferred to France. Living on France's elite Left Bank, Julia learned French cooking methods at the Cordon Bleu, world-famous culinary school founded in 1895, and studied privately under Max Bugnard, a Belgian chef. A friend, Simone "Simca" Beck, helped Julia launch Le Cercle des Gourmettes and L'Ecole des Trois Gourmandes, exclusive cooking schools held in Julia's flat.

- The outgrowth of Julia's study was her first book, *Mastering the Art of French Cooking* (1961), a best-seller among travelers and gourmet diners during the heady Kennedy years, when noted guests to the White House inspired Americans to notice European food preparation and service.

- After Paul's retirement, the Childs settled in Cambridge, Massachusetts, where Julia penned articles for *House and Garden* and *House Beautiful* and a weekly column in the *Boston Globe*.

- Following a guest stint on Boston's WGBH-TV in 1963 to make an on-air omelette, Julia agreed to appear regularly as "The French Chef," which soon spread to 100 stations. She gave her audiences confidence to try difficult recipes requiring fresh ingredients, appropriate utensils, and attention to explicit instructions and timing.

- The sequel, "Dinner at Julia's," earned her the 1965 George Foster Peabody award, honorary degrees, and an Emmy.

- Television pay was small, but the proceeds from Julia's books paid for a second home outside Nice, France, and a condo near Santa Barbara, California.

- She influenced Rosalyn Carter to modernize White House menus and addressed Aspen's elite Food and Wine Classic.

- Because of changes in American attitudes toward diet and health, Julia altered her fare to less complicated, lower fat, and lighter menus and joined Robert Mondavi, James Beard, Alice Waters, Jeremiah Tower, and Richard Graff in founding the American Institute of Wine and Food (A.I.W.F.), a league of restaurateurs promoting quality in food and wine.

- Her productions have included a column in *McCall's* and *Parade* magazines from 1982–1986, as well as appearances on "Good Morning, America," and the publication of *The French Chef Cookbook* (1968), *From Julia Child's Kitchen* (1975), *Julia Child & Company* (1978), *Julia Child & More Company* (1979), *The Way to Cook* (1989), and *Cooking at Home with the Master Chefs* (1993).

Complete the presentation with a demonstration or samples of some of Child's famous chocolate cake or paté.

Budget: $$$$

Sources:

Coffey, Roberta Wallace. "Julia and Paul Child: Their Recipe for Love." *McCall's,* October 1988, 96–99.

Grandee, Charles. "Grandee at Large." *House and Garden.* June 1989, 174.

"A Holiday Bird and a Free-Range Chat with Julia." *Life,* December 1989, 95–100.

"Julia's Crusade." *Boston Herald,* March 5, 1989.

Mather, Robin. "Child's Play." *Detroit News,* October 4, 1989.

Rennert, Amy. "The West Interview: Julia Child." *San Jose Mercury News,* March 30, 1986.

Stephen, Beverly. "Cosmo Talks to Julia Child." *Cosmopolitan,* May 1990, 246–48.

Weddell, Leslie. "Renowned Cook Rises to Defense of Food as Gastronomic Bliss." *Colorado Springs Gazette Telegraph,* June 29, 1990.

Alternative Applications: Ask local amateur chefs to hold a series of sessions devoted to examining Julia Child's early recipes from *Mastering the Art of French Cooking* (1961). Which of her techniques have become outdated with the shift in American eating and dining habits over the past 30 years? Record the group's alterations or substitutions in the original recipes.

Cooks *and the* Civil War

Age/Grade Level or Audience: Middle or high school home economics or history class; history or preservation society program; home demonstration monograph; United Daughters of the Confederacy project; media foods page feature; museum brochure.

Description: Compile a series of historically based recipes that feature dishes created from limited ingredients.

Procedure: Select recipes and substitutions that women used during the Civil War when supplies ran low or when there was no money to pay inflated prices for imported goods. Recipes recycled a small list of staples, which were often in season for a short time and had to be dried or preserved in salt, both labor-intensive tasks:

- grains: cornmeal, grits, hominy, flour, dry beans

- meat and fish: pork sidemeat, ham, wild birds and game, freshwater and ocean fish, shellfish

- nuts: peanuts, walnuts, pecans, hazel nuts, pine nuts, hickory nuts, chestnuts

- tubers and root vegetables: sweet potatoes, yams, Jerusalem artichokes, radishes, onions, shallots, beets

- other vegetables: green beans, peas, cauliflower, squash, pumpkin, winter squash, peppers, edible flowers (particularly nasturtiums and squash blossoms), asparagus, okra

- greens: wild cress, dandelion, lettuce, mustard, savory, parsley, peppergrass, spinach, herbs

- berries and fruit: huckleberries, blackberries, dewberries, gooseberries, blueberries, strawberries, apples, wild plums, quince, cherries, crabapples, damsons, apricots, peaches, persimmons

- sweeteners: molasses, maple syrup, fruit leather, cider, preserves

Use the following authentic Southern recipes as a start on your collection:

Bean Soup

Soak a cup of navy beans in cold water 8–12 hours. Rinse, cover with fresh water, parboil, and drain. Add 2 quarts water, ¾ tablespoon salt, and a ham or beef bone; simmer 4 hours. Add chopped onion, cubed turnips, parsnips, acorn squash, and white potatoes. Stir in 2 tablespoons of minced green herbs, dandelion greens, or beet tops. Cook until tender. Thicken with 1 tablespoon of flour, crushed crackers, or bread crumbs. Serve with a generous topping of coarsely ground peppercorns or chopped hot pepper.

Baked Beans

Soak 1 pound of navy beans in cold water 8–12 hours. Rinse, cover with fresh water, parboil, and drain. Simmer 2 hours. Add drained beans, 1 cup of ham or salt pork chunks, and ½ cup of chopped onion or scallions. Blend in a tablespoon of ground mustard seed, three bay leaves, a half cup of molasses, salt, coarsely ground peppercorns, and a cup of water. Top with strips of salt pork or streak-a-lean. Bake uncovered in a medium oven for 2 hours.

Field Peas and Ham Hock

Soak 2 cups of field peas overnight. Bring to a boil, drain, and cover with 2 quarts of water. Add a ham hock, coarse salt, and black and red pepper to taste. Simmer gently 4 hours. Serve with chowchow, fried squash blossoms, drop biscuits, and cornbread.

Fried Squash Blossoms

Gently spread a dozen squash blossoms and press into a thin batter of corn meal and milk. Shake off excess. Fry in bacon grease no more than a minute on each side. Drain on brown grocery paper, salt, and serve hot.

Herbed Sauerkraut

Chop a head of green cabbage into fine slivers. Sprinkle with coarse salt and pack into a stone crock or glass jar. Top with cheesecloth and weight with a plate and brick. Place crock in a warm room. Skim the brackish foam every three days for two weeks. Drain and rinse for less salty kraut. Before heating, sprinkle with dill weed or dill seed. Serve fried with sidemeat or fried squirrel.

Sweet Potato Supreme

Peel 6 baked yams or sweet potatoes. (Substitute persimmons and a cup of sugar if necessary.) Slice into one-inch chunks. Alternate rows of potatoes with slices of apple or pineapple. Dot with butter and cinnamon. Drizzle with 4 tablespoons of lemon or pineapple juice. Top with ½ cup of white sugar and crushed pecans or pecan halves. (Substitute hickory nuts or walnuts if necessary.) Brown for 10 minutes. Serve as a vegetable or dessert.

Rebel Hash

Mince leftover beef or pork. Boil 4 large potatoes. Chop potatoes with 1 onion. Brown meat in hot lard or butter; add chopped vegetables. Season with salt, pepper, and horseradish, sage, or parsley. Cook until mixture browns on both sides. Serve slices with creamed horseradish or mornay sauce.

Buttermilk Cornbread

Blend 2 cups self-rising corn meal, 1 cup flour, 3 tablespoons of lard or bacon drippings, 2 eggs, and 2 cups buttermilk into a batter. (The addition of ½ cup of white sugar is optional.) Drizzle bacon drippings in a skillet, pour in batter, and bake in a hot oven for 40 minutes. Serve leftover slices split and fried in bacon drippings.

Yam Pudding

Boil 6 yams for 30 minutes. (Substitute sweet potatoes, acorn squash, or pumpkin if necessary.) Add 3 eggs, 1 cup sugar, 2 tablespoons lime or lemon juice with the zest, and 1 teaspoon of nutmeg, allspice, or cinnamon. Dot the top with pecan halves or pieces. Bake ½ hour in a moderate oven.

Indian Pudding

Heat 3 cups of milk to a bubble. Stir in ½ cup cornmeal and cook for fifteen minutes. Add 1 egg, 3 tablespoons of lard or butter, and ½ cup molasses. Blend and bake in a pudding pan for 40 minutes at medium temperature. Serve with cottage cheese, clotted cream, or whipped cream.

Fish Gumbo

Cut fresh or salt fish into cubes, roll in meal or flour, and fry in lard or butter until brown on all sides. Add ½ pound okra slices and cover with boiling water. Cook 10 minutes, then add salt, cayenne pepper, sassafras powder or fillée. Cook for 5 minutes. Serve over grits, hominy, or rice.

Calves' Foot Jelly

Clean and boil 4 hooves in salted water. Skim and strain through cheesecloth. Chill and remove fat. Place mixture, 4 sticks of cinnamon, 3 cloves, and the zest and juice of 3 limes or lemons in a dutch oven. Beat crushed shells and whites of 4 eggs with a cup of cold water. Blend in ½ pound of sugar, a pint of cider, and a pint of sherry. Simmer five minutes. Strain through cheesecloth. Set in molds.

Budget: $$

Sources:

Davis, William C. *The Civil War Cookbook.* Courage Books, 1993.

Haskell, E. L., ed. *Civil War Cooking: The Housekeeper's Encyclopedia.* R. L. Shepherd, 1992.

Mickler, Ernest M. *White Trash Cooking.* Jargon Society, 1986.

The Women's Exchange Cookbook. Wimmer Brothers, 1994.

Alternative Applications: Make a chart of items that Civil War-era women substituted for ingredients that were either scarce, too expensive, unavailable because of the destruction of farm land, rationed for military use only, or restricted by port blockades, particularly spices, rum, sherry, coffee, and tea. Begin with these makeshift ingredients:

- coffee—toasted okra seeds, chicory
- tea—spearmint, peppermint, chamomile, tansy, lemon grass
- fresh greens—dandelion greens, beet tops, nasturtium flowers and leaves, poke salad, wild cress, parsley
- vegetables—rutabagas, parsnips, acorn squash, jerusalem artichokes, pumpkin, carrots
- red meat—rabbits, birds, squirrels, ground peanuts or chestnuts, turkey, duck or guinea eggs, catfish, mussels, alligator, turtle, ground pecans or walnuts
- desserts—clotted cream or cottage cheese sweetened with honey or molasses, candied violets, sweet potatoes and yams, wild berries, dried apples and apricots, carob, pear honey
- spices and condiments—ground or grated horseradish root, pine nuts, juniper berries, wild onions

The food/diet boomerang

Age/Grade Level or Audience: Middle school or high school economics or health database; home demonstration presentation; women's studies public forum; hospital or women's clinic newsletter.

Description: Create a time line that delineates how food has continued to be an obsession for some American women.

Procedure: Impress on participants how food and weight loss have increasingly encroached on the lives of American women by having groups provide dates and trends. Organize on a wall chart, database, or series of posters these facts and events:

135

- **1961** Julia Child publishes *Mastering the Art of French Cooking*.

- **1963** Julia Child inaugurates the television series "The French Chef," ignoring calories in her concentration on French cuisine, which is rich with cream sauces. The sequel, "Dinner at Julia's," airs in 1965. That same year, Jean Nidetch establishes Weight Watchers, which, with 600,000 members, still holds first place thirty years later in an inflated weight-loss industry.

- **1967** The publication of Dr. Irwin Stillman's *The Doctor's Quick Weight Loss Diet* presses for menus rich in protein and for a daily regimen of eight glasses of water to cleanse the body. Meanwhile, Twiggy graces the fashion runways of America, helping to foster America's obsession with slimness.

- **1972** Five years after Stillman's protein diet, Dr. Atkins encourages a control of carbohydrates but allows plenty of saturated fat.

- **1976** Nathan Pritikin reduces the risk of heart disease by stressing exercise, fiber, and no more than 10% fat in the diet.

- **1977** The year after the Pritikin diet, Slim-fast introduces powder protein, which consumers mix with skim milk. The number of deaths connected with this drastic alteration in nutrition ends the flurry of look-alike protein powders.

- **1978** Jean Nidetch sells Weight Watchers to H. J. Heinz for $72 million.

- **1979** Herman Tarnower cashes in on diet trends with *The Complete Scarsdale Medical Diet*.

- **1981** Judy Mazel's *The Beverly Hills Diet* makes unsubstantiated claims that pineapple and papaya enzymes burn fat. That same year, Stouffer's markets Lean Cuisine, which is a runaway success among young singles and working women.

- **1982** Nutri/System buys Body Contour and begins promoting chain weight-loss centers.

- **1985** Jenny and Sid Craig, former owners of Nutri/System, bring the Jenny Craig centers to the U.S. Another couple, Harvey and Marilyn Diamond, publish a food-combinant system, *Fit for Life*.

- **1988** Oprah Winfrey claims to have lost 67 pounds on Optifast's liquid diet.

- **1989** Actress Ann Jillian poses for an upgraded Slim-fast program.

- **1990** Oprah Winfrey regains the weight she lost.

- **1991** Consumers became wary of the spiels of diet plans, pills, powders, food additives, diet centers, and diet books.

- **1992** Nabisco moves into the weight-loss competition with SnackWell crackers and cookies.

- **1993** Winfrey's more sensible approach to dieting brings her down to 150 pounds. A *Consumer Reports* study of dieters finds readers more contented with Weight Watchers than with contract chain programs. The Federal Trade Commission accuses the leading contenders in the weight-loss industry with false claims and deceptive advertising. Nutri/System declares bankruptcy.

- **1994** Kathleen Sullivan becomes a pitchwoman for Weight Watchers. Oprah's cook, Rosie Daley, publishes *In the Kitchen with Rosie*. Susan Powter makes product history by selling $50 million in diet goods and videos in her program *Stop the Insanity*. She allies with Nutri/System, heads a chain of Susan Powter Centers, and publishes *Food*.

Budget: $$

Sources:

Balch, James F., and Phyllis Balch. *Prescription for Cooking and Dietary Wellness*. P. A. B. Books, 1993.

Deeb, Richard G. *The Longevity Equation: How to Eat as Much as You Like and Still Live over 100 Years to Tell about It!* Long Life Press, 1992.

Santillo, Humbart. *Intuitive Eating*. Hohm Press, 1993.

Stephen, Beverly. "Cosmo Talks to Julia Child." *Cosmopolitan,* May 1990, 246–48.

Vreeland, Leslie. "Lean Times in Fat City." *Working Woman,* July 1995, 46–51, 73–74.

Alternative Applications: Moderate a seminar on a radio or television program focusing on the historic relationship between women and weight. Allow an open-mike segment during which physicians and nutritionists answer questions from local girls and women who are disillusioned with trendy diets, special meals, vitamins and herbs, exercise programs, weight-training centers, smoking to lose weight, aerobics, and failure. Discuss how fickle fashion and media have historically encouraged girls and women to emulate often unattainable or unrealistic body types. Offer recipe brochures featuring healthful foods and meal-planning tips.

Historic *American cooks*

Age/Grade Level or Audience: High school or college home economics or nutrition seminar; home demonstration presentation; women's studies theme; civic club program; media open forum; video or televised cooking show.

Description: Discuss women's role in the evolution of regional American nutrition, cooking styles, and eating habits.

Procedure: Present an interactive group study of women's roles in foods and cooking. Divide the group into teams to work on the following questions:

- What did American settlers learn from Native Americans about ash cake, which colonists called hoecake or johnny cake? How do Aztec cooks flavor **atolli** cereal? How do Native American cooks vary bean bread with squash seeds, sweet potato, chestnuts, and juniper berries? Why was acorn **chemuck** a difficult dish to prepare? How did pioneer cooks adapt the Hopi **chukuviki** loaves, which Native Americans bake in horno ovens?

- What did Martha Washington add to American cuisine with *Martha Washington's Booke of Sweetmeats* (1749) and *Booke of Cookery* (1749)?

- What recipes from Marjorie Kinnan Rawlings's kitchen represent the Florida back country? What use does she make of local game, fowl, herbs, fruit, and greens?

- How have food and nutrition changed since World War II? What effect did the war have on demand for French cuisine? How does Julia Child's work illustrate post-war taste, style, and preference for fine wines and continental menus?

- For what style of cuisine is Fannie Farmer best known? How does her style of preparation and presentation vary from that of Irma Romauer, Marion R. Becker, Natalie Dupree, or Julia Child? Which of the four chefs is most centered in American lore and native foods, particularly:

arrowroot	manioc	quinoa
avocado	maple syrup	samp
blueberries	persimmons	seaweed
chocolate	piki bread	squamash
corn	pinole nuts	succotash
leather breeches beans	posole	terrapin

- How could a local group demonstrate the distinct tastes and cooking styles of America's best female chefs? What recipes would you choose for a public sampling? What ingredients would you feature, for example, tomatillos, jerked chicken, or avocado dip with piki chips? What style of cooking would you depict?

- Examine the cookbooks authored by women over the last several centuries. How do food preparation and meal planning techniques illustrate a shift from home-centered living to more complex living arrangements? What basic advice cuts preparation time for most meals? Consider some of the innovations in kitchen technology and their effect on the lives of women.

Budget: $$

Sources:

Bailey, Bonnie S. *Remembrances of Things Passed.* Highland Gourmet, 1993.

Banner, Lois W. *American Beauty.* University of Chicago Press, 1984.

Belote, Julianne. *The Compleat American Housewife.* Mariposa Press, 1974.

Cadits, Judith. *Recipes for a Healthy Life: Low Cholesterol, Low Fat, Low Sodium, No Added Sugar.* Center for the Partially Sighted, 1992.

Chelf, Vicki R. *Arrowhead Mills Natural Foods Cookbook: Healthy Homestyle Cooking from America's Heartland.* Avery Publications, 1993.

Davis, William C. *The Civil War Cookbook.* Courage Books, 1993.

Dupree, Natalie. *Natalie Dupree Cooks for Family and Friends.* Morrow, 1991.

Farmer, Fannie. *The Boston Cooking School.* Gordon Press, 1972.

Fritz, E. Mae. *Prairie Kitchen Sampler.* Prairie Winds Press, 1988.

Luchetti, Cathy. *Home on the Range.* Willard Books, 1993.

Newman, Jacqueline M. *Melting Pot.* Garland, 1993.

Rawlings, Marjor Kinnan. *Cross Creek Cookery.* Macmillan, 1971.

Rombauer, Irma S., and Marion R. Becker. *Joy of Cooking.* E. P. Dutton, 1989.

Shapiro, Laura. *Perfection Salad.* Farrar, Straus and Giroux, 1986.

Smith, Barbara. *Barbara Smith's Entertaining and Cooking For Friends.* Artisan, 1995.

Alternative Applications: Conclude a study of America's most notable female chefs with a buffet dinner. Utilizing historic Native American, Hispanic, regional American, and African American recipes, create a menu specializing in foods of the United States: avocado salad, taco appetizers, jerked chicken, baked beans, corn on the cob, chocolate pudding, iced tea, and sweet potato souffle. Decorate tables with drawings of the chefs and calligraphied recipe cards for diners to share with others or keep as souvenirs. Offer a cookbook of local adaptations of recipes from America's female chefs.

Pasta *spellers*

Age/Grade Level or Audience: Kindergarten, preschool, or elementary crafts activity; after school art program; home-school program; Brownie Scout or 4-H project.

Description: Spell out the name of a heroine from history.

Procedure: Choose a woman from history to honor; for example, Dr. Elizabeth Blackwell, the first woman doctor, or Lucy Stone, a champion of women's rights. Place different kinds of pasta on cardboard to spell out the last name or the whole name, depending on the space and the skill of the participant. Glue each piece into place. Create a background formed from aquarium rock, dried beans and peas, colored laundry powder, broken pasta, confetti, glitter, or cut up bits of colored magazines. Glue the background into place. Mold clay or weave strips of paper into a frame. Place completed pasta pictures in a Women's History Month display case.

Budget: $$$

Sources:

Buckingham, Sandra. *Stencil It!* Firefly Books, 1995.

Bulloch, Ivan. *Play with Models.* Lerner Group, 1996.

Clark, Judith Freeman. *Almanac of American Women in the Twentieth Century.* Prentice Hall, 1987.

Ellis, Vernoica Freeman. *Afro-Bets First Book about Africa: An Introduction for Young Readers.* Just Us Books, 1989.

Great American Women. Knowledge Unlimited, n.d. (Posters)

Hughes, Phyllis. *Indian Children Paper Dolls.* Red Crane, 1990.

Sattler, Helen Roney. *Recipes for Art and Craft Materials.* Lothrop, Lee & Shepard, 1987.

Women's History. Cowles Media Company, 1995.

"Women Who Dare." National Women's History Project, 1995. (Calendar)

Zyromski, Page. "Wycinanki." *Cobblestone,* June 1995, 24–25.

Alternative Applications: Explain the process of making a science mosaic. Demonstrate how students can honor Women's History Month by drawing a simple female shape entering a space capsule or a woman performing surgery or checking results in a test tube. To complete the mosaic, have the participants arrange pieces of foil, glitter, confetti, or aquarium rock into areas of the shape and glue them into place. The background should reflect a contrasting color, for example, crushed dyed eggshell or colored sand glued to the area. Present these mosaics, along with a paragraph explaining their significance, at a PTA meeting, open house, parents' night gathering, library or science museum display case, fall carnival, or church school program.

Save *me a place!*

Age/Grade Level or Audience: Elementary school art activity; home-school cooperative project; scout or 4-H frieze.

Description: Draw a place setting for a favorite woman from history.

Procedure: Select a woman from the past who best exemplifies courage, strength, intelligence, dedication to family, wit, or kindness. For example, from history consider Indira Gandhi, Helen Keller, or Winnie Mandela; from politics select Queen Victoria or Mamie Eisenhower;

from literature, choose Louisa May Alcott, George Sand, or Mary Shelley. Draw a life-size table setting, showing mat, napkin, plate or bowl, teapot or pitcher, cup or glass, chopsticks, and utensils. The place mat should include symbols that represent her life, drawings or pictures of her, and a short biographical sketch. Add a napkin, place card with the honoree's name in large letters, and some drawings of appropriate foods; for example, foo-foo and coconut milk for Winnie Mandela, or bowls of vegetable curry and ghee for Indira Gandhi. Join the other members of the class in displaying place settings on a long table, wall display, or bulletin board.

Budget: $$

Sources:

Ashby, Ruth, and Deborah Gore Ohrn. *Herstory: Women Who Changed the World.* Viking, 1995.

Chicago, Judy. *The Dinner Party: A Symbol of Our Heritage.* Anchor Books, 1979.

Cogan, Nancy, and Roni Akmon. *Come to My Teaparty.* Eclectic Oregon, 1993.

Dlugosch, Susan. *Table Setting Guide.* Brighton Publications, 1990.

Hazen, Barbara. *Hello, Gnu, How Do You Do.* Doubleday, 1990.

Lunardini, Christine. *What Every American Should Know About Women's History.* Bob Adams, 1994.

To stimulate choices from a wide range of women, have participants discuss whom they admire most and where they learned about the person. Suggest stories from recreational reading, story hour, television, movies, or history lessons.

Alternative Applications: At the end of a nonfiction reading, have participants draw a table, centerpiece, chair, and place setting to depict a memorable female character from favorite stories, particularly Eleanor Coerr's *Sadako and the Thousand Paper Cranes* or Laura Ingalls Wilder's *Little House on the Prairie.* At the side, print an appropriate menu; for example, foods common to the prairie for Laura or a hospital meal for Sadako.

Sweet *hearts*

Age/Grade Level or Audience: K-4 art class; summer library program; home-school activity; Brownie Scout or 4-H project.

Description: Bake valentines for favorite women from history or literature.

Procedure: Select a woman from history, movies, or literature. For example, choose Joan of Arc, Harriet Tubman, or Annie Oakley. Roll out packaged sugar cookie dough or baking clay. Use a heart-shaped cookie cutter to make heart shapes. Pierce each near the top. Bake, cool, then decorate with acrylic paint or tubes of colored icing by outlining the name on both sides of the cookie. String hearts through the opening with ribbon, colored twine, yarn, or florist wire. Suspend from a Women's History Month clothesline, branch, or tree along with origami figures, tinsel, paper chains, and other ornaments. Save a heart for your own name or for a woman in your town who deserves a thank-you.

Budget: $$

Sources:

Arthur: Myth and Reality. Scholar's Bookshelf, n.d. (Video)

Avis, Jen, and Kathy Ward. *Just for Kids.* Avis & Ward, 1990.

Clark, Judith Freeman. *Almanac of American Women in the Twentieth Century*. Prentice Hall, 1987.

Elizabeth R. Critics' Choice Video. (Video)

Ellis, Vernoica Freeman. *Afro-Bets First Book about Africa: An Introduction for Young Readers*. Just Us Books, 1989.

Ferdinand and Isabella. Schlessinger, 1995. (Video)

Fire over England. Time Warner Viewer's Edge, n.d. (Video)

Great American Women. Knowledge Unlimited. (Posters)

Griffin, Lynne, and Kelly McCann. *The Book of Women: 300 Notable Women History Passed By*. Bob Adams, 1992.

Hoven, Kendall. *Amazing American Women: 40 Fascinating 5-Minute Reads*. Libraries Unlimited, 1995.

Kings and Queens I and II. Scholar's Bookshelf, n.d. (Video)

Mills, Kay. *From Pocahontas to Power Suits*. Plume, 1995.

Sherr, Lynn, and Jurate Kazickas. *Susan B. Anthony Slept Here*. Random House, 1994.

The Windsors. Pacific Arts Publishing, n.d. (Video)

"Women Who Dare." Women's History Project, 1995. (Calendar)

Alternative Applications: Cover a wall with poster paper or a long strip for a frieze. Have participants use markers, chalk, crayon, and tempera to make hearts of a variety of colors, sizes, and shapes. Leave enough room to print the name of the historical, biblical, movie, or literary character who most deserves honor. Appoint a committee to complete the display with a catchy phrase (Nobel notable; our favorite writer; grand lady) and a colorful border suggesting basketry, stitchery, carving, or fantasy shapes.

Who's *coming to dinner?*

Age/Grade Level or Audience: Elementary or middle school interdisciplinary art and history activity; home-school program; scout or 4-H project; after-school drama presentation; Women's History Month presentation.

Description: Create a dinner scenario of favorite women from history.

Procedure: Draw invitations and a map to your house. Address envelopes to favorite women from history or sports—Pocahontas, Queen Victoria, Calamity Jane, Kristi Yamaguchi, Jackie Joyner-Kersee. Create a menu suitable to the tastes of a diverse group of women. Prepare a seating chart pairing women who share similar interests, for example Georgia O'Keeffe and Annie Oakley who both loved the American Southwest. Compose several questions or comments to start the dinner conversation. For example:

- What teachers influenced your lives?
- How would you educate a girl to take your place?
- What is your favorite way to spend private time?
- For what ideas or events do you want to be remembered?
- What famous woman would you like to meet at this dinner party?

Budget: $

Sources:

Cogan, Nancy, and Roni Akmon. *Come to My Teaparty.* Eclectic Oregon, 1993.

Ellis, Veronica Freeman. *Afro-Bets First Book about Africa: An Introduction for Young Readers.* Just Us Books, 1989.

Hay, Susannah. *The Women's Heritage Scrapbook.* Caillech Press, 1992.

Hazen, Barbara. *Hello, Gnu, How Do You Do.* Doubleday, 1990.

Medearis, Angela Shelf. *Dancing with the Indians.* Holiday House, 1991.

Milne, A. A. *Winnie-the-Pooh's Teatime Cookbook.* Dutton Child Books, 1993.

"Women Who Dare." National Women's History Project, 1995. (Calendar)

Alternative Applications: Select a group of girls to actually act out the dinner party, taking on the roles of famous women from history. Begin by making polite introductions, making sure to comment on highpoints in the lives of the "guests:"

- Mrs. Roosevelt, I would like you to meet Princess Michiko of Japan. Princess Michiko, this is Mrs. Eleanor Roosevelt, former First Lady of the United States and one of the founders of the United Nations Human Rights Commission.

- Dr. Chinn, this is our guest of honor, anthropologist Mary Leakey. Dr. Leakey, I am pleased to introduce you to Dr. May Chinn, Harlem's foremost public health doctor.

- Ms. Bethune, this is Marian Edelman, one of the twentieth century's noted educators. Ms. Edelman, I want you to meet Mary McLeod Bethune, a leader of education for African Americans.

- Ms. Cleary, please welcome Laura Ingalls Wilder, a pioneer who taught school and wrote books about her childhood. Mrs. Wilder, this is Beverly Cleary, one of the most popular children's authors in America.

Have participants use the "ice-breaker" questions as a jumping off point to further dinner discussion.

Women's *recipes*

Age/Grade Level or Audience: High school or college home economics or nutrition study; desktop publishing exercise; home demonstration presentation; women's studies or civic club project; media feature; church bazaar item.

Description: Compile a series of traditionally inspired recipes that feature women's names as creators or inspirations.

Procedure: Select a group of recipes that were named for their creators or for famous women, for example:

- chicken Tetrazzini, a pasta entree honoring opera diva Luisa Tetrazzini

- crêpes Suzette, a flaming French dessert commemorating Suzette, an unidentified paramour of Edward, Prince of Wales

- Jenny Lind Cake, named for the early twentieth-century Swedish soprano

- Kitty Green's hoppin' jon, a traditional Louisiana recipe made popular by a twentieth-century New Orleans chef

- madeleines, a bite-size dessert cake named for Madeleine Paumier, a nineteenth-century pastry chef
- peach Melba, an ice cream topped with berry sauce named for Nellie Melba
- Zephyr Wright's shrimp curry, commemorating Zephyr Wright's service in the White House kitchen during Lyndon Johnson's administration

Form a database of heirloom recipes and women's biographies. Publish on-line or in a monograph as a money-raising project. Include the following:

Zephyr Wright's Shrimp Curry

Steam 2 pounds of shelled shrimp five minutes. To ½ cup minced onion sautéed in butter, stir in 6 tablespoons flour, 1 teaspoon salt, ¼ teaspoon ginger powder, and 1 teaspoon sugar. Dissolve a chicken bouillon cube in 1 cup boiling water; stir in 2 cups milk. Add liquid to dry ingredients. Top with shrimp and ½ cup mirin or sherry, 1 teaspoon of lemon juice, and the zest of 1 lemon. Serve over rice.

Peach Melba

Boil ½ cup currant jelly with one cup raspberries. Blend a ½ cup sugar with 1 teaspoon cornstarch. Stir into berry sauce. Serve cold over a generous scoop of vanilla ice cream covered with peach slices.

Martha Washington Fudge

Blend 2 boxes fine powdered sugar with 1 can condensed milk, ¼ cup melted butter, 2 teaspoons vanilla, and 3 cups chopped walnuts or pecans. Form by tablespoonfuls into balls and chill. Prepare icing by melting 2 packages semi-sweet chocolate bits and 1 cup of paraffin in a double boiler. Drop chilled balls into chocolate and coat. Remove with tongs and dry on waxed paper. Makes 5 pounds of fudge balls.

Aunt Bee's Mayberry Fried Chicken

Whip 2 eggs with salt. Dip 8 chicken pieces in egg mixture and roll in flour. Fry in a skillet in one inch hot melted shortening. Turn pieces several times, then cook on low for 20 minutes. When juices run clear and coating is brown, cover skillet and cook 20 minutes on low. Serves four.

Budget: $$

Sources:

Beck, Ken, and Jim Clark. *Aunt Bee's Mayberry Cookbook*. Rutledge Hill Press, 1991.
Betty Talmadge's Lovejoy Plantation Cookbook. Peachtree, 1995.
Child, Julia. *Cooking with Master Chefs*. Alfred Knopf, 1993.
David, Elizabeth. *An Omelette and a Glass of Wine*. Viking, 1990.
———. *Summer Cooking*, Viking, 1988.
Davis, William C. *The Civil War Cookbook*. Courage Books, 1993.
Fischer, Lynn. *Healthy Indulgences*. Hearst Books, 1995.
Rosso, Julee. *Great Good Food*. Crown Publishing Group, 1993.
Rosso, Julee, and Sheila Lukins. *The New Basics Cookbook*. Workman, 1989.
Sanders, Dori. *Country Cooking*. Algonquin Books, 1995.
Shriver, Jerry. "Marcella Hazan Carefully Crafts New Cookbook." *USA Today*, July 31, 1995, D1, 2.

Smith, Barbara. *B. Smith's Entertaining and Cooking for Friends.* Artisan Sales, 1995.

Weber, Judith Eichler. *Melting Pots.* Silver Moon Press, 1995.

Wilkins, Sharron E. "The President's Kitchen." *African-American History,* spring 1995, 56–58.

Alternative Applications: Create recipes to suit the role of famous women, both real and fictional. For example, make a dip, nourishing soup, or pie from these recipes:

Lucy Van Pelt's Simple Dill Pickle Dip

Soften an 8 ounce block of cream cheese. Blend with a large dill pickle in a food processor at high speed. Top with dill weed. Serve with crackers or chips.

Florence Nightingale Chicken Soup

Boil 3 chicken breasts in 1 quart of salted water. Chop with kitchen shears and return to broth. Cook with 1 cup rice, cup water, ½ cup finely slivered carrots, a half cup finely sliced celery tops or hearts, salt, and a generous amount of black pepper. Serve hot with crackers or buttered toast points.

Leona Helmsley's Rich Chocolate Pie

Bake 2 deep-dish pie shells and set aside to cool. Make 1 large package of cooked chocolate or dark chocolate pudding according to instructions on the box. To the hot mixture add 1 heaping teaspoon instant coffee powder and 1½ cups of finely minced bittersweet chocolate. Stir briskly until smooth. Pour into shells and cool. Top with whipped cream and sprinkles of bittersweet chocolate.

Foreign *language*

Balulalow

Age/Grade Level or Audience: High school or college middle English or Chaucer research topic; choral performance program notes; post-graduate music or literature seminar on medieval liturgical music; interdisciplinary language lecture.

Description: Conduct a round table discussion of the speaker in "Balulalow."

Procedure: Study the point of view of the speaker in "Balulalow," an original medieval lullaby adapted by Benjamin Britten as a soprano solo with harp and chorus accompaniment in his *A Ceremony of Carols.*

Balulalow

O my deare hert, young Jesu sweit,
Prepare thy creddil in my spreit,
And I sall rock thee to my hert,
And never mair from thee depart.

But I sall praise thee evermoir
With sanges sweit unto thy gloir;
The knees of my hert sall I bow,
And sing that richt Balulalow.

Ask the following questions:

- What are several possibilities for the identity of the speaker?

- Why do these possibilities strongly indicate that she is female? A mother? The Virgin Mary?

- What image suggests that the speaker intends to remain humble before Jesu?

- What modern terms mean the same as *creddil, spreit,* and *mair*?

- What does this intimate lullaby add to a Christmas oratorio?

- Why would the singer choose a lullaby that is *richt*?

Budget: $

Sources:

Britten, Benjamin. *A Ceremony of Carols.* Boosey & Hawkes, 1948.

Carpenter, Humphrey. *Benjamin Britten: A Biography.* Macmillan, 1993.

Johnson, Kevin Orlin. *Expression of the Catholic Faith.* Random House, 1994.

Lockyer, Herbert. *All the Women of the Bible.* Zondervan, 1988.

Metzger, Bruce M., and Michael D. Coogan, eds. *The Oxford Companion to the Bible.* Oxford University Press, 1993.

Wright, G. Ernest, ed. *Great People of the Bible and How They Lived.* Reader's Digest Association, 1974.

Alternative Applications: Lead a comparison of the middle English of "Balulalow" with similar language in "Adam Lay Y-bounden," "As Dew in Aprille," "That Yongë Child," and "Spring Carol," all part of Benjamin Britten's *A Ceremony of Carols.* Note the archaic terms in these phrases:

a maiden that is makèles	doth be wrong
God's purvayance for sustenance	her son she ches
his moder's bour	it gan weep
nought thereto	passèd alle minstrelsy
to hear iwis	lay y-bounden
ne had the appil také bin	we maun singen

Discuss the emphasis on Mary as a mother and Jesus as an infant rather than as deities or divine figures worthy of veneration. How does this festival of carols fit into the history of Mariology? Why are middle English lines mixed with such Latin liturgical phrases as *deo gracias?*

Claudia's *tombstone*

Age/Grade Level or Audience: High school or college Latin lesson; Latin club program; creative writing contest; calligraphy project.

Description: Translate and discuss the epitaph of Claudia.

Procedure: Present an ornately lettered version of Claudia's eight-line tomb inscription, a famous tribute dating to 135–120 B.C. from a monument or pillar that has since been lost. Distribute the epitaph either untranslated or accompanied by this interlinear translation:

Hospes, quod deico paullum est; asta ac pellege.
Guest, what I have to say is little; stand and read it.
Heic est sepulcrum hau pulcrum pulcrai feminae.
This is the unlovely tomb of a lovely woman.
Nomen parentes nominarunt Claudia.
Her parents called her Claudia.
Suom maritom corde deilexit souo.
She loved her husband with all her heart.
Gnatos duos creavit, horunc alterum
She bore two sons, one now
in terra linquit, alium sub terra locat.
Left behind on the earth, the other dead.
Sermone lepido, tum autem incessu commodo.
She spoke sweetly; her behavior was seemly.
Domum servavit, lanam fecit. Dixi. Abei.
She guarded her home, she made wool. I have spoken. Go away.

Have students translate and discuss the worth of a good wife as described by the monument maker.

- Who is speaking? What is significant about the "paullum" that the speaker has to say?
- What does this terse description say about the brevity and quality of Claudia's life?
- Why is it important to know that the speaker thinks that Claudia was beautiful, but her tomb is not?
- Why does the speaker consider gentle speech and modesty important assets in a wife?
- Why is it important that she "loved her husband with all her heart?"
- What family members does the speaker refer to? How does the description of her two sons suggest that Claudia suffered tragedy before her death?
- Why does the speaker conclude that Claudia "kept her home and made wool?"

Explain the surly, incourteous tone of the speaker, who adds at the end, "I have spoken. Go away."

Budget: $

Sources:

Snodgrass, Mary Ellen. *Auctores Latini*. Amsco School Publications, 1993.

Warmington, E. H., ed. and trans. *Remains of Old Latin*. Harvard University Press, 1967.

Alternative Applications: Contrast the monument to Claudia with the Roman monument to Pompeia, from around the second century B.C. Present it either untranslated or accompanied by this interlinear translation:

> **Primae Pompeiae ossua heic.**
> Prima Pompeia's bones lie here.
> **Fortuna spondet multa multis, praestat nemini;**
> Lady Luck teases many, but she is faithful to none;
> **Vivi in dies et horas, nam propriam est nihil.**
> Live in your days and hours, for nothing is really yours.
> **Salvius et Heros dant.**
> Salvius and Hero give this tomb.

How does the tone of the monument contribute to the distaste of the speaker for eulogizing young women who died in the fullness of youth. Why does the speaker describe Prima Pompeia as "bones?" Explain why the speaker urges the reader to "live in your days and hours." Why does the speaker insist that "nothing is really yours?"

Mariology *in verse*

Age/Grade Level or Audience: High school or college French class; Alliance Française presentation; oral interpretation of French poetry.

Description: Summarize the depiction of the Virgin Mary in verse.

Procedure: Distribute copies of Pierre Villete's "Hymne à la Vierge," either untranslated or accompanied by this interlinear translation:

Hymn à la Vierge

O toute belle Vierge Marie
O most beautiful Virgin Mary.
Votre âme trouve en Dieu
Your soul finds in God
Le parfait amour.
A perfect love.
Il vous revêt du manteau de la Grâce
He dresses you in a mantle of grace
Comme une fiancée
As a fiancé
Parée de ses joyaux. Alleluia.
Decks herself in jewels. Alleluia.
Je vais chanter ta louange, Seigneur,
I will sing your praise, Lord,
Car tu as pris soin de moi,
Because you have cared for me,
Car tu m'as enveloppée du voile de l'innocence.
Because you have cloaked me in a veil of innocence.

Vous êtes née avant les collines
You were born before the hills
O sagesse de Dieu
O wisdom of God
Porte de Salut.
Gateway to salvation.
Heureaux celui qui marche dans vos traces
Happy is the person who walks in your steps
A la voix de vos conseils. Alleluia.
Led by the word of your counsel. Alleluia.
Je vais chanter ta louange, Seigneur,
I will sing your praise, Lord,
Car tu m'as faite, avant la jour,
Because you created me, before the day,
Car tu m'as faite précéder la jaillissement des sources.
Because you created me before the gush of springs.

Avant les astres vous étiez présente
Before the stars you were proclaimed
Mère du Créateur
Mother of the Creator
Au profond du ciel.
To the depths of the sky.
Quand Dieu fixait les limites du monde
When God established Earth's limits
Vous partagiez son coeur
You resided in his heart
Etant à l'oeuvre avec lui. Alleluia.
And were a part of his work. Alleluia
O Toute belle Vierge Marie.
O most beautiful Virgin Mary.

Lead a discussion group in expressing the poet's intention in placing the Virgin Mary so prominently in creation. How does God honor her? What aspects of God's work does she influence? How does the speaker intend to show gratitude to God and the Virgin Mary?

Budget: $$

Sources:

Benko, Stephen. *The Virgin Goddess: Studies in the Pagan and Christian Roots of Mariology.* E. J. Brill, 1993.

Jameson, Anna B. *Legends of the Madonna as Represented in the Fine Arts.* Omnigraphics Inc., 1990.

Jones, Lois S. *Madonna and Child: The Development of Christian Symbolism.* Jones Preston, 1992.

The Madonna. Palisades Home Video. (Video)

The Many Faces of Mary. Servant, 1992.

Michelis, Dennis. *Mary of Nazareth.* Holy Cross Orthodox, 1992.

Much Ado about Nothing. Sony Music Entertainment Inc., 1993. (CD)

Rotelle, John E. *Mary's Yes: Meditations on Mary Through the Ages.* Servant, 1990.

Villette, Pierre. "Hymne à la Vierge Marie" in *French Choral Music.* Meridian Records, 1988. (CD)

Walsh, Maria J. *Titles of Mary.* Franciscan University Press, 1991.

Alternative Applications: Study and discuss numerous works of mariology from different times and places in a comparison with the creation poem by Villette. Consider these:

cantatas	paintings	stained glass
fresco	poems	statuary
hymns	religious jewelry	tapestry
litanies	songs	

Contrast the romanticized view of the Virgin Mary with descriptions found in the biblical books of Matthew and Luke and with "Pardon Goddess of the Night," from the 1993 Kenneth Branagh film version of *Much Ado about Nothing.* Determine how the elevation of the Virgin affects the worshipper's attitude toward the faults of human women.

The Mystery *of Sappho*

Age/Grade Level or Audience: High school literature, history, or Latin research topic; college classics or humanities lecture; book club presentation; poetry or reading circle.

Description: Introduce the work of Sappho (ca. 613–508 B.C.), poet, educator, and philosopher.

Procedure: Provide participants with a hand-out and map delineating Sappho's life and times, poetic works, and political and religious ties. Include these facts:

- Although her name is known worldwide and her songs still sung, she left few clues to her real identity. Whether she was called Psappho or Phsappho or Sappho, she was the bright, energetic, charismatic daughter of Cleïs and Scamandronymus, born on the island of Lesbos, off the coast of Asia Minor, although other islands claim her.

- Sappho was short with dark hair and eyes. She enjoyed a comfortable life, education, and privileges not usually accorded to Greek women of her day. Her background and writing indicates an intimate knowledge of the Mediterranean, its lifestyles, and its social and political concerns.

- After her father died when she was six, Sappho depended on her mother and three brothers—Larychus, Charaxus, and Eurygius—for care. Charaxus may have been her favorite.

- Sappho appears to have favored Hera and Aphrodite, the goddesses of marriage and passion. She was wooed by Alcaeus but married Cercolas, a merchant from Andros, and gave birth to a fair-haired girl, Cleïs, probably named after Sappho's mother and evidently quite spoiled by her own adoring mother.

- Sappho may have participated in political intrigue against the tyrant Pittacus and was exiled to Sicily from 604–595 B.C., a time of vigorous creativity as demonstrated by her original song, marriage hymns, and romantic verse in the Aeolian dialect.

- Sappho operated a girls' school or academy on Lesbos for local girls and boarding students from Ionia during a time when most males were involved in war and women were left to make their own decisions and agendas. Among her pupils were her pets, Anactoria, Atthis, and Gongyla; she was less fond of Andromeda, possibly a rival or sulky student.

- She may have died from intentional drowning in the Ionian Sea off the island of Leucra after being spurned by Phaon, a conceited ferryman, although this story appears to have sprung up in the legends that developed around her centuries after she lived.

Budget: $

Sources:

Bowder, Diana, ed. *Who Was Who in the Greek World*. Washington Square Press, 1982.

Bowie, Angus M. *The Poetic Dialect of Sappho and Alceus*. State Mutual Book and Periodical Service, 1989.

Davenport, Guy. *Thasos and Ohio*. North Point Press, 1985.

DeJean. *Fictions of Sappho*. University of Chicago Press, 1989.

Fithian, Theodore. *Where Sappho Sang*. Vantage, 1992.

Rayor, Diane. *Sappho's Lyre: Archaic Lyric and Women Poets of Ancient Greece*. University of California Press, 1991.

Robinson, David M. *Sappho and Her Influence*. Cooper Square, 1963.

Smyth, Herbert Weir. *Greek Melic Poets*. Biblo and Tannen, 1963.

Alternative Applications: Provide comparative hand-outs or give readings from various translations of Sappho's works. Comment on the addition of thought, image, or innuendo to the basic meaning of lines such as these:

- Like a rosy apple on a high branch is the maiden; the pickers have forgotten her—no, not forgotten: they have simply not been able to reach her.

- Awed by her splendor, stars near the lovely moon cover their own bright faces when she is roundest and light earth with her silver.

- You may forget but let me tell you this: someone in some future time will think of us.

- I loved you once long ago, Athis . . . you seemed to me a small, ungainly child.

- The moon has set, and the Pleiades; it is midnight, and time passes, and I sleep alone.

- Sweet mother, I cannot ply the loom, vanquished by desire for a youth through the work of soft Aphrodite.

- Hesperus, you herd homeward whatever Dawn's light dispersed: you herd sheep—herd goats—herd children home to their mothers.

- Death is an ill; 'tis thus the Gods decide: For had death been a boon, the Gods had died.

- No honey for me if it comes with a bee.

- I know not what to do; my mind is divided.

- Handsome horses O shiver and admire, long ships and symmetries of archers, but black earth's fine sight for me is her I love.

- Anaktoria so far away, remember me, who had rather hear the melody of your walking and see the torch flare of your smile than the long battle line of Lydia's charioteers, round shields and helmets.

- Love—bittersweet, irrepressible—loosens my limbs and I tremble.

- Although they are only breath, words which I command are immortal.

Draw conclusions about alternate perceptions of Sappho as classical scholar, philosopher, educator, writer, leader of women, iconoclast, lesbian, sybarite, and romantic poet. Cite poets who have imitated her imagery and cadence, particularly Catullus.

Readings *from the Peace Corps*

Age/Grade Level or Audience: Middle school or high school literature, history, or language reading; book or travel club presentation; reading circle or improvisational drama class.

Description: Read aloud from the past and present experiences of women in the Peace Corps.

Procedure: Comment on significant phrases that Peace Corps workers have needed to know to appreciate culture, geography, foods, and other aspects of a distant setting, particularly in these and other male-female settings: a marketplace, school, post office, clinic, hospital, depot, cafe, or government building. Consider director Carol Bellamy's comment in evaluating her experience in Guatemala that corps members have distinguished themselves by being adaptable, tough, and resilient. Discuss with listeners how courtesy and a quick ear for slang and idiomatic language are essential. Consider these models:

- Lora Parisien's experiences in Tunisia, described in "YSWF . . . Living in an Arab World," where she travels by moped through the *medina* and learns quick-witted retorts such as "Rude bellick, Allah bish yhizz Isaanik" (Be careful or Allah's gonna yank out your tongue!). She also learns to recognize the spelling of *Quran* for Koran and such everyday phrases as *shkoon* (Who is it?) and *fisa, fisa* (hurry, hurry).

- As explained in Tina Martin's "Under the Tongan Sun," she concentrates on being *anga lelei* (good-natured), a means of endearing herself to South Pacific islanders.

151

- In Jacqueline Francis's "'H' Is for Hopsi," she emphasizes the Nepalese *hopsi* (Negro), the single word that described the Asian community's response to her black skin and features.

- As Victoria Derr expresses in "Reasons for Joy," life in Gambia, West Africa, puts her at the mercy of Mandinka natives who introduce her with a local name, *Neema Biyaay,* spend *butut* (local currency), and demand as a test of her patience *M foo alimetoo* (I want a match.)

- A significant part of Kathleen Coskran's "So This Is Paris" utilizes Ethiopian terms, especially *ferenj* or *ferenjis* (foreigner or foreigners), *tej* (beverage), *birilla* (drinking glass), and the pejorative *shankalla* (slave) for Hamid, a black-skinned student who is defeated in a school election.

- Susan Rich, a corps volunteer in Niger, West Africa, notes in a poem, "Mariama," the traditional greeting, *Sanu, sanu* (How are you? How are you?) and *magani* (love potion), which Mariama jokes about because she is old by Niger's standards for an unmarried woman. Mariama's advice to Susan was also doubled for effect: *Sai hankuri, sai hanku,* (Have patience, have patience.)

Budget: $

Sources:

Bellamy, Carol. Introduction to *To Touch the World: The Peace Corps Experience*. Peace Corps, 1995.

Benjamin, Medea. *The Peace Corps and More: One Hundred and Fourteen Ways to Work, Study and Travel in the Third World*. Seven Locks Press, 1991.

Coleman, Carol, and Steve Smith. *Life as a Peace Corps Volunteer in the Federated States of Micronesia*. Development through Self-Reliance, 1986.

Lowrette, Susan. *Under the Neem Tree*. University of Washington Press, 1993.

Schwarz, Karen. *What You Can Do for Your Country inside the Peace Corps—A Thirty Year History*. Doubleday, 1993.

Alternative Applications: Have volunteers explain why phrases connected with daily courtesies and male-female relations help outsiders adapt to local ways and win friends without misleading others as to intent or purpose. Make a prioritized list of useful phrases in English, Tagalog, Spanish, French, Italian, Portuguese, Arabic, Korean, German, Bantu, Swahili, Nepalese, Urdu, or another language. Supply a pronunciation guide for each. List greetings, simple questions about place and time, introductions, names for currency and foods, and references to transportation, lodging, toilet facilities, fresh water, illness, and emergencies.

Walking *across Pompeii*

Age/Grade Level or Audience: Elementary or middle school history and writing activity; summer library project; home-school design project; museum display.

Description: Describe the city of Pompeii from a woman's perspective.

Procedure: Have participants select a female persona to assume. Guide visiting family members from Rome over this cool, pleasant coastal getaway, pointing out names of areas and objects in Latin. Provide commentary on the fast-food *tavernae;* shops selling chilled *vina; theatra et templa; coqui* making *panem* and *crustulli;* and jewelers hammering *aurum et argentum.* Point out the most appealing architecture: the Herculaneum *Portus, palaestra,* *amphitheatre, forum,* Hall of *Duoviri,* Stabian *Portus,* Inn of Aselina, *domus* of the Vettii, Cicero's *Villa,* Diomede's *Villa, Templum Fortunae Augustae, Fasilica, Via Abbondonza,* and *Templum* of Isis. Make pointed comments on the importance of the Egyptian cult of Isis on local Romans and visitors. Save the *Villa* of Mysteries for the final stop of your tour.

Portray yourself as a guide when *Mons Vesuvius* begins to cloud over and spout *fumos.* Before *cineres* begin to rain on your *hostes* and the *aeres* grows thick and hot, lead the way from *oppidum* and east to *salutatem* in the *montes.* Observe the devastation of the beach and the disappearance of Pompeii.

Budget: $$

Sources:

Andrews, Ian. *Pompeii.* Lerner Publications, 1980.

Biel, Timothy L. *Pompeii.* Lucent books, 1989.

Mau, August. *Pompeii.* Caratzas, 1984.

Wallace-Hadrill, Andrew. *The Roman Social Habitat: Studies of Housing at Pompeii and Herculaneum.* Princeton University Press, 1993.

Alternative Applications: List the jobs of the *domina* of a vacation *domus* in Pompeii. Describe the difficulty of maintaining a *casa* in *Roma* and a *domum secundum* nearer Italy's southwestern coast. Comment on the availability of artisans to inlay the *atrium,* build a *fontem* and *nymphaeum,* and construct a cool, breezy *triclinium* for informal summer *cenas.* Name your favorite *cibi* available in Pompeiian markets; for example, fresh *pisces* and shellfish to be marinated in *vino* and charbroiled on a grill at the *mensam.* Comment on the quality of melons, olives, pears, and *altera frumenta.* Conclude with your feelings of safety and contentment away from the hustle and political turmoil of *Roma.*

Women *in the news*

Age/Grade Level or Audience: High school or college French class; Alliance Française presentation.

Description: Discuss articles concerning women's history and women's rights as described in French journals and newspapers.

Procedure: Distribute current copies of books, newspapers, *Paris Match, Elle,* or the special women's edition of *Notre Histoire: 16e–20e siècle.* Have groups summarize and present in the target language information about these religious and secular topics:

- les femmes et l'eglise en France et Belgique
- Mere Thérèse: une modele liturgique
- les oeuvres des feministes
- les danseuses populaires
- les feministes and le théâtre moderne
- les femmes et l'eglise
- les actrices au cinéma aujourd'hui
- les femmes et de sucre de Guadeloupe
- la catholique moderne vs. des clercs and des hommes en général

- les femmes et la distribution de l'eucharistie
- Jeanne Aubert, la première jociste de France
- Isabeau, bergère prophétesse
- la réforme au féminin
- la sculptrice Camille Claudel
- l'education des filles avant "la révolution"
- témoins de le temps difficile
- les femmes sous les soviets
- des rôles nouveaux pour les femmes
- la foi de Jeanne d'Arc
- Québec et les aventurières des femmes
- les pensees de Simone de Beauvoir

Include sidebars defining these terms:

anabaptistes	novices
baptistes	ordres
bérulle	piétisme
blocus continental	presbytériens
camisards	prêtres religieuses
canoniste	prêtres séculiers
cîteaux	puritains
clunisien	quakers
congrégationalisme	quiétisme
convers	refuge
darbystes	régulier
devotio moderna	réviel
diaconie	révocation de l'édit de Nantes
diaspora	sages-femmes
encyclique	Saint-Cyr
eschatologique	sorcières de Salem
evangélique	sovietiques
femmes catéchistes	synodale période
Jansénisme	synode
libertin	Tiers ordre
lumières	Trente, Concile de
méthodisme	unitariens
militantes	vielle-catholique
moniales	voeux solonnels

Budget: $$$

Sources:

"Avec les femmes de la Bible." *Prier.* Paris: Prier/VPC, 1995. (CD-ROM and cassette)

Hébrard, Marc. *Féminité dans un nouvel âge de l'humanité.* Paris: Droguet et Ardant, 1993.

Hildesheimer, F. *Le jansénisme: l'histoire et l'héritage.* Paris: DDB, 1992.

"L'eglise aime-t-elle les femmes?" *Notre Histoire.* Numero 116, Novembre 1994.

"L'histoire de france au cinéma, 1895–1995." *CinémAction.* Condë-sur-Noireau: Notre Histoire et CinémAction, 1995.

Notre Histoire: 16e–20e siècle. Numero 121, Avril 1995.

Thomas, Lyn. "Twentieth-Century France." *Bloomsbury Guide to Women's Literature.* Prentice-Hall, 1992.

Tunc, Suzanne. *Les femmes au pouvoir.* Paris: Cerf, 1995.

Vallet, Gerarde. *Femmes et religions.* Paris: Gallimard, 1994.

Alternative Applications: Have participants add to a time line or capsule history of women's rights in France and its former and current territories. Include Switzerland, Monaco, Luxembourg, Belgium, Québec, Tahiti, Martinique, Guadeloupe, St. Martin, St. Barts, and north Africa. Include the experiences of these women:

Marie Antoinette	Annie Leclerc
Jeanne d'Arc	Thérèse Lisieux
Jeanne Aubert	Martine Millet
Simone de Beauvoir	Suzanne Necker
Catherine Cadiére	Edith Piaf
Marie Cardinal	Christine de Pisan
Marie-Thèrése Cheroutre	Mère Saint-Claude
Colette	Saint-Gildas en Bretagne
Juana Inés de la Cruz	Madeleine de Saint-Maximin
Madeleine Delbrel	Sophie Scholl
Assia Djebar	Sophie Swetchine
Marie de France	Simone Weil

Women *in opera, oratorio, and chorale*

Age/Grade Level or Audience: High school or college foreign language poetry study; chorale society presentation; foreign language club monograph; newsletter.

Description: Contrast the women described or revealed in original lyrics and English translations of operas, operettas, folk songs, hymns, chorales, anthems, or oratorios.

Procedure: Provide participants with segments of lyrics in the target language. Listen to recordings of the lyrics or videos of the performances and note musical stress, phrasing, repetition, and prosody. Discuss the original implication as it compares or contrasts with English translation. Consult dictionaries for explicit definitions. Note obvious anachronism, connotation, nuance, errors, additions, or deletions. Use the following example as a model:

Czecho-Slovak

"Waters Ripple and Flow," folksong harmonized by Deems Taylor

Tece voda, tece,	Waters ripple and flow,
cez Velecky majir	Slowly passes each day;
Nechal si ma, nechal,	Faithless lover of mine,
stare davny frajir;	Stay no longer away;
Nechal si ma, nechal,	Faithless lover of mine,
staro davny frajir.	Stay no longer away.
Nechal som t'a, nechal	Dear one, well dost thou know
dobre ty vies komu;	Why fond lovers must part:
Coty reci nosi,	Wherefore falters thy faith?
do naseho domu;	Why so timid thy heart?
coty reci nosi,	Wherefore falters thy faith?
do naseho domu.	Why so timid thy heart?
vrat' sa, mily, vrat' sa,	Dearest lover, come back;
od Kysuckej vody,	End the vigil I keep.
Odnie sols mi klucik,	Thine, the key to my heart,
Od mojej slobody!	Mine, without thee to weep.
Odnie sols mi klucik,	Thine, the key to my heart,
Od mojej slobody!	Mine, without thee to weep.
Skur sa stara Tura,	When the mountain shall turn,
Slobodenka moja,	Then my happiness dawns,
t'a sa minavrati;	Then shall freedom be mine;
Slobodenka moja,	Then my happiness dawns,
t'a sa minavrati.	Then shall freedom be mine.
Uz sa stara Tura,	Lo, the mountain has turn'd,
u kolecko obraca;	Now the vict'ry is thine;
. slobodenka moja	Now my happiness dawns,
t'a sa minavraca;	Now shall freedom be mine;
Slobodenka moja,	Now my happiness dawns,
t'a sa mi navraca,	Now shall freedom be mine,
t'a sa minavraca!	Now shall freedom be mine!

Budget: $

Sources:

Commins, Dorothy Berliner. *Lullabies of the World*. Random House, 1967.

Fifty Art Songs from the Modern Repertoire. G. Schirmer, 1939.

Mayer, Mariana. *Turandot*. Morrow Junior Books, 1995.

Simon, Henry W., ed. *A Treasury of Grand Opera*. Simon & Schuster, 1946.

Also, sheet music, CDs, cassettes, disk recordings, and videos of operas, chorales, liturgical music, folk songs, and oratorios.

Alternative Applications: Study vocal or choral recordings in the target language. Discuss the role of women in the major operas, operettas, chorales, and oratorios, including:

Aida	Puccini's *Madame Butterfly*
La Boheme	*The Magic Flute*
Carmen	Bach's *Magnificat*
Dido and Aeneas	*The Marriage of Figaro*
Don Giovanni	Schubert's *Mass in G*
Bach's *Easter Oratorio*	*The Merry Widow*
Faust	*The Messiah*
Die Fledermaus	*Orfeo*
Vivaldi's *Gloria*	*Pagliacci*
Heloise et Abelard	Faure's *Requiem*
Handel's *Judas Maccabeus*	John Rutter's *Requiem*
Lohengrin	*Der Ring des Nibelungen*
Lucia di Lammermoor	*Tosca*

For English classes, study the vocal rhythms and sentiments of the female characters in Sigmund Romberg's *The Student Prince,* Jerome Kern's *Show Boat,* Leonard Bernstein's *Mass,* or George Gershwin's *Porgy and Bess,* America's first folk opera.

Organize a study of patriarchy in such common motifs as the forced or feudal marriage, elopement, abandonment, separation from a lover, yearning for love, isolation, religious ecstasy, theft of a child, infanticide, and royal edicts against women. Determine the marital, social, religious, and governmental pressures that force the women of song into desperate solutions, including depression, asylums, pleas for mercy, suicide, murder, infanticide, flight from abuse or arranged marriage to unsuitable mates, immurement in a convent, self-exile, or martyrdom.

Geography

Anne *Frank's long road*

Age/Grade Level or Audience: Middle school or high school literature or history research; school library bulletin board; synagogue Holocaust Day program; history club presentation; preface to cinema study of *The Diary of Anne Frank*.

Description: Trace the journey of Anne Frank on a map.

Procedure: Read aloud from the famous diary, which opens June 14, 1942, with introductory comments to "Kitty," imaginary confidante of Anne Frank, a teenager who became a Jewish death-camp victim. Using several research sources, have readers follow her short life from birth to death. Include these data:

- birth in Frankfurt, Germany, June 12, 1929, to Otto and Edith Hollander Frank

- Anne, along with her sister Margot and their mother, stayed in Aachen, Germany, at the home of her maternal grandmother from summer 1933 to early 1934

- the family flight from Germany and resettlement in February 1934 in Amsterdam, Holland, where Anne attended a Montessori school

- vacations to Zandvoort aàn Zee

- from July 6, 1942–August 4, 1944, spent in hiding from Gestapo occupation forces in close quarters in an annex of her father's spice import office, Opekta-Works, at 236 Prinsengracht Canal. Anne lived with Hermann Van Pels (renamed Putti Van Daan), Otto Frank's business partner; Auguste (renamed Petronella Van Daan), his wife; fifteen-year-old Peter; and Mouschi, the Van Pels's cat. The group depended upon supplies smuggled in by Miep Gies, Mr. Frank's secretary; her husband, Henk; a clerk named Elli; and Johannes Kleiman and Victor Kugler, Mr. Frank's business associates, whom Anne renamed Koophuis and Kraler

- discovery by Gestapo agents on August 4, 1944, three days after Anne's last entry and transport by covered truck to an interrogation center and holding cell

- boarded a train and traveled northeast of Amsterdam to Westerbork, a work camp

- separated from others in early September 1944, when the group joins 1000 internees; traveled by cattle-car to Auschwitz-Birkenau, Poland, a notorious death camp and crematorium currently known by its Polish name, Oswiecim

- reassignment to Bergen-Belsen, located outside Celle in north-central Germany, October 30, 1944, after the infamous Dr. Josef Mengele selected women for extermination at Auschwitz and lists others to be shipped to Germany. Anne and Margot were transported separately from Mrs. Van Daan to Bergen-Belsen and died of typhus in late February or early March 1945, two months before Holland's liberation

Include side commentary on Queen Wilhelmina's flight to England May 10, 1940, when the Nazis occupied Holland. Add to the map battles in Czechoslovakia, England, and the D-Day beaches on the north shores of Normandy, France, all of which the group experienced vicariously while listening to a contraband radio. Add specific details about the fate of Anne's parents and six fellow internees:

- Miep's dentist, Dr. Fritz Pfeffer, who had joined the group in hiding in late 1942, shuttled from Auschwitz to a concentration camp at Neuengamme, Germany, where he died December 20, 1944

- Edith and Otto Frank and the Van Pels, imprisoned at Auschwitz

- Mrs. Auguste Van Pels's death at about the same time as Margot and Anne Frank died, although no date or cause was recorded

- Hermann Van Pels, gassed in fall of 1944

- Edith Frank's death of an unidentified illness, January 6, 1945

- Peter, transported to Mauthausen in north-central Austria and gassed May 5, 1945, three days before camp liberation

- Otto, an inmate in the infirmary, the only survivor when the Russians liberated prisoners in February 1945. Routed by ship through Odessa on the Black Sea to Marseilles, France, and back to Holland, Otto Frank returned home and reclaimed Anne's diary, which Miep had retrieved from a rubbish pile. He lived for a time with his mother, Alice Frank-Stern, in Basel, Switzerland. As a memorial to Anne, Margot, and their mother, Otto published the diary in 1947. An unexpurgated volume of her diary was published in 1995.

Budget: $$

Sources:

The Apparatus of Death. Time-Life, 1991.

Gutman, Yisrael, ed. *Encyclopedia of the Holocaust.* Macmillan, 1990.

Friesel, Evyatar. *Atlas of Modern Jewish History.* Oxford University Press, 1990.

Gies, Miep, and Alison L. Gold. *Anne Frank Remembered: The Story of the Woman Who Helped to Hide the Frank Family.* Simon & Schuster, 1988.

Jacobs, Gloria. "The Unabridged Anne Frank." *Ms.,* May/June 1995, 75.

Lange, Nichoas de. *Atlas of the Jewish World.* Facts on File, 1984.

Leitch, Michael. *Slow Walks in Amsterdam: A Visitor's Companion.* HarperCollins, 1991.

Schnabel, Ernst. *Anne Frank: A Portrait in Courage.* Harbrace, 1958.

van der Rol, Ruud, and Rian Verhoeven. *Anne Frank: Beyond the Diary.* Puffin Books, 1995.

Alternative Applications: Keep a map on a computer mapping program while a group reads the play version of *The Diary of Anne Frank* or screens the 1959 black-and-white film, starring Millie Perkins as Anne. Note that the movie won an Academy Award for William C. Mellor's photography and nominations for best picture, direction, music, and the acting of Shelley Winters.

Designing *women*

Age/Grade Level or Audience: Middle school art or geography interdisciplinary study; museum bulletin board; summer library project.

Description: Create a gender-balanced array of national emblems and monuments.

Procedure: Assign each participant a country to provide with gender-balanced symbols, figureheads, monuments, shoulder patches, letterhead stationery, money, stamps, flags, banners, national seals, passports, and other official documents. Offer Jane Addams, Lucy Stone, Dr. Elizabeth Blackwell, Emily Dickinson, and Patsy Cline as examples that balance Thomas Jefferson, Dr. George Washington Carver, Robert Irving, and Elvis Presley as individuals featured on United States postal stamps. Use Haiti, Martinique, Guadaloupe, St. Martin, St. Barts, Tahiti, or another French-speaking country as a model: have participants select figures from history to represent on coins, scrip, stamps, and legal tender. Include appropriate French slogans to appear on each type of currency, particularly "Vive la France!" and "Liberté, Egalité, Fraternité." Create a national monument or crest from the figure of Marianne, the national revolutionary emblem of France.

Budget: $$

Sources:

Buckingham, Sandra. *Stencil It!* Firefly Books, 1995.

Bulloch, Ivan. *Play with Models.* Lerner Group, 1996.

Mixed Media: Masks and Face Coverings. Crystal, n.d. (Video or filmstrip with audiocassettes)

Moxley, Susan. *Play with Papier-Mâché.* Lerner Group, 1996.

"Women Who Dare." National Women's History Project, 1995. (Calendar)

Also almanacs, encyclopedias, coin collectors' catalogs, history books, and *National Geographic, Travel,* and *Smithsonian* magazines.

Alternative Applications: Set up a group to create a hypothetical country or nation on a distant planet. Name the country and create a gender-balanced representation of offices, governing bodies, currency, flags, monuments, street signs, maps, legislative seal, capital city, focal statue, and other national groups and symbols. Or, base your creations on a location from a work of science fiction, such as Doris Lessing's *Canopus in Argos* or Margaret Atwood's *The Handmaid's Tale.*

A Life *map of Esther Forbes*

Age/Grade Level or Audience: Middle school literature class project; school library display; National Education Week wall map; Women's History Month frieze.

Description: Portray on a life map the career of young adult fiction writer Esther Forbes, juxtaposed against the settings of her historical novels.

Procedure: Create a fantasy map of the life of Esther Forbes, possibly set on a map of Massachusetts or on an imaginary odyssey. Also mark the settings and travels of the characters in her popular works of historical fiction. Include the following data:

- As antiquarian and historian, Esther Forbes's accomplishments ranged far beyond the capabilities her family expected for someone with poor vision and a rheumatic heart. Following the example of her mother, Harriette Marrifield Forbes, an author in the meticulous, exacting New England tradition, Forbes studied the Salem witch trials and the American Revolution in journals, letters, diaries, maps, interviews, court records, and histories. While compiling a genealogy, she discovered a Forbes relatives who died in a Cambridge, Massachusetts, jail with other incarcerated women awaiting trial for witchcraft.

161

- In 1918, after studying at Bradford Junior College and the University of Wisconsin, Forbes abruptly abandoned formal education without completing a degree. Absorbed in research and writing, she accepted a job editing for Houghton Mifflin in Boston. Her husband, attorney Albert Learned Hoskins Jr., urged her to write historical fiction. In 1937 she published *Paradise,* set during King Philip's War.

- After a divorce, Forbes returned to her family's home, set up a regular study alcove in the Worcester library, and researched apprentice-master relations in colonial Massachusetts, a subject that formed the background of *Johnny Tremain,* the story of a fictional character who participates in the Boston Tea Party and Paul Revere's ride.

- Still writing her impressions of colonial New England at the time of her death in 1967, Forbes left notes for *The Year of the Witches—1692.* Her awards include a Pulitzer Prize, Newbery Medal, O. Henry award for "Break Neck Hill," and numerous honorary doctorates. Walt Disney produced her story *The Running of the Tide* in 1957; *Rainbow on the Road* ran on Broadway in 1969. Forbes's consuming interest in the Salem trials resulted in *A Mirror for Witches,* a Broadway play and ballet performed nine years after her death.

Budget: $

Sources:

Benet's Reader's Companion to American Literature. HarperCollins, 1993.

Erskine, Margaret. "Esther Forbes." Monograph for the Worcester Bicentennial Commission, Worcester, Massachusetts, 1976.

Forbes, Esther. "Acceptance Speech." *Horn Book,* July–August 1944.

More Junior Authors. H. W. Wilson, 1963.

Oxford Companion to American Literature. Oxford University Press, 1983.

The Oxford Illustrated Literary Guide to the United States. Oxford University Press, 1982.

Spear, Marilyn W. "Distinguished Worcester Authoress Dies at Age 76." *Worcester Sunday Telegram,* August 13, 1967, 5B.

Twentieth Century Authors: A Biographical Dictionary of Modern Literature. H. W. Wilson, 1942.

Twentieth Century Children's Writers. St. Martin's Press, 1978.

Alternative Applications: Follow the action that takes place in Esther Forbes's *Johnny Tremain.* On a tourist map of the Boston area, mark significant landmarks of the American Revolution, including Paul Revere's workshop, Wharf district, route to Lexington and Concord taken by the Minute Men, and Old North Church.

A map of *True Grit*

Age/Grade Level or Audience: Elementary or middle school literature or geography graphics; Friends of the Library display; history or cinema club review.

Description: Complete a map contrasting Arkansas and the Indian Territory as revealed in the novel and film *True Grit.*

Procedure: Read aloud Charles Portis's *True Grit* over a period of weeks. Have students sketch settings while they listen. Organize an interdisciplinary study of the fictional westward journey of Mattie Ross from the family farm in Dardanelle, Arkansas, to Fort Smith and across the state line into Choctaw territory in search of her father's murderer. Locate these important landmarks:

Arkansas River	Mount Nebo	Sebastian County
Jonesboro	Poteau River	Waco
McAlester	Russellville	Winding Stair Mountains
Memphis	San Antonio	Yell County
Mount Magazine	San Bois Mountains	

Note the rail lines in existence during the novel's time span. Conclude with a summary of how the land affected women's lives as rancher, female banker, boarding house manager, horse buyer, invalid, and traveler by rail and on horseback.

Budget: $$

Sources:

Ashmore, Henry S. *Arkansas: A History*. W. W. Norton, 1984.

Berry, Fred, and John Novak. *The History of Arkansas*. Rose Publishing, 1987.

Ferrell, Robert H., and Richard Natkiel. *Atlas of American History*. Facts on File, 1987.

Foner, Eric, and John A. Garraty, eds. *The Reader's Companion to American History*. Houghton Mifflin, 1991.

Portis, Charles. *True Grit*. Dutton, 1995.

Steckmesser, Kent L. *Western Outlaws: The 'Good Badman' in Fact, Film, and Folklore*. Regine Books, 1983.

Underhill, Lonnie E. *Outlaws in the Indian Territory*. Roan Horse Press, 1985.

Alternative Applications: Have students create an annotated itinerary and maps for a tour group or video crew retracing the route of the fictional Mattie Ross. Apply a similar study to other journey motifs featuring these strong female characters:

- Anna Leonowens in Margaret Landon's biography *Anna and the King of Siam*
- Annie Sullivan in the biographical play *The Miracle Worker*
- Blanca in Isabel Allende's *The House of the Spirits*
- Jeanne Kawashima House in the autobiographical *Farewell to Manzanar*
- Esther Hautzig in the autobiographical *The Endless Steppes*
- title character in Avi's *The True Confessions of Charlotte Doyle*
- Winnie Louie in Amy Tan's *The Kitchen God's Wife*
- Zlata Filipovich, writer of *Zlata's Diary*
- Yoko and Ko in *So Far from the Bamboo Grove*

Name *that place*

Age/Grade Level or Audience: Elementary school art or geography database; bulletin board; summer library project; ongoing home-school study.

Description: Locate geographical towns, cities, areas, and landmarks that bear women's names.

Procedure: Have participants study maps and globes for places named for women, such as Adelaide, Australia; Columbia, Missouri; Christiana, South Africa; or Helena, Montana. Learn more about the place-name by answering these questions:

- Was the area named for a real woman? For example Victoria Falls was named for Queen Victoria, and Virginia and West Virginia honor Queen Elizabeth I, the Virgin Queen.

- Does the female name suggest a saint, as with Santa Barbara, Saint Catherine Point, or Saint Kilda?

- Are there additives to the name, as, for instance, Elizabeth*ton* and Mary*land?*

- Do the names attach to picturesque tourist spots like Peggy's Cove, Martha's Vineyard, Alice Springs, and the Marianas Trench?

- Were the places named for deities or mythological figures, as with Europe, Dianium, and Athens?

- Was a feminine place-name used in ancient times, for example, Lutetia or Lutece, now called Paris, France?

Distribute reference materials—almanacs, geographical dictionaries, maps of the ancient world, and atlases. Have groups fill a database with more examples and place a few sentences beneath each entry to describe the genesis of the name, location, and terrain. Include information about important products, battles, local heroes, and geographical facts. For example, the Marianas Trench is the deepest point in the Pacific Ocean.

Budget: $$

Sources:

Asante, Molefi K., and Mark T. Mattson. *Historical and Cultural Atlas of African Americans.* Macmillan, 1992.

Bayly, Dr. Christopher, gen. ed. *Atlas of the British Empire.* Facts on File, 1989.

Dickerson, Brenda. "Panna Maria, Texas." *Cobblestone,* June 1995, 13–16.

Ferrell, Robert H., and Richard Natkiel. *Atlas of American History.* Facts on File, 1990.

Waldman, Carl. *Atlas of the North American Indian.* Facts on File, 1985.

Webster's New Geographical Dictionary. Merriam-Webster, 1988.

Also, almanacs, encyclopedias, geography books, *National Geographic, Traveler,* and other magazines.

Alternative Applications: Set up a group to design a salt map or wall-size map. Draw in geographical locations named for women. Place symbolic markers on each locale: a star for a capital, flag for a tourist attraction, crossed swords or a cannon for a battlefield, profile for a famous person born in or connected with the area, waves for a waterway or lake, and a leaf for a nature trail or animal habitat.

National *fireworks*

Age/Grade Level or Audience: Elementary geography or civics focus; summer or after-school library activity; history club's international festival.

Description: Connect cities around the world with the work of major female politicians and social activists.

Procedure: Create an oversized world map and place names of female politicians and activists at significant spots; for example, Margaret Thatcher in London, Gloria Steinem in New York, Henrietta Szold in Jerusalem, and Winnie Mandela in Johannesburg. Include these names along with a small flag naming their effort or accomplishment, as with Petra Kelly's creation of Green Peace or Aung San Suu Kyi's 1991 Nobel Peace Prize:

- **Argentina:** Eva Peron

- **Australia:** Enid Lyons, Annabelle Rankin

- **Bangladesh:** Khaleda Zia

- **Bulgaria:** Lyudmila Zhirkova

- **Burma:** Aung San Suu Kyi

- **Canada:** Flora MacDonald, Louise McKinney, Jeanne Sauvé

- **China:** Barbara Castle, Chi'u Chin, Kang Keqing, Ching Ling Soong

- **England:** Margot Asquith, Beatrice Webb Nancy Astor, Emily Pankhurst

- **France:** Edith Cresson, Françoise Giroud, Simone Weil

- **Germany:** Marie Juhacz, Petra Kelly, Louise Schroeder, Helene Weber

- **Iceland:** Vigdis Finnbogadottir

- **India:** Rani Gaidinliu, Indira Gandhi, Vijaya Lakshmi Pandit

- **Ireland:** Mairead Maguire, Mary Robinson, Maud MacBride, Betty Perkins, Bernadette Devlin, Constance Gore-Booth

- **Italy:** Teresa Noce

- **Japan:** Takako Doi, Fusaye Ichikawa

- **Malta:** Agatha Barbara

- **New Zealand:** Mabel Howard

- **Norway:** Gro Harlem Brundtland, Eva Kolstad

- **Pakistan:** Benazir Bhutto, Fatima Jinnah

- **Palestine:** Hanan Ashrawi

- **Portugal:** Maria de Lourdes Pintassilgo

- **Romania:** Ana Pauker

- **Russia:** Ekaterina Alexeyevna Furseva, Alexandra Kollontai

- **South Africa:** Dorothy Nyembe, Helen Suzman, Winnie Mandela

- **Spain:** Dolores Ibarruri

- **Sri Lanka:** Sirimavo Bandaranaika

- **Sweden:** Alva Myrdol, Gertrud Sigurdsen

- **United States:** Pat Schroeder, Miriam Amanda Ferguson, Patricia Roberts Harris, Ella Grasso, Elizabeth Holtzman, Jeannette Rankin, Carol Moseley Braun

- **Vietnam:** Nguyen Thi Binh

Budget: $$$

Sources:

Martin, Jean, gen. ed. *Who's Who of Women in the Twentieth Century.* Crescent Books, 1995.

Smith, Jessie Carney. *Epic Lives.* Visible Ink Press, 1993.

Wheelwright, Julie. *Amazons and Military Maids.* Pandora, 1989.

Alternative Applications: Invite participants to a women's history "spot on the map" dinner. Have each guest bring food representing a particular cuisine:

- **America:** posole, piki, cranberry sauce, baked beans
- **Argentina or New Zealand:** mutton
- **Britain:** bangers and mash
- **China:** egg rolls or sesame chicken
- **France:** petit fours and crepes suzette
- **Germany:** sauerbraten
- **Holland:** coldcuts with Edam cheese
- **India:** tandoori chicken
- **Italy:** manicotti and polenta
- **Japan:** sushi and sashimi
- **Morocco:** stuffed pita
- **Pakistan:** curry
- **Philippines:** skewered meat
- **Russia:** borscht
- **Thailand:** noodles

Cluster dishes of food near a flag of the country and a list of names of women who have fought for liberty, better health conditions, equal pay, education, religious rights, the vote, property ownership, or full rights as citizens. Compare the changes in women's social and political situations within these countries over the past two centuries.

Seeing *the sights*

Age/Grade Level or Audience: High school art appreciation activity; travel club focus; art museum workshop; library display; civic exhibit; travel column or local arts newsletter feature.

Description: Compose an itinerary for a trip to famous art collections that feature women models.

Procedure: Compile a list of art collections in the world's largest cities. Suggest places where visitors can experience the best collection of art focusing on women in history. Begin with these:

- Florence, Italy—The Uffizi Gallery, donated by Cosimo de' Medici in 1560 and famous for Da Vinci's *The Annunciation;* Michelangelo's *Holy Family;* Raphael's *Madonna of the Goldfinch;* and Tintoretto's *Leda and the Swan.*

- Rome, Italy—The Borghese Gallery, which displays *Paolina Borghese,* a silken reclining statue famous for its lifelike skin and luxurious satin cushion. Also renowned for its collection is the Vatican Museum, repository of statuary, tapestries, portraits, and art treasures of a variety of religious and secular subjects.

- London, England—The Tate Gallery, built by Sir Henry Tate in the late nineteenth century and worth visiting for a view of Dante Gabriel Rossetti's *Beata Beatrix;* Auguste Renoir's *The First Outing;* Peter Lely's *Two Ladies of the Lake Family;* and *Madame Suggia* by Augustus John. A second required stop is the National Gallery, which features Jean August Dominique Ingres's *Madame Moitessier.*

- Madrid, Spain—The Prado Museum, an eighteenth-century edifice built by King Charles III. This museum features Murillo's *Immaculate Conception* and *The Holy Family of the Little Bird;* Velasquez's *Las Meninas;* Bosch's *The Adoration of the Magi;* and Goya's *Family of Charles IV, The Clothed Maja,* and *The Naked Maja.*

- Amsterdam, Holland—The Rijksmuseum, location of Rembrandt's *The Jewish Bride* and Vermeer's *Maidservant Pouring Milk* and *Woman in Blue Reading a Letter.*

- Leningrad, Russia—L'Hermitage, a palatial setting featuring Titian's *Mary Magdalene,* Giogione's *Judith,* Rubens's *Perseus and Andromeda,* Raphael's *Virgin and Child with St. Joseph* and *Conestabile Madonna,* and Fra Angelico's *Virgin and Child with Saints Dominic and Thomas Aquinas.*

Budget: $$

Sources:

Barcelona. Crystal, n.d. (Videodisc)

Danto, Eloise. *Museums of Paris.* Eldan, 1987.

———. *Undiscovered Museums of Florence.* Surrey Books, 1991.

Edson, Gary, and David Dean. *The Handbook for Museums.* Routledge, 1993.

Latino Art and Culture in the United States. Crystal, 1995. (Video or slide kit)

The National Gallery of Art. Crystal, n.d. (Laserdisc)

Pearce, Susan. *Museums and the Appropriation of Culture.* Humanities, 1993.

Pearce, Susan, ed. *Museums and Europe.* Humanities, 1992.

Shapiro, Michael S., and Louis W. Kemp, eds. *The Museum: A Reference Guide.* Greenwood, 1990.

World Wide Web sites for this activity include:

- the Electronic Exhibitions (http://www.uky.edu/Artsource/exhibitions.html)
- Artsource's home page (http://www.uky.edu/Artsource/artsourcehome. html)
- the Electric Gallery (http://www.egallery.com/egallery)

Also, travel guides, AAA maps, illustrated brochures, art encyclopedias, posters, and art prints.

Alternative Applications: Compose a categorical overview of artworks featuring female poses in the museums of major North American cities, including:

- Duchamp's *Nude Descending a Stair* in the Philadelphia Museum of Art

- National Gallery in Washington, D.C., featuring Whistler's *The White Girl* and Renoir's *Portrait of Madame Henriot.*

- Picasso's *Guernica* and *Les Demoiselles d'Avignon* at the Museum of Modern Art in New York City

- Picasso's *Seated Woman* in Toronto's Art Gallery of Ontario

- Rembrandt's *Toilet of Bathsheba* in the National Gallery of Canada in Ottawa

Add American holdings at museums located in Chicago, Houston, Richmond, Boston, Los Angeles, Denver, Key West, Atlanta, and San Francisco.

Third *world women*

Age/Grade Level or Audience: Middle school history or geography current events study; book club newsletter; library display; museum program; religious women's month theme; video series for educational television or radio.

Description: Depict the living conditions around the globe by studying the historic struggles of women and children in under developed countries.

Procedure: Organize a multimedia bulletin board, museum, or library display of women's living situations and conditions in under developed countries around the world. Cover the following problems:

- aggression and genocide (Bosnia, Rwanda)

- coercive marriage laws (South Africa, Islamic countries)

- customs encouraging female circumcision (much of Africa, Islamic countries)

- customs requiring veils, dark colors, head coverings (Islamic countries)

- disenfranchisement (Cuba, South Africa)

- inadequate educational offerings for women (Uganda, Pakistan, Malaysia)

- laws or customs enforcing birth control or supporting female infanticide (China)

- laws prohibiting inheritance and land ownership (Cuba)

- limited life expectancy (Honduras, Pakistan, Kurds, Angola, Rwanda)

- unequal pay scales for women (almost anywhere in the world)

- unfair burden on refugee women and children (Ethiopia, Haiti, Kurds, Romania, Somalia, Rwanda)

Include graphs, maps, charts, photos, copies of articles and chapters from books, and taped interviews with women, missionaries, journalists, and UN authorities.

Budget: $$

Sources:

Acierno, Maria Armengol. *Children of Flight Pedro Pan*. Kaleidoscope Press, 1994. (English or Spanish version.)

Morgan, Robin, ed. *Sisterhood is Global*. Doubleday, 1984.

Ngo, Shelly, and Bruce Brander. "Should We Cut off Africa?" *World Vision Partners,* spring 1995, 2–4.

Women Today Series. Rourke, 1992.

Also almanacs, census figures, encyclopedias, and newsletters.

Alternative Applications: Have participants list positive steps toward increasing the life expectancy of people in difficult situations. Begin with the volunteer work done by CARITAS, UNICEF, Letters for Peace, *Medicins sans Frontieres,* Amnesty International, Save the Children Fund, Red Cross, or the Salvation Army. Catalog transportation, housing, food, seeds, tools, medicine, prenatal care, inoculations, clean drinking water, jobs, school supplies and teachers, and markets for crafts and homemade goods. Discuss the changing living conditions of women in light of the following positive steps:

- end of aggression in Mozambique

- end of communism in Cuba and Russia

- improved educational opportunities in Uganda

- opportunities for good jobs in the Philippines

- peace in most parts of the world

- world attention on Bosnia and Haiti

- restoration of Native American tribal rights and cultural awareness

- safety for children and families in Rwanda

- schools for children in India, Brazil, and Malaysia

Traveling *with Joy*

Age/Grade Level or Audience: Middle school English or geography oral report; book club project; summer reading exercise; PTA or traveler's club program.

Description: Present a chalk talk or guided map tour of Joy Adamson's *Born Free.*

Procedure: Provide listeners with blank maps of Kenya and surrounding countries. Summarize Joy Adamson's travels with Elsa the lioness whom Joy reintroduces to the wild after raising Elsa from an orphaned cub to maturity. Include references to the movie and its award-winning theme song, "Born Free," by John Barry. Point out scenic wonders of the area using photographs from *National Geographic,* books, slides, filmstrips, videos, or printed travel materials. Follow this chronological model:

- Traveling along the north frontier of Kenya on February 1, 1956, George Adamson, a game warden, shoots a lioness, whose death leaves three motherless cubs. Adamson drives home to Isiolo and leaves the cubs for his wife Joy to feed and train. She names them Big One, Lustica, and Elsa, the runt. The Adamsons give the larger two lionesses to the Rotterdam-Blydorp Zoo and keep Elsa to raise as a pet.

- During a family camping trip on the banks of the Uaso Nyiro, the Adamsons introduce Elsa to the wild.

- The next year, the family takes a vacation on the Kenya-Somali border, where Elsa delights in climbing and hunting, and swims in the Indian Ocean. She returns home with hookworm.

- After her recovery, George allows Elsa to ride along on a business trip to Merti and is gone for three and a half weeks.

- When Elsa reaches maturity, the Adamsons take her on a two-month safari to the Kaisut Desert and nearby Mount Marsabit. On rambles to the Huri Hills, Chalbi

Desert, North Horr Oasis, and Lake Rudolf, they introduce Elsa to a variety of topography. They reach Loyongalane, from which they scale Mount Kulal, where cool air chills Elsa.

- At age two, Elsa grows restless. In May, Joy and George take her to the Great Rift Valley in hopes of teaching her lion ways and establishing her with a pride of wild lions. This journey and the trips that follow fail to end Elsa's love for Joy as her mother.

- Visits to the wild press Elsa into an ambivalent state. She locates a mate; on December 20, 1958, she gives birth to her first litter. On February 25, 1959, Joy separates permanently from her pet lion.

Videotape the report before a live audience of young listeners. Invite them to participate in the telling of the story by making appropriate jungle noises, clapping for Elsa's triumphs, and waving goodbye. Ask a volunteer to summarize the whole story. Point on the map to varied terrain, including lava flows, seawater, hill country, mountains, desert, highlands, veldt, lakes, savanna, oases, and urban areas.

Budget: $$$

Sources:

Adamson, George. *My Pride and Joy*. Ulverscroft, 1988.

Adamson, Joy. *Born Free*. Vintage, 1974.

———. *The Searching Spirit*. Ulverscroft, 1982.

Amin, Mohamed, et al. *Kenya: The Magic Land*. Trafalgar Square, 1989.

Born Free. Columbia, 1966. (Video)

Gess, Denise. *Kenya*. Chelsea House, 1987.

Pease, Alfred E. *The Book of the Lion*. St. Martin's Press, 1986.

Walker, John, ed. *Halliwell's Film Guide*. HarperCollins, 1994.

Alternative Applications: Compare the life of Joy Adamson to that of animal rights activist and conservationist Dian Fossey. Begin by screening the film *Gorillas in the Mist* (1988), an adaptation of Fossey's 1983 book of the same title. Trace Fossey's journey from her birth in San Francisco to her death in the Parc National des Volcans in Rwanda. Conclude the presentation with a discussion of Fossey's findings about gorillas (their behavior, patterns of communication, and eating habits). Compare Joy Adamson's attitudes to those of Fossey toward the interdependence of animals, plants, and human beings.

Women *on the map*

Age/Grade Level or Audience: Family vacation or day trip; school field trip; travel club program; genealogical society map study; garden club presentation.

Description: Study a museum, historical site, or residence that demonstrates the accomplishments of women.

Procedure: Take a map-based, real, or imagined tour of a significant historic structure; for example:

Africa

- site of Cleopatra's palace or tomb, Alexandria, Egypt
- location of Queen Sheba's realm, Ethiopia

Asia

- Empress Theodora and Emperor Justinian's palace, Istanbul, Turkey
- Taj Mahal, honoring Mumtaz, wife of Shah Jehan, Agra, India

Australia

- aboriginal camp in Australia's outback
- waystation operated by women in southern Australia

Canada

- Anne of Green Gables's house, Prince Edward Island
- statue to Evangeline, Acadian heroine, Nova Scotia

Europe

- George Sand's country estate, Nohant, France
- office of Mary Robinson, president of Ireland
- Follies Bergere, the first can-can club, Paris, France
- Anne Frank Museum in Amsterdam, Holland
- pirate and mercenary Grace O'Malley's hideout, Rockfleet Castle, Connaught, Ireland
- Temple of Vesta, Rome, Italy
- colonnade of the Vestal Virgins, Roman Forum, Italy

United States

- Walker Building, monument to entrepreneur Sarah Walker, Indianapolis, Indiana
- justice-of-the-peace Esther Morris's cabin, South Pass City, Wyoming
- palace of Queen Liliuokalani, Honolulu, Hawaii
- Beaumont, Texas, museum honoring double gold medalist of the 1932 Olympics, Babe Didrikson Zaharias
- home of first female astronomer Maria Mitchell, Nantucket, Massachusetts
- site of Susan B. Anthony's arrest, Rochester, New York
- inn of first federal contractor, Nellie Trospey Neal Lawing, Lawing, Alaska
- Bayou Bend Collection and Gardens of philanthropist Ima Hogg, Houston, Texas
- Horseshoe Falls, New York, where Annie Edson Taylor became the first woman to go over Niagara Falls and survive
- birthplace of Juliette Gordon Low, founder of Girl Scouts, Savannah Georgia
- reconstructed Indian village, Jamestown, Virginia
- pueblo potter's market at San Ildefonso, New Mexico
- Black History Museum, Omaha, Nebraska
- fishing village on Daufuskie, Kiawah, or other of the Sea Islands

Organize a one-day trip to an historical site important for women; for example, a one-room school, grist mill, country store, dispensary, church, or other place where women have aided communities. During the trip or tour, make notes, take photographs and videotapes, sketch herb beds and kitchen gardens, or make tombstone and plaque rubbings to preserve the spirit and data of the journey. Afterwards, discuss the location visited and its similarities to the studied location. Publish findings in a family or travel club newsletter, scrapbook, Friends of the Library or travel club presentation, history club or genealogical society news bulletin, or online network. Stress the work at which women excelled and the way in which their activities uplifted families, churches, schools, and communities.

Budget: $$$$$

Sources:

Abeel, Erica. "A Revolutionary's Retreat: George Sand at Nohant." *On the Issues,* summer, 1995, 45–47.

Butterfield, Laura, et al. "A Fourth Grade's Architectural Journey." Teaching K–8, October 1994, 46–48.

China for Women. Feminist Press, 1995.

Emert, Phyllis Raybin, ed. *Women in the Civil War: Warriors, Patriots, Nurses, and Spies.* Discovery Enterprises, 1995.

Hansen, Ellen, ed. *The Underground Railroad: Life on the Road to Freedom.* Discovery Enterprises, 1993.

Jeffares, A. Norman, and Anna MacBride White, eds. *The Autobiography of Maud Gonne: A Servant of the Queen.* University of Chicago, 1995.

Sherr, Lynn and Jurate Kazickas. *Susan B. Anthony Slept Here.* Random House, 1994.

———. "Where Women Made History." *USA Weekend,* June 26, 1994, 16.

Also, collect material from travel agencies, libraries, American Automobile Association, and magazines such as *American Heritage, Islands, Traveler, National Geographic,* and *Realm.*

Alternative Applications: Study videos, films, books, magazines, and other sources about historic points of interest and significance in women's history that you would like to visit. Create a time line of your imaginary journey along with maps showing what routes you would take and where you would stop for photos, information, study, or amusement. Consider these hypothetical treks:

- the Bozeman Trail

- Lewis and Clark's journey, guided by Sacajawea, from the Dakota hills to the state of Washington and back

- the setting of Queen Malama's rule in Lahaina, Hawaii

- the flight of women and children from Nanking west after the Japanese invasion and bombings in the late 1930s

Women *tall and mighty*

Originator: Gary Carey, writer and editor, Lincoln, Nebraska.

Age/Grade Level or Audience: Photography club project; women's history scrapbook; historical society or travel club presentation; art club activity.

Description: Photograph or sketch statues and bas-reliefs of significant female figures and display as a group study.

Procedure: Invite participants to donate photographs, post cards, travel brochures, slides, and sketches of statues and bas-reliefs of famous women. Use these examples as a beginning:

- Belle Starr and Indian Woman statue, Woolaroc Museum, Bartlesville, Oklahoma

- bas-reliefs on the doors of the Library of Congress, Washington, D.C.

- Emma Sansom Monument, Gadsden, Alabama

- Gertrude Stein statue, Bryant Park, New York, New York

- Laura Smith Haviland memorial, Adrian, Michigan

- Nurses Memorial, Arlington, Virginia

- Phillis Wheatley statue at the Phillis Wheatley Memorial, Jackson, Mississippi

- Pioneer Woman statue, Ponca City, Oklahoma

- Queen Liliuokalani statue, Honolulu, Hawaii

- Statues of Sacajawea, Alice Brown Davis, and Roberta Campbell Lawson, National Hall of Fame for Famous American Indians, Route 62, Oklahoma

- Sharon Lane Memorial, Canton, Ohio

- Suffrage Monument, Capitol, Washington D.C.

- Vietnam Women's Memorial, Washington, D.C.

Budget: $$$$$

Sources:

Griffin, Lynne, and Kelly McCann. *The Book of Women: 300 Notable Women History Passed By.* Bob Adams, 1992.

The Lewis and Clark Expedition. Knowledge Unlimited, n.d. (Video)

"Salute to the Military." *Daughters of the American Revolution Magazine,* November 1990, 852–53.

Sherr, Lynn, and Jurate Kazickas. *Susan B. Anthony Slept Here: A Guide to American Women's Landmarks.* Random House, 1994.

Alternative Applications: Begin a fund to establish a statue, bas-relief, plaque, or monument to honor a local heroine. Consider an educator, founder of a midwives' society, freedom fighter, explorer, writer, artist, philanthropist, or civil rights activist, such as Viola Gregg Liuzzo, whose work a fountain in Montgomery, Alabama, recognizes. Select an open area where anyone can enjoy the monument free of charge. Commission a female sculptor to design the work.

Women *and the* Underground Railroad

Age/Grade Level or Audience: Middle school history or geography graphics activity; book club presentation; library display; museum program; newsletter theme; lecture series for educational television or radio.

Description: Illustrate the paths used by Harriet Tubman and other conductors on the Underground Railroad.

Procedure: Create a series of maps illustrating the flight of men, women, and children from plantations in Southern slave states to free Northern states and beyond. Illustrate the following information:

- slave states included Alabama, Arkansas, Florida, Georgia, Kentucky, Louisiana, Maryland, North Carolina, South Carolina, Tennessee, Texas, and Virginia. Slaves chose a variety of escape routes such as: across the Rio Grande River into Mexico; through Florida to Chickasaw, Choctaw, or Seminole Indian camps; across the Caribbean Sea to Cuba or other islands; by sea to New England or further north into Canada; or west to Kansas, Minnesota, or into Indian territory.

- Underground Railroad agents were inspired by abolitionist Quakers and Mennonites who, on February 18, 1688, issued the first anti-slave document.

- In 1799 New York State agreed to manumit slaves born after July 4 by setting women free at age 25 and men free at age 28.

- Later growth of the anti-slavery movement derived strength from these and other women:

feminist Susan B. Anthony	editor Sarah Grimké
editor Mary Ann Shadd Cary	activist Lucretia Mott
ex-slave Ellen Craft	abolitionist Amy Post
Lydia Marie Child, publisher of *The National Anti-Slavery Standard*	novelist Harriet Beecher Stowe
	orator Frances Walling Titus
feminist Josephine Griffin	orator Sojouner Truth
editor Angelina Grimké	agent Harriet Tubman

- The Grimké sisters published *American Slavery as It Is* in 1839, thus exposing the degradation and misery that some whites refused to believe existed.

- Harriet "Moses" Tubman, one of the outstanding participants in the escape system. The granddaughter of an African, she was born about 1820, hired out for manual labor, and beaten regularly. Tubman was also seriously injured when her master threw a heavy weight that struck her skull. She married John Tubman in 1844, then fled bondage in Maryland in her late twenties. After working in Philadelphia for two years, she returned to find her husband remarried. In her work on the Underground Railroad, and traveling mostly in winter, Tubman gathered escapees late on Saturdays, so they would not be missed and pursued until Monday. After 1850 it was necessary for her to lead groups north beyond the U.S.-Canadian border. In 1857 she rescued her own parents from slavery. A year later, she collaborated with John Brown on his notorious failed raid on Harpers Ferry. 1860 saw her final run on the Underground. In 1865, the *New England Freedmen's Aid Society* honored her with an article.

- In 1850, Sojourner Truth, pseudonym of Isabella "Belle" Van Wagener, a former slave and agent, published her autobiography, *Narrative of Sojourner Truth: A Southern Slave;* the next year, she addressed the Women's Rights Convention in a stirring speech, "Ain't I a Woman?"

- A further agitation was the popularity of Harriet Beecher Stowe's *Uncle Tom's Cabin,* published in 1852.

- In 1864, Abraham Lincoln autographed Sojourner Truth's *Book of Life.*

- In 1994 Toni Morrison won a Nobel Prize for her novel *Beloved,* a tribute to the people who fled bondage along the routes of the Underground.

Budget: $$

Sources:

Abrahams, Roger D. *Singing the Master.* Pantheon, 1992.

Bernard, Jacqueline. *Journey toward Freedom.* Feminist Press, 1990.

Chittenden, Elizabeth F. *Profiles in Black and White: Stories of Men and Women Who Fought against Slavery.* Scribner's, 1973.

Freedman, Florence B. *Two Tickets to Freedom.* P. Bedrick Books, 1989.

Hansen, Ellen, ed. *The Underground Railroad: Life on the Road to Freedom.* Discovery Enterprises, 1993.

Hooks, Bell. *Ain't I a Woman?* South End Press, 1991.

McClard, Megan. *Harriet Tubman: Slavery and the Underground Railroad.* Silver Burdett Press, 1990.

McKissack, Patricia C., and Fredrick McKissack. *Sojourner Truth: Ain't I a Woman.* Scholastic, 1992.

Taylor, M. W. *Harriet Tubman: Antislavery Activist.* Chelsea House, 1991.

Venet, Wendy Hamand. *Neither Ballots nor Bullets.* University Press of Virginia, 1991.

Alternative Applications: Make an audio map-guide accompaniment to a visual map study or a computer graphic presentation featuring Susan B. Anthony, the Grimké sisters, Harriet Tubman, Sojourner Truth, Harriet Beecher Stowe, and other women who helped end slavery. Point out cities and rivers where Quaker and Mennonite station masters led runaway slaves to safety and comment on the types of landscape (fields, forest, hills, riverbeds) that could either hasten or impede the progress of men, women, and children in their flight. Conclude with the logical move from anti-slavery to women's suffrage, a movement interwoven in the history of slavery and bondage.

Women *who dared*

Age/Grade Level or Audience: Middle school and high school history or geography frieze; book club presentation; library display; museum program; newsletter feature series; lecture series for educational television or radio.

Description: Map the world and mark areas discovered or explored by women.

Procedure: Create a number of unconventional views of the world by rotating a globe, diagram of the universe, or map template to present destinations that avoid placing the American point-of-view at the center. Draw an oversized series of maps to span a classroom, lunchroom, gymnasium, library, hallway, entrance, or auditorium. Pin to significant points index cards containing a precis of the studies, transportation methods, travels, and insights of these women:

- Amelia Earhart, Kansan who flew solo over the Atlantic Ocean and disappeared on a flight over the Pacific

- Amy Johnson, Englishwoman who flew to Australia, Japan, and South Africa

- Annie Smith Peck, Rhode Islander who scaled mountains in Peru and published *A Search for the Apex of America*

- Beryl Markham, Englishwoman who flew the Atlantic Ocean and wrote a bestseller, *West with the Night*

- Daisy Bates, who lived in South Australia and wrote *The Passing of the Aborigines*

- Delia Akeley, American traveler who studied Zaire's pygmies

- Fanny Bullock Workman, New Englander who traveled Asia

- Florence Baker, a Romanian explorer of Africa's Lake Albert and the Nile River

- Gertrude Bell, an English traveler to Arabia and the Middle East

- Isabella Bird, English writer who journeyed through Asia, the Middle East, and North America and published *The Yangtze River and Beyond*

- Jeana Yeager, Texan who co-piloted the *Voyager* nonstop around the world

- Lady Anne Blunt, Egyptian native who visited Arabia and studied the Bedouins of Iraq

- Louise Arner Boyd, a Californian expert on glaciers and fjords of Greenland who also led expeditions to the Arctic and published original photography in *National Geographic*

- Margaret Mead, Pennsylvania anthropologist who studied Pacific Islanders and wrote *Coming of Age in Samoa,* a landmark volume on evolving adulthood

- Mary Douglas Leakey, Londoner who studied archeology in France and East Africa

- Mary Kingsley, Englishwoman who wrote of her journeys to West Africa and published *Travels in West Africa*

- Sacajawea, Shoshone trader and translator on the Lewis and Clark expedition from North Dakota to the Pacific Ocean

- Sally Ride, Californian who flew aboard the space shuttle *Challenger*

- Susie Carson Rijhnhart, Canadian missionary to Lhasa, Tibet

- Svetlana Savitskaya, Russian astronaut

- Valentina Tereshkova, Russian astronaut and the first woman in space

Follow this model or develop another method of encapsulating detailed information into precise form to aid browsers in a brief examination:

- Sacajawea or Sacagawea, born 1786 in the Rocky Mountains. Kidnapped and enslaved by the Hidatsa at age 13 until she was passed to a trader as a gambling prize.

- Accompanied Lewis and Clark and her husband, Toussaint Charbonneau, and their newborn son, whom she carried in a cradleboard while on an overland and river exploration west to the Pacific Ocean.

- Reunited with her brother, Cameahwait, in Montana before reaching the Pacific, November 7, 1805.

- Returned to North Dakota. Received no pay for her role as translator, guide, and horse trader; her husband received $500.

Budget: $$

Sources:

Abdullah, Morag Murray. *My Khyber Marriage.* Octagon Press, 1995.

———. *Valley of the Giant Buddhas.* Octagon Press, 1995.

Adnan, Etel. *Of Cities and Women: Letters to Fawwaz.* Post-Apollo Press, 1993.

Blanchet, M. Wylie. *The Curve of Time.* Seal Press, 1995.

Bond, Marybeth. *Traveler's Tales: A Woman's World.* Travelers' Tales, 1995.

Castiglia, Julie. *Margaret Mead.* PLB, 1989.

Desai, Anita, ed. *The Turkish Embassy Letters of Lady Mary Worley Montagu.* Virago Press, 1995.

Emert, Phyllis Raybin, ed. *All that Glitters: The Men and Women of the Gold and Silver Rushes.* Discovery Enterprises, 1995.

Graham, Robin Lee, and Derek Gill. *Dove.* HarperPerennial, 1972.

Helmericks, Constance. *Down the Wild River North.* Seal Press, 1995.

Jansz, Natania, and Miranda Davies, eds. *More Women Travel.* Rough Guide, 1995.

Kaye, Evelyn. *Amazing Traveler; Isabella Bird, The Biography of a Victorian Adventurer.* Blue Penguin Publications, 1995.

Lambert, Lisa A. *The Leakeys.* Rourke, 1993.

Markham, Beryl. *West with the Night.* North Point Press, 1983.

Mazel, David. *Mountaineering Women: Stories by Early Climbers.* Texas A&M University Press, 1995.

Mead, Margaret. *Coming of Age in Samoa.* Morrow, 1971.

Odell, Scott. *Streams to the River, River to the Sea.* Fawcett, 1986.

Olds, Elizabeth Fagg. *Women of the Four Winds.* Houghton Mifflin, 1985.

Rogers, Susan Fox, ed. *Another Wilderness: New Outdoor Writing by Women.* Seal Press, 1995.

Schriber, Mary Suzanne, ed. *Telling Travels: Selected Writings by Nineteenth-Century American Women Abroad.* Northern Illinois University Press, 1995.

Stefoff, Rebecca. *Women of the World: Women Travelers and Explorers.* Oxford University Press, 1992.

Stephens, Autumn. *Wild Women.* Conari Press, 1992.

Tinling, Marion. *Women into the Unknown: A Sourcebook on Women Explorers and Travelers.* Greenwood Press, 1989.

We Proceeded On: Expedition of Lewis and Clark. Instructional Video, 1991. (Video)

Alternative Applications: Create a progressive time line or database of daring women by integrating the dates when female explorers studied, traveled, photographed, sketched, interviewed, sailed, worked, homesteaded, or navigated. Keep your source open for regular additions from news items, trivia, and data from almanacs, histories, microfiche, and CD-ROM encyclopedias. Use this method or adapt one to your needs:

1373	Margery Kempe	Holy Lands
1716	Mary Wortley Montagu	Europe, Turkey
1805–1806	Sacajawea	Pacific Ocean
1850s	Mary Jane Megquier	New York, Panama, Acapulco, San Blas, San Diego, California
1851	Elizabeth Gunn	South America, Central America, and California
1862–1864	Florence Baker	East Africa
1873	Isabella Bird	the American West
1877–1880	Anne Blunt	Arabia
1885–1908	Annie Smith Peck	Matterhorn, Mount Huascaran, Peru, Bolivia

177

1893–1894	Mary Kingsley	West Africa
1894–1902	Susie Carson Rijnhart	China, Tibet
1895	Isabella Bird	China
1895–1906	Fanny Workman	Africa, Middle East, Greece, Java
1904	Carrine Gafkjen	Dakotas
1905	Isobel Knowles	Florida, Canada
1905–1911	Delia Akeley	East Africa
1910–1927	Alexandra David-Neel	India, Tibet, Lhasa
1912	Dora Keen	Mount Blackburn, Alaska
1913	Gertrude Bell	Arabia
1925–1926	Margaret Mead	Samoa
1926	Louise Arner Boyd	Arctic
1928	Amelia Earhart	flight to Newfoundland
1928	Beryl Markham	flight to Kenya, Sudan
1930–1936	Amy Johnson	Pakistan, Thailand, Singapore, Australia, South Africa
1931–1940	Louise Arner Boyd	Greenland, Arctic
1937	Amelia Earhart	flight to Hawaii
1937	Mary Douglas Leakey	East Africa
1963	Valentina Tereshkova	space
1978	Irene Miller and Vera Komarkova	Annapurna, Nepal
1978–1980	Arlene Blum	Himalayas, Gangotri Glacier
1982	Svetlana Savitskaya	space
1983	Sally Ride	space
1986	Jeana Yeager	around the world nonstop
1986	Christa McAuliffe	space
1995	Alison Hargreaves	Mt. Everest
1995	Liv Arnesen	Antarctica

Government

Betty *Ford: the president's wife*

Age/Grade Level or Audience: High school history research assignment; library reference or online exercise; history society newsletter; bulletin board display.

Description: Detail the job of First Lady as performed by Betty Ford.

Procedure: Outline, chronologically, the stages by which Betty Ford advanced via her husband's career to become First Lady. List the challenges she faced as a president's wife, namely:

- gave up her more carefree lifestyle when she met and married Yale law school graduate Gerald Ford, then a candidate for Congress

- moved to Georgetown in 1948 to learn about the Washington social scene and let Bess Truman, Muriel Humphrey, and Lady Bird Johnson instruct her in the role of congressman's wife and wife of the House Minority Leader

- found herself the wife of a vice president unexpectedly, after Spiro Agnew's resignation in October 1973

- moved to the White House as First Lady Betty Ford after President Nixon resigned and Gerald Ford assumed Nixon's remaining time in office in August 1974

- championed early treatment for cancer after the loss of a breast from the disease

Conclude with the post-First Lady phase of Ford's life: In 1978, after her husband's defeat for reelection, she acknowledged dependence on liquor and drugs, freed herself of addiction, and started the Betty Ford Center.

Budget: $

Sources:

Angel, Sherry. "This Ford Has a Future." *50 Plus,* September 1986, 24–27.

Current Biography. H. W. Wilson, 1975, 133–35.

Ford, Betty, and Chris Chase. *Betty: A Glad Awakening.* Doubleday, 1987.

———. *The Times of My Life.* Ballantine, 1979.

Fortino, Denise. "No One Wants to Think of Herself as an Alcoholic." *Harper's Bazaar,* September 1981, 313–16.

Simpson, Kathleen. "Betty Ford: A Lesson in Caring." *Good Housekeeping,* May 1981, 108–112.

Steinem, Gloria. "Betty Ford Today: Still Speaking Out." *Ms.,* April 1984, 41–45.

Alternative Applications: Compare Betty Ford's advocacy of proper women's health care with the activities of other First Ladies:

- Lady Bird Johnson's dedication to highway cleanup

- Jackie Kennedy's restoration of historical furniture and decor in the White House

- Barbara Bush's children's reading program

- Nancy Reagan's "Just Say No" anti-drug campaign

- Hillary Clinton's support for health insurance for all Americans

Crowned *heads*

Originator: Gary Carey, writer and editor, Lincoln, Nebraska.

Age/Grade Level or Audience: Elementary or middle school history study sheet; home-school activity; scouts or 4-H cooperative project; bulletin board; library research quiz; book club presentation.

Description: Organize a game describing the famous female rulers of history.

Procedure: Either orally or on a study sheet, present data describing famous women rulers such as the Empress Theodora, wife of Justinian and rescuer of the empire from mob rule, or Semiramis, the legendary Assyrian queen. Have students take brief notes and then match information on a questionnaire such as the one provided below:

_____ 1. last czarina of Russia and mother of Princess Anastasia

_____ 2. wife of King David of Israel and mother of his successor, King Solomon

_____ 3. mother of Queen Elizabeth II and brave supporter of England's volunteer effort during World War II

_____ 4. Empress of India during its colonial period

_____ 5. queen guillotined during the French Revolution

_____ 6. ruler of Egypt under the protection of Julius Caesar

_____ 7. glamorous visitor to King Solomon's court

_____ 8. leader of the Netherlands before the Nazi takeover

_____ 9. queen of Egypt during the mid-fourteenth century

_____ 10. queen of England during voyages to the New World

_____ 11. twentieth-century dowager empress who helped reform China

_____ 12. financier of Christopher Columbus's voyage to the New World

A. Queen Mary   G. Queen Victoria

B. Queen Isabella   H. T'zu-Hsi

C. Marie Antoinette   I. Cleopatra

D. Alexandra   J. Bathsheba

E. Queen Wilhelmina   K. Elizabeth I

F. Queen of Sheba   L. Nefertiti

ANSWERS:

1. D	5. C	9. L
2. J	6. I	10. K
3. A	7. F	11. H
4. G	8. E	12. B

Budget: $$

Sources:

Anne of the Thousand Days. The Video Catalog, 1969. (Video)

Arthur: Myth and Reality. Scholar's Bookshelf, n.d. (Video)

Baudicca, Queen of the Iceni. Scholar's Bookshelf, n.d. (Video)

Becket. The Video Catalog, 1964. (Video)

Bridge, Antony. *Theodora: Portrait in a Byzantine Landscape.* Academy Chicago Publishers, 1993.

Bruce, Evangeline. *Napoleon and Josephine: An Improbable Marriage.* Scribners, 1995.

Cook, Petronile. *Queen Consorts of England.* Facts on File, 1993.

Elizabeth R. Critics' Choice Video, n.d. (Video)

Ferdinand and Isabella. Schlessinger, 1995. (Video)

Fire Over England. Time Warner Viewer's Edge, n.d. (Video)

Griffin, Lynne, and Kelly McCann. *The Book of Women: 300 Notable Women History Passed By.* Bob Adams, 1992.

Henry VIII and His Six Wives. Scholar's Bookshelf, n.d. (Video)

Jackson, Guida. *Women Who Ruled.* ABC-Clio, 1990.

Kings and Queens I [and] II. Scholar's Bookshelf, n.d. (Video)

The Last Emperor. The Video Catalog, 1987. (Video)

The Lion in Winter. Critics Choice, 1968. (Video)

Martin, Jean, gen. ed. *Who's Who of Women in the Twentieth Century.* Crescent Books, 1995.

Nicholas and Alexandra. Pacific Arts Publishing, 1971. (Video)

Seagrave, Sterling. *Dragon Lady: The Life and Legend of the Last Empress of China.* Vintage, 1992.

The Silk Road. The Video Catalog, n.d. (Video)

The Six Wives of Henry VIII. The Video Catalog, n.d. (Video)

St. Aubyn, Giles. *Queen Victoria: A Portrait.* Sinclair-Stevenson, 1991.

The Windsors. Pacific Arts Publishing, n.d. (Video)

Alternative Applications: Have a group of volunteers draw appropriate crowns or headgear and supply enough clues to identify each ruler named in the quiz above. Give students time to work in groups, with reference materials, to identify each ruler, mate or consort, country, and the style of clothing and royal emblems appropriate to each historic period; for example, the royal insignia and domed crown worn by Cleopatra and the crown, orb, and scepter of Elizabeth I.

First *ladies of the land*

Age/Grade Level or Audience: Middle school or high school history quiz; library research exercise; historical society handout; newspaper feature; bulletin board display.

Description: Some U.S. first ladies—like Nancy, Abigail, Jackie, Martha, Eleanor, Ladybird, Rosalynn, Betty, Mamie, Dolly, Pat, and Hillary—are so familiar that they readily connect with surnames, i. e., Reagan, Adams, Kennedy, Washington, Roosevelt, Johnson, Carter, Ford, Eisenhower, Madison, Nixon, Clinton. Other given names of First Ladies are less well known because they received less notoriety or made their achievements after their husbands' terms of office.

Procedure: Select the patronyms that connect the first names of First Ladies in the list that follows. Beside each, describe the achievement or influence that marked each woman's contribution during her husband's presidency. For instance:

- Ladybird Johnson supported a strong clean-up campaign along national highways.

- Hillary Clinton fought for improved health care.

- Jackie Kennedy organized a rigorous remodeling and redecorating campaign to preserve historical authenticity in the White House.

- Pat Nixon encouraged women to have regular mammograms and to join the fight against breast cancer.

- Eleanor Roosevelt campaigned against race prejudice by traveling and making personal appearances in the place of her husband, a victim of polio who was confined to a wheelchair.

- Rosalynn Carter joined her husband in a drive for international human rights. After leaving the White House, she took an active role in Habitat for Humanity, a charity that helps the poor become first-time homeowners.

- Nancy Reagan helped establish the "Just Say No" campaign against drugs, alcohol, and tobacco in American public schools by making public appearances, testifying before Congressional hearings on addictive behavior, and making television appeals to children to stay away from dangerous and addictive substances.

Adams	Harding	Pierce
Bush	Hayes	Polk
Carter	Harrison	Reagan
Cleveland	Hoover	Roosevelt
Clinton	Johnson	Taft
Coolidge	Kennedy	Taylor
Eisenhower	Lincoln	Truman
Fillmore	Madison	Tyler
Ford	McKinley	Van Buren
Garfield	Monroe	Washington
Grant	Nixon	Wilson

_____ 1. Letitia _____

_____ 2. Edith _____

_____ 3. Florence _____

_____ 4. Lucy _____

_____ 5. Mary _____

_____	6. Frances
_____	7. Lou
_____	8. Sarah
_____	9. Bess
_____	10. Hannah
_____	11. Jane
_____	12. Louisa

ANSWERS:

1. Tyler	5. Lincoln	9. Truman
2. Wilson	6. Cleveland	10. Van Buren
3. Harding	7. Hoover	11. Pierce
4. Hayes	8. Polk	12. Adams

Budget: $

Sources:

Anthony, Carl S. *First Ladies: The Saga of the Presidents' Wives and Their Power.* Morrow, 1992.

Caroli, Betty B. *First Ladies.* Oxford University Press, 1988.

Brooks, Lee. *First Ladies of the White House: Washington Through Nixon.* Hallberg Publishing Corp., 1969.

Hillary Rodham Clinton—Changing the Rules. Instructional Video, 1994. (Video)

Jackson, Guida. *Women Who Ruled.* ABC-Clio, 1990.

Jacqueline Kennedy Onassis. Instructional Video, 1991. (Video)

Klapthor, Margaret B. *First Ladies.* White House Historical Association, 1990.

Alternative Applications: Create a bulletin board list of queens, consorts, princesses, maharani, empresses, and other royal women. Summarize each woman's role in history. For example:

- Queen Noor of Jordan, an American originally named Lisa Hallaby, has influenced her husband, King Hussein, to become a peacemaker to end the hostility between Jews and Arabs in the Middle East.

- Czarina Alexandra Romanov, an English princess who became the wife of Nicholas II, the last czar of Russia, supported open relations between Russia and Western Europe to improve the quality of her subjects' lives and to import advanced technology.

- Theodora, wife of the Emperor Justinian, ruler of the eastern Roman Empire, strengthened her husband and his palace guard against a hostile takeover and championed the rights of humble and oppressed women.

- Empress Nagako, wife of Japan's Emperor Hirohito, remained with her family during the bombing of World War II and assisted in humanitarian aid to Hiroshima and Nagasaki.

- Queen Nefertiti, wife of Egypt's King Akhenaton, helped establish the worship of one god, Aton the sun god, and thus end polytheism.

- Queen Elizabeth, wife of King George VI of England, remained in London with Princesses Elizabeth and Margaret during the Blitz as a symbol of courage and determination in the war against Nazi Germany.

- Queen Liliuokalani of Hawaii attempted to strengthen the island's monarchy as a means to avoid colonization.

Accompany each entry with a map, time span, and royal insignia.

A geneology *of Elizabeth II*

Age/Grade Level or Audience: Middle school or high school drafting, math, or computer project; history term paper; women's studies bulletin board; Women's History Month handout or monograph; media or newsletter illustration.

Description: Research and publish the genealogy of a female royal.

Procedure: Using graphics software or a genealogy program, create a genealogy of a royal woman. Use as an example Elizabeth II, Queen of England. Present entries on the family tree in this form:

A Genealogy of Elizabeth II

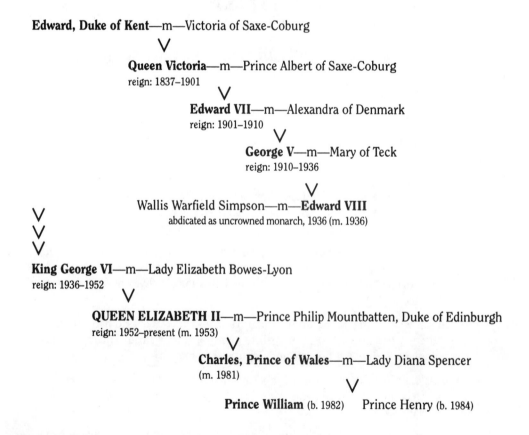

Edward, Duke of Kent—m—Victoria of Saxe-Coburg

V

Queen Victoria—m—Prince Albert of Saxe-Coburg
reign: 1837–1901

V

Edward VII—m—Alexandra of Denmark
reign: 1901–1910

V

George V—m—Mary of Teck
reign: 1910–1936

V

Wallis Warfield Simpson—m—**Edward VIII**
abdicated as uncrowned monarch, 1936 (m. 1936)

V
V
V

King George VI—m—Lady Elizabeth Bowes-Lyon
reign: 1936–1952

V

QUEEN ELIZABETH II—m—Prince Philip Mountbatten, Duke of Edinburgh
reign: 1952–present (m. 1953)

V

Charles, Prince of Wales—m—Lady Diana Spencer
(m. 1981)

V

Prince William (b. 1982)   Prince Henry (b. 1984)

Budget: $$

Sources:

Acton, Lord. "A Curtsy for the Queen." *British Heritage,* October/November 1994, 31–39.

Massie, Robert K. *Nicholas and Alexandra.* Atheneum, 1967.

Meacham, Jon, and Daniel Pedersen. "Was Queen Victoria a Bastard?" *Newsweek,* July 24, 1995, 56.

Parker, Michael St. John. *Britain's Kings and Queens.* Pitkin, 1994.

Alternative Applications: Compare the lineage of Elizabeth II with that of her strong female predecessor, Queen Victoria, who gave birth to nine children, suffered lasting grief after her husband's death from typhoid fever, and spent her old age finding suitable royal wives and husbands for her offspring. Draw a lineage chart that links Victoria's family with notable European family trees, including the tragic Romanov line, which ended with the murder of Czar Nicholas II, Czarevich Alexis, the young Grand Duchesses Olga, Tatiana, Anastasia, and Marie, and Empress Alexandra, who was Victoria's granddaughter.

Golda *Meir, prime minister of Israel*

Age/Grade Level or Audience: Middle school speech or writing assignment; home-school audio tape; bulletin board data; library research topic; League of Women Voters or book club presentation.

Description: Compose a speech on Golda Meir's dedication to Israeli history and Zionism.

Procedure: Create a speech outline around these topics from the life of Golda Meir:

- the push for a free state of Israel
- Zionism and Palestine
- the role of the Israeli prime minister
- the Hebrew Immigrant Aid Society
- Meir's interest in socialism
- anti-Semitism and the mission of the Socialist-Zionist Poale Zion
- Meir's proselytizing more Jews for Zionism
- life in a Kibbutz
- the Women's Worker's Council and Zionist feminism
- Meir and the labor committee of Histadrut
- Meir and Jordan's King Abdullah, the Jews' only ally in the Middle East
- Meir's role in the Knesset and the department of labor
- strength for the labor party through political coalition
- Meir as interim premier
- "Our Golda"

Conclude with a summary of the world's acceptance of Golda Meir as a leader and spokesperson for Jews and for Israel.

Budget: $$

Sources:

Amdur, Richard. *Golda Meir: A Leader in Peace and War.* Fawcett, 1990.

Martin, Ralph G. *Golda Meir: The Romantic Years.* Scribner's, 1988.

McAuley, Karen. *Golda Meir.* Chelsea House, 1985.

Meir, Golda. *A Land of Our Own.* G. P. Putnam, 1973.

————. *My Life.* G. P. Putnam, 1975.

Twentieth Century Heroes. Knowledge Unlimited, 1990.

Alternative Applications: Have students compose an appropriate epitaph to Golda Meir to mark a park, playground, public works project, kibbutz, temple, or school that she established. Select words that display her courage, drive, religious faith, and confidence in a free Jewish State.

Governing *Vermont*

Age/Grade Level or Audience: Middle school history or writing assignment; home-school activity; computer class database; library research quiz; League of Women Voters or book club presentation.

Description: Organize a study of the style and accomplishments of female governors, as exemplified by Madeleine Kunin.

Procedure: Present an overview of the rise of Madeleine Kunin to three-time governor of Vermont. Summarize these data:

- A service-oriented governor, Kunin has spoken against eroded farm-land values, acid rain, homelessness, hardships for the poor, oversized military budgets, neglect of the handicapped, and mediocre schools.

- A native of Zurich, Switzerland, Kunin was born September 28, 1933. In 1936, Kunin's widowed mother spent the last of her money to bring her children, Madeleine and Edgar, to New York, taking in sewing and teaching French to support her family.

- A naturalized citizen at age fourteen, Madeleine Kunin majored in history at the University of Massachusetts and earned a master's degree from Columbia School of Journalism in 1957. She was writing for the Burlington, Vermont, *Free Press* two years later when she met and married Dr. Arthur S. Kunin, a kidney specialist.

- After the births of her children, Julia, Peter, Adam, and Daniel, she involved herself in local politics by lobbying for Medicare. Kunin completed a second master's degree in English at Trinity College in 1967 and started a career in freelance public relations and technical writing.

- After losing a local election for alderwoman, she won a seat in the Vermont House of Representatives. Working briefly on a radio talk show before running for higher office, she became Vermont's first woman governor. Her main thrusts—balancing the budget while protecting the environment and Vermont's fragile ski industry—required diplomacy. To win local support, she championed the state's art, crafts, fashions, maple syrup, dairy products, lamb, and beers and boosted college and local school expenditures.

- Reelected to a second term, Kunin became active in the National Governors' Association. In 1988, her third term compromised her pro-environment stance. With no other way to end a long and honorable public career and remain in office, she withdrew, returned to her Burlington home, and waited for opportunities in future liberal administrations.

Contrast the governance of Madeleine Kunin with that of Dixy Lee Ray of Washington or Christine Whitman of New Jersey.

Budget: $

Sources:

Current Biography. H. W. Wilson, 1987.

Daley, Yvonne. "Her Long Journey to Power." *Daily Herald* (Rutland, Vermont), April 4, 1990.

Day, Nancy. "Madeleine Kunin." *Working Woman,* July, 1986, 74–77.

Garcia, Guy. "Ten Routes to the American Dream." *Time,* July 8, 1985, 63.

"Governors Tell Washington the Word from Home." *U.S. News and World Report,* March 11, 1985, 49–50.

Hoffman, Jack. "Kunin Will Step Down."*Daily Herald* (Rutland, Vermont), April 4, 1990.

Rossant, Colette. "A Visit with Vermont's Governor." *McCall's,* January, 1988, 82–83.

Runnion, Marge. "Once a Refugee from Nazi Europe, Madeleine Kunin Takes Charge as Vermont's First Woman Governor." *People Weekly,* April 1, 1985, 102–106.

"The Way Back: Ideas from Two Democrats." *U.S. News and World Report,* November 26, 1984, 31–35.

Alternative Applications: Have students work in groups to study varied references, works, almanacs, and online sources to create a time line of female governorships along with sidebars summarizing contributions to their states.

Indira *and India*

Age/Grade Level or Audience: Middle school outlining or writing assignment; home-school reference exercise; monograph; library research topic or bulletin board display; civic club or book club presentation.

Description: Outline the major influences on the career of Indira Gandhi.

Procedure: Study the life of Indira Gandhi. Place in chronological order the background and educational experiences that enabled her to rise to power and lead India. Begin with these events:

- born to a family of prestigious nationalists, including a crusading pro-West grandfather, Motilal Nehru; her attorney father, Jawaharlal Nehru; and her aunt Vijaya Lakshmi Pandit, president of the United Nations General Assembly

- learned asceticism and meditation from her mother, Kamala, a devout Hindu, and studied activism as depicted by her parents' involvement in Indian affairs

- remembered national and family crises from early childhood and learned to honor multiple points of view

- profited from the example of family friend Mohandas K. Gandhi, India's noted leader and martyr

- acquired patience while awaiting the release of her parents who served prison sentences for anti-colonial activities

- recognized the need for compassion toward the poor and challenged political action that worsened life for the lowest class

- espoused pacifism and attempted to find logical, non-violent solutions to problems

- studied history at Somerville College in Oxford, England

- proudly emulated her family tradition by serving time in prison for championing her beliefs

- in 1947 aided her father by serving as first lady of India in place of her deceased mother

- joined the Congress party to aid women and families and worked as a representative of UNICEF

- formed a civil defense network to support soldiers and their dependents

- accepted the post of Minister of Information and Broadcasting

- became India's third Prime Minister in 1966 and handled the business of the atomic energy commission, agriculture, birth control, and international relations

- opened a training center for indigent students in Delhi, nationalized banks, and demoted maharajahs to a ceremonial role by cancelling their government stipends

- kept peace with Pakistan by organizing border surveillance

- returned to power in 1978 and, in 1980, began her second term as Prime Minister

Conclude with a summary of the personal tragedies that diminished Gandhi's final months in office—the death of her son in a plane crash and her assassination October 31, 1984.

Budget: $

Sources:

Abbas, K. A. *Indira Gandhi: The Last Post*. Asia Book Corp., 1985.

Alexander, P. *My Years with Indira Gandhi*. South Asia Books, 1991.

Fishlock, Trevor. *Indira Gandhi*. Trafalgar, 1991.

Jayakar, Pupul. *Indira Gandhi: An Intimate Biography*. Pantheon, 1993.

Malik, Yogendra K., and Dhirendra K. Vajpeyi, eds. *India: The Years of Indira Gandhi*. E. J. Brill, 1988.

Alternative Applications: Contrast the life of Indira Gandhi and her controversial political family to that of another ruler faced with both the tension of political intrigue and the pressing needs of their populace. Choose from these:

Czarina Alexandra	Princess Grace Kelly	Queen Semiramis
Queen Anne	Queen Liliuokalani	Queen Shub-ad
Corazon Aquino	Chief Wilma Mankiller	Princess Sirikit
Benazir Bhutto	Imelda Marcos	Empress Theodora
Eleanor of Aquitaine	Princess Michiko	Empress Tz'u-Hsi
Queen Esther	Queen Noor	Queen Wilhelmina
Queen Guinevere	Susan La Flesche Picotte	Sarah Winnemucca

Kitty *Dukakis and the high price of notoriety*

Age/Grade Level or Audience: High school social studies research; League of Women Voters presentation; library reference or online exercise; Women's History Month newsletter or bulletin board.

Description: Explore the pressures faced by women in the political scene by focusing on the life of Kitty Dukakis, wife of former Massachusetts Governor and presidential candidate Michael Dukakis.

Procedure: Comment on the changes in the life of Kitty Dukakis caused by public notoriety and political pressure. Make note of the events that altered her adult life and pushed her into despair:

- tried to please a demanding mother by being prim, slim, and ladylike

- briefly modeled and served on the fashion board of Filene's Department Store

- attended Pennsylvania State University and majored in dance; after a difficult marriage and divorce, entered Lesley College

- married Michael Dukakis, a Swarthmore law student, June 13, 1963; lived in Brookline, Massachusetts; and, after a miscarriage, gave birth to two daughters

- assumed the role of governor's wife in 1974

- argued in private with Dukakis over her dependence on drugs

- suffered the deaths of her mother and father-in-law

- after several trips to Israel and a rebirth of religious faith, served on the Holocaust Memorial Council

- returned to the position of governor's wife and, in 1982, admitted that she needed help in controlling her addiction to anti-depressants

- remained stalwart during her husband's failing campaign against George Bush in 1988, then increased her dependence on alcohol

- came close to death after an exceptional incident of intoxication; continued to fight the manic depressive cycle that threatened her life

Compare the struggles of Kitty Dukakis's life with those similarly faced by other politicians' wives: Mary Todd Lincoln, Mamie Eisenhower, Betty Ford, Martha Jefferson, and Eleanor Roosevelt.

Budget: $

Sources:

Dukakis, Kitty, with Jane Scovell. *Now You Know.* Simon & Schuster, 1990.

Kenney, Charles, and Robert L. Turner. *Dukakis: An American Odyssey.* Houghton Mifflin, 1992.

Locy, Toni. "Dukakis Writes of Her Pain." *Boston Globe,* August 9, 1990.

Reidy, Chris. "Kitty Dukakis Fled 'Depression' in Binges, Book Says." *Boston Globe,* August 26, 1990.

Roberts, Eleanor. "Book Tour a Tough Test for Kitty." *Boston Herald,* August 19, 1990.

Williams, Marjorie. "The Chilling Chapters of Kitty Dukakis." *Washington Post,* September 9, 1990.

Alternative Applications: Compose an introduction to Kitty Dukakis's autobiography in which you acknowledge and describe the pressures that pushed her into a life of drug and alcohol dependence. Comment on her courage in facing the media, who divulged her most humiliating faults. Contrast her circumstances with those of other "high profile" political wives, such as Mary Todd Lincoln.

Sarah Winnemucca, freedom fighter

Age/Grade Level or Audience: Middle school history research or desktop publishing exercise; home-school composition topic; library or museum bulletin-board display; travel club presentation.

Description: Summarize the influence of Sarah Winnemucca on government leaders of her time.

Procedure: Produce a monograph featuring Sarah Winnemucca's importance in the fight for Native American rights. Add maps, charts, illustrations, tribal symbols, and historical data to this list of facts:

- Named Tocmetone, or Shellflower, at her birth in 1844 near Humboldt Lake, Nevada, Sarah Winnemucca came from a noble lineage of Paiute chiefs and decision-makers.

- Captain Truckee, Sarah's grandfather, wanted his girls to learn English; in 1856, he found a place for them at the home of Major and Mrs. William Ormsby. With the help of Margaret Ormsby, Sarah and her sister Elma learned to read and write.

- Before Captain Truckee died in 1857, he asked that the girls go to San Jose to study under the direction of nuns at the Sisters of Notre Dame School. The two sisters got off to a good start until racist parents objected to their presence. The nuns had to remove the Winnemucca girls from the school.

- During the Civil War, Sarah observed firsthand the laziness, theft, and corruption of people hired by the government to provide clothing, food, and shelter for the Paiutes.

- After her mother died, Sarah moved to Pyramid Lake to be near her brother, Natchez. During negotiations with whites, officials sent and received communications through Sarah, who was the only English-literate Paiute.

- A scholar and peacemaker, Sarah spoke English, Spanish, Paiute, Washoe, and Shoshone and served as chief translator at Fort McDermitt, where she met and was briefly married to Lt. Edward Bartlett.

- The Paiutes continued to suffer hunger and mistreatment under corrupt government agents. In 1875 conditions began to improve at Malheur Reservation, Oregon, when Sarah began working as an interpreter.

- During good times and bad, Sarah served as an intermediary between whites and Native Americans and was the first to learn that her tribe was being moved to the Yakima reservation in Washington State. Her eyes blazed with anger when she learned that the Paiutes would have to travel in snow.

- Father Wilbur, a trusted ally, attempted to shelter the Paiutes through the winter. Because the government failed to deliver her pay or promised supplies, Sarah lectured to whites on the starvation of American Indians and wrote letters to local newspapers about the Paiutes' predicament at the Yakima reservation.

- Father Wilbur proved false by tricking Sarah into taking a government post at Fort Vancouver to stop her activism on behalf of the Paiutes. Far from family and tribe, she determined to expose the Bureau of Indian Affairs for its duplicity. She married Lambert Hopkins, but her happiness was dimmed because of her concern for the Paiutes' difficulties.

- Sarah set out on her own for Boston to launch a lecture tour and collect contributions for her people. Dressed in brilliant ceremonial beaded buckskins, leggings, and headdress, she moved listeners to tears and gained credence from those who had traveled west and could corroborate her testimony from their own firsthand experience.

- With the help of Mary Peabody Mann, in 1883 Sarah Winnemucca became the first Native American to publish in English when she completed her autobiography, *Life Among the Piutes: Their Wrongs and Claims,* which blames the Bureau of Indian Affairs for cheating Indians and failing to keep their promises.

- The end of Sarah's story details repeated misfortunes: she was robbed of her savings and lost her teaching job. Her husband, ill with tuberculosis, required much care. The one bright spot of her later years was the donation of 160 acres of land outside Lovelock, Nevada, where her brother Natchez built a school for Sarah.

- In 1887, after her husband's death, Sarah retired and visited her sister, Elma Smith. Sarah died of exhaustion and tuberculosis October 17, 1891. Through the efforts of her benefactor, Elizabeth Peabody, she was remembered and revered as educator, welfare worker, and champion of all Native Americans.

Conclude with more information about the Paiutes and their circumstances when they no longer had Sarah as champion.

Budget: $$

Sources:

Canfield, Gae W. *Sarah Winnemucca of the Northern Paiutes.* University of Oklahoma Press, 1988.

Morrow, Mary F. *Sarah Winnemucca.* Raintree, 1990.

Scordato, Ellen. *Sarah Winnemucca.* Chelsea House, 1992.

Winnemucca, Sarah. *Life Among the Piutes: Their Wrongs and Claims.* Chalfant, 1992.

Alternative Applications: Have volunteers set up a life map of Sarah Winnemucca, following her from her birthplace in the Great Basin to Yakima, Washington, and east to Boston and Washington, D.C. On each site of importance to her biography, have participants list details and dates of her speeches, jobs, and lobbying efforts on behalf of the Paiutes. Note the importance of her grandfather, sister, brother, and father to her work as tribal supporter.

Women *rulers*

Age/Grade Level or Audience: High school history research; home-school computer or online activity; library or museum bulletin board or reference quiz; travel club presentation.

Description: Use the search for female rulers as an introduction to a wide range of print and electronic reference sources.

Procedure: Employing databases, reference books, online services, and newspapers, organize a search for former and current queens and empresses, female chieftains, prime ministers, governors, presidents, and tribal leaders with whom students are less familiar, such as:

Aethelthryth, seventh-century East Anglian princess

Anne, Queen of Brittany

Anne, Queen of England

Beatrix, Queen of Holland

Nita Barrow, Governor-General of Barbados

Benazir Bhutto, Prime Minister of Pakistan

Boadicea (or Boudicca), Queen of Britain

Violetta Barrios de Chamorro, President of Nicaragua

Mary Eugenia Charles, Prime Minister of Dominica

Tansu Ciller, Prime Minister of Turkey

Eire, Queen of Ireland

Eugénie, Empress of France

Esther, Queen of Persia

Farah, Princess of Iran

Vigdis Finnbogadottir, President of Iceland

Haiulani, Princess of Hawaii

Hathshepsut, Queen of Egypt

Himiko, Queen of Japan

Kaahumanu, Queen of Hawaii

Kapiolani, Queen of Hawaii

Deborah Kapule, Queen of Hawaii

Kung Sheng, Empress of China

Liliuokalani, Queen of Hawaii

Livia of Rome

Margrethe II, Queen of Denmark and Greenland

Messalina of Rome

Michiko, Princess of Japan

Noor, Queen of Jordan

Olympias, Queen of Macedon

Maria Liberia Peters, Premier of the Netherlands Antilles

Renee, Duchess of Parma

Mary Robinson, President of Ireland

Emma Rooke, Queen of Hawaii

Roxane, Princess of Bactria

Ruth, Princess of Hawaii

Sangwal Mahidol, Princess Mother of Thailand

Semiramis, Queen of Assyria

Shub-ad, Queen of Ur

Sirikit, Queen of Thailand

Theodora, Empress of Byzantium

Catherine Tizard, Governor-General of New Zealand

Toyo, Queen of Japan

Trung Nhi of Vietnam

Trung Trac of Vietnam

Tz'u-Hsi, last Empress of China

Budget: $$

Sources:

Bridge, Antony. *Theodora: Portrait in a Byzantine Landscape.* Academy Chicago, 1993.

Bruce, Evangeline. *Napoleon and Josephine: An Improbable Marriage.* Scribner, 1995.

Elizabeth R. Critics' Choice Video, n.d. (Video)

Ferdinand and Isabella. Schlessinger, 1995. (Video)

Ferrero, Guglielmo. *The Women of the Caesars.* Barnes & Noble, 1993.

Fire Over England. Time Warner Viewer's Edge, n.d. (Video)

Griffin, Lynne, and Kelly McCann. *The Book of Women: 300 Notable Women History Passed By.* Bob Adams, 1992.

Guinness Book of World Records. Grolier, 1995. (CD-ROM)

Jackson, Guida. *Women Who Ruled.* ABC-Clio, 1990.

The Lion in Winter. Critics Choice, 1968. (Video)

Martin, Jean, gen. ed. *Who's Who of Women in the Twentieth Century.* Crescent Books, 1995.

Mills, Kay. *From Pocahontas to Power Suits.* Plume, 1995.

1995 Information Please Almanac. Houghton Mifflin, 1995.

Szulc, Tad. "We Cannot Turn Back." *Parade,* April 2, 1995, 4–6.

Whitman, Ruth. *Hatshepsut, Speak to Me.* Wayne State University Press, 1992.

Alternative Applications: Assign small groups an individual female ruler to study. Have volunteers summarize the lifestyle in the ruler's native land. Describe palaces, terrain, major products, international conflicts, and population and religion statistics appropriate to the time. Account for the ruler's accession to power. For example, mention the incestuous pairing of brother and sister on Egypt's throne and Cleopatra's revolt against her brother Ptolemy, whom she had killed. Add that Cleopatra reputedly bore children to both Julius Caesar and Mark Antony. After Octavius marched on her realm, Cleopatra committed suicide to spare herself torment as a captive queen. The Romans murdered her heir, Caesarion.

Health

Champions *of women's health*

Age/Grade Level or Audience: Middle school or high school science, health, or biology project; science and history club oral report; Women's History Month newsletter; hospital or women's clinic bulletin board; newspaper feature.

Description: Summarize the alteration in women's reproductive health and freedom of choice as a result of the work of women scientists and activists.

Procedure: Introduce the status of birth control and abortion before safe medical solutions replaced botched home abortions, indiscriminate dosages of Seneca snakeroot or juniper berries, deliberate trauma or falls, caustic douches, and strong purgatives as methods of ending pregnancy. Present information on the work of the following champions of women's rights to have control over their bodies and to the choice families have whether or not to produce children. Include these:

- Dr. Elizabeth Blackwell, founder of lying-in clinics, lecturer, and writer on the subject of feminine hygiene, safe delivery, exercise, diet, and birth control as it applies to length and quality of life

- Dr. Mary Steichen Calderone, supporter of the Sex Information and Education Council of the United States (SIECUS)

- Mary Ware Dennett, crusader for open access to family planning information and author of *The Sex Side of Life*

- Crystal Eastman, orator and crusader for sex information and devices without the intervention of male doctors

- Dr. Joycelyn Elders, former U.S. surgeon general and supporter of sex education as a deterrent to teen pregnancy and AIDS

- Martha May Eliot, chief of the U.S. Children's Bureau and activist for maternal and infant health

- Emma Goldman, radical pacifist and champion of women's civil rights, who went to jail for distributing birth control information

- Estelle Griswold, director of Planned Parenthood and activist against Connecticut's ban on birth control

- Patricia Maginnis, founder of the Society for Humane Abortion

- Margaret Sanger, creator of a chain of health clinics that dispensed birth control to the poor

- Faye Wattleton, leader of Planned Parenthood during the height of the struggle for reproductive choice

- Sarah R. Weddington, president of the National Abortion Rights Action League (NARAL)

Use as an example of leadership a prepared handout on the career and dedication of Dr. Marie Carmichael Stopes, best-selling author, inventor of the cervical cap, and proponent of the sponge and spermicide as a reliable contraceptive for women. Summarize these facts:

- Born October 15, 1880, in Edinburgh, Scotland, Stopes was one in a family of strong women. Her mother, a university graduate and Elizabethan scholar, taught Marie at home until she entered private school at age twelve. Stopes attended University College and vacillated between chemistry and botany as potential majors. Upon graduation in 1902 with honors in both botany and geology, she furthered her studies with a doctorate in paleobotany from Munich University's Botanical Institute.

- The first woman to teach science at Manchester University and the youngest scientist with a Ph.D. in Britain, she was acknowledged by a fellowship from the Royal Society. For ten years she furthered her knowledge of ancient plants and published three scholarly works on the formation of coal. An unsuccessful marriage to Reginald Ruggles Gates resulted in a book on human sexuality, a novelty in 1918. During her second marriage, to publisher Humphrey Verdon Roe, she produced an illustrated book on birth control that recommended the cervical cap, which she introduced to working-class women through a monograph called "A Letter to Working Mothers."

- Dr. Stopes's unflinchingly realistic marriage manuals, plus the opening of a birth control clinic in London in 1921, brought her into conflict with religious leaders. A bitter lawsuit against Halliday Sutherland, a Catholic physician, took more than ten years to complete and left her paranoid on the subject of church interference with women's rights. Although newspapers refused to mention her name or causes, the unfavorable publicity generated by lawsuits against her garnered increasing public appeal for Stopes.

- During this period, her personal life was beset with the difficulties of a stillbirth and the cesarean delivery of her son Harry. Her last years reverberated with lost causes, family disappointments, and self-imposed exile, but Stopes, a pioneer in the field of women's right to health education, never stopped supporting women's clinics staffed with nurse-midwives rather than male doctors. Suffering from breast cancer, she died October 2, 1958.

Conclude with an open study of pros and cons of a variety of procedures common in the practice of women's health care. Summarize the arguments for and against routine cesarean sections, the availability of birth control, and methods of ending dangerous or unwanted pregnancies. Contrast the points of view of NARAL, NOW, Planned Parenthood, ACLU, the religious right, and the Catholic Church as depicted in the media and through brochures, mailings, and media campaigns. Include data about the government's involvement in lessening the availability of abortion, particularly to teenagers and poor women. Debate the wisdom of allowing individuals to decide for themselves the safety and necessity of undergoing specific medical procedures.

Budget: $

Sources:

Apple, Rima D. ed. *Women, Health, and Medicine in America.* Garland, 1990.

Benderly, Jill. "Margaret Sanger." *On the Issues,* spring 1990.

Benson, Michael D. *Coping with Birth Control.* Rosen, 1992.

Cadoff, Jennifer. "The Pill over 40." *Mirabella,* September 1991.

Caruana, Claudia. *The Abortion Debate.* Millbrook Press, 1992.

Ehrenreich, Barbara, and Deirdre English. *For Her Own Good: 150 Years of the Experts' Advice to Women.* Doubleday, 1989.

Elias, Marilyn. "The Pill Turns 35: A New Era for Women Was Born, Too." *USA Today,* May 4, 1995, D1–2, 4.

From Danger to Dignity: The Fight for Safe Abortion. Concentric Media, 1995. (Video)

Huston, Perdita. *Motherhood by Choice.* Feminist Press, 1995.

Larkin, Jack. *The Reshaping of Everyday Life—1790–1840.* HarperCollins, 1988.

Mucciolo, Gary. *Everything You Need to Know about Birth Control.* Rosen, 1990.

Parsons, Judith. "Marie Stopes." In *The Great Scientists,* Frank Magill, ed., Grolier, 1989.

Rubin, Eva R., ed. *The Abortion Controversy: A Documentary History.* Greenwood Press, 1994.

Teen Pregnancy. Rosen, 1994. (Video)

Teen Sexuality. Rosen, 1994. (Video)

Wertz, Richard W. and Dorothy C. Wertz. *Lying-In: A History of Childbirth in America.* Yale University Press, 1989.

Alternative Applications: Create a chalkboard time line of events that have revolutionized women's health care and increased women's life spans, particularly in impoverished and patriarchal countries. Note these topics:

- acceptance of a "morning after" pill such as RU-486

- adoption, *in vitro* fertilization, and artificial insemination

- increased publicity of female mutilation through circumcision, genital mutilation, and infibulation

- increased availability of safe and inexpensive methods of contraception

- government programs aiding women in selecting a reliable method of birth control

- liberalization of the wife's role in decision making

- significance of religious teachings

- single mothers who have no choice but work

- social and familial attitudes toward family size

- women's need of work outside the home or farm

Determine how these forces affect the lives of women and their families.

Colonial *soap*

Age/Grade Level or Audience: Middle school or high school chemistry or biology class; history or preservation society program; home demonstration presentation; women's studies or civic club project; media feature; museum handout.

Description: Create soap from colonial recipes.

Procedure: Set up a demonstration booth or laboratory experiment and make soap as American women did before it was manufactured commercially.

Colonial Soap

Store wood ashes and straw in a barrel and add boiling water. To a cup of the resulting lye or sifted wood ash add a tablespoon of cooking fat. Boil the mixture in a deep pan, stirring carefully until the ingredients blend. Stir in ½ cup of salt and bring to a boil. Pour the finished mixture into molds or a rectangular pan. Melt, stir in chopped mint, rose petals, or lavender, and re-cool mixture. Cut into bars.

Ask participants how so non-specific a recipe could be altered by using different types of wood ash and varied types of fat, fragrances, and herbs. Explain why buying soap from Europe was not an alternative, especially during the American Revolution.

Budget: $$

Sources:

Bracken, Jeanne Munn, ed. *Life in the American Colonies: Daily Lifestyles of the Early Settlers.* Discovery Enterprises, 1995.

Colonial America. Knowledge Unlimited, 1995. (Filmstrips)

Davis, William C. *The Civil War Cookbook.* Courage Books, 1993.

Encyclopedia of the North American Colonies. Scribners, 1993.

Hawke, David Freeman. *Everyday Life in Early America.* Harper & Row, 1988.

Stenson, Elizabeth. *Early Settler Activity Guide.* Crabtree, 1993.

Tunis, Edwin. *Colonial Craftsmen and the Beginnings of American Industry.* Thomas Y. Crowell, 1965.

Warner, John F. *Colonial American Home Life.* Franklin Watts, 1993.

Washburne, Carolyn Kott. *A Multicultural Portrait of Colonial Life.* Marshall Cavendish, 1994.

Alternative Applications: Discuss toiletries, candles, and other goods that colonial women made and traded on market days for these and other goods or services: tuition at a dame school, dried leather breeches beans strung on cord, bread, butter, feathers and down for mattresses and pillows, midwifery, tooth drawing, or fine stitchery. Print recipes for scented candles and potpourri, which were blended with lemon mint, rosemary, orris root, and chamomile. Describe how women mixed scent with rainwater to make a rinse for hair or to remove the lye residue of homemade soap from household linens, kitchen towels, blouses, cloth bonnets, nightgowns, swaddling and baby clothes, and lingerie. Comment on gifts of "startings" of herbs, which families and friends shared and sent along with those leaving for homesteads in the West.

Dr. Cicely *Saunders and hospice*

Age/Grade Level or Audience: High school and college sociology or humanities study; Hospice volunteers' introductory lecture or handout; nursing or theology research topic; Kindermourn seminar; medical society symposium; Friends of the Library or local Women's History Month monograph.

Description: Present the role of Dr. Cicely Saunders in formalizing England's Hospice program.

Procedure: Compile a brochure concerning the growth of "death with dignity" programs and Cicely Saunders's role in initiating a British hospice program. Emphasize these facts:

- Dr. Saunders, director of St. Joseph's Hospice, was influenced by the research of Elisabeth Kubler-Ross—*On Death and Dying* (1967)—and sought to allay clients' fears by providing personalized care and support for the dying and their families through a multi-disciplinary team of caregivers.

- Because of Dr. Saunders's initiative, the Douglas Macmillan Fund began underwriting hospices, creating appropriate protocols of palliative treatment, and training health-care providers to relieve pain and reassure dying people that they could live out their time in dignity and with a reasonable amount of comfort.

- The positive response to Dr. Saunders's work resulted in over one hundred care homes throughout the United Kingdom and over 170 visiting nurse programs providing in-home treatment.

- As a result of broader demands, Dr. Saunders founded St. Christopher's Hospice in Sydenham, England, and began planning an international hospice and children's hospice network.

Conclude with a comparison of England's hospice with parallel programs in the United States and Canada.

Budget: $$$

Sources:

Corr, C. A., and D. M. Corr. *Hospice Approaches to Pediatric Care*. Springer, 1985.

Kastenbaum, Robert. *Death, Society, and Human Experience*. Charles E. Merrill, 1986.

———. *Encyclopedia of Death*. Avon, 1989.

Kubler-Ross, Elisabeth. *On Death and Dying*. Macmillan, 1969.

Levy, M. H. "Pain Control Research in the Terminally Ill." *Omega,* 1987–1988, No. 18, 265–80.

Mor, V. *Hospice Care Systems*. Springer, 1987.

Mor, V., D. S. Greer, and Robert Kastenbaum. *The Hospice Experiment*. Johns Hopkins University Press, 1988.

Mother Frances Domina. "Reflections on Death in Childhood." *British Medical Journal,* No. 294, 108–110.

Saunders, Cicely. *The Management of Terminal Disease*. Hospital Medical Publications, 1967.

Twycross, R. G. *Pain Relief and Cancer*. Saunders, 1984.

Zimmerman, J. *Hospice: Complete Care for the Terminally Ill*. Urban & Schwarzenberg, 1981.

Alternative Applications: Contrast the work of Dr. Cicely Saunders with that of Ann Wickett, co-founder of the Hemlock Society, and of Elisabeth Kubler-Ross, pioneer in the study of death and dying. Comment on the talents and energy of Saunders, who transformed a philosophy into an international service.

Freedom *and the pill*

Age/Grade Level or Audience: High school science, health, or biology overview; science club project; Women's History Month newsletter or monograph; hospital or women's clinic bulletin board.

Description: Compose a summary of changes in women's lives over the past thirty-five years caused by the creation of safe oral birth control.

199

Procedure: Feature facts about contraception on a bulletin board, poster, wall chart, or newsletter. Express these early forms of birth control in cartoon, headline, or graphic style:

- condoms created by the Inuit from fish skins or intestines

- wool plugs and honey spermicide described on Egyptian papyri

- ancient Greek use of olive oil to decrease sperm motility

- Roman prescriptions for pennyroyal, Queen Anne's lace, juniper, and asafetida and the creation of linen condoms

- Hebrew women's preference for sponge barriers

- Indian mixtures of *ghee* (goat milk butter) and honey

- Minoan condoms for women made from sheep's bladders

- Shoshone reliance on powdered stoneseed

Bring the study of contraception to more recent times by contrasting ancient methods with these events:

- In 1917 police vice-squad raided the first U.S. birth control clinic in Brooklyn, New York. Twenty years later, the American Medical Association recognized birth control as a legitimate role of the medical profession. A method introduced in 1947—temperature-based abstinence, which allowed women to keep track of ovulation and to avoid intercourse as a means of birth control—was the only method countenanced by the Catholic Church.

- The synthetic progesterone pill resulted from the combined efforts of Min-Chueh Chang, Gregory Pincus, and Dr. John Rock and was manufactured for G. D. Searle and Company under the trade name Enovid. In 1955 philanthropist Kathleen Dexter McCormick joined forces with Margaret Sanger to commission research on a birth control pill, a drug that would mimic pregnancy. Sanger sought to honor her mother, dead at age fifty from eighteen pregnancies and seven miscarriages. Trials were performed on Puerto Rican volunteers, who lined the sidewalks to acquire a simple, cheap, and dependable method of birth control. The FDA approved Enovid on May 4, 1960. As a result, women achieved more autonomy, control, and choice in their lives, education, and work. Many postpone childbearing until much later in life than their ancestors. The U.S. Supreme Court legalized the use of birth control in 1965. Medicaid began providing contraception for poor women at regional health clinics and from visiting nurses.

- In the 1960s, Dr. Jack Lippes provided an alternative to the pill—a plastic, steel, or copper intrauterine device, which remains in the vagina and prevents conception. A development in the 1970s—the spermicide nonoxynol-9—was made available in foam, cream, suppository, jell, or sponge as an alternative or break from the pill or a backup to the IUD, cervical cap, and other barrier methods.

- By 1970, abortion became more available in New York; Congress funded family-planning research and education. A landmark decision legalized abortion in 1973 with the famed Roe vs. Wade case, pressed by Norma McCarvey as a class-action suit to benefit all women.

- In 1984 President Ronald Reagan rescinded budget items to aid the poor with family planning. Three years later, women's control over reproduction lessened after Reagan refused to allow federally funded clinics to mention abortion as an option and the Supreme Court upheld states' rights to restrict abortion. In 1990, the Supreme Court displayed more conservatism by allowing states to require parental notification. The next year, the Court upheld the gag rule for federally funded clinics.

- Wyeth-Ayerst Laboratories' Norplant, a subcutaneous device releasing progesterone directly into the bloodstream, was approved for distribution in 1990. Another alternative to the earlier hormone contraceptive was Depo-Provera, developed in the 1970s, but stalled by the Federal Drug Administration because of links with osteoporosis and cancer until 1992.

- Later developments, not in use long enough to prove their value and safety, include the female condom, which the FDA approved in 1993, and the abortifacient RU 486, which began clinical trials in 1994.

Budget: $

Sources:

Adler, T. "Pill Ups Cancer Risk in Young Women." *Science News,* June 10, 1995, 356.

Asbell, Bernard. *The Pill: A Biography of the Drug that Changed the World.* Random House, 1995.

Ehrenreich, Barbara, and Deirdre English. *For Her Own Good: 150 Years of the Experts' Advice to Women.* Doubleday, 1989.

Elias, Marilyn. "The Pill Turns 35: A New Era for Women Was Born, Too." *USA Today,* May 4, 1995, D1–2, 4.

Gordon, Linda. *Women's Body, Women's Right.* Viking, 1990.

James, Peter, and Nick Thorpe. *Ancient Inventions.* Ballantine, 1994.

McCorvey, Norma. *I Am Roe: My Life, Roe v. Wade and Freedom of Choice.* HarperPerennial 1995.

Travers, Bridget, ed. *World of Invention.* Gale Research, 1994.

Alternative Applications: Using graphing software or graph paper, create a pie chart, flow chart, or vertical graph indicating the types of contraception preferred by couples who actively practice birth control. Consider these facts and choose a graphing style and appended commentary to suit each:

- Of the women who take the pill, 61% are in their late teens; 11% are in their late thirties. Only one woman in fourteen has an unwanted pregnancy while taking the pill, compared with one in six who rely on condoms. More than a half of married couples opt for sterilization.

- The pill reduces the risk of ovarian cancer, drops ovarian cancer rates by 40%, and endometrial cancer by 50%. It also decreases chances of PID (pelvic inflammatory disease) and benign breast growths, and wards off rheumatoid arthritis. On the negative side, the pill may cause fatal blood clots and migraine headaches. It also increases chances of heart problems for smokers over 35 or drug interaction for women taking anti-convulsants or the antibiotic Rifampin. Researchers also suspect a link between oral contraception and breast cancer in women under age 35, which appears to rise 40% as compared to women 35–44, who experience no more breast cancers than non-users of the pill. For women 44–54, the risk of breast cancer drops 10% with use of the pill. Overall, the benefits to older women may make oral contraception a plus for longevity and health.

- Other side effects of oral contraception include breakthrough bleeding, tender breasts, queasiness, a perception of weight gain or bloating, mild headaches, and a one-month delay in return of ovulation after stopping the pill. Also, smokers over 35 are discouraged from taking the pill. The National Women's Health Network in Washington, D.C., cautions that a lifetime of taking the pill followed by hormone replacement in menopause exposes women to decades of artificial body control.

- 34.3% of women 15 to 44 chose some form of birth control other than surgery in 1990. Of this group, 49% chose the pill, 31% the condom, 13% rhythm method, abstinence, or withdrawal, 5% the diaphragm, and 2% the IUD.

- One set of figures places failure rates of contraception in this order, from least to greatest: male sterilization 0.15%, Norplant 0.2%, female sterilization 0.4%, progestogen injections 0.3%, oral contraceptives 3%, intrauterine device 3%, condom with spermicide 12%, diaphragm with spermicide 18%, sponge 18%, abstinence or rhythm method 20%, spermicide alone 21%, no contraception 85%.

The history *of nursing*

Age/Grade Level or Audience: Middle school and high school health, vocational, and biology lecture; health or civic clubs monograph; career or college forum; Women's History Month presentation; medical society program.

Description: Present an historical overview of the contributions of women to patient care.

Procedure: Give a chalk talk about nursing as an innovative profession led by people seeking to comfort and heal in a variety of situations—doctors' offices, medical centers, home care, rehabilitation centers, hospices, hospitals, day clinics, nurseries, industries, nursing homes, institutions for the handicapped, independent practice, mission work, and mobile health facilities. Impress on the audience that nursing is still labeled "woman's work": over 97% of nurses are female, even though many men who trained and served in the Korean, Vietnam, and Persian Gulf wars returned to civilian life with appropriate skills and interest in the profession. Provide a transparency of memorable facts. Include these:

- According to Hippocrates' *On Decorums,* in ancient times Mediterranean women served as midwives and wetnurses; temple priestesses doubled as medical attendants, especially during epidemics, but only males were allowed to learn the healing mysteries or rituals.

- The Bible lauds Deborah and other nurse-midwives (Exod. 1:15, Ezek. 16:4), who used birthing stools and cleaned and swaddled Israelite newborns.

- Chinese sources depict nutritionists, veterinarians, internists, acupuncturists, and village doctors accompanied by nurse assistants, perhaps to attend to minor dressings, washing of instruments, or compounding medications from the highly sophisticated pharmacopeia of ancient China.

- Likewise, specific information about the early Xhosa of Africa includes mention of the role of midwives in administering warm-water massage and infusions to women undergoing protracted labor.

- Islamic hospices and hospitals followed religious teachings and utilized male and female attendants to care for the sick, whom administrators separated via a complex system of triage. Because Arab nurses performed the work of Allah, medical training and care were free of charge.

- During the Roman Empire, local sick and wounded veterans chose between care by temple priest practitioners and slave healers in the *valetudinaria,* or Roman hospitals, which were usually suites of rooms surrounding a cloister or colonnade. Nurse slaves, who applied hot cloths and therapeutic soaks in mineral baths, were sometimes knowledgeable in the treatments and skills of Galen and Hippocrates. Medical manuals list forceps, tongs, probes, clips, scalpels, and other innovations, which disappeared from use with the fall of the empire.

- By the Christian era, sophisticated knowledge of Roman hospital staffs brought about the draining of the Pontine Marsh to halt malaria and the introduction of prosthetic limbs for amputees. Ordained deaconesses, heeding Christian injunctions to help the less fortunate, performed social work, including washing and burying the dead. The first nurse that Paul mentions by name is Phoebe of Cenchrea (Rom. 16:1–2). Two—Praxides and Pudentiana—devoted their ministrations to prisoners. One of Paul's converts, Thecla of Iconium, deserted her fiancé and set up a healing clinic for women in a cave near Seleucia in Asia Minor.

- After hearing St. Jerome and converting to Christianity, Marcella (4th century A.D.), a wealthy Roman scholar and the first Christian nursing instructor, opened her home to nursing students. More important in the history of nursing is Fabiola, a contemporary of Marcella, who founded the Western world's first hospital, or *nosokomia,* in Rome in A.D. 390. The complex of suites treated lepers in the contagious ward, the insane in another private ward, and accident victims in a separate wing. Later hospitals offered nurse care for the elderly at numerous *gerokomia,* a form of rest home.

It was during the Middle Ages that female nurses began receiving specific mention in medical histories, letters, and journals. Consider the works and contributions of these women:

- Brigit of Kildare (A.D. 450–525), who taught nursing and received all comers to her dispensary at the convent she established in Ireland.

- In Siena, St. Catherine (1347–1380) dedicated her outreach to loathsome diseases—leprosy, scrofula, and deformities—that other hospitals rejected. For her devotion to plague victims, she earned the title of patron saint of nursing.

- In 1854, Dr. Elizabeth Blackwell hired nurse-midwife Marie Zakrzewska and trained other nurses at the women's dispensary in New York City.

- On the battle scene at Scutari, Italy, from 1854–1856, Florence Nightingale made stringent demands on the British military that included requiring sanitary conditions to control rampant cholera, a 24-hour kitchen, clean bedding, and heat. Her tenets of hospital care proved successful—she reduced military deaths from 42% to 2%. In 1859 she founded a hospital of lay nurses in Lausanne, Switzerland; the next year, she opened London's Nightingale Training School for Nurses, the prototype of the modern hospital.

- In 1863, Nurse Adah Thomas pressed both the Red Cross and U.S. Army hierarchy to accept black nurses. In January 1863, sixteen-year-old Susie King Taylor, a slave, helped nurse casualties of the 33rd U.S. Colored Troops. In 1886 she organized the Women's Relief Corps to provide visiting nurses to aid veterans.

- The first licensed nurse-midwife was Carolyn Vanblarcom, born in 1879, the year that Mary Eliza Mahoney graduated as the first black registered nurse.

- Still active after her Civil War efforts, Clara Barton cajoled Congress into supporting the Red Cross in 1882. Seven years later, she led the group's flood relief in Johnstown, Pennsylvania; the following year she oversaw flood and hurricane relief in Galveston, Texas.

- Dr. Anita Newcomb McGee established the Army Nurse Corps on February 2, 1901, with Dita H. Kinney as chief of operations.

203

- World War II brought an urgent need for nurses. Captain Annie Fox received the first Purple Heart, earned during the bombing of Pearl Harbor, December 7, 1941. The military high-command put WAAC and WAVE nurses on the front lines. Two hundred died in battle. On March 13, 1942, nurse Julia Otteson Flikke became the first military nurse to earn a rank (colonel). In 1943 reaction against women in the military put a 2% cap on participation, limited participation to transport vehicles, and halted advancement beyond commander or lieutenant colonel.

- Two navy nurses earned certificates for studying submarine escape measures in New London, Connecticut in 1943. On December 28, 1944, Lt. Aleda E. Lutz of the Army Nurse Corps received the Distinguished Flying Cross. That same year, Lt. Cordelia Cook became the first military nurse to be awarded a Bronze Star. A year later, Captain Sue Dauser earned the Distinguished Service Medal. In 1947, the Army-Navy Nurse Act established a permanent position for nurses in the military. Col. Florence A. Blanchfield became the first female U.S. soldier to hold a regular commission; Lt. Comm. Bernice Rosenthal Walders was the first female soldier assigned to a ship, the *Consolation*.

- By the end of the war, health care demands increase the hiring of nurses in hospitals, where more than half were employed. During the polio epidemics of the late 1940s, Sister Elizabeth Kenny revolutionized the care of victims with a simple system of hot packs and muscle manipulation. Her program saved many from a life of crutches, iron lungs, and wheelchairs.

- In response to the government's low quotas for black nurses, Mabel Stampers, in February 1948, founded the National Council of Negro Women and pressed for inclusion into the American Nurses Association.

- Four nurses earned Purple Hearts in Vietnam in 1965. Nine died during the conflict. In 1967 Congress lifted the cap on women enlisting in the nurse corps and opened the way to higher rank. The next year, Lt. Jane A. Lombardi evacuated a Danang hospital and earned the Bronze Star, the first combat citation awarded to an American woman. On June 8, 1969, Sharon Lane died in action in Vietnam and was commemorated by a statue in her hometown of Canton, Ohio. By 1970 General Anna Mae Hayes had become the highest-ranking nurse in the army, followed by Jeanne Holm, Alene B. Duerk, and Elizabeth Hoisington. On May 5, 1970, Sister Nancy Ann Eagan became the first commissioned nun in the military and worked with the aeromedical airlift team. Nurse Duerk became the first female Admiral in Naval history on April 27, 1972.

- In 1971, in a move to end nursing's women-only stereotype, Justice Sandra Day O'Connor wrote the majority statement that nursing schools should admit men.

- In 1986 Congress set up the National Center for Nursing Research.

- Onnie Lee Logan, Mobile midwife, published *Motherwit: An Alabama Midwife's Story* in 1989, a reflection on her half century of service.

Budget: $$$

Sources:

Bullough, Vern L., Olga Maranjian Church, and Alice P. Stein. *American Nursing: A Biographical Dictionary*. Garland, 1988.

Cosner, Shaaron. *War Nurses*. Walker and Co., 1988.

Cytron, Barry, and Phyllis Cytron. *Myriam Mendilow: Mother of Jerusalem*. Lerner Books, 1994.

Daniels, Doris Groshen. *Always a Sister: The Feminism of Lillian D. Wald*. Feminist Press, 1995.

Ehrenreich, Barbara, and Deirdre English. *Witches, Midwives, and Nurses: A History of Women Healers*. Feminist Press, 1995.

Emert, Phyllis Raybin, ed. *Women in the Civil War: Warriors, Patriots, Nurses, and Spies.* Discovery Enterprises, 1995.

Flanagan, Lyndia. *One Strong Voice: The Story of the American Nurses Association.* ANA, 1976.

Garey, Diane, and Lawrence R. Hott. *Sentimental Women Need Not Apply: A History of the American Nurse.* 60 min. Florentine Films, 1988. (Film)

Griffin, Lynne, and Kelly McCann. *The Book of Women: 300 Notable Women History Passed By.* Bob Adams, 1992.

Hine, Darlene Clark. *Black Women in White: Racial Conflict and Cooperation in the Nursing Profession 1890–1950.* Indiana University Press, 1989.

Hurmence, Belinda. *Before Freedom: 48 Oral Histories of Former North and South Carolina Slaves.* Mentor Books, 1990.

Kalisch, Philip A., and Beatrice J. Kalisch. *The Advance of American Nursing.* Lippincott, 1986.

Kenny, Sister. *And They Shall Walk.* Ayer, 1980.

Leavitt, Judith Walzer. *Brought to Bed: Childbearing in America 1750–1950.* Oxford University Press, 1986.

Mellish, J. M. *A Basic History of Nursing.* Durban, South Africa: Butterworths, 1984.

Melosh, Barbara. *The Physician's Hand: Work, Culture and Conflict in American Nursing.* Temple University Press, 1982.

Pryor, Elizabeth Brown. *Clara Barton: Professional Angel.* University of Pennsylvania Press, 1987.

"Salute to the Military." *Daughters of the American Revolution Magazine,* November 1990, 852–53.

Stoddard, Martha. "Program Delivers Birth Support." *Lincoln Star,* June 23, 1995, 1, 8.

Straubing, Harold Elk. *In Hospital and Camp: The Civil War through the Eyes of Its Doctors and Nurses.* Stackpole Books, 1993.

Zalumas, Jacqueline. *Caring in Crisis: An Oral History of Critical Care Nursing.* University of Pennsylvania Press, 1995.

Alternative Applications: Screen the movie *Sister Kenny* (RKO, 1946). Have volunteers study the role played by Rosalind Russell, who dramatized the thinking, decision-making side of nursing. Help participants compose scenes from exciting times in the history of women's health care. Suggest that one group describe the crusades of Margaret Sanger for birth control centers in poor neighborhoods. Have another group portray Florence Nightingale's midnight walks among wounded soldiers, an act that earned her the nickname of "The Lady of the Lamp." A worthy subject for a diorama are the coordinated efforts of volunteers and professionals like Clara Barton to staff makeshift field hospitals and rehabilitation centers during the Civil War. Use desktop publishing to compose a brochure accompanying the skits and explaining the qualities and skills that brought nursing out of the convent and brothels and into respectable hospitals, neighborhood clinics, and nurse-care facilities. Perform the finished program for a history club, civic club convention, or school.

Medicine *women, curanderas, and women doctors*

Age/Grade Level or Audience: Middle school and high school health, history, and biology research; school newspaper feature; civic club presentation; career or college forum; Women's History Month lecture; medical society program.

Description: During Women's History Month, present an extended definition of "medicine woman" and *curandera* in the Native American and nature-centered tradition.

Procedure: Give a chalk talk outlining the contributions of female healers. Emphasize the importance of woman-centered healing, such as that practiced at the clinic outside Old Fort, North Carolina, and staffed by Wind Trees, R.N., a Cherokee healer following the tradition of her father, Chief Two Trees. Define the *curandera* (healer), *sobordora* (masseuse), *curandera total* (general practitioner), *yerbera* (herbalist), and *partera* (midwife) in terms outside an American Medical Association standard. Include these facts:

- Native healers expect their oneness with God to lead them to answers to pain and suffering and to reestablish the patient's harmony with nature. This animistic concept calls for attention to belief systems and emotions and a restoration of essential body rhythms.

- Traditionally, Native practitioners have relied on quinine, willow bark, and coca for suppression of fever and pain and on stoneseed as a natural contraceptive. All these natural substances they taught to the European and Hispanic newcomers to North America.

- Native counselors stress non-competitive living, acceptance of others, strong individuality, humility, and sharing as a means of restoring oneness in both a tribe and a diseased body or spirit.

Mention by name and location these native medicine women and southwestern healers, past and present. Discuss the variety of backgrounds and methods they have brought to women's health care:

- Annie Kahn, a Navaho herbalist in Lukachukai, Arizona, regarded as having been born with the "Blessingway" or gift of healing

- *Curandera* Josephita Ortiz y Davis, who utilized the cycles of the heavens with healing plants to increase the potency of medicines and potions

- *Curandera* Juanita Sedillo, a New Mexican visiting healer who blends medical skill with Catholic faith

- *Curandera y partera* Jesusita Aragon of Las Vegas, New Mexico, who trusts in the saints to help her deliver healthy infants and to train others in midwifery

- *Curandera y sobardora* Gregorita Rodriguez of northern New Mexico, who applies a love of people through her healing hands, which locate and massage *empacho,* or impactions in the stomach

- *Curandera y yerbera* Sabinita Herrera of Truchas, New Mexico, who learned *remedios* or herbal cures from her father

- Dhyani Yhwahoo, priestess of the Cherokee and student of a culture that teaches meditation, dance, music, and healing through veneration of crystals and through a method of scratching the skin to restore the balance of energy

- Dr. Josette Mondanaro of Santa Cruz, California, who honors the native methods as well as modern medicine

- Dr. Molly Radford Ward of Los Piñones, New Mexico, who headed a well-baby clinic and the state department of gerontology

- Dr. Stirling Puck of Santa Fe, New Mexico, geneticist and practitioner of female-centered healing

- Tu Moonwalker, an Apache healer and descendent of Mangas Coloradas who weaves healing into her baskets

Budget: $

Sources:

Anaya, Rudolfo. *Bless Me, Ultima*. Tonitiuh International, 1972.

Lewis, Dale. "Woman Is Medicine: An Interview with CheQweesh Auh-Ho-Oh." *Woman of Power,* winter 1987.

Muina, Natalia. "To Make Whole." *Woman of Power,* winter 1987.

Perrone, Bobette, H. Henriette Stockel, and Victoria Krueger. *Medicine Women, Curanderas, and Women Doctors.* University of Oklahoma Press, 1989.

Stoddard, Martha. "Program Delivers Birth Support." *Lincoln Star,* June 23,1995, 1, 8.

Alternative Applications: Create a wall chart or collage blending the beliefs and traditions of medicine women and *curanderas* with the work of AMA doctors, Lamaze trainers, and La Leche instructors. Stress compassion, the healing touch, respect for nature and wholeness, knowledge of anatomy and plants, and a genuine desire to end suffering.

Our *bodies, our own*

Age/Grade Level or Audience: Health, human sexuality, and biology summary; women's studies time line; civic club program; League of Women Voters public forum; Planned Parenthood series; media feature.

Description: Discuss changing attitudes toward women and the power struggle over sexual awareness and reproductive rights.

Procedure: Introduce a brief overview of women's rights to information on birth control, the right to privacy, and control of the body. Discuss the influence of women like Dr. Marie Stopes, Dr. Elizabeth Blackwell, Margaret Sanger, Faye Wattleton, Emma Goldman, and Dr. Joycelyn Elders in assuring women that their bodies and reproductive capabilities belong to them and not to the church or state. Present a handout or taped reading of the events in the life of sex therapist Dr. Ruth Westheimer, a strong voice for access to reproductive and sexual information and the strengthening of male-female relationships through knowledge. Use this framework as a starter:

- Karola Ruth Siegel, a native of Frankfurt, Germany, was born to a middle-class family June 4, 1928. When the Nazis menaced Jews, Ruth's family planned to move away, but her grandmother, who lived with them in their four-room apartment, refused to go. The SS arrested Ruth's father, Julius Siegel; Ruth joined 300 Jewish children in a last-minute flight to a school in Switzerland and never learned the fate of her family, who probably died at Auschwitz.

- As a charity case, Ruth learned menial tasks while coping with schoolgirl squabbles. She repudiated orthodox Judaism and, in 1945, joined Zionists on an Israeli kibbutz, then moved to Haifa to support Haganah, the Jewish freedom-fighters, and to study early childhood education. During an Arab attack, she sustained injury to her ankles and feet.

- Graduated in 1949, she taught in Yemen, married a Romanian soldier, and settled the next year in Paris. She studied psychology at the Sorbonne and directed a preschool program. Her marriage failed.

- In 1956 she remarried and moved to Manhattan. She began a master's degree program in sociology at the New School for Social Research. Her second marriage ended in 1958; on a maid's wages, Ruth attempted to support herself and daughter Miriam. The Jewish Family Service assisted until she earned a doctorate in education from Columbia University.

- In 1961 Ruth married communications engineer Manfred Westheimer and gave birth to Joel Westheimer in 1964. As project director at the Harlem Planned Parenthood clinic, she chose a specialty in sex therapy. After three years of post-graduate work, she received a Ph.D. in 1970 and lectured at Lehman College in New York.

- Influenced by Dr. Helen Singer Kaplan, Ruth earned her certification as a sex therapist and opened a private practice. While lecturing to newscasters about sexual ignorance, she accepted an invitation from Betty Elam to speak on a Sunday morning radio broadcast. Her brief show, "Sexually Speaking," earned a faithful following and covered numerous topics: sex therapy, contraception, individual needs, and misinformation.

- By 1981 Dr. Ruth's show had expanded to an hour of call-ins from her quarter of a million fans. The show emphasized explicit sexual information and covered traditional values, birth control, monogamy, religion, sex education, and abortion rights. The next year, she initiated a monthly column in *Playgirl* and spoke on television and at colleges while maintaining private counseling and therapy sessions at Bellevue Hospital and West Point.

- Her best-seller, *Dr. Ruth's Guide to Good Sex,* led to her corporation, Karola, Inc., a *Good Sex* board game, home video, and a burst of publications, some written with co-authors: *Loving Couples* (1986), her autobiography, *All in a Lifetime* (1987), *Sex and Morality* (1988), *Dr. Ruth's Guide for Married Lovers* (1992), *Dr. Ruth's Guide to Erotic and Sensuous Pleasures* (1992), *The Art of Arousal* (1992), and *Dr. Ruth's Encyclopedia of Sex* (1994).

Budget: $

Sources:

Another Woman for Choice. American Civil Liberties Union, 1995.

Benson, Michael D. *Coping with Birth Control.* Rosen, 1992.

Bosworth, Patricia. "Talking with Doctor Goodsex." *Ladies' Home Journal,* February 1986, 82, 84, 167.

Connell, Steve. "Dr. Ruth Answers Her Critics." *Union* (Sacramento, California), May 13, 1987.

Dawidziak, Mark. "Dr. Ruth, Sexual Guru." *Beacon Journal* (Akron, Ohio), March 1, 1987.

Ehrenreich, Barbara, and Deirdre English. *For Her Own Good: 150 Years of the Experts' Advice to Women.* Doubleday, 1989.

Gindhart, Mary A. M. "Sex Life: Dr. Ruth Advocates Lasting Education." *Arizona Republic* (Phoenix), June 3, 1987.

Lichtenstein, Robin. "Dr. Ruth: Sex, Aging Are Compatible." *Trenton Times* (New Jersey), November 16, 1989.

Mano, D. Keith. "Good Sex!" *People,* April 15, 1985, 109–112.

Martin, Emily. *The Woman in the Body.* Beacon Press, 1987.

The Nature of Sex: Sex Research 1700–1860. Research Publications, 1995. (Microfilm)

No Way Out: Young, Pregnant, and Trapped by the Law. American Civil Liberties Union, 1991.

Schaefer, Stephen. "Dr. Ruth Makes Film Debut." *Boston Herald,* April 3, 1987.

Shattering the Dreams of Young Women: The Tragic Consequences of Parental Involvement Laws. American Civil Liberties Union, 1990.

Sheehy, Gail. *New Passages*. G. Merritt, 1995.

Westheimer, Dr. Ruth. *All in a Lifetime*. Warner Books, 1987.

Alternative Applications: Contrast the work of twentieth-century supporters of sex education. Include the views of the people mentioned above plus information gleaned from these writers:

- Lonnie Barbach's *For Yourself: Fulfillment of Female Sexuality and Guide to Orgasmic Response* (New American Library, 1976)

- Joyce Canterbury's *Time We Talk: The Pre-Teen Years* (Hoffman, 1993)

- Shere Hite's *The Hite Report* (Dell, 1987) and *Women in Love* (St. Martin, 1989)

- Peter Mayle's *What's Happening to Me?* (L. Stuart, 1975)

- *The New Our Bodies, Ourselves* (Touchstone, 1992)

- Alexandra Penney's *How to Make Love to a Man . . . Safely* (Dell, 1993)

- Frances Younger's *Five Hundred Questions Kids Ask about Sex and Some of the Answers* (C. C. Thomas, 1992)

Determine the parameters of public opinion on women's vulnerability vs. their right to control and enjoy their sexuality and reproductive powers.

Women *healers*

Age/Grade Level or Audience: Elementary school science or health project; medical careers program; science club cooperative study; Women's History Month newsletter or bulletin board; history club presentation.

Description: Celebrate women's role as healers with an illustrated scrapbook.

Procedure: Search through reference works and summarize the contribution of female healers. Have participants list famous healers and their contributions on pages of a scrapbook. Consider these as possible additions to the collection:

- Dr. Sara Josephine Baker, worker for inoculations for children

- Sister Elizabeth Kenny, creator of a treatment for polio

- Myriam Mendilow, a gerontologist who designed programs for the elderly

- Susan La Flesche Picotte, who established an itinerant nurse care program on Indian reservations

- Dr. Margaret Sanger, founder of America's first birth control clinic

- Dr. Marie Stopes, creator of the cervical cap as a birth control device

Budget: $$$

Sources:

American Men and Women of Science. R. R. Bowker, 1989.

Crofford, Emily. *Healing Warrior: A Story about Sister Elizabeth Kenny*. Lerner Books, 1989.

Cytron, Barry and Phyllis Cytron. *Myriam Mendilow: Mother of Jerusalem*. Lerner Books, 1994.

Ferris, Jeri. *Native American Doctor: The Story of Susan LaFlesche Picotte*. Lerner Books, 1991.

Golob, Richard, and Eric Brus, eds. *The Almanac of Science and Technology*. Harcourt Brace Jovanovich, 1990.

Griffin, Lynne and Kelly McCann. *The Book of Women: 300 Notable Women History Passed By*. Bob Adams, 1992.

Haber, Louis. *Black Pioneers of Science and Invention*. Harcourt Brace Jovanovich, 1992.

James, Edward T., et al., eds. *Notable American Women, 1607–1950*. Belknap Press, 1971.

Magill, Frank N., ed. *Great Events from History II: Science and Technology Series*. Salem Press, 1991.

Martin, Jean, gen. ed. *Who's Who of Women in the Twentieth Century*. Crescent Books, 1995.

McGrew, Roderick E. *Encyclopedia of Medical History*. McGraw-Hill, 1985.

Veglahn, Nancy J. *Women Scientists*. Facts on File, 1991.

Alternative Applications: Design individual leaflets on female healers featuring their creative ideas and enthusiasm for medical work. Use this abbreviated form as a model:

Florence Nightingale (1820–1910). Born to the upper middle class, she refused to marry and dismayed her family by insisting on becoming a nurse. Using connections with military leaders, she insisted on taking medical care to the battlefield rather than transport wounded soldiers back to England. Settled in a ramshackle monastery in Scutari, Italy, from 1854–1856, she scrubbed floors, walls, and ceilings with carbolic acid; sterilized bedding; and established an around-the-clock kitchen. By hiring only competent, professional women, she produced the first battlefront staff and reduced military deaths from 42% to 2%. By 1860 her ideas had grown in influence both in London and around the world, wherever communities were willing to pay for and supervise a modern hospital.

Women's *health fair*

Age/Grade Level or Audience: Civic or industrial health fair; health and biology class project; media campaign; local medical society outreach.

Description: During Women's History Month, establish a central clearinghouse, health fair, phone bank, library reference table, or other sources of free women's health information.

Procedure: Foster improved lives and prevention of disease by organizing a woman-centered health fair. Impress on women that, because of advanced techniques and a change in attitude toward the value of women to society, our current generation has a better chance of living a long, healthy, and useful life than has any past generation. Follow these procedures:

- Provide posters indicating the availability of free health information. Include free transportation or bus routes.

- Spread the message through all media, including letters from PTA groups, door-to-door campaigns, media features and columns.

- Use club assistance in collecting groups of women to speak on topics significant to women.

- Target all areas of a town, county, or rural community. If necessary, create a traveling health show by bus, van, or truck.

Stress significant points from the female perspective and give details of the history of women who have championed the cause of birth control, safe abortions, child care, better schools, supervised play areas, healthy diets, clean and safe work conditions, and fair wages. Celebrate these:

Virginia Apgar	Florence Nightingale
Dr. Josephine Baker	Mary Nutting
Dr. Elizabeth Blackwell	Margaret Sanger
Mary Brewster	Pat Schroeder
Edith Cavell	Helene Schweitzer
Florence Crittenden	Rhena Schweitzer-Eckart
Dorothea Dix	Dr. Marie Stopes
Emma Goldman	Lillian Wald
Rose Lathrup	Faye Wattleton

All of these historic figures gave selflessly: some were imprisoned and scorned for their outspoken support of women's entitlement to a good life or the right of a female to study nursing or midwifery; others were silenced, arrested, shot, tortured, or killed in combat. One, Pat Schroeder, continues to support women's needs in the home and workplace and adequate health care for families.

Budget: $$$$$

Sources:

A.D.A.M.: The Inside Story. A.D.A.M. Software. 1995. (CD-ROM)

Apple, Rima D., ed. *Women, Health and Medicine in America*. Garland, 1990.

Batt, Sharon. *Patient No More: The Politics of Breast Cancer*. Ragweed Press, 1994.

Doress-Worters, Paula B., and Diana Laskin Siegal. "Managing Menopause." *Modern Maturity*, May–June 1995, 40–42, 76–77.

————. *The New Ourselves, Growing Older: Women Aging with Knowledge and Power*. Simon & Schuster, 1994.

Ehrenreich, Barbara, and Deirdre English. *For Her Own Good: 150 Years of the Experts' Advice to Women*. Doubleday, 1989.

The Family Doctor. Creative Multimedia, 1995. (CD-ROM)

Gearing, Sylvia. *Female Executive Stress Syndrome: The Working Woman's Guide to a Balanced and Successful Life*. Summit, 1995.

Love, Dr. Susan. *Dr. Susan Love's Breast Book*. Addison-Wesley, 1995.

Moe, Barbara. *Everything You Need to Know about PMS*. Rosen, 1995.

The New Our Bodies, Ourselves: A Book by and for Women. Simon & Schuster, 1984.

The PDR Family Guide to Women's Health and Prescription Drugs. Medical Economics, 1994.

Raloff, Janet. "Drug of Darkness." *Science News*, May 13, 1995, 300–301.

Sheehy, Gail. *New Passages*. G. Merritt, 1995

Sher, Elizabeth. *Approaching the Fourteenth Moon*. Landmark Media, Inc., 1995. (Video)

Wallis, Claudia. "The Estrogen Dilemma." *Time*, June 26, 1995, 46–53.

White, Evelyn C., ed. *Black Women's Health Book: Speaking for Ourselves*. Seal Press, 1994.

Contact your city hall, county commissioners, health department, and women's clinics for free brochures. Also, enlist these organizations:

American Cancer Society
777 Third Ave.
New York, NY 10017
212-371-2900

American Heart Association
7272 Greenville Ave.
Dallas, TX 75231-4596
800-242-8721
FAX: 214-691-6342

Depression After Delivery
P.O. Box 1282
Morrisville, PA 19067
215-295-3994

March of Dimes
Birth Defects Foundation
P.O. Box 1657
Wilkes-Barre, PA 18703

National Osteoporosis Foundation
P.O. Box 96173
Washington, DC 20077

National Women's Health Network
1325 G St. NW
Washington, DC 20005
202-347-1140

Office of Cancer Communications
National Cancer Institute
9000 Rockville Pike
Bldg. 31, Rm. 10A24
Bethesda, MD 20892
800-422-6237

National Black Women's
    Health Project
1237 Gordon St. SW
Atlanta, GA 30310
404-753-0916
FAX: 404-752-6756

National Center for Education in
    Maternal and Child Health
2000 15th St., North, Ste. 701
Arlington, VA 22201
703-524-7802

National Council on Patient
    Information and Education
666 Eleventh St, NW, Ste. 810
Washington, DC 20001
202-347-6711

The People's Medical Society
462 Walnut St.
Allentown, PA 18102
800-624-8773
215-770-1670

Women's Health Exchange
CIBA
P.O. Box 549188
Miami, FL 33054-9188
800-776-CIBA, ext. LB95

Alternative Applications: Organize a distribution point for brochures or online services to answer questions about women's concerns. Select a point available to all classes of people, such as a mall kiosk, bus terminal, public library, or post office. Post notices of free clinics, self-help groups, and private consultations. If your area lacks these groups, establish a center at a church, civic center, or Salvation Army hall where women's groups may meet informally to discuss the possibility of starting needed groups.

History

Eleanor *Roosevelt and the United Nations*

Age/Grade Level or Audience: Junior high or high school writing or history study; library research exercise; history or literary society lecture; museum or library display; newsletter or media feature.

Description: Outline the influence of Eleanor Roosevelt on the United Nations.

Procedure: Have participants make a topic or sentence outline of the work done by Eleanor Roosevelt on the incipient United Nations. As a start, include these data:

- Eleanor Roosevelt, wife of President Franklin D. Roosevelt, performed significant social and altruistic work among deprived women, workers, blacks, and immigrants while serving as First Lady.

- Returned to her home in Hyde Park, New York, after her husband's death on December 31, 1945, she accepted appointment by President Harry Truman to the United Nations. The only woman representative, she used her bilingual skills in French and English to demand human rights and helped compose the United Nations Charter Committee's initial mission statement on relieving suffering of women and children. The passage of the Universal Declaration of Human Rights on December 10, 1948, brought her a standing ovation from admiring committee members, even those with whom she disagreed.

- The eight paragraphs of the preamble to the Universal Declaration of Human Rights affirms that rights are "a common standard of achievement for all peoples and all nations," and shall "promote respect for these rights and freedoms and by progressive measures, national and international, to secure their universal and effective recognition and observance." Subsequent articles assert dignity and conscience and inveigh against slavery, torture, degradation, discrimination, arbitrary exile or imprisonment, and compulsory belief systems. Separate remarks govern the entitlements of women and children, especially in regard to education and culture expression.

- During the fifties, after President Eisenhower relieved her of the U.N. appointment, Roosevelt championed the state of Israel, returned to writing a regular newspaper column entitled "My Day," taught at Brandeis University, and set the tone of women's objections to the McCarthy hearings.

- Under President Kennedy, Roosevelt resumed her post at the United Nations and chaired a women's status commission that preceded passage of the Equal Pay Act of 1962. During this period, she produced her autobiography, which preceded her death from tuberculosis in 1962.

Budget: $

Sources:

Collier, Peter. *The Roosevelts: An American Saga.* Touchstone, 1995.

Goodwin, Doris Kearns. *No Ordinary Time: Franklin and Eleanor Roosevelt.* Simon & Schuster, 1994.

Weatherford, Doris. *American Women's History.* Prentice Hall, 1994.

Yearbook of the United Nations, 1948–1949. New York, 1950, 535–37.

Alternative Applications: Have participants read aloud from the Universal Declaration of Human Rights. Determine whether the text is still applicable to these and other situations:

- capricious detainment
- clothing that conceals the entire body
- feudal or patriarchal marriage
- flight of refugees from disease and genocide
- genital mutilation of young girls
- house arrest
- infanticide of female infants
- inhumane treatment of female prisoners
- mass rape of captured females
- religious and cultural taboos excluding women from full involvement in a community
- unlawful search and seizure

Famous *mothers*

Age/Grade Level or Audience: Elementary computer or current events activity; home-school study; scout or 4-H list or bulletin board; library research quiz; book club topic.

Description: Create a database of famous women whose children have done well as a result of parental guidance.

Procedure: Present a list of famous women who have succeeded in their own right while producing successful children. Use these examples as models:

- Christy Wood, mother of author Catherine Marshall and subject of her book *Christy*
- composer Mary O'Kelley Peacock, mother of Dr. Diane Peacock Jezic, teacher and musicologist
- Suffragist Elizabeth Cady Stanton, mother of Harriot Blatch Stanton, women's suffrage leader
- Helene Schweitzer, wife of Albert Schweitzer and mother of medical technologist Rhena Schweitzer-Eckart
- pioneer Jane Reno, mother of Attorney General Janet Reno
- Laura Ingalls Wilder, journalist and diarist, mother of journalist and collaborator Rose Wilder Lane

- Lillian Carter, Peace Corps volunteer and mother of President Jimmy Carter

- Marie Curie, physicist and mother of physicist Irene Joliot, both Nobel Prize winners

- Mary Bell Washington, widowed mother of five, including George Washington

- Monica, mother of church scholar St. Augustine, whom she converted to Christianity

- Queen Olympias of Macedonia, wife of King Philip of Macedon and mother of Alexander the Great

- Theodora Kroeber, author whose daughter Ursula Le Guin is one of America's finest female science fiction writers

Budget: $$

Sources:

Bell, Joseph N. "Shirley Temple: Her Movies, Her Life." *Good Housekeeping,* February 1981, 114–115, 185–90.

Biography Today. Omnigraphics, September 1993.

Black, Shirley Temple. *Child Star.* McGraw-Hill, 1988.

Cadden, Vivian. "Return to Prague." *McCall's,* April 1990, 60–66.

Clement, J., ed. *Famous Deeds of American Women.* Corner House, 1975.

Griffin, Lynne, and Kelly McCann. *The Book of Women: 300 Notable Women History Passed By.* Bob Adams, 1992.

"Happy Birthday, Shirley Temple Black!" *McCall's,* April 1982, 58.

Her Mother Before Her: Winnebago Women's Stories of Mothers and Grandmothers. Instructional Video, 1992. (Video)

Hoven, Kendall. *Amazing American Women: 40 Fascinating 5-Minute Reads.* Libraries Unlimited, 1995.

"The Joys of Being a Grandmother." *McCall's,* December 1983, 102–108.

Koppelman, Susan, ed. *Between Mothers and Daughters.* Feminist Press, 1995.

Meachum, Virginia. *Janet Reno, United States Attorney General.* Enslow, 1995.

"Mutiny on the Lollipop." *Time,* October 31, 1988, 59.

Pflaum, Rosalynd. *Marie Curie and Her Daughter Irene.* Lerner Publications, 1993.

Yorkshire, Heidi. "Shirley Temple Black Sets the Record Straight." *McCall's,* March 1989, 88–94.

Alternative Applications: Summarize the value of a strong mother, as demonstrated by the guidance of Gertrude Temple in the life of her daughter, Shirley Temple Black, who has been Chief of White House Protocol, delegate on African Refugee Problems, and member of a United Nations group studying Law of the Seas, a U.N. Conference on Human Environment, President's Council on Environmental Quality, and U.S. Commission for UNESCO.

- The third child and first daughter of Gertrude Krieger Temple and financier Francis George, Shirley Temple was born April 23, 1928. Gertrude wanted her third child to be a girl so much that, before giving birth, she set her thoughts on music, art, and nature to get her unborn baby off to a good start.

- Gertrude introduced three-year-old Shirley to tap dance at Ethel Meglin's children's dance studio. There, Charles Lamont, a talent scout for Educational Studios, selected Shirley from the other dancers. From the beginning, Gertrude

215

Temple accompanied her daughter to all rehearsals and performances and controlled all interviews and auditions.

• At age four, Shirley starred in *Stand Up and Cheer;* by age six, at the depths of the Depression, she earned $1,250 a week; by age eight, the amount rose to $3,500 for such starring roles as *Little Miss Marker, Rebecca of Sunnybrook Farm, Baby Take a Bow, Bright Eyes, Curly Top, Poor Little Rich Girl, The Blue Bird, The Little Princess, Wee Willie Winkie,* and *The Little Colonel.* The steady income paid for the family's move from their stucco bungalow to a new Brentwood residence. Meanwhile, Twentieth-Century Fox built Shirley a four-room playhouse on the movie lot.

• Gertrude insisted that the studio hire private tutors for Shirley until she reached age twelve, when she enrolled in the Westlake School for Girls while filming *Since You Went Away, Kiss and Tell,* and *The Bachelor and the Bobby-Soxer.* To keep her daughter from losing touch with reality, Gertrude reminded her that people loved the illusion of her forty major movies rather than the real Shirley Temple.

• In the late 1940s, Shirley's career faltered after her unsuccessful marriage to John Agar. Accompanied by her own daughter Susan, Shirley vacationed in Hawaii and met Charles Alden Black, whom she married that December. The family settled in San Francisco and produced sons Lori and Charles Jr.

• During her own parenthood, Shirley diverted some of her energies to worthy causes—the National Wildlife Federation, AIDS research programs, programs for homeless people, the Equal Rights Amendment, the pro-choice movement, and the National Multiple Sclerosis Society. As U.S. ambassador to Ghana, she built strong relations with black Africans.

• After a mastectomy at age 44, Shirley accepted a post at the Czechoslovakian Embassy and smoothed the way for Vaclav Havel's emergence as leader.

• Like Gertrude, Shirley Temple Black takes satisfaction in her own children: Susan Black Falaschi, journalist and science fiction writer; Charles Jr., employee of the Department of Commerce; and Lori, a photographer.

• Shirley credits many of her accomplishments to self-discipline and pragmatism, qualities Gertrude fostered during her daughter's early childhood.

The Hiroshima *Maidens*

Age/Grade Level or Audience: Elementary school English or history summary; library research project; museum or library focus; United Nations Day program or media release.

Description: Summarize the joint effort of nations to help the Hiroshima Maidens.

Procedure: Read aloud to participants the stories of Michiko Yamaoka and the other Hiroshima Maidens, a group of young girls whose physical scarring and deformities stirred American journalist, critic, and philanthropist Norman Cousins.

In 1949, Cousins visited victims of the World War II bombing of Hiroshima, when an atomic weapon was dropped from the Enola Gay, an American warplane. Guided by Reverend Kioshi Tanimoto, who would later be fictionalized in John Hersey's *Hiroshima,* Cousins saw the deplorable filth and squalor of Japanese hospitals. With assistance from the American Friends Service Committee, in August 1953, he organized a rescue operation of 400 orphans and, from these, brought the 24 healthiest females to New York. Cousins's employer, *Saturday Review,* paid for treatment and plastic surgery to restore them to a normal life. He paralleled his humanitarian efforts by similarly assisting the "Ravensbruck Lapins," 35 victims of medical experimentation.

Ask participants to determine why Cousins and his fellow Americans showed pity to young girls rather than a cross-section of victims, including males, old people, and young children.

Budget: $

Sources:

Barker, Rodney. *The Hiroshima Maidens.* Penguin, 1985.

Hersey, John. *Hiroshima.* Vintage, 1973.

————. "Hiroshima: The Aftermath." *New Yorker,* July 15, 1985, 37–62.

Hiroshima Survivors. National Public Radio, n.d. (Audiocassette)

Japanese-American Survivors of the A-Bomb. National Public Radio, n.d. (Audiocassette)

Lifton, Betty J. *A Place Called Hiroshima.* Basic Books, 1985.

Miner, Jane C. *Hiroshima and Nagasaki.* Franklin Watts, 1984.

Moritz, Charles, ed. "Norman Cousins." *Current Biography.* H. W. Wilson, 1978.

Sanders, David. *John Hersey.* Twayne, 1967.

Wyden, Peter. *Day One: Before Hiroshima and After.* Simon & Schuster, 1994.

For more information, consult these agencies:

Committee of Atomic Bomb
    Survivors in the U.S.
1109 Shellgate Pl.
Alameda, CA 94501
510-523-5617

Friends of Hibakusha
1759 Sutter St.
San Francisco, CA 94115
415-567-7599

Alternative Applications: Make a written report on the Hiroshima Maidens, including a time line of the atomic bomb. Note at what point the media concentrated on the Maidens. Discuss the contrast between the Japanese men who bombed Pearl Harbor and the Japanese women who received free surgical care from New York doctors. Conclude with comments on the American response to a Hiroshima display held at the Smithsonian Institution in 1995.

Lucy: *who, what, why, where, when, and how*

Age/Grade Level or Audience: Junior high and high school history or biology biographical sketch; college anthropology or anatomy project; library research exercise; science club fact sheet; historical society newsletter; bulletin board display.

Description: Characterize Lucy, the oldest human skeleton ever discovered.

Procedure: Write a brief account of Lucy's life, death, and discovery. Include answers to simple questions:

- Who was she?
- What percent of her skeleton remains?
- What parts of her skeleton are missing?
- Where was she found? by whom? when?

217

- What were the circumstances of her death?

- In what medium were her remains preserved?

- Why is her recovery so significant to anthropologists?

- How did she get her name?

- What evidence proves that she is female?

- How do researchers estimate her size, posture, and age?

- How does her finder's work compare to similar studies made by Louis Leakey, his wife Mary Leakey, and their son, Richard Leakey?

- What controversy arose from expert evaluations of Lucy?

- Why did her finder assume that an extinct ancestor remains unknown?

- Why did he insist that Lucy cannot be labeled human?

- How do the terms *allometry* and *dimorphism* apply to Lucy?

- What is special about her jaws and teeth?

- Do her remains tell us anything about her life?

Conclude with a comparison of other finds, particularly these:

- Donald Johanson's 1994 unearthing of a complete male skeleton

- female from the La Brea tar pits in Los Angeles

- Mary Leakey's study of prehistoric footprints in Laetoli, Tanzania

- Yael Rak's discovery of the skull of a contemporary of Lucy in Hadar, Ethiopia

Budget: $

Sources:

Ardrey, Robert. *African Genesis*. Atheneum, 1961.

Cove, John J. *What the Bones Say: Tasmanian Aborigines, Science and Domination*. Carleton University Press, 1995.

Friend, Tim. "New Skull Illuminates Early Man." *USA Today,* March 31, 1994, D1–2.

Johanson, Donald. *Lucy's Child: The Discovery of a Human Ancestor*. Avon, 1990.

Johanson, Donald, and James Shreeve. *Lucy's Child: The Search for Our Origins*. Morrow, 1989.

Johanson, Donald, and Kevin O'Farrell. *Journey from the Dawn: Life with the World's First Family*. Random House, 1990.

Johanson, Donald, and Maitland Edey. *Lucy: The Beginnings of Humankind*. Touchstone, 1981.

Morgan, Elaine. *The Scars of Evolution: What Our Bodies Tell Us about Human Origins*. Oxford University Press, 1990.

Nova: In Search of Human Origins. Pacific Arts Publishing, n.d. (Video)

Alternative Applications: For a newsletter, bulletin board, or handout for an advanced study of Donald Johanson's find, create an enlarged bio sheet on Lucy, including drawings of her remains. Give approximate date of birth, sex, length of life, cause of death, size, anomalies, posture, teeth, location, and particulars of her life, including diseases, motherhood, and her relationships to these classifications:

A. Africanus	Meganthropus
A. boisei	Neanderthal
Australopithecus afarensis	Ouranopithecus

Australopithecus Hadarensis	Paranthropus
Australopithecus laetolensis	Peking Man
Cro-Magnon	Pithecanthropus
Dryopithecidae	Plesianthropus
East African homo	Pongidae
East African robustus	Praeanthropus
Gigantopithecus	Proconsul
Hispanopithecus	Ramapithecus
hominids	Rangwapithecus
homo erectus	Rudapithecus
homo sapiens	Sivapithecus
homo habilis	South African gracile
Java man	South African robustus
Limnopithecus	Steinhein man

Name *the husband*

Age/Grade Level or Audience: Middle school or high school history research; home-school activity; scouts or 4-H list or bulletin board; library research quiz; book club puzzle; table favor or place mat quiz; newsletter feature.

Description: Make a list of famous women to match the names of their husbands.

Procedure: Present a list of famous women from Western history and the Bible. Have participants pick from a list of men's names the appropriate husband or husbands. For example, Caesar Augustus/Livia; Edward VII/Wallis Warfield Simpson; Queen Elizabeth II/Prince Philip

_____	1. Abigail	_____	10. Esther
_____	2. Alexandra	_____	11. Isabella
_____	3. Anne Boleyn	_____	12. Jezebel
_____	4. Anne of Cleve	_____	13. Katherine von Bora
_____	5. Bathsheba	_____	14. Leah
_____	6. Calpurnia	_____	15. Michal
_____	7. Catherine	_____	16. Nefertiti
_____	8. Cleopatra	_____	17. Olympias
_____	9. Eleanor of Aquitaine	_____	18. Rachel
		_____	19. Rebekah

_____ 20. Roxane	_____ 23. Queen Victoria
_____ 21. Sarah	_____ 24. Xanthippe
_____ 22. Theodora	_____ 25. Zipporah

Mountbatten; Virgin Mary/Joseph; or Mumtaz/Shah Jihan. Note that some answers appear more than once and some not at all:

Abraham, Ahab, Ahasureus, Akhenaten, Albert, Alexander the Great, Amenhotep, Buddha, Charles I, Charles Martell, Confucius, Croesus, David, Edward VII, Ferdinand, Genghis Khan, George VI, Henry II, Henry VIII, Isaac, Jacob, John Calvin, John Wesley, Josephus, Julius Caesar, Justinian, Louis VII, Luke, Martin Luther, Mohammed, Moses, Nero, Nicholas II, Paul, Philip of Macedon, Plato, Ptolemy XIV, Shaka, Socrates, Uriah, Xerxes

ANSWERS:

1. David	14. Jacob
2. Nicholas II	15. David
3. Henry VIII	16. Amenhotep or Akhenaten
4. Henry VIII	17. Philip of Macedon
5. David	18. Jacob
6. Julius Caesar	19. Isaac
7. Henry VIII	20. Alexander the Great
8. Ptolemy XIV, Julius Caesar	21. Abraham
9. Louis VII, Henry II	22. Justinian
10. Ahasureus	23. Albert
11. Ferdinand	24. Socrates
12. Ahab	25. Moses
13. Martin Luther	

Add to the puzzle with lists of notables from Africa, China, Japan, the Pacific, and the Americas. Include a variety of races and periods of time; for example, Charbonneau/Sacajawea; Hirohito/Nagako; Henry Tibbles/Susette La Flesche; and Kamehameha I/Keopuolani.

Budget: $

Sources:

Clark, Gillian. *Women in Late Antiquity: Pagan and Christian Lifestyles.* Oxford University Press, 1993.

Dennis, Denise. *Black History for Beginners.* Highsmith, 1992.

Fantham, Elaine, et al. *Women in the Classical World.* Oxford University Press, 1994.

Great Lives from History: American Women Series. Salem Press, 1995.

Renault, Mary. *The Nature of Alexander.* Pantheon, 1975.

Trager, James. *The People's Chronology.* Henry Holt, 1992.

Alternative Applications: Select a famous pair of mates from history. Make a Venn diagram by overlapping two circles or ovals. Indicate to the far left and right the accomplishments of each mate. In the center, name the achievements the couple completed together. Use this pair as a model:

Eleanor of Aquitaine

queen of France
supporter of the arts
ruler of Aquitaine

parents of Richard
the Lion-Hearted
and of John, signer
of the Magna Carta

Henry II

king of England
uniter of England
and France

Names *to know*

Age/Grade Level or Audience: Middle school or high school world history work sheet; newspaper feature; bulletin board focus; library research quiz; book club.

Description: Some well-known women achieve instant recognition with a single name, paired names, nickname, or pair of names, as is the case with these figures from history, legend, the Bible, opera, sports, and literature:

single name

Boadicea, Sappho, Scheherazade, Sacajawea, Esther, Marilyn, Pocahontas, Theodora, Sheba, Messalina, Bathsheba, Nefertiti, Carmen, Aida, Esmeralda, Svetlana, Heloise, Scarlet, Ruth, Twyla, Isadora, Hypatia, Enya, Midori, Hildegarde, Iman, Twiggy

name with title

Mrs. Simpson, Madame Chiang, St. Joan, Queen Noor, Princess Michiko, Queen Wilhelmina, Dear Abby, Queen Beatrice, Empress Eugénie, Princess Caroline

nickname

Flo-Jo, Liz, the Divine Miss M, Good Queen Bess, Jackie-O, the Jersey Lily, Cleo, Grandma Moses, the "It" Girl, the Queen Mum, Bubbles, the Lady with the Lamp

[athlete Florence Griffith-Joyner, actress Elizabeth Taylor, singer Bette Midler, Elizabeth I of England, Jacqueline Beauvier Kennedy Onassis, Lillie Langtry, Queen Cleopatra of Egypt, painter Anna Mary Moses, actress Clara Bow, Queen Mary of England, opera singer Beverly Sills, and nurse Florence Nightingale]

pair of names

the Captain and Tenille, Tarzan and Jane, Hero and Leander, Priscilla and Aquila, Romeo and Juliet, Bonnie and Clyde, Victoria and Albert, Ike and Tina, Ike and Mamie, Peaches and Herb

Procedure: Complete the following single clues with the appropriate given names and patronyms of famous women. To the right, name the contribution or achievement of each.

1. Cher _____   _____

2. Hillary _____   _____

3. _____ Capucine   _____

4. Queen Elizabeth II _____   _____

5. Madame _____ Tussaud   _____

6. _____ Colette   _____

7. Charro _____   _____

8. Madonna _____   _____

9. Queen Guinevere _____   _____

10. Diana _____   _____

11. _____ Chanel   _____

12. _____ Makarova   _____

13. _____ Pavlova   _____

14. Queen Victoria _____   _____

15. Anaiis _____   _____

16. Isadora _____   _____

17. _____ Garbo   _____

18. Princess Anastasia _____   _____

19. Mother Teresa _____   _____

20. Selena _____   _____

21. Gypsy _____   _____

22. Bernadette of _____   _____

23. _____ Bernhardt   _____

24. Leona _____   _____

25. Princess Grace _____   _____

26. Dr. Ruth _____   _____

27. Mother _____ Hale   _____

28. Zsa-Zsa _____   _____

29. Coretta _____   _____

30. Empress Josephine _____   _____

31. _____ Bardot   _____

32. "Lady Day" _____   _____

ANSWERS:

1. Cher Bono, singer

2. Hillary Clinton, attorney

3. Germaine Lefebvre Capucine, actor

4. Elizabeth Windsor, Queen of England

5. Madame Marie Tussaud, founder of London's waxworks

6. Sidonie-Gabrielle Colette, diarist

7. Charo Martinez, singer

8. Madonna Ciccone, entertainer

9. Guenevere Pendragon, legendary Queen of Camelot

10. Diana Spencer, Princess of Wales and supporter of arts and charities

11. Coco Chanel, couturier

12. Natalia Makarova, dancer

13. Anna Pavlova, dancer

14. Victoria of Saxe-Coburg, Queen of England

15. Anaiis Nin, writer

16. Isadora Duncan, dancer

17. Greta Garbo, actress

18. Anastasia Romanov, Russian princess

19. Agnes Gonxha Bojaxhiu, missionary and settlement worker

20. Selena Quintanilla, singer

21. Gypsy Rose Lee, vaudeville entertainer and author

22. Bernadette of Lourdes, religious visionary

23. Sarah Bernhardt, actor and singer

24. Leona Helmsley, hotel owner

25. Princess Grace Kelly, actress and wife of Prince Rainier Grimaldi of Monaco

26. Dr. Ruth Westheimer, sex therapist

27. Mother Clara Hale, child-care expert

28. Zsa-Zsa Gabor, actress

29. Coretta Scott King, director of the Martin Luther King Museum

30. Empress Josephine Beauharnais, wife of the Emperor Napoleon Bonaparte

31. Brigitte Bardot, actress and animal rights activist

32. Billie "Lady Day" Holiday, jazz singer

Budget: $

Sources:

Bailey, Brooke. *The Remarkable Lives of 100 Women Artists.* Bob Adams, 1994.

———. *The Remarkable Lives of 100 Women Healers and Scientists.* Bob Adams, 1994.

———. *The Remarkable Lives of 100 Women Writers and Journalists.* Bob Adams, 1994.

Griffin, Lynne, and Kelly McCann. *The Book of Women: 300 Notable Women History Passed By.* Bob Adams, 1992.

Hoven, Kendall. *Amazing American Women: 40 Fascinating 5-Minute Reads.* Libraries Unlimited, 1995.

Alternative Applications: Create a game of one-name charades. Have participants act out the name by demonstrating the central achievement of the person. For example, for Makarova or Pavlova, perform a ballet pose or series of dance steps; for Princess Di or Princess Fergie, act out the role of the royal bride. For Sacajawea or Pocahontas, depict Sacajawea's role of guide for the Lewis and Clark expedition from the Dakotas to Washington State or Pocahontas's rescue of Captain John Smith. To characterize Flo-Jo, demonstrate the skill that won track star Florence Griffith-Joyner an Olympic medal.

Pass *the hat*

Age/Grade Level or Audience: K–4 drama or art activity; home-school project; scout or 4-H game; frieze or series of posters; library research quiz.

Description: Initiate a women's history lesson with a game of Pass the Hat.

Procedure: Have participants draw hairstyles, hats, or decorations to fasten to a hat to illustrate the activities and achievements of famous women. Consider some of these contributors to women's history:

nurse's cap	Clara Barton, Civil War nurse and supporter of the Red Cross
Girl Scout hat	Juliette Low, founder of the American Girl Scouts
Egyptian headdress	Nefertiti, Queen of Egypt
braids, tumpline	Sacajawea, leader and translator on the Lewis and Clark expedition
crown	Queen Elizabeth II of England

Budget: $$

Sources:

Bailey, Brooke. *The Remarkable Lives of 100 Women Artists*. Bob Adams, 1994.
———. *The Remarkable Lives of 100 Women Healers and Scientists*. Bob Adams, 1994.
———. *The Remarkable Lives of 100 Women Writers and Journalists*. Bob Adams, 1994.
Griffin, Lynne, and Kelly McCann. *The Book of Women: 300 Notable Women History Passed By*. Bob Adams, 1992.
Hay, Susannah. *The Women's Heritage Scrapbook*. Caillech Press, 1992.
Hoven, Kendall. *Amazing American Women: 40 Fascinating 5-Minute Reads*. Libraries Unlimited, 1995.
Mills, Kay. *From Pocahontas to Power Suits*. Plume, 1995.

Alternative Applications: Alter the hat game by creating a mural or series of posters on which participants draw hats, hairstyles, or decorations. Have each player point to a hat and provide three clues to help other players guess the mystery woman's identity. Conclude by having each player write the owner's name above the hat.

Witches: *fact and fiction*

Age/Grade Level or Audience: High school interdisciplinary activity; library research exercise; historical society banner; book club presentation; women's club newsletter; media feature; bulletin board display; Women's History Month handout.

Description: Have volunteers compare historical and literary works detailing the events of the Salem witch trials.

Procedure: Post a time line of historical facts. Begin with these:

1620	Colonists arrived, already certain that evil existed in human form and justifying their beliefs on the strength of Exod. 22:18: "Thou shalt not suffer a witch to live."
1647–1663	Fifteen witches were hanged; two were husbands of women executed for practicing the occult.

1662	Hartford, Connecticut, experienced a rash of charges against witches.
1680	Puritan authorities studied evidence of witchcraft in New England.
1689	Rev. Cotton Mather published *The Wonders of the Invisible World*, a work revealing the influence of four young witches in Boston.
1691–1692	Abigail Williams, Elizabeth Parris, Elizabeth Hubbard, and Ann Putnam came under the influence of Tituba, a Barbadian slave and palm reader, in Danvers, Massachusetts. The girls became hysterical after reading books on witchcraft. The uproar spread to nearby Salem, where eyewitnesses claimed to have seen witches.
1692	Increase Mather published *Cases of Conscience Concerning Evil Spirits*, a study of witchcraft trials in Boston.
1692	In Salem, the brunt of the mass hysteria fell on aged, ill, or isolated women, especially those who kept pets. On February 29, women suspected of being witches faced an all-male panel of Puritan judges.

- **March 1** Nineteen women, including Tituba, Sarah Osborne, and Sarah Good, were arrested. As a result of Tituba's influence, Mr. Parris, her owner, forfeited her papers. She was sold.

- **March 21** The court examined suspected witch Martha Corey.

- **March 29** Sarah Good implicated Sarah Osborne. Additional witnesses implicated George Burroughs, Martha Corey, Bridget Bishop, Susanna Martin, and Rebecca Nurse.

- **June** Sir William Phips, governor of the Massachusetts Bay Colony, appointed Samuel Sewall, John Hathorne, and William Stoughton as judges to try the accused.

- **early June** The panel condemned Bridget Bishop.

- **June 30** Mary Warren swore to a deposition that John Proctor tortured her, Mercy Lewis, John Indian, and Miss Pope.

- **July 19** Rebecca Nurse was acquitted, but the court overturned the verdict and hanged her, along with Sarah Good, Susanna Martin, and three other women. For refusing to comply with the witch hunt, Martha Corey, Mary Easty, and Deputy Constable John Willard were also executed. A Mrs. Cary from Charlestown attended the trial as a spectator and was arrested but not punished.

- **August 19** George Burrough, John Willard, and others from Andover were condemned for conducting a Black Mass. Willard was defrocked by a state court.

- **August 29** William Barket confessed.

- **mid-September** Giles Corey refused to acknowledge the court request for a plea and was pressed to death with rocks. He was 80 years old.

- **September** Mary Easty petitioned the court for clemency.

- **October** Governor Phips halted the witch hunt.

| 1693 | Governor Phips appointed a new court. Public opinion turned against John Parris. The courts freed all condemned prisoners still held in jail. |

1696	On December 17, the court made a formal recantation of its errors.
1697	On January 14, Samuel Sewall publicly atoned for the court's faulty reasoning.
1711	Heirs of the victims received court compensation on behalf of those wrongly accused and executed.

Divide a group into reading circles to study the facts and contrast them with fictional accounts; for example, Hilary Weisman's *The Salem Witch Hunt* (one-act play). Determine how fiction embroiders on fact, yet provides readers with accurate pictures of how justice is distorted when individuals fear to come forward with the truth.

Budget: $

Sources:

Fowler, Samuel P. *Salem Witchcraft*. Heritage Books, 1992.

Miller, Arthur. *The Crucible*. Bantam, 1959.

Perrone, Bobette, H. Henriette Stockel, and Victoria Krueger. *Medicine Women, Curanderas, and Women Doctors*. University of Oklahoma Press, 1989.

Petry, Ann. *Tituba of Salem Village*. HarperCollins, 1991.

Richards, Jeffrey J. *The Cry at Salem*. Paladin House, 1992.

Six Centuries of Witchcraft. Research Publications, 1995. (Microfilm)

Three Sovereigns for Sarah. N.p., n.d. (Video)

Trask, Richard B., compiler. *Salem Village and the Witch Hysteria*. Jackdaw Publications, n.d.

Weisman, Hilary. *The Salem Witch Hunt*. Discovery Enterprises, 1995. (Play)

The Witches of Salem: The Horror and the Hope. Columbia University, 1972. (Video)

Alternative Applications: Summarize facts about witch trials in England and America. Post data on a bulletin board or present as a media feature, bulletin board display, or club newsletter. Stress the political nature of witch hunts aimed at victimizing women—especially women who owned or inherited property. Present a summary of the activities of Wicca. Conclude the study with a screening of the film *Three Coins for Sister Sarah*.

Women *and the Holocaust*

Age/Grade Level or Audience: Junior high and high school humanities focus; library research exercise; literary society discussion; museum or library display; church school or synagogue Holocaust Day presentation.

Description: Summarize the qualities that helped a significant number of women survive the Holocaust.

Procedure: Have participants evaluate the strengths and strategies of women sought by Hitler's SS for extermination in death camps such as Auschwitz and Treblinka. Note common motifs in their struggles against laws curtailing rights of Jews and other identifiable groups, and their experiences in regard to medical experimentation, forced labor, euthanasia of children with birth defects, murder, sexual bondage, and other forms of genocide. Stimulate interest by screening films such as *Julia, The Music Box, Shoah, Sophie's Choice, Holocaust, Schindler's List,* and *Playing for Time.* Arrange a library reference table of notable works by survivors of the Holocaust. Extend the study of the Jewish Holocaust with comparisons to these incidents:

- eyewitness accounts of atrocities against black female slaves by Ku Klux Klan members and other racist attackers in the American South, Caribbean, and other parts of the world

- genital mutilations and curtailment of human rights of women in Muslim countries

- genocide in Bosnia-Herzogovina and subsequent rape, murder, and displacement of Muslim women and children

- Japanese mistreatment or forced prostitution of Korean "comfort girls" during World War II

- slaughter or mutilation of American Indian women and children at Wounded Knee

- summary executions of females during the My Lai Massacre in Vietnam

Conclude with a reading of the United Nations Commission on Human Rights statement guaranteeing the dignity of all people.

Budget: $

Sources:

Amatenstein, Sherry. "A Rescue Mission with a Time Clock." *USA Weekend,* May 5–7, 1995, 4–5, 7.

Brecher, Elinor J. *Schindler's Legacy: True Stories of the List Survivors.* Plume Books, 1994.

Chicago, Judy. *The Holocaust Project: From Darkness to Light.* Penguin Books, 1993.

Cornwall, Claudia. *Letter from Vienna: A Daughter Uncovers Her Family's Jewish Past.* Canada: Douglas & McIntyre, 1995.

The Diary of Anne Frank. Critics Choice, n.d. (Video)

Eichengreen, Lucille. *From Ashes to Life: My Memories of the Holocaust.* Mercury House, 1994.

Fenyvesi, Charles. "A Child's View of War's End." *U. S. News and World Report,* May 15, 1995, 74.

Frank, Anne. *The Diary of a Young Girl.* Doubleday, 1995.

Griffin, Lynne, and Kelly McCann. *The Book of Women: 300 Notable Women History Passed By.* Bob Adams, 1992.

Hautzig, Esther. *The Endless Steppe.* Harper Keypoint, 1968.

Holocaust. Pacific Arts Publishing, n.d. (Video)

Keneally, Thomas. *Schindler's List.* Simon & Schuster, 1982.

Rol, Ruud van der, and Rian Verhoeven. *Anne Frank: Beyond the Diary.* Puffin Books, 1995.

Shire, Amy. "Jewish Women Now: The Holocaust as Seen by Women." *Jewish Currents,* July–August 1994, 24–25.

Song of Survival. Palisades Home Video, n.d. (Video)

Styron, William. *Sophie's Choice.* Bantam, 1982.

Sutin, Jack, and Rochelle Sutin. *Jack and Rochelle: A Holocaust Story of Love and Resistance.* Graywolf Press, 1995.

ten Boom, Corrie. *The Hiding Place.* Bantam, 1971.

Zyskind, Sara. *Struggle.* Lerner Books, 1989.

For information connecting Holocaust survivors with other survivors, contact Survivors of the Shoah, 1-800-061-2092.

Alternative Applications: Have English or journalism students create a method of interviewing elderly survivors of the Holocaust. Stress quandaries faced by women. Use these questions as models:

- Why did so many women avoid pregnancy, give away infants to Christian families or orphanages, or seek abortions?

- What coping mechanisms helped women overcome separation from or the arrest and murder of their children?

- How did networking enable women to find places to hide their children in other countries, in orphanages and boarding schools, or with Gentile families until the end of World War II?

- What agencies and individuals, such as Nazi-hunter Simon Wiesenthal, humanitarian Elie Wiesel, or Survivors of Shoah, assist people in determining the fate of families?

- What torture methods were designed specifically to terrorize women, such as the threat of gang rape or sexual mutilation by Nazi officials, doctors, capos, and guards?

- What role did sex play in the salvaging of lives; for example, the bartering of sexual favors in exchange for a lighter work assignment or the placement of attractive women in the homes of high-ranking officials to work as entertainers, escorts, waiters, or call girls?

- What bonds of sisterhood helped women overcome fear and weakness, particularly during Dr. Josef Mengele's dreaded selection of those allowed to work vs. those deemed unfit, who were immediately executed and cremated in gas ovens?

- What unusual ruses saved women, including posing as Catholics, dressing in men's clothing, or feigning expertise in important jobs and professional skills such as nursing, food preparation, or office management?

- What role did Hannah Senesh, Haviva Reik, and Zivia Lubetkin play in the fight to stop fascism and genocide?

Women *and war*

Age/Grade Level or Audience: Junior high and high school English or history speech; library research exercise; literary society report; museum or library display; newsletter and media series.

Description: Report on the women who have fought bravely as insurgents or those noncombatants injured during wartime or in political hostilities that victimized women and children.

Procedure: Have participants summarize on audiocassette the achievements and patriotism of women during political hostilities. Include these examples:

- Anna Warner Bailey, Groton, Connecticut
- Martha Brae, Jamaica
- Molly Brant, Mohawk
- Edith Cavell, England

- Anson Chan, Hong Kong

- Zlata Filipovich, Bosnia

- Milly Hayo Francis, Creek-Seminole

- Anne Frank, Holland

- Irma Hadzimuratovic, Bosnia

- Jean Wakatsuki Houston, Japanese-American

- Joan of Arc, France

- Golda Meir, Israel

- Rigoberta Menchu, Guatemala

- Jehan Sadat, Egypt

- Corrie ten Boom, Holland

- Nancy Ward, Cherokee

- Yoko Kawashima Watkins, Japan

Give details of each person's sacrifice or daring. Use this model:

- Five-year-old Irma Hadzimuratovic suffered spinal and abdominal paralysis from a shrapnel injury during the Serbian shelling of Bosnia on July 30, 1993. After being airlifted to London ten days later and pictured on worldwide news networks, she served as an example of botched United Nations efforts to provide care for wounded children. As a result, she was honored by "Operation Irma," a multinational effort to spare children injured by the protracted Bosnian War.

Use as a longer model for a presentation or formal program these facts about actress and activist Chiang Ch'ing:

- Born Li Chin to a carpenter's concubine in March 1914 in Chu-Ch'ing, Shantung Province, Chiang studied the Confucian virtues of self-discipline and respect. Chiang's father, an alcoholic, beat and cursed her, her mother, and her siblings. Her mother took the children and fled to Tsinan and supported them with menial work. Chiang Ch'ing lived unsupervised and fed herself off scraps and garbage.

- The family moved to the home of Chiang's grandfather, where Chiang attended public school. She became obsessed by the violence and want in China. In 1929 she withdrew from her political concerns and began to study opera, drama, and piano at the Shantung Provincial Experimental Art Theater.

- Two years later, when economic depression forced her mother to consider selling her, Chiang ran away to Tsingtao University, where she worked as a librarian's assistant and taught Chinese to pay her tuition. She entered the Seaside Drama Society, a wandering troupe that lived on meager returns from performances.

- When the Japanese invaded Manchuria, Chiang joined an idealistic band of rebels. At the age of twenty, she was imprisoned in Nanking for eight months. By February 1935, malnutrition had depleted her body.

- Playing Nora in Henrik Ibsen's *A Doll's House* under the stage name of Li Yun-ho, Chiang gave up revolution and remained immersed in her career until 1937. Employed by the Lien Hua Motion Picture Company in Shanghai, she took a new name—Lan P'ing or "Blue Apple"—to disguise her identity in leftist films such as *Blood on Wolf Hill* and *Wang Lao Wu* and was favorably compared to vamp Greta Garbo. For a brief time, she was married to critic T'ang Na.

229

- After the Japanese seized Shanghai in 1937, Chiang resettled in Chunking and taught drama at Lu Hsun Art Academy. Two years later, she proclaimed herself a member of the Chinese Communists. Mao Tse-Tung, hero of the Long March four years earlier, invited her to one of his speeches.

- That spring, Mao, divorced for the third time, married Chiang Ch'ing. As his mate and secretary, she again changed her name, this time to "River Azure," or Chiang Ch'ing (now spelled Jiang Qing). The party insisted that she end her film career and live in obscurity to spare Mao the embarrassment of media claims that he deserted a loyal mate and married a trophy wife twenty years his junior. In July 1944 Mao broke the ban on public appearances by waltzing with her during a state visit by Franklin Roosevelt.

- In Yenan, Chiang Ch'ing kept house at army headquarters, which was a cave. She cared for Mao's son and daughter and in 1940 gave birth to Li Na. Her life consisted of various forms of manual labor that served as a model to communist collectives.

- On March 12, 1947, the Japanese intensified bombing; Chiang was driven south by jeep through snow banks and rode horseback for five months in search of safe quarters. Her frail health deteriorated; she was dispatched to Moscow and Yalta for surgery and treatment of respiratory and urinary problems. After the Chinese Revolution in 1949, Chiang Ch'ing took an active part in promoting propagandist cinema while undergoing radiotherapy for cervical cancer. In 1956 she received cobalt treatment, which brought her near death.

- In the 1960s, Chiang Ch'ing recovered and influenced art reform, introducing her Communistic revisions of *The Taking of Tiger Mountain, The Red Lantern, Sentinels under Neon Lights,* and *A Great Wall Along the Southern Coast,* and a ballet, *The Red Detachment of Women.*

- In 1962 she began to seek an active part in the political hierarchy. Two years later, she made a speech at the Peking Opera Festival. When anti-Maoism threatened her husband's hold on China's Community party, Chiang Ch'ing contributed to a severe purge of Western influences. To secure her position, she avoided rich dress and wore proletarian garb.

- By November 1966, Chiang Ch'ing was second in command of the Cultural Revolution, a virulent anti-West display and a stage for the Maoist cult, buoyed by the publication of *The Quotations from Chairman Mao.* Her organization of youth brigades gave the impression that the people loved and supported Mao.

- The most notorious of Chiang Ch'ing's excesses was a purge of anti-Maoist officials, some of whom were executed. World reaction led to a softening of Chiang Ch'ing's role. By March 1968, she returned to artistic influence and stressed innovation and involvement of rural culture. During a state visit to China, President and Mrs. Richard Nixon attended one of her stage productions on February 22, 1972.

- Two years later, Mao could no longer hide his advanced age and physical deterioration. Upon his death on September 9, 1976, Chiang went into formal mourning. In October 1976 she was arrested as one of the "gang of four" and hanged in effigy. In January 1981 the new cabal sentenced her to death. Recognizing her advanced aged and waning strength, they allowed house arrest in her daughter's home in Beijing. On May 14, 1991, suffering throat cancer, she hanged herself.

Budget: $

Sources:

Bruhn, Sheila. *Diary of a Girl in Changi, 1941–1945*. Kangaroo Press, 1994.

Buel, Joy Day, and Richard Buel, Jr. *The Way of Duty: A Woman and Her Family in Revolutionary America*. W. W. Norton, 1995.

A Change in Attitude: Women, War and Society 1914–1918. Research Publications, 1995. (Microfilm)

"Deaths Elsewhere: Irma Hadzimuratovic." *Sacramento Bee,* April 3, 1995, B5.

Ellett, Elizabeth. *The Women of the American Revolution*. Corner House, 1995.

Emert, Phyllis Raybin, ed. *Women in the Civil War: Warriors, Patriots, Nurses, and Spies*. Discovery Enterprises, 1995.

Figner, Vera. *Memoirs of a Revolutionist*. Northern Illinois University Press, 1995.

Fox-Genovese, Elizabeth. "A New World for Women and Blacks?" *The World and I,* June 1995, 44–53.

Gates, Betsey. *The Colton Letters: Civil War Period 1861–1865*. McLane, 1993.

Gioseffi, Daniela. "Women on War and Survival." In *Women on War,* Touchstone Books, 1990.

"Guilty Verdict: The Gang of Four." *Time,* February 2, 1981.

Holley, David. "Mao's Widow Jiang Qing, Radical Leader, Dead at 77." *Los Angeles Times,* June 5, 1991.

Huong, Duong Thu. *Novel without a Name*. William Morrow, 1995.

Lief, Louise. "Second Class in the Israeli Military." *U. S. News and World Report,* May 22, 1995, 47–48.

Mary Silliman's War. Heritage Films, 1994. (Video)

"Milestones." *Time,* June 17, 1991, 73.

Moore, Molly. *A Woman at War: Storming Kuwait with the U.S. Marines*. Scribner's, 1993.

Pelka, Fred. "Mothers in the Fatherland." *On the Issues,* fall 1990, 26–28, 36–39.

Piturro, Marlene C. "First Chinese, First Woman." *On the Issues,* summer 1995, 35–37.

Reynoldson, Fiona. *Women and War*. Thomson Learning, 1993.

Salmonson, Jessica Amanda. *The Encyclopedia of Amazons: Women Warriors from Antiquity to the Modern Era*. Paragon, 1991.

Smedley, Agnes. *Portraits of Chinese Women in Revolution*. Feminist Press, 1995.

Terrell, Ross. *The White-Boned Demon: A Biography of Madame Mao Zedong*. Morrow, 1984.

Witke, Roxane. *Comrade Chiang Ch'ing*. Little, Brown, 1977.

"Women in World War II." University Publications of America, 1994. (Microfilm)

Woodward, C. Vann, ed. *Mary Chesnut's Civil War*. Yale University Press, 1981.

Alternative Applications: Create a "Women and War" map noting girls and women who have involved themselves in behind-the-scenes efforts. For example: Molly Pitcher, Clara Barton, Edith Cavell, Chiang Ch'ing, Audrey Hepburn, Christiane Amanpour, Belle Boyd, Joan of Arc, the widows of the Khmer Rouge and martyrs of Tianenmen Square, Winnie Mandela, Corrie ten Boom, and Rigoberta Menchu. Add information about women who have served near battlefields in the Red Cross, French Resistance, UNICEF, Caritas, *Medicins sans Frontieres,* Peace Corps, news bureaus, and other agencies providing relief, transportation, and medical care.

Humor

Guerrilla *Girls*

Age/Grade Level or Audience: Adult art or history class; art museum or library symposium; PTA or civic club program.

Description: Present data on the Guerrilla Girls.

Procedure: Display posters, overlays, lists, and handouts on the efforts of the Guerrilla Girls to increase exposure to women's art and to encourage young female artists to expect a living wage from their work on par with male artists. Comment on the humorous antics, masks, costumes, and outrageous behavior used by the group to gain entry to the media and thus advertise the historic quandary of male-dominated galleries and foundations in support of the arts, which currently allot ten percent of their time and efforts to women's work. Note that less than a quarter of art reviews and feature writing pertains to women's art.

Budget: $$

Sources:

Confessions of the Guerrilla Girls. HarperCollins, 1995.

Hackett, Regina. "Guerrilla Girls Go Bananas for Equality in Art." *Montreal Gazette,* May 29, 1995, 3D.

Martin, Jean, gen. ed. *Who's Who of Women in the Twentieth Century.* Crescent Books, 1995.

Alternative Applications: Use Guerrilla Girls tactics to support women's art in your area. Invite girls and women to collect all types of expression—poetry, drawing, mural, portrait art, photography, interior design, dressmaking, dance, video, sculpture, drama, architecture, and landscaping—to put on display during Women's History Month. Offer prizes for the best in show and in category. Distribute business cards and brochures of creative businesses and the women who own them.

Laughing *at the movies*

Age/Grade Level or Audience: Film appreciation topic; Women's History Month movie-rama; women's studies symposium; history research paper; newspaper or magazine film column.

Description: Discuss the importance of energy and humor in comedies starring female actors.

Procedure: Focus on the study of energy and humor as motivators of women's films and as vehicles of women's screen success, as is evident with Prissy, Aunt Pittypat, and Mammy in

Gone with the Wind. Select these roles and actors for study: a group of films starring Doris Day, Carole Lombard, Lucille Ball, Martha Raye, Mae West, Rosalind Russell, or Marjorie Main. Apply the following questions to each title:

- Why is energy important to a comic role?

- How does female energy differ from male energy onscreen?

- How do women carry comedy to the edge of tragedy in more contemporary films such as *'Night Mother, Used People, Crimes of the Heart, Steel Magnolias,* and *Fried Green Tomatoes*?

Conclude with a discussion of expectations for women's humor as opposed to patterns set by male comics.

Budget: $$$

Sources:

McDougal, Stuart Y. *Made into Movies: From Literature to Films.* Harcourt Brace, 1985.

Stones, Barbara. *America Goes to the Movies.* National Association of Theatre Owners, 1993.

Towers, Deidre, ed. *Dance Film and Video Guide.* Princeton, 1991.

Walker, John, ed. *Halliwell's Film Guide.* HarperPerennial, 1995.

Alternative Applications: Select a favorite comedy and analyze the role of the female comic. List characteristic gestures, speech patterns, dress, hair, posture, and interaction with male and female characters. For example, study the comic structure of *His Girl Friday,* starring Rosalind Russell. Summarize the gestures, actions, poses, words, and looks that indicate guile, ridicule, or good-natured fun. Complete the study with a summary of why the character earns laughs and why the audience complies.

Let *them eat cake*

Age/Grade Level or Audience: Middle school or high school creative writing or business project; after-school community center activity; women's studies seminar.

Description: Create a women's humor magazine.

Procedure: Have participants set up a mock first issue of a women's humor magazine entitled *Let Them Eat Cake.* Include cover design with a comic shot of Marie Antoinette wielding a tray laden with cupcakes. Design a masthead, slogan, table of contents, and advertising strategy. Include humorous episodes in the lives of Dorothy Parker, Clara Bow, Zelda Fitzgerald, Mary Pickford, Mae West, Isadora Duncan, and Mother Jones. Compose a focal series on dance by introducing the scandals caused by can-can clubs and by flappers doing the black bottom, Charleston, and Big Apple. Supply movie and book reviews, regular columns by Molly Ivins and Florence King, and cartoons by Barbara Brandon.

Budget: $$$$$

Sources:

Barreca, Regina. *New Perspectives on Women and Comedy.* Gordon and Breach, 1992.

Ivins, Molly. *Molly Ivins Can't Say That, Can She?* Random, 1991.

———. *Nothing But Good Times Ahead.* Random, 1993.

King, Florence. *Confessions of a Failed Southern Lady.* Bantam, 1986.

———. *The Florence King Reader*. St. Martin's Press, 1995.

———. *Reflections in a Jaundiced Eye*. St. Martin's 1989.

Levenson, Dorothy. *Women of the West*. Franklin Watts, 1973.

Martin, Jean, gen. ed. *Who's Who of Women in the Twentieth Century*. Crescent Books, 1995.

Miller, Brandon Marie. *Buffalo Gals: Women of the Old West*. Lerner Group, 1996.

Stephens, Autumn. *Wild Women*. Conari Press, 1992.

Wheelwright, Julie. *Amazons and Military Maids*. Pandora, 1989.

Alternative Applications: Using a word processor, compose a letter to the editor of *Let Them Eat Cake* in which you request articles on your favorite funny women. Include Carol Burnett, Roseanne Arnold, Holly Hunter, Shirley MacLaine, Whoopi Goldberg, Bette Midler, and Teri Garr. Extol the virtues of these funny ladies and express what qualities make them your favorites.

Shady *ladies and notorious women*

Age/Grade Level or Audience: Middle school or high school chorus, band, or music composition assignment; library summer project; music club workshop; scout or 4-H exercise; women's studies seminar.

Description: Create a sheaf of songs that capture the spirit of notorious women and shady ladies.

Procedure: Have participants select a familiar tune ("Yankee Doodle," "Passing By," "On Top of Old Smoky," "I've Been Workin' on the Railroad") or compose an original melody to accompany a simple multi-verse song about a legendary or real woman of questionable character or actions. Before beginning the writing phase, have lyricists study the history of these women:

- poisoner Agrippina, wife of Rome's Emperor Claudius
- alluring actresses Clara Bow and Mae West
- arsonist Anne Bonny, who burned her father's plantation after he disinherited her
- Bonnie Parker, notorious bank robber
- counterfeiter Mary Butterworth
- the daring Russian empress Catherine the Great
- Elizabeth "Madam Alex" Adams, the Hollywood procurer
- Eva Braun, mistress of Adolf Hitler
- Lizzie Borden, suspected ax murderer of her parents
- Lucrezia Borgia, famed poisoner of her enemies
- outlaw Molly "Moll Cutpurse" Frith
- pioneer and outlaw Belle Starr
- Sally Rand, exotic dancer
- saloon performer Diamond Lil

- spy Mata Hari

- stage robber Pearl Hart

- "Typhoid Mary" Mallon, spreader of disease

- uninhibited dancer Isadora Duncan

- wartime D.J.s Tokyo Rose, Hanoi Hannah, Seoul City Sue, Hanoi Hattie, and Axis Sally

Encourage writers to seek wit rather than ridicule in adding to the body of legend surrounding each character. Invite a guitarist or pianist to accompany a performance of the best "Shady Lady" songs.

Budget: $$$

Sources:

Gamse, Albert, ed. *World's Favorite Folk Songs*. Ashley Publications, 1961.

The Golden Book of Favorite Songs. Schmitt, Hall & McCreary, 1951.

Griffin, Lynne, and Kelly McCann. *The Book of Women: 300 Notable Women History Passed By*. Bob Adams, 1992.

Martin, Jean, gen. ed. *Who's Who of Women in the Twentieth Century*. Crescent Books, 1995.

Narkiewicz, Beverly S. "Yuma Prison." *Wild West*, August 1995, 63–69.

Raymer, Steve. "'Hanoi Hannah' Was Propaganda Voice of North Vietnam." *Montreal Gazette*, April 30, 1995, C4.

"Transition." *Newsweek*, July 24, 1995, 63.

Alternative Applications: Study folk lyrics or poems that question the behaviors, beliefs, and morals of various female characters. Include insinuating limericks and the poems "La Belle Dame sans Merci," "Guinevere," "Christabel," and "Barbara Frietchie." Research the words of these songs: "Frankie and Johnny," "Mademoiselle from Armentiers," "Mack the Knife," "The Lady Is a Tramp," and "Sadie Was a Lady." Discuss the humor directed at "Clementine," "She Sells Seashells," "She'll Be Comin' Round the Mountain," "The Star of the County Down," and "Won't You Marry Me?" Conclude whether the lyrics would be humorous, accurate, or interesting if the situation were applied to a male character.

Women *in song*

Age/Grade Level or Audience: Any-age music assembly; library summer project; piano or music club; synagogue or church exercise; women's studies seminar; retirement-home activity.

Description: Lead a program of folk songs that celebrate women by name.

Procedure: Present song sheets, overhead projector, or chalkboard lyrics to accompany piano tunes or recorded music on tape, record, or CD. Stress the dramatic moment or characterization of the girl in the song, for example, the anonymous singer in "Oh, Dear, What Can the Matter Be?" Discuss the composer's purpose in giving the focal character a name or personality, as with the calypso favorite "Marianne," the teasing "Little Annie Rooney," the Renaissance classic "Greensleeves," the Irish ballad "Molly Malone," or the British ballad "Barbara Allen." Why do songs omit specific names of loved ones, as with "Comin' Through the Rye," "Black is the Color of My True Love's Hair," "The Yellow Rose of Texas," "Tie a Yellow Ribbon Round the Old Oak Tree," "She'll Be Comin' Round the Mountain," "Beautiful Dreamer," "Buffalo Gals," "Dark Eyes,"

"The Girl I Left Behind Me," "Du, Du, Liegst Mir im Herzen," "The Last Rose of Summer," "Won't You Marry Me?," the Czech love song "Waters Ripple and Flow," and "O Waly Waly"?

Choose among these songs for program material. Suit the titles to the audience's interests and musical background:

"Annie Laurie"	"Li'l Liza Jane"
"Aura Lee"	"My Bonnie Lies Over the Ocean"
"Darling Nellie Gray"	"My Darling Clementine"
"Delia Gone"	"Nelly Was a Lady"
"Flow Gently, Sweet Afton"	"Oh Susanna"
"Gentle Annie"	"Reuben and Rachel"
"Go Tell Aunt Rhody"	"Sally in Our Alley"
"Go to Sleep, Lena Darling"	"Seeing Nellie Home"
"Good Night, Irene"	"Skip to My Lou"
"I'll Take You Home Again Kathleen"	"The Skye Boat Song"
"Jeanie with the Light Brown Hair"	"Sweet Genevieve"
"Juanita"	"Sweet Marie"
"Kathleen Mavoureen"	'Sweet Molly Malone"

Arrange the group in SATB order for harmony. Record or videotape the sing-along to share with clubs, church organizations, the home-bound, or retirement centers.

Budget: $$$

Sources:

Gamse, Albert, ed. *World's Favorite Folk Songs*. Ashley Publications, 1961.

The Golden Book of Favorite Songs. Schmitt, Hall & McCreary, 1951.

Wenner, Hilda E., and Elizabeth Freilicher. *Here's to the Women: 100 Songs For and About American Women*. Feminist Press, 1995.

Alternative Applications: Comment on the historic, religious, and social context of folk music. Note that "Aura Lee" was a Civil War favorite on both sides of the conflict. As to be expected from lonely men in wartime, soldiers sang of pleasures and comforts that were missing from the battlefield. Aura Lee, a lovely, light-hearted "maid with golden hair," recalls the girls with fresh-bathed skin, fragrant hair, and smiling eyes who wait at home for the return of their brothers, husbands, cousins, lovers, friends, and neighbors. In contrast, soldiers know a daily life of hunger, vermin, dirty clothes, tedium, marching, fighting, and death. How did the singing of an idealized love relieve tensions and replace grim reality with pleasant illusions? How are women portrayed in folk songs from other cultures and in other moments from history, as in Robert Louis Stevenson's "Skye Boat Song"?

Women *in the 'toons*

Age/Grade Level or Audience: High school journalism or creative writing composition; college journalist or communications research topic; scout or 4-H project; women's studies seminar; school newspaper column; open forum; radio or television feature.

Description: Analyze the female character roles in comic strips.

Procedure: Have participants work in pairs to determine what female roles dominate the most popular comic strips of today and yesterday. Suggest a list of questions to help readers systemize their research. Continue the study over a period of weeks so that current-cartoon readers can get a feel for the female roles they are summarizing. Include these queries and suggested figures to study for answers:

- Does this cartoon depict a stereotype, a strong individual, or a group of women or girls who weakly mimic real life? (overreacting adult women in "Baby Blues," the mother in "Mother Goose and Grimm," secretary in "Judge Parker," female shoppers in "Cathy," Honey in "Doonesbury," Lucy van Pelt or Peppermint Patty in "Peanuts")

- Do women form a strong image of home life as mothers, wives, workers, and community leaders? ("Sally Forth," "Lu Ann," "Jump Start," "Rose Is Rose," "Blondie")

- Do girls grow up in nurturing, supportive atmospheres where they feel free to be themselves? (most women in "Doonesbury," students in "Safe Havens," women in "Funky Winkerbean," Hilary in "Sally Forth," April and Elizabeth in "For Better or Worse")

- Are there negative qualities that overbalance or overwhelm the positive aspects of female images, particularly predictable responses or overdone caricatures and facial features? (medieval women in "Real Life Adventures" and "The Wizard of Id," women in "That's Jake," mother and daughter in "9 Chickweed Lane," General Halftrack's secretary in "Beetle Bailey," Jon's veterinarian and infrequent dates in "Garfield," clothing and posture of comic women in "Close to Home")

- Is there an intentional absence of women or girls in the strip? ("Frank and Ernest," "Ziggy," "Garfield," "The Amazing Spiderman," "Beetle Bailey," "The Born Loser," "Marvin," "Mark Trail")

- Is there an air of unreal, comic, or snide humor that prevents the character from escaping a one-dimensional life or an outdated lifestyle? (mother in "Baby Blues," "Listen, Honey . . .," "Suburban Cowgirls," "Nancy," "The Lockhorns," workers in "Mary Worth," the wife in "Andy Capp," Verandah Tadsworth in "Kudzu," boyish anti-feminism in "Fox Trot," the mother in "The Family Circus," the mother of "Dennis the Menace," women in "Ernie" and "Grin and Bear It")

- Has the comic strip outlived its use in mirroring an effective, thought-provoking character or taken on a soap-opera quality? (most females in "Rex Morgan M.D.," "Nancy," "Hagar," female tourists in "Grin and Bear It," Peppermint Patty in "Peanuts," medieval maidens in "Prince Valiant," the title character in "Mary Worth," helpless female victims in "The Amazing Spiderman," "Mickey Mouse")

Consider others from this list:

mother and girls	"Hi and Lois"
Brenda Starr	"Brenda Starr"
Gladys	"The Born Loser"
Sally	"Peanuts"
Minnie Mouse	"Mickey Mouse"
Mrs. Wilson	"Dennis the Menace"
Loretta	"The Lockhorns"

housewives	"Close to Home"
brides	"Kudzu"
king's mother, Rodney's girlfriend	"The Wizard of Id"
mother, salesclerks	"Cathy"
wife and secretary	"Beetle Bailey"
secretary	"Judge Parker"
mother	"Curtis"
medieval maidens	"Prince Valiant"
cavewomen	"B.C."
female friends	"Where I'm Coming From"

Budget: $$

Sources:

"Cathy Guisewite." *Biography Today*. Omnigraphics, 1993.

Herman, Valli. "Sure, 'Cathy' Cartoon Is Obsessed with Fashion." *Charlotte Observer*, February 5, 1995, 1E, 5E.

Robbins, Trina. *A Century of Women Cartoonists*. Kitchen Sink, 1993.

Sheridan, Martin. *Comics and Their Creators: Life Stories of American Cartoonists*. Hyperion, 1993.

Alternative Applications: Apply this study to other characterizations of women in comedy. Study female roles individually and as an interrelated group on television sitcoms. Look for stereotypes, worn-out humor, invisible female roles, predictable responses, caricature, and overacting. How have women's characters evolved over long-running situation comedies like *I Love Lucy, The Mary Tyler Moore Show,* or *All in the Family*? Include a look at contemporary shows such as *Murphy Brown,* or *Cybill* as well as syndicated programs like *MASH, Cheers, The Jeffersons, Happy Days, The Carol Burnett Show,* and *The Brady Bunch.*

Interdisciplinary *activities*

A day *in the colonies*

Age/Grade Level or Audience: Playschool, home school, kindergarten or elementary history dramatization; 4-H or scout activity; PTA program; civic presentation; children's improvisational theater scenarios.

Description: Organize groups of students to present a typical day in the life of a girl or woman living in the American Colonies.

Procedure: Have students join in groups of appropriate size to present activities common to the lives of female colonists, including Native Americans, citizens, visitors, indentured servants, and slaves. Allow students to select any method of presentation. Suggest the following models:

- Act out a day at market with housewives and servants purchasing fowl, eggs, herbs, yard goods, shot, powder, sewing thread, hoop skirts, ribbons, shoe buckles, medicine, green vegetables, fruit, tea, coffee, hardtack, and other necessities. Make change from British coinage or trade goods for goods; for example, homemade brushes and brooms or fine embroidery for ink and homemade paper, or trade goods for services, such as babysitting, singing lessons, use of a breeder horse or bull, or goat milk for a year in exchange for a set of betty lamps, wicks, and fuel. Barter with Native Americans for corn, pumpkins, and wild cherry bark to supply the family with cough medicine.

- Help the youngest children at a dame school learn to count, cipher, and draw letters on a slate. Assist the second level of students in writing letters with quill pens and pokeberry ink on parchment. Supervise older students in sewing samplers with homilies taken from the *Book of Common Prayer, New England Primer, Poor Richard's Almanack,* or John Bunyan's *Pilgrim's Progress.* Lead the entire group in singing the Doxology or reciting Psalm 8 or 121. Conclude with a group activity; for example, the recitation of a favorite poem by Phillis Wheatley or a game of Simon Says.

- Supervise the work of indentured servants and slaves in the preservation of summer fruit, particularly apples for cider, scuppernongs for wine, grapes for raisins, and rings of pumpkin or winter squash dried in the sun as a base for stew, soup, or succotash. Help participants thread waxed cording through a needle to string leather breeches beans to be dried over a hearth. Assign workers to draw water from the common well, hull corn, stir kettles of hominy, melt tallow for dipping candles, salt meat and fish, and boil down maple syrup. With the help of Native Americans, bind sweet grass and tie herbs in small bunches to hang upside down from the rafters and be crushed later into grease or oil to make salves and poultices. Supervise the repair of wattle-and-daub walls and the storage of wood splits in the lean-to for easy access to the hearth.

- Greet an incoming schooner bearing relatives from England. Welcome them to homes where plump feather mattresses and warm woolen coverlets await and friends taking meals at the trestle table renew old acquaintances. Retire to the common room to ask questions about life under Oliver Cromwell's Puritan rule in the English Commonwealth (1649–1660) or the glorious return of the monarchy with the coronation of Charles II in 1660. Conclude the dinner with mulled cider in pewter flagons which are warmed at the fireside with a plunge of a hot poker and passed around like a loving cup. Join in singing the "Doxology" or "Blessed Be the Tie That Binds."

- Present a colonial recipe album such as Paul Revere's *The Frugal Housewife* (1772), containing detailed descriptions of succotash, one-dish stews and boiled dinners, persimmon pudding, cottage cheese, samp, journeycake, crullers, hasty pudding, and beer. Record recipes in this form:

Home-Churned Butter

Take new milk, strain into a kettle, and let settle until it thickens. Churn and pour off whey. Rinse butter in four changes of water. Stir in salt and flavorings, herb seeds, or dried dill leaves. Beat; let stand for an hour; beat again. Layer into a butter pot and cover with a generous topping of rock salt.

Peas Porridge

In a kettle of boiling salted water pour an equal amount of green peas, sidemeat, and a twist of dried mint. Season with coarse pepper. Thicken with a ball of butter dipped in flour. Stir to a full boil, then pour in two quarts of milk or cream. Remove mint and serve with crusty sourdough loaves.

Hasty Pudding

Boil salted water in a kettle before drizzling in handfuls of cornmeal. Stir until the mixture thickens. Dot with butter and ladle into bowls. Serve with a splash of molasses or syrup and a dusting of ground nutmeg.

Pilgrim Cake

Cut two tablespoons of butter into a quart of flour. Add enough cold water to form a stiff dough. Roll out an inch thick and dust top and bottom with flour. Place in hot ashes and cover with coals. Cook until dry to the touch.

- Prepare your family for a spring departure through Indian territory to a farm beyond the Allegheny Mountains in Lenni Lenape land. Check the wagon for tight axle fittings, sound wheels, cookware, dried goods, salt, medicine, blankets, firearms, and utensils. As you depart from your dwelling in the colonies, say farewell to the people who have been faithful friends and neighbors. Leave behind items too fragile to carry, such as a spinet, framed portrait, rocking chair, or window glass.

Budget: $$

Sources:

Bracken, Jeanne Munn, ed. *Life in the American Colonies: Daily Lifestyles of the Early Settlers*. Discovery Enterprises, 1995.

Encyclopedia of the North American Colonies. Scribner's, 1993.

Hawke, David Freeman. *Everyday Life in Early America.* Harper & Row, 1988.

Miller, Arthur. *The Crucible.* Vintage, 1954.

Petry, Ann. *Tituba of Salem Village.* HarperCollins, 1964.

Revere, Paul. *The Frugal Housewife.* N.p., n.d.

Richter, Conrad. *The Light in the Forest.* Bantam, 1953.

The Scarlet Letter. PBS, n.d. (Video)

Speare, Elizabeth George. *The Sign of the Beaver.* Dell, 1983.

————. *The Witch of Blackbird Pond.* Dell, 1958.

Stenson, Elizabeth. *Early Settler Activity Guide.* Crabtree, 1993.

Three Sovereigns for Sister Sarah. N.p., n.d. (Video)

Washburne, Carolyn Kott. *A Multicultural Portrait of Colonial Life.* Marshall Cavendish, 1994.

Alternative Applications: Have participants work together to compose letters home from overworked colonial women to friends, authorities, relatives, or neighbors. Tell the most interesting facts about life in the colonies, for example, relations with the Lenni Lenape, scarlet fever, sugaring off the maples, celebrating the new year, worship in a new chapel, schooners entering the harbor, buying ribbons at the market, and listening to the beadle read proclamations from George III encouraging the colonists to work hard and establish trade in hides, corn, rum, molasses, tobacco, and slaves. Inquire about dentists, coopers, printers, and tinkers who might want to immigrate and set up practice in the colonies. Discuss why colonial parents encouraged males either to enter colleges to learn professions (medicine, law, ministry) or to sign apprentice papers to study skills needed in the New World. Comment on the need for engineers and doctors.

Comment on the outlook for a young girl's future and education. Describe the difficulties unique to the female colonist due to the lack of plumbing, pure water, midwives, health care, labor-saving devices, and suitable sewing materials. Explain how families spend anxious days in the fort when there is danger of Indian attack. Name games that children and parents play to pass the time—making cornshuck dolls, stringing seeds and nuts into jewelry, practicing archery and bowls, dancing the Virginia Reel or gavottes, and playing shovelboard, draughts, nine man's morris, kitty-in-the-corner, and I Spy.

Dressed *in pants and fighting like men*

Age/Grade Level or Audience: Middle school or high school history database; genealogy or history presentation; term paper on a military topic; media column or miniseries focus; map study.

Description: Organize a data search on women who entered the military in the guise of male warriors and spies.

Procedure: Have students divide into groups to list and collect data on women who fought as men in various wars. Include these:

- Deborah Sampson, Revolutionary War patriot who earned a veteran's pension in 1818

- Lyons Wakeman (Sarah Rosetta Wakeman), who died at age 21 after seeing action in Louisiana, one of 400 female Union and Confederate soldiers among three million males

- Private Franklin Thompson (Emma E. Edwards), who composed "Nurse and Spy," a journal of her role in the 2nd Michigan Volunteers

Locate information on other female soldiers. Name the five who fought at Antietam. Note that one died in action and two were wounded. Read aloud from letters and diaries in which the women report steady wages to support their families. Name other reasons for taking on the guise of a male soldier, including patriotism, urge for adventure, economic independence, and nearness of brothers and mates in battle. Comment on methods of concealing their identity by binding their breasts, lowering their voices, and concealing their gender until death (treatment in field hospitals, or pregnancy gave away their secrets.) Create a multidisciplinary tribute to female soldiers, including a diorama, skits, outdoor drama, brochure, or local festival. Hold annual contests for children to depict battle scenes, create special medals of honor, or make speeches honoring women willing to hide their gender to fight for their country.

Budget: $$$$$

Sources:

Colman, Penny. *Spies! Women in the Civil War.* Betterway Books, 1992.

Emert, Phyllis Raybin, ed. *Women in the Civil War: Warriors, Patriots, Nurses, and Spies.* Discovery Enterprises, 1995.

Griffin, Lynne, and Kelly McCann. *The Book of Women: 300 Notable Women History Passed By.* Bob Adams, 1992.

Hall, Richard. *Patriots in Disguise.* Paragon House, 1993.

Middleton, Lee. *Hearts of Fire.* Lee Middleton, 1993.

Wheelwright, Julie. *Amazons and Military Maids.* Pandora, 1989.

Alternative Applications: Using desktop publishing, compose an illustrated study of a famous cross-dressing soldier such as Lyons Wakeman, the alias of Sarah Rosetta Wakeman. Mention these details:

- Born in 1843 on a farm near Afton, New York, Wakeman served in the 153rd New York State Volunteers as a private from 1862–1864, guarding her secret by keeping her hair cropped and her breasts bound. A daguerreotype pictures her in uniform with official bandolier, rifle, and bayonet.

- The Wakemans needed the money Sarah sent them from her pay, but were so humiliated by her adventuresome spirit that not even her brothers and sisters knew of her military service.

- Wakeman performed well at the battle of Pleasant Hill and wrote in her letter of August 1863 that she was not afraid to die in battle and that she preferred never to return home to a woman's identity because she enjoyed the freedom of pretending to be male.

- After the Red River campaign, she died near New Orleans, Louisiana, of dysentery and is buried in Chalmette National Cemetery alongside other soldiers under a simple plaque that gives no clue to her secret identity.

Experiencing *womanhood*

Age/Grade Level or Audience: Middle school or high school writing or humanities interdisciplinary oral report; book club or literary society activity; Friends of the Library summer reading project; local panel discussion celebrating Women's History Month; religious study.

Description: Organize a month-long individualized study of contemporary women's lives.

Procedure: Assign participants a single twentieth-century life to study from many angles as a preface to an oral report. Choose, for example:

politician Corazon Aquino	social worker Mother Teresa
physician Jean Auel	journalist Deborah Norville
singer Kathleen Battle	professor Lotsee Patterson
runner Zola Budd	classicist Mary Renault
philanthropist Louise M. Davies	fiction writer Jane Smiley
novelist Lucille Elliott	autobiographer Yoko Kawashima Watkins
actress Audrey Hepburn	psychologist Jane Wheelwright
potter Jacomena Maybeck	actress Suzy Wong

Encourage each presenter to use diverse methods: fictional interview, biographical handout, filmstrip, video, CD, and posters. Follow this model or adapt your own method of demonstrating the female experience of syndicated columnist and author Erma Bombeck:

1. *Summarize early influences*
Erma Louise Bombeck, born February 21, 1927, in Dayton, Ohio, learned the art of compromise before the age of ten. After her father died in 1936, her mother worked in a factory and remarried, adding a half-sister, Thelma, to the family.

2. *Preparation for a career*
Longing to be a writer, Erma attended Patterson Vocational High School, studied the humorists of her day, and worked as copy girl for the Dayton *Journal-Herald*. A degree in English from the University of Dayton moved her to feature writer for the women's section, the usual role of women in journalism at that time. She married sportswriter Bill Bombeck, adopted daughter Betsy, and gave birth to two boys, Andy and Matthew. Into the 1950s, she lived the suburban stereotype in Centerville, Ohio.

3. *Note pivotal moments*
At age 37, Bombeck initiated a humor column for the Kettering-Oakwood *Times,* then returned to the *Journal-Herald.* Her columns, now carried by 200 newspapers, burgeoned into a syndicated feature.

4. *Results*
A forthright writer with name recognition and a unique voice that is both witty and satiric, she accepted a slot on Arthur Godfrey's radio program and appeared on the *Tonight* show. By the 1970s, writing from a garage studio in Phoenix, Arizona, she was a major player in the women's humor market.

5. *Reading*
At this point, the presenter could read aloud from one of Bombeck's books or columns or present a video clip or audio reading that captures the quick-draw drollery that is the author's trademark.

6. *Outlook*
Still producing columns and volumes of humor, Bombeck remains a household friend, the voice that puts into quip the raw edge of female work-a-day frustration.

7. *Handout*
The presenter may want to offer aphorisms, a time line, or a list of titles available in book stores or libraries in print, video, or audiocassette.

Budget: $$$

Sources:

Bailey, Brooke. *The Remarkable Lives of 100 Women Artists.* Bob Adams, 1994.

———. *The Remarkable Lives of 100 Women Healers and Scientists.* Bob Adams, 1994.

———. *The Remarkable Lives of 100 Women Writers and Journalists.* Bob Adams, 1994.

Battelle, Phyllis. "Erma Bombeck: Worries Behind Her Wit." *Woman's Day,* January 21, 1986, 75–80.

Bombeck, Erma. *Aunt Erma's Cope Book.* McGraw Hill, 1979.

———. *Family: The Ties That Bind . . . and Gag!* McGraw Hill, 1987.

———. *I Lost Everything in the Post-natal Depression.* Doubleday, 1970.

———. *I Want to Grow Hair, I Want to Grow Up, I Want to Go to Boise.* Harper & Row, 1989.

———. *If Life Is a Bowl of Cherries—What Am I Doing in the Pits?* McGraw Hill, 1978.

———. *Just Wait Till You Have Children of Your Own!* Doubleday, 1971.

———. *Motherhood: The Second Oldest Profession.* McGraw Hill, 1983.

———. *When You Look Like Your Passport Photo, It's Time to Go Home.* Caedmon, 1994. (Audiocassette)

Current Biography. H. W. Wilson, 1979.

Griffin, Lynne, and Kelly McCann. *The Book of Women: 300 Notable Women History Passed By.* Bob Adams, 1992.

Mills, Kay. *From Pocahontas to Power Suits.* Plume, 1995.

Painter, Charlotte. *Gifts of Age.* Chronicle Books, 1985.

A Salute to Historic Black Women. Empak Enterprises, 1984.

Skow, John. "Erma Bombeck: Dingbat Neighbor Supreme." *Reader's Digest* (Canadian Edition), February, 1985, 65.

———. "Erma in Bomburbia: For a Survivor of Housework and Motherhood, Laughter Is Still the Best Revenge." *Time,* July 2, 1981, 56–63.

———. "Erma Bombeck: Syndicated Soul of Suburbia." *Reader's Digest,* February, 1984, 39–46.

Alternative Applications: Form a group and assign a study of a woman's life. Conduct a panel or group session during which participants discuss five topics:

1. early influences
2. preparation for a career
3. pivotal moments
4. successes and failures
5. outlook

Invite participants to present any evidence of uniqueness in their studies, including readings, photos, art, film, videos, recordings, interviews, or personal appearances. Contrast the subject with others in the same class or age, for example suffragists, scientists, artists, politicians, rulers, inventors, or athletes.

Marjory *Stoneman Douglas: defender of nature*

Age/Grade Level or Audience: Elementary school Earth Day celebration; school or community library presentation; zoo or museum seminar; garden club program; women's studies newsletter; media column; civic or neighborhood Women's History Month event; Sierra Club or local ecology project.

Description: Celebrate the life, writings, and work of Marjory Stoneman Douglas.

Procedure: Hold a recognition ceremony on Earth Day or May Day to discuss the goals and methods of Marjory Stoneman Douglas, writer, editor, traveler, and preserver of Florida's Everglades. Note that as assistant editor of the *Miami Herald,* she made Americans appreciate the tenuous balance of life threatened by human intrusion, traffic, herding, run-off, hurricanes, and overdevelopment. Appoint presenters to describe various stages of Douglas's crusade to preserve the wilds of southern Florida. Comment on these facts about her life:

- Marjory Douglas treasured the Everglades as a rare home of animals since her first visit to Tampa, Florida, by train and ship in 1894, when she first saw and heard these:

alligator	diamondback rattler	panther
bald eagle	great white heron	raccoon
black bear	kite	roseate spoonbill
bobcat	liguus tree snail	snowy egret
box turtle	limpkin	turkey vulture
brown deer	manatee	white-tailed deer
brown pelican	opossum	wood ibis
buzzard	osprey	woodpecker
cougar	otter	wood stork

- Also, she wanted to preserve the watery habitats of plants and trees such as these:

custard apple	mangrove	strangler fig
cypress tree	orchid	succulents
duckweed	palmetto	waterlily
gumbo limbo	river hyacinth	wax myrtle
mahogany	saw grass	willow

Douglas loved Lake Okeechobee in all its moods: from the thin trickle in the north during high summer drought to the roar of the Gulf of Mexico in the south in hurricane season.

Before beginning individualized projects, clear up questions by defining difficult words, such as woody hammock, interaction, conservation, deterioration, wetlands, and ecology. Have participants choose to work alone or in groups to create a thank-you to Marjory Stoneman Douglas. Suggest several possibilities, including these:

- animal mobile of endangered species
- library table decoration depicting a ride in a dugout, pirogue, or airboat
- mobile of Everglades birds and ducks
- mural depicting how asphalt parking lots and overdevelopment bring more people to an area than nature can provide for
- series of bookmarks featuring plants and animals of the wild
- shadow box depicting Seminole life on the lagoon

- terrarium holding plants common to the Everglades
- topographical map of Florida and the Keys

Present the finished thank-yous at a PTA parents' night meeting, Friends of the Library session, or school assembly period.

Budget: $$$

Sources:

Bryant, Jennifer. *Marjory Stoneman Douglas: Voice of the Everglades.* Twenty-First Century Books, 1992.

Douglas, Marjory S., and John Rothchild. *Marjory Stoneman Douglas: Voice of the River.* Pineapple Press, 1987.

Morgan, Cheryl. *Everglades.* Troll, 1990.

Sawyer, Kem Knapp. *Marjory Stoneman Douglas: Guardian of the Everglades.* Discovery Enterprises, 1994.

Alternative Applications: Have students divide Marjory Stoneman Douglas's life into segments and discuss these and other influences that empowered her: childhood rambles and reading, study at Wellesley, suffragist activism, bicycling the wilds, journalism, entering the Navy during World War I, Red Cross volunteer work, meeting refugees, visiting the Balkans, editing the *Miami Herald,* founding Fairfield Tropical Garden, traveling the Tamiami Trail, assisting the poor in Coconut Grove, writing short stories, stopping egret poaching, meeting Calusa and Tequesta Indians, tracing the journeys of Ponce de Leon, sailing in the Keys, visiting Seminoles, interviewing Jesuits in Cuba, touring Florida before writing an official history, directing the University of Miami Press, and being named Conservationist of the Year.

Mythic *women*

Age/Grade Level or Audience: Elementary reading or language listing; summer reading project; computer database.

Description: Organize a study of the female mythic prototype, which undergirds much of literature, film, art, and social interaction.

Procedure: Have students isolate the essential data of a mythic prototype. Use these models from Greek, Roman, and Hebrew mythology as starting points:

- Aphrodite/Venus—goddess of passion and romance
- Artemis/Diana—goddess of nature and the hunt
- Athene/Minerva—goddess of wisdom and war
- Demeter/Ceres—goddess of the hearth and grain, goddess of the cycle of the seasons
- Hera/Juno—goddess of married love and childbirth
- Nemesis—embodiment of recompense or punishment
- Pandora/Eve—curious meddler who brought unhappiness to a perfect world
- Psyche—embodiment of the soul, longing, and desire

Ask students to apply the personal traits, foibles, and misdeeds of each goddess to characters in a current movie, television program, or book. For example, discuss how blaming the Pandora/Eve figure for human sin constitutes scapegoating, thus settling on the shoulders of females the problems inherent in all human behavior.

Balance the study of Pandora with an examination of Demeter/Ceres, the Earth mother who searches Earth and the underworld for Persephone/Proserpina, her kidnapped daughter. Narrate how Demeter/Ceres refuses to adorn Earth with green growing things while her daughter is kept prisoner in the underworld.

Budget: $

Sources:

Bell, Robert. *Women of Classical Mythology.* ABC-Clio, 1991.

Bulfinch, Thomas. *Bulfinch's Mythology.* Harper, 1959.

Campbell, Joseph. *Myths to Live By.* Bantam, 1984.

Cavendish, Marshall, ed. *Man, Myth, and Magic.* Marshall Cavendish, 1970.

Feder, Lillian. *The Meridian Handbook of Classical Literature.* New American Library, 1986.

Hamilton, Edith. *Mythology.* New American Library, 1969.

Larrington, Carolyn, ed. *The Feminist Companion to Mythology.* Pandora Press, 1992.

Rosenberg, Donna. *World Mythology.* Passport Books, 1992.

Alternative Applications: Have groups act out pivotal scenes involving male-female relationships in mythology. Ask observers to note stereotypes in reactions, prejudices, and social roles. Begin with these models:

- Echo's pursuit of the handsome Narcissus

- Leda's seduction by Zeus, who comes to her in the form of a handsome swan

- Psyche's curiosity about Cupid, her mysterious lover

- Medea's mystical powers of Jason

- Arachne's explanation of a way out of the labyrinth

- Aphrodite's unfairness at the judgment of Paris

New *books for old*

Age/Grade Level or Audience: High school desktop history publication; summer library or after-school project

Description: Design a woman-centered book on the Civil War.

Procedure: Organize a textbook or reference work on the Civil War as seen through the eyes of women. Include significant shifts from the usual male-centered work as exemplified in:

- recipes such as ground okra coffee and sugarless cracker-crumb pies created to make the most of local supplies during blockades and shortages

- maps of the underground railroad movement and locations of major nursing centers, aid stations, and rehabilitation hospitals

- pictures of typical garments worn by laundresses, female cooks, plantation managers, nurses, innkeepers, mill owners, child-care providers, wetnurses, and women passing as soldiers

249

- summaries or excerpts from letters, journals, diaries, and interviews with women, including slave narratives and details of women tackling civic, business, transportation, agricultural, parish, and management jobs

- popular songs that featured women, particularly "Lorena," "Gentle Annie," and "Aura Lee," one of the most popular love songs of the mid-1800s

- speeches, encomiums, poetry, novels, and short stories by and about women

- eyewitness accounts of battles, routs, training, aid stations, dispossessed families, and night riders

- General Butler's proclamation that the women of New Orleans were to respect Union occupation troops

- photos, sketches, or descriptions of art, sculpture, needlework, and architecture designed or built for and by women

- school curricula taught by women, especially those lessons offered to illiterate slaves

Include short biographies of women who achieved fame by daring to compete in a male-dominated era. Include these:

author Louisa May Alcott	religious leader Catherine Ferguson
journalist Myrta L. Avary	stagecoach driver Mary Fields
nurse Clara Barton	diarist Charlotte Forten
chronicler Fannie Beers	secessionist Rose O'Neal Greenhow
nurse Mary Ann Bickerdyke	volunteer Victoria Henderson
spy Belle Boyd	First Lady Mary Todd Lincoln
teacher Sophronia Bucklin	abolitionist Hannah Ropes
diarist Mary Boykin Chesnut	publisher Mary Ann Shadd
administrator Kate Cumming	novelist Harriet Beecher Stowe
soldier Pauline Cushman	preacher Sojourner Truth
diarist Maria Lydia Daly	spy Harriet Tubman
soldier Sarah Emma Edmonds	banker Maggie Walker

Comment, in a preface or overview, on the vacuum left by men gone to war and the jobs that women had to undertake to keep day-to-day life as normal as possible while also supplying men with shoes, food, armaments, letters, and emotional support.

Budget: $$$

Sources:

Davis, William C. *The Civil War Cookbook*. Courage Books, 1993.

Emert, Phyllis Raybin, ed. *Women in the Civil War: Warriors, Patriots, Nurses, and Spies*. Discovery Enterprises, 1995.

Historical Atlas of the United States. National Geographic, 1993.

Jordan, Robert Paul. *The Civil War*. National Geographic, 1969.

Mitchell, Margaret. *Gone with the Wind*. Warner Books, 1993.

Morrison, Toni. *Beloved*. New American Library, 1987.

Paulsen, Gary. *Nightjohn*. Doubleday, 1993.

Stowe, Harriet Beecher. *Uncle Tom's Cabin*. HarperCollins, 1965.

Alternative Applications: Audiotape daily dispatches from the front that cover the activities and work of women on the Civil War battlefield. Alternate voices from South and North. Comment on the pragmatism of nurses, volunteers, and cooks who had to improvise shelter and cook and care for the wounded and whose daily existence was threatened by imminent invasion, shelling, disease, starvation, rape, or execution.

The New *England bluestocking*

Age/Grade Level or Audience: High school drama improvisation; literary club seminar; school or community library presentation; Unitarian Universalist convention; women's studies topic; media column; civic or neighborhood celebration of Women's History Month.

Description: Hold a seminar on the importance of Margaret Fuller, the key female transcendentalist.

Procedure: Organize a multimedia study of transcendentalism. Follow these suggestions as exercises, springboards to discussion, or areas of research:

Begin with an extended definition of these terms:

bluestocking	Immanuel Kant	oversoul
commune	intellectualism	philosophical romanticism
epistemology	intuition	transcendentalism
idealism	Lyceum	unitarianism
idyll	mysticism	

Describe the Transcendental Club and the work of these and other members:

Bronson Alcott	Ralph Waldo Emerson	Mariana Ripley
Louisa May Alcott	Sarah Margaret Fuller	Sophia Willard Ripley
Ellery Channing	Elizabeth Palmer Peabody	Henry David Thoreau

Read aloud the journal overview of Brook Farm written by Kate Sloan Gaskill in June 1843 when she and her widowed mother moved to Pilgrim House, a commune that became their residence for three years. Comment on the break with traditional dress in women's bloomers, men's tunics, and brimmed hats adorned with wild flowers.

Express the ideals of Margaret Fuller in her weekly sessions held at Elizabeth Peabody's bookstore on West Street in the 1840s. Note contributions from the female perspective in *The Dial* (edited by Fuller), *The Western Messenger, Boston Quarterly Review, Spirit of the Age, Harbinger, The Present, Aesthetic Papers,* and *The Massachusetts Quarterly Review* as well as Margaret Fuller's 1848 feminist classic *Woman in the Nineteenth Century.*

Express the influence of transcendentalism on the poetry of Emily Dickinson and the theology of Mary Baker Eddy.

Discuss the role of abolitionism and the beginning of the Civil War in fueling controversy and ending the Transcendentalist Club.

Budget: $

Sources:

Balducci, Carolyn. *Margaret Fuller*. Bantam, 1991.

Blanchard, Paula. *Margaret Fuller: From Transcendentalism to Revolution*. Addison-Wesley, 1987.

Hansen, Ellen, ed. *The New England Transcendentalists: Life of the Mind and of the Spirit*. Discovery Enterprises, 1993.

Stern, Madeleine. *The Life of Margaret Fuller*. Greenwood, 1991.

Wilson, Ellen. *Margaret Fuller: Bluestocking, Romantic, Revolutionary*. Farrar, Straus and Giroux, 1977.

Alternative Applications: Express in a collage the basic elements of transcendentalism. Include the concepts of freedom from ritual and governmental interference, development of the individual, respect for manual labor, encouragement of education for women, and support of abolitionism and women's suffrage. Cite lines from Elizabeth Fuller's works, for example:

- The character and history of each child may be a new and poetic experience to the parents, if he will let it.

- No temple can still the personal griefs and strifes in the breasts of its visitors.

- A house is no home unless it contain food and fire for the mind as well as for the body.

- Man is not made for society, but society is made for man. No institution can be good which does not tend to improve the individual.

- A great work of art demands a great thought, or a thought of beauty adequately expressed. Neither in art nor literature more than in life can an ordinary thought be made interesting because [it is] well dressed.

- Male and female represent the two sides of the great radical dualism. But, in fact, they are perpetually passing into one another. Fluid hardens to solid, solid rushes to fluid. There is no wholly masculine man, no purely feminine woman.

Who *was Mona Lisa?*

Age/Grade Level or Audience: Middle school or high school interdisciplinary unit; book club or literary society study; Friends of the Library presentation; local panel discussion celebrating Women's History Month.

Description: Organize a thorough study of Mona Lisa.

Procedure: Appoint a task force to research the most enigmatic female model in art history. Study the various interpretations of the life of Leonardo da Vinci and his association with the model who posed for the portrait of Mona Lisa. Note these few data:

- Leonardo fled Milan in 1499 during an attack by the French on the Sforza family and returned to Florence, where he was born. From 1503–1506, he worked at the "Mona Lisa" as a portrait of Lisa del Giocondo, a 24-year-old middle-class woman, the wife of Francesco di Bartolommeo del Giocondo, a local merchant.

- The unfinished work, which the French call "La Gioconda," is named for an elision of "Madonna" Lisa, meaning "My Lady." Treasured and much imitated, the portrait is housed in the Louvre Museum in Paris. Because of its subtlety, perspective, aerial mastery, and hazy, dreamlike sfumato effect, the portrait is considered one of the complex oil masterworks of all time.

- Critics continue to puzzle over Da Vinci's concept of womanhood and the intriguing sensuality and faint disdain in her facial expression. The intensely detailed background suggests an Edenic setting, thus implying that Mona Lisa is Eve, the quintessential mythic female who tempted her mate to defy God.

Budget: $

Sources:

Boorstin, Daniel J. *The Creators: A History of Heroes of the Imagination.* Vintage Books, 1992.
Lepsky, Ibi. *Leonardo Da Vinci.* Barron, 1992.
McMullen, Roy. *Mona Lisa: The Picture and the Myth.* Da Capo, 1977.
Nat King Cole: All-Time Greatest Hits. Creative Concepts. (Recording)
Wallace, Robert. *The World of Leonardo, 1452–1519.* Time-Life Books, 1966.

Alternative Applications: Compare the artistic representation of Mona Lisa to other portraits by da Vinci, particularly "Ginevra de' Benci," which predates "Mona Lisa" by two decades. Also, compare the model for "Mona Lisa" with the woman in the song by the same name, which Jay Livingston and Ray Evans wrote and Nat King Cole popularized as the Academy Award-winning best song of 1949. Answer these questions about the lyrics:

- Why does lyricist Jay Livingston set the study in a villa in a small Italian town?
- Why does the song's subject resemble the "lady with the mystic smile"?
- To what does the speaker attribute her "strangeness"?
- Why does the speaker assume her heart is broken?
- Why do dreams cease to flourish at her doorstep?
- If she is beautiful, why is she lonely?
- Why does the speaker suspect that she is not real?

A woman-to-woman family tree

Age/Grade Level or Audience: Any-age community activity; 4-H and scout focus; PTA program; family project.

Description: Organize a group study of strong women in a family, neighborhood, church, synagogue, or community.

Procedure: Begin by having a discussion about what constitutes "strength." Ask participants to brainstorm about the characteristics a "strong" woman would affect. Have participants work with tape recorder, camcorder, questionnaires, genealogies, archives, local church and civic records, photo albums, and other sources of information to locate strong women in their backgrounds. Help participants sift through information and locate verifiable claims of important contributions, for example:

- foundation of women's shelters and day care centers
- support of women's rights

- assistance at a women's health care center

- creation of schools and workshops or craft centers for the handicapped

- activist for integration, voter registration, and busing

- record keeping, whether in diaries, letters, film, photographs, journals, books, or formal histories

- support groups and rehabilitation center volunteers during wartime

- creator of murals, quilts, sculpture, beautification projects, herb gardens, bird sanctuaries, playgrounds, or parks

- establishment of businesses, including book shops, catering, hair care, tutoring, job placement, tax preparation, domestic service, or home health care

Use as an example the combined efforts of Clara Hale and her daughter to create Hale House, a shelter for children of alcoholics, drug addicts, and AIDS victims. Depict the combined strengths of females in a single family or community networks by drawing history webs, genealogies, and cause-and-effect charts.

Budget: $$$$

Sources:

"Aids for Genealogical Research." National Archives, 1995.

Benberry, Cuesta. *Always There: The African-American Presence in American Quilts.* Museum of History and Science, 1992.

Doane, Gilbert H., and James B. Bell. *Searching for Your Ancestors: The How and Why of Genealogy.* University of Minnesota Press, 1992.

"Family Folklore." Folklife Programs, Smithsonian Institution.

"Family Folklore: Interviewing Guide and Questionnaire." U.S. Department of Commerce, Bureau of the Census, U. S. Government Printing Office, 1990.

Hay, Susannah. *The Women's Heritage Scrapbook.* Caillech Press, 1992.

Helmbold, F. Wilbur. *Tracing Your Ancestry: A Step-by-Step Guide to Researching Your Family History.* Oxmoor House, 1976.

Ki-Zerbo, Joseph. "Oral Tradition as a Historical Source." *UNESCO Courier,* April 1990, 43–46.

"Our Family, Our Town: Essays on Family and Local History Sources in the National Archives." National Archives and Records Administration, n.d.

Alternative Applications: Arrange in chronological order a group of family or community photos displaying the skills and strengths of women of all ages and interests. Create a video by photographing the photos against a background of appropriate music and captions or against a recorded voice-over telling who and what is important or worthy of celebration. Include these and other events: military swearing-in, the arrival of immigrants at airports or port authority, graduations or entrance into training programs, uniforms and hands at work, social committees, neighborhood improvement projects, political campaigns, anniversaries, church socials, building projects, assistance to the poor and needy, and recreation or sports programs for the handicapped.

Women *volunteers*

Age/Grade Level or Audience: City-wide celebration; civic club symposium; Friends of the Library activity; local Women's History Month media release or poster.

Description: Highlight local women's groups and organizations that have historically benefitted the community and honor newly formed groups that carry on the torch.

Procedure: Have groups join in a city-wide celebration of women who volunteer in established and newly formed organizations. Use these models:

- moonlight serenade by a barbershop quartet at the home of a pro-choice activist or women's clinic volunteer

- mass mailing of thank-you notes to grade mothers and guidance department volunteers

- candy kisses distributed to women who serve meals and snacks or entertain at an AIDS clinic or veteran's hospital

- billboard signed by grateful recipients of volunteer aid from a women's auxiliary of the fire or police department or rescue squad

- book marks, tray mats, lapel buttons, and bumper stickers proclaiming the work of a women's shelter, genealogical societies, Gray Ladies, Friends of the Library, or hospice

- proclamation of Women of Mercy Week for foster mothers and volunteers to the handicapped, invalids, refugees, and orphanages

- concerted effort to include all girls in Take Our Daughters to Work Day by spreading information well in advance, offering transportation for disadvantaged girls, opening military academies to the project, opening online information about careers for women, and pairing disabled girls with suitable job possibilities.

Budget: $$$

Sources:

Angus, Susan G. *Invest Yourself: the Catalogue of Volunteer Opportunities.* Community Voluntary Service and Action, 1993.

Bayh, Marvella, with Mary Lynn Kotz, ed. "My Fight Against Cancer." *Life,* October 1978, 54.

Bayh, Marvella, with Mary Lynn Kotz. *Marvella: A Personal Journey.* Harcourt Brace Jovanovich, 1979.

"Girls Around the World." *Montreal Gazette,* April 24, 1995, E3.

Kelly, Joyce. "CHA Project House Call." *Chicago Tribune,* June 25, 1995, Sect. 6, 3.

Woodworth, David. *The International Directory of Voluntary Work.* Peterson's Guides, 1993.

Zuger, Abigail. *Strong Shadows: Scenes from an Inner City AIDS Clinic.* W. H. Freeman, 1995.

Alternative Applications: Publish in a newspaper column or as a media feature the contributions of Marvella Bayh, champion of early cancer detection and treatment. Stress these facts:

- Marvella Hern Bayh was born February 14, 1933, in rural Lahoma, Oklahoma. A prize student orator, she won the governorship of Oklahoma at Girls' State. After her marriage to Birch Bayh on August 24, 1952, she ran a 450-acre farm while earning degrees in social studies and secondary education.

- Suffering a hormone deficiency and chronic insomnia, Bayh took estrogen, thyroid extract, and tranquilizers, which helped her cope with her father's alcoholism and the demands of being the wife of a U.S. Senator. At age 38, Marvella underwent extensive surgery for breast cancer and began daily radium treatments and eighteen months of chemotherapy.

- In keeping with her education in social service, she agreed to interviews for *Today's Health, Medical Tribune,* and the *National Enquirer* and championed early detection for the American Cancer Society in a televised feature, *The Marvella Bayh Story*. In 1977, as consultant for the Society, she joined Joe Califano, HEW Secretary, in denouncing tobacco products as carcinogens. The American Society of Surgical Oncologists presented her with the James Ewing Memorial Award.

• A year later, cancer metastasized to her upper chest bones. Bayh continued fighting the tobacco lobby and published an autobiography. Weeks before her death on April 24, 1979, she received the Hubert H. Humphrey Inspirational Award for Courage.

Journalism

Extra! *get your history news!*

Age/Grade Level or Audience: Elementary or middle school desktop publishing project; creative writing activity; PTA program; summer library project; teacher education seminar.

Description: Create a newspaper filled with articles about women's historical events.

Procedure: Divide a group into staff members for a history newspaper. Collect data for features, news, lead stories, updates, political cartoons, weather maps, comic strips, book reviews, kid's page, society events, sports, business, and a crossword puzzle. Follow these suggestions:

- Compose a lead story on a suffrage march on Washington, D.C. Follow up with an interview with President Woodrow Wilson concerning his and the First Lady's response to pressures from female citizens for the right to vote. Interview Edith Wilson about her interest in politics.

- Cover cultural events that involve entertainer Lola Montez, painter Ammi Phillips, singer Enya, vocal group Sweet Honey in the Rock, operatic star Leontyne Price, folk singer Buffy Sainte-Marie, actor Mary Pickford, ballerina Marjorie Tallchief, choreographer Pearl Primus, designer Jane Jacobs, architect Gae Aulenti, or sculptor Kathe Kollwitz.

- Summarize important events in women's sports, for example, Zola Budd's unusual running style, Gloria Chadwick's move from skiing to serving as delegate to the women's Olympics, or Carol Lewis's preparations for a winning track event.

- Make a two-page spread of photos and maps detailing the transatlantic flight of Amelia Earhart. Include a before and after flight interview.

- Present fashions from the 1890s. Comment on hobble skirts, corsets, soutache and braid trim, and wide-brimmed plumed hats as well as demure styles in ribbons, dimity, and plissé for young girls.

- Create a comic strip featuring a family living in a boardinghouse in California during the Gold Rush. Describe uproar from claim jumpers, theatrical performances, and general clamor to make California a state.

Round out the newspaper with a variety of appealing photos, drawings, maps, weather reports, and other information from a favorite historical period.

Budget: $$$$$

Sources:

Balcziak, B. *Newspapers*. Rourke, 1989.

Crisman, Ruth. *Hot off the Press*. Lerner, 1990.

Fleming, Thomass. *Behind the Headlines.* Walker & Co., 1989.

Sears Roebuck Catalog, 1897. Chelsea House, 1993.

Walters, Sarah. *How Newspapers Are Made.* Facts on File, 1989.

See also *Old News,* 400 Stackstown Rd., Marietta, PA 17547 (717-426-2212)

Alternative Applications: Make up a mock newspaper or broadside for your town or county as it was a hundred years ago. Emphasize the women who worked, performed, raised families, sold products, or made headlines. Feature an advice column and advertisements for women's needs, particularly laundry products, kitchen devices, child-care products, and sewing needs.

The five w's: *who, what, where, when, why (and how)*

Age/Grade Level or Audience: High school journalism or logic activity; school or public library handout or brochure; writers club presentation; women's studies class; Toastmaster's Club; Women's History Month presentation; women's civic society; pro-choice rally.

Description: Collection and organize data concerning *Roe vs. Wade.*

Procedure: Read a variety of materials on *Roe vs. Wade,* the landmark court decision that decriminalized abortion and allowed women the right to make decisions concerning their own bodies. Preface reading by listing questions that fall under these six categories:

Who:

Who pressed the charge?

Who is Jane Roe?

What attorney backed the plaintiff?

What judge presided over the final decision?

Who wrote the deciding opinion?

What:

What were the facts in the case?

What happened to Roe's pregnancy?

What were the reactions of notable figures, including the President, the Pope, and the head of Planned Parenthood?

What pressure groups took sides?

What media presentations featured the case?

What "litmus test" was applied to politicians?

Where:

Where did Roe live?

Where was the father of her child?

Where was the final decision made?

Where did she seek an abortion?

In what states had abortion been illegal?

When:

When did Roe become pregnant?

When was she denied an abortion?

When did the case first come to trial?

When did the high court make its decision?

Why:

Why did Roe conceal her identity?

Why was she denied an abortion?

Why did the case reach the Supreme Court?

Why did religious and political leaders take sides in the matter?

How:

How did the Supreme Court determine that abortion should be legal?

How did pressure groups make their case for or against Roe?

How did Roe react to the decision?

How has public opinion altered since the Roe decision?

Add to the list of questions as additional reading suggests more angles of inquiry. Organize your data in outline form and compose a short editorial setting forth a viewpoint based on factual information.

Budget: $

Sources:

Faux, Marian. *Roe vs. Wade: The Untold Story of the Landmark Supreme Court Decision that Made Abortion Legal.* Macmillan, 1988.

McCorvey, Norma. *I Am Roe.* HarperCollins, 1993.

Miller, Patricia G. *The Worst of Times.* HarperCollins, 1993.

Schambelan, Bo. *Roe vs. Wade: The Most Controversial Ruling of Our Time.* Running Press, 1992.

Alternative Applications: Make a list of open-ended survey questions to ask a variety of people on the issue of *Roe vs. Wade.* Include a gynecologist, judge, journalist, politician, law enforcement officer, women's health clinic staff member, nurse, child care worker, priest, minister, abortion recipient, social worker, humanities teacher, feminist, father, mother, grandparent, adoption agent, public defender, teenagers of both sexes, pro-choice activist, and pro-life activist. Consider these models:

- Who should decide whether women receive privacy when making decisions concerning health and child-bearing?

- How can groups justify stalking, harassment, and violence against abortion providers?

- Does Roe deserve privacy?

- How does the law affect abortion, women's health, civil rights, and marital rights?

- What cultural practices or religious beliefs enter into the discussion of women's right to choice?

• When does a fertilized egg become a life?

• What should doctors learn about abortion during training?

• What situations would justify an abortion? Rape? Incest? Severe birth defects?

Getting *the news online*

Age/Grade Level or Audience: High school or college current-events online research; women's studies newsletter; newspaper column or open forum; radio or television presentation.

Description: Study women's news by reading newspapers online.

Procedure: Introduce students to women's issues by studying such newspaper and news magazine online services as these:

Aspen Times	*New York Times*
Atlanta Constitution & Journal	*News York Newsday*
Chicago Tribune	*Raleigh News & Observer*
Dallas Morning News	*San Francisco Chronicle*
Irish Times	*San Francisco Examiner*
London Sunday Time	*San Jose Mercury*
London Telegraph	*St. Petersburg Times* (Russia)
Los Angeles Times	*Tampa Tribune*
Miami Herald	*U.S. News Online*

Have students compile a database, bulletin board, or in-house news release of information about women and such women's issues as affirmative action, abortion rights, health care, jobs, civil rights, and legislation. Discuss how up-to-the-minute availability of news is useful in studying women's issues and how such information in the past was not readily available to the general public.

Budget: $$$

Sources:

Lancaster, F. W., and E. G. Fayen. *Information Retrieval On-Line.* Books Demand, 1994.

Outing, Steve. *Jupiter Online Newspaper Report.* N.p., n.d.

———. "Newspapers Online." *USAir Magazine,* 50, 52.

Alternative Applications: Introduce students to online news by utilizing these services:

• America Online (800-827-6364) $9.95/mo., addition of NewsHound $4.95/mo.

• CompuServe (800-510-4247) $9.95/mo.

• Delphi UK (44-171-757-7150) $10–$20/mo.

• Prodigy (800-792-LINK) $9.95/mo. + $4.95 per newspaper or $6.95 for news only

• Internet (800-818-NEWS) $15–$30/mo.

• Women's Wire (800-210-8998) $15/mo.

Appoint volunteers or participants to locate articles and data for a report on women's interests as represented via computer networks. Search for special interest sections, business, career opportunities, sports, cinema, books, science, travel, and names in the news. Determine what percent of online news from each service pertains to women.

Interviewing *women*

Age/Grade Level or Audience: High school journalism or creative writing assignment; young-adult book club presentation; scout or 4-H project; women's studies theme; newspaper column, open forum, or media feature.

Description: Study the art of interviewing by collecting information about journalist and feminist Gloria Steinem.

Procedure: Act out a serious mock-interview session. Before attempting to contact Gloria Steinem, study her life and prepare a list of questions that would allow her to elaborate on pertinent topics. Use these as a beginning:

- What, in your own life, provoked you to form, in 1971 along with Brenda Fasteau, the Women's Action Alliance? and *Ms.* magazine, the following year?

- I have read in interviews that, early in your career, a common praise you received was, "You write like a man." How did that make you feel? Would this sentiment ever be uttered today? What changes in your profession have occurred in the past two decades?

- How have your sensibilities and/or expectations changed in the past several decades?

- At what point in your life have you felt most creative, productive, respected, and fulfilled?

- What changes do you anticipate for the next two decades? How will women's roles in the workplace and in the family be different?

Budget: $$

Sources:

Daffron, Carolyn. *Gloria Steinem*. Chelsea House, 1988.

The Decade of Women: A Ms. History of the Seventies in Words and Pictures. Paragon, 1980.

The Education of a Woman: Gloria Steinem. Bantam, 1995.

Hite, Shere. "Bringing Democracy Home." *Ms.*, March/April 1995, 54–61.

Powell, Dannye Romine. *Parting the Curtains: Interviews with Southern Writers*. John F. Blair, 1994.

"Radio Days." *People,* April 24, 1995.

Raymer, Steve. " 'Hanoi Hannah' Was Propaganda Voice of North Vietnam." *Montreal Gazette,* April 30, 1995, C4.

Shenon, Philip. "Hanoi Hannah Looks Back with Few Regrets." *New York Times,* November 4, 1994.

Alternative Applications: Prepare questions for a mock-interview with "Hanoi Hannah," the public name of Trinh Thi Ngo, who read propaganda statements over Vietnamese radio from 1965–1973. Prepare questions that follow these models:

261

- Where did you learn English? Why did you take a job as a wartime propagandist?

- What cultural information did you employ in your broadcasts? Why did you include names, American editorials, and articles from *Stars and Stripes?*

- How did your program compare to that of Seoul City Sue, Hanoi Hattie, Axis Sally, or Tokyo Rose?

- What was your reaction to the American bombing of Hanoi in December 1972? Where did citizens go during the assault? Did your program cease during the height of the bombing?

- What medals did you win for your work? Were you well paid? Would you do this work again? Why have you moved south to Saigon? What is the focus of your current work as news editor for Saigon television?

Mother *Hale, a human-interest classic*

Age/Grade Level or Audience: High school or college journalism or sociology model; Business and Professional Women's League or small business association newsletter; media column or feature; Women's History Month forum; educational radio or television presentation; women's religious group study; civic club talk.

Description: Present a model human-interest feature based on the work of a female altruist.

Procedure: Model a human interest story by presenting these facts about the work of Mother Clara Hale and Hale House. Keep in mind the type of publication it would appear in: newspaper, women's magazine, etc. Use these facts:

- In 1932 Hale, a widow, took in foster children at her Harlem flat and opened a home child-care facility for parents who worked out of town. A year after she retired, her daughter, child specialist Dr. Lorraine Hale, helped her open a home for heroin addicts. Word spread that mothers with addicted infants could find lodging without sermons. The Hales filled the cramped apartment with baby beds for over a year and functioned without help from social organizations.

- As a model halfway house from 1979 to 1980, Hale House provided for children who arrived in pitiful condition, often crying from withdrawal pains, hungry, and unused to personal attention. When the mothers were rehabilitated, they were reunited with healthy, smiling children who had become accustomed to adequate food and clothing, medical care, and love and affection over an average stay of eighteen months.

- The advent of designer drugs produced a new challenge to Hale: an increase in the number of crack babies whose problems ranged from low birth weight to respiratory distress, poor concentration, and learning disabilities among the 88% who survived birth.

- Percy Sutton, a Manhattan official, joined the support for Hale House and secured donations and city, state, and federal funds. In 1975 Hale bought a five-story brownstone at the corner of 122nd Street and Adam Clayton Powell Jr. Boulevard, and rebuilt it to include dining room, kitchen, playroom, and nursery. Out of the first 500 children, only twelve were put up for adoption and eleven were placed in foster homes; the remaining 477 returned to their mothers.

- In his State of the Union Address in January 1985, President Ronald Reagan honored Hale for creating a receiving-home for unwanted infants of every type: handicapped, HIV-positive, or those addicted to alcohol and drugs. John Jay College of Criminal Justice awarded an honorary doctorate to Hale; she also received the Truman Award for Public Service.

Budget: $

Sources:

Bidel, Susan. "When Mom's a Hard Act to Follow." *Woman's Day,* May 22, 1990, 86–90.

Carcaterra, Lorenzo. "Mother Hale of Harlem." *People,* March 5, 1984, 211–14.

"Chronicle—Clara Hale." *New York Times,* December 5, 1990.

"Clara Hale to Get Truman Award for Public Service." *Jet,* March 20, 1989, 23.

Coles, Robert. *Dorothy Day: A Radical Devotion.* Addison-Wesley, 1987.

Day, Dorothy. *The Long Loneliness: An Autobiography.* Harper & Row, 1981.

Elisberg, Robert, ed. *Dorothy Day: Selected Writings.* Orbis, 1992.

"Fifty Thousand Dollars Rehabs House for Cocaine-Addicted Babies." *Jet,* January 25, 1988, 23.

Hacker, Kathy. "Mother Hale: A Savior and Her Growing Mission." *Philadelphia Inquirer,* May 7, 1986.

"Hale Receives $1.1 Million to Expand Home for Babies." *Jet,* May 19, 1986, 26.

Johnson, Herschel. "Clara (Mother) Hale: Healing Baby 'Junkies' with Love." *Ebony,* May 1986, 58–61.

Kastor, Elizabeth. "The Hour of the Heroes." *Washington Post,* February 8, 1985.

Klejment, Anne and Alice Klejment. *Dorothy Day and the Catholic Worker.* Garland Publications, 1985.

Lanker, Brian. *I Dream a World.* Stewart, Tabori, and Chang, 1989.

Lanker, Brian, and Maya Angelou. "I Dream a World." *National Geographic,* August 1989, 206–26.

Miller, William D. *All Is Grace: The Spirituality of Dorothy Day.* Doubleday, 1987.

"Ordinary Women of Grace: Subjects of the 'I Dream a World' Photography Exhibit." *U.S. News & World Report,* February 13, 1989, 54.

"Reagan Cites Clara Hale as a 'Hero' in Union Address." *Jet,* February 25, 1985, 6.

Roberts, Nancy L. *Dorothy Day and the Catholic Worker.* State University of New York Press, 1985.

Safran, Claire. "Mama Hale and Her Little Angels." *Reader's Digest,* September 1984, 49–54.

Stanley, Alessandra. "Hale House Fights City Hall for Babies' Fate." *New York Times,* September 23, 1990.

Winter, Annette. "Spotlight." *Modern Maturity,* October–November 1988, 18.

Alternative Applications: Compose a similar piece of writing about Dorothy Day, co-founder of the Catholic Worker Movement, who believed that Christianity demands care for poor, oppressed, or dispossessed people. Use these data as a model:

- Born in Brooklyn, New York, Dorothy Day received no religious training at home, but the family maid took her to Catholic mass. From early childhood, Dorothy became lonely and introspective after dealing with poverty, frequent moves, and family instability.

- At the University of Illinois at Urbana, she worked as a governess, housekeeper, and waitress. In class, she studied labor history, unions, voting rights, and sexual freedom and joined the Socialist party. While writing for the socialist periodical

Call, Day developed close alliances with notable leftists Emma Goldman, Jack Reed, and Max Eastman and went to jail for fighting at a suffrage rally.

- While writing for *Masses* and *Liberato,* Day studied nursing at Kings County Hospital during the great influenza epidemic. The experience introduced her to charity work. Conversion to Catholicism came in 1927, shortly before the birth of daughter Tamar Teresa; Dorothy then joined a Catholic volunteer program. She met writer Peter Maurin, a Catholic layman, and inaugurated the *Catholic Worker,* which reached a circulation of 150,000 with articles on racism, employment controversies, and women's issues.

- She opened a store, apartments, and a settlement house on Jackson Square for the homeless, abused, and hungry. From her experiences, she transformed the *Catholic Worker* into a voice for social change. In the late 1940s Day protested nuclear proliferation and was jailed along with fellow "peaceniks." In 1965 she visited the Vatican peace council; at the tomb of Saint Priscilla, she fasted for ten days while studying the writings of Martin Luther King, Jr.

- Day's hospitality house and the 23-acre Peter Maurin Farm and two cottages at Pleasant Plains, Staten Island, formed a complex of social services by 1968. In the early 1970s she supported César Chávez at a farm workers' strike and was jailed. Upon her death, many recipients of her kindness came to honor a long life devoted to altruism.

Newsgatherers

Age/Grade Level or Audience: Elementary writing assignment; book club presentation; scout or 4-H project; women's studies banners; newspaper column; open forum; radio or television feature.

Description: Celebrate women as newsgatherers with a brief compendium of women journalists.

Procedure: Create a poster series or frieze featuring the work of a famous female journalist, commentator, or newsgatherer. Include a symbol to indicate the focus of each person's work. Begin with these models:

- a hard hat for **Christiane Amanpour,** who rejected a helmet and flak jacket during her extensive coverage of the Bosnian War

- a feathered headdress for **Nelly Bly,** who dressed like a can-can dancer to get a story for *The New York World*

- a map of India and flash camera to honor the work of **Margaret Bourke-White,** who followed the dramatic rise of Gandhi's pacifist movement in colonial India

- a Spanish/English dictionary for **Kitty Coleman,** first female North American war correspondent, who covered the Spanish-American War

- an ocean liner for **Margaret Fuller,** who served as America's first female European correspondent when she wrote for the *New York Tribune* in the 1840s

- a masthead for **Katharine Graham,** who took over the *Washington Post* after the death of her husband and led the paper to national success

- barbed wire for **Marguerite Higgins,** who reported from Dachau before its liberation from Nazi death camp operators and won a Pulitzer Prize for her coverage of the Korean War

- a PBS logo for **Charlayne Hunter-Gault,** who serves as a national correspondent for *The MacNeil-Lehrer NewsHour*

- an AP press pass for **Ruth Cowan Nash,** overseas reporter with French forces on the front during the Battle of the Bulge

- a veil for **Helen Thomas,** whom men in the National Press Club forced to cover political speeches from the balcony, which she dubbed "purdah"

- a map of Germany for **Dorothy Thompson,** who denounced fascism in the mid-1920s in reports to the *Philadelphia Public Ledger* and warned of Hitler's fanaticism

- a map of Charleston in flames for **Elizabeth Timothy,** Rotterdam native who published the *South Carolina Gazette* from 1734–1741. During her tenure with the paper, she formed a command post to locate people missing in the great fire of 1740

- a suffragist banner for **Carrie Chapman Catt,** Iowa journalist turned crusader

Budget: $$

Sources:

Brady, Kathleen. *Ida Turbell: Portrait of a Muckraker.* Seaview/Putnam, 1989.

Daffron, Carolyn. *Margaret Bourke-White.* Chelsea House, 1988.

Ehrlich, Elizabeth. *Nellie Bly.* Chelsea House, 1989.

Freeman, Barbara M. *Kit's Kingdom: The Journalism of Kathleen Blake Coleman.* Carleton University Press, 1995.

Hetter, Katia, and Dorian Friedman. "The Animating Role of Women Pundits." *U.S. News & World Report,* August 7, 1995, 33–34.

Hinds, Patricia Mignon, ed. *Essence: 25 Years Celebrating Black Women.* Abrams Books, 1995.

Watson, David. Margaret Fuller: An American Romantic. *St. Martin's Press, 1988.*

Alternative Applications: Post a wall chart honoring the following Pulitzer Prize-winning female journalists; include the dates, and subjects of their reportage:

- Ada Louise Huxtable, 1970, critical commentary

- Anne O'Hare McCormick, 1937, European correspondence

- Hazel Brannon Smith, 1964, controversial editorials

- Lucinda Franks, 1971, life of Diana Oughton

- Madeleine Blais, 1980, feature

- Marguerite Higgins, 1951, Korean War

- Mary McGrory, 1975, commentary

- Minna Lewinson, 1918, newspaper history

- Miriam Ottenberg, 1960, used-car scams

- Mrs. Walter Schau, 1954, amateur photograph of a rescue

- Signe Wilkinson, 1992, editorial cartoons

Reviewing *a book or film*

Age/Grade Level or Audience: High school journalism or creative writing assignment; book or cinema review column; cinema or writer's club presentation; women's studies theme; civic club commentary; open forum; radio or television feature.

Description: Review a book with an overt feminist theme.

Procedure: Prepare a review of a nonfiction work on women, for example, Miriam Ali's *Without Mercy.* Include commentary that helps readers decide if the work is worth reading. Note these aspects in the review:

- shocking opener: two British girls, Zana and Nadia Muhsen, kidnapped from Birmingham, England, by their father, Muthana Muhsen, and sold as brides in Yemen

- descriptions of dramatic photographs, one of which could appear with the review

- details of their marriage to unknown men to whom they have since borne children

- the amount of money their father earned for selling them: £1,300 for each girl

- Yemen's insistence that birth to a Yemeni father and British mother did not free the girls from Yemeni law

- Mother Miriam's continued travel to Yemen and her legal maneuvers to free the girls from patriarchal bondage and arranged marriage

- a flashback to Miriam's reasons for marrying Muhsen, who years earlier had taken Leila and Ahmed at ages three and four and never returned them from Yemen

- details of Miriam's life as a cafe manager who trusted her husband and believed his lies about her children's fate

- details of Zana's return alone—without her children, whom her Yemeni husband retains in substandard quarters

Note that in 1992, 1,100 girls were abducted from England and forced into Yemeni slavery.

Budget: $

Sources:

Ali, Miriam, and Jana Wain. *Without Mercy.* Little, Brown, 1995.

Black, Ayanna. "About Desire, Memory, Longing and Death." *Toronto Star,* March 12, 1995.

"Book Reviews." *Workforce,* winter 1994, 62.

Chambers, Veronica. "Review: 'Tailspin: Women at War in the Wake of Tailhook,'" *Ms.,* July/August 1995, 76.

Driscoll, Margarette. "Lock Up Your Daughters . . ." *Sunday Times* (London), March 5, 1995, sect. 7, 10.

"Jefferson and Sally: Affair Lives On." *Parade,* March 26, 1995, 16.

Lumpkins, Barbranda. " 'Wedding' Marries Issues of Race, Class." *USA Today,* March 1, 1995 8D.

Also, read or watch guest reviews as well as syndicated book critics and commentators.

Alternative Applications: Using a model from a local newspaper, review a film, video, or television program that exemplifies a feminist theme, for example, *Norma Rae* or the television miniseries *Calamity Jane.* Present facts, details, and data that support your conclusion. Comment on photography, production and pre-performance data. Note how this work depicts certain groups of women; for example, workers, mothers, single parents, professionals, travelers, religious groups, and taxpayers.

Women *make headlines*

Age/Grade Level or Audience: Elementary or middle school journalism or creative writing activity; newspaper column; radio or television feature; word processing assignment; writers or press club presentation; teacher training project.

Description: Teach headline writing using events from women's history.

Procedure: Instruct participants in headline writing with a demonstration of banner, single deck, double deck, triple deck, subhead, no count, and counted heads. Follow these models drawn from the life and political career of Corazon Aquino:

Corazon Aquino Assumes Role;
Leads Filipino Freedom Fight
Begun by Husband Benigno

Time Names Philippine Leader "Woman of the Year"

Aquino's Knowledge of Foreign Languages
Impresses International Community

Far Eastern University Honors Famous Alumna, President Aquino

Aquino Battles Corruption of Marcos's Nacionalista Party
Fears Terrorism, Crime, and Strike Preface Anarchy, Takeover

Aquino Begs Help of President Carter
for Humane Intervention to Address
Husband Benigno's Heart Disease

Corazon Aquino Not Present at Scene of Husband's Assassination;
Prays with Her Children at Their Temporary Quarters in Boston

Widow Energized to Avenge Public Assassination of Mate

Aquino Selects Yellow;
"L" Laban Party Insignia

Crowds Demand "Cory, Cory, Cory";
55 Million Filipinos Rally for Aquino

Display finished headlines in a variety of typefaces, sizes, and styles: italic, Roman, sans serif, all caps, down style, and tabloid style. Discuss the best choices of diction and style to meet the needs of the general public, political leaders, academics, young adults, and other groups of news readers.

Budget: $

Sources:

Carlson, Peter. "A Matter of Family Honor." *People Weekly*, March 17, 1986, 34–40.
Cooper, Nancy. "The Remarkable Rise of a Widow in Yellow." *Newsweek*, March 10, 1986, 32–36.

Crisostomo, Isabelo T. *Cory: Profile of a President.* Branden, 1987.

Current Biography. H. W. Wilson, 1986.

Komisar, Lucy. "Cory Aquino: The Story of a Revolution." *New York Review of Books,* June 11, 1987, 10–13.

Losee, Stephanie. "The Billionaires." *Fortune,* September 7, 1992, 86–138.

Paul, Anthony. "Triumph of the Widow in Yellow." *Reader's Digest,* June 1986, 93–98.

Valenzuela, Luisa, and Joe Conason. "Woman of the Year: Corazon Aquino." *Vogue,* May 1986, 288–92.

Wheeler, Jill. *Corazon Aquino.* Abdo & Daughters, 1991.

"The World's Ten Most Important Women." *Ladies Home Journal,* November 1987, 133–40.

Wurfel, David. *Democracy in the Philippines? The Precarious Aquino Regime.* Westview, 1993.

Alternative Applications: Select a single news story; for example, coverage of the contributions of one of the four choices for the 1994 Sara Lee Frontrunner Awards:

- Ardis Krainik, general director of Chicago's Lyric Opera

- Barbara Jordan, ethicist and chair of the Commission on Immigration Reform

- Dr. Susan Love, director of the UCLA Breast Center

- Jill Barad, President of Mattel

Present the same facts in a variety of journalistic styles: editorial commentary, column, lead news story, women's page feature, sidebar, letter to the editor, or political cartoon with caption. Write appropriate headlines for each.

Writing *captions*

Age/Grade Level or Audience: Elementary school writing assignment; history club presentation; women's studies theme.

Description: List a series of captions to describe pictures celebrating the life of Princess Ka'iulani of Hawaii.

Procedure: Organize a study of the life of Princess Ka'iulani of Hawaii. Write a series of orders to a newspaper, magazine, or television photography crew. Supply captions for pictures of the most important scenes in the princess's life. Begin with these:

- Princess Ka'iulani, Hawaii's last princess, was born October 16, 1875, to Archibald Cleghorn and Princess Miriam Likelike, sister of King Kalakaua.

- After talking with the dying Likelike, at age eleven, the princess accepted her role as an *ali'i,* or noblewoman, and agreed to attend school at Great Harrowden Hall in England.

- Before Princess Ka'iulani sailed from home, her friend Robert Louis Stevenson comforted her and dedicated a poem to her voyage.

- Seated in the parlor before a fire while snow peppered the window, Princess Ka'iulani read disturbing news that white usurpers were stealing Hawaiian businesses and land and interfering in island government.

- In 1887, the king died, leaving Princess Ka'iulani to fend for herself against enemies of the royal family.

- At age seventeen Princess Ka'iulani visited President Grover Cleveland, who promised to investigate the situation.

- With pomp and celebration, Princess Ka'iulani returned home on November 9, 1897, to find her people abject and defeated.

- The next year, Congress annexed the island cluster; by August 12, 1898, Hawaii was a protectorate with no need for a queen.

- Despairing, Princess Ka'iulani died March 6, 1899, and was buried with honors appropriate to the islands' last princess.

Vary this exercise with other historical figures, for example, the last flight of Amelia Earhart, the departure of the last Empress of China from the throne, Indira Gandhi's reelection as prime minister of India, or the selection and training of Christa McAuliffe for her NASA flight. If possible photocopy actual photographs or drawings that follow their achievements. Compose captions that express detailed information to clarify figures in the pictures and note the date and location of each.

Budget: $

Sources:

D'Anglade, M. G. Bosseront. *A Tree in Bud: The Hawaiian Kingdom, 1889–1893.* University of Hawaii Press, 1987.

Daws, Gavan. *Shoals of Time: A History of the Hawaiian Islands.* University of Hawaii Press, 1968.

Mrantz, Maxine. *Hawaii's Tragic Princess—The Girl Who Never Got to Rule.* Aloha Graphics, 1980.

Rayson, Potter Kasdon, et al. *The Hawaiian Monarchy.* Bess Press, 1983.

Stanley, Fay, and Diane Stanley. *The Last Princess: The Story of Princess Ka'iulani of Hawaii.* Macmillan, 1991.

Tabrah, Ruth. *Hawaii: A Bicentennial History.* W. W. Norton, 1980.

Zambucka, Kristin. *Princess Kaiulani: The Last Hope of Hawaii's Monarchy.* Mana Publishing, 1982.

Alternative Applications: Select a year for "Year in Review." Write detailed orders to a photographer or film crew of the photos you want for a newspaper, magazine, or television spread. Select some of these eventful timespans:

- 1848—the first Women's Rights Convention meets in Seneca Falls, New York.

- 1862—Women and children join the move West to escape the Civil War.

- 1890—The Battle of Wounded Knee pits heavily armed cavalry against women and children.

- 1919—Women respond to the dangers of alcohol by supporting the Volstead Act; Frances Willard establishes the Women's Christian Temperance Union.

- 1919–20—Women press for the right to vote.

- 1993–94—Title IX encourages women athletes to take part in a wide variety of competitions.

- 1995—More women desert factories and offices to go into business for themselves.

Writing *a column*

Age/Grade Level or Audience: High school journalism model; writer's club presentation; women's studies theme; civic club demonstration; seminar topic; radio or television feature.

Description: Present a column about women's history or achievements.

Procedure: Distribute, play tapes, or read aloud to a journalism class several columns highlighting important events in women's history. Study this essay on Toni Morrison's Nobel Prize as a model:

As I was driving to town, a news announcer on WDAV heralded welcome words: "Toni Morrison has been awarded the Nobel Prize for literature."

"It's about time," I shrieked and pounded the steering wheel, severely alarming the driver in the next lane.

If only I could tell that driver what a terrific writer Morrison is, what an unshakable voice for women, for blacks, for humanity.

If only I could read aloud to him the revelations in *Beloved*.

When I studied Morrison's masterpiece, I had my difficulties reweaving the circular narrative—a round-and-round dispersal of shreds of truth from varied points of view.

The fictionalized history of a real fugitive from slavery, *Beloved* tells of Sethe, a pregnant mother of two sons and a toddler.

After a courier of the Underground Railroad rescues the children from plantation misery, Sethe hurries to reclaim them, but her plans are found out.

Two white youths hold her down and suck out her breast milk, a most unsettling, perverse act of degradation.

Sethe escapes and travels straight to her children. A month later, when slave-catchers come for her family, she snatches up the toddler and hacks her throat with a saw, a jarring act of grace sparing another female from slavery's breeding pens.

The action radiates so swift and sure from Sethe's hand that it justifies as mercy killing the sacrifice of a just-crawling girl-child.

After I was assigned to explain this powerful novel for Cliffs Notes, I realized that I needed expert advice before I could interpret it.

From Warren Hutton, a local attorney, I discovered the fault in my creation of the term "mammary rape." Warren explained that rape is an act of penetration and that the assault on Sethe would have to be labeled according to state statutes governing sexual abuse.

When I pondered the status of Kentucky laws to protect female slaves, I cut to the heart of Morrison's focus—when people become the equivalent of farm animals, there are no laws, no courts, no justice to circumvent torment.

Next, I had to account for the fact that Sethe's breasts continue to well with milk after a severe lashing, the hanging and burning of her friend, separation from her husband, and the premature birth of her fourth child in a semi-submerged boat on the Ohio River opposite Cincinnati.

I turned to my medical guru, Dr. Frank Wilson, who assured me that the inhuman trauma that Sethe endured would in all likelihood interfere with milk production.

Slowly, I pieced together the rest of *Beloved,* growing more attuned to Morrison's quiet mastery and benevolence toward her determined, defiant central character, and the significance of the healing touch and forgiveness, the bedrock on which the story is founded.

The characters, all of whom have suffered some degree of bestial treatment, relearn that they are worthy and good and respectable.

Morrison's bold choice of so repulsive a situation proves her value to American literature, especially the branch that recovers what we have lost from the past—our awareness of the irreparable harm done by slavery's devaluation of life.

Congratulations, Toni. You bring honor to the prize.

[Used with permission of the *Charlotte Observer,* October 24, 1993, V1]

Achieve a balance of political, humorous, reflective, muckraking, and whimsical columns. Contrast the tone, focus, and other structural details used by each writer. Compile a database, cassette library, or scrapbook of models that students can turn to for assistance. Caption each according to type.

Budget: $$$$

Sources:

Carter, Jimmy. "Rights? Not for Women." *USA Today,* March 8, 1995, 9A.

Goodman, Ellen. *At Large.* Summit Books, 1981.

Hetter, Katia, and Dorian Friedman. "The Animating Role of Women Pundits." *U.S. News & World Report,* August 7, 1995, 33–34.

Kincaid, Jamaica. "Putting Myself Together." *New Yorker,* February 20, 1995, 93, 98–101.

Randolph, Laura B. "Working Women." *Ebony,* March 1995, 20.

Wolf, Naomi. "Are Opinions Male?" *New Republic,* November 29, 1993, 20–26.

Also, read or watch guest columnists as well as syndicated writers and commentators, especially these:

Christian Amanpour (CNN news)	Ann Landers (syndicated columnist)
Joan Beck (*Chicago Tribune*)	Mary Matalin (CNBC's "Equal Time")
Erma Bombeck (syndicated columnist)	Kathy Moos (CNN News)
Donna Britt (*Washington Post*)	Dee Dee Myers (CNBC's "Equal Time")
Linda Chavez (syndicated columnist)	Deb Price (*Detroit News*)
Hillary Clinton (syndicated columnist)	Diane Rehm (syndicated public radio)
Ellen Goodman (*Boston Globe*)	Lesley Stahl (CBS "60 Minutes")
Molly Ivins (*Fort Worth Star Telegram*)	Mary Tillotson ("CNN & Co.")

Alternative Applications: Assign groups of students to study the work of various types of female columnists, both liberal and conservative. Use print, audio, and video models that display command of tone and language, compassion, control of delivery and gestures, and knowledge of the subject matter. Have students state the value of columns discussing contemporary issues from the female point of view as well as works by different races, religions, and cultural groups. Offer a list of fiction and nonfiction essayists for study as models of persuasive, compelling writing.

Writing *a memorial*

Age/Grade Level or Audience: Middle or high school journalism or creative writing assignment; general interest column; writer's club presentation; women's studies theme; civic club commentary; open forum focus; radio or television feature.

Description: Compose an epitaph or memorial to a famous woman.

Procedure: Write a succinct, yet moving memorial to a notable woman who died recently. Summarize the qualities that make that woman memorable. Capture significant events, decisions, and attitudes that colored the woman's life, such as the following data about Jackie Kennedy Onassis:

- Former news photographer and First Lady, Jacqueline Kennedy Onassis, who lived in Manhattan and worked as an editor and publicist, died in May 1994.

- Her decades as an American icon cover her term as First Lady, while husband John F. Kennedy served as president of the United States, and her widowhood, when she turned to her own affairs, remarried, divorced, and returned to publishing as meaningful work.

- Despite her popularity and compassionate gestures as First Lady, she was the object of hoaxes, rumors, and outlandish legends that sprang up immediately after her husband's election to the White House and again during the public mourning after his assassination.

- Significant to her service to America were the many gatherings and receptions that she hosted and her ability to charm and welcome foreign dignitaries, often by conversing knowledgeably in French or Italian on matters of state, the arts, and current affairs.

- Her redecoration of the White House brought historical accuracy to period details such as wallcoverings, lighting, window treatments, landscaping paintings, *objets d'art,* and furnishings.

- At her death, people from all walks of life mourned her passing and wept at the tomb of a lovely, unselfish woman whose grace enhanced a significant era of American history.

Flesh out generalizations with specific details of her life; for instance, her poise at the gravesite of her stillborn son Patrick, the self-control that marked her response to her husband's assassination, and the wistful pose of widow and mother as she escorted her children to John Kennedy's casket. Conclude with a strong statement on the subject's most meaningful or most unusual contributions and achievements.

Budget: $

Sources:

Anthony, Carl Sferrazza. ". . . Love, Jackie." *American Heritage,* September 1994, 90–101.
Dixon, Oscar. " 'Skeeter' Took Fame in Stride." *USA Today,* November 14, 1994, 1–2C.
Gwynne, S. C. "Death of a Rising Star." *Time,* April 10, 1995, 91.
Heymann, David C. *A Woman Named Jackie.* New American Library, 1990.

Alternative Applications: Using a model from a newspaper or magazine, compose a memorial to a woman now dead that you admire for personal reasons: for example, a strong role model such as Edith Cavell, a British nurse who was executed during World War I for helping prisoners escape, or the late Jacqueline Baker, exotic dancer and stage performer. Remain objective as you list the qualities that made the person memorable. Expand on aspects of education or experience that led that person to perform extraordinary deeds.

Language

"Fill'er *up, lady?*"

Age/Grade Level or Audience: Adult word game; women's center newsletter; adult literacy library research.

Description: Study common phrases and titles by identifying and explaining the female reference involved in each.

Procedure: Present participants with the following puzzle. Have them provide expressions like *Little Women, There is nothing like a dame,* or *Girl of my dreams* to fill each blank, which completes a common phrase, person or character's name, title of a song or work of literature, or name of a television show or movie:

1. _____ luck

2. _____ Nature

3. The _____ of Amherst

4. _____ for a day

5. The Blue _____

6. My Gal _____

7. the _____ of mercy

8. "I'm gonna buy a paper _____ that I can call my own"

9. _____ magazine

10. an Ivory _____

11. _____ Marple

12. _____ Mame

13. "You must have been a beautiful _____

14. grass _____

15. June _____

16. _____ bunch

17. sob _____

18. The _____ of Sigma Chi

19. _____ from Armentiers, parley-vous?

20. I am _____ , hear me roar.

ANSWERS:

1. lady luck	6. Sal	11. Miss	16. honey
2. Mother	7. sisters	12. Auntie	17. sister
3. Belle	8. doll	13. baby	18. sweetheart
4. queen	9. *Ms.*	14. widow	19. Mademoiselle
5. Angel	10. girl	15. bride	20. woman

Budget: $

Sources:

Jacobs, Dick, and Harriet Jacobs. *Who Wrote That Song?* Writers Digest Books, 1994.

Roget's International Thesaurus. 4th edition. Harper & Row, 1984.

Urdang, Laurence. *The Oxford Thesaurus.* American Edition. Oxford University Press, 1992.

Alternative Applications: Have participants make up lists of famous couples from song, movies, television, history, or literature, leaving the female's name blank. For example, use Adam and Eve, Helen and Annie, David and Bathsheba, Gertrude and Alice, Susan and Elizabeth, Bill and Hillary, or Ozzie and Harriet. Organize a swap of puzzles until each person has had an opportunity to see everyone's list. Note the number of repeated pairings of familiar couples.

The name's *the same*

Age/Grade Level or Audience: High school English or vocabulary lesson; book club handout; library quiz; school or office bulletin board; newsletter contest.

Description: Compile a worksheet of eponyms referring to or naming women.

Procedure: Many eponyms derive from the names of real women; for example, the Kenny method of treating polio, bloomers, Pandora's box, pythian, psychic, philomel, rolfing technique, malapropism, medusa, Tony award, Sally Lunn cake, Typhoid Mary, xanthippe, atheneum, Bacitracin, curie, Electra complex, fedora, grace, grundyism, hebephrenia, cloth, and iris. Consider the derivation of these terms:

- *madeleine,* a shell-shaped cake named for Madeleine Paumier, a mid-nineteenth-century pastry chef

- a *cinderella,* a person whose life shows little promise, then attains the height of fame and fortune

- the *Tony,* short for the Antoinette Perry Award in theater production

- a *jezebel,* a wanton, unprincipled temptress

- a *lady bountiful,* a generous person, named for a character in the play *The Beaux' Strategem*

- *melba toast,* derived from Nellie Melba

- an *abigail,* a maid named in the Bible

- *mother hubbard,* a muumuu or dress named from a nursery rhyme character

- *victoria,* a carriage derived from the English queen

- *junoesque,* stately, like the Greek Goddess Juno

- *niobium,* a chemical element named for the Greek mythological character, Niobe

Fill in the blanks below with female eponyms. To the right, list the category or person from which each derives.

1. _____ a perpetual optimist _____

2. _____ same as #1 _____

3. _____ cheap or gaudy _____

4. _____ traitor _____

5. _____ rainbow-colored _____

6. _____ any type of spider _____

7. _____ life vest _____

8. _____ northern lights _____

9. _____ carnival organ _____

10. _____ southern state _____

11. _____ brand of chocolates _____

12. _____ meretricious spy _____

13. _____ puppet _____

14. _____ non-alcoholic drink _____

15. _____ porridge _____

16. _____ spring month _____

17. _____ traditional month of weddings _____

18. _____ reverberation _____

19. _____ day of the week _____

20. _____ cannon _____

ANSWERS:

1. Little Mary Sunshine (literature)

2. pollyanna (literature)

3. tawdry (corruption of St. Audry)

4. Delilah (biblical character)

5. iridescent (Iris, from Greek mythology)

6. arachnid (Arachnis, from Greek mythology)

7. Mae West (actress in films starring W. C. Field)

8. aurora borealis (Aurora, Greek goddess of the dawn)

9. calliope (one of the three Greek Muses)

10. Virginia (real person—Queen Elizabeth I, the "Virgin Queen")

11. Godiva (real person)

12. Mata Hari (World War I spy for the Germans)

13. marionette (literally "little Mary," Jesus' mother)

14. Shirley Temple (actor and Ghanian diplomat)

15. cereal (Ceres, Greek goddess of grain)

16. May (Maia, Greek goddess of spring)

17. June (Juno, Greek goddess of marriage and childbirth)

18. echo (mythological character)

19. Friday (Frigga, Norse goddess and wife of Thor)

20. big bertha (real person)

Budget: $

Sources:

Beeching, Cyril L. *A Dictionary of Eponyms.* Oxford University Press, 1988.

Boycott, Rosie. *Batty, Bloomers and Boycott: A Little Etymology of Eponymous Words.* Hutchinson, 1982.

Douglas, Auriel. *Webster's New World Dictionary of Eponyms.* Simon & Schuster, 1990.

Dunkling, Leslie, and William Gosling. *The New American Dictionary of Baby Names.* Penguin, 1983.

McArthur, Tom, ed. *The Oxford Companion to the English Language.* Oxford Press, 1992.

Alternative Applications: Have participants study the origin and meaning of the given names of famous women. Create a list including translation or meaning, original language, and the name holder's area of achievement. Use the following examples as a model:

1. Margaret Thatcher (pearl, Greek)	prime minister of England
2. Zora Neale Hurston (dawn, Slavic)	folklorist, novelist
3. Hillary Clinton (cheerful, Latin)	attorney, activist for health and child care
4. Renee Richards (reborn, French)	tennis player and coach
5. Joanna Spyri (John, Latin)	author of *Heidi*
6. Eileen Ferrell (Helen, Irish)	opera singer
7. Emma Goldman (all-embracing, German)	orator and activist for women's rights
8. Abigail Adams (my father rejoices, Hebrew)	supporter of women's rights
9. Ivy Baker Priest (plant, German)	U.S. postmaster general
10. Jeanne Wakatsuki Houston (John, French)	autobiographer, novelist

New *day, new pronouns*

Age/Grade Level or Audience: Middle school language or vocabulary discussion; English-as-a-second-language research; GED or adult literacy training.

Description: Discuss a new set of third person pronouns that avoids sexism.

Procedure: Write on a chalkboard or overhead projector examples of grammatical situations in which masculine or feminine pronouns are inappropriate. Explain the favoritism in these models:

1. A cyclist should pack tools, water, first aid kit, and his name and address in case of an accident.

2. Educational benefits for a former soldier should provide him with tuition, housing allowance, and a monthly stipend to cover the cost of his books and incidentals.

Have participants discuss the need for a gender-free third person pronoun to apply to both male and female examples. Use the proposed s/he as a possible replacement. Ask the following questions:

- How will this replacement solve the problem of the objective case (him/her), possessive case (his/hers), and reflexive pronouns (himself/ herself)?

- What other methods free language of gender favoritism? For example, how can rewriting remove the problem by removing the pronoun? Consider the restatement of the former examples:

1. A cyclist should pack tools, water, first aid kit, and name and address in case of an accident.

2. Educational benefits for a former soldier should provide tuition, housing allowance, and a monthly stipend to cover the cost of books and incidentals.

Extend the discussion of pronouns to the title Ms. and the mock humorous change of history to herstory.

Budget: $

Sources:

Maggio, Rosalie. *The Dictionary of Bias-Free Usage: A Guide to Nondiscriminatory Language.* Oryx, 1991.

————. *The Nonsexist Word Finder: A Dictionary of Gender-Free Usage.* Beacon Press, 1988.

Miller, Casey, and Kate Swift. *The Handbook of Nonsexist Writing.* Harper & Row, 1988.

Mills, Jane. *Womanwords.* Macmillan, 1989.

Snodgrass, Mary Ellen. *The English Book.* Perma-Bound, 1991.

Alternative Applications: Have grammar students study both current news broadcasts, newspapers, magazines, and movies and those from twenty years ago for examples of gender bias in pronouns and other grammatical structure. What are the shifting trends; what existed twenty years ago that doesn't exist today; what hasn't changed. Experiment with different methods of removing such bias, i.e., rewriting and substituting. Compile a list on a bulletin board or use models as a guide to forms, structure, and rhetoric to avoid in speaking and writing.

Scramble *aboard*

Age/Grade Level or Audience: K–3 school spelling lesson; Women's History Month newsletters or bulletin board.

Description: Create a trainload of names and words to unscramble.

Procedure: Place a cut-out train on the bulletin board or a wall mural or draw a train on the chalkboard. On each car, present a creation or accomplishment of a famous woman. Scramble

chalkboard. On each car, present a creation or accomplishment of a famous woman. Scramble a key word or name in each entry. Call out the sentence in which the word belongs. Have participants spell each term in the correct blank on the answer sheet. Offer a happy face or star sticker for each correct answer sheet. Use this model:

- Sarah Knight created a machine that makes **asbg.** (bags)

- Astronaut Sally **dier** flew into space. (Ride)

- Fanny Crosby wrote many **shmny.** (hymns)

- Dr. May **nhnic** brought medicine to the poor in Harlem. (Chinn)

- **sneru** Clara Barton started the American Red Cross. (Nurse)

- Harriet Tubman earned the name **messo.** (Moses)

- Beverly Cleary wrote The **oesmu** and the Motorcycle. (Mouse)

- Emma Lazarus wrote the poem on the **esautt** of Liberty. (Statue)

- Eleanor Roosevelt helped establish the U.N.'s **anmhu** rights declaration. (human)

- Kristi Yamaguchi won an Olympic **dealm** in skating. (medal)

Budget: $

Sources:

Aaseng, Nathan. *Twentieth-Century Inventors*. Facts on File, 1991.

American Men and Women of Science. R. R. Bowker, 1989.

Ashby, Ruth, and Deborah Gore Ohrn, eds. *Herstory: Women Who Changed the World*. Viking, 1995.

Bailey, Brooke. *The Remarkable Lives of 100 Women Healers and Scientists*. Bob Adams, 1994.

Haber, Louis. *Black Pioneers of Science and Invention*. Harcourt Brace, 1992.

MacDonald, Anne L. *Feminine Ingenuity: Women and Invention in America*. Ballantine, 1992.

Martin, Jean, gen. ed. *Who's Who of Women in the Twentieth Century*. Crescent Books, 1995.

McHenry, Robert, ed. *Famous American Women: A Biographical Dictionary from Colonial Times to the Present*. Dover Publications, 1980.

Veglahn, Nancy J. *Women Scientists*. Facts on File, 1991.

"Women Inventors." *Cobblestone*. June 1994.

Alternative Applications: Repeat the sentences listed above and indicate which word students are to spell in each, e. g., *machine, space, wrote, medicine, cross, earned, motorcycle, rights, poem,* and *skating.* Then have students write new sentences about each of the focal names, e. g., Sarah Knight and her machine, Sally Ride in space, and Fanny Crosby's hymns.

Signs *of equality*

Age/Grade Level or Audience: Elementary or middle school language demonstration; book club activity; library handout; school or office bulletin board; media feature; educational television series.

Description: Teach the basics of signing by demonstrating a vocabulary of words applicable to women.

Procedure: Teach young students about Alice Cogswell, the nine-year-old girl for whom Thomas Gallaudet created the American Sign Language. Demonstrate how to spell useful words and phrases, including those that give a positive image to womanhood: sister, niece, girlfriend, nun, friend, aunt, mother, grandmother. Extend the difficulty of each session by adding these and other famous names to the list: Eleanor Roosevelt, Sally Ride, Princess Michiko, Florence Nightingale, Sarah Winnemucca, Laura Ingalls Wilder, Rosa Parks, Helen Keller, and Queen Hatshepsut. Have students model names or words of their choice for a group to decipher. Have the audience write their answers. Score points for the person identifying the most examples.

Budget: $

Sources:

Brown, Michele, and Ann O'Connor. *Woman Talk*. MacDonald & Co., 1985.

Maggio, Rosalie. *The Beacon Book of Quotations by Women*. Beacon Press, 1992.

"Making Choices." *American Girl,* May/June 1995, 26–29.

Sign Language Primer. Nelson, 1993.

"To Sign or Speak." *American Girl,* May/June 1995, 30–31.

Also consult: HiP magazine, 1563 Solano Ave., Berkeley, CA 94707 (510-527-8993).

Alternative Applications: Initiate a high school or adult group into the intermediate level of American Language for the Deaf by using quotations from famous females from history as models. Consider the following citations on women and equality:

- The only question left to settle now is, are women persons? (activist Susan B. Anthony)

- I march every day in my heart. (singer Pearl Bailey)

- The feminine mystique has succeeded in burying millions of American women alive. (Betty Friedan)

- Revolution is the festival of the oppressed. (Germaine Greer)

- All human life on the planet is born of woman. (Adrienne Rich)

- No woman can call herself free who does not own and control her body. (Margaret Sanger)

Terms *from the wardrobe*

Age/Grade Level or Audience: Elementary and middle school language or vocabulary activity; school library research; English-as-a-second-language demonstration; GED or adult literacy training oral presentation.

Description: Define idiom with examples from women's fashions.

Procedure: Explain how idioms evolve from situations that require words to take on special meanings in particular situations, as with *spick and span* (adjective), *make haste* (verb), *grass widow* (noun), *whoa Nellie* (interjection). Appoint individuals to make a poster illustrating each of these idiomatic phrases and terms from women's historical fashions and the garments, objects, or situations they bring to mind:

- armed with a hatpin
- handle with kid gloves

- kept it under her hat

- lost her bloomers

- mules

- pannier

- play drop the handkerchief

- put a bee in her bonnet

- rings on her fingers and bells on her toes

- slipshod

- straitlaced

- tied to her apron strings

Budget: $

Sources:

Kalman, Bobbie. *Settler Sayings*. Crabtree, 1995.

Maggio, Rosalie. *The Dictionary of Bias-Free Usage: A Guide to Nondiscriminatory Language*. Oryx, 1991.

Mills, Jane. *Womanwords*. Macmillan, 1989.

Roget's International Thesaurus. 4th edition. Harper & Row, 1984.

Urdang, Laurence. *The Oxford Thesaurus*. (American edition). Oxford University Press, 1992.

Alternative Applications: Extend the study with group participation in a rebus or scrambled word game naming women's wear. Include bonnet, corset, handkerchief, bloomers, laces, gloves, clog, calaash, bodice, muff, farthingale, shoes, cape, weskit, mules, slippers, camisole, petticoat, leotard, and reticule.

That's *my name*

Age/Grade Level or Audience: K–4 handwriting unit; English-as-a-second-language drill; daycare project.

Description: Pair female students' first names with famous women from history who have the same name.

Procedure: Have participants copy the letters of their first names on a sheet of paper. Discuss with each the name of someone who shares that first name and who is well known or who has made worthwhile achievements. Use these as models:

Alice	Alice Walker, Pulitzer Prize-winning author
Clara	Civil War nurse Clara Barton
Diane	Dian Fossey, conservationist and researcher
Elizabeth	Elizabeth Blackwell, first woman doctor in America
Esther	historian and writer Esther Forbes
Jacqueline	tap dancer Jacqueline Baker

Jane	Jane Alexander, actor; Jane Goodall, zoologist
Josafina	playwright Josafina Lopez
Julia	hymn writer Julia Ward Howe
Lois	Lois Lowry, author of *The Giver*
Margaret	birth control advocate Margaret Sanger
Marguerite	Marguerite Johnson, real name of writer Maya Angelou
Marie	Marie Curie, physicist who discovered radium
Molly	Molly Brant, native American peacemaker
Rachel	biologist and author, Rachel Carson
Sally	astronaut Sally Ride
Sandra	Sandra Day O'Connor, United States Supreme Court Justice
Victoria	Victoria, England's queen in the last century

Have participants cut out a symbol of achievement, such as a space capsule for Sally Ride or tap shoes for Jacqueline Baker. Inscribe each with the famous first name and attach them to a makeshift clothesline, wall, or window panes.

Budget: $

Sources:

Tuten-Puckett, Katharyn E. *My Name in Books: A Guide to Character Names in Children's Literature.* Libraries Unlimited, 1993.

Also, encyclopedias, history books, magazines, and newspapers.

Alternative Applications: Have each participant keep an open database, scrapbook, bulletin board, or collection of memorabilia that commemorate people with the same first name. Make time each day to ask if anyone heard a name in the news or in their reading or saw a picture of someone who belongs on one of the lists, for example, Elizabeth George, Pequot activist on the Connecticut reservation, or Pat Schroeder, U.S. Congresswoman who demanded more government action in the fight to prevent breast cancer. Help students share information to increase each other's collection of famous namesakes.

Using a Spanish dictionary

Age/Grade Level or Audience: Elementary and middle school reading assignment; summer book club library display; museum program; lecture series for educational television or radio.

Description: Study Maria Armengol Acierno's *Children of Flight Pedro Pan* by translating crucial terms from the story.

Procedure: Read aloud Maria Armengol Acierno's story of ten-year-old Maria, a fictional character representing the child refugees who fled the communist control that halted personal freedom of travel in Cuba in 1961. Assist participants in selecting important words in the story that appear in Spanish. Distribute Spanish-English dictionaries to small groups. Have each group elect a scribe to write the word, with its diacritical marks, and add a definition that fits the sentence from which the word is taken. Write some of these models on the chalkboard or distribute on handouts as examples:

a Dios	to God
bizcochos	cookies
cafe con leche	coffee with milk
caña	sugarcane
cerdo	pig
empanadas	pastry filled with meat or fish
gracias	thanks
hermanito	little brother
jojo	yo-yo
leche frita	white fudge
mi amor	my love
nacimiento	nativity scene
natilla	custard
negro	black
nervosa	nervous
niña	little girl
niño	little boy
niños	children
No mires para atras	Don't look back
Pedro Pan	Peter Pan
pelota	ball
pistolas	pistols
playa	beach
por favor	please
si	yes
soldado	soldier
zafra	harvest

Ask students to look for cognates, words that look the same in both English and Spanish. For example: *nervosa*/nervous, *Pedro Pan*/Peter Pan, *pistolas*/pistols, *soldado*/soldier. Have students name other pairs of words that bear no resemblance to each other, as with *si*/yes, *playa*/beach, *por favor*/please, *zafra*/harvest, and use an English dictionary to find clues to their derivation.

Budget: $

Sources:

Acierno, Maria Armengol. *Children of Flight Pedro Pan*. Kaleidoscope Press, 1994.

Bucuvalas, Tina. *South Florida Folklife*. University Press of Mississippi, 1993.

Gernand, Reneé. *Cuban Americans*. Chelsea House, 1988.

Santana, Francisco. *Cuban Roots*. Arca Publications, 1987.

Alternative Applications: Have participants retell Maria's story. Ask the following questions about her experience:

- Why does the escape seem like the flight of Peter Pan?

- What feelings and experiences does Maria share with Wendy Darling, the girl who supervises Peter's gang in J.M. Barrie's *Peter Pan?*

- How does Maria display her concern about the plight of people left behind in Cuba?

- What role does Maria's mother play in soothing her fears?

- What does Maria learn from the experience of flight that will make her stronger and less fearful?

- What kind of adult will Maria become?

What's *in the closet?*

Age/Grade Level or Audience: High school history or vocabulary assignment; college fashion or design research topic; women's study database; book club historical fashion show; newspaper column; library reference quiz; museum brochure.

Description: Compile an illustrated list of items from historic women's fashions.

Procedure: The blend of *haute couture,* fads, crazes, and sensible design in women's fashions began long before the war between midis and minis or the dance of the seven veils. For centuries, clothing styles have been hallmarks of what a culture believes about women and how women perceive both themselves and their aspirations. Thus, a study of women's garments, jewelry, and hairstyles—from corsets and lockets to farthingales, fringe, flounced petticoats, jumpers, stomachers, Merry Widows, and tiaras—is a revealing glance at history.

Create a database, glossary, or pronouncing gazetteer of unique items of fashion from many countries, such as the *ao dai,* the native costume in Vietnam, or the Polynesian *pareu,* a square or oblong scarf tied into a sarong or skirt. Note the era when the item was popular, what raw materials went into the costume, how it was adorned and detailed, and other important points of identity and use, such as the social class, religion, marital status, or level of education of the wearer, or a special purpose, as with Girl Scout, WAAC, and WAVE uniforms. Include these terms:

A-line skirt	gorget	pareu
amouti	huarache	parka
anorak	huipilli	pattens
barbette	kimono	pauluk
bathing cap	koteny	peignoir
boa	kuspeck	picture hat
boater	labret	pinafore
burberry	lei	robe
caftan	mackinaw	ruff
camisa	maniakis	sari
chador	mantilla	sarong
chiton	maxtli	shirtwaist

choker	mitts	snood
cloche	mob cap	stola
collet monté	moccasin	stomacher
corset	muff	surcote
cowl	mukluk	toque
dirndl	obi	tumpline
fibula	parasol	zarape

Add to the list other confining, shaping, or socially delineating styles that you find in your reading or in cinema or television.

Budget: $$

Sources:

Barber, Elizabeth Wayland. *Women's Work: The First 20,000 Years.* W. W. Norton, 1994.

Bentley, Toni. *Costumes by Karinska.* Abrams Books, 1995.

Fashions of a Decade, 1920s–1990s. Series edited by Valerie Cumming and Elane Feldman. Facts on File, various dates.

Kalman, Bobbie. *Colonial Life.* Crabtree, 1992.

———. *18th Century Clothing.* Crabtree, 1993.

———. *19th Century Clothing.* Crabtree, 1993.

Kennett, Frances. *Ethnic Dress.* Facts on File, 1995.

Lynton, Linda. *The Sari: Styles, Patterns, History, Technique.* Abrams Books, 1995.

Müller, Claudia. *The Costume Timeline.* Thames & Hudson, 1992.

Paterek, Josephine. *Encyclopedia of American Indian Costume.* ABC-Clio, 1994.

Yarwood, Doreen. *The Encyclopedia of World Costume.* Bonanza, 1986.

Alternative Applications: Organize a bulletin-board display of sketches that reveal how women's fashion has shaped women and their place in the family and society. Another use of this fashion panorama is a booklet or monograph arranged by era, country of origin, or category of garment, e. g., hats, ceremonial dress, nightwear, shoes, hair adornments, holiday or performance costumes, ritual jewelry, or purses and carryalls. Use a variety of source material to answer the following questions:

• Why have women followed social convention and worn or submitted to uncomfortable, disabling, humiliating, and disfiguring garments and adornments such as foot binding, waist cinch, labret, tattoo, chastity belt, panty girdle, burka, chador, veil, garter belt, and scarification?

• Which garments are worn as an enhancement of the body's natural curves, particularly the pannier, bustle, padded bra, laced corset, basque jacket, peplum, leg-of-mutton sleeve, bridal garter, rat, shoulder pads, empire waist, and pointed-toe shoes? Which garments detract from the natural female shape?

• What details symbolize marriage status, religious devotion, and political persuasion, as with the wimple, squash blossom hairdo, patching, mask, apron, habit, body paint, flower in the hair, tattoo, cradleboard, widow's weeds, mourning veil, wedding band, engagement ring, bridal knot, or train?

• What styles derive strictly from climate, terrain, and work and child care responsibilities, such as the cowl, snood, amouti, maternity smock, pareu, sarong, overalls, tunic, sling, backpack, parasol, leggings, jumpsuit, Mao jacket, padded vest, pinafore, jumper, nurse's cap, habit, wimple, stewardess's uniform, and slacks?

What's *in a name?*

Age/Grade Level or Audience: Elementary and middle school language or vocabulary lesson; English-as-a-second-language exercise; GED or adult literacy model.

Description: Introduce students to the concepts of denotation and connotation in reading, writing, and speech by exploring terms historically associated with women.

Procedure: Divide participants into groups of three to five and assign them a list of words to categorize by connotation or unstated meaning. Present words that have historically been applied to women, such as diva, chanteuse, meretrix, and meter maid, which describe professions—superior artists, the coaching prostitute from classical drama or comedy, and a female patrol officer issuing parking fines. Consider these terms:

amah	dowager	lady-in-waiting	old maid
angel	duenna	ladylove	parlor maid
au pair	empress	lass	princess
ayah	*frau*	lassie	queen
babe	*fraulein*	the little woman	*rani*
better half	gal	*madame*	scullery maid
bimbo	gentlewoman	*mademoiselle*	*senora*
chambermaid	girl	*maharani*	*senorita*
charlady	girlfriend	maid	siren
charwoman	goddess	maiden	sister
chatelaine	godmother	maidservant	sob sisters
chick	governess	mate	spinster
cleaning lady	grandmother	*materfamilias*	squaw
cleaning woman	grass widow	matron	stewardess
coquette	hag	minx	vamp
crone	handmaiden	miss	vixen
dame	helpmeet	the missus	waitress
darling	honey	mistress	war bride
divorcee	honey bunch	mother	wetnurse
doll	housekeeper	ms.	widow
domestic	hussie	nurse	wife
doña	ingenue	nursemaid	witch
donna	lady	old lady	witch woman

- Have participants create extensive headings, for example, relatives, workers, servants, joking terms, terms of endearment, insults or racial slurs, words that could apply to either gender, patronization, marital status, rank, criminality, and obsolete or foreign terms.

- Note words that could be on several lists, for example, *sugar, sugar babe, doll baby, dolly,* or *doll* could be an insult and term of endearment to a child, friend, or lover; likewise, *honey* can be a loving name or a patronizing term for a clerk or woman in business.

- Identify commonly used terms that usually exclude women, as with these:

bachelor	fisherman	paperboy
chairman	G-man	serviceman
company man	he-man	shipmaster
fellowship	man-hours	tradesman
ferryman	master-at-arms	underclassman
fireman	master-of-ceremonies	watchman

- Also identify words with the historically exclusive connotation of the female gender, such as these:

actress	huntress	old maid
aviatrix	laundress	patroness
beautician	majorette	prima donna
equestrienne	nanny	saleswoman
executrix	nun	schoolmarm
hostess	nurse	waitress

Notice that some terms are changing, as with *server* for *waitress* and *Worker's Compensation* for *Workman's Compensation*.

Assign individuals to keep an open database throughout the year as they glean new terms from their reading, viewing, and listening.

Budget: $

Sources:

Maggio, Rosalie. *The Dictionary of Bias-Free Usage: A Guide to Nondiscriminatory Language.* Oryx, 1991.

Mills, Jane. *Womanwords.* Macmillan, 1989.

Roget's International Thesaurus. 4th edition. Harper & Row, 1984.

Snodgrass, Mary Ellen. *The English Book.* Perma-Bound, 1991.

Urdang, Laurence. *The Oxford Thesaurus* (American edition). Oxford University Press, 1992.

Alternative Applications: Extend the study of connotative and denotative language by supplying categories and having students fill in words applying to the feminine gender. Conclude the study with a pairing of terms of both genders, as with these:

wild animals: buck/doe; lion/lioness or she-lion; wolf/she-wolf; fox/vixen; tiger/tigress; bear/she-bear; **domestic animals:** ram/ewe; bull/cow, bossy, heifer, or milk cow; stallion or stud/mare, nag, filly, dam, jade, or brood mare; billy/nanny or she-goat; boar/shoat or sow; peacock/peahen; jack/jenny; rooster or cock/hen or biddy; turkey cock/turkey hen; gander/goose.

Continue the study of paired terms for male and female with legal terms, employment terminology, and other categories.

Women *in Rome*

Age/Grade Level or Audience: Elementary Latin lesson; cooperative art project; home school activity.

Description: Make a collage honoring women from history who have Latin names.

Procedure: Have participants study Latin texts, history books, reference works on women's history and given names, and other sources for women's names that derive from Latin words. Use these as models:

- California Senator Barbara Boxer (*barbara* = foreign woman)
- COBOL computer language inventor Grace Hopper (*gratia* = thanks)
- actor Sylvia Sidney (*sylva* = forest)
- Red Cross founder Clara Barton (*clara* = bright)
- athlete Florence Griffith-Joyner (*flores* = flowers)

Continue this exercise with these:

Ava (bird)	May (spring)	Stella (star)
Bonnie (good)	Mina (smallest)	Terra (land)
Flavia (blonde)	Patricia (noblewoman)	Vera (true)
Lucy (light)	Regina (queen)	Virginia (maiden)

Also, match with real people some Latin given names, e. g. Julia, Lydia, Celia, Cornelia, Maria, Marcia, Paula, Lavinia, Marian, and Anna. Collect enough to make a wall hanging, door decoration, or rice paper window art.

Budget: $$

Sources:

Buckingham, Sandra. *Stencil It!* Firefly Books, 1995.

———. *Papiér-Mâché for Kids.* Firefly Books, 1995.

Traupmann, John C. *Latin Is Fun.* Amsco, 1989.

Alternative Applications: Clip articles about notable women from the newspaper or copy from textbooks. Underline these and other names that derive from Latin:

Ann Tallent	Julie Andrews	Marian Anderson
Anna Leonowens	Lucy Stone	Marie Curie
Clarissa Howe	Marcia Gillespie	Mary Brant
Cornelia Otis Skinner	Margaret Mitchell	Pauletta Pearson

Make a scrapbook or bulletin board of your collection. Indicate the work or accomplishment of each model. For example, Anna Leonowens was a tutor in Siam, Julie Andrews is an actor and singer, and Marcia Gillespie is a writer and the editor of *Ms.* magazine.

Law *and civil rights*

Anita *Hill: speaking out*

Age/Grade Level or Audience: High school history or civics class discussion; college introductory law study; library or online research exercise; bar association presentation; newsletter column or bulletin board display.

Description: Summarize the role of Anita Hill in illustrating the difficulties women have had in pressing suit against sexual harassment.

Procedure: Begin by presenting and defining sexual harassment in the workplace. Cite these and other examples of behaviors that are not appropriate:

- humiliating women with suggestive language
- demanding dates from employees
- touching, fondling, or brushing against women
- display or discussion of pornographic material

Have participants create three sets of details stemming from the Anita Hill controversy: facts, falsehoods, and questionable statements or situations. Include information that the panel supervising the Clarence Thomas hearings suppressed; particularly the testimony of other women charging Thomas with lewd or inappropriate anatomical comments, touching, remarks about pornographic material, and requests for dates. Suggest ways that the panel could have allayed the public's fears that Thomas brings dishonor to his role on the Supreme Court. Conclude with a discussion of the public's reaction if a similar situation had occurred ten, forty, or even eighty years ago.

Budget: $

Sources:

Bouchard, Elizabeth. *Everything You Need to Know about Sexual Harassment.* Rosen, 1995.

Fox, Ken. *Everything You Need to Know about Your Legal Rights.* Rosen, 1995.

Goldstein, Leslie Friedman, ed. *Feminist Jurisprudence: The Difference Debate.* University Press, 1992.

Larkin, June. *Sexual Harassment: High School Girls Speak Out.* Second Story Press, 1994.

The Legal Status of Women. Research Publications, 1995. (Microfiche)

Martin, Jean, gen. ed. *Who's Who of Women in the Twentieth Century.* Crescent Books, 1995.

Nicholas, Susan Cary, et al. *Rights and Wrongs: Women's Struggle for Legal Equality.* Feminist Press, 1995.

Sex and Justice—The Highlights of the Anita Hill/Clarence Thomas Hearings. First Run Films, 1993.

Alternative Applications: Suggest ways that Anita Hill and other women might protect themselves in a court battle from a stalemate of "he said/she said." Name these methods:

- keep a journal of comments, date, place, time, and witnesses

- acquire affidavits from witnesses shortly after incidents occur

- acquire photographic or taped evidence

- keep superiors informed of complaints

- make strong negative replies where witnesses can hear them

- utilize company-sanctioned grievance procedures

- insist that superiors make a fair assessment of the situation

Farewell *to Manzanar*

Age/Grade Level or Audience: Middle school, high school, or college history or civics class, history club, civic or library presentation or lecture series.

Description: Determine the political purpose and public and private ramifications of the internment of Japanese-American men, women, and children during World War II.

Procedure: Present the facts undergirding Jeanne Wakatsuki Houston and James Houston's *Farewell to Manzanar:*

- On December 7, 1941, the Japanese attacked American military posts and ships by an early-morning bombing run over Pearl Harbor, Hawaii.

- President Franklin Roosevelt declared war on December 8. On February 19, 1942, he issued Executive Order 9066, by which 700 Japanese-Americans suffered an unwarranted and unconstitutional arrest.

- FBI agents arrested Jeanne Wakatsuki Houston's father Ko, a fisherman, for allegedly supplying the enemy with fuel ferried out of Long Beach, California, on his fishing boat. Ko spent nearly nine months in a prison at Fort Lincoln, North Dakota, where he suffered frostbite and developed an addiction to alcohol.

- Ko's family was interned at Camp Manzanar on the Mojave Desert in northeastern California from April 1942 to October 1945, at which time the Wakatsukis were released and resettled in Cabrillo Homes, a flimsy housing project in Long Beach. Ko was unable to reassume his role as head of household. He died in 1957.

- The Americans bombed Hiroshima, Japan, on August 6, 1945. Three days later, a second bomb destroyed Nagasaki. On August 15, 1945, the Japanese signed an official surrender aboard the U.S.S. *Missouri*. On December 1, 1945, all internment camps were officially closed.

- At age 38, Jeanne Wakatsuki Houston, suffering emotional turmoil, returned with her husband and three children to the remains of Camp Manzanar, which had been virtually reclaimed by the desert. She found mementos of human occupation in the ruins of the artificial village in which she had grown up.

Have participants comment on the personal point of view in Jeanne Wakatsuki Houston's book, which she co-authored with her husband James. Discuss the devastation of the patriarchal family, Jeanne's inability to settle into a traditional lifestyle, and the growing strength of Riku,

Jeanne's resourceful and hard-working mother. Account for Jeanne Houston's unassuaged shame and grief in her adult years.

Budget: $

Sources:

Baker, Lillian. *Redress and Reparations Demands by Japanese-Americans.* Webb Research, 1991.

Bosworth, Allan R. *America's Concentration Camps.* Norton, 1967.

Bryant, Dorothy. "The School Yearbook with the Barbed-Wire Design." *Nation,* November 9, 1974, 469.

Cohen, Elie. *Human Behavior in the Concentration Camp.* Greenwood, 1984.

Ding, Loni. *The Color of Honor.* National Asian American Telecommunications Association, 1992. (Video)

Houston, Jeanne Wakatsuki, and James Houston. "Other Days of Infamy." *Mother Jones,* February/March, 1976.

Humanaka, Sheila. *The Journey: Japanese Americans, Racism and Renewal.* Orchard Books, 1990.

Sone, Monica. *Nisei Daughter.* University of Washington Press, 1979.

Uchida, Yoshiko. *The Invisible Thread.* Beech Tree, 1995.

"The War at Home." *Humanities,* March/April 1995, 320–35.

Weglyn, Michi. *Years of Infamy: The Untold Story of America's Concentration Camps.* Morrow, 1978.

Yamauchi, Wakako. *Songs My Mother Taught Me.* Feminist Press, 1995.

Yoshida, Michael, and Jenni Morozumi. *Concentrated Americans.* National Asian American Telecommunications Association, 1985. (Audiocassette)

Alternative Applications: Have students study *Farewell to Manzanar* along with these and other autobiographical views of World War II:

- Anne Frank's *The Diary of a Young Girl*

- Esther Hautzig's *The Endless Steppe*

- Carrie ten Boom's *The Hiding Place*

- Yoko Kawashima Watkins's *So Far from the Bamboo Grove*

Include the semi-autobiographical study in Amy Tan's *The Kitchen God's Wife* or *The Joy Luck Club* and Bette Greene's young-adult classic *The Summer of My German Soldier.* Present information on the noncombatant as a victim of hunger, disease, prejudice, racism, violence, displacement, upheaval, loss of property, disenfranchisement, and genocide. Compare the female survivor's behaviors as parent, worker, student, nurse, entrepreneur, inmate, underground member, accomplice, and refugee. Contrast Jeanne Wakatsuki Houston's emotional turmoil with the physical uprooting and menace suffered by other female victims.

Women *and integration*

Age/Grade Level or Audience: Junior high history or civics database; League of Women Voter's program; NAACP brochure; college introductory law study; library research exercise; historical society handout; newsletter; bulletin board display.

Description: Present a series of short oral biographies that underscore women's historic sympathies with other disenfranchised people, particularly during the movement to integrate public schools.

Procedure: Compose short essays on the role of female activists in the integration process. Stress these names and deeds alongside action shots from newspapers, magazines, and film clips:

- In 1896, a half century before civil rights marches began, Mary Church Terrell formed the National Association of Colored Women.

- On March 2, 1955, Claudette Colvin was arrested for her refusal to surrender her seat to a white passenger on a Montgomery, Alabama, public bus. On December 1, 1955, Rosa Parks suffered the same fate as Claudette Colvin for refusing to leave her bus seat.

- Dorothy Counts, the first black student to enroll at a public school in Charlotte, North Carolina, entered the building on September 9, 1957, amid taunts and jeers from white students and parents. Because of threats, her parents withdrew her from Harding High the next week.

- That same year, Elizabeth Eckford enrolled in Little Rock's Central High, where Arkansas Governor George Wallace's belligerent stand forced the federal government to dispatch federal marshals to assure student rights.

- Women's organizations sought peace in union: Ella Baker founded the Southern Christian Leadership Conference in 1957. Angela Davis supported the work of Black Panthers and other radical groups who spurred lagging integration movements to action. Civil rights activist Fannie Lou Hamer, who was arrested and beaten in June 1963 in Winona, Mississippi, continued her work and formed the Mississippi Freedom Democratic Party in 1964.

- Violence prevailed in some areas. On September 15, 1963, assassins bombed the Sixteenth Street Baptist Church of Birmingham, Alabama, and killed four black girls. While driving activists to nearby Selma on March 25, 1965, Viola Liuzzo was murdered by Ku Klux Klan members.

Budget: $

Sources:

Beals, Melba Pattillo. *Warriors Don't Cry: A Searing Memoir of the Battle to Integrate Little Rock's Central High*. Washington Square Press, 1994.

Garrow, David J., ed. *The Montgomery Bus Boycott and the Women Who Started It*. The University of Tennessee Press, 1987.

Griffin, Lynne, and Kelly McCann. *The Book of Women: 300 Notable Women History Passed By*. Bob Adams, 1992.

Levine, Ellen, ed. *Freedom's Children*. Avon, 1993.

Moody, Anne. *Coming of Age in Mississippi*. Dell, 1968.

Spirit to Spirit: Nikki Giovanni. Direct Cinema Ltd, n.d. (Video)

Strossen, Nadine. "75 ACLU Greatest Hits." *Civil Liberties,* spring 1995, 1–4.

The Struggle for Civil Rights. Knowledge Unlimited. (Posters)

Ward, Sam. "Milestones in Desegregation and Affirmative Action, 1954–1995." *USA Today,* June 13, 1995, 5A.

Webb, Sheyann, and Rachel West Nelson. *Selma, Lord, Selma: Girlhood Memories of the Civil Rights Days*. University of Alabama Press, 1980.

Women of Hope: African Americans Who Made a Difference. Knowledge Unlimited. (Posters)

Alternative Applications: Study the historic role of female activism in other areas of interest. Include voter registration, settlement work, suffrage, health care, abortion rights, day care, the abolition of slavery, pollution control, AIDS outreach, environmental concerns, shelters for the homeless, birth control, counseling for runaways, prohibition, MADD, anti-drug campaigns, and rape crisis and spouse abuse centers. Make a scrapbook of these attempts to improve life for minorities. Add photocopies or pictures of women currently in action in your community or state.

Women *and the law*

Age/Grade Level or Audience: Middle school civics banner; high school law study; library posters; literary society presentation; American Constitution Week newsletter or bulletin board display.

Description: Draw a banner or series of posters celebrating historic court cases that expanded women's rights.

Procedure: Decorate a classroom, library or courthouse wall, museum display, or women's history fair. Stress these cases from the last three decades that have advanced the cause of women:

- **1961** *Poe v. Ullman,* an unsuccessful, but highly publicized assault on Connecticut's ban of contraceptive sales, which Justice John Harlan declared an invasion of privacy

- **1965** *Griswold v. Connecticut,* an invalidation of the Connecticut law halting use of contraception, thereby violating marital privacy

- **1967** *Loving v. Virginia,* the defeat of Virginia's anti-miscegenation laws that violate rights to choose marital partners

- **1968** *King v. Smith,* which established that states cannot withhold welfare to children whose mothers maintain a common-law marriage

- **1971** *Reed v. Reed,* a reversal of preferential selection of men as executors of estates, a clear example of sex bias

- **1971** *U.S. v. Vuitch,* which expanded abortion rights by declaring that the health of a patient includes psychological as well as physical considerations

- **1972** *Eisenstadt v. Baird,* the defeat of a Massachusetts law refusing contraceptive devices to unmarried women

- **1973** *Frontiero v. Richardson,* which altered the status of male dependents of women in the armed forces so that spouses of all soldiers can claim dependent status

- **1973** *Roe v. Wade,* a landmark decision upholding women's right to control their own bodies and the defeat of state laws criminalizing abortion

- **1978** *In re* Primus, which allows an ACLU lawyer to encourage females on welfare to sue the state for requiring sterilization

- **1992** *Planned Parenthood v. Casey,* which overturned Pennsylvania's restrictive laws criminalizing abortion

- **1993** *J. E. B. v. T. B.,* which guaranteed the rights of both sexes to serve on juries

Budget: $$

Sources:

Century of Women: Sexuality and Social Justice. Instructional Video, 1994. (Video)

Dickerson, Marla. "Affirmative Action: A Question of Fairness." *Detroit News,* July 14, 1995, 11A.

Finkelman, Paul, gen. ed. *Abortion Law in the United States.* Garland, 1995.

Friedman, Jane. *America's First Woman Lawyer: Myra Bradwell.* Prometheus, 1993.

Goldstein, Leslie Friedman, ed. *Feminist Jurisprudence: The Difference Debate.* University Press, 1992.

Johnson, John W., ed. *Historic U.S. Court Cases, 1690–1990.* Garland, 1995.

Katz, Montana, and Veronica Vieland. *Get Smart!* Feminist Press, 1994.

Landmark Documents in American History. Facts on File, 1995. (CD-ROM)

The Legal Status of Women. Research Publications, 1995. (Microfiche)

Marshall, Steve. "Megan's Law Upheld." *USA Today,* July 26, 1995, 2A.

Nicholas, Susan Cary, et al. *Rights and Wrongs: Women's Struggle for Legal Equality.* Feminist Press, 1995.

Perry, Nancy J. "If You Can't Join 'Em, Beat 'em." *Fortune,* September 21, 1992, 58–59.

The Rights of Women: The Basic ACLU Guide to Women's Rights. American Civil Liberties Union, 1993.

Shannon, Elaine. "Skirts and Daggers." *Time,* June 12, 1995, 46–47.

Strossen, Nadine. "75 ACLU Greatest Hits." *Civil Liberties,* Spring 1995, 1–4.

Wortman, Marlene Stein, ed. *Women in American Law: From Colonial Times to the New Deal.* Holmes & Meier, 1985.

Alternative Applications: Create a bulletin board composed of original political cartoons, caricatures, or comic strips of women lawyers on the job. Show volunteer attorneys interviewing poor and disenfranchised clients for the Legal Aid Society. Depict the plight of female migrant workers, deportees, immigrants, illegal aliens, victims of spousal abuse, and workers suffering sexual harassment or job discrimination. Carry your drawings through mediation, lawsuits, and adjudication, with these actual examples:

- In 1994 Col. Margarethe Cammermeyer, winner of a bronze star in Vietnam, won reinstatement in the Army Nurse Corps after being discharged for admitted homosexuality.

- August 7, 1994, feminist writer Taslima Nasrin eluded a charge of religious offense in Bangladesh, where officials charged her with blasphemy for writing *Shame,* a novel lambasting Muslim fanatics for persecuting Hindus, and for demanding a revision of the Koran.

- June 2, 1995, exotic dancers lost their appeal against charges of prostitution.

- June 27, 1995, Susan Thibaudeau lost her case against the taxation of child-support payments in Canada's Supreme Court.

Women *and slavery*

Age/Grade Level or Audience: Middle school and high school English or history study; women's studies topic; NAACP seminar; library research exercise; literary society symposium; museum or library display; newsletters and media miniseries.

Description: Summarize the situations that influenced women's views of enslavement.

Procedure: Have participants contribute to a study of women during slave times. Look in reference works, databases, diaries, journals, family records, letters, and interviews for answers to these questions:

- How did black slave women become trusted healers and midwives? Where did they learn about herbs and naturopathic treatment?

- Why did black and white herders and field workers in cane, indigo, tobacco, rice, and vegetables have low status?

- Why were house slaves valued above field hands? How did they utilize books and conversations as methods of learning?

- Why did plantation owners hire out press gangs to industries such as tanneries, brickyards, mines, shipyards, cigarette factories, ironworks, and quarries?

- Who tended the children of women serving on press gangs? How were these caretakers chosen?

- Why were the wetnurse and nanny significant in white families? What role did the wetnurse play in the life of the black infant?

- Why did plantation owners frequently sell slave children in infancy or early childhood?

- Why were pregnant slaves protected from overwork and severe discipline, such as starvation, whipping, mutilation, or solitary confinement?

- How did women relax on holidays or weekends when they were free from duties? Why was this a good time to escape?

- What did female slaves recall about the coming of freedom? How did their lives change with added opportunity, but also with the added responsibility of caring for their families by earning a wage or working as sharecroppers?

Budget: $

Sources:

Black Americans of Achievement: Harriet Tubman. Instructional Video, 1992. (Video)

Black Americans of Achievement: Sojourner Truth. Instructional Video, 1992. (Video)

Dudden, Faye E. *Serving Women: Household Service in Nineteenth-Century America.* Wesleyan University Press, 1983.

A History of Slavery in America. Instructional Video, 1994. (Video)

Lester, Julius. *To Be a Slave.* Scholastic, 1968.

Morrison, Toni. *Beloved.* New American Library, 1987.

"Slavery in Ante-Bellum Southern Industries." University Publications of America, 1995. (Microfilm)

Southern Women and Their Families in the Nineteenth Century: Papers and Diaries. University Publications of America, 1995. (Microfilm)

Sterling, Dorothy. *Ahead of Her Time: Abby Kelley and the Politics of Antislavery.* W. W. Norton, 1991.

Straight, Susan. *I Been in Sorrow's Kitchen and Licked out All the Pots.* Doubleday, 1993.

Yellin, Jean Fagan. *Women & Sisters: The Antislavery Feminists in American Culture.* Yale University Press, 1989.

Alternative Applications: Explain why slavery for women carried an extra burden—the birth of mixed-race children sired by white owners, slavers, and overseers. Discuss the predicament of hating the conception, but loving the unborn child. Learn how enslaved women aborted their own children or trusted their lives to medicine women, who used primitive methods and potions to cause an abortion. Also discuss with a small group what enslaved parents might have felt for children whom the mother was forced to bear and subsequently lose when the children were sold as excess field hands or traded to repay debts.

Women *making law*

Age/Grade Level or Audience: Middle school biographical outline; college political science lecture; history database; library research exercise or card file; historical society presentation; newsletter feature; bulletin board display.

Description: Outline the life and influence of female lawmakers.

Procedure: Create an annotated outline or time line depicting the significant female lawmakers in America. Stress how they arrived at positions of importance and the legislation they promoted. Use Senator Pat Schroeder as a model:

- Born in Portland, Oregon, on July 30, 1940, Patricia Scott Schroeder graduated Phi Beta Kappa, Magna Cum Laude, from the University of Minnesota and earned a law degree from Harvard in 1964. As a practicing attorney in Denver, she served the National Labor Relations Board and as a proponent of working women at the Colorado Department of Personnel and Planned Parenthood.

- Running on an anti-Vietnam War platform in 1972, she won both a congressional seat and a reputation for her vocal, sometimes humorous, feminism. As chair of a subcommittee of the House Armed Services Committee, Schroeder fought for tighter control of Pentagon spending.

- The first woman to wield power in military matters, Schroeder has also championed gender and family issues: the availability of abortion and testing of abortifacients, discrimination against homosexuals in the military, poor treatment of military wives, women's health allocations, child support, family leave, and women in combat.

Apply this model to the lives of Sadie Alexander, Carol Moseley-Braun, Jeanne Kirkpatrick, Barbara Boxer, Dianne Feinstein, Nancy Kassebaum, Kay Bailey Hutchison, Patty Murray, Madeleine Kunin, Irma Vidal Santaella, Christine Whitman, Madeleine Albright, and Barbara Mikulski.

Budget: $

Sources:

Brill, Alida, ed. *A Rising Public Voice: Women in Politics Worldwide.* Feminist Press, 1995.

Fireside, Bryna J. *Is There a Woman in the House . . . or Senate?* Albert Whitman & Co., 1993.

"A Freshman in the Weapons Club." *Nation,* November 5, 1973.

Le Veness, Frank P., and Jane P. Sweeney. *Women Leaders in Contemporary U.S. Politics.* Lynn Rienner Publishers, 1987.

McElwaine Sandra. "Front and Center." *USA Weekend,* Marsh 11, 1994, 4–6.

Morris, Celia. *Storming the Statehouse.* Scribner's, 1992.

Schroeder, Patricia. *Champion of the Great American Family.* Random House, 1989.

———. "Toward Effective and Family-Friendly National Policies for U.S. Children and Their Families." *Denver University Law Review,* 1992, 303–14.

Witt, Linda, et al. *Running as a Woman: Gender and Power in American Politics.* Free Press, 1993.

Alternative Applications: Establish a database or card file of female legislators and their proposals for equality, health care, and support for families. Include such U.S. senators, congresswomen, and lobbyists as Barbara Mikulski and Carol Moseley-Braun and these women from other countries: Mary Robinson (Ireland), Diane Abbot (England), Gloria Bonder (Argentina), Eugenia Charles (Dominica), Hanna Beate Schoepp-Schilling (Germany), Rigoberta Menchu (Guatemala), Talima Nasrin (Bangladesh), and Wu Qing (China). Report on the percentage of voters who support them and the media's response to their humanistic agendas.

Library *research*

Book *of the week*

Age/Grade Level or Audience: Reading guide for all ages; checklist of exemplary titles in women's literature; weekly newspaper feature.

Description: Publish a monthly list of works by women in a single genre.

Procedure: Supply library patrons or a local newspaper column with titles of books by women in categories such as children's literature, books on tape, videos, reference works and data-bases, large print books, and journals as well as novels, short fiction, mysteries, westerns, poetry, and drama. Mix current bestsellers with reissued works and annotated volumes of classics. Place new books on racks at the ends of rows or mark them with a ribbon or gold star.

Budget: $$

Sources:

Bailey, Brooke. *The Remarkable Lives of 100 Women Writers and Journalists.* Bob Adams, 1994.

Bauermeister, Erica, Jesse Larsen, and Holly Smith. *500 Great Books by Women.* Penguin Books, 1994.

"Celebrate Reading Together." *Instructor,* May/June 1995, 24.

Skow, John. "Books: Cops with Machisma." *Time,* October 3, 1994, 43.

"Spotlight on the Playwright." *On the Issues,* spring 1995, 32.

Also, newspaper and journal book columns, *Publishers Weekly, New York Review of Books, Mystery Readers Journal, VOYA, ARBA, Booklist,* and other review services.

Alternative Applications: Use desktop publishing to create brochures, bookmarks, wall charts, or paper fans listing library holdings in particular areas by or about women. Keep a lively, varied offering of works such as these:

Biography

- *Anne Frank: The Diary of a Young Girl*
- Lewis L. Gould, ed., *American First Ladies: Their Lives and Their Legacy*
- Brooke Kroeger's *Nellie Blye: Daredevil, Reporter, Feminist*
- Patricia McMahon's *Chi-Hoon, a Korean Girl*

Books on Tape

- Margaret Atwood's *The Handmaid's Tale*
- Avi's *The True Confessions of Charlotte Doyle*
- Rita Dove's *Selected Poems*

Crime Novels

- Patricia Cornwell's *The Body Farm*
- Carol O'Connell's *Mallory's Oracle*
- April Smith's *North of Montana*

Essays

- Sally Alexander's *History Workshop*
- Florence King's *The Florence King Reader*

Historical Fiction

- Jennifer Owings Dewey's *Cowgirl Dreams*
- Ching Yeung Russell's *First Apple*
- Fred Trump's *Lincoln's Little Girl*
- Alice Walker's *The Color Purple*

History

- Elizabeth Barber's *Women's Work*
- Bobbie Kalman's *Colonial Life Series*
- Jo Ann Levy's *They Saw the Elephant: Women in the California Gold Rush*
- Erlene Stetson and Linda David's *Glorying in Tribulation: The Lifework of Sojourner Truth*
- Martha Vicunus, ed., *Hidden from History*

Interviews

- Dannye Romine Powell's *Parting the Curtains*

Magazines

- *American Girl*
- *City Family*
- *Cobblestone*
- *On the Issues*
- *Ms.*
- *Working Woman*

Memoir

- Zlata Filipovich's *Zlata's Diary*
- Brenda Ueland's *Me: Me A Memoir*

Multicultural

- Anne O. Freed's *The Changing Worlds of Older Women in Japan*
- Zohl de Ishtar's *Daughters of the Pacific*
- Soyini Madison's *The Woman That I Am*
- Bharati Mukherjee's *The Holder of the World*
- Emily Nasrallah's *A House Not Her Own: Stories from Beirut*

Celebrating *women's history*

Novels

- Isabel Allende's *The House of the Spirits*
- Valerie Martin's *The Great Divorce*
- Terri McMillan's *Mama*
- Toni Morrison's *Beloved*
- E. Annie Proulx's *The Shipping News*
- Susan Straight's *I Been in Sorrow's Kitchen and Licked Out All the Pots*

Plays

- Jane Campion's *The Piano*
- Carolyn Gage's *The Second Coming of Joan of Arc and Other Plays*
- Sharon Pollock's *Blood Relations*
- Ntozake Shange's *for colored girls who have considered suicide/when the rainbow is enuf*

Poetry

- Anna Akmatova's *The Italics Are Mine*
- Stella and Frank Chipasula, eds, *African Women's Poetry*
- Chrystos's *Fire Power*
- Carolyn Forchés's *Gathering the Tribes*
- Tess Gallagher's *Portable Kisses*

Read-aloud books for preschoolers

- Virginia L. Kroll's *Naomi Knows It's Springtime*
- Christine San José and Debrah Santini's *Cinderella*
- Pegi Deitz Shea's *The Whispering Cloth*
- Laura E. Williams's *The Long Silk Strand*
- Jane Breskin Zalben's *Miss Violet's Shining Day*

Reference

- Kimberly Colen's *Peas and Honey: Recipes for Kids*
- Cathy N. Davidson and Linda Wagner-Martin, eds, *The Oxford Companion to Women's Writing in the United States*
- Paul J. Dubeck, ed., *Women and Work: A Handbook*

Religion

- Christina Buchmann and Celina Spiegel's *Out of the Garden: Women Writers on the Bible*
- Shahin Gerami's *Women and Fundamentalism: Islam and Christianity*
- Elaine Pagels's *The Origin of Satan*
- Swami Sivananda Radha's *Mantras: Words of Power*

Science

- Jennifer Owings Dewey's *Wildlife Rescue: The Work of Dr. Kathleen Ramsay*

- Elaine Morgan's *The Scars of Evolution: What Our Bodies Tell Us about Human Origins*

Short Fiction

- Sandra Cisneros's *The House on Mango Street*

- Frieda Forman and Ethel Raicus's *Found Treasures: Stories by Yiddish Women Writers*

- Sue Thomas, ed., *Wild Women: Contemporary Short Stories by Women Celebrating Women*

- Diana Vélez, ed., *Reclaiming Medusa: Short Stories by Contemporary Puerto Rican Women*

Videos

- *Babette's Feast*

- *Daughters of the Dust*

- *Impromptu*

- *Little Women*

Young Adult Fiction

- Lois Lowry's *The Giver*

- Cynthia Rylant's *Missing May*

Overcoming *the odds*

Age/Grade Level or Audience: Any-age writing contest; women's studies project, school or public library exercise; teacher education research model; civic club competition.

Description: Sponsor a contest that honors women who have overcome physical or mental disabilities.

Procedure: Ask a civic club, Friends of the Library, or Chamber of Commerce to celebrate Women's History Month by sponsoring a writing or speech contest honoring women who have succeeded despite disabilities. Use this model of Chris Costner Sizemore, the real woman behind *The Three Faces of Eve*, as an example of pre-writing:

- born April 4, 1927, to tenant farmer Acie Costner and Zueline Hastings near Wallace, North Carolina

- early traumas—deaths of neighbors, a cousin, an uncle and aunt, and a grandmother; dissociative memories and sleepwalking

- from early childhood—multiple personality syndrome brought on by repressed memories and rage at the birth of her three siblings

- security from living close to grandparent; loss of security after the family moved

- in the early forties, emergence of the Freckle Girl, the Blind Girl, the Liar, and the Singing Girl, all fragmented selves incapable of superseding the aliases

- unpredictable outbursts that preceded fainting, headaches, and unexplained blindness; an abrupt conclusion to a first love and an attempted suicide

- emergence of the Big-Eyed Girl; quit school and worked in a factory sewing uniforms

- married stunt driver Al Thorne, an abusive husband; settled briefly in Augusta, Georgia, before returning home

- more physical anomalies preceding marriage to Ralph White and the birth of daughter Taffy Acieline January 9, 1948; a traumatic miscarriage of a second child

- treatment at Augusta University Hospital from Dr. Corbett H. Thigpen, who introduced Chris's unusual mental state at the American Psychiatric Association in Los Angeles and published an article about it in the *American Weekly*

- evolved Chris White and Chris Costner, alter egos who battled for control

- marriage to Don Sizemore December 19, 1953, and continued corresponding with Dr. Thigpen

- filming of *The Three Faces of Eve* and publication of *The Final Face of Eve*

- birth of Bobby in 1959; illness, accident, and the failing health of her parents

- treatment by Dr. Tony A. Tsitos of Annandale, Virginia, in 1975, when 22 personalities ultimately swirled in Chris's mind

- writing a definitive study of the dissociative nightmare and reliving of repressed memories; peace in her tormented spirit

- receipt of the Clifford W. Beers and the National Mental Health Bell of Hope awards in 1982

Consider these women and their obstacles and achievements as possible subjects for research:

- activist Marvella Bayh, cancer

- actor and diplomat Shirley Temple Black, cancer

- Iditarod winner Susan Butcher, dyslexia

- historian and young-adult author Esther Forbes, sight impairment

- actor Marlee Matlin, deafness

- author and playwright Carson McCullers, alcoholism and stroke

- actor Patricia Neale, stroke

- Helen Keller, deafness and blindness

- Kitty O'Neil, deafness

- short fiction writer and novelist Flannery O'Connor, lupus

- athlete Wilma Rudolf, polio

- teacher Annie Sullivan, trachoma and partial blindness

Budget: $$$$

Sources:

Bhalerao, Usha. *Eminent Blind Women of the World.* Sterling Publishers, 1988.

Holcomb, Mabs, and Sharon Wood. *Deaf Women: A Parade through the Decades.* DawnSign-Press, 1989.

Lancaster, Evelyn, with James Poling. *The Final Face of Eve.* McGraw-Hill, 1958.

Rousso, Harilyn. *Disabled, Female, and Proud! Stories of Ten Women with Disabilities.* Exceptional Parent Press, 1988.

Sizemore, Chris Costner. *A Mind of My Own*. William Morrow, 1989.

Sizemore, Chris Costner, and Elen Sain Pittillo. *I'm Eve*. Doubleday, 1977.

Van Biema, David. "Three Faces of Eve Told Her Story." *People Weekly*, March 27, 1989, 79–82.

Alternative Applications: Create a poster honor roll for a hospital, rehabilitation center, veteran's home, museum, library, or school on which you record a brief statement of the accomplishments of prestigious disabled women. Use this brief data sheet on Helen Keller as a model:

- Helen Adams Keller, blinded and deafened in early childhood by an outbreak of scarlet fever in 1882 in Tuscumbia, Alabama; until age seven, the pampered, uncontrollable child of Kate Adams and Arthur Keller, a Confederate officer

- student of Annie Mansfield Sullivan, a partially blind teacher; learned that abstract movements against her skin were code for thoughts, emotions, and objects; entered Boston's Horace Mann School for the Deaf; completed a sociology degree from Radcliffe College

- brilliant writer and lecturer, suffragist, champion of the handicapped; volunteer at veterans' hospitals and convalescent homes during World War II; traveler and author of autobiographies; creator of the American Foundation for the Blind in 1924

Reader's *circle*

Age/Grade Level or Audience: All-ages reading list; summer reading program.

Description: Compile a multi-faceted reading and story-hour program to introduce readers to works that have strong women as characters and that portray resilient ties among females in the community.

Procedure: Select a list of poems, plays, biographies, autobiographies, nonfiction, and speeches that express strength, character, and action on the part of admirable females. Consider these possibilities, which represent the writing of both male and female authors from a cross-section of world literature:

Preschool

Angela's Airplane, Michael Martchenko

Anna in the Garden, Diane Dawson Hearn

Avalanche in the Alps, Betsy Loredo

Moira's Birthday, Robert Munsch

My Mother the Mail Carrier/Mi Mama la Cartera, Inez Maury

The Tinker of Salt Creek, Susan Hand Shetterly

Primary

Agatha's Feather Bed, Carmen Agra Deedy

Anastasia at Your Service, Lois Lowry

Are You There, God? It's Me, Margaret, Judy Blume

The Castle of Pictures: A Grandmother's Tale, George Sand

Charlotte's Web, E. B. White

The Farolitos of Christmas, Rudolfo Anaya

From the Mixed-Up Files of Mrs. Basil E. Frankweiler, E. L. Konigsburg

The Legend of the Bluebonnet, Tomie de Paola

Los Niños Alfabéticos, Lourdes Ayala and Margarita Isona-Rodríguezs

Pippi Longstocking, Astrid Lindgren

Sadako and the Thousand Paper Cranes, Eleanor Coerr

Elementary

Abuelita's Paradise, Carmen S. Nodar

The Anne of Green Gables Storybook, L. M. Montgomery

Buffalo Gals: Women of the Old West, Brandon Marie Miller

Family Celebrations, Diane Patrick

The Hundred Dresses, Eleanor Estes

Little House on the Prairie, Laura Ingalls Wilder

Manya's Story: Faith and Survival in Revolutionary Russia, Bettyanne Gray

The Secret Garden, Frances Hodgson Burnett

Tuck Everlasting, Natalie Babbitt

Middle School

Allegra Maud Goldman, Edith Konecky

A Book of Americans, Stephen Vincent Benet and Rosemary Benet

Camilla, Madeleine L'Engle

Daughter of the Mountain/Un Cuento, Edna Escamill

Deenie, Judy Blume

The Earth-Sea Trilogy, Ursula Le Guin

Editha's Burthar, Frances Hodgson Burnett

The Enchanted Raisin, Jacqueline Balcells

Forbidden Friendship, Judith Eichler Weber

Julie of the Wolves, Jean Craighead George

Golden Quest, Bonnie Bader

Missing May, Cynthia Rylant

Singing Softly/Cantando Bajito, Carmen de Monteflores

A Thief on Morgan's Plantation, Lisa Banim

A Wrinkle in Time, Madeleine L'Engle

Zlata's Diary, Zlata Filipovic

High School

The Diary of a Young Girl, Anne Frank (1995 edition)

The Good Earth, Pearl Buck

Happy Endings Are All Alike, Sandra Scoppettone

     Journey toward Freedom: The Story of Sojourner Truth, Jacqueline Bernard

     A Raisin in the Sun, Lorraine Hansberry

     Sally Wister's Journal

     Short Stories of Katherine Mansfield

Mature Advanced Readers

     Camille, Alexandre Dumas Fils

     The Good Mother, Sue Miller

     Red Azalea, Anchee Min

     The Robber Bride, Margaret Atwood

     Steel Guitar, Linda Barnes

     Through the Arc of the Rain Forest, Karen Tei Yamashita

     True and False Romances, Ana Lydia Vega

Budget: $$

Sources:

Use a general catalog, particularly these:

- Harper Audio Caedmon, 10 E. 53rd St., New York, NY 10022
  800-242-7737, FAX: 800-822-4090

- Listening Library, One Park Ave., Old Greenwich, CT 06870-1727
  800-243-4504, FAX: 204-698-1998

- Perma-Bound, Vandalia Rd., Jacksonville, IL 62650
  800-637-6581, FAX: 217-243-7505

- Recorded Books, 270 Skipjack Rd., Prince Frederick, MD 20678
  800-638-1304, FAX: 410-535-5499

Alternative Applications: Include non-readers or disadvantaged readers in a skill-building program that pairs works with tapes. Utilize the following titles from these lists. Conclude with a "tape" or film festival featuring one of these favorite titles:

Preschool or Primary

     Are You My Mother?, P. D. Eastman

     Cam Jansen and the Mystery of the Dinosaur Bones, David A. Adler

     A Chair for My Mother, Vera B. Williams

     Linnea in Monet's Garden, Ludwig Bemelmans

     Ramona Quimby, Beverly Cleary

Elementary

     Anastasia Krupnik, Lois Lowry

     Anne of Green Gables, L. M. Montgomery

     Dear Mr. Henshaw, Beverly Cleary

     A Gathering of Days, Joan W. Blos

Middle School

Dicey's Song, Cynthia Voigt

The Face on the Milk Carton, Caroline B. Cooney

Robert Frost in Recital

Sing down the Moon, Scott O'Dell

A Tree Grows in Brooklyn, Betty Smith

The True Confessions of Charlotte Doyle, Avi

Zia, Scott O'Dell

High School

The Caedmon Treasury of Modern Poets Reading Their Own Poetry

A Child's Christmas in Wales, Dylan Thomas

Poems from Black Africa

The Talking Earth, Jean Craighead George

Mature Reluctant Readers

The Autobiography of Miss Jane Pittman, Ernest Gaines

Medicine Woman, Lynn V. Andrews

Woman Warrior, Maxine Hong Kingston

Hispanic Readers

Caperucita Roja, F. Boada

El Gato Ensombrerado, Dr. Seuss

Eres Tu Mi Mama?, P. D. Eastman

Yaci Y Su Muneca, C. Zendrera

Tracking *famous women*

Age/Grade Level or Audience: High school library exercise or board game; public library handout; research model for written or oral presentation; women's studies warm-up exercise.

Description: Introduce a research project with a puzzle on famous women.

Procedure: In conjunction with a study of notable women in history have participants move from **Start** to **Finish** by linking seventy blocks either vertically or horizontally, but not diagonally. The clues will lead the way. [For puzzle grid see p. 478]

Questions:

1. Who served as medical technologist at Lambaréne, Gabon?

2. Who championed the cause of human treatment of the insane?

3. Who founded soup kitchens and homeless shelters and edited the *Catholic Worker?*

4. Who opened a New York foster home to crack babies and children with AIDS?

5. Who revolutionized painting with vivid desert scenes and close-up drawings of flowers?

6. Who wrote "The New Colossus," inscribed now on the Statue of Liberty?

7. Who lived alone and communicated through vivid imagist verse and letters?

8. What black poet is known as "the ninth Muse?"

9. Who petitioned her husband to think of women as he and other males drafted the Constitution?

10. Who championed rights for women and children during the formation of the United Nations?

11. Who restored genteel dining and tasteful redecoration of the White House?

12. Who studied sculpture under Auguste Rodin and created numerous works rivaling his masterpieces?

13. Whose mother and child portraits added a feminine perspective to impressionist art?

14. Who became the first Native American prima ballerina?

15. Who made baskets and sold them as works of art?

16. Who was elected head of the Cherokees?

17. Who studied primates?

18. Who defended apes in the wild from poachers?

19. Who studied the Olduvai Gorge for evidence of early civilization?

20. Who was the first American woman in space?

21. What Native American woman sat for a portrait in England?

22. What social worker defended the rights of Native Americans to own land?

23. Who studied adolescent Samoans?

24. Who isolated radium?

25. Who treated polio victims with hot packs and exercise?

26. Who led her own dance troupe and choreographed a tribute at the 1984 Olympics?

27. What dancer made her stage reputation on one performance of "Cry?"

28. What housekeeper turned humor into a syndicated column?

29. What female interviewer earned recognition on CBS's "60 Minutes?"

30. What female journalist co-anchored with Dan Rather?

31. What singer-actor pioneered television talk shows?

32. What actress was known as "the first lady of the American stage?"

33. What pilot was suspected of espionage?

34. What congresswoman joined in the public airing of Anita Hill's testimony against Clarence Thomas?

35. What law professor insisted that sexual harassment is a serious crime?

36. What cabinet member served as Secretary of Health and Human Services in the Clinton administration?

37. What writer-activist founded and edited *Ms.* magazine?

38. What writer of the 1960s published *The Feminine Mystique?*

39. What novelist wrote *The Kitchen God's Wife,* a fictional memoir of wife abuse and unjust imprisonment during World War II?

40. What Caribbean author earned fame in the young adult market?

41. What South American was immortalized in the Broadway musical *Evita?*

42. What female Russian divulged the secrets of the Stalin years?

43. What champion of birth control and abortion rights led Planned Parenthood?

44. What Georgian woman oversaw the Martin Luther King Museum?

45. What singer released an album of duets with her father?

46. What rock star fought spouse abuse?

47. What chef introduced French cooking on televised broadcasts?

48. What cosmetics manufacturer excelled in business and trendsetting?

49. What widow established a cosmetics line sold door-to-door?

50. What pacifist tried to study the Vietnam War from both sides?

51. What designer became rich by creating cosmetics and fashions for the elite woman?

52. What country singer recorded the hit "Crazy?"

53. What country performer helped rehabilitate Johnny Cash?

54. What New England governor showcased Vermont's products?

55. What Texas governor helped bring down the Bush administration?

56. What singer/composer/movie producer starred in *Yentl?*

57. What autobiographer produced her life story in five volumes?

58. What actor earned acclaim for her appearance as the maid in *Driving Miss Daisy?*

59. What black exotic dancer found acceptance in Paris?

60. What choreographer influenced the early career of Betty Ford?

61. What comedian headed an entertainment complex?

62. What actor became a European princess?

63. What singer gave a public performance before the Lincoln Memorial?

64. What gospel singer performed at Martin Luther King's funeral?

65. What widow of a Middle East leader became a lecturer at an American college?

66. What politician became the first major party candidate for vice-president?

67. What African freedom fighter was accused of kidnapping and obstructing police investigations?

68. What Asian prime minister fought unsubstantiated accusations of corruption?

69. What chemist became a prime minister?

70. What wife of a Filipino activist was elected president?

Budget: $$

Sources:

Bailey, Brooke. *The Remarkable Lives of 100 Women Artists*. Bob Adams, 1994.

————. *The Remarkable Lives of 100 Women Healers and Scientists*. Bob Adams, 1994.

————. *The Remarkable Lives of 100 Women Writers and Journalists*. Bob Adams, 1994.

Bataille, Gretchen M. *Native American Women: A Biographical Dictionary*. Garland, 1993.

Griffin, Lynne, and Kelly McCann. *The Book of Women: 300 Notable Women History Passed By*. Bob Adams, 1992.

Hay, Susannah. *The Women's Heritage Scrapbook*. Caillech Press, n.d.

Hine, Darlene Clark. *Black Women in American*. 2 vols. Carlson, 1993.

James, Edward T., ed. *Notable American Women: A Biographical Dictionary*. Belknap, 1973.

Salem, Dorothy C. *African American Women: A Biographical Dictionary*. Garland, 1993.

Sherr, Lynn, and Jurate Kazickas. *Susan B. Anthony Slept Here*. Random House, 1994.

Smith, Jessie Carney. *Notable Black American Women*. Gale Research, 1992.

Telgen, Diane, and Jim Kamp, eds. *Notable Hispanic American Women*. Gale Research, 1993.

Weatherford, Doris. *American Women's History*. Prentice Hall, 1994.

Alternative Applications: Present the quiz matrix to groups of researchers. Have them create their own rules and write their own questions for alternate games of "Tracking Famous Women." Organize a separate group of game-makers to write a new set of names from a particular era, movement, or country. For example, produce similar games for "Tracking Famous Women Scientists," "Tracking Famous Roman Women," "Tracking Famous Female Characters," "Tracking Hollywood's Illustrious Actresses," "Tracking Women Leaders," or "Tracking Female Artists and Musicians."

Who *am I?*

Age/Grade Level or Audience: Middle school library research or scrambled word game; Women's History Month civic-center bulletin board game; book club warm-up activity or place-mat quiz; women's studies database; newspaper column or series.

Description: During Women's History Month sponsor a daily contest to identify a notable woman from history.

Procedure: Have participants study a daily presentation of facts, photos, and other clues to the identity of the woman of the day. Tabulate answers and award prizes to the person with the most correct answers. Follow these models:

1. While studying astronomy, math, and philosophy in Alexandria, Egypt, during the 5th century A.D., I invented the hydroscope and astrolabe.

2. Although not much is known about my life, I was the first child of European ancestry born in North America. Historians believe I lived with the Croatoan Indians after my village was struck by disease and famine.

3. As labor organizer of the United Mine Workers, I earned the honorary title of "Mother" and joined other female union leaders to assure equal pay and better working conditions for women.

4. With my daughter's help, I took in the children of drug and alcohol addicts and HIV-positive children and established a model for foundling homes in New York.

5. After my husband died at the Battle of Monmouth, I took his post as a patriot soldier and received General Washington's praise.

6. With the publication of my book, *Life among the Piutes,* in 1883 I became the first Native American to publish in English.

7. I founded the Philadelphia Female Anti-Slavery Society and in 1848 joined Elizabeth Cady Stanton to establish the first Women's Rights Convention in Seneca Falls, New York.

8. My name is synonymous with the women's rights movement. As the first editor of *Ms.* magazine, I launched a series of publications that have boosted the position of women as wage-earners, caregivers, and individuals.

9. While working as director of nurses for the Union Army, I began a drive to establish the Red Cross in America and pushed Congress to ratify the Geneva Convention, an international accord that guarantees the rights of refugees, women, children, and people in need of medical care.

10. I became famous as a photojournalist and joined the colony of pacifists who followed Mohandas Gandhi.

ANSWERS:

1. Hypatia	6. Sarah Winnemucca
2. Virginia Dare	7. Lucretia Mott
3. Mary Jones	8. Gloria Steinem
4. Clara Hale	9. Clara Barton
5. Molly Pitcher	10. Margaret Bourke-White

Budget: $$

Sources:

Clement, J., ed. *Famous Deeds of American Women.* Corner House, 1975.

Dennis, Denise. *Black History for Beginners.* Highsmith, 1992.

Fantham, Elaine, et al. *Women in the Classical World.* Oxford University Press, 1994.

Great Lives from History: American Women Series. Salem Press, 1995.

Harrison, Cynthia, ed. *Women in National Politics.* University Publications of America, 1995.

Karlekar, Malavika. Introduction to *Changing Lives: Life Stories of Asian Pioneers in Women's Studies.* Feminist Press, 1995.

Alternative Applications: Divide participants into groups to comb reference sources and draw up lists for the "Who Am I?" game. Present names in categories. For example:

• Native Americans: Sarah Winnemucca, Wilma Mankiller, Datsolali, Susette La Flesche, Sacajawea, Molly Brant, Martha Brae, Shawnawdithit, Catherine Tekakwitha, Nancy Ward

- African-Americans: Rosa Parks, Coretta King, Mahalia Jackson, Jacqueline Baker, Lena Horne, Mary McLeod Bethune, Barbara Jordan, Shirley Chisholm, Clara Hale

- government leaders: Madeleine Kunin, Christine Whitman, Frances Perkins, Ivy Baker Priest, Madeleine Albright, Eleanor Roosevelt, Elizabeth Dole, Ann Richardson, Jeanne Fitzpatrick, Ada Deer, Carol Moseley-Brown

Continue grouping names and contributions under these headings: healers, artists, designers, entertainers, scientists, soldiers, and writers. Appoint volunteers to phrase a question for each name.

Women of the Harlem Renaissance

Age/Grade Level or Audience: High school or college seminar; Women's History Month library display; teacher education research model for written or oral presentation.

Description: Organize a seminar on women of the Harlem Renaissance.

Procedure: Have participants select a topic about the women of the Harlem Renaissance and their contributions to the culture of the 1920s. Consider the following themes:

- a biographical study of Zora Neale Hurston in *I Love Myself When I Am Laughing: A Zora Neale Hurston Reader*
- the collaborative efforts of Langston Hughes and Zora Neale Hurston on *Mule Bone*
- the correspondence of novelist Nella Larsen
- Dorothy West's reflections on the Harlem Renaissance
- feminist themes in Georgia Douglas Johnson's *The Heart of a Woman* and *Bronze*
- folklore in the PBS video *Zora*
- memoirs of Dorothy West, the Harlem Renaissance "Kid"
- middle-class black women in Jessie Redmon Fauset's *The Chinaberry Tree* and *Comedy, American Style*
- *Mule Bone* on Broadway
- oral tradition in *Tell My Horse* and *Dust Tracks on the Road*
- Zora Neale Hurston's sociological essays about the Caribbean

Combine research efforts into a multi-phase project including notes, interviews, drawings, taped readings, videotaped skits, biography, and a map of significant sites in Harlem.

Budget: $$

Sources:

Gibaldi, Joseph, and Walter S. Achtert. *MLA Handbook for Writers of Research Papers.* Modern Language Association of America, 1995.

Harlem Renaissance. Empak Publishing Co., n.d. (Filmstrip)

Hurston, Zora Neale. *Their Eyes Were Watching God.* HarperPerennial, 1990.

Lumpkins, Barbranda. "The Harlem Renaissance Lives on in Dorothy West." *USA Today,* March 1, 1995, 8D.

"Sisters of the Harlem Renaissance." National Women's History Project. (Postcard Set)

Skow, John. "The Second Time Around." *Time,* July 24, 1995, 67.

Smith, Jessie Carney. *Notable Black American Women.* Gale Research, 1992.

Walker, Alice, ed. *I Love Myself When I Am Laughing: A Zora Neale Hurston Reader.* Feminist Press, 1979.

Watson, Steven. *The Harlem Renaissance: Hub of African-American Culture, 1920–1930.* Random House, 1995.

West, Dorothy. *The Living Is Easy.* Feminist Press, 1982.

The Wedding. Doubleday, 1995.

Alternative Applications: Join in a group effort to encircle a room or hall with an oversized horizontal time line of women's roles in the Harlem Renaissance. Highlight events and publications with photos, walking tours of Harlem, book jackets, women's clothing styles, maps of Zora Neale Hurston's fact-finding travels in Florida and the Caribbean, quotations, and/or drawings of the Cotton Club, Savoy Ballroom, and lavish mansion of Madame C. J. Walker.

Women *and reference works*

Age/Grade Level or Audience: College or graduate school bibliography study; teacher education exercise; research model for written or oral presentation; women's studies focus; ministerial association discussion topic.

Description: Hold a seminar to discuss gender bias in reference works.

Procedure: Have participants select a group of current reference works to study for examples of bias or under-representation or for negative or outmoded images of women. Organize small groups to study these types of works:

- databases and microfiche—Infotrac, ProQuest, Africa Watch, ERIC, Silver Platter, and Newsbank

- encyclopedias—*World Book, Encarta, Grolier, Funk and Wagnall's, Academic American, Merit, Compton's, Britannica,* and *Americana*

- English dictionaries—*Merriam Webster Collegiate Dictionary, The American Heritage College Dictionary, The Concise Oxford Dictionary, The Shorter Oxford English Dictionary*

Assess thesauruses, almanacs, compendia, yearbooks, art histories, grammatical desk references, teacher's guides, catalogs, biographical collections, audio-visual holdings, picture files, monographs, journals, genealogies, and historical overviews. Appoint a small group to compile a list of terms, illustrations, and items of interest that help determine which works are unbiased. Look for inclusion of the following concerns:

- ecofeminism, midwifery, nurse-practitioners, National Women's Political Caucus, Pro-Choice, Wicca, care-giving, NOW, MADD

- medical inquiry into PMS, menopause, heart disease, osteoporosis, and cancer in women, pharmaceutical testing and normative procedures on women

- female accomplishments in the military, law enforcement, government, medicine, science, religion, space engineering, politics, finance, and business

- illustrations, photos, and drawings that depict activities, significant social roles, work performed by women of varied races

313

- acknowledgment of patriarchy or over-protection in government, education, business, religion, finance, medical care, and family

- a balanced picture of women's contributions to society in all nations during all historical periods

- fair and balanced gender representation in medical compendia, congressional yearbooks, investment, and the arts

- an avoidance of stereotypes of women by age, dress, parenthood, behavior, status, race, religion, education, or social class

Budget: $$

Sources:

Consult and compare critical commentary in *ARBA, Booklist, Publishers Weekly, Choice, VOYA, School Library Journal,* and other independent studies of new publications.

Alternative Applications: Present a book fair or informational booth about gender prejudice in reference books. Propose a list of questions parents, ministers, teachers, principals, educational supervisors, readers, scout leaders, school board members, and the media may use as a test of the equality in data sources. Offer an independently prepared list of suspect reference works and textbooks that denigrate, ignore, or devalue women.

Women's *history term paper*

Age/Grade Level or Audience: High school term paper; sociology or psychology study; library handout; research model for written or oral presentation.

Description: Help students develop research skills by having them select a topic on women's history and complete a detailed group study, oral report, or term paper.

Procedure: Present the following words of advice and methods of finding and utilizing information for a research project on women's history:

1. Understand all elements of the assignment by asking questions or requesting a private conference with the teacher. Use approved topics such as these:

   - contrasting female characters in Pearl Buck's *The Good Earth*

   - trends in women-owned businesses

   - changes in prevention of osteoporosis

   - women in the Anglican church hierarchy

   - studies linking birth control pills and breast cancer

   - women in the Psalms

   - cloisters of the Middle Ages

   - women's historic impact on the U.S. legislature

   - the influence of Mary Baker Eddy on religion and legislation

   - Florence Nightingale and the modern military hospital

   - female influence and the longhouse tradition

2. Examine your topic and thesis statement for research clues—an historical period, person, literary work, social situation, religious influence, or scientific discovery. Cluster secondary ideas. For example, if you are writing about the speeches of Susan B. Anthony, list additional topics that might provide insight, such as the women's movement, suffrage, voting rights, post-abolitionistic fervor, and women in nineteenth-century American history. Search library shelves in the general area for likely books. Apply the same numbers to the archives and special collections, reference room, audio tapes, disk recording collection, microfische, microfilm, databases, photo collections, and videocassettes.

3. For valuable critical information, read the introduction, footnotes, and afterword of several editions of the same primary work or the jacket on related recordings, audiocassette or videos. If relevant to your topic, search books on legends surrounding women like Calamity Jane, Joan of Arc, Maid Marian, Pocahontas, or Lady Godiva; occult practices, such as the Salem witch trials; goddess studies, such as the goddess in art and bas-relief as listed in Marshall Cavendish's *Man, Myth, and Magic* or Robert Bell's *Women in Classic Mythology.* For social topics, such as ecofeminism, hormones and aging, voting patterns among young urban females, and survival rates of women in underdeveloped countries, refer to specific sociological compendia, particularly *SIRS* (*Social Information Resource Series*) as well as almanacs, databases, the Library of Congress, and the U.S. Bureau of Census.

4. Use comprehensive sources for individual topics. For example, for information about female jazz stars and composers, refer to the *Grove Dictionary of Music and Musicians;* for "Take Your Daughter to Work Day," refer to the *American Book of Days;* for data on scientists like Barbara McClintock and Agnes Chase, refer to the *Encyclopedia of Science and Technology* or *Famous Deeds of American Women.* Other standard sources of specific information include *Great Lives from History: American Women Series, Oxford Companion's to Women's Writing in the United States, Women in National Politics,* and *Changing Lives: Life Stories of Asian Pioneers in Women's Studies.*

5. Take notes on a single subject on each card. For instance, for a paper on women in space, make notes on Sally Ride on one card, and on Christa McAuliffe on another card. For a paper on the career of activist Barbara Jordan or Cherokee Chief Wilma Mankiller, divide information chronologically to cover family influence, education, experience, work history, and elected positions. Rephrase the main source in your own words. Underline key phrases on photocopies. Transfer information to cards, noting page numbers from the source.

6. If you choose to quote, select sentences that stand out for their originality and succinctness, as with lines from a speech by Eleanor Roosevelt or a musical phrase from Zora Neale Hurston's *Mule Bone.* Copy the words carefully, using three dots to indicate segments that you have deleted. A shortened version of Brooke Medicine Eagle's comment in Joan Halifax's *Shamanic Voices: A Survey of Visionary Narratives* would appear as follows: "Being Indian is an attitude, a state of mind, a way of being in harmony with all things and all beings. It is allowing the heart to be the distributor of energy. . . ." Photocopy sections you want to quote; note publisher, date of publication, and page numbers of sources.

7. Interview local experts on your topic. Mark video or audio tape with name of subject, date, and location.

8. Be prepared to fill in gaps and strengthen research with more details. Keep an open mind about the topic. Be prepared to find varying interpretations, particularly of controversial topics, such as how to end ageism or "starve the wife" divorce settlements, the purpose of affirmative action in the workplace, improving women's outlook on math education, or the purpose of a Vietnam memorial honoring nurses.

Budget: $$

Sources:

Gibaldi, Joseph, and Walter S. Achtert. *MLA Handbook for Writers of Research Papers.* Modern Language Association of America, 1995.

Lee, Henry. *How Dry We Were—Prohibition Revisited.* Prentice-Hall, 1963.

Levenson, Dorothy. *Homesteaders and Indians.* Franklin Watts, 1971.

———. *Women of the West.* Franklin Watts, 1973.

Snodgrass, Mary Ellen. *The English Book.* Perma-Bound, 1991.

Alternative Applications: Prepare models of group presentations, oral reports, convocation speeches, sales campaigns, and other formal research on women's issues. Make a strong impression on your audience by following these methods:

- Assess the age, needs, gender, background, marital status, and educational level of the audience. Use suitable tone, diction, and gestures.

- If the subject is complicated, as with a study of changes in workplace safety equipment or an analysis of women's health care by state, county, or region, supply charts, photos, a chalkboard demonstration, posters, film or video, diagrams, filmstrips or film loops, dramatization, slides, overhead projections, diagrams, or live models.

- Select a topic that suits the needs of the occasion. For a Fourth of July speech to the city council, emphasize the positive qualities of women in the community by naming pioneers, activists, civic club leaders, and volunteers. List women's groups that have made a positive impact on civic improvements; for example, women's religious groups that have supported day-care and safe streets, branches of NOW or American University Women, or League of Women Voters political campaigners. Pause for audience reaction, applause, or corroborative nods and laughter.

- Focus on a single purpose. Determine whether you intend to entertain, persuade, or pass along crucial data, as with a travelogue on women in Outward Bound, women in typically male professions, or the effects of HMO's on women's postnatal recovery or La Leche training in breastfeeding.

- Deliver a clear statement of intent. Arrange facts logically in chronological order or least-to-greatest progression. Support each addition with fact. Strive to leave the strongest point last for your audience to carry away with them, as with the importance of raising standards for the health and well being of women and children to break the cycle of welfare and entitlements.

- Rehearse with a variety of tone, gestures, nods, and other physical displays of emphasis. Speak with confidence and a variety in volume, speed, pitch, intensity, and pronunciation. Maintain an upright, flexible posture by placing one foot slightly in front of the other. Sweep the audience with your eyes to display your interest in their reaction.

Women's *research and achievement*

Age/Grade Level or Audience: Middle school or high school oral report; women's studies focus; school or public library bulletin board; teacher education model for written or oral presentation.

Description: Present a study of women and their historic contributions to research and achievement in a variety of fields.

Procedure: Have participants make group presentations on various areas of endeavor in which women have distinguished themselves. Summarize the work of these people in the following fields:

- abolitionism—Angelina Grimke, Sarah Grimke, Harriet Beecher Stowe, Sojourner Truth

- anthropology—Elizabeth Barber, Mary Leakey, Elaine Morgan

- architecture—Julia Morgan, Maya Lin

- arts—Jane Alexander, Mine Okubó, Jackie Onassis

- astronomy—Maria Mitchell, Antonia Caetana de Paiva Pereira

- aviation—Bessie Coleman, Amelia Earhart, Beryl Markham, Ruth Nichols

- botany—Emma Lucy Braun, Agnes Chase

- business—Mary Provoost Alexander, Sarah Knight, Rebecca Lukens, Madame C. J. Walker

- choral music—Wihla Hutson, Jane Marshall

- choreography—Isadora Duncan, Katharine Dunham, Martha Graham, Judith Jamison, Helen Tamiris, Twyla Tharp

- ecology—Rachel Carson, Marjory Stoneman Douglas, Wangari Maathai

- education—Mary McLeod Bethune, Sister Julia, Mary Lyon, Maria Montessori, Alice Putnam, Martha Schofield, Annie Sullivan, Martha Carey Thomas

- geology—Elizabeth Fisher, Julia Anna Gardner, Winifred Goldring, Eleanora Frances Bliss Knopf

- folklore—Zora Neale Hurston, Nancy Roberts

- government—Oveta Culp Hobby, Patsy Mink, Alice Paul, Pat Schroeder

- history—Mary Beard, Fawn Brodie, Clara Driscoll, Ida Husted Harper, Barbara Tuchman

- human rights—Margarethe Cammermayer, Lydia Maria Child, Martha Cotera, Jennifer Harbury Everardo, Abigail Kelley Foster, Anna Thompson Ickes, Coretta Scott King, Rigoberto Menchu, Clarina Nichols, Graciela Olivarez, Rosa Parks, Susan La Flesche Picotte, Katherine Russell, Fannie Williams, Sarah Winnemucca

- humor—Lucille Ball, Erma Bombeck, Molly Ivins, Florence King

- international relations—Jane Addams, Olympia Brown, Selena Butler, Vera Dean

- journalism—Nellie Bly, Ellen Goodman, Anna Quindlen, Ida Tarbell

- labor—Emily Greene Balch, Louise Brown, Emma Goldman, Dolores Huerta, Frieda Miller, Leonora O'Reilly, Maud Younger

- law—Annette Adams, Ruther Bader Ginsburg, Anita Hill, Barbara Jordan, Sandra Day O'Connor, Charlotte Ray

- literature—Joyce Carol Oates, Flannery O'Connor, Toni Morrison, Beatrix Potter, Eudora Welty, Edith Wharton, Yoshiko Uchida

- medicine—Josephine Baker, Elizabeth Blackwell, Joycelyn Elders, Gertrude Elion, Alice Hamilton, Madge Macklin, Louise Pearce, Sarah Stevenson, Lillian Welsh

- military—Sybil Ludington, Belle Starr, Dorothy Stratton

- music—Sarah Caldwell, Wihla Hutson, Jane M. Marshall, Florence Price

- Native American rights—Anna Mae Aquash, Angie Debo, Susette La Flesche, Wilma Mankiller, Red Bird, Muriel Wright

- nursing—Clara Barton, Edith Cavell, Florence Nightingale, Isabel Stewart, Suzie King Taylor, Adah Thomas

- paleontology—Mary Leakey

- philosophy—Hannah Arendt, Simone de Beauvoir, Ayn Rand

- photography—Diane Arbus, Margaret Bourke-White, Dorothea Lange

- primate research—Jane Goodall, Dian Fossey

- prison reform—Jessie Hodder

- psychiatry—Elisabeth Kübler-Ross

- psychology—Dorothea Dix, Anna Freud, Karen Horney

- religion—Mary Baker Eddy, Marija Gimbutas, Georgia Harkness, Anna Howard, Anna Spencer, Mother Teresa

- sex and reproduction—Mary Calderone, Shere Hite, Margaret Sanger, Dr. Marie Stopes, Faye Wattleton

- sociology—Ruth Benedict, Dorothy Day, Theodora Kroeber, Alice Higgins Lothrop, Margaret Mead, Barbara Meyerhoff

- space exploration—Mae Jemison, Christa McAuliffe, Sally Ride, Valentina Tereshkova

- sports—Susan Butcher, Gertrude Ederle, Chris Evert, Althea Gibson, Martina Navratilova

- women's rights—Bella Abzug, Susan B. Anthony, Carrie Chapman Catt, Matila Joslyn Gage, Martha Griffiths, Lucretia Mott, Mary Church Terrell

Budget: $$

Sources:

Bailey, Brooke. *The Remarkable Lives of 100 Women Artists.* Bob Adams, 1994.

———. *The Remarkable Lives of 100 Women Healers and Scientists.* Bob Adams, 1994.

———. *The Remarkable Lives of 100 Women Writers and Journalists.* Bob Adams, 1994.

Griffin, Lynne, and Kelly McCann. *The Book of Women: 300 Notable Women History Passed By.* Bob Adams, 1992.

Hay, Susannah. *The Women's Heritage Scrapbook.* Caillech Press, 1992.

Alternative Applications: Make a time chart from the present back through 1776. List American women who have won significant recognition for their published work or research. Compile an honor roll of publications by noteworthy women:

Ruth Benedict's *Patterns of Culture*

Rachel Carson's *Silent Spring*

Anna Botsford Comstock's *The Handbook of Nature Study*

Betty Friedan's *The Feminine Mystique*

Margaret Fuller's *Women in the Nineteenth Century*

Marija Gimbutas's *The Civilization of the Goddess*

Sarah Grimké's *Letters on the Equality of the Sexes*

Edith Hamilton's *Mythology*

Jane Jacobs's *The Death and Life of Great American Cities*

Elisabeth Kübler-Ross's *On Death and Dying*

Maggie Kuhn's *No Stone Unturned*

Lois Lowry's *The Giver*

Barbara McClintock's *The Dynamic Genome*

Margaret Mead's *Coming of Age in Samoa*

Elaine Morgan's *The Descent of Woman*

Toni Morrison's *Beloved*

Leontyne Price's *Aida*

Gail Sheehy's *Passages*

Gloria Steinem's *Revolution from Within*

Barbara Tuchman's *The Guns of August*

Maintain an open database of women winners of the Nobel Prize, Pulitzer Prize, Woodrow Wilson fellowship, Academy Award, Coretta Scott King Award, Scott O'Dell Award, Rhodes Scholarship, *Time* magazine's Woman of the Year award, National Endowment for the Humanities grant, Spingarn Medal, and other acclaim.

Literature

Analyzing *women's poetry*

Age/Grade Level or Audience: High school literary analysis assignment; library hand-out; book club study.

Description: Introduce poetic analysis via a study of women's verse.

Procedure: Present a written handout explaining how to analyze poetry. Have participants follow this series of steps as they apply to a work by a female poet:

- Who wrote the poem? When was it written? In what language? In what country? Is it a part of a special collection, for example, one of Elizabeth Barrett Browning's *Sonnets from the Portuguese?* Does it reflect a particular period, such as the Romantic Era, Victorian Age, Chivalric Era, post-modern, or Harlem Renaissance?

- Describe the style in one of these categories:

  long poem about a great heroine, such as "Joan of Arc" [epic]

  short, musical verse [lyric], like Sappho's love poems

  narrative, e.g., the book of Ruth in the Bible

  Is it a three-line verse of seventeen syllables [haiku] or some other identifiable measure like limerick, terza rima, or dramatic monologue, as with Amy Lowell's "Patterns"?

- What meaning does the title convey? Is it obvious, e.g., H. D.'s "Pear Tree," or does it imply deeper meaning, e.g., Emma Lazarus's "The New Colossus"? Note words, phrases, or verses that are repeated. Decide what sounds, rhythms, or information deserves repetition, as in Maya Angelou's *Now Sheba Sings the Song.*

- Concentrate on the opening and closing lines. For instance Gwendolyn Brooks's "We Real Cool" begins "We real cool" and ends with "We die soon." Why and how does the poet place significance in these crucial places? Does the poet intend to end with a particular emotion or impression?

- What is the poet's tone? Is it humorous, satiric, serious, mock serious, playful, somber, or proud, as are many of the poems of Nikki Giovanni? Does the poet admire, agree with, or condemn the speaker? Summarize by looking for a pattern. Has the poet described an intense experience or defined something? Is the poet telling a story? Does the poet want to sway opinion? How has the poet made an impression? Why?

Budget: $

Sources:

Angelou, Maya. *Now Sheba Sings the Song.* Dutton, 1988.

Giovanni, Nikki. *Sacred Cows and Other Edibles.* Quill, 1988.

Hindley, Meredith. "The Furious Flower: Black Poets Discuss Their Craft." *Humanities,* September/October 1994, 28–30.

Mazer, Norma Fox, ed. *Waltzing on Water.* Laurel-Leaf Library, 1989.

Rozakis, Dr. Laurie. *How to Interpret Poetry.* Macmillan, 1995.

Alternative Applications:

Prepare a choral reading of a notable work by a female author, particularly these works:

- Maya Angelou's *Now Sheba Sings the Song*
- Elizabeth Barrett Browning's *Sonnets from the Portuguese*
- Gabriel Mistral's "Rocking"
- Amy Lowell's "Patterns"
- Christina Rossetti's *The Goblin Market*
- Nelly Sachs's "The Swan"
- Sappho's poems and fragments

Also consider poems by Claribel Alegría, Carolyn Forché, Emily Dickinson, Audre Lorde, Naomi Shihab Nye, Gertrude Stein, and Daisy Zamora.

Book *reports on famous women*

Age/Grade Level or Audience: Elementary or middle school publishing project; ESL or GED composition.

Description: Compose a brochure describing a book about an admirable female character from history.

Procedure: Have participants select a worthy book that expresses each person's idea of someone to admire and emulate. Then have them follow these instructions:

- Make a construction-paper folder with the title and author printed dramatically on the front and a cover illustration that continues to the back. For example, for *Abbie Burgess, Lighthouse Keeper* written by Dorothy Holder Jones, depict the stalwart Abbie peering from her lighthouse.

- Mark the page number that describes the action you are picturing. Summarize the height of the plot in a caption, preferably via a scene that demonstrates the best qualities of the main character.

- On the first page of your report, list the title, your name, and the number of pages in the book. A good selection for a report is *Amelia's Flying Machine,* by Barbara Shook Hazen, a story based on the childhood of aviator Amelia Earhart.

- Make a character list, followed by descriptions of looks, dress, beliefs, and actions that figure prominently in the book. For example, if you are considering the title character in Patricia Clapp's *I'm Deborah Sampson: A Soldier in the War of the Revolution,* describe both Deborah's civilian and military garb.

- Summarize the beliefs and qualities that helped the person act bravely or courteously or inventively in the most crucial situations. If you are summarizing Cornelia Meigs's *Invincible Louisa*, explain how Louisa May Alcott remains strong even during her family's most dire hardships.

- List problems that characters face, such as hunger, poverty, doubt, fear, harsh weather, war, disillusionment, loss, or loneliness. Beside each, note the most effective way in which the character combats the problem. A good choice for young readers is *My First Little House Books: Going to Town,* by Laura Ingalls Wilder, where you could characterize Laura and Mary's apprehensions as they make their first journey to town.

- Copy a list of phrases from the book that capture the style and speaking voice of the character, particularly dialect, wit, and kind words, such as the language of the title character in *Sojourner Truth,* by Patricia C. McKissack and Fredrick McKissack.

- Contrast the character to people living now. Do women still have the same problems? Are the problems worse now? Are more recent problems replacing the old problems? A good choice for comparison is the photo biography *Anne Frank: Beyond the Diary,* by Ruud van der Rol and Rian Verhoeven with an introduction by journalist Anna Quindlen.

- Copy a few lines of dialogue. Add your own part as though you were a character in the scene. What would you like to tell or advise the main character? How would you be of service in difficult times?

- List any terms that were new to you or that you did not recognize in use, as with technical or manufacturing terms in Frank Gilbreath and Ernestine Gilbreath Carey's *Cheaper by the Dozen* or descriptions of Native American culture in Jeri Ferris's *Native American Doctor,* the biography of Susan La Flesche Picotte.

- Describe the type of person who would like this book and learn from it. Describe the kind of person to whom you would recommend this book.

Budget: $

Sources:

Select a variety of non-fiction works from Parents' Choice, VOYA, ARBA, Booklist, IRA- or ALA-approved lists, Caldecott or Newbery winners, and biographies for children available through your local library.

Alternative Applications: Have participants make a list of scenes, costumes, lighting, music, props, and actors they would need to turn their selected book into a ballet, miniseries, television sitcom, drama, movie, musical comedy, or outdoor drama. Decide which treatment would best capture the characters' expressions of emotion. What actors would you choose to play the parts? Which part would you save for yourself or write into the story?

History *into legend*

Age/Grade Level or Audience: Middle school creative writing assignment; library handout; book club presentation.

Description: Define legend by studying how real women have passed from the pages of history into mysticism or legend.

Procedure: Have students study several women whose achievements have transformed them from historical figure into negative stereotype, martyr, or saint: for example, Monica of Rome, Katherine the Great, Ida Wells, Aimee Semple MacPherson, Katharine Hepburn, Mother Teresa, Kay Boyle, Eleanor Roosevelt, Maud Gonne, Kay Boyle, Mary Todd Lincoln, Maria von Trapp, Winnie Mandela, Clara Hale, Carry Nation, Sarah Winnemucca, and Dorothy Parker. Use these models as examples:

- *Cleopatra,* queen of Egypt, exalted in film, art, dance, and sculpture as daring, romantic, sultry and beautiful, seductive, unusually gifted in foreign languages, was unable to defy the will of her late father, Ptolemy XIII, who decreed that she should marry her fourteen-year-old brother and rule jointly. To elude her brother's vengeful advisers, in the summer of 48 B.C., Cleopatra was reputedly carried to court to lure Julius Caesar to take her part against Ptolemy XIV. The presentation of royalty rolled in a rug apparently worked. After Caesar's death, Mark Antony, drawn to her beauty and wit, remained at her side to defend Caesarion, the child of Caesar and Cleopatra. In 38 B.C., Cleopatra could no longer hold Antony from his Roman obligations; the next year, he fought at Actium, Greece, and departed from the battle to live out his remaining years with his Egyptian queen. Skilled with poisons, the legendary Cleopatra eventually committed suicide rather than live as the captive of the Emperor Augustus.

- *Pocahontas* (1595–1617), daughter of Chief Powhatan and an 18-year-old English hostage. Pocahontas is credited with saving the first English colony from hunger and death and, at age 12, with saving Captain John Smith near Jamestown, Virginia. Legend depicts her as brave, willing to die for her love, and extremely fascinating to the English court of James I, whom she visited in 1616 after her marriage to planter John Rolfe. An oil portrait from this era preserves a likeness of her in English lace collar and steeple-crown hat. In 1617, before her son's second birthday, Pocahontas, or Lady Rebecca Rolfe as she was known after her conversion to Christianity, died during a return voyage to Virginia. According to Captain John Smith's version, *Generall Historie* (1624), her remains were returned to England and buried at Gravesend.

Demonstrate the extremes of legend by comparing historical references from reliable sources with movies, television miniseries, filmstrips, historical markers, entablatures, posters, and historical fiction. Have participants discuss the differences between the "real" women and the characters into which they evolve due to the passage of time.

Budget: $

Sources:

Brandon, William. *The Last Americans.* McGraw-Hill, 1974.

DeCosta-Willis, Miriam. *The Memphis Diary of Ida B. Wells.* Beacon, 1995.

Fritz, Jean. *The Double Life of Pocahontas.* Puffin, 1983.

Goodrich, Norma Lorre. *Heroines: Demigodesses, Prima Donna, Movie Star.* Harper, 1993.

Johnson, Steve. "Real Life." *Chicago Tribune,* June 26, 1995, sect. 5, 3.

Klar, Arthur. *Cleopatra.* National Publishers, 1963.

Lourdes: Pilgrimage and Healing. Palisades Home Video, n.d. (Video)

"Pocahontas, for Real." *U.S. News & World Report,* June 19, 1995, 61–64.

Rasmussen, William, and Robert Tilton. *Pocahontas: Her Life and Legend.* Virginia Historical Society, 1994.

Rountree, Helen. *Pocahontas's People: The Powhatan Indians of Virginia through Four Centuries.* University of Oklahoma Press, 1990.

Salins, Marshall. *Islands of History.* University of Chicago Press, 1985.

Wloszczyna, Susan. "Great Expectations Greet Pocahontas." *USA Today,* May 22, 1995, 4D.

Alternative Applications: Have students create a three-column list of events, qualities, or relationships from the chronicled lives of such fabled women as these:

Susan B. Anthony	Flora Macdonald
Ma Barker	Carry Nation
Bernadette of Lourdes	Annie Oakley
Calamity Jane	Bonnie Parker
Cleopatra	Pocahontas
Diamond Lil	Queen of Sheba
Eleanor of Aquitaine	Empress Alexandra Romanov
Maud Gonne	Grand Duchess Anastasia Romanov
Guinevere	Sojourner Truth
Joan of Arc	Belle Starr
Princess Kaiulani	Mother Teresa
Queen Liliuokalani	Madame C. J. Walker

Assist participants in placing details under the headings of fact, probability, and legend. Discuss the use of corroborating details; for example, the distance a character would have to travel within the time period allowed to take part in an event, as is the case with pirates Anne Bonney and Grace O'Malley, who are cited as being in numerous places during the same week and whose exploits extend beyond their lifespans.

Kate *Chopin and The Awakening*

Age/Grade Level or Audience: High school or college English literature lecture; women's studies report; library handout; book club presentation; Women's History Month presentation.

Description: Substantiate the contribution of Kate Chopin to an honest portrayal of female characters in fiction.

Procedure: As a preface to a study of *The Awakening* and other of the author's works, present an overview of the life of Kate Chopin. Include these facts:

• From girlhood in St. Louis, Missouri, Katherine "Kate" O'Flaherty Chopin (February 8, 1851–August 22, 1904), studied literature, especially the short works of Guy de Maupassant, Walt Whitman's verse, and Sarah Orne Jewett's fiction. A member of a socially prominent family, she and her family suffered the death of Kate's brother during the Civil War and also the accidental death of her father. Kate was educated at the Academy of the Sacred Heart, and studied piano, French, and traditional deportment with her grandmother, Madame Victoria Charleville. Influenced by St. Louis's mix of Creole and Cajun customs, Kate served briefly as companion to an opera singer living in New Orleans.

• Kate married financier and buyer Oscar Chopin, enjoyed the standard European honeymoon, and became a supporter of the arts in New Orleans, where the

Chopins settled. She displayed uncharacteristic female behavior by walking unchaperoned, traveling alone, and smoking in public.

- In 1879, severe financial losses forced the couple to move to the Cane River. Swamp fever killed Oscar Chopin in 1883, leaving Kate to support herself and six children. She moved to her grandmother O'Flaherty's home in St. Louis; five years later, the death of Kate's grandmother brought Kate to the brink of a nervous breakdown from worry and overwork. On a doctor's advice, she began writing and initiated a regular Thursday salon. She sold her first novel, *Bayou Folk,* and published short stories in *America, Atlantic Monthly, Vogue, Youth's Companion, Criterion, Harper's Young People,* and the *St. Louis Dispatch.*

- Critics were scandalized by the sensuality, unladylike behavior, and feminism of protagonist Edna Pontellier following publication of *The Awakening* in 1899. Readers also objected to the fictional heroine, a headstrong New Orleans artist who drowns herself in the Gulf of Mexico at the end of a failed affair. The media characterized Chopin as a pornographer and exhibitionist. Her major publications—*The Complete Works of Kate Chopin* (1959), *Kate Chopin: The Awakening and Other Stories* (1970), *The Storm and Other Stories* (1974), and *A Kate Chopin Miscellany* (1979)—found respect among feminist critics, however, who laud her as a visionary ahead of her time. Subsequent interest in her fiction made Chopin's residence in Cloutierville a shrine to feminism.

Budget: $

Sources:

Bloom, Harold. *Kate Chopin.* Chelsea House, 1987.

Bonner, Thomas, Jr. *The Kate Chopin Companion.* Greenwood, 1988.

Boren, Lynda S., and Sara D. Davis, eds. *Kate Chopin Reconsidered: Beyond the Bayou.* Louisiana State University Press, 1992.

Christ, Carol P. *Diving Deep and Surfacing: Women Writers on Spiritual Quest.* Beacon Press, 1980.

Jewitt, Sarah Orne. *The Only Rose and Miss Tempy's Watchers.* Commuters Library, 1995. (Audiocassette)

Jones, Ann Goodwyn. *Tomorrow Is Another Day: The Woman Writer in the South, 1859–1936.* Louisiana State University Press, 1981.

Koloski, Bernard, ed. *Approaches to Teaching Chopin's the Awakening.* Modern Language Association, 1988.

Martin, Wendy, ed. *New Essays on The Awakening.* Cambridge University Press, 1988.

Papke, Mary E. *Verging on the Abyss: The Social Fiction of Kate Chopin and Edith Wharton.* Greenwood Press, 1990.

Skaggs, Peggy. *Kate Chopin.* Macmillan, 1985.

Toth, Emily. *Kate Chopin: A Life of the Author of The Awakening.* William Morrow, 1993.

Wharton, Edith. *The Eyes, The Other Two, and The Mission.* Commuters Library, 1995. (Audiocassette)

Alternative Applications: Have participants discuss aspects of *The Awakening* which shocked polite nineteenth-century society on its publication. Include the failed love affair with a younger man, the return to Grand Isle, and flirtations with Victor and Alcée. Contrast Edna's individuality with the blossoming of these characters:

- Nora in Henrik Ibsen's *A Doll's House*

- Winnie in Amy Tan's *The Kitchen God's Wife*

- the title character in Terry McMillan's *Mama*

- Clara in Isabel Allende's *House of the Spirits*

- women in Sarah Orne Jewett's *The Only Rose and Miss Tempy's Watchers*

- wives in Edith Wharton's *The Eyes, The Other Two, and The Mission of Jane*

Discuss the roll of artistic expression, sexual intimacy, female networking, and privacy in the rejuvenation of housebound women of movies such as *The Piano, Crimes of the Heart, Out of Africa, Like Water for Chocolate, Babette's Feast, Places in the Heart,* and *The Group.*

Ask a volunteer to read aloud passages from these works or from Chopin's short stories that capture a positive emotion, especially love, delight, pleasure, comfort, self-expression, or welcome. Compose a list of these and other details that undergird Edna's attraction: honesty, natural grace, and curiosity. Discuss the reasons for Léonce Pontellier's inability to appreciate or alleviate Edna's inner unrest and disaffection for her role as wife and mother. Explain how her nourishment of self benefited both body and spirit.

Milestone *books*

Age/Grade Level or Audience: Library newsletter; book-club handout; media column; education class discussion topic; basic library reading list.

Description: Compile a list of the most important works of literature by female authors.

Procedure: Invite participants to draw up a list of the most significant works of literature by women, including works for children and young adults. Present the list to local libraries and emphasize the titles that should be on the women's shelf and among the works selected for audiocassette and large print. Include these works from the canon of women's literature:

- Louisa May Alcott's *Little Women*

- Isabel Allende's *House of Spirits*

- Maya Angelou's *I Know Why the Caged Bird Sings*

- Willa Cather's *My Antonia*

- Kate Chopin's *The Awakening*

- Sandra Cisneros's *The House on Mango Street*

- Marilyn French's *The Women's Room*

- Betty Friedan's *The Feminine Mystique* and *The Fountain of Age*

- Germaine Greer's *The Female Eunuch*

- Radclyffe Hall's *The Well of Loneliness*

- Barbara Ward Jackson's *Spaceship Earth*

- Ruth Prawer Jhabvala's *Heat and Dust*

- Terry McMillan's *Waiting to Exhale* and *Mama*

- Toni Morrison's *The Bluest Eye* and *Beloved*

- Harriet Beecher Stowe's *Uncle Tom's Cabin*

- Mary Wollstonecraft Shelley's *Frankenstein*

- Alice Walker's *Possessing the Secret of Joy*
- Yoko Kawashima Watkins's *So Far from the Bamboo Grove*

Budget: $

Sources:

Bauermeister, Erica, Jesse Larsen, and Holly Smith. *500 Great Books by Women*. Penguin Books, 1994.

Kenyon, Olga, ed. *Eight Hundred Years of Women's Letters*. Penguin, 1994.

Martin, Jean, gen. ed. *Who's Who of Women in the Twentieth Century*. Crescent Books, 1995.

"People." *U.S. News & World Report,* July 10, 1995, 12.

Alternative Applications: Coordinate a local or civic club effort to supply public and school libraries with copies of classic women's literature, especially books, tapes, and videos in which female characters behave in assertive, logical fashion. Canvass secondhand book dealers, book finders, and donors for titles by the strongest voices in women's literature, both fiction and nonfiction. Hold a fund raiser or book fair to purchase the materials necessary to bring the library's holdings up to a standard of excellence on the subject of women. Include read-along with tapes, large print, foreign language, adult literacy, and other special needs categories. For help in your endeavor contact the Michigan Women's Studies Association, 213 W. Main St., Lansing, MI 48933, or phone 517-372-9772.

The Nineteenth-*century literary conscience*

Age/Grade Level or Audience: High school or college term paper; women's history speech or forum; Women's History Month presentation; medical society or missionary program.

Description: Summarize the work of one of literature's female altruists.

Procedure: Compose a term paper, lead a symposium, or give a chalk talk or formal speech on the impact of female writers on social reform, especially during the nineteenth century. Consider these writers and their works:

- Charlotte Brontë's *Shirley* (1849)
- Elizabeth Barrett Browning's *The Cry of the Children* (1844)
- Elizabeth Gaskell's *Mary Barton* (1848) and *North and South* (1889)
- Frances Trollope's *Michael Armstrong, the Factory Boy* (1840)
- Louisa May Alcott's *Little Women* (1868)

Contrast the level of social significance in these works with that of Harriet Beecher Stowe's *Uncle Tom's Cabin*.

Budget: $$

Sources:

Hay, Susannah. *The Women's Heritage Scrapbook*. Caillech Press, 1992.

Martin, C. *The Brontës*. Rourke, 1990.

Alternative Applications: As a club project, publish a monograph featuring nineteenth-century woman-sponsored settlement work, nurse care, or activism on behalf of abolition, suffrage, or the crusade for better living conditions for the poor. Concentrate on biographies, letters, journals, speeches, and autobiographies of these women:

- Josephine St. Pierre Ruffin, journalist, women's club activist, and suffragist

- Caroline Fliedner, nursing instructor at the Kaiserwerth Institute

- Lucy Parsons, co-founder of International Working People's Association

- Clara Barton, founder of the American Red Cross

- Elizabeth Fry, Quaker prisoner worker

- Florence Nightingale, superintendent of the Institution for the Care of Sick Gentlewomen in Distressed Circumstances and military nurse administrator

- Frederika Münster, founder of the Kaiserwerth Institute for the Training of Deaconesses

- Jane Addams, settlement worker and suffragist

- the lectures and writings of Dr. Elizabeth Blackwell on the subject of women's health, exercise, and hygiene

Shakespeare's *women*

Age/Grade Level or Audience: High school or college English literature or drama worksheet; women's studies quiz; book club activity; library or museum handout; program filler for playbill for one of Shakespeare's plays; book page feature; education radio call-in contest.

Description: Present a series of lines spoken by Shakespeare's most memorable female characters.

Procedure: As an exercise in characterizing Shakespeare's women, have participants supply speaker, play, and person being addressed in each of these lines from Shakespeare's plays. For example, Gertrude says "Sweets to the sweet" in *Hamlet* as she addresses Ophelia's corpse as it is lowered into the grave. Place your answers in the blanks:

1. If then true lovers have been ever cross'd
   It stands as an edict in destiny.
   Then let us teach our trial patience,
   Because it is customary cross,
   As due to love as thought and dreams and sighs,
   Wishes and teas, poor fancy's followers.

a. _____ b. _____ c. _____

2. Tell me your counsels, I will not disclose 'em.
   I have made strong proof of my constancy,
   Giving myself a voluntary wound
   Here, in the thigh; can I bear that with patience,
   And not my husband's secrets?

a. _____ b. _____ c. _____

3. He took me by the wrist, and held me hard,
   Then goes he to the length of all his arm,
   And with his other hand thus o'er his brow,
   He falls to such perusal of my face
   As 'a would draw it. Long stay'd he so.

a. _____ b. _____ c. _____

4. The poor soul sat by a sycamore tree,
   Sing all a green willow;
   Her hand on her bosom, her head on her knee,
   Sing willow, willow, willow.

a. _____ b. _____ c. _____

5. Think you to walk forth?
   You shall not stir out of your house to-day.

a. _____ b. _____ c. _____

ANSWERS:

1. Hermia, *A Midsummer Night's Dream,* Lysander
2. Portia, *Julius Caesar,* Brutus
3. Ophelia, *Hamlet,* Polonius
4. Desdemona, *Othello,* Emilia
5. Calpurnia, *Julius Caesar,* Caesar

Conclude with a discussion of the type of speaker—round, flat, or stereotyped—and the meaning of the passage.

Budget: $

Sources:

Bartlett, John. *Bartlett's Familiar Quotations.* Little, Brown, 1992.

Belpusi, Peter A., and Nathalie B. Belpusi. *Shakespeare Yesterday–Today: Student Classics.* Globe Publications, 1990.

Bentley, Gerald E. *Shakespeare: A Biographical Handbook.* Yale University Press, 1961.

Boyce, Charles. *Shakespeare A to Z.* Facts on File, 1990.

Chute, Marchette. *An Introduction to Shakespeare.* E. P. Dutton, 1951.

———. *Shakespeare of London.* E. P. Dutton, 1949.

Muir, Kenneth, and Samuel Schoenbaum. *A New Companion to Shakespearean Studies.* Cambridge University Press, 1971.

Shakespeare, William. *The Riverside Shakespeare.* Houghton Mifflin, 1974.

Wright, Courtni Crump. *The Women of Shakespeare's Plays.* University Press, 1992.

Alternative Applications: Contrast situations in Shakespeare's histories, comedies, and tragedies that depict a patriarchal society which discounts or stifles women's individuality. Determine the following:

- the status of women in Shakespeare's day
- Shakespeare's awareness of patriarchal constraints

- the role of fathers, particularly those of Juliet and Ophelia

- expectations for such brides as Kate, Hermia, and Hero

- the reason for quarreling with husbands, particularly Titania and Kate

- the role of power in internal strife, as found in *Macbeth, Hamlet, King Lear, As You Like It, Othello,* and *Romeo and Juliet*

- the untimely deaths of female characters, including Brutus's wife Portia, Lady Macbeth, Lady Macduff, Juliet, Hero, Cleopatra, Cordelia, Ophelia, and Desdemona

Short *stories by and about women*

Age/Grade Level or Audience: High school creative writing lesson; term paper or library research topic; book club or women's studies presentation; radio or television reading; oral interpretation.

Description: Contrast female characters and actions in short stories by and about women.

Procedure: Have volunteers select a short story to study in depth. Begin the study with these literary elements:

- plot—the events or actions, thoughts, dreams, visions, or hallucinations, as found in works by Ursula LeGuin, or Angela Carter, or in fantasies, e.g., the dreams of Cress Delahanty, protagonist in short stories by Jessamyn West

- character—all creatures, human as well as animal or supernatural, who participate in the action: for example, robots, aliens, humanoids, and such fantasy creations as a mouse riding a motorcycle, the focus of Beverly Cleary's "The Mouse and the Motorcycle"

- setting—place and time in which the events occur; for instance, Amy Tan's "The Moon Lady," which gives clues to time and place through dress, history, and inventions

- theme—the dominant idea that the story illustrates, such as youth, loss, renewal, patriotism, death, or love. The children's tale "Little Red Riding Hood," is a story about obedience; "Goldilocks," on the other hand, depicts curiosity.

- mood—the dominant emotion (cheerful, brooding, mysterious, hopeful, or negative). In Eudora Welty's "A Worn Path," the focal character, Aunt Phoenix, maintains a positive outlook against impossible odds.

- tone—the author's attitude toward the story. The Bible narrative of Queen Esther, for example, demonstrates that the author is in sympathy with the Hebrew heroine and does not regret the death of her wicked accuser.

Consider other possible influences on analysis: Is the story translated from a foreign language, as is the case with Isak Dinesen's "The Pearls"? Does the story belong to a particular period or, like Shirley Jackson's "The Lottery," seem unattached to time? Does the story fit a particular category, like Katherine Ann Porter's character study "The Jilting of Granny Weatherall," or Toni Cade Bambara's "Blues Ain't No Mockin' Bird," an intense recreation of negative emotion. Before reaching a conclusion, determine whether the author is entertaining, alarming, or creating a mental picture; for example, the contrast between rich and poor in Katherine Mansfield's "The Garden Party."

Budget: $$

Sources:

Booth, Marilyn. *Stories by Egyptian Women*. University of Texas Press, 1993.

Cisneros, Sandra. *The House on Mango Street*. Vintage, 1989.

McLoughlin, Pat. *Woman's Hour Book of Short Stories*. Parkwest Publications, 1993.

Stephenson, Glennis, ed. *Nineteenth-Century Stories by Women*. Broadview Press, 1994.

Alternative Applications:

Select a short story depicting a crucial decision in the life of one woman. Compose an extensive character study of the woman indicating these conflicts:

- difficult decisions or choices

- unfavorable self-image

- test of courage

- analysis of family problems

- loss of belief system

- national crisis, such as war or famine

Conclude with a succinct statement of the author's purpose in showing a woman applying logic to a difficult situation.

Women *in epic and heroic literature*

Age/Grade Level or Audience: High school or college English composition topic; Latin, Greek, or drama research paper; women's studies lecture; book club presentation; library or museum focus; journal feature.

Description: Summarize the strengths and weaknesses of female figures in epic and heroic literature.

Procedure: Identify the individual qualities of female figures—including human and divine—in epic and heroic literature. For example, enumerate these significant female personae in Homer's *Iliad* and *Odyssey:* Penelope, Cassandra, Hecuba, Helen, Andromache, Briseis, Calypso, Athena, Hera, Eurycleia, and Nausicaa. Determine whether their strengths come from inherited power, money, fame, beauty, intelligence, prestige, guile, or supernatural power. Apply this same study to other female characters:

- Dido, Andromache, Venus, Juno, Creusa, Helen, Anna, Amata, the Cumaean Sybil, and Lavinia in Virgil's *Aeneid*

- Ygraine, Guinevere, Morgan le Fay, Lynette, Lady Lyonors, and Elaine in Arthurian lore, especially Sir Thomas Malory's *Le Morte d'Arthu,* Mary Stewart's Merlin trilogy, and Alfred, Lord Tennyson's *Idylls of the King*

- Eve and Urania in John Milton's *Paradise Lost*

- Swanhild, Sigrdrifa, Gudrun, Ran, Sigrlinn, Skadi, Svava, Freyja, Grimhild, Borghild, and Oddrun in the *Edda*

- Beatrice, Myrrha, Potiphar's wife, Dido, Medusa, Thais, Virgin Mary, Deidamia, the harpies, and Helen in Dante Alighieri's *Divina Commedia*

- Miriam, Zipporah, Levi's wife, and Pharaoh's daughter in *Exodus*

Extend the exercise with female personae from *El Cid, Le Chanson de Roland, Niebelungen-lied, Luciad, Kalevala, Beowulf, The Song of Hiawatha, Gilgamesh, The Birth of Cú Chulainn, The Epic of Qayak,* and *Mahabharata.* Conclude why the role of women in epic and heroic lore tends to overstep or violate reality.

Budget: $

Sources:

Cantor, Norman F. *The Medieval Reader.* HarperCollins, 1994.

Daly, Pierrette. *Heroic Tropes: Gender and Intertext.* Wayne State University Press, 1993.

Jackson, Guida M. *Encyclopedia of Traditional Epics.* ABC-Clio, 1994.

Markale, Jean. *Women of the Celts.* Inner Traditions International, 1986.

Oman, Lela Kiana. *The Epic of Qayak.* Carleton University Press, 1995.

Poems of the Elder Edda. University of Pennsylvania Press, 1990.

Snodgrass, Mary Ellen. *Encyclopedia of Utopian Literature.* ABC-Clio, 1995.

The Transformation of Hera. Rowman, 1993.

Alternative Applications: Characterize the male-female relationships from epic and heroic literature. For example, note these qualities:

- Odysseus's dependence on Athena

- Aeneas's acceptance of the god's order to abandon Dido

- Arthur's horror at his incestuous affair with his half-sister

- Miriam's protection of her infant brother Moses

- Gilgamesh and the alewife Siduri

Determine how these relationships function to enhance or detract from the reader's overall evaluation of the hero's significance, humanity, godliness, obedience, commitment, and loyalty.

Women *in sagas*

Age/Grade Level or Audience: High school or college composition; women's studies assignment; book club presentation; literary society lecture.

Description: Compose an extended definition of saga by presenting the actions and interrelations of women in a single title or series.

Procedure: Have participants read Tsao Hsueh-Chin's *Dream of the Red Chamber,* China's most popular saga novel, which Tsao left unfinished at his death on February 1, 1764. The work details the decline of the debauched, self-absorbed aristocracy of the Ching Dynasty and the resultant fall of the feudal system, a patriarchy causing women needless misery and initiating their conniving and manipulation as a means to gratification. Assign groups to list qualities of a saga as represented in the novel. Consider stereotype and individuality in the work's numerous female characters:

- Aunt Hsueh, member of the Wang family and mother of Hsueh Pao-Chai and Hsueh Pan, a villain and ne'er-do-well

- Granny Liu, a distant relative of Lady Wang of peasant stock who offers a pragmatic view of the spendthrift Chia lifestyle

- Hsueh Pao-chai or "Precious Virtue," devoted wife of Chia Pao-Yu and follower of feudal expectations for noble wives

333

- Hsia Chin-Kuei, merchant-class wife of Hsueh Pan who torments her husband's concubine Hsiang-ling and accidentally ingests poison while trying to kill the concubine

- Hsi-Chun or "Compassion Spring," daughter of the noble ascetic Chia Tai-Hua and Madame Yu; sister of the spoiled and vice-ridden Chia Chen; and a friend of the nun Miao-Yu and potential novice

- Lady Dowager, the family matriarch and widow for many years, who supervises her grandchildren's education

- Lady Hsing, the discontented, envious wife of Chia Sheh and daughter-in-law of the Lady Dowager

- Lin Tai-Yu or "Black Jade," the delicate, wistful daughter of Lin Ju-Hai, and Chia Pao-Yu's love

- Li Wan, widow of Chia Chu and daughter-in-law of Chia Ching, who indulges her son, Chia Lan, to the exclusion of all other interests

- Shih Hsiang-Yun or "River Mist," the pet and frequent visitor to her grandmother, the Lady Dowager

- Tan-Chun or "Quest Spring," Chia's Ching's daughter and rebel against feudalism

- Wang Hsi-Feng or "Phoenix," manipulative wife of Lady Hsing's grandson, daughter of Chiao-chieh, and expert housekeeper

- Ying-Chun or "Welcome Spring," daughter of Chia Sheh and his concubine; a misguided girl with poor judgment

- Ying-Lien or "Lotus," Chen Shih-Yin's daughter, who is kidnapped and forced into Hsueh Pan's bed

- Yuan-Chun, Chia Cheng's daughter and the emperor's concubine

Apply the overall texture of intrigue, passions, and antipathies to the action and to the political and social milieu that erodes national and personal values. Contrast the women in the work with those in other sagas such as:

- Aeschylus's *Oresteia*

- William Faulkner's *The Hamlet, The Town,* and *The Mansion*

- John Galsworthy's *The Forsyte Saga: The Man of Property, In Chancer, To Let,* and *A Modern Comedy*

- Thomas Mann's *Joseph and His Brothers*

- William Morris's *Sigurd the Volsung*

- Laura Ingalls Wilder's *Little House on the Prairie* series

- Mary Stewart's *The Crystal Cave, The Hollow Hills,* and *The Last Enchantment*

- Jung Chang's *Wild Swans*

- Isabel Allende's *The House of the Spirits*

Budget: $

Sources:

The Emigrants. Critics Choice, n.d. (Video)

Feng, Yuan-Chun. *A Short History of Classical Chinese Literature.* Foreign Language Press, 1959.

Hsia, Chih-Tsing. *The Classic Chinese Novel.* Columbia University Press, 1968.

Jian Bozan, Shao Xunzheng, and Hu Hua. *A Concise History of China.* Foreign Language Press, 1981.

Little House on the Prairie Series. Critics Choice, n.d. (Video)

Liu, Meng-Xi. *Selected Essays on the Story of The Dream of the Red Chamber.* Tientsin: Hundred Flower Press, 1984.

Lu Hsun. *A Brief History of Chinese Fiction.* Peking: Foreign Language Press, 1959.

Miller, Lucian. *Masks of Fiction in Dream of the Red Chamber: Myth, Mimesis, and Persona.* University of Arizona Press, 1975.

The New Land. Critics Choice, n.d. (Video)

Ping-Leung Chan. "Myth and Psyche in Dream of the Red Chamber." In *Critical Essays on Chinese Fiction.* Hong Kong: The Chinese University Press, 1980.

Plak, Andrew H. *Archetype and Allegory in the Dream of the Red Chamber.* Books Demand, 1994.

Qayaq, Lela Kiana. *The Epic of Quayaq.* Carleton University Press, 1995.

Tsao Hsueh-Chin. *Dream of the Red Chamber.* Anchor Books, 1958.

You, Kuo-en, ed. *The History of Chinese Literature.* Peking: People's Literature Press, 1984.

Alternative Applications: Compare the women of different ages and social levels in Tsao Hsueh-Chin's *Dream of the Red Chamber.* Determine if changes in social expectation, broadened opportunities, liberal education, and freedom of choice in marriage alter the behavior patterns of certain pairs, notably these:

wife/husband	wife/concubine
sister/brother	mother/daughter
mother/son	mother/grandchildren
mother/daughter-in-law	woman/female servants
woman/female relatives	woman/female friends
empress/daughters	empress/daughters-in-law

Contrast the experiences of these pairs with characters found in Isabel Allende's *The House of the Spirits* or Lela Kiana Oman's *The Epic of Qayak.*

Women's *rhetoric*

Age/Grade Level or Audience: High school or college literary handbook database; desktop publishing project, teacher education model.

Description: Discuss the style and elements of literary genres by applying them to female characters or scenes and descriptions of or by women. Present these as models:

Elements of Fiction

- character—Melanie Hamilton in Margaret Mitchell's *Gone With the Wind*
- circular narrative—Toni Morrison's *Beloved*
- conflict—experiences in Tiananmen Square in Ding Xiaoqi's *Maidenhome*
- first person—Celie in Alice Walker's *The Color Purple*

- plot—events in Jessamyn West's *Except for Me and Thee*
- setting—early twentieth-century China in Pearl Buck's *The Good Earth*
- story talk—Maxine Hong Kingston's *The Woman Warrior*
- theme—a noncombatant's inner war in Phyllis Walker's *Jubilee*

Types of Poetry

- confessional poetry—Anne Sexton's *To Bedlam and Part Way Back*
- epic poetry—Lela Qiana Oman's *The Epic of Qayak*
- lyric poetry—fragments by Sappho
- narrative poetry—Christina Rosetti's *The Goblin Market*

Types of Comedy

- comedy of manners—Anita Loos's *Auntie Mame*
- drawing room comedy—Enid Bagnold's *The Chalk Garden*
- tragicomedy—Winnie's final assault on her husband in Amy Tan's *The Kitchen God's Wife*
- humor—Florence King's columns for *Southern Magazine*
- parody—Stella Gibbons's *Cold Comfort Farm*
- pun—the title of Margaret Atwood's *The Handmaid's Tale*
- romantic comedy—Esther McCracken's *Quiet Weekend*
- satire—Molly Ivins's *Molly Ivins Can't Say That, Can She?*
- wit—aphorisms by Gertrude Stein

Oratory

- speech—Toni Morrison's Nobel Prize acceptance speech
- address—Barbara Jordan's address to the 1992 Democratic Presidential Convention
- harangue—Sojourner Truth's *Ain't I a Woman?*

Nonfiction

- memoir—diaries of Anaïs Nin
- biography—Fawn Brodie's life of Thomas Jefferson
- autobiography—Maya Angelou's *I Know Why the Caged Bird Sings*
- diary—Anne Frank's *The Diary of a Young Girl*
- column—Eleanor Roosevelt's "My Day"

Procedure: Have volunteers create a database of lines, titles, characters, action, and dialogue drawn from their favorite works, portfolios, or personal journals. Make the project ongoing.

Budget: $

Sources:

Cuddon, J. A. *A Dictionary of Literary Terms*. Penguin Books, 1982.

Gledhill, Christine. *Home Is Where the Heart Is: Studies in Melodrama and Women's Film*. BFI, 1987.

Holman, C. Hugh, and William Harmon. *A Handbook to Literature.* Macmillan, 1992.

Jordan, Rosan A., and Susan J. Kalcik, eds. *Women's Folklore, Women's Culture.* University of Pennsylvania Press, 1985.

Kenyon, Olga, ed. *Eight Hundred Years of Women's Letters.* Penguin, 1994.

Alternative Applications: Have participants study literary works by female authors and locate models of literary devices, versification, and genre. Create a literary reference chapbook for a library, creative writing class, book club, or museum. Begin with these models:

GENRE

Fiction

- novella—Edith Wharton's *Ethan Frome*
- detective novel—Ellen Raskin's *The Westing Game*
- thriller novel—Agatha Christie's *Ten Little Indians*
- psychological novel—Margaret Atwood's *The Robber Bride*
- utopian novel—Marge Piercy's *Woman on the Edge of Time*
- stream-of-consciousness—Margaret Atwood's *The Handmaid's Tale*
- epistolary novel—Alice Walker's *The Color Purple*
- novel of manners—Jane Austen's *Pride and Prejudice*
- gothic novel—Charlotte Brontë's *Jane Eyre*
- realistic novel—Willa Cather's *My Antonia*
- regional novel—Shirley Ann Grau's *The Condor Passes*
- science fiction—Ursula LeGuin's *The Lathe of Heaven*
- short story—Toni Cade Bambara's "Blues Ain't No Mockin' Bird"
- young adult novel—Natalie Babbitt's *Tuck Everlasting*
- coming-of-age novel—Judy Blume's *Are You There God? It's Me, Margaret*

Nonfiction

- autobiography—Yoko Kawashima Watkins's *So Far from the Bamboo Grove*
- eyewitness to history—Anne Moody's *Coming of Age in Mississippi*
- legend—Pocahontas, Annie Oakley
- hagiography—legends of St. Bernadette
- folklore—Annie Oakley, Calamity Jane
- fairy tale—Snow White and Rose Red, Rapunzel
- myth—Ceres and Persephone

LITERARY DEVICES

- alliteration—"Great self-destruction follows upon unfounded fear," Ursula Le Guin's *The Lathe of Heaven*
- aphorism—Susan Straight's *I Been in Sorrow's Kitchen and I Licked Out All the Pots.*
- dialect—Gwendolyn Brooks's "We Real Cool"

337

- grotesque—the monster in Mary Shelley's *Frankenstein*

- image—silver in H.D.'s "Pear Tree"

- irony—*The Awakening*

- melodrama—Little Eva's death in Harriet Beecher Stowe's *Uncle Tom's Cabin*

- metonymy—Elizabeth I as "the crown"; Indira Gandhi as "a voice for unity"

- palindrome—Ava, Eve

- personification—Lady Luck

- pseudonym—George Eliot (Mary Ann Evans)

Maintain the database or keep a journal of phrases, titles, characters, settings, or scenes that typify a rhetorical device.

Writing *a woman's story*

Age/Grade Level or Audience: High school or college comparative literature topic; book club presentation; women's studies lecture; newspaper column; formal debate.

Description: Contrast female characters and situations from the perspective of two different writers, one male and one female.

Procedure: Have volunteers select a male and female writer who each presents a single aspect of womanhood, such as coping skills, coming of age, establishing a career, coping with a handicap, or establishing a family. Consider these pairs:

- the mother as typified in Terry McMillan's *Mama* and Richard Wright's *Black Boy*

- the farm wife in Willa Cather's *My Antonia* and Robert Frost's "The Death of the Hired Man"

- the innocent girl in Toni Morrison's *The Bluest Eye* and Randall Jarrell's "Lady Bates"

- the victim of war in Amy Lowell's "Patterns" and Allan Gurganous's *The Oldest Living Confederate Widow Tells All*

- the elderly woman in Eudora Welty's "A Worn Path" and Truman Capote's "A Christmas Memory"

- wartime privations in Jung Chang's *Wild Swans* and Lillian Hellman's *Julia*

- the unmarried woman in Annie Proulx's *Post Cards* and Isaac Singer's "Yentl"

- the self-absorbed woman in Maxine Hong Kingston's *Woman Warrior* and Thornton Wilder's *The Bridge of San Luis Rey*

- coming of age in Betty Smith's *A Tree Grows in Brooklyn* and James Vance Marshall's *Walkabout*

Budget: $

Sources:

Agatha's Christie's Miss Marple. Pacific Arts Publishing, n.d. (Video)

Carpenter, Angelica Shirley, and Jean Shirley. *Frances Hodgson Burnett: Beyond the Secret Garden.* Lerner Books, 1990.

Chadwick, Roxanne. *Anne Morrow Lindbergh: Pilot and Poet.* Lerner Books, 1987.

Collins, David R. *The Country Artist: A Story about Beatrix Potter.* Lerner Books, 1989.

Dixon, Oscar. " 'Skeeter' Took Fame in Stride." *USA Today,* November 14, 1994, 1C.

Feingold, Michael. "Terms of Medeament." *New York Theatre Critics' Reviews,* No. 5, 1994, 79–80.

Mitchell, Barbara. *Between Two Worlds: A Story about Pearl Buck.* Lerner Books, 1988.

Sprechman, Ellen Lew. *Seeing Women As Men: Role Reversal in the Novels of Thomas Hardy.* University Press, 1995.

Twain, Mark. *Joan of Arc: Personal Recollections.* Gramercy, 1995.

Alternative Applications: Arrange a panel discussion of paired plays, poems, novels, articles, short stories, essays, interviews, studies, songs, hymns, anthems, television miniseries, biographies, or screenplays by male and female authors. Pose these questions as impetus to commentary:

- What attitudes color the objectivity, curiosity, purpose, literary style, and humanity of each author?

- How do contrasting writers delineate values, spiritual growth, emotional maturity, and beliefs?

- What hindrances to self-fulfillment spring from society and which derive from the media or institutions, particularly school and church?

- What burdens stem from overt sexism, harassment, low self-esteem, law, custom, or prejudice?

- How do female protagonists use wit, guile, humor, and coping skills to ease trauma or to facilitate difficult decisions and choices?

- What personal experiences and historical events promote growth and self-worth?

- How do the female characters compare with male characters in terms of thorough delineation, intelligence, courage, ambition, and dedication to goals?

- How do dialogue, dreams, thoughts, diaries, journals, and unspoken words reveal repressed hopes and desires?

- What aspects of the female personality remain untapped, particularly sexuality, oppression, maternal hunger, depression, and rage?

Mathematics *and* computers

Database *time line*

Age/Grade Level or Audience: High school or women's history computer database; term paper or library research topic; book club handout; Women's History Month celebration table runner or frieze.

Description: Using a computer create a broad-based overview of women's accomplishments by years or eras. For more advanced computer users, determine what sorts would be useful in constructing the data file, such as: date, surname, nationality, genre, etc.

Procedure: Have participants conduct ongoing readings, literary and historical research, and other study of women's accomplishments. Establish a time-line database; log these accomplishments into it:

- **ca. 2000 B.C.** Priestess Enheduanna composed the world's first poetry volume, by which she reverenced the goddess Inanna.

- **fifth century B.C.** Artemisia of Halicarnassus became the first female ship's captain and fleet commander by taking her husband's place after his death and backing Xerxes's fleet near Marathon, Greece.

- **31 B.C.** Cleopatra, Egypt's last queen, chose death rather than be displayed as an ornament among Octavian's captured booty.

- **370 A.D.** Hypatia of Alexandria, Egypt, studied mathematics with Plutarch and philosophy, designed a hydroscope and astrolabe, and taught geometry, algebra, and astronomy at the University of Alexandria.

- **610** Khadimah, Mohammed's wife, supported the prophet with her mercantile business while he completed his religious mission.

- **855** Pope Joan, under the name John VIII, remained in office in the Vatican until the birth of her child, for which she was stoned to death in 858.

- **ca. 1000** Lady Murasaki Shikibu published *The Tale of Genji,* a Japanese adventure tale considered the first novel. An anonymous female Japanese author produced *The Diary of a May-Fly.*

- **1619** Isabella, the first black female slave, arrived in Jamestown, Virginia, aboard a Dutch trader.

- **1779** At the Battle of Monmouth, Molly Pitcher took her husband's place after he died. She earned a commendation from General Washington. Likewise, Margaret Corbin replaced her husband at Fort Washington and was wounded. In July Congress awarded her disability pay and one suit of clothes.

- **1848** Lucretia Mott and Elizabeth Cady Stanton convened the first Women's Rights Convention in Seneca Falls, New York.

- **1852** Harriet Beecher Stowe's *Uncle Tom's Cabin* ignited the abolitionist cause and precipitated talk of a civil war.

- **1860** Susan B. Anthony pressed for the enactment of the Women's Property Act, which granted divorced women rights to property and to their children.

- **1865** Lucy Stone and Julia Ward Howe established the American Woman Suffrage Association in Boston.

- **1878** The first black female doctor, Caroline Virginia Anderson, began practicing medicine.

- **1881** Clara Barton established the American Red Cross. The next year Congress ratified the Geneva Convention to strengthen the position of the Red Cross during war.

- **1890** Headed by Anna Howard Shaw and Carrie Chapman Catt, the National Woman Suffrage Association merged with the Equal Rights Association and allied with women's clubs and the Woman's Christian Temperance Union in a mass rally for voting rights.

- **1890** Wyoming became the first state to give women the vote.

- **1905** Bertha von Suttner became the first female Nobel Prize winner.

- **1910** Pacifist attorney Crystal Eastman published *Work Accidents and the Law,* an influential work that led to her drafting of the first U.S. workers' compensation law. Two years later, she helped found the National Woman's Party.

- **1917** Inessa Armand, Clara Zetkin, and Nadezhda Krupskaya pressured Russian officials to sanction International Women's Day.

- **1917–1919** Pacifist Jeannette Rankin served her first term as the first U.S. Congresswoman; she would serve again from 1941–1943.

- **1919** Crystal Eastman organized the First Feminist Congress, which supported the Equal Rights Amendment. The Volstead Act forbade the sale of alcohol, a law influencing Frances Willard's establishment of the Women's Christian Temperance Union (WCTU).

- **fall 1919** First Lady Edith Wilson assumed presidential powers for eighteen months after Woodrow Wilson suffered a stroke.

- **1920** Jane Addams, Jeannette Rankin, Elizabeth Gurley Flynn, and Helen Keller helped establish the American Civil Liberties Union.

- **1923** The National Woman's Party (now known as the League of Women Voters) pressed for the Equal Rights Amendment.

- **1925** Nellie Tayloe Ross was elected governor of Wyoming.

- **1950** Poet Gwendolyn Brooks won a Pulitzer Prize.

- **December 1, 1955** In Montgomery, Alabama, Rosa Parks refused to give her bus seat to a white passenger and willingly went to jail in protest of racial discrimination on public transportation.

- **1959** Lorraine Hansberry became the first female playwright to win the coveted New York Drama Critics Circle Award, for the Broadway run of *A Raisin in the Sun.*

- **1961** Congresswoman Jessica Weis sponsored the equal rights amendment.

- **1962** Betty Friedan launched new-wave feminism with the publication of *The Feminine Mystique.*

- **1966** To press for passage of the Equal Rights Amendment, Betty Friedan sponsored NOW, the National Organization of Women.

- **1970** Maggie Kuhn organized the Gray Panthers.

- **1972** Barbara Jordan of Texas became the first black female to chair a state legislature.

- **1972** Gloria Steinem inaugurated her fifteen-year editorship of *Ms.* magazine.

- **1973** Norma McCorvey, officially known as "Roe," sued the state of Texas for the right to an abortion.

- **September 1992** Mae Jemison left her medical practice and became the first black woman in space.

- **1993–1994** Title IX requirements raised the number of women participating in basketball, cross country, diving, fencing, field hockey, golf, gymnastics, lacrosse, rifle, skiing, soccer, softball, swimming, tennis, track, and volleyball in the United States.

- **January 1993** President Bill Clinton commissioned Maya Angelou to compose a poem for his inauguration.

- **1994** The women inducted into the Women's Hall of Fame in Seneca Falls, New York, included former Congresswomen Geraldine Ferraro and Bella Abzug, entertainer Oprah Winfrey, Olympic runner Wilma Rudolph, first female surgeon general Dr. Antonia Novello, ERA supporter Catherine East, financier Muriel Siebert, and the Reverend Betty Bone Schiess, first female Episcopal priest.

- **February 1995** Myrlie Evers-Williams advanced to the presidency of the NAACP.

- **March 1995** Gertrude Mongella of Tanzania headed the U.N. Conference on Women in Beijing. President Clinton appointed Marjorie Margolies-Mezvinsky to head the American delegation.

- **June 22, 1995** President Bill Clinton and Hillary Rodham Clinton broke ground at Arlington Cemetery for a semi-circular monument and reflecting pool, to be tended by curator Kathryn Sheldon. The memorial, designed by Marion Gail Weiss and Michael Manfredi, honors the 1.8 million women who served the military since 1776, of whom 350,000 are active, 200,000 are dead and 1.2 million are veterans.

- **July 11, 1995** Nobel Peace prize winner and freedom fighter Aung Suu Kyi of Burma ended six years of house arrest.

Budget: $$

Sources:

Axelrod, Dr. Alan, and Charles Phillips. *What Every American Should Know About American History*. Bob Adams, 1992.

Clark, Gillian. *Women in Late Antiquity: Pagan and Christian Lifestyles*. Oxford University Press, 1993.

Clark, Judith Freeman. *Almanac of American Women in the Twentieth Century*. Prentice Hall, 1987.

Clement, J., ed. *Famous Deeds of American Women*. Corner House, 1975.

Dennis, Denise. *Black History for Beginners*. Highsmith, 1992.

Fantham, Elaine, et al. *Women in the Classical World*. Oxford University Press, 1994.

Franck, Irene, and David Brownstone. *Women's World: A Timeline of Women in History*. HarperCollins, 1995.

Great Lives from History: American Women Series. Salem Press, 1995.

Griffin, Lynne, and Kelly McCann. *The Book of Women: 300 Notable Women History Passed By.* Bob Adams, 1992.

Hampton, Henry, and Steve Fayer. *Voices of Freedom: An Oral History of the Civil Rights Movement from the 1950s through the 1980s.* Bantam Books, 1990.

Harrison, Cynthia, ed. *Women in National Politics.* University Publications of America, 1995.

Karlekar, Malavika. Introduction to *Changing Lives: Life Stories of Asian Pioneers in Women's Studies.* Feminist Press, 1995.

Levenson, Dorothy. *Homesteaders and Indians.* Franklin Watts, 1971.

———. *Women of the West.* Franklin Watts, 1973.

Lunardini, Christine A. *What Every Woman Should Know About Women's History.* Bob Adams, 1994.

Olsen, Kirstin. *Chronology of Women's History.* Greenwood Press, 1994.

Ovington, Mary White. *Black and White Sat Down Together: The Reminiscences of an NAACP Founder.* Feminist Press, 1995.

Trager, James. *The Women's Chronology.* Henry Holt, 1994.

Alternative Applications: Select an era and appoint groups to determine trends in gender equality by constructing a database, being careful to note setbacks as well as victories. Add entries for the creation of female civic, business, and community leadership posts that occurred during the Civil War when there were no men to take the jobs, and similar promotions of women to major positions in industry, as in World War II. If relevant, append a map noting pockets of activism and success and areas which show little or no growth in civil rights or gender fairness.

The geometric *roman doll*

Age/Grade Level or Audience: Middle school geometry activity; after-school program; home-school design project; history display.

Description: Design a female Roman doll from geometric figures.

Procedure: Begin design with a schematic drawing of a female torso from a rectangle 4" x 1¼" x ⅜". Insert ⅜" arcs at the upper right and left edges where the arms will join the shoulders. Add two ⅜" arcs at the bottom of the rectangle where the legs will fit. Attach a rectangle ¼" x ⅜" x ¼" to serve as a neck. Using a pattern cut from the schematic drawing, mold the torso out of clay. Pierce on outer points of each arc and insert a thin strip of wire. Bake clay or harden in the sun.

Form a head and hair freehand to suit the neck and body of the doll. Form upper legs from a cylinder of clay 1½" x ⅜". Attach by wire to a lower leg that is 1" x ¼". Mold feet freestyle and add to lower leg. Pierce hips to receive torso wires. Bake or harden pieces and attach to wires. Using similar proportions, form upper and lower arms and hands that taper to ⅛" thick. Bake and attach.

Complete female doll by painting on a face and jewelry and by cutting a strip of thin white cloth the width of the doll from shoulder to knee and long enough to wrap the body loosely. Fasten the strip into a tube with small stitches at the ends. Close up the shoulder seams with stitches. At the hem and neckline, paint on the Greek key or meander. Use a rich aqua, the color of the Mediterranean Sea, or purple, a popular color derived from shellfish and preferred by royalty in ancient times.

Budget: $$

Sources:

Andrews, Ian. *Pompeii*. Lerner Publications, 1980.

Brown, Charlene, and Carolyn Davis. *Clay Fun*. W. Foster, 1989.

Handbuilt Clay Sculpture. Crystal, 1995. (Video)

McGraw, Sheila. *Dolls Kids Can Make*. Firefly Books, 1995.

Purdy, Susan, and Cass R. Sandak. *Ancient Greece*. Franklin Watts, 1982.

Sapiro, Maurice. *Clay: Handbuilding*. Davis Mass, 1983.

Alternative Applications: Make or draw a family of Roman female dolls, including a younger and older sister, mother, housekeeper, and slave girl. Provide them with historically accurate objects and tools: ladle, winnowing basket, loom, pull toys, scroll books, wax tablet and stylus, hanging lamp, comb, curling iron, or flute and lyre to entertain or teach the girls about music. Include a Roman bride, who dressed in yellow with a flammeum or flame-red veil over her braided hair.

Geometry *and design*

Age/Grade Level or Audience: Middle school drafting project; mathematics term paper; desktop publishing exercise; women's studies oral report; bulletin board feature; Women's History Month handout; media or newsletter illustration.

Description: Publish a study about the Women's Memorial in Arlington National Cemetery.

Procedure: Organize groups to discuss the shape of the Women's Memorial, a project spearheaded by retired Air Force Brig. Gen. Wilma Vaught, one of America's most decorated women and a veteran of Vietnam. Collect critiques from different types of visitors, including veterans, widowers, children of female veterans, nurses, legislators, the media, and tourists from all nations. Comment on the patriotism of Navy pilot Lt. Kara Hultgreen, killed in an F-14 fighter jet off California; retired Brigadier General Hazel Johnson-Brown; and Dorothy Manfredi, Army nurse in World War II. Present the following figures denoting women's role in past wars, according to the Women in Military Service for America Memorial Foundation, Inc.:

Civil War	6,000
Spanish-American War	1,500
World War I	34,000
World War II	400,000
Korean War	22,000
Vietnam War	7,500
Grenada	116
Panama	1,300
Persian Gulf	37,213
Total	**509,629**

Note that the estimated total for all military involvement since the American Revolution is 1.8 million American women. Have groups work together with geometric shapes—semicircles, squares, triangles, circles, hexagons—to define the monument and its focus. Include doorways, rooflines, entrances, courts, reflecting pools, walls, staircases, parapets, and decorative touches. Summarize the architectural effect of the building as a whole.

Budget: $$$

Sources:

Moss, Desda. "For Military Women, Pride Knocked Down the Barrier." *USA Today,* June 23, 1995, 10A.

"Women's Memorial Under Way." *Chicago Tribune,* June 23, 1995, Section 1, 3.

Or contact The Women's Memorial Foundation, Dept. 560, Washington, D.C. 20042-0560; 800-222-2294.

Alternative Applications: Lead a discussion or compose a survey of different views of the Women's Memorial. Contrast the design geometrically and aesthetically to the Washington Monument, Jefferson Memorial, Lincoln Memorial, and Vietnam Memorial. Propose other geographical locations for women's memorials, for example, a commemoration of pioneer women along the Oregon Trail or Cumberland Gap or a statue grouping women and children at Wounded Knee or on the Long Walk or the Trail of Tears. Have participants draft a preliminary site plan showing their proposed monument's design, construction, and public access.

Graphing *the works*

Age/Grade Level or Audience: High school desktop publication; history term paper; library research topic; open database; women's studies compilation; bulletin board focus; newspaper column; Women's History Month monograph.

Description: Publish a brochure detailing significant trends in women's lives, jobs, families, education, and attitudes.

Procedure: Instruct participants on the various types of graphing. Encourage them to combine artistic presentation with the most effective method of presenting meaningful data, particularly information from national census figures. Consider these charts:

Horizontal

Projection on Women Entering Menopause

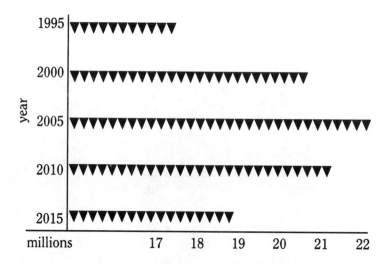

(SOURCE: Gail Sheehy, *New Passages.* New York: G. Merritt, 1995.)

Vertical

Political Concerns

(Women marked by X; men by 0)

```
      25%   0
            0
      20%   0   X                           0
            0   X                   0        0
      15%   0   X           X       0        0   X
            0   X           X       0   X    0   X
      10%   0   X       0   X       0   X    0   X
            0   X       0   X       0   X    0   X
       5%   0   X       0   X       0   X    0   X
            0   X       0   X       0   X    0   X
       0%   0   X       0   X       0   X    0   X
         unemployment  cost of living  deficit   taxes
```

percentage

Columnar

Female French Catholics

	secular priests	religious priests	women in the church	female catechists
1990	25,000	67,000	25,000	200,000

(SOURCE: Langlois, Claude, "19e siècle: religieuses et laïques à la tâche," *Notre Histoire,* April 1995, 28.)

Budget: $$$

Sources:

Jensen, Rita Henley. "Welfare." *Ms.,* July/August 1995, 50–61.

Morgan, Robin. *Sisterhood is Global.* Anchor Books, 1984.

Schmittroth, Linda, ed. *Statistical Record of Women Worldwide.* Gale Research, 1991.

Woods, Harriett. "Trendicators." *Working Woman,* May 1995, 26.

Alternative Applications: Using the models above as suggestions for graphing, create a package of raw data for computer or math classes to study and present in a pleasing, eye-catching format. Apply the following data to a variety of graphs:

Failed marriages in 1905:

nation	1 in 12
San Francisco	1 in 3
Washington	1 in 4

Montana	1 in 5
Colorado	1 in 6
Texas	1 in 6

(SOURCE: Dorothy Levenson, *Homesteaders and Indians.* New York: Franklin Watts, 1971.)

Pregnancies

Unwed Mothers per 1,000 white women

	ages 20-24	ages 15-44
1980	25.1	18.1
1982	26	18.5
1984	28	20.1
1986	33.5	23.8
1988	39	27.5
1990	47.5	32
1992	52.7	35.2

(SOURCE: *Charlotte Observer,* June 7, 1995, 1C.)

Use of Free Time

Cooking—men, 15%, women 81%

Repairs—men 91%, women 14%

Cleaning—men 7%, women 78%

Shopping—men 18%, women 87%

Paying bills—men 35%, women 63%

(SOURCE: Patricia Edmons. "Double Shift for Women: Work, Home," *USA Today,* April 10, 1995, 4A.)

Cancer

Women:

   lung cancer—new cases, 75,000; deaths, 58,000

   breast cancer—new cases, 180,000; deaths, 48,000

Men:

   lung cancer—new cases, 85,000; deaths, 80,000

   prostate cancer—new cases, 240,000; deaths, 46,000

(SOURCE: "Dying in Disgrace," *Harvard Health Letter,* August 1995, 4–5.)

The Greek cook

Age/Grade Level or Audience: Elementary school cooking demonstration; summer library program; home-school activity; Brownie Scout or 4-H metrics project.

Description: Combine the study of females in the Greek culture with a lesson in measurements.

Procedure: Introduce students to unusual flavors and to the protocol of a formal recipe with these directions for a Greek salad:

"Fit for a Goddess" Greek Salad

Wash and pat or spin dry a variety of greens—arugula, Boston lettuce, leaf lettuce, romaine, spinach, or chicory. Tear two quarts of greens into bite-sized pieces and place in a deep four-quart bowl. In a shallow cup, crumble a cup of dry feta cheese. Sprinkle feta cheese on top of greens. Add a half cup of Greek kalamata olives, a half teaspoon of shredded basil leaves, a quarter teaspoon of oregano leaves, and a quarter cup of packaged seasoned bread crumbs. Toss ingredients to blend. In a cruet, pour two tablespoons vegetable oil and the juice and zest of one lemon. Shake vigorously. Pour over salad. Serve immediately with breadsticks, butter, and sparkling grape juice. Serves six.

At the end of the sampling, have older participants copy the recipe and directions. For advanced students, require measures to be converted into metric units.

Budget: $$

Sources:

Andersson, Billie V. *Simple and Classic: Greek Elegance for the Everyday Cook*. Andesign, 1991.

Purdy, Susan, and Cass R. Sandak. *Ancient Greece*. Franklin Watts, 1982.

Zane, Eva. *Greek Cooking for the Gods*. Cole Group, 1992.

Alternative Applications: Collect several Greek recipes and combine into a "Fit for a Goddess" cookbook of rotisserie meats, fish, entrees, breads, cheeses, fruit dishes, appetizers, desserts, and beverages. List all measures in metric units. Decorate pages with Greek cooks carrying amphorae, baskets, and wooden trenchers and dressed in traditional upswept hairdos, chitons or tunics, armbands, and sandals.

Inside *radium*

Age/Grade Level or Audience: Middle school physical science, project; history or science library research topic; women's studies class presentation; bulletin board; Women's History Month media feature.

Description: Publish a drawing of the configuration of a radium atom and include side notes on the pioneers in the study of radiation science.

Procedure: Using desktop publishing or design graphics, draw several views of the radium atom. Include sidebars explaining what Marie and Pierre Curie discovered about radium, and the work of their daughter, Irene Joliot, who, in 1939, worked with her husband to simulate radioactivity. Also present biographical information on Lise Meitner, who clarified nuclear fission, and on radiologist Edith Quimby, who standardized the dosage of radiation for use in medical treatments of the human body. Name women who died from exposure to radiation while studying radium and its uses.

Budget: $$

Sources:

American Men and Women of Science. R. R. Bowker, 1989.

Ashworth, William. *The Encyclopedia of Environmental Studies*. Facts on File, 1991.

Clark, Judith Freeman. *Almanac of American Women in the Twentieth Century*. Prentice Hall, 1987.

Golob, Richard, and Eric Brus, eds. *The Almanac of Science and Technology*. Harcourt Brace Jovanovich, 1990.

James, Edward T., et al., eds. *Notable American Women, 1607–1950*. Belknap Press, 1971.

Magill, Frank N., ed. *Great Events from History II: Science and Technology Series*. Salem Press, 1991.

Martin, Jean, gen. ed. *Who's Who of Women in the Twentieth Century*. Crescent Books, 1995.

Montgomery, Mary. *Marie Curie*. Silver Burdett, 1990.

Stanley, Autumn. *Mothers and Daughters of Invention: Notes for a Revised History of Technology*. Scarecrow Press, 1993.

Veglahn, Nancy J. *Women Scientists*. Facts on File, 1991.

Yenne, Bill. *100 Inventions That Shaped World History*. Bluewood Books, 1993.

Alternative Applications: Use a similar design method to depict the work of these and other scientists:

- Marjorie Ferguson Lambert, excavator of Pueblos

- Mary Whitney, calculator of orbits for asteroids, comets, and double stars

- Katherine Foot, the first researcher to photograph through a microscope

- Cicely Williams's work with the protein-calorie fault causing kwashiorkor disease

Label parts of schematic drawings or layouts and present on an overhead projector along with an oral report.

Keepers *of the purse*

Age/Grade Level or Audience: College economics, civics, or computer class; economics or history oral presentation; women's studies class lecture; bulletin board book review; Women's History Month handout or display; media or newsletter illustration.

Description: Predict how women will affect finance in coming generations.

Procedure: Summarize the trends in Patricia Aburdene and John Naisbitt's *Megatrends for Women*. Organize groups to discuss the impact that the movement toward attaining equal rights for women has made in all sectors of the financial world throughout history. Discuss the following predictions:

- the future of women in computer science

- the coming liberation of women from pink collar jobs

- the end of the glass ceiling

- the integration of home and career for both parents

- the significant role of women in politics

- alterations in affirmative action

Conclude with a discussion of how more choices for women has and will continue to affect the family and national prosperity.

Budget: $

Sources:

Aburdene, Patricia, and John Naisbitt. *Megatrends for Women.* Random House, 1992.

Darling, Jan. *Outclassing the Competition: The Up-and-Comer's Guide to Social Survival.* St. Martin's, 1986.

Faludi, Susan. *Backlash: The Undeclared War Against American Women.* Crown Publishing Group, 1992.

Alternative Applications: Compose a canvass or mail-in survey of a cross-section of your community. Determine how women are currently influencing financial trends, home ownership, buying, saving, and investing. Question men on their trust in women as entrepreneurs, professionals, or office holders. Consider the following questions for your questionaire:

- What did your mother do for a living?

- How involved were your grandmothers and mother in family finance?

- Who controls most of the expenditures in your household?

- For what reasons do you admire women entrepreneurs?

- How do you feel about women as financiers and planners?

- Where do you feel women do the best job in your community government? school system? church? volunteer agencies?

Online *for jobs*

Age/Grade Level or Audience: High school or college guidance; term paper or library research topic; communications or women's studies newsletter; newspaper column series; radio or television presentation.

Description: Explore new alternatives for women in the computer age by searching the job market via online services.

Procedure: Offer women an electronic window on the SAT, college scene, job market, geographic settings for specialized fields, career services, and openings for applicants at all levels of expertise. Present excerpts of current literature on jobs of the future, standards and skills, and emerging fields of interest for women. Note the availability to job seekers of online information, college and job fairs, résumé models, and job listings. Summarize the following data for a newsletter, bulletin board, handout, or online entry:

- America Online, info@occ.com, 800-827-6364

- CompuServe, info@occ.com, 800-848-8199

- Delphi Internet Service, 800-695-4005

- eWorld (Macintosh format), 800-775-4556

- GEnie, 800-638-9636

- IBM Internet Connection, 800-455-5056

- Internet (gopher msen.com)

- Mindvox, 800-646-3869

- Online Résumé Service, 1713 Hemlock Ln., Plainfield, IN 461668

- Prodigy, info@occ.com
- Women's Wire, 800-210-8998

Budget: $$

Sources:

Dalgarn, Melinda K. *Smart Start.* McGraw-Hill, 1994.

Dixon, Pam. *Be Your Own Headhunter: Go Online to Get the Job you Want.* Random House, 1995.

————. "Job Searching in Cyberspace." *Careers and Colleges,* Spring 1995, 42–45.

Guilden, Paul. "Go Forth and Succeed." *Careers and Colleges,* Spring 1995, 42–45.

Harrington, Charles, and Joseph Elliot. *Tooth and Nail: A Novel Approach to the New SAT.* Harcourt Brace, 1994.

Miller, Leslie. "More Women Find a Niche on the Internet." *USA Today,* July 11, 1995, 6D.

Alternative Applications: Study online offerings for women. Compose a critique for a newspaper column, in-house newsletter, convention booth, or computer company brochure. Include these:

- Aliza Sherman's Cybergrrl Page, (http://www.interport.net/-asherman/). Domestic violence, breast cancer, and other social science topics.

- Amy Goodloe's Site, (http//www.best.com/-agoodloe/home.html) Women's e-mail. Includes women-info and internet-women-info (majordomo@best.com).

- English Server at Carnegie Mellon University (http://English-www.hss.cmu.edu/Feminism.html) for women's studies.

- Georgia Tech (http://www.cc.gatech.edu/gvu/user'surveys/) for women's studies.

- Interactive Publishing Alert, (http://www.netcreations.com/ipa/) for women's studies.

- Matrix Information and Directory Services, (http://www.mids.org) for women's studies.

- Systers (systers-admin2systers.org)

- University of Maryland's Women's Studies Database (http://www.inform.umd.edu:8080/EdRes/Topic/WomensStudies/) for feminist data.

- Voices of Women World, (http://www.voiceofwomen.com) Scope limited to the Virginia and Maryland area.

- Women's Wire (800-210-8998) Women-oriented information.

- WomensNet, (http://www.igc.apc.org/womensnet/) Covers world news relevant to women.

Who's *on first*

Age/Grade Level or Audience: High school computer database; book or history club presentation; genealogical society display; county fair booth; women's studies frieze; newspaper column; museum monograph.

Description: Create a broad-based database of female pioneers—the first women in particular fields or arenas.

Procedure: Have participants collect data on famous female firsts, such as Theodate Pope Riddle, America's first major female architect; Margaret Chase Smith, the first woman to serve both the U.S. Senate and House and the first female presidential candidate from a major party; Mary Kingsley, first English women to travel Africa without a male escort; Jacqueline Auriol, first woman to fly the Concorde SST; Dr. Louise Pound, first female president of the Modern Language Association; Jacqueline Cochran, first woman to break the sound barrier; Junko Tabei, first woman to climb Mt. Everest; and Louise Boyd, first woman to fly over the North Pole. Feature these examples:

- **1660** Margaret Hughes, England's first actress to appear onstage in London

- **1715** Mrs. Sibilla Masters, the first American patenter with her Tuscorora Rice, a dietary cure for tuberculosis

- **1792** Mary Wollstonecraft's *The Vindication of the Rights of Women,* the first European feminist doctrine

- **Mid-1800s** Maria Mitchell, the first American female astronomer

- **1870** Esther Morris Cabin, the first female U.S. justice of the peace

- **1874** Mary Ewing Outerbridge, first female U.S. tennis player

- **1893** Queen Liliuokalani of Honolulu, America's first deposed queen

- **1900** Madam C. J. Walker, America's first female millionaire

- **1903** Dame Ethel Mary Smyth's opera *Der Wald* is the first written by a woman to be performed at the Metropolitan Opera House, New York City; Maggie Lena Walker, the first woman bank president

- **1905** May G. Sutton, the first American woman to win at Wimbledon

- **1910** A. S. Wells, the first woman police officer

- **1915** Nellie Lawing, the first female federal contractor

- **1917** Bacteriologist Alice Catherine Evans, the first woman scientist employed by the Bureau of Animal Industry

- **1918** Opha May Johnson, the first woman to join the U.S. Marine Corps

- **1920** Bessie Coleman, the world's first licensed black female aviator

- **1920s** Dr. Sara Josephine Baker, America's first public health nurse

- **1925** Florence Sabin, the first woman member of the National Academy of Science

- **1932** Hattie Wyatt Caraway, the first woman elected to the U.S. Senate

- **1947** Frances Xavier Cabrini, the first American canonized by the Vatican

- **1953** Jacqueline Cochran, first woman to break the sound barrier in an F-86

- **1959** Lorraine Hansberry, first woman to win the New York Drama Critics Circle Award

- **1978** Louise Brown, the first human infant conceived outside the womb

- **1979** Joan Benoit, the first woman to finish the Boston Marathon

- **1984** Geraldine Ferraro, the first candidate for vice president from a major party (Democrat)

- **1990** Violetta Chamorro, Nicaragua's first female president

- **1995** Rebecca Elizabeth Marier, first female West Pointer to graduate at the head of her class

- **1995** Muriel Siebert, first woman owner of a seat on the New York Stock Exchange

Utilizing desktop publishing software, have participants create unusual presentations, for example, a calendar of firsts, a color-coordinated time line, frieze, banner, table runner, or window display.

Budget: $$

Sources:

Deen, Edith. *Great Women of the Christian Faith.* Barbour Books, 1959.

Grolier Encyclopedia Grolier, 1993. (CD-ROM)

Martin, Jean, gen. ed. *Who's Who of Women in the Twentieth Century.* Crescent Books, 1995.

Read, Phyllis J., and Bernard L. Witlieb. *The Book of Women's Firsts.* Random House, 1992.

Alternative Applications: For a Women's History Month banquet, workshop, career day, or community celebration, collect data on the first women in the city, county, or region who achieved in these areas:

- filed for a patent

- led expeditions

- opened health clinics

- owned businesses or opened factories

- performed original music or dance

- pioneered farming techniques

- supervised police or firefighters

- taught school or became principals or administrators

- won election to town boards or the mayoralty

Name every woman in your area who put the area on the map or had cities or buildings named for them, as with the Sarah Walker Building in Indianapolis, Indiana. Urge historical societies to place markers or plaques to honor these achievers.

The woman *behind Halley's comet*

Age/Grade Level or Audience: High school physical science or mathematics project; history or science library research topic; women's studies class presentation; Women's History Month media feature.

Description: Uncover the usually anonymous female associates behind some of the world's most well-known mathematical discoveries.

Procedure: Invite participants to investigate the history behind general theories and concepts of mathematics. Ask them to be on the lookout for female associates who are generally left out of the "history books." Use as an example the life of German mathematician Amalie Emmy Noether, who succeeded in mathematically generalizing Albert Einstein's theory of relativity:

- born in 1882, daughter of mathematician Max Noether

- although German educational policy barred women from becoming a full-fledged university student, Noether still attended lectures in language and mathematics

- she was eventually granted an exception and received her doctorate in 1907

- Noether pursued the newly emerged study of abstract algebra

- because she was a woman, Noether was restricted from pursuing a teaching position, however, she continued independently in her research

- in 1922 Noether was finally granted an associate professorship at Göttingen University

- Noether's formulations comprised a significant body of work on the ring theory and concept of ideals—a theory that lended itself to the basis of abstract algebra

Consider other female mathematicians such as Nicole-Reine Etable de la Brière Lepaute, who along with Alexis Clairaut and Joseph Jerome de Lalande, mathematically computed the correct return time of Halley's comet. Share findings in a newsletter or post biographies of such noteworthy women on a math or science bulletin board showcase.

Budget: $

Sources:

Abbott, David, ed. *Mathematicians*. Peter Bedrick Books, 1985.

Bailey, Martha J. *American Women in Science*. ABC-Clio, 1994.

Cook, Cynthia Conwell. *The Ages of Mathematics*. Doubleday, 1977.

Ogilvie, Marilyn Bailey. *Women in Science: Antiquity Through the Nineteenth Century*. MIT Press, 1986.

Travers, Bridget. *World of Scientific Discovery*. Gale Research, 1994.

Veglahn, Nancy J. *Women Scientists*. Facts on File, 1991.

Alternative Applications: Ask participants to post-mortem their research efforts. How easy was it to find the information they were seeking? Was it enough to go to very general sources, or did they have to seek specialized reference material? What types of sources had the most equal coverage of men and women? In what areas of study did they have the most trouble locating information? What areas, if any, were fairly brimming with facts? How successful were on-line searches? Have participants compile a database of female scientific pioneers, complete with biographies, timelines, and reliable resource material to make the job easier for the next researcher.

Women's *statistics*

Age/Grade Level or Audience: High school or college statistics or graphing project; term paper or library research; demographic study.

Description: Design an annual almanac of women's statistics.

Procedure: Have participants work with a small group to create an annual almanac of women's statistics, both of historical significance and current relevancy. Determine the scope: racial, tribal, city, statewide, countywide, national, or international. Set up the parameters of each chapter. Use this model as a starting point:

Table of Contents

Age Distribution

Birth Control and Abortion

Causes of Death

Death Rate

Education

Financial Status

Health

Leisure

Marital Status

Preference for Male Children

Size of Families

Work

Have participants choose sections and determine where to seek data on relevant topics, such as the number of women in each age or racial group who have completed high school, college, and graduate school in 1895 vs. 1995. Name the sources available for up-to-date information. Consider the USA Information number (800-347-1997), almanacs, online sources, newspaper files, Bureau of Census, and other library or governmental sources. Discuss the best way to keep the almanac current and available at a low cost. Name these and other locations where the information will be most useful and accurate: demographics offices, government planning boards, and health departments.

Budget: $

Sources:

"American Households." *American Demographics Desk Reference Series,* No. 3, July 1992.

Blonston, Gary. "Women Focus of Population Summit." *Charlotte Observer,* August 28, 1994, 1A, 16A.

Braus, Patricia. "Women of a Certain Age." *American Demographics,* December 1992, 44–49.

Grigsby, Jill S. "Women Change Places." *American Demographics,* November 1992, 46–50.

We, the American Woman. Ethnic and Hispanic Statistics Branch, 1995.

Women: The New Poor. Women Make Movies, Inc., 1994. (Video)

Alternative Applications: Write introductory paragraphs for each chapter in a women's almanac or for a work covering female citizens of a foreign country. Broaden the study to include religion, arranged marriage, sequestering or veiling, and such ethnic or cultural events as tattooing, body piercing, or female circumcision or genital mutilation. Comment on the tasks of the United Nations Conference on Population and Development held September 5–13, 1995, in Cairo, Egypt.

Music

The best of Aretha Franklin

Age/Grade Level or Audience: Middle school or high school music appreciation class; piano or music club study; civic club presentation; women's studies research topic; arts and commentary column; Women's History Month open-forum discussion; educational radio or television series.

Description: Salute the long-lived fame and career of vocalist Aretha Franklin.

Procedure: Present a program of music interspersed with facts about the rise and success of singer Aretha Franklin. Note these facts:

- Born in 1942, Aretha Franklin grew up in a family of five headed by her father, the Rev. C. L. Franklin, after her mother deserted them in 1948 and later died.

- She grew up under the influence of Mahalia Jackson, Clara Ward, and Dinah Washington—all frequent houseguests of her father.

- Franklin sang her first solo in her father's church, New Bethel Baptist Church in Detroit, Michigan; Franklin's first solo recording came at age fourteen, with Chess Records.

- In 1960 Franklin began a five-year contract with Columbia Records in New York City; she eventually moved to the Atlantic label.

- In 1967 Franklin won her first Grammy award—best rhythm and blues recording for "Respect," which would eventually become an anthem embraced by all women.

- Franklin has maintained a steady flow of quality live and recorded performances for over three decades. Her works contain a variety of vocal and instrumental accompaniments: bass, conga, flute, guitar, keyboard, oboe, percussion, thumb piano, tympani, and vibraphone.

- Presented the Kennedy Center Honor in 1994, Franklin, the first female in the Rock and Roll Hall of Fame, continues to maintain the image of the "Queen of Soul."

Conclude with selections from Aretha Franklin's album *I Never Loved a Man*. Summarize her choice of songs reflecting the many faces of love and longing—"Respect," "Who's Zoomin' Who," and "I'm the Girl." Note Franklin's ability to add punch and drive, as with the fervid, "No Tears in the End."

Budget: $$

Sources:

Bego, Mark. *Aretha Franklin: Queen of Soul.* St. Martin, 1989.

Franklin, Aretha. *Who's Zoomin' Who.* Arista, 1985. (CD)

Randolph, Laura B. "Aretha Talks About Men, Marriage, Music and Motherhood." *Ebony,* April 1995, 28–34.

Alternative Applications: Compose a fan letter to Aretha Franklin. Compare her works to those of other twentieth-century soul and rhythm and blues greats, such as Bessie Smith, Billie Holiday, and Roberta Flack. Conclude with an analysis of Aretha Franklin's strengths as a performer and her role as an inspirational model for young listeners. Comment on the reasons behind her staying power with the American public.

Black *women composers*

Age/Grade Level or Audience: High school or college chorus program; women's religious group study; women's studies or liturgical music seminar; voice or music club newsletter; synagogue or church song sheet.

Description: Study the words and music of secular and religious works by black female composers and arrangers.

Procedure: Organize a varied program of study including the biographies of black female composers, presented along with lyrics or music from CDs, cassettes, and records of their works and their performances or arrangements of traditional spirituals, anthems, and hymns. Feature these works:

- Florence Price (1888–1953): "My Dream"; "My Soul's Been Anchored in the Lord"; "Night"; "Song to a Dark Virgin"

- Undine Smith Moore (1904–1989): "Come Down Angels"; "I Am in Doubt"; "Is There Anybody Here That Loves My Jesus"; "Let the Wind Cry . . . How I Adore Thee"; "Watch and Pray"

- Margaret Bonds (1913–1972): "Dry Bones"; "He's got the Whole World in His Hand"; "Lord I Just Can't Keep from Cryin'"

- Julia Perry (1924–1979): "The Negro Speaks of Rivers"; "Three Dream Portraits"

Budget: $

Sources:

Andrews, Dwight. Liner notes to *Note on Watch and Pray.* Koch International Classics, 1994. (CD)

Green, Mildred Denby. *Black Women Composers: A Genesis.* Twayne, 1983.

Jezic, Diane Peacock. *Women Composers: The Lost Tradition Found.* Feminist Press, 1994.

Singing the Living Tradition. Beacon Press, 1993.

Alternative Applications: Make a card file for the public library music or audio-visual room. Follow these examples:

Bonds, Margaret (1913–1972)

Education:	Northwestern University; Juilliard School of Music; private study with Roy Harris, Florence Price, and Robert Starer.
Career:	founder and director of Allied Arts Academy in Chicago (1930s).

Awards:	Wanamaker competition.
Fields:	art songs, spiritual arranging

King, Betty Jackson (1928–   )

Education:	private study with Gertrude Smith Jackson; Roosevelt University; Peabody Conservatory; Westminster Choir College
Career:	accompanist and teacher at University of Chicago Laboratory School, Dillard University, Wildwood High school; choir director
Fields:	cantata, choral anthems, spiritual solo arrangements

Female *hymn writers*

Age/Grade Level or Audience: College musicology research; library summer project; piano or music club presentation; synagogue or church exercise; women's religious group study; women's studies seminar.

Description: Research the influence of women on hymnody.

Procedure: Divide participants into groups to study the feminist and humanistic influence or collaboration of women in the composition, collection, or translation of hymns or anthems. Use these as models:

Sara Flowers Adams	"Nearer My God to Thee"
Mary A. Bachelor	"Go Bury Thy Sorrow"
Katherine Lee Bates	"America the Beautiful"
Fanny J. Crosby	"I Am Thine, O Lord"
Lizzie DeArmond	"Who Will Our Pilot Be?"
Emily Dickinson	"If I Can Stop One Heart from Breaking"
Charlotte Elliott	"Thy Will Be Done"
Mabel Frost	"Come Home"
Katherine Hankey	"I Love to tell the Story"
Frances Ridley Havergal	"I Know I Love Thee Better, Lord"
Fannie E. S. Heck	"The Woman's Hymn"
Julia Ward Howe	"The Battle Hymn of the Republic"
Annie B. Russell	"Wonderful, Wonderful Jesus"
Dorothy Caiger Senghas	"We Gather Together"
Barbara Zanotti	"We'll Build a Land"

Have participants match groupings of women's hymns that could serve as music for a worship service, matins, evensong, ordination, baptism, wedding, funeral, communion, fellowship dinner, Christmas Eve mass, Thanksgiving or Easter service, ecumenical gathering, or dedication of self to God.

Budget: $$$

Sources:

The Broadman Hymnal. Broadman Press, 1940.

Grossman, Cathy Lynn. "Updates Strive to Cleanse Hymns of Bias." *USA Today.* D1–2.

The Hymnal of the United Church of Christ. United Church Press, 1974.

The New Century Hymnal. N. p. 1995.

Singing the Living Tradition. Beacon Press, 1993.

Alternative Applications: Present an instrumental tribute to women composers, collectors, harmonizers, and arrangers. Coordinate handbells, autoharp, piano, organ, guitar, string quartet, flute, brass, and percussion to present the melodies of these hymns:

Betsy Jo Angebrandt	"View the Starry Realm," "Where Gentle Tides Go Rolling By," "When All the Peoples on This Earth"
Lucy Broadwood	"O Thou Who by a Star Didst Guide"
Flora Hamilton Cassell	"Mother Knows," "Loyalty to Christ"
Mary E. Grigola	"I Know This Rose Will Open"
Alice Hawthorne	"Whispering Hope"
Libby Larsen	"Nay, Do Not Grieve," "Wild Waves of Storm"
Jane Manton Marshall	"What Gift Can We Bring," "Sovereign and Transforming Grace," "The Harp at Nature's Advent"
Joyce Poley	"One More Step"
Cecily Taylor	"Our World Is One World"
Mrs. J. G. Wilson	"When We All Get to Heaven"
Betty A. Wylder	"Light One Candle," "Let It Be a Dance"

Get *your programs!*

Age/Grade Level or Audience: High school music history project; computer class activity; piano or music club presentation or recital selections; women's studies seminar.

Description: Organize a program to showcase the works of female composers.

Procedure: Divide participants into groups to design a balanced program of music for a choral concert, symphony performance, recital, or women's history celebration. Complete the finished programs with appropriate front-page logo or symbol, internal commentary on composers, and lettering in dignified type. Consider some of these groupings:

Choral Festival

Hildegard of Bingen's *Kyrie*

Louise Reichardt's *Heir liegt ein Spielmann*

Rebecca Clark's *Psalm*

Julia Ward Howe's *The Battle Hymn of the Republic*

Ruth Schonthal's *The Young Dead Soldiers*

Marga Richter's *Seek Him*

Judith Lang Zaimont's *Sacred Service for the Sabbath Evening*

Orchestral Performance

Isabella Leonarda's *Sonata*

Anna Amalia of Prussia's *Serenata*

Fanny Mendelssohn *Hendel's Overture in C Major*

Judith Lang Zaimont's *Chroma—Northern Lights*

Operetta

Louise Pauline Marie Héritte-Viardot's *Lindoro*

Ballet

Francesca Caccini's *Rinaldo Innamorato*

Oratorio

Anna Amalia, Duchess of Saxe-Weimar's *Oratorio*

Opera

Maria Theresia von Paradis's *Ariadne auf Naxos*

Organ Concert

Fanny Mendelssohn Hensel's *Prelude in F Major*

Piano Recital

Louise Dumont Farrenc's *Air Russe Varié*

Cécile Chaminade's *Album des Infants*

Lila Boulanger's *D'un jardin clair*

Amy Marcy Cheney Beach's *By the Still Waters*

Chamber Musicale

Katherine Hoover's *Medieval Suite*

Ellen Taaffe Zwilich's *Prologue and Variations for String Orchestra*

Barbara Kolb's *Three Place Settings*

Marga Richter's *Pastorale*

Budget: $$

Sources:

American Catholic Who's Who. National Catholic News Service, 1979.

Cohen, Aaron. *International Discography of Women Composers.* Greenwood Press, 1984.

Drexel, John, ed. *Encyclopedia of the Twentieth Century.* Facts on File, 1991.

Drinker, Sophie. *Music and Women: The Story of Women in Their Relation to Music.* Feminist Press, 1995.

Drucker, Ruth, and Helen Strine, eds. *A Collection of Art Songs by Women Composers.* HERS Publishing, 1988.

Green, Mildred Denby. *Black Women Composers: A Genesis.* Twayne, 1983.

Jezic, Diane Peacock. *Women Composers: The Lost Tradition Found.* Feminist Press, 1994.

Lindeman, Carolyn, compiler. *Women Composers of Ragtime.* Theodore Presser, 1985.

McClary, Susan. "Of Patriarchs . . . and Matriarchs, Too." *Musicology Today,* June 1994, 364–69.

Pendle, Karen, ed. *Women and Music: A History.* Indiana University Press, 1991.

Singing the Living Tradition. Beacon Press, 1993.

Alternative Applications: Complete a database by title, author, and style covering women's compositions from early times to the present. Include hymnologists and liturgists and works by these composers:

Raffaella Alcotti	Bertha Terry Donahue	Clare Shore
Vittoria Alcotti	Vivian Fine	Nancy Van de Vate
Judith Shatin Allen	Jane Frasier	Elizabeth Vercoe
Mary van Appledorn	Winifred Hyson	Jane Vieu
Lyle de Bohun	Anna Larson	Maria von Trapp
Harriet Bolz	Ruth Lomon	Gwyneth Walker
Jane Brockman	Frances Thompson McKay	Vally Wiegl
Ann Callawa	Alexandra Pierce	Eileen Wieniawska
Emma Lou Diemer	Ruth Schonthal	

Learning *from Jane Marshall*

Age/Grade Level or Audience: College music history lesson; vocal pedagogy project; music club presentation or recital selection; synagogue or church program; women's studies seminar.

Description: Analyze the style of Jane Manton Marshall, organist, conductor, and choral composer.

Procedure: Present a brief biography of Jane Marshall, born December 5, 1924, in Dallas, Texas, and student of conducting, organ, piano, and voice at Southern Methodist University, where she taught for seven years. Note her receipt of the American Guild of Organists award for composition in 1957. Select Marshall's "My Eternal King" as an introduction to choral music and vocal pedagogy. Ask participants to answer these questions:

- In what key is the piece written?

- From what era did translator Edward Caswell take the words?

- What irregularities of rhythm present a challenge to the conductor?

- Explain these Italian abbreviations and other musical notations:

a tempó	*molto espressivo*	*ppp*
allarg.	*mp*	*rit.*
ff	*p*	*sosten.*
fff	*poco rit.*	*sotto voce*
maestoso	*pp*	*ten.*

Conclude with a summary of how this work can best be performed by a chorus with piano or organ accompaniment. Comment on difficulties in prosody, for example, the caesura in the line beginning "Why, oh why." Contrast Marshall's use of personalized Christian ethics in this work and in "He Comes to Us."

Budget: $$

Sources:

The Alfred Burt Carols. Shawnee Press, 1985.

Cohen, Aaron. *International Discography of Women Composers*. Greenwood Press, 1984.

Drinker, Sophie. *Music and Women: The Story of Women in Their Relation to Music*. Feminist Press, 1995.

Drucker, Ruth, and Helen Strine, eds. *A Collection of Art Songs by Women Composers*. HERS Publishing, 1988.

Jezic, Diane Peacock. *Women Composers: The Lost Tradition Found*. Feminist Press, 1994.

Lindeman, Carolyn, compiler. *Women Composers of Ragtime*. Theodore Presser, 1985.

Marshall, Jane M. *My Eternal King*. Carl Fischer, Inc., 1954.

————. *What Gift Can We Bring?* Hope Publishing, 1982.

Pendle, Karen, ed. *Women and Music: A History*. Indiana University Press, 1991.

Singing the Living Tradition. Beacon Press, 1993.

Who's Who of American Women. A. N. Marquis Co., 1967.

Alternative Applications: Apply a similar study technique to Jane Marshall's most popular anthems and hymns:

"Awake, My Heart"	"He Comes to Us"
"Blessed Is the Morn"	"Praise the Lord"
"God's Own People"	"Sovereign and Transforming Grace"
"The Harp at Nature's Advent"	"What Gift Can We Bring?"

Contrast these works with more traditional anthems and carols as well as those by Wihla Hutson, lyricist for the Alfred Burt Carols.

Making *a joyful noise*

Age/Grade Level or Audience: Elementary or middle school composition class; piano or music club; synagogue or church exercise; women's religious group study; women's studies seminar.

Description: Compose songs that reflect the spirit, curiosity, and adventures of real American female pioneers.

Procedure: Present a brief overview of the life of a famous American pioneer woman. A worthy example is Laura Ingalls Wilder, who traveled west with pioneers, taught in a frontier school, helped build houses and barns, and worked outdoors with her family raising food and domestic animals. Make a handout, overhead outline, or chalkboard summary of these facts:

- Born February 7, 1867, in Lake Pepin, Wisconsin, Laura and her older sister Mary were the daughters of Charles Philip and Caroline Lake Quiner Ingalls. Although petite and small of frame, Laura survived the rigors of pioneer travel to Independence, Kansas, and enjoyed evenings with neighbors and family when her father played his violin. When the first move proved unsatisfactory, Caroline and Charles chose to move on to Walnut Grove, west of Springfield in Indian Territory, where Laura's sister Carrie was born. Three years later, the Ingalls moved back to Lake Pepin, where Laura attended Barry Corner School.

- In 1873 the family resettled in a dugout at Plum Creek, Minnesota, where Laura's brother Freddie was born. Caroline taught the girls at home; Charles hired out to earn cash for family needs. The whole family attended church at Walnut Grove. Two years later, the town opened a school. One spring, Laura made a heroic journey across a flooded creek to get help for her mother, who was ill. Charles suffered dismal crops and other setbacks and chose to move to relative Peter Ingalls's farm on the Mississippi River. Caroline remained frail; Freddie died in August. The Ingalls family managed the Masters Hotel, where they boarded, along with guests, before moving to a brick residence.

- Grace Pearl Ingalls was born in May 1877, when the family returned to Plum Creek. Laura blossomed in school, but Mary was blinded by scarlet fever and a stroke. The family boarded a wagon for Dakota Territory and lived first on Silver Lake, then in De Smet, South Dakota, and finally near the Big Slough. In 1881, the year that Mary enrolled at an eastern school for the blind, Laura met Almanzo "Manly" Wilder—she was fourteen and he was twenty-four. She moved closer to the school where she taught, and boarded with a local family. Disillusioned with her job, Laura married Manly on August 25, 1885.

- After their daughter Rose's birth on December 5, 1887, Manly struggled to support them by adopting progressive farming methods. They suffered a series of setbacks—the barn burned and diphtheria struck both Laura and Manly, who suffered a stroke and partial paralysis. In 1889 the family's second child died in infancy and their home burned. The Wilders had little choice but to move in with Manly's parents in Spring Valley, Minnesota, before settling in Westville, Florida. Three years later, the couple tried once more to live in De Smet to be near the Ingalls's. Manly searched for odd jobs; Laura worked as a seamstress and kept a journal.

- Two years later, the Wilders bought Rocky Ridge Farm outside Mansfield, Missouri. Laura sponsored clubs for rural women and wrote for the local newspaper; Rose became a journalist. In 1915 Laura visited the Panama-Pacific International Exposition in San Francisco. Fifteen years later, she began writing about her travels and experiences: *Little House in the Big Woods* (1932), *Farmer Boy* (1933), then her best-seller, *Little House on the Prairie* (1935). At age 70, Laura produced *On the Banks of Plum Creek* (1937), followed by *By the Shores of Silver Lake* (1939), *The Long Winter* (1940), *Little Town on the Prairie* (1941), and *These Happy Golden Years* (1943).

- Still vigorous in old age, Laura survived Carrie and Grace and weathered Manly's death in 1946. A local storyteller and noted author, she continued her warm relationship with daughter Rose. At Laura's death on February 10, 1957, she was buried in the family plot in Mansfield Cemetery. Rose added *On the Way Home* (1962) to her mother's saga of the Ingalls and Wilder families's stories.

Organize groups of three or four participants to write a short ballad commemorating significant moments when Laura experiences challenge, loss, triumph, hard work, and serenity. Select a standard American tune—"Turkey in the Straw," "Down in the Valley," "Yankee Doodle," "Beautiful Dreamer"—or have a volunteer compose a melody to be played on piano, autoharp, or guitar. Conclude with a written and illustrated copy of the song to be placed in a local scrapbook, sung for a PTA assembly, or performed with skits at a civic celebration of Women's History Month.

Budget: $$

Sources:

Blair, Gwenda. *Laura Ingalls Wilder*. Putnam, 1981.

Ehrlich, Eugene, and Gorton Carruth. *The Oxford Illustrated Literary Guide to the United States*. Oxford University Press, 1982.

Giff, Patricia. *Laura Ingalls Wilder: Growing Up in the Little House*. Viking, 1987.

Lasky, Kathryn, and Meribah Knight. *Searching for Laura Ingalls: A Reader's Journey*. Macmillan, 1993.

Spaeth, Janet. *Laura Ingalls Wilder*. Macmillan, 1987.

Wheeler, Jill. *Laura Ingalls Wilder*. Abdo & Daughters, 1992.

Wilder, Laura Ingalls. *Little House in the Ozarks: A Laura Ingalls Wilder Sampler, the Rediscovered Writings*. G. K. Hall, 1993.

————. *West from Home: Letters of Laura Ingalls Wilder, San Francisco 1915*. HarperCollins, 1976.

Wilder, Laura Ingalls, and Rose Wilder Lane. *A Little House Sampler*. University of Nebraska Press, 1988.

Williams, Jane A. *Laura Ingalls Wilder and Rose Wilder Lane: Their Writings*. Blackstocking Press, 1994.

Zochert, Donald. *Laura: The Life of Laura Ingalls Wilder*. Henry Regnery Co., 1976.

Alternative Applications: Have participants compose an American Women's History Month anthem containing verses commemorating a variety of notable women. Include these famous women:

- Clara Barton, founder of the American Red Cross
- botanist Agnes Chase
- U.S. Olympic soccer star Mia Hamm
- opera star Leontyne Price
- singer and troop entertainer Martha Raye
- Margaret Chase Smith, noted congresswoman
- Civil War surgeon Mary Edwards Walker
- inventor and cosmetician Madame C. J. Walker

Musicals *and women characters*

Age/Grade Level or Audience: All-ages public performance; piano or music club group study; women's studies research project; newspaper music history series.

Description: Present a group of songs that capture the action, longings, joys, and predicaments of female characters from the grand tradition of American musical drama.

Procedure: Introduce the audience to women in classic musicals and movies by arranging a concert series featuring a chorus and soloists. Begin with these songs:

- "Don't Cry for Me Argentina," *Evita*
- "Don't Rain on My Parade," *Funny Girl*
- "Hello Young Lovers," *The King and I*
- "I Could Have Danced All Night," *My Fair Lady*
- "I Don't Know How to Love Him," *Jesus Christ Superstar*
- "I'm Gonna Wash That Man Right Out of My Hair," *South Pacific*
- "I'm Just a Girl Who Can't Say 'No,'" *Oklahoma*
- "Love Me or Leave Me," *Love Me or Leave Me*

Include in the program background information on the musical—when it was first performed; who was in the original cast; who are the composers. Also, if applicable, include biographical information for the woman whose life serves as the basis for the play; for example Eva Peron/*Evita*, Fanny Brice/*Funny Girl* and *Funny Lady*, and Gypsy Rose Lee/*Gypsy*.

Budget: $$$$

Sources:

Cabaret Songbook. Hal Leonard Publishing, 1991.

70s & 80s Showstoppers. CPP/Belwin, Inc., 1993.

Alternative Applications: Present a placemat or handout quiz of fill-ins. Include these examples of related words, divided into four items: show tune, singer, character, and show or movie title:

1. "Anything You Can Do, I Can Do Better," Betty Hutton, _____ , *Annie Get Your Gun*

2. "Cabaret," _____ , Sally Bowles, *Cabaret*

3. "People Will Say We're in Love," Shirley Jones, Laurie, _____

4. "Make Believe," _____ , Magnolia, *Showboat*

5. "Edelweiss," Julie Andrews, _____ , *The Sound of Music*

6. "If They Could See Me Now," Shirley MacLaine, _____ , *Sweet Charity*

7. "Don't Rain on My Parade," _____ , Fanny Brice, *Funny Girl*

8. "I Ain't Down Yet," Debbie Reynolds, Molly Brown, _____

9. "I _____ ," Natalie Wood, Maria, *West Side Story*

10. "I Don't Know How to Love Him," Yvonne Elliman, _____ , *Jesus Christ, Superstar*

ANSWERS:

1. Annie Oakley	6. Charity
2. Liza Minelli	7. Barbra Streisand
3. *Carousel*	8. *The Unsinkable Molly Brown*
4. Kathryn Grayson	9. Feel Pretty
5. Maria von Trapp	10. Mary Magdalene

Rug *concert*

Age/Grade Level or Audience: Preschool or kindergarten music class; library summer project; piano or music club activity; children's religious group study; music educators' seminar.

Description: Introduce students to various musical instruments as played by talented female musicians.

Procedure: Present a music series devoted to instrumental music played by female performers. Begin with the piano or drum and add more complex examples from strings, woodwinds, brass, and percussion. Have students examine how the sound is produced and what stops, breath control methods, mute, brushes, damper pedal, or other mechanisms alter the sound; for example, the drone on a bagpipe or the holes on an ocarina. Allow students to familiarize themselves with small instruments (harpsichord, flute, piccolo, recorder, viola, violin, triangle, oboe, clarinet) and ask questions of the performer about lessons, cost of an instrument, and possibilities for a career in music performance, production, or instruction. Conclude with a visit to an orchestra or bell choir which has women performers or conductor or to a pipe organ recital given by a female organist.

Budget: $$$

Sources:

Antonia: A Portrait of the Woman. Direct Cinema, n.d. (Video)

Celtic Twilight. Hearts of Space, 1994. (CD)

Deferred Voices: Organ Music by Women. Public Radio Musicsource, n.d. (CD)

Emily Lowe Singers. *Choral Tapestries: An Anthology of Contemporary American Choral Music.* Northeastern Records, 1991. (CD)

Martin, Jean, gen. ed. *Who's Who of Women in the Twentieth Century.* Crescent Books, 1995.

Also, records, tapes, or CDs of orchestral music, or demonstrations of the zither, sitar, thumb piano, maracas, panpipes, finger cymbals, tabor, rebec, synthesizer, shakere, accordion, banjo, or other unusual instruments.

Alternative Applications: Present a series of lessons featuring recordings of the world's most famous female instrumentalists. Include these:

- Maria Kalaniemi, Sharon Shannon (accordion)
- Eileen Ivers (banjo)
- Jacqueline DuPré, Ofra Harnoy (cello)
- Maire Breatnach, Eileen Ivers, Natalie MacMaster, Mairéad Ni Mhaonaigh (fiddle)
- Bobbi Humphrey, Radhika Miller, Anne Stackpole, (flute)
- Elizabeth Cotton (guitar)
- Yolanda Kondonassis, Anna Lelkes, Carol Thompson, Grainne Yeats, Naoko Yoshino (harp)
- Wanda Landowska (harpsichord)
- Joanie Madden (Irish whistle)
- Alexa Zirbel (oboe)
- Amy Beach, Edith Borroff, Fanny Mendelssohn, Christa Rakich (organ)
- Kim Atkinson, Evelyn Glennis (percussion)

367

- Lillian Hardin Armstrong, Martha Argerich, Alicia de la Rocha, Elaine Elias, Myra Hess, Natalie Hinderas, Marguerite Long, Christina Ortiz, Germaine Tailleferre, Mary Lou Williams (piano)

- Loreena McKennitt (synthesizer)

- Midori (violin)

Have volunteers study the careers of these musicians and present a summary of their achievements:

- Marianne Faithfull, Eva Jessye, Carole King, Elizabeth Lutyens, Ethel Smyth, Williametta Spencer, Ellen Taaffe Zwilich (composers)

- Nadia Boulanger, Antonia Brico, Sarah Caldwell, Thea Musgrave (conductors)

- Grace Bumbry, Kirstin Flagstad and Montserrat Caballé, Lotte Lehmann, Birgit Nilsson, Leontyne Price (opera singers)

- Patsy Cline, Linda Childs, Celia Cruz, Ella Fitzgerald, Aretha Franklin, Emmylou Harris, Umm Kulthum, Loretta Lynn, Pauletta Pearson, Sarah Vaughan, (pop, folk, gospel, soul, classical, and country and western vocalists)

Women *and folk music*

Age/Grade Level or Audience: Middle school music appreciation activity; women's religious group study; women's studies research project; recorded music media critique; educational radio or television series.

Description: Present a collection of traditional music by female folk singers from around the world.

Procedure: Introduce the audience to a major folk singer or group; for example, Janis Ian, Sweet Honey in the Rock, Judy Collins, Angelique Kidjo, Tish Hinojosa, Le Mystere des Voix Bulgares, Mary Black, Clannad, Mary Travers, Kate Wolf, Linda Hirschhorn, Sheila Chandra, Chaba Fadela, Nanci Griffith, Miriam Makeba, Maire Breatnach, or Joan Baez. As part of the program, summarize the performer's life and achievements, present live and recorded music, and identify the performer's role as a political activist. Mention these data on Joan Baez as a model:

- Of Scottish-Mexican descent, Joan Chandos Baez was born January 9, 1941, in Staten Island, New York, the middle of three sisters. From childhood, Joan was introspective, moody, and shy. Her father, a physicist, taught at Cornell University; her mother influenced her childhood with Quaker philosophy.

- At age ten, the family moved to Baghdad after Al Baez took a job with UNESCO. Far from American affluence, Joan commiserated with the Iraqi's poverty. A year later, the family settled in Redlands, California. Joan, recovering from hepatitis, missed school for yet another reason—she didn't fit in with Anglo or Hispanic children.

- While a student at Palo Alto High School, Baez studied music and became enthralled with the humanism of Martin Luther King Jr., who spoke to her school on racial equality. A family friend and fellow Quaker, Ira Sandperl, introduced her to the pacifism of Gandhi.

- Joan developed an unusually sweet, pliant three-octave range, studied the ukulele and guitar, and began singing professionally and making friends with local folksingers. After a move to Boston, her father took her to Tulla's Coffee Grinder, where she observed some of the best singers of her era. Leaving academia behind following an unsuccessful semester at Boston University, she launched her forty-plus year career with a variety of pop, gospel, spiritual, folk, and original songs.

- Working briefly at the Perkins Institute for the Blind, Joan evolved a laid-back lifestyle. No longer fearful or shy, she sang at a Newport, Rhode Island, festival on the same program as the Weavers, Pete Seeger, Harry Belafonte, John Jacob Niles, Flatt and Scruggs, and Odetta.

- Her first album, *Joan Baez,* sold exceptionally well. In 1964 she published *The Joan Baez Songbook,* toured college campuses, and introduced her signature titles in eight gold recordings, among which are *Rare, Live and Classic, Diamonds and Rust, The First Ten Years,* and *Play Me Backwards.*

- As "Queen of Folk," Baez remained unfettered by social obligations and limited herself to public engagements at the Hollywood Bowl, Hanoi war zones and southeast Asian refugee camps, the Mormon Tabernacle, Madison Square Garden, Carnegie Hall, and Milan's Teatro Lirico and L'Arena. Her humanist politics allied her with human rights activists, nuclear disarmament, Vietnam War protests, tax revolt, and pacifism. She willingly served time in 1967 in Santa Rita Rehabilitation Center for supporting draft protesters.

- At home in Big Sur, California, in 1961, she kept her private life separate from hordes of fans and media curiosity seekers. She married fellow war protester David Harris and gave birth to her only child, Gabriel. In 1974, Baez divorced Harris and wrote two reflective autobiographies.

- During a thirtieth-anniversary tour in 1989, she continued her outspoken pacifism, supported controversial movements, and bonded with audiences who bought her albums and thronged to her concerts.

Conclude each segment with the artist's best-known works: e.g., "Wildwood Flower," "All My Trials," "Diamonds and Rust," "Pilgrim of Sorrow," "Barbara Allen," and "The House of the Rising Sun." Provide song sheets and invite listeners to sing along.

Budget: $$

Sources:

Baez, Joan. *And a Voice to Sing With.* Summit Books, 1987.

———. *Coming Out.* Bantam Books, 1971.

———. *Daybreak.* Dial Press, 1968.

Elizabeth Cotten. Rounder Records, n.d. (Video)

Green, Ann. "Joan Baez: At Ease, at Last." *Durham Morning Herald,* November 17, 1989.

Hentoff, Nat. "A Passionate Survivor." *Progressive,* February 1983, 52–53.

Holden, Stephen. "The All-American Voice." *High Fidelity,* July 1980, 87.

Joan Baez. Schlessinger, 1995. (Video)

Melich, Nancy. "Joan Baez Returns." *Salt Lake City Tribune,* October 20, 1989.

Romandetta, Julie. "Baez Continues to Mix Politics and Music in New LP 'Dreams,'" *Boston Herald,* November 13, 1989.

Sager, Mike. "Joan Baez," *Rolling Stone,* November 5, 1987, 163–64.

Sanoff, Alvin P. "How the Times They Are A-changin'." *U.S. News and World Report,* June 29, 1987, 60.

Wilder, Sherri. "Joan Baez Still Sings for Justice." *Capital Times,* November 2, 1989.

For a full selection of folk music from many countries, refer to Ladyslipper, Inc., P.O. Box 3124-R, Durham, NC 27715, 800-634-6044.

Alternative Applications: Discuss the influence folk-singing and traditional instrumental music has on the popular perception of society's ills. Explore its role both as a mirror of common concerns and a platform to air grievances. Use, as a model, Joan Baez's intense refusal to play to middle-class audiences without pressing them to respond to her concerns over poverty, isolation, racism, war, and political corruption. List lyrics from folk songs that support her consciousness-raising efforts; for example, the simple sorrow of a lover whose mate has died in war as expressed in her "Where Have All the Flowers Gone?," Miriam Makeba's "Soweta Blues," or Janis Ian's plaintive "At Seventeen."

Women *in the spotlight*

Age/Grade Level or Audience: College chorus music-history presentation; vocal or music club recital selections; liturgical music program; women's studies seminar.

Description: Analyze the great recitatives, arias, solos, duets, and trios written for female voices.

Procedure: Present a lecture on the great classical and liturgical works written for women. Play recorded versions of these titles:

- "Agnus Dei," (soprano, bass, chorus), Franz Schubert's *Mass in G*
- "Behold, God Hath Sent Elijah," (soprano), Felix Mendelssohn Bartholdy's *Elijah*
- "Domine Deus, Agnus Dei," (contralto), Antonio Vivaldi's *Gloria*
- "Esurientes Implevit Bonis," (alto), Johann Sebastian Bach's *Magnificat*
- "Holy Is God the Lord," (contralto, quartet, and chorus), Felix Mendelssohn Bartholdy's *Elijah*
- "Laudamus Te," (soprano duet), Antonio Vivaldi's *Gloria*
- "O Rest in the Lord," (contralto), Felix Mendelssohn Bartholdy's *Elijah*
- "Pie Jesu," (soprano, mezzo-soprano), Gabriel *Fauré's Requiem*
- "Qui Sedes ad Dexteram," (contralto), Antonio Vivaldi's *Gloria*
- "Suscepit Israel," (soprano I and II, alto), Johann Sebastian Bach's *Magnificat*

Have vocal participants select works for practice, taping, or public performance. Record or videotape recitals and keep for future class study or for use in a school or public music library.

Budget: $$$

Sources:

Drinker, Sophie. *Music and Women: The Story of Women in Their Relation to Music*. Feminist Press, 1995.

Drucker, Ruth, and Helen Strine, eds. *A Collection of Art Songs by Women Composers*. HERS Publishing, 1988.

Jezic, Diane Peacock. *Women Composers: The Lost Tradition Found*. Feminist Press, 1994.

Pendle, Karen, ed. *Women and Music: A History*. Indiana University Press, 1991.

Singing the Living Tradition. Beacon Press, 1993.

Thompson, Randall. *The Testament of Freedom.* E. C. Schirmer, 1976.

Alternative Applications: Present solos or duets written for tenor and bass, but sung by female voices. Select "We Have Counted the Cost," "I Shall Not Die Without Hope," or "We Fight Not for Glory" from Randall Thompson's *The Testament of Freedom,* the musical setting of four American Revolutionary War passages by Thomas Jefferson.

Women *who make music*

Age/Grade Level or Audience: High school chorus, band, or music appreciation lesson; piano or music club study; women's studies focus; newspaper column; open forum commentary; educational radio or television series.

Description: Present a songfest featuring female music-makers.

Procedure: Introduce a varied group of recordings, audiotapes, or music videos that feature music written and/or performed by female singers, instrumentalists, or choral groups. Provide information about stand-out performances such as these:

- Aretha Franklin's album *The Very Best of Aretha Franklin*
- Barbra Streisand's album *Classical Barbra*
- Billie Holiday's "Fine and Mellow"
- conductor Sarah Caldwell's debut
- Edith Piaf's "La Vie en Rose"
- fiddler Maire Breatnach's album *The Voyage of Bran*
- Jessye Norman's "Give Me Jesus" and "Amazing Grace"
- Janis Joplin's *Pearl*
- Joan Baez's *One Day at a Time*
- Joanie Madden on the album *Celtic Twilight*
- Judy Collins's "Both Sides Now"
- Lena Horne's *Lady and Her Music*
- Mahalia Jackson's gospel solo at the funeral of Martin Luther King Jr.
- Maria Callas's "Mio Caro Babbio"
- Marian Anderson's solo "America the Beautiful"
- Nanci Griffith's "Goodnight to a Mother's Dream"
- Patsy Cline's "Crazy" and "I Fall to Pieces"
- Jennifer C. Paz's role in *Miss Saigon*
- Rosa Purim's jazz
- Yoko Mine's karaoke songs

Budget: $$$

Sources:

Bufwack, Mary A. and Robert K. Oermann. *Finding Her Voice: The Saga of Women in Country Music.* Crown Publishers, 1993.

"Carly Conquers Grand Central, Stage Fright." *USA Today,* May 18, 1995, 12D.

Cecile Kayirebwa: Music from Rwanda. Multicultural Media, n.d. (CD)

Celtic Twilight. Hearts of Space, 1994. (CD)

Chiba, Hitoshi. "Songs for the Town of Flowers." *Look Japan,* July 1994, 33.

Corliss, Richard. "Viva the Divas!" *Time,* August 7, 1995, 72–73.

Ella Jenkins: Live at the Smithsonian. Multicultural Media, n.d. (Video)

Ferris, Jeri. *What I Had Was Singing: The Story of Marian Anderson.* Lerner Books, 1994.

Herdman, Priscilla. *Stardreamer.* Alcazar, 1995. (CD)

Janis: The Way She Was. Pacific Arts Publishing, n.d. (Video)

"Jennifer C. Paz: Lead Actress and Singer in Miss Saigon Musical." *Heritage,* summer 1995, 14–15.

Joan Baez. Schlessinger, n.d. (Video)

Knight, Richard. "Folk Lore." *Chicago Tribune,* June 25, 1995, Sect 6, 2.

Mahalia Jackson: Give God the Glory. Palisades Home Video, n.d. (Video)

Margareth Menezes: Bahian Music. Multicultural Media, n.d. (Video)

Rogers, Sally. *What Can One Little Person Do?* Alcazar, 1995. (CD)

Say Amen, Somebody. Palisades Home Video, n.d. (Video)

Severson, Molly, ed. *Performing Artists.* UXL, 1995.

Spirituals. Polygram Classics, 1978. (CD)

Spirituals in Concert. Palisades Home Video, n.d. (Video)

Svetlana: Russian Songs. Multicultural Media, n.d. (CD)

Sweet Honor in the Rock: All for Freedom. Multicultural Media, n.d. (CD)

Wild Women Don't Have the Blues. Knowledge Unlimited, 1995. (Video)

Alternative Applications: Design program notes for the following series:

- The Best in Female Country and Western
- An Evening with the Classics
- Women Performing Jazz
- Women Sing the Top 40
- Art Songs By Women
- Gospel from the Finest Female Vocalists
- Hymns and Liturgical Music by Women of Faith

Create separate program entries to accompany groupings of female vocalists, instrumentalists, lyricists, directors, arrangers, translators, and composers.

Women's *songs for the season*

Age/Grade Level or Audience: High school chorus music-history unit; background music for a Women's History Month reception or open house; piano or music club; synagogue or church exercise; women's religious group presentation; St. Cecilia program; women's studies seminar.

Description: Select a group of CDs or tapes to offer a full spectrum of music sung by women or honoring their place in history.

Procedure: Present a varied program of music to characterize the many moods and melodies by and about women. Consider these:

- *Essential Opera*, featuring *Carmen, Tosca, La Boheme, Aida,* and *Madame Butterfly,* and showcasing Kiri Te Kanawa and Joan Sutherland

- *Ave Gracia Plena; Music in Honour of the Virgin Mary,* from the Lady Chapel at Ely, *a cappella* praises sung by John Rutter's Cambridge Singers

- *Bach, Brahms, Schubert Recital,* a classic collection including the *Brahms Alto Rhapsody,* sung by contralto Marian Anderson

- *Masterpieces of the French Baroque,* featuring Lisa Crawford, the Philharmonia Virtuosi, and the Oberlin Baroque Ensemble in rococo music dating from 1660 to 1742

- *Offenbach: Gaité Parisienne,* a potpourri of *Geneviève de brabant, Les belles américaines,* and cancan played by the Cincinnati Pops Orchestra

- *Villa-Lobos: Bachianas Brasileiras,* a blend of folk and classical featuring the soprano of Barbara Hendricks with the Royal Philharmonic

- *Vive Ibert!,* flutist Eugenia Zukerman and the Manhattan Chamber Orchestra

- *Five Heroines,* lead parts from *Lucia di Lammermoor, Madame Butterfly, Tosca, La Traviata,* and *Norma* sung by soprano Maria Callas

- *Chamber Works by Women Composers,* showcasing the Macalester Trio in instrumental works by Clara Schumann, Amy Beach, Fanny Mendelssohn, Cecile Chaminade, Germaine Tailleferre, Lili Boulanger, and Teresa Carreño

- *Reverie,* pianist Carol Rosenberger's performance of tone poems by Debussy, Chopin, and Liszt

- *The Prima Donna Collection,* soprano Leontyne Price's performance of 47 pieces ranging from Gianni Schicchi, Semele to Purcell's "When I Am Laid in Earth"

Budget: $$$$

Sources:

Minnesota Communications Group
P.O. Box 64502
St. Paul, MN 55164-0502
800-949-9999
FAX: 612-659-4495

Alternative Applications: Select a few works sung or composed by female musicians during a historic musical epoch; e.g., Romantic. Present them to a small group for discussion and comparison to the male composers and singers of the same period. Discuss the musical canon's treatment of female talent. Describe subtle trends and differences in women's operatic roles; for example, the play on acquiescence to or rebellion against overbearing husbands and fathers or the flirtatious and simple-witted lyrics written by male composers to illustrate such stereotypical female behavior.

Religion

Bible *pairs*

Age/Grade Level or Audience: Children's church festival skits; bulletin board duos; church school or Bible camp contest; holiday gatherings; stage readings; radio or television presentations; church bulletin or newsletter; newspaper column.

Description: Organize reenactments of important scenes from the Bible that feature women.

Procedure: Have participants improvise or pantomime important biblical scenes involving women. Choose from these:

Bathsheba's attempts to find happiness among David's many wives

Mary and Elizabeth's contemplation over Mary's impending motherhood

Mary and Martha's debate over the place of women in the home versus the role of women in religious study

Miriam's report to her mother on the infant Moses' safety in Pharaoh's house

Naomi's discussion of widowhood with her three daughters-in-law

Rachel and Leah's tent squabbles with their serving women

Sarah's confrontation with her servant Hagar

Budget: $

Sources:

Feminist Interpretations of the Bible. Westminster Press, 1985.

Graham, Sheila. "Jesus and Women." *Plain Truth,* July 1994, 14–18.

Kam, Rose Sallberg. *Their Stories/Our Stories: Women of the Bible.* Continuum, 1995.

Newsome, Carol, and Sharon Ringe, eds. *The Women's Bible Commentary.* Westminster/John Knox, 1992.

Stanton, Elizabeth Cady. *The Woman's Bible.* Coalition Task Force on Women and Religion, 1986.

Telushkin, Rabbi Joseph. *Jewish Literacy.* William Morrow, 1991.

Alternative Applications: Have participants select two women from different biblical eras to study in a Venn diagram. Overlap two circles. Place in the far left the unique qualities of one woman; place in the far right the unique qualities of the women to be compared. Place in the overlap qualities that they share.

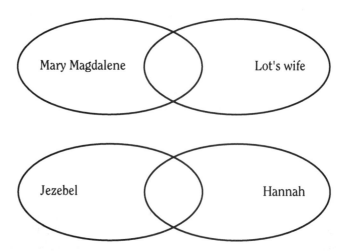

Corrie *ten Boom*

Age/Grade Level or Audience: Any-age participant at a church, mosque, or synagogue festival; history lecture on world religion or World War II; bulletin board or media feature; Holocaust memorial presentation; stage reading; church bulletin focus; newsletter subject.

Description: Using Corrie ten Boom as a model, lead a seminar on the manner in which simple talents can be applied to philanthropic or altruistic work.

Procedure: Introduce participants to the contribution made by Corrie ten Boom and her family and network of Protestant friends in saving Jews from the SS during World War II. Begin by summarizing her family life, war role, and post-war efforts to heal combatants and victims. Mention these facts:

> A native of Bloemendaal, Holland, Corrie, born April 15, 1892, followed in the trade of her father Casper, a clockmaker and watch repairer. In the family's shop on the corner of Barteljorisstraat in Haarlem, she kept accounts, opened a church school for retarded parishioners, and nursed her mother during a severe illness.

> After Queen Wilhelmina withdrew from Holland in 1940, Dutch citizens surrendered to Nazi occupation forces and the imposition of dehumanizing curfews, rationing, and anti-Semitic laws calling for Jews to identify themselves by wearing a yellow star. Corrie and other underground agents attended meetings of anonymous "Smits" and scoured the area for hiding places for Jews until they could safely depart by sea. The ten Booms concealed refugees in a secret alcove built behind Corrie's bed on the third floor of their house. She organized a system of stolen ration cards and saved over 700 people from conscription and possible death in extermination camps. On February 28, 1944, an informer led the Gestapo to the ten Boom house. The troopers confiscated the family's illegal radio and arrested Corrie, her sister and father, and 35 Jews. During the investigation that followed, Casper died at The Hague. Corrie repeated to herself the biblical belief that God is "a hiding place," a phrase that would become the title of her book recounting her World War II experiences.

> Corrie and sister Betsie occupied separate cells in Scheveningen, a cheerless penitentiary. Outsiders made incarceration more bearable by smuggling in soap, safety pins, and the first four books of the Bible, which Corrie hid in a bag around her neck and read during periods of physical hardship in solitary confinement. The

experience brought on pleurisy and tuberculosis. She received a packet containing a sweater, cookies, vitamins, needle and thread, towel, and the encouraging secret message that the Jews they were hiding had escaped arrest. In May 1944, Corrie underwent intense interrogations by Lieutenant Rahms, who wanted the particulars of the political underground, black marketing, refugee hiding places, and names of agents. Corrie's Christian principles moved Rahms to deeper faith in God. That June, he allowed her time with her brother Willem.

On D-Day, June 6, 1944, the SS reunited Corrie and Betsie for their evacuation by train south to Vught, near Brabant, where Corrie worked at the Phillips factory assembling radios. The foreman, also a prisoner, showed her how to sabotage the product to keep information from the Nazis. Later transported to Ravensbruck, a German extermination camp for women, Corrie slept on straw, fought vermin, and tolerated rain-soaked ground in makeshift quarters. To maintain her sanity and fight despair, Corrie continued praying for others and singing hymns of faith.

In permanent quarters by October, Corrie and Betsie worked the loading docks at the Siemens factory. In winter, they were switched to road work. On December 14, 1944, Betsie's health began to fail; starved, exhausted, and chronically ill, she died in the infirmary. Two weeks later, with no prior warning, authorities released Corrie. On January 1, 1945, Corrie, sick and hungry, traveled to Berlin and scavenged for food. At Uelzen, a railway employee put her on a train to Groningen, Holland. She remained at a hospital for ten days, ate well, recovered, and was then reunited with Willem in Hilversum.

Back at work at the ten Boom shop, Corrie mourned the deaths of her father and sister. To assuage her loneliness, she put her energy into helping Haarlem's retarded citizens. Beginning in early spring of 1945, Corrie also ministered to war victims. Mrs. Bierens de Haan, a wealthy matron, offered a 56-room mansion to house people traumatized by the war. By May, the city was again free of Nazis. That summer, hundreds migrated to the ten Boom rehabilitation center, including combatants on both sides and the despised Dutch collaborators. The next year, Corrie established a second center at Darmstadt. Until 1950, the ten Boom house continued to welcome all who needed counseling and rest. At a church in Munich, Germany, Corrie locked eyes with an SS guard who had brutalized women at Ravensbruck and forced herself to forgive him.

In 1959, Corrie honored the 96,000 female inmates of Ravensbruck Prison and realized how close she had come to being exterminated. In memory of Betsie, she founded Christians Incorporated, which she financed with proceeds from her many books and lectures and the movie version of her autobiography, *The Hiding Place*, starring Julie Harris as Betsie and Jeannette Clift as Corrie. Her missionary efforts extended to Cuba, Africa, England, and Russia. In poor health from a stroke in 1978, she accepted an invitation to live with friends in Placentia, California, where, five years later, at age 93, she died.

Select a group to list and evaluate Corrie ten Boom's strongest personal and spiritual strengths. Have another group make a similar list of Betsie ten Boom's qualities. Compare the lists to determine how the two women worked together to evangelize and uplift women in prison.

Budget: $$

Sources:

Biography Index. H. W. Wilson, 1984.

Drexel, John, ed. *Facts on File Encyclopedia of the Twentieth Century.* Facts on File, 1991.

Graham, Billy, and Corrie ten Boom. *To God Be the Glory.* Walker & Co., 1985.

Poley, Hans. *Return to the Hiding Place.* LifeJourney Books, 1993.

ten Boom, Corrie. *Amazing Love.* Christian Literature, 1959.

———. *Common Sense Not Needed.* Christian Literature, 1969.

———. *Corrie ten Boom's Prison Letters.* N.p., 1975.

———. *Defeated Enemies.* Christian Literature, 1962.

———. *Each New Day.* Baker Books, 1977.

———. *This Day Is the Lord's.* Baker Book, 1990.

ten Boom, Corrie, and Jamie Buckingham. *Tramp for the Lord.* Baker Books, 1974.

ten Boom, Corrie, and John Scherrill. *The Hiding Place.* Bantam, 1971.

Alternative Applications: Screen *The Hiding Place* and *Schindler's List.* Note the similarities and differences in the method by which two people risked their lives to save Jews. Have a panel answer the following questions:

> How do refugees show their appreciation of both Corrie ten Boom and Oskar Schindler?
>
> How does life change for both heroes after the war?
>
> What method does Oskar Schindler use to maintain friendship with the SS?
>
> Which rescuer has the most at stake in his or her attempt to save Jews from gas ovens?
>
> Why is Corrie's Christian faith significant to her longevity? to the people she rescues? to informers for the SS?
>
> Why is Corrie's meeting with a former guard of significance in terms of her ability to recover emotionally from her ordeal? to forgive?

Deborah

Originator: Dr. Carol S. Blessing, assistant professor of literature, Point Loma Nazarene College, San Diego, California.

Age/Grade Level or Audience: Any-age church or synagogue festival; improvisational theater; church school or Bible camp activity; holiday skit or choral reading; radio or television presentation.

Description: Organize a dramatic reading, dramatization, or oral interpretation detailing the lives of women in the Bible.

Procedure: Assemble volunteers to act out the lives of famous women from the Bible. Present significant information about these women:

Abigail	Jezebel	Phoebe
Anna	Leah	Potiphar's wife
Bathsheba	Lydia	Priscilla
Delilah	Martha	Rachel
Dinah	Mary (Jesus' mother)	Rebekah

Dorcas	Mary (Martha's sister)	Ruth
Elizabeth	Mary Magdalene	Sarah
Esther	Michal	Sheba
Eve	Miriam	woman at the well
Hannah	Naomi	Zipporah

One of the rarities of biblical females is Deborah, a judge who stands on her own, without relying on power, money, or authority from her husband. Use this overview as a guide to the multiple roles women played in the Bible and to the strength of their faith in Yahweh:

Around 1125 B.C., Deborah was a judge in a largely patriarchal society, where she served as prophet, wife, mother, and military leader during threatening times. Her personal qualities and talents gave her wisdom, administrative skills, and the ability to speak, command, and persuade.

As the wife of Lappidoth, she apparently fulfilled the expected role of the Hebrew woman. As Israeli leader, she also prophesied and served as mediator from her customary seat under a palm on the hill of Ephraim, between Bethel and Ramah.

In her home in Canaan, Deborah and her followers lived under the threat of the ten thousand troops of King Jabin of Hazor, whose commander-in-chief was Sisera. The situation was so dangerous that, for twenty years, travelers and caravans had ceased to pass their way. When Sisera and his Canaanites led a party against Israel, Deborah, at the request of Barak, her military strongman, joined her prudence with Barak's strength to create a beneficial and highly effective coalition of charisma and battlefield savvy.

Before accepting the unaccustomed role of field commander, Deborah warned Barak that, because he hesitated to fight without her help, she would claim her rightful honor. At the plain of Esdraelon, Israelites faced 900 Canaanite chariots, archers, and infantry wearing shields, helmets, and breastplates and armed with spears. With their bronze daggers, swords, bows and arrows, and slings, the ill-clad Israelis fell in behind General Barak, a seasoned warrior, and met with the best of luck—heavy rains that sidelined Sisera's chariots in an overflow of the river Kishon near Megiddo. The plucky Canaanites killed every enemy soldier except Sisera, who abandoned his iron-wheeled chariot and fled on foot.

Leaving the carnage behind, Sisera approached the Kenite camp, where Yael, the leader's wife, persuaded him to rest, treated him to milk and curd, and pulled a coverlet over him, then impaled the unwary soldier with a tent stake through the skull and into the ground below his pillow. At Sisera's home, his mother peered through a latticed window in anticipation of the spoils of war—handmaids for the men and embroidered goods for her and the other women.

In the ancient style, a singer composed a paean to the God-given victory, one of the oldest victory songs in the Bible. In it the poet thanks Zebulon, Naphtali, Ephraim, Benjamin, and Issachar for backing Barak in so one-sided a battle. To Reuben, Asher, and Dan, the singer utters a humiliating reprimand for their failure to lend aid to the other tribes. These lines suggest that Deborah herself may have written the poem.

Crying out in the first person at the end of a series of verses describing a successful campaign, her admirer calls her a mother of Israel and exclaims: "That the leaders led in Israel, that the people volunteered, Bless the Lord! Hear, O Kings; give ear, O rulers! I—to the Lord, I will sing, I will sing praise to the Lord, the God of Israel" (Judges 5:2—3). Deborah's song stands out as a thanksgiving to Yahweh, who had broken the Hazorite stranglehold over Israel and brought forty years of peace to Canaan. Historically, the victory is significant for a second reason: Sisera's kinsman, Akiva, became an influential Hebrew scholar.

Conclude the presentation with additional passages from various translations. Comment on the contrast between the prose account of the event and the parallel poetic version. Note as a conclusion that the song of Deborah pictures three types of women: Deborah, the assertive decision-maker; Yael, the wily loner; and Sisera's overconfident, materialistic mother, who counts nonexistent spoils at the same time that her son lies dead, ambushed by a Canaanite woman.

Budget: $

Sources:

Blessing, Dr. Carol. "Judge, Prophet, Mother: Learning from Deborah." Daughters of Sarah, winter 1995, 34–37.

Chamberlin, Ann. *Tamar*. Forge Books, 1993.

Feminist Interpretations of the Bible. Westminster Press, 1985.

Great Women of the Bible in Art and Literature. Eerdmans, 1995.

Hughes, Ingrid. "The Strength of Tamar." *Lilith*, summer 1994, 26–30.

Kam, Rose Sallberg. *Their Stories/Our Stories: Women of the Bible*. Continuum, 1995.

Mary Magdalen. Palisades Home Video, n.d. (Video)

Newsome, Carol, and Sharon Ringe, eds. *The Women's Bible Commentary*. Westminster/John Knox, 1992.

Telushkin, Rabbi Joseph. *Jewish Literacy*. William Morrow, 1991.

Alternative Applications: Have participants in a Women's History Month celebration give dramatic readings from sections of the Bible that detail the lives of famous women characters. Consider the following possibility for oral interpretation:

> Hannah's prayer in the tabernacle, which follows a momentous event—the first silent communication with God in the Judaeo-Christian worship tradition (I Sam. 12:1–10). As a result of Hannah's faith that God would grant her a child, she returned to give thanks for Samuel, her first-born, and speak her hymn of thanksgiving, which parallels the Magnificat of the Virgin Mary: "My heart exults in the Lord; my strength is exalted in the Lord. My mouth derides my enemies, because I rejoice in thy salvation."

Hannah concludes her testament to God's strength:

> "He will guard the feet of his faithful ones; but the wicked shall be cut off in darkness; for not by might shall a man prevail. The adversaries of the Lord shall be broken to pieces; against them he will thunder in heaven. The Lord will judge the ends of the earth; he will give strength to his king, and exalt the power of his anointed."

Goddesses

Age/Grade Level or Audience: High school or college religion lecture; bulletin board series; book club presentation; Friends of the Library monograph; women's studies series; ecumenical consortia.

Description: Organize a week-long unit on ancient goddess cultures.

Procedure: Initiate a study of goddess worship through a study of myth, archetypes, architecture, prehistoric art, and sculpture. Explore the following questions:

What evidence proves that early cultures worshipped goddesses or earth mothers; for example, the statue of the multi-breasted Diana Multimamma in the Villa d'Este outside Rome?

Why were these religions agriculture-centered? Why do Wiccans divide their year into four agricultural seasons?

How did the use of herbal cures and naturopathic medicine increase the prestige of female priestesses and sages?

Does this evidence prove that the cultures were themselves woman-centered or matriarchal? What conclusions could be drawn about these herbalists and their powers to heal?

What aspects of drawings and sculptures—broad hips, rounded bellies, and full breasts—suggest that these cultures revered procreation?

Why did these cultures embrace female deities? Did women offer something vital to their existence?

What changes in ancient society quelled goddess worship and replaced it with male deities?

How was the development of iron weapons and the lust for territory a boost to the warlike gods?

Are such female icons as Marianne, the Statue of Liberty, Our Lady of Guadalupe, the Black Madonna, and Blind Justice an outgrowth of goddess worship?

Why do revivals of goddess worship, such as Wicca, alarm and dismay religious fundamentalists?

What is the position on female deities in religions such as Buddhism, Shintoism, Islam, Confucianism, Zen, Christianity, Hinduism, Mormonism, and Sikhism?

Does patriarchal faith subconsciously or overtly denigrate or devalue women?

Why were the Salem witch trials and similar hysterical outbreaks in Europe aimed primarily at women?

Is the subjugation of women crucial to some faiths? Why?

Summarize the outlook for women in countries where patriarchy remains dominant. Include information about child marriage, clitoral mutilation, infibulation, suttee, female infanticide, early death rates, and other hostilities toward women.

Conclude the fifth session with commentary from participants about the future of organized religions and their disinclination toward empowering women.

Budget: $

Sources:

Biaggi, Christina. *Habitations of the Great Goddess.* Knowledge, Ideas, and Trends, 1994.

Bolen, Jean Shinoda. *Goddess in Everywoman.* HarperCollins, 1985.

Gimbutas, Marija. *The Civilization of the Goddess: The World of Old Europe.* Harper, 1991.

Goodrich, Norma Lorre. *Heroines: Demigoddesses, Prima Donna, Movie Star.* Harper, 1993.

Fantham, Elaine, et al. *Women in the Classical World.* Oxford University Press, 1994.

381

Imel, Marth Ann, and Dorothy Myers Imel. *Goddesses in World Mythology.* Oxford University Press, 1995.

Leeming, David, and Jake Page. *Goddess: Myths of the Feminine Divine.* Oxford University Press, 1995.

Lomperis, Linda, and Sara Stanbury. *Feminist Approaches to the Body in Medieval Literature.* University of Pennsylvania Press, 1993.

Matossian, Lou Ann. "Re-Imagining God: Are We Made in Her Image?" *On the Issues,* spring 1995, 33–35.

O'Brien, Joan. *The Transformation of Hera.* University Press, 1993.

Ruth, Sheila. *Take Back the Light.* University Press, 1993.

Stein, Diane. *The Goddess Book of Days.* Crossing Press, 1992.

Torjesen, Karne Jo. *When Women Were Priests.* HarperCollins, 1993.

Alternative Applications: Select a goddess from early times and categorize the myths, miracles, and powers attributed to her. For example, explore the variations of mythology that cling to Selene/Artemis, also called Hecate the witch. Determine why the chaste moon goddess evolved into a fearful deity. Contrast her style of evil with that of Hera, the jealous wife, or Venus, the unprincipled temptress who offered Paris the gift of Helen of Troy, the world's most beautiful woman.

Holy *woman quiz*

Age/Grade Level or Audience: Middle school or high school research project; bulletin board game; book club handout; Friends of the Library presentation; media column.

Description: Identify goddesses, madonnas, and holy women from all cultures and the holidays and feast days with which they are associated.

Procedure: Organize a study of goddesses and holy women and the traditional holidays and feast days with which they are associated. Have participants use religious research materials to answer questions about female deities and their power. Underline the answer to each question. If more than one name applies, make several selections:

1. German New Year's goddess (**Juno, Tara, Bertha, Hera, Erzulie, Devi, Spider Woman, Gaia, Lachesis**)

2. Saint of Lourdes (**Ishtar, Aida, Santeria, Kwan Yin, Mari, Isis, Wedo, Bernadette, Yemaya**)

3. Roman "Good Goddess" (**Maia, Rhea, Fauna, Lei, Bona Dea, Diana Multimamma, Guinevere, Demeter**)

4. Goddess of grain (**Demeter, Hel, Shiva, White Shell Woman, Eurydice, Ceres, Corn Woman, Oya**)

5. Hawaiian goddess worshipped through sacrifice at a volcano (**Capistrano, Scorpio, Lilith, Pele, Copper Woman, Astarte**)

6. Irish deities celebrated on All-Saints Day (**Banshees, El Dia de las Muertes, Samhain, Wicca, Tarot**)

7. Hopi healers (**Sun Sisters, Earth Mother, Maidens of the Four Directions, Buffalo Calf Women, Semele**)

8. Costa Rica's Our Lady of Angels (**Wyrd, Leto, Quetzocoatl, Aphrodite, the Virgin of Guadalupe, the Black Madonna**)

9. Honored mother of the Immaculate Conception (**Mary, Hestia, Freya, Anne, Tara, Brunhilde, the Goddess of Light, Crow Mother**)

10. honoree of the Epiphany (**Adonis, La Befana, Tammuz, Lucia, the Virgin of Salambao, Luna**)

ANSWERS:

1. Bertha
2. Bernadette
3. Bona Dea
4. Demeter, Ceres, Corn Woman
5. Pele
6. Banshees
7. Maidens of the Four Directions
8. Black Madonna
9. Anne
10. La Befana, Lucia

Budget: $

Sources:

Gimbutas, Marija. *The Civilization of the Goddess: The World of Old Europe.* Harper, 1991.
Goodrich, Norma Lorre. *Heroines: Demigoddesses, Prima Donna, Movie Star.* Harper, 1993.
Fantham, Elaine, et al. *Women in the Classical World.* Oxford University Press, 1994.
Stein, Diane. *The Goddess Book of Days.* Crossing Press, 1992.

Alternative Applications: Have students create a calendar of goddesses with drawings that depict the province of each deity. Use these as models:

Artemis, moon
Athena, spear
Baba Yaga, grandmother
Bean Maiden, black beans
Gaia, earth
Isis, births
Juno, weddings
Lachesis, spinning wheel
Monica, thorn tree
Yamuna, river

Decorate the edges of each page with a suitable motif; for example, laurel branches, stars, spider webs, phases of the moon, waves, blossoms, flames, farm implements, rings, weapons, or signs of the Zodiac.

Issues *of faith*

Age/Grade Level or Audience: Any-age participant at a church, mosque, or synagogue symposium; history class studying world religious practices; bulletin board, women's studies series; newspaper column or media presentation; Women's History Month handout.

Description: Organize a newsletter, online database, or brochure detailing women's concern for religious rights during the twentieth century.

Procedure: Outline the differences of opinion that have occurred in the past century between women and religious authorities over a variety of concerns:

abortion

arranged marriage

birth control

church elections

circumcision (male and female)

female leadership

divorce and remarriage

dress, hair, and makeup

homosexual ministers

homosexual participation in religious services

infibulation (ritual pinning of the labia)

interpreting scripture

ordination of women

patriarchy

sexist hymns and liturgy

Discuss the role of the United Nations in granting political asylum to women and girls who flee genital mutilation, forced marriage, polygamy, concubinage, incest, child slavery, and other civil rights violations. Explain why civil rights take precedence over religious practice or customs.

Budget: $$$

Sources:

Barad, Elizabeth. "Haiti Dances to a Different Drummer." *Dance Magazine,* August 1994, 38–41.

Block, Irwin. "Feminists at Odds." *Montreal Gazette,* June 2, 1995, 8D.

Curnutte, Mark. "Women's Issues Key to Group: Presbyterians Promote Feminist Theology." *Cincinnati Enquirer,* July 20, 1995, 1C.

Mahmoody, Betty. *For the Love of a Child.* St. Martin, 1992.

Sigurdsson, Rev. Rupert. "The Shakers." *National Spiritualist Summit,* July 1995, 29.

Stone, Andrea. "Southern Baptists 'Repent' Past." *USA Today,* June 20, 1995, 3A.

Weaver, Mary Jo, and R. Scott Appleby, eds. *Being Right: Conservative Catholics in America.* University of Indiana Press, 1995.

Alternative Applications: Present the video *Not Without My Daughter* (MGM/Pathé, 1991) or readings from Betty Mahmoody's *For the Love of a Child* (St. Martin, 1992). Lead a group discussion of the author's continued crusade against Islamic spousal abuse, child kidnapping, and child abuse. Describe the emasculating forces that drove Mahmoody's husband away from his hospital job in the United States and back to the security of fundamentalistic Islam in his native land. Explain why imperiled women like Betty rely on an underground network as a method of escape. Compare the network described in her account to the underground railroad. Discuss Mahmoody's alternatives to flight and kidnapping. Why does she maintain her property rights in the United States? Express the film's purpose. To what audience does it appeal?

Mother *Teresa*

Age/Grade Level or Audience: Any-age participant; world religion biography; bulletin board, church school or Bible camp topic; in-house newsletter or media presentation; church newsletter focus; newspaper column; Women's History Month handout.

Description: Create a brochure honoring Mother Teresa, one of the modern world's most treasured women.

Procedure: Introduce Mother Teresa's journey from anonymity in Yugoslavia to her status as a world icon of religious devotion and compassion. Begin with these facts:

> One day to be known as "The Saint of the Gutters," Mother Teresa, a grocer's daughter, was born in Yugoslavia in 1911 and named Agnes Gonxha Bojaxhiu. In 1923 she heard stories of India's poverty and decided to become a nun to serve the world's poorest people.

> A diminutive woman, Mother Teresa took on all-but-impossible tasks: She joined an Irish mission in Calcutta and aided lepers and the poor who lay ill and spurned by passersby in the streets. At age 39 she became a citizen of India. In 1965, her work spread to troubled spots all over the globe, where her workers, dressed in white saris and living simply, staff 500 convents in 87 countries.

> Mother Teresa's selfless example earned her the Nobel Peace Prize in 1979. At her acceptance speech she denounced abortion as the world's greatest destroyer. Opponents question her dogmatic stance against birth control and the right to choice, which could relieve India of its burden of unwanted children. Others challenge her to become more political and to speak against family violence, racism, and sexism.

> Mother Teresa suffered heart problems in 1994. She came to the United States in 1995 to make appearances in Atlanta, Georgia, where she visited Atlanta's House of Grace, a refuge for homeless women suffering from AIDS. She spoke in Charlotte, North Carolina, where nuns have followed her example and opened a simple convent in a poor neighborhood and live a spartan life in service to others.

Budget: $$$

Sources:

Chawla, Navin. *Mother Teresa*. Transaction, 1994.

Garfield, Ken. "Mother Teresa's Lesson to Us All." *Charlotte Observer*, June 11, 1995, 1A, 14A.

Laszlo, Caroline. *Mother Teresa*. Macmillan, 1993.

Mother Teresa. Palisades Home Video, n.d. (Video)

Pond, Mildred. *Mother Teresa*. Chelsea House, 1992.

Alternative Applications: Contrast Mother Teresa's prayer, "Radiating Christ," with the Lord's Prayer or the Prayer of St. Francis of Assisi. Decorate a banquet hall, parochial school library, clinic, soup kitchen, or religious retreat with her thoughts:

> Dear Jesus, Help us to spread your fragrance everywhere we go. Flood our souls with your spirit and life. Penetrate and possess our whole being so utterly that our lives may only be a radiance of yours. . . .

> Let us preach you without preaching, not by words but by our example. By the catching force, the sympathetic influence of what we do, the evident fullness of the love our heart bears to you. Amen.

Plain *women*

Age/Grade Level or Audience: Womens' ecumenical symposium; middle school or high school world religion unit; library or museum bulletin board; church school or Bible camp study; holiday gatherings; church bulletin or newsletter; newspaper column.

Description: Read aloud the testimony of women who have adopted the Amish philosophy.

Procedure: Read articles, testimonies, histories, columns, memoirs, and descriptions of the lives of Amish women. Initiate a discussion concerning the choice to live in the plain, Amish way. Ask these questions:

> Does living in an Amish community discourage individuality? Why is the individual considered to be less worthy than the group as a whole?
>
> How does the church influence marriage and family? What voice do Amish women have in the selection of a mate?
>
> How do Amish community members express disapproval? Are their methods legal?
>
> How do intelligent, sensitive Amish women express rebellious thoughts and feelings?
>
> Why do Amish women turn against technology, modern dress, tourism, commercialism, and contact with the world?
>
> What do Amish women fear most about being modern? Do they have reason to be afraid? Would modern thinking threaten the continuation of their culture?

Budget: $

Sources:

Gingerich, Orland. *The Amish of Canada.* Books Demand, 1994.

Good, Phyllis Pellman. *A Mennonite Woman's Life.* Good Books, 1993.

Kaiser, Grace H. *Dr. Frau: A Woman Doctor Among the Amish.* Good Books, 1986.

Skees, Suzanne. "The Last of the Shakers?" *Ms.,* March/April 1995, 40–45.

Stoltzfus, Louise. *Amish Women: Lives and Stories.* Good Books, 1994.

———. *Two Amish Folk Artists: The Story of Henry Lapp and Barbara Ebersol.* Good Books, 1993.

Wasilchick, John V. *Amish Life.* Outlet Books, 1991.

Alternative Applications: Contrast the lives of Amish women with these and other religious groups:

Advent Christians	Hindus	Quakers
Bahai	Jehovah's Witnesses	Shakers
Buddhists	Jews	Taoists
Catholics	Mormons	Unitarians
fundamental Christians	Muslims	

Discuss which groups have been open to liberal roles for women in education, lifestyle, and worship? Which have welcomed women into the role of spiritual leader? Which prefer that women remain in a secondary role?

Saints *and their specialties*

Age/Grade Level or Audience: Middle school or parochial school quiz; any-age church study session; confirmation worksheet; bulletin board activity; church school or Bible camp lecture; book club presentation; Friends of the Library handout; ecumenical consortia; radio or television series; Women's History Month seminar.

Description: Honor female saints with a "Who Am I" quiz.

Procedure: Have participants utilize reference works and databases to answer the following questions. Distribute a copy of the quiz to each participant and have him or her underline the area identified with each saint or display a copy on a chalkboard or overhead projector for oral or written selection of the correct answer.

1. Agatha (cleanliness, breast disease, poverty)
2. Agnes (lambs and geese, shy people, young girls)
3. Aldegonda (cancer, diners, traveling women)
4. Anne (investments, spiritual weakness, pregnancy)
5. Apollonia (toothache, scholarship, female companions)
6. Barbara (lightning, banking, ships at sea)
7. Bernadette (springs and fountains, handicapped children, shepherds)
8. Bibiana (hangovers, weavers, basketmakers)
9. Bridget of Sweden (dreamers, seekers of comfort, healing)
10. Catherine of Alexandria (separated lovers, grandparents, millers)
11. Catherine of Siena (artists, cloth sellers, fire)
12. Cecilia (fishers and divers, music, night prayers)
13. Dymphana (insanity, fighters, armor makers)
14. Elizabeth of Portugal (war, scientists, gardeners and orchard keepers)
15. Faith (gentle people, pilgrims, martyrs)
16. Felicity (mothers of sons, childless parents, lonely women)
17. Genevieve (the prayerful, cooks, disaster)
18. Gertrude (fear of rats, lepers, the deaf)
19. Justa and Ruffina (printers, potters, teachers of young children)
20. Lucy (blindness, loss of wealth, public speakers)

ANSWERS:

1. Agatha, breast disease
2. Agnes, young girls
3. Aldegonda, cancer
4. Anne, pregnancy
5. Apollonia, toothache
6. Barbara, lightning

7. Bernadette, shepherds

8. Bibiana, hangovers

9. Bridget of Sweden, healing

10. Catherine of Alexandria, millers

11. Catherine of Siena, fire

12. Cecilia, music

13. Dymphana, insanity

14. Elizabeth of Portugal, war

15. Faith, pilgrims

16. Felicity, mothers of sons

17. Genevieve, disaster

18. Gertrude, fear of rats

19. Justa and Ruffina, potters

20. Lucy, blindness

Budget: $

Sources:

Attwater, D. *The Penguin Dictionary of Saints.* Penguin, 1984.

Bentley, J. *A Calendar of Saints: The Lives of the Principal Saints of the Christian Year.* Facts on File, 1986.

Farmer, D. H. *The Oxford Dictionary of Saints.* Oxford University Press, 1993.

Hallam, Elizabeth, gen. ed. *Saints: Who They Are and How They Help You.* Simon & Schuster, 1994.

Head, T. *Hagiography and the Cult of Saints.* Cambridge University Press, 1990.

Walsh, M., ed. *Butler's Lives of Patron Saints.* Harper & Row, 1991.

Alternative Applications: Use sainthood as a research topic, either from a historical, religious, or artistic point of view. Follow these suggestions:

- Study film versions of saints' lives, including The Lark, Saint Joan, and The Song of Bernadette, as well as sculptures, mosaics, statuary, paintings, and tomb effigies portraying sainted figures.

- Discuss how cinema and art blend the real with the spiritual or supernatural to create an aura of otherworldliness and a communion with forces of goodness and love.

- Express the importance of devotion, faith, and prayer to saints during periods of inspiration, miracles, examination, doubt, torture, and threat of death.

- Enumerate the stages of beatification and canonization and the requirements at each level. Note changes in the canonization process through the years. Name women currently being considered for sainthood.

- Differentiate between martyrdom, natural death, and execution.

- Discuss the importance of relics and monstrances to the veneration of saints.

Conclude with religious, historical, and psychological justification for the veneration of saints.

Wiccans *and witches*

Age/Grade Level or Audience: High school sociology class; any age history lecture; bulletin board focus; book club presentation; Friends of the Library seminar; ecumenical consortia; Wiccan monograph.

Description: Explore the definition of Wicca and its relationship to the stereotype of the witch.

Procedure: Have participants utilize reference works and databases to answer the following questions differentiating between the stereotypical Halloween witch and the practitioner of Wicca:

Why does Wicca attempt to open an inner consciousness? Why does the Wiccan consider psychic powers inborn?

What rituals do Wiccans employ? To what purpose?

Why does Wicca divide its deities into four categories: fire, earth, water, and air?

What are Wiccan ethics? Why do they relate to the ancient Celtic worship of Epona the nature goddess and Belenos the hunter?

Why do Wiccans characterize God as "the unknowable"?

Of what significance is the five-pointed star within three concentric circles in honoring God? How do the circles move the spirit toward God? What are the five inroads?

How does this pentangle differ from the five-pointed star of Satanism or the six-pointed Mogen David?

Why did the Catholic Church outlaw the "old ways"? How does orthodoxy differ from nature worship?

Why were the sixteenth and seventeenth centuries called the 'burning times'?

Why do Wiccans doubt the existence of karma and hell? Why are they agnostic?

Why were early Wiccans strongly feminist?

Why do Wiccans contend, "If it harm none, do what you will"?

Conclude with a description of the founding of witchcraft and a discussion of the Wiccan belief system: "Walk tall. Walk in balance. Follow your path." Compare this system with Zen Buddhism, Celtic agricultural gods, and Native American animism.

Budget: $

Sources:

Frost, Gavin, and Yvonne Frost. *Who Speaks for the Witch?* Godolphin House, 1992.

Lecture 1: Basic Precepts and Definitions. Godolphin House, 1991.

Meyer, Marvin, and Richard Smith, eds. *Ancient Christian Magic.* N.p., 1995.

Mills, Jane. *Womanwords.* Macmillan, 1989.

Alternative Applications: Collect facts about Wicca and create a glossary to explain the following terms and activities:

Samhain, the harvest festival held on the full moon closest to November 1

sabbat, a holy day

flamen and *flamenca,* male and female spiritual leaders

handfasting, Wiccan marriage

wiccaning, welcoming and blessing an infant

dedication, accepting witchcraft as a lifestyle

initiation, affirming that the dedicatee is ready to follow the Wiccan path

Imbolc, the spring festival held on the full moon closest to February 1

Beltane, the summer festival held on the full moon closest to May 1

Lugnaasad, the first fruits festival held on the full moon nearest to August 1

Women *in the Bible*

Age/Grade Level or Audience: Adult church or synagogue seminar; bulletin board or newsletter quiz; church school or Bible camp activity; place mat or poster for holiday gatherings; stage readings with audience participation.

Description: Identify female Bible characters from scriptural citations.

Procedure: Present the following lines from scripture and have participants identify the character:

<u>Old Testament</u>

_____ 1. [She] looked through a window and saw King David leaping and dancing before the Lord; and she despised him in her heart.

_____ 2. And the dogs shall eat [her] in the portion of Jezreel, and there shall be none to bury her.

_____ 3. And they were both naked, the man and his wife, and were not ashamed.

_____ 4. And when she had opened it, she saw the child: and, behold, the babe wept. And she had compassion on him. . .

_____ 5. But his wife looked back from behind him, and she became a pillar of salt.

_____ 6. . . . Cast out this bondwoman and her son: for the son of this bondwoman shall not be heir with my son, even with Isaac.

_____ 7. And Jacob heard that he had defiled . . . his daughter: now his sons were with his cattle in the field: and Jacob held his peace until they were come.

_____ 8. And Moses was content to dwell with the man: and he gave Moses . . . his daughter.

_____ 9. Now it came to pass on the third day, that [she] put on her royal apparel, and stood in the inner court of the king's house, over against the king's house: and the king sat upon his royal throne in the royal house, over against the gate of the house.

_____ 10. [She] therefore took new ropes, and bound him therewith, and said unto him, the Philistines be upon thee. . . .

ANSWERS:

1. Michal
2. Jezebel
3. Eve
4. Pharaoh's daughter
5. Lot's wife

6. Hagar
7. Dinah
8. Zipporah
9. Esther
10. Delilah

<u>New Testament</u>

_____ 1. But [she] was cumbered about much serving, and came to him, and said, Lord, dost thou not care that my sister hath left me to serve alone?

_____ 2. And when they were departed, behold, the angel of the Lord appeareth to Joseph in a dream, saying, arise, and take the young child and his mother, and flee into Egypt, and be thou there until I bring thee word: for Herod will seek the young child to destroy him.

_____ 3. But a certain man named Ananias, with . . . his wife, sold a possession, and kept back part of the price, his wife also being privy to it, and brought a certain part, and laid it at the apostles' feet.

_____ 4. And after those days his wife . . . conceived, and hid herself five months, saying, Thus had the Lord dealt with me in the days wherein he looked on me, to take away my reproach among men.

_____ 5. After these things Paul departed from Athens, and came to Corinth; and found a certain Jew named Aquila, born in Pontus, lately come from Italy, with his wife . . . .

_____ 6. And certain women, which had been healed of evil spirits and infirmities, [she] out of whom went seven devils . . . .

_____ 7. It was that [woman] which anointed the Lord with ointment, and wiped his feet with her hair, whose brother Lazarus was sick.

_____ 8. And there came a certain poor [woman], and she threw in two mites, which make a farthing.

_____ 9. And a certain woman . . ., a seller of purple, of the city of Thyatira, which worshipped God, heard us:

whose heart the Lord opened, that she attended unto the things which were spoken of Paul.

_____ 10. I commend unto you . . . our sister, which is a servant of the church which is at Cenchrea: That ye receive her in the Lord, as becometh saints, and that ye assist her in whatsoever business she hath need of you: for she hath been a succourer of many, and of myself also.

ANSWERS:

1. Martha	6. Mary Magdalene
2. Mary	7. Mary
3. Sapphira	8. widow
4. Elisabeth	9. Lydia
5. Priscilla	10. Phoebe

Budget: $

Sources:

Feminist Interpretations of the Bible. Westminster Press, 1985.

Great Women of the Bible in Art and Literature. Eerdmans, 1995.

Kam, Rose Sallberg. *Their Stories/Our Stories: Women of the Bible.* Continuum, 1995.

Newsome, Carol, and Sharon Ringe, eds. *The Women's Bible Commentary.* Westminster/John Knox, 1992.

Stanton, Elizabeth Cady. *The Woman's Bible.* Coalition Task Force on Women and Religion, 1986.

Telushkin, Rabbi Joseph. *Jewish Literacy.* William Morrow, 1991.

Alternative Applications: Make a chalk talk about the women in the Old and New Testaments. Comment on the greater diversity and description of women in the Old Testament. Note that the New Testament concentrates on the actions and importance of men. List minor figures in both segments of the Bible who remain nameless (the woman of Samaria, Pilate's wife, Potiphar's wife) and those who receive little description (Priscilla, Joanna, Zipporah). Ask volunteers to create character sketches and vignettes based on what they know of these women.

Women *of faith and wisdom*

Age/Grade Level or Audience: Church monograph; world religion unit; stage readings; radio or television presentations; church bulletin focus; newsletter or handout.

Description: Organize a newsletter, online database, or brochure honoring women who have influenced world faith, health, family life, humanitarianism, or holistic spirituality.

Procedure: Outline the contributions of such important activists, thinkers, leaders, and philosophers as Mary Baker Eddy, founder of the Christian Science movement. Summarize her studies and meditations by following this model:

Born in Bow, New Hampshire, in 1821, Mary Baker Eddy suffered a debilitating spinal ailment. In home study supervised by her brother Albert, she learned the

Westminster Catechism, as well as philosophy, ethics, Hebrew, Greek, and Latin. She developed independence by strengthening her own beliefs about right and wrong.

After marrying George Washington Glover in 1843, Eddy moved to Boston and joined the abolitionist movement to end slavery. When her husband died, she freed the family's slaves. Returning to her family's home, she gave birth to a son and relapsed into poor health. When Eddy recovered her strength, she taught school and wrote news articles.

After marrying Daniel Patterson, she began studying home remedies that would end her dependence on doctors and came under the influence of a faith healer, Phineas P. Quimby. Restored to health, she lectured on methods of spiritual healing. In 1866 a slip on the ice renewed her frailty and dependence on doctors. After studying the Bible for three years, she determined that faith could cure the sick. She named her system Christian Science and taught followers how to help others who suffered spiritual weakness.

Eddy wrote *Science and Health with a Key to the Scriptures,* a significant work of philosophy that influenced her sect. In 1879 she established the First Church of Christ, Scientist, in Boston. During the 1880s she taught her system of healing at Massachusetts Metaphysical College. Mary Baker Eddy's prolific publications of speeches and advice evolved into the *Christian Science Monitor, Christian Science Sentinel, Herald of Christian Science,* and *Christian Science Journal.* Her influence is still strongly felt by the followers who study, worship, and visit Christian Science reading rooms around the world.

Add other worthy female evangelists, preachers, healers, and religious philosophers. Include these:

Elizabeth Barton	Maria Goretti	Carry Nation
Birgitta of Sweden	Clara Hale	Essie Parrish
Antoinette Blackwell	Hannah	Anna Howard Shaw
Nannie Helen Burroughs	Anne Hutchinson	Starhawk
Catherine of Siena	Joan of Arc	Catherine Tekakwitha
Clare of Assisi	Susette La Flesche	St. Teresa de Jesus of Spain
Lillian Brooks Coffey	Ann Lee	Theresa of Lisieux
Mary Daly	Amy Semple MacPherson	Sojourner Truth
Dorothy Day	Mechthild of Magdeburg	Teresa Urrea
Deborah	Monica	Katherine Von Bora
Elizabeth of Hungary	Mother Seton	Narcissa Whitman
Esther	Mother Teresa	Lucy Wright

Differentiate aspects of lore, legend, and history; for example, the conversion of Aethelthryth, a seventh-century East Anglian princess, to Saint Audrey, founder of an abbey in Ely, England. Distribute the finished product to interested groups, give readings at a meeting of the Friends of the Library, share by Internet or online bulletin board, or place copies in church or school libraries, museums, mosques, or synagogues.

Budget: $$$

Sources:

Behind the Veil: Nuns. Palisades Home Video, n.d. (Video)

Brides of Christ. Palisades Home Video, n.d. (Video)

Carpenter, Gilbert C., Sr., and Gilbert C. Carpenter Jr. *Mary Baker Eddy: Her Spiritual Footsteps.* Pasadena Press, 1985.

Cazden, Elizabeth. *Antoinette Brown Black: A Biography.* Feminist Press, 1995.

Clement, J., ed. *Famous Deeds of American Women.* Corner House, 1975.

Dawkins, Mary. "Utopia at Oneida Lake." *Daughters of the American Revolution Magazine,* May 1990, 173–77.

Deen, Edith. *Great Women of the Christian Faith.* Barbour Books, 1959.

Greenberg, Blu. *On Women and Judaism: A View from Tradition.* Jewish Publication Society, 1981.

Hildegard of Bingen. Palisades Home Video, n.d. (Video)

Hutterites: To Care and Not to Care. Instructional Video, 1993. (Video)

The Inn of the Sixth Happiness. Critics Choice, n.d. (Video)

Lachance, Paul. *Angela of Foligno: Complete Works.* Paulist Press, 1993.

Mills, Jane. *Womanwords.* Macmillan, 1989.

The Miracle. Critics Choice, n.d. (Video)

Mother Teresa. Palisades Home Video, n.d. (Video)

Mother Wove the Morning. Palisades Home Video, n.d. (Video)

Powell, Lyman P. *Mary Baker Eddy: A Life Size Portrait.* Christian Science Publishing Society, 1950.

Sered, Susan Star. *Priestess, Mother, Sacred Sister: Religions Dominated by Women.* Oxford University Press, 1994.

Sigurdsson, Rev. Rupert. "The Shakers." *National Spiritualist Summit,* July 1995, 29.

Smaus, Jewel Spangler. *Mary Baker Eddy: The Golden Days.* Christian Science Publishing Society, 1966.

Story of a Soul. Palisades Home Video, n.d. (Video)

Thérèse: The Little Flower of Jesus. Palisades Home Video, n.d. (Video)

Thomas, Robert David. *With Bleeding Footsteps: Mary Baker Eddy's Path to Religious Leadership.* Alfred A. Knopf, 1994.

Vernoff, Edward, and Rima Shore. *The International Dictionary of 20th Century Biography.* New American Library, 1987.

von Mehren, Joan. *Minerva and the Muse: A Life of Margaret Fuller.* University of Massachusetts Press, 1995.

Zweig, Stefan. *Mental Healers: Franz Anton Mesmer, Mary Baker Eddy, Sigmund Freud.* Frederick Ungar, 1990.

Alternative Applications: Create a time line for a bulletin board, database, poster, frieze, newspaper column, brochure, or handout. Enter at each century the works and achievements of these and other women of faith:

- Monica, mother of St. Augustine who encouraged her son to become a Christian in the third century a.d.

- Hypatia, philosopher and mathematician who attempted to counter religious fanaticism with reason and neoplatonic compassion

- first archeologist Helena, mother of Constantine and Empress of Rome in the early 4th century

- Marjery Kempe, pilgrim to the Holy Lands in 1373

- Quaker martyr Mary Dyer, executed in 1660 for her faith

- Isabella Graham, distributor of Bibles and creator of an orphanage in New York in 1806; with her associate, Sarah Hoffman, founder of a relief center for widows

- Margaret Barrett Prior, who managed the New York Orphan asylum and provided soup for the poor during the winter of 1818–1819

- Jarena Lee, first black female minister, ordained by the AME Church in 1824

- Reverend Penny Ellis, chaplain, University of Chicago

- Lydia Sigourney, a Christian crusader from Hartford, Connecticut, who in 1828 collected money and clothing to aid the women of Greece during the Greek Revolution

- Helene Bresslau Schweitzer, missionary and helpmate to her husband, Albert Schweitzer, at their clinic in Lambarene, Gabon

- Rhena Schweitzer-Eckart, medical technologist with her parents at Lambarene, Gabon

- the Fox Sisters, Shakers who tried to incorporate spiritualism into communal worship and faith

- Nobel Prize-winning altruist and evangelist Mother Teresa

- Amanda Smith, black missionary and evangelist of the early twentieth century

- Pandita Ramabai, Bible translator and evangelist in India

- Mrs. Charles Jones Soong, advocate of Christian education in China

Place a star by women who have earned such worldwide recognition as a statue, shrine, sainthood, *Time* Woman of the Year, MacArthur Award, Springarn Medal, Pulitzer Prize, Freedom Medal, National Geographic Medal, National Book Award, National Institute of Arts and Letters fellowship, American Academy of Arts and Letters fellowship, French Academy honor, Eleanor Roosevelt Award, Legion of Honor, Albert Lasker Award, or the Nobel Prize.

Science

Ecofeminism *week*

Age/Grade Level or Audience: All-ages garden clubs; civic clean-up campaigns; ecology drives; health or biology focus; media series.

Description: During Women's History Month, establish an Ecofeminism Week to stress the interdependence of all living things and to honor female pioneers in the field of ecology.

Procedure: Organize a female-engineered ecology awareness week to consist of media features honoring ecofeminists such as Petra Kelly, Marjory Stoneman Douglas, Lady Bird Johnson, Mollie Beattie, and Octavia Hill. Include coverage of women in your own town who battle pollutants. Use as an example a pioneer in the field of ecology such as Rachel Carson:

- born May 27, 1907, in Springdale, Pennsylvania; Carson's love of nature began early on; by 1917 she was submitting nature articles to *St. Nicholas* magazine

- Carson received a B.A. in science from the Pennsylvania College for Women; an M.A. from Johns Hopkins in 1932

- in 1936 Carson was hired as an aquatic biologist by the U.S. Bureau of Fisheries

- her books include *Under the Sea* (1941), *The Sea Around Us* (1951), *Edge of the Sea* (1955), and *Silent Spring* (1962)

- the release of *Silent Spring* brought to the fore the debate over the use of chemical pesticides such as DDT; Carson was thrust into the spotlight and became an international spokesperson on environmental issues

- in 1963 Carson testified before a Senate Committee on the Chemical Pesticides Coordination Act; this legislation led to the placement of warning labels on chemical products

Throughout the week put into action a clean-up and recycling campaign of roadsides, picnic and recreation areas, children's playgrounds, schools, day-care facilities, downtown areas, and other problem spots. Have a telephone bank enlist groups of 8–12 people to organize litter collection and recycling of usable salvaged materials. Follow these procedures:

- Appoint an adult to supervise groups with children.

- Provide posters indicating meeting spots.

- Target all areas of town or a rural community.

- Spread the clean-up over areas frequented by all ages and interests.

- For roadside clean-up, provide orange vests to protect workers near streets and highways.

- Recycle reusables, particularly glass, cardboard, newspaper, and plastics. Place grass, leaves, and branches in a compost heap.

Budget: $$$

Sources:

Bigwood, Carol. *Earth Muse: Feminism, Nature and Art.* Temple University Press, 1993.

Diamond, Irene, and Gloria Orenstein. *Reweaving the World: The Emergence of Ecofeminism.* Sierra, 1990.

Gaard, Greta, ed. *Ecofeminism: Women, Animals, Nature.* Temple University Press, 1993.

Gaia and God: An Ecofeminist Theology of Earth Healing. Harper, 1992.

Gartner, Robert. *Working Together Against the Destruction of the Environment.* Rosen, 1994.

Harlan, Judith. *Sounding the Alarm: A Biography of Rachel Carson.* Dillon Press, 1989.

Jezer, Marty. *Rachel Carson.* Chelsea House, 1988.

Johnson, Elizabeth. *Women, Earth and Creator Spirit.* Paulist Press, 1992.

Mies, Maria, and Vanana Shiva. *Ecofeminism: Reconnecting a Divided World.* Humanities, 1993.

Norwood, Vera. *Made from This Earth: American Women and Nature.* University of North Carolina Press, 1993.

Alternative Applications: Organize a unified girls' and women's clubs week to encourage public assistance in restoring the local environment. Contact officers of church groups, 4-H and scout troops, nature clubs, camping and outdoors enthusiasts, teachers' unions, and local women's magazines and newsletters, newspapers, radio, and television to spread information about pollution, toxic wastes, erosion, and litter.

Eve, *mother of all*

Age/Grade Level or Audience: High school or college research paper topic; science club presentation; media feature.

Description: Present a paper on the DNA study that speculates on the possibility of a single mother of the human race.

Procedure: Present on overhead projector, handout, monograph, or scholarly abstract the study of the Y chromosome, which leads some genome researchers to consider the possibility that modern humanity sprang from a female or small group of females living about 198,000 B.C. Define terms, particularly these:

combinants	primate
DNA sequence	X chromosome
evolution	Y chromosome
genetic information	zinc finger Y genes

Contrast the results of the study with accepted evolutionary findings regarding humankind's origins. Note that the basis for the study, the ZFY or zinc finger Y gene, is in the very early stages and requires a great deal more study of primates.

Budget: $

Sources:

Carlisle, Thomas J. *Eve and After: Old Testament Woman in Portrait.* Eerdmans, 1984.

Dorit, Robert L. "Lineage of Y Chromosome Boosts Eve Theory." *Science News,* May 27, 1995, 326.

Duseau, Janice A. *Eve: Woman in God's Image.* Word Power, 1989.

Alternative Applications: Contrast the biblical account of Eve with the scientific study above. Make an oral report on the difference between mythic earth-mother and human progenitor. Focus on these issues:

- In what respect are both versions of the first woman flawed?

- Why is the Christian version compared to the myths of Lilith and Pandora?

- What do scientists hope to gain from locating evidence of a "first mother"?

- How does the study of a single mother of the human race reflect on X-linked disease?

Inventions *and bright ideas*

Originator: Thea Sinclair, author and biologist, Hickory, North Carolina.

Age/Grade Level or Audience: Elementary school science class; library club project; Women's History Month newsletter; city hall bulletin board; history club frieze.

Description: Celebrate women's historic role in invention and creativity by mapping out a walk of fame.

Procedure: Summarize on waterproof placards the inventions or revolutionary ideas of famous women, such as oil geologist Elizabeth Fisher, mathematician and inventor Hypatia of Alexandria, naturalists Ruth Harris Thomas and Amelia Lasky, and social economist and Nobel Prize winner Emily Greene Balch. Post the placards along a popular walking tour, bike route, or hiking trail. Mark each placard with a symbol of the woman's achievement: for example, a coffee filter for inventor Melitta Bentz or a window sash for Margaret Knight. Use the following data about inventor and entrepreneur Sarah Breedlove Walker as a model:

- An orphan at age six, Sarah Breedlove Walker lived with her sister in Vicksburg, Mississippi, and worked as a hotel laundress to support herself and her daughter A'Lelia. In the early 1900s, Walker revolutionized the process of straightening hair by developing a hot comb and pomade. From this beginning she expanded to a line of skin and hair products and fragrances, a system of direct demonstrations and sales to women's clubs, and a beauty school to teach the Walker Process. Aware that her success as America's first black female millionaire rested on the support of her clients, Walker donated generously to black causes and established halfway houses in Indianapolis and St. Louis.

Include the work of these famous inventors:

- Carmenta—the 15-letter Latin alphabet, which she based on Phoenician writing

- Alchemist Miriam the Prophetess—the bain-marie, or double boiler; three-stage distillation; and the condenser (1st–2nd century B.C.)

- Mathematician and philosopher Hypatia—commentaries on Ptolemy's astronomy and existing mathematical systems (5th century A.D.)

- Mrs. Sibilla Masters—Tuscorora rice as a cure for tuberculosis; a corn grinder; and a hat-making machine (1715)

- Midwife Marie Gillain Boivin—pelvimeter and vaginal speculum to monitor the heartbeat of an unborn child (1812)

399

- Ann Harned Manning—mowing machine (1831)
- Mathematician Augusta Ada King, Countess of Lovelace—computer program (1842)
- Sarah Mather—submarine light and telescope (1845)
- Margaret E. Knight—safety stop for looms; a machine to make square-bottom paper bags; leather cutters and sewing machines for the shoe industry; sash windows; barbecue spit; treaded tires; sleeve-valve engine; and numberer (1850–1914)
- California farmer Harriet Strong—irrigation devices (1887)
- Wilhelmina Fleming—system of star classification (1890)
- Helen Augusta Blanchard—split needle (1896)
- Anna Wessels Williams—antitoxins for diphtheria and rabies (late 1890s)
- Sorbonne professor and Nobel Prize-winner Dr. Marie Skladowska Curie—isolation of pure radium (1906)
- Melitta Bentz—drip-brew coffee filter from recycled notebook paper (1908)
- Henrietta Leavitt—variations in Cepheids (1912)
- Catherine Kuhn-Moos—slide fastener, the forerunner of Whitcomb Judson's zipper (1913)
- Mary Phelps Jacob—bra (November 1914)
- Scottish microbiologist Mary Steele Bruce—identified bacteria in goat's milk (1920s)
- Bertha Thompson—"tommy iron" or shaping iron (1921)
- Melanie Klein—proposed an anti-Freud, pro-female psychology (1921)
- Bacteriologist Gladys Dick—test for scarlet fever (1924)
- Annie Jump Cannon—catalogue of stars (1924)
- Marjorie Joyner—permanent wave machine (1928)
- Dorothy Harrison Wood Eustis—Seeing Eye dog school (1929)
- Barbara McClintock and Harriet Creighton—research on chromosomes (1929)
- Biologist Wanda Farr—plant production of cellulose (1930s)
- Anna Freud—egalitarian ego psychology movement (1937)
- Katherine Burr Blodgett—nonreflecting or "invisible" glass and a plane wing de-icer (1938)
- Dr. Dorothy H. Andersen—cystic fibrosis syndrome (1938)
- Irene Joliot, daughter of Marie and Pierre Curie—artificial radioactivity (1939)
- Lise Meitner—identified nuclear fission (1939)
- Rebecca Craighill Lancefield—classified streptococci (1940)
- Karen Horney—gender-neutral study of the human mind (1941)
- Hedy Lamarr—secret coded communication system and remote-control torpedo (1942)

- Dr. Helen Taussig—arterial bypass to cure infant cyanosis (1944)

- Nobelist Dr. Gerty Thersa Cori—study of enzymes (1947)

- Captain Grace Hopper—COBOL, a computer language (1951)

- Barbara McClintock—movable gene theory (1951)

- Rosalind Franklin—DNA theory (1951)

- Dr. Virginia Apgar—the Apgar Score, a method of evaluating the viability of newborns by assessing color, response, pulse, breathing, and muscle tone (1952)

- Typist Bette Nesmith Graham—Mistake Out (1957)

- Chien-Shiung Wu—study of subatomic particles (1960s)

- Hattie Alexander—meningitis antiserum (1960s)

- Marguerite Perey—Francium (1962)

- Nobelist Maria Goeppert-Mayer—quantum electrodynamics (1963)

- Nobelist Dorothy Hodgkin—analysis of crystals (1964)

- Dr. Rosalyn S. Yalow—radioimmunoassay (1976)

- Dr. Maria Bustillo—ova transplant (1980)

- Ann Moore and Lucy Aukerman—Snugli infant carrier (1983)

- Dr. Riba Levi-Montalcini—study of cell biology (1986)

- Nobelist Gertrude Elion—AZT (1988)

- Rosalind Franklin—an x-ray diffraction study of DNA (1990)

- Jeanie Low, the youngest U.S. patent holder—folding stool (1992)

Add entries on AIDS geneticist Mathilde Krim, archaeologists Lily Ross Taylor and Iris Love, biologist Ethel Browne Harvey, chemist Emma Perry Carr, botanist Alice Eastwood, molecular spectroscopist Reiko Kuroda, physicist Marie Gertrude Rand, and geologist Winifred Goldring.

Budget: $$$

Sources:

Aaseng, Nathan. *Twentieth-Century Inventors.* Facts on File, 1991.

"African-American Inventors." *Cobblestone,* February 1992.

American Men and Women of Science. R. R. Bowker, 1989.

Annie and the Stars of Many Colors. CfA Publications, n.d. (Video)

Ashworth, William. *The Encyclopedia of Environmental Studies.* Facts on File, 1991.

Bailey, Brooke. *The Remarkable Lives of 100 Women Healers and Scientists.* Bob Adams, 1994.

Bailey, Martha. *American Women in Science: A Biographical Dictionary.* ABC-CLIO, 1994.

Bonta, Marcia Myers, ed. *American Women Afield: Writings by Pioneering Women Naturalists.* Texas A&M University Press, 1995.

Clark, Judith Freeman. *Almanac of American Women in the Twentieth Century.* Prentice Hall, 1987.

"Entrepreneurs of the Past." *Cobblestone,* May 1989.

Etori, Akio. "The Difference between Shoes and Socks." *Look Japan,* April 1994, 20–21.

Freeman, J. *A Passion for Physics.* IOP Publishing, 1991.

Golob, Richard, and Eric Brus, eds. *The Almanac of Science and Technology.* Harcourt Brace Jovanovich, 1990.

Griffin, Lynne, and Kelly Mccann. *The Book of Women: 300 Notable Women History Passed By.* Bob Adams, 1992.

Haber, Louis. *Black Pioneers of Science and Invention.* Harcourt Brace Jovanovich, 1992.

Healey, James R. "Control Panel Designer Achieves the Right Touch." *USA Today,* June 19, 1995, 4B.

———. *Mary Leakey: In Search of Human Beginnings.* W. H. Freeman, 1995.

James, Edward T., et al., eds. *Notable American Women, 1607–1950.* Belknap Press, 1971.

James, Portia P. *The Real McCoy: African-American Invention and Innovation, 1619–1930.* Smithsonian Institution, 1989.

Kass-Simon, G., and Patricia Farnes. *Women of Science: Righting the Record.* Indiana University Press, 1990.

Klein, Aaron E., and Cynthia L. Klein. *The Better Mousetrap.* Beaufort Books, 1982.

Lafferty, Peter. *The Inventor Through History.* Thompson Learning, 1993.

Macdonald, Anne L. *Feminine Ingenuity: Women and Invention in America.* Ballantine Books, 1992.

Magill, Frank N., ed. *Great Events from History II: Science and Technology Series.* Salem Press, 1991.

Martin, Jean, gen. ed. *Who's Who of Women in the Twentieth Century.* Crescent Books, 1995.

McGrew, Roderick E. *Encyclopedia of Medical History.* McGraw-Hill, 1985.

McHenry, Robert, ed. *Liberty's Women.* G. & C. Merriam, 1980.

Montgomery, Mary. *Marie Curie.* Silver Burdett, 1990.

Ogilvie, Marilyn Bailey. *Women in Science: Antiquity Through the Nineteenth Century.* MIT Press, 1990.

Patton, Phil. *Made in the USA.* Grove Weidenfeld, 1992.

Richardson, Robert O. *The Weird and Wondrous World of Patents.* Sterling, 1990.

Stanley, Autumn. *Mothers and Daughters of Invention: Notes for a Revised History of Technology.* Scarecrow Press, 1993.

Sterling, Dorothy. *We Are Your Sisters: Black Women in the Nineteenth Century.* W. W. Norton, 1984.

Travers, Bridget, ed. *World of Scientific Discovery.* Gale Research, 1994.

Urry, C. Megan, et al. *Women at Work: A Meeting on the Status of Women in Astronomy.* STSci, 1992. (Available on email: cmu@stsci.edu.)

Van Doren, Charles, and Robert McHenry, eds. *Webster's American Biographies.* G. & C. Merriam, 1974.

Vare, Ethlie Ann, and Greg Ptacek. *Mothers of Invention: From the Bra to the Bomb, Forgotten Women and Their Unforgettable Ideas.* William Morrow, 1988.

Veglahn, Nancy J. *Women Scientists.* Facts on File, 1991.

"Women Inventors." *Cobblestone,* June 1994.

Yenne, Bill. *100 Inventions That Shaped World History.* Bluewood Books, 1993.

Alternative Applications: Establish a miniature inventor's museum. Display models, schematic drawings, photos, or actual equipment or devices designed by women alongside brief descriptions of how each idea works to save or improve life. Feature Margaret E. Knight, inventor of a safety stop for looms, the square-bottomed paper bag, cutters and sewing machines for the shoe industry, sash windows, barbecue spit, sleeve-valve engine, and automatic numberer. Highlight these designs and inventions:

Virginia M. Ammons's fireplace camper tool

Dr. Virginia Apgar's score sheet for evaluating infants

Henrietta Bradbury's torpedo discharger

Marie Van Brittan Brown's home security system

Meredith Gourdine's paint spray-gun and smoke control

Dorothy Hoover's aeronautical devices

Dr. Helen Taussig's arterial shunt

Mary Phelps Jacob's silk and ribbon brassiere

Marie Gillain Boivin's pelvimeter and vaginal speculum

Wanda Farr's study of cellulose

Katherine Burr Blodgett's nonreflecting glass

Dr. Maria Bustillo's plan for implanting ova in infertile women

Bessie Cary Evinrude's motor designs

bacteriologist Alice Catherine Evans's study of brucellosis

microbiologist Mary Steele Bruce's study of goat's milk

Countess Augusta Ada King's computer program

Dr. Marie Curie's diagrams of the radium molecule

Catherine Kuhn-Moos's slide fastener

Sibilla Masters's Tuscorora rice

alchemist Miriam the Prophetess's double boiler, three-stage still, and condenser

midwife Mary Donally's method of performing cesarian sections

chemist Mary Engle Pennington's frozen food containers

Lydia Estes Pinkham's vegetable compound

radiologist Edith Quimby's studies of radiology

Nevenka Schumaker's revolutionary dashboard for the 1996 Ford Taurus

Patsy Sherman's Scotchguard process

Melitta Bentz's coffee filter

Ida Hyde's microelectrode

Florence Sabin and slides of tuberculosis and syphilis bacteria

The laparoscope *and female anatomy*

Age/Grade Level or Audience: High school health or biology oral presentation; science club demonstration; women's history week newsletter or bulletin board.

Description: Present an oral overview of the invention of the laparoscope and its revolutionary application to female diseases and treatment.

Procedure: Summarize the creation and use of fiber optics for internal examination and biopsy. Present an overview of the shape, technical advances, and use of the laparoscope. Describe its application to these and other procedures on female patients: study of suspicious uterine tissue, tubal ligation, treatment of blocked fallopian tubes, and examination of fibroid tumors, endometriosis, and cervical cancer. Briefly describe the experience of undergoing such treatment prior to the development of the laparoscope. Contrast the extent and cost of a laparoscopic procedure to midline surgery.

Budget: $

Sources:

Aaseng, Nathan. *Twentieth-Century Inventors.* Facts on File, 1991.

American Men and Women of Science. R. R. Bowker, 1989.

Golob, Richard, and Eric Brus, eds. *The Almanac of Science and Technology.* Harcourt Brace Jovanovich, 1990.

"Inventive Women Poster Set." National Women's History Project, 1993.

Lafferty, Peter. *The Inventor Through History.* Thompson Learning, 1993.

Magill, Frank N., ed. *Great Events from History II: Science and Technology Series.* Salem Press, 1991.

McGrew, Roderick E. *Encyclopedia of Medical History.* McGraw-Hill, 1985.

Alternative Applications: Have students suggest other ways in which prevention and treatment of female reproductive diseases and anomalies have changed throughout the history of medicine. Project how new developments in technology, especially the use of laser microsurgery, transderm patch, time-release medication, bionic surgery, and in vitro fertilization, will change the future of treating female patients.

Male-*female anatomical differences*

Age/Grade Level or Audience: Middle school or high school anatomy or biology discussion; science fair display; medical careers program; science club symposium; Women's History Month newsletter or bulletin board article; newspaper feature or media series.

Description: Research historical studies into the differences between the male and female anatomy.

Procedure: Assign pairs of participants to research differences in male and female anatomy. Include obvious differences in reproductive organs and hormones, but also expand to include studies on:

- aging
- brain function
- center of gravity
- communication skills
- eye-hand coordination
- learning capabilities
- metabolis

- muscle-to-bone ratio
- perception
- rate of maturation
- sexual needs
- stamina and agility
- susceptibility to disease
- viability at birth

Discuss anatomical differences in light of evolution and human development. Propose explanations for differences between men and women, e.g., women's relative longevity.

Budget: $

Sources:

Gorham, Christine. "How Gender May Bend Your Thinking." *Time,* July 17, 1995, 51.

Lubens, Pualine. "Girls in Women's Bodies." *Detroit Free Press,* J1, 3.

Weiss, Rick. "Race of the Sexes." *Charlotte Observer,* March 27, 1995, 1–2E.

Alternative Applications: Create a year-by-year wall chart contrasting the average male and female in terms of physical development, hormonal and metabolic changes, and aging. Note differences and similarities. Draw conclusions regarding areas of greatest variances, such as use of the right and left hemispheres of the brain for problem solving, participation in high-contact sports, decoding written messages, concentration, spatial and kinesthetic orientation, and nonverbal communication.

The mother *of the atom*

Age/Grade Level or Audience: Middle school or high school physical science or chemistry activity.

Description: Introduce students to a study of the atom, isotopes, and/or the periodic table of the elements through the work of Nobel Prize winner Maria Goeppert-Mayer.

Procedure: Begin a study of the structure of the atom by having students create basic models using materials such as different colored clay to represent protons and neutrons. Expand the activity to include different elements and/or isotopes using the periodic table as a guide. Discuss the contributions of physicist Maria Goepppert-Mayer, whose theory of nuclear shells explains why certain isotopes are unusually stable; all of these isotopes had 2, 8, 20, 28, 50, 82, or 126 protons or neutrons. These numbers came to be known as magic numbers. Include in the lesson additional biographical facts:

- born June 28, 1906, in Kattowiz, Upper Silesia, then a part of Germany

- barred from public school, Goeppert-Mayer enrolled at the Frauenstudium, a small all-girl's private school operated by suffragists

- in 1924 she entered the University of Göttingen; began the study of mathematics, but changed her major to physics due to the influence of Professor Max Born

- earned doctorate in 1930; married Joseph Mayer, an American studying in Germany

- husband accepted position at Johns Hopkins University in Baltimore; Goeppert-Mayer refused position due to university policy forbidding the hire of both husband and wife

- first teaching position in 1941 as half-time instructor at Sarah Lawrence

- during World War II she worked on Columbia's Substitute Alloy Material Project developing processes for uranium isotope separation for use in atomic bombs

- shortly after World War II, she attained a full-time position as professor of physics at the University of Chicago

- she received the 1963 Nobel Prize for physics for her theory of nuclear shells

Budget: $$

Sources:

Kass-Simon, G., and Patricia Farnes. *Women of Science: Righting the Record.* Indiana University Press, 1990.

McGrayne, Sharon Bertsch. *Nobel Prize Women in Science.* Carol Publishing, 1992.

Ogilvie, Marilyn Bailey. *Women in Science: Antiquity Through the Nineteenth Century.* MIT Press, 1990.

Travers, Bridget, ed. *World of Scientific Discovery.* Gale Research, 1994.

Alternative Applications: Incorporate the study of other female Nobel Prize winners such as Marie Curie or Dorothy Crowfoot Hodgkin (1963), who developed the procedure of X-ray crystallography. Discuss the fact that Hodgkin used a wire-based model of the B-12 molecule and ordinary light to simulate her study, thus determining the easiest way to discover the molecular structure of crystals. Further the discussion by inviting students to compile statistics on female Nobel Prize winning scientists; for example, the first recipient in each field (physics, chemistry, astronomy, biology, medicine), the total number of female recipients, the percentage of women recipients compared with the number of women working within each field, as well as the number of female recipients versus the number of male recipients.

A rose *is a rose*

Age/Grade Level or Audience: Preschool and kindergarten naming activity.

Description: Create a learning center composed of seeds, plants, shrubs, and trees bearing famous female first names.

Procedure: Introduce participants to plants bearing famous female first names by assembling seed catalogs and plant identification books. Make a seedling or plant-cutting center by filling egg cartons, used seedling trays, milk cartons, or paper cups with potting soil and planting seeds or cuttings under a grow-light or on a sunny window sill. Cover with plastic wrap or glass until plants develop at least one set of leaves. Open and sprinkle lightly with water when soil dries.

Make a list of notable women who share some of the same names as plants. Also discuss the tradition of imbuing flowers with certain personality characteristics, e.g., Amaryllis=Pride; Bluebell=Constancy. Use these as examples:

- dianthus (photographer Diane Arbus)
- belladonna (adventurer Belle Starr or feminist Bella Abzug)
- black-eyed susan (activist and feminist Susan B. Anthony)
- helenium (Helen of Troy)
- laurel (writer Laura Ingalls Wilder)
- rose (Kennedy matriarch Rose Kennedy)
- violet (Violette Neatly Anderson, first black woman to practice law before the U.S. Supreme Court)

Compose a poster or chalkboard list spelling other female flower names and connect them with traditional storybook characters and nursery rhyme figures. Cut out pictures from seed catalogs of these:

- camellia
- daphne
- delphinia
- emilia
- florabunda
- heather
- holly

- ione
- iris
- ivy
- jasmine
- lily
- marguerite
- marigold

- myrtle
- olive
- rose
- ruta
- valeria
- veronica
- violet

Expand word recognition to the names of these plants, some of which are common and some rare:

acacia	cassia	gilia	pansy
alona	cherry	hazel	petunia
althea	chloe	iolanthe	prunella
amaryllis	clematis	laelia	rhoda
andromeda	clivia	linnea	saffron
asteria	dahlia	michaelia	stellaria
azalia	erica	mina	tansy
calla lily	fern	nandina	viola

Distribute paper and crayons for participants to color and label pictures of common flowers and plants, particularly the daisy, fern, cherry, and petunia.

Budget: $$

Sources:

Anatta, Ivan. *Flowers*. Child's World, 1993.

Dobelis, Inge N., ed. *Magic and Medicine of Plants*. Reader's Digest, 1986.

Greenaway, Kate. *Kate Greenaway's "Language of Flowers."* Grammercy, 1978.

Holmes, Anita. *Flowers for You: Blooms for Every Month*. Macmillan, 1993.

Macoboy, Stirling. *What Flower Is That?* Portland House, 1988.

Wren. *Flowers in Hawaii Coloring Book*. Bess Press, 1992.

Alternative Applications: Have participants create a collage of plants with women's names by these methods:

- Cut pictures from seed catalogs or garden magazines and paste into a collage.

- Press fresh flowers in a book to dry; then glue to heavy board in a pattern.

- Draw blossom shapes on tissue or typing paper.

- Cut flowers from colored sheets of paper or cellophane.

- Glue thin bits of voile, organza, or batiste to wire or pipe cleaners. Add green stems.

Collect the finished flowers in a bulletin board display, in May baskets, or mount on windows so sunlight shines through them, illuminating the colors. Display the finished projects at a library, museum, school, retirement or convalescent home, hospital, store windows, or mall. Have a garden or woman's club or junior league hold a contest and select the best flower picture.

Science *and* biography

Age/Grade Level or Audience: Middle school writing lesson; medical careers program; science club project; school newspaper series; civic club presentation.

Description: Introduce interdisciplinary writing skills in science.

Procedure: Conduct a lesson in research and composition for science students by assigning participants to write a biography of a famous female scientist. Introduce students to standard sources of information: *Current Biography, Who's Who,* biographies, autobiographies, *Newsbank, ProQuest,* and the *Reader's Guide to Periodical Literature.* Use the life of astronomer Joycelyn Bell Burnell as a model:

- Born July 15, 1943, in a rural section outside Belfast, Ireland, Joycelyn Bell Burnell studied in a small local school and performed poorly. Intrigued by the Armagh Observatory, she became interested in the stars and read about famous astronomers.

- In her teens, she chose radioastronomy as a career because the job can be performed in daylight. Her father sent her to Mount School in York, England, where her academic performance improved. At the University of Glasgow, she majored in physics and studied geology, chemistry, and mathematics as sidelines. She graduated with honors in 1965 and began graduate work in astronomy at Cambridge University.

- Under the mentorship of Antony Hewish, she utilized a radio telescope to locate unidentified lights or pulsars. Two years into study with a high-speed recorder, she and Hewish traced the anomaly, which Bell Burnell labeled Belisha beacons. Under worldwide scrutiny, Bell Burnell presented evidence of what may be earth's first record of extraterrestrial signals. Credit for the project won Hewish the 1974 Nobel Prize in astrophysics; although he was credited for making his achievements with the help of "others," the committee made no specific mention of Bell Burnell's massive studies.

- In 1982, Bell Burnell joined the Royal Observatory staff in Edinburgh, where she studied infrared views of galaxies. In 1991 she managed a space observatory. She has received numerous prizes and awards and published learned articles.

Present completed biographies at a public forum on women's history or bind into a notebook for use in a science class, laboratory, or school or public library.

Budget: $$

Sources:

Annals of New York Academy of Sciences. 302: 685, 1977.

Bailey, Brooke. *The Remarkable Lives of 100 Women Healers and Scientists.* Bob Adams, 1994.

Bailey, Martha. *American Women in Science: A Biographical Dictionary.* ABC-CLIO, 1994.

Beatty, Kelly. "They Touch the Future." *Parade,* July 16, 1995, 4–5.

Bigwood, Carol. *Earth Muse: Feminism, Nature and Art.* Temple University Press, 1993.

Current Biography. H. W. Wilson, 1995.

Diamond, Irene, and Gloria Orenstein. *Reweaving the World: The Emergence of Ecofeminism.* Sierra, 1990.

Gaard, Greta, ed. *Ecofeminism: Women, Animals, Nature.* Temple University Press, 1993.

McGrayne, Sharon Bertsch. *Nobel Prize Women in Science.* Carol Publishing, 1992.

Alternative Applications: Select an area of science in which women have made significant contributions; for example:

- **applied science** (Reta Beebe, Rachel Fuller Brown, Annie Jump Cannon, Gerty Cori, Imke de Pater, Gertrude Belle Elion, Williamina Fleming, Dian Fossey, Erna Gibbs, Heidi Hammel, Grace Hopper, Melissa McGrath, Antonia Maury, Maria Goeppert-Mayer, Barbara McClintock, Lucy McFadden, Maria Mitchell, Carolyn Shoemaker, Chien-Shiung Wu, Rosalyn S. Yalow)

- **ecology** (Rachel Carson, Caroline Dorman, Ann Haven Morgan, Ynes Mexia, Marjory Stoneman Douglas, Ruth Benedict)

- **engineering** (Edith Clarke, Lillian Moller Gilbreth, Irmgard Flügge-Lotz)

- **medicine** (Virginia Apgar, Clara Barton, Elizabeth Blackwell, Lydia Folger Fowler, Alice Hamilton, Sister Elizabeth Kenny, Dorothy Reed Mendenhall, Ann Preston, Florence Sabin, Virginia Apgar, Lillian D. Wald)

- **mental health** (Joyce Brothers, Augusta Fox Bronner, Dorothea Dix, Anna Freud, Karen Horney, Elisabeth Kubler-Ross, Ruth Westheimer)

- **mathematics** (Hilda Geiringer, Ada Lovelace, Amalie Emmy Noether, Anna Pell Wheeler)

Create a card file, database, wall chart, or timeline acknowledging the place of women in science. Accompany each entry with a capsule biography.

Space-age women

Age/Grade Level or Audience: Elementary school earth science project; science club wall chart; children's science museum bulletin board.

Description: Compose a star chart of women who have contributed to space exploration and study.

Procedure: Center a bulletin board, newsletter, montage, or mobile with a model of the solar system. Around it group the names and achievements of women in all areas of the space program:

- Dr. Evelyn Anderson, whose studies of the hypothalamus and pituitary glands help control human reaction to weightlessness

- Ann Eckels Bailie, mathematician, who tracked Vanguard I and discovered evidence of variations in the earth's gravitational pull

- Ellen Baker, flight specialist and physician, who tested the Mir crew in the Atlantis spacelab during its June–July 1995 flight

- Julie Beasely, whose knowledge of G-forces elucidated the study of human behavior in space

- Dr. Jimmie Blume, who examines how stress in space could lower immunity to disease and allergies

- Annette Chambers, mathematician, who programs computers to guide manned spacecraft

- Marcelline Chartz, NASA supervisor, who writes computer programs for the Ames Research Center to speed data analysis

- Alice King Chatham, sculptor and expert in anatomy, the developer of space beds, test dummies, and pressurized suits and helmets for fighter pilots

- Merna Dawson, analytical chemist at Edward Air Force Base Rocket Site, who increased flight speed of rocket ships by analyzing and refining fuels

- Bonnie Dunbar, biomedical engineer and Russian language expert, who staffed the Atlantis flight in cooperation with the Russian Mir crew in the June–July 1995 team effort

- Beatrice Finkelstein, nutritionist for NASA space missions

- Elizabeth Guild, one of the first women to be commissioned in the WAACs and to apply the science of sound to supersonic flight

- Mary Hedgepeth, a mathematician for Edwards Air Force Base and head of the data assessment group that oversees research aircraft

- Mae Jemison, physician and the first black woman astronaut, member of the first joint US/Japan space mission

- Dorothy B. John, a mathematician studying digital differential at Wright-Patterson Air Force Base

- Helen Mann, who tracked missiles and predicted impact on their landing

- Dr. Mildred Mitchell, creator of bionic parts and analyst of sleep-deprivation syndrome at the Air Force Avionics Laboratory, Wright-Patterson Air Force Base

- Ellen Ochoa, physicist and astronaut, led a research group working on optical systems for automated space exploration

- Lieutenant Dee O'Hara, the world's first space nurse

- Edith Olson, army chemist, who reduced the size of rocket parts to save weight and space and promote greater use of fuel and who devised a tiny ceramic chip for storing electronic systems

- Eleanor Pressly, NASA mathematician, who integrates the operations for sounding rockets and plans for moon observatories and space platforms

- Rita Rapp, inventor of a survival kit including an automatic hypodermic needle to inject pain reliever through a space suit

- Lee Curry Rock, researcher at Wright-Patterson Air Force Base and inventor of protective coverings for space suits

- Laurel van der Wal Roennau, head of bioastronautics at the Space Technology Laboratories, Inc., and assessor of weightlessness on mice lodged in missile nose cones

- Dr. Nancy Grace Roman, NASA astronomer, who oversees experiments carried by orbiting satellites

- Pat Rydstrom, a researcher in the study of speech in space and the effects of extremes of temperature and vibrations on the body

- Margaret Rhea Seddon, member of both the Discovery 1981 team and the Columbia 1991 team

- Barbara Short, NASA aerospace engineer, who studied aerodynamic stability by photographing small-scale models and studying the resulting shadowgraphs for details to aid in increasing the precision of trajectories

- Marjorie Townsend, a NASA electronic engineer who designs orbiting weather satellites
- Dr. Tsu-tzu Tsai, chemist at Wright-Patterson Air Force Base, who studies the reaction of synthetic alloys to differing temperatures

Budget: $

Sources:

Abell, George. *Exploration of the Universe*. Saunders College Press, 1991.

"Atlantis and Mir: Together at Last." *Birmingham Post-Herald*, June 30, 1995, B2.

Hoversten, Paul. "Shuttle Aloft; Docking Ahead." *USA Today*, June 28, 1995, 1, 11A.

Hoyt, Mary Finch. *American Women of the Space Age*. Atheneum, 1966.

Martin, Jean, gen. ed. *Who's Who of Women in the Twentieth Century*. Crescent Books, 1995.

Williams, Janis. "Women with the Right Stuff." *Vital*, September–October 1981, 20–24.

Alternative Applications: Assign a team to create a mock-interview with female workers launching and analyzing the aims and results of space missions. Create a list of questions to ask women workers and trainees such as Mary Cleave, Bonnie Dunbar, Anna Fisher, Shannon Lucid, Judy Resnik, Rhea Seddon, and Kathryn Sullivan, questions such as:

- when they became interested in science, math, astronomy, medicine, flight, or engineering
- what childhood hobbies developed into adult studies, for example, astronomy and rocketry
- what advice successful female scientists, medical technicians, engineers, astronomers, inventors, and mathematicians would give young girls who want careers in space technology

Conclude the study by using desktop publishing software to create a brochure to distribute in a guidance counselor's office, PTA workshop, careers and jobs fair, science museum, or public library.

Women *and disease*

Age/Grade Level or Audience: High school health or biology class; medical careers program; science fair entry.

Description: Present a unit of study on women and disease.

Procedure: Conduct a thorough reference study of disease as it has historically impinged on the lives of women. Research data and draw graphs detailing the number of women affected by HIV, AIDS, heart disease, breast and ovarian cancer, fibromyalgia, degenerative hip disorders, alopecia, clinical depression, bipolar mood swings, PMS, and other debilitating physical conditions. Comment on such trends as the rise in AIDS among heterosexual women and the perplexing nature of fibromyalgia in female joint ailments as well as advances in medicine that have lessened the mortality rate for conditions such as breast cancer. Describe diagnoses, prevention, and treatment for each.

Budget: $

Sources:

A.D.A.M.: The Inside Story. A.D.A.M. Software, 1995. (CD-ROM)

Adler, Tina. "Pill Ups Cancer Risk in Young Women." *Science News,* June 10, 1995, 356.

———. "Progestin Fails to Cut Breast Cancer Risk." *Science News,* June 17, 1995, 375.

Cornacchia, Cheryl. "Across the Divide." *Montreal Gazette,* June 12, 1995, 1–2D.

"Depression's Birth in Poor Women." *Science News,* June 17, 1995, 381.

Doress-Worters, Paula B., and Diana Laskin Siegal. "Managing Menopause." *Modern Maturity,* May–June 1995, 40–42, 76–77.

Fackelmann, Kathleen. "Variations on a Theme: Interplay of Genes and Environment Elevates Cancer Risk." *Science News,* May 6, 1995, 280–81.

Hassibi, Mahin, M.D. "Why Change the World . . . When You Can Have a Prozac Moment?" *On the Issues,* summer 1995, 28–40, 57.

"Implant Fiasco: A Case of Putting Safety Last." *USA Today,* May 17, 1995, 12A.

Marsa, Linda. "Can Vitamin Creams Combat Wrinkles?" *Health,* May–June 1995, 49–51.

"No Harm in Adding a Little Testosterone." *Science News,* May 13, 1995, 294.

Painter, Kim. "Women in 40s Overestimate Breast Cancer Risk." *USA Today,* May 17, 1995, 4D.

Payer, Lynn. "Hell Week." *Ms.,* March 1989, 28, 30–31.

Rees, Gillian. "Dying of Perfection: Overcoming Chronic Fatigue Syndrome." *Yoga International,* March–April 1995, 13–16.

Wallis, Claudia. "The Estrogen Dilemma." *Time,* June 26, 1995, 46–53.

Alternative Applications: Compose an oral report on the interrelation between mental health and physical ailments. Differentiate between emotional causes for PMS and bipolar mood swings or physical or environmental causes; for example, light deprivation in winter or water retention and its effects on brain tissue in women suffering from PMS. Discuss how the recent diagnosis of PMS has changed traditional public perception of the "moodiness" characteristic of some women, now known to have its cause in a physiological hormone imbalance.

Women *in the stars*

Age/Grade Level or Audience: Elementary mythology unit; astronomy, Latin, or science club presentation; bulletin board focus.

Description: Present a program on constellations denoting mythic women.

Procedure: Present a map, handout, or transparency of the heavens and note names and astronomical symbols or abbreviations that denote women or female creatures in mythology. Invite volunteers to account for each name and its importance to astronomers. Include these:

Andromeda, the chained woman	Hydra, the water monster
Bellatrix, the amazon	Libra, the woman holding the scale
Cassiopeia, the woman in the chair	the Pleiades
Coma Berenices, Bernice's hair	Virgo, the maiden

Explain the circumstances of each myth; for example, who was Andromeda, why and where was she chained, and who set her free.

Budget: $

Sources:

Constellations. Running Press, 1993.

Feldman, Susan, ed. *The Story-Telling Stone.* Laurel, 1965.

Fraser, Frances. *The Bear Who Stole the Chinook.* Douglas & McEntyre, 1990.

Galant, Roy A. *The Constellations: How They Came to Be.* Macmillan, 1991.

Lovi and Tiron. *Men, Monsters, and the Modern Universe.* Willmann-Bell, 1989.

Motz, Lloyd, and Carol Nathanson. *The Constellations: An Enthusiast's Guide to the Night.* Doubleday, 1988.

Sanford, John. *Observing the Constellations.* Simon & Schuster, 1990.

Seiger, Barbara. *Seeing Stars: A Book and Poster about the Constellations.* Putnam Group, 1993.

Sesti, Giuseppe M. *The Glorious Constellations.* Abrams, 1991.

Verdet, Jean-Pierre. *The Sky: Mystery, Magic and Myth.* Abrams, 1992.

Zigel, F. *Wonders of the Night Sky.* Beekman Publications, 1994.

Alternative Applications: Have students create a bulletin board, mobile, posters, or wall hanging depicting women in constellations from numerous mythologies, including the Chinese Spinning Maid, the Blackfoot tale of the moon and seven singers, and the Arapaho girl who wanted to touch the sky.

Social *science*

Anti-female *taboos*

Age/Grade Level or Audience: High school women's studies research; media feature; women's religious group lecture; civic club presentation; public library focus.

Description: Explore traditional taboos against women from customs around the globe.

Procedure: Present facts on anti-female taboos through history. Lead a discussion on the causes and results of these practices:

- advertisement of girls for marriage
- banishment from religious observances during menstruation
- female castration, genital mutilation, and infibulation
- humiliation, banishment, and divorce of barren women
- huts for "unclean" women during their menstrual periods
- infanticide of female infants
- ostracism and excommunication of "fallen women"
- purda or harems confining women from free movement or contact with strangers
- ritual bathing for menstruating women
- scalding or murder of women who give birth to female infants
- taboos against women touching weapons
- terrifying puberty rites
- veils or burkhas covering the face, head, arms, legs, and hair

Budget: $

Sources:

Abrahamsen, Valerie A. *Women and Worship at Phillippi.* Astarte Shell Press, 1995.

Ahmed, Leila. *Women and Gender in Islam.* Yale University Press, 1995.

Brooks, Geraldine. *Nine Parts of Desire: The Hidden World of Islamic Women.* Doubleday, 1995.

Divakaruni, Chitra Banerjee. *Arranged Marriage.* Anchor, 1995.

Fritsch, Julie, and Sherokee Ilse. *The Anguish of Loss.* Wintergreen Press, 1992.

Goodwin, Jan. *Price of Honor: Muslim Women Lift the Veil of Silence on the Islamic World.* Little, Brown, 1995.

Lorch, Donatella. "Unsafe Abortions Take Toll." *New York Times,* June 5, 1995, n.p.

Our Feet Walk the Sky: Women of the South Asian Diaspora. Feminist Press, 1995.

Shaarawi, Huda. *Harem Years.* Feminist Press, 1995.

Winnifrith, Tom. *Fallen Women in the Nineteenth-Century Novel.* St. Martin, 1994.

Alternative Applications: Lead a what-if scenario: a discussion of a system of reproduction by which both parents possess wombs, both parents menstruate, and either parent can choose to gestate and give birth to a child. Consider other variations, for example, colorless menstrual fluids or transparent wombs through which parents can watch their infant grow from a fertilized embryo to labor and delivery. Discuss how taboos against girls and women would alter and how men would value the gift of creating life.

Bonding *as friends*

Age/Grade Level or Audience: High school sociology discussion; media feature; college sociology lecture; women's studies research topic; civic club presentation; stress management or women's shelter course.

Description: Compose a series of lectures or essays on women friends.

Procedure: Collect audiotapes, interviews, historic letters or journal entries, or essays from women who have maintained a close association with female friends. Enumerate the value of a woman-to-woman network or support system. Mention these benefits:

- sounding board for frustration, grief, or stress
- source of applause and encouragement for achievements
- mirror of feelings and misgivings about age and aging
- repository of memories and humor
- gift to the self

Conclude the collection with a monograph or scrapbook honoring lengthy friendships between women in history such as Susan B. Anthony and Elizabeth Cady Stanton or Jane Addams and Ellen Gates Starr. Make your work available at a women's center, public library, women's study class, hospital, hospice, or nursing home.

Budget: $$$

Sources:

Blieszner, Rosemary. *Adult Friendship.* Sage, 1992.

Boyd, Julia. *Girlfriend to Girlfriend: Everyday Wisdom and Affirmations from the Sister Circle.* E.P. Dutton, 1995.

Faber, Doris. *Love & Rivalry: Three Exceptional Pairs of Sisters.* Viking Press, 1993.

Shanley, Mary K. *She Taught Me to Eat Artichokes: The Discovery of the Heart of Friendship.* STA-Kris, 1993.

Welty, Eudora, and Ronald A. Sharp, eds. *The Norton Book of Friendship.* W. W. Norton, 1991.

Alternative Applications: Draw up a list of requirements or expectations from an imaginary best friend in whom to confide personal thoughts and feelings. Like Anne Frank and the persona of Kitty, her diary, express imagined views on events and changes in everyday life during a historic era, such as the Civil War. Round out the activity by replying in the voice and spirit of the imaginary friend.

The descent *of woman*

Age/Grade Level or Audience: Middle school social studies unit; college anthropology and sociology research topic; formal women's history symposium.

Description: Present a woman-centered view of early human life.

Procedure: Using Elaine Morgan's *The Descent of Woman* as a text, have volunteers read aloud significant passages stressing Morgan's ideas on the importance of females to nomadic neolithic tribes. Emphasize the following points from the introduction:

- Tribes valued fertility and procreation as a means of self-preservation. Tribal goddess figures featured prominent hips, bellies, and breasts as symbols of strong womanhood, tribal strength, and blessings from the gods.

- The birth of healthy, strong infants promised a secure future to the group. A tribe on the move to better hunting grounds or warmer winter quarters would have moved no faster or farther than could pregnant women, lactating women, and women carrying or leading toddlers.

- The value of women could never be supplanted by a male-focused tribe orientation because early people understood that both genders played a vital role in group survival.

Assign individual chapters to groups for reading, discussion, summary, and presentation to the group. Question group leaders about possible stereotyping and misconceptions in male-centered theories. Discuss the contention that no society can devalue either sex without risking a skewed social system, unnatural growth pattern, and discontent.

Budget: $

Sources:

Leakey, Lewin. *Origins Reconsidered.* Doubleday, 1991.

Leakey, L. S., et al., eds. *Adam or Apes: A Sourcebook of Discoveries About Early Man.* Schenkman Books, 1982.

Leakey, Mary, et al., eds. *The Olduvai Gorge.* Cambridge University Press, 1993.

Leakey, Richard E. *Origin of Humankind.* BASC, 1994.

———. *Origins Reconsidered: In Search of What Makes Us Human.* Doubleday, 1992.

Leakey, Richard E., and Roger Lewin. *Origins: What New Discoveries Reveal about the Emergence of Our Species and Its Possible Future.* Viking Penguin, 1991.

———. *People of the Lake.* Avon, 1979.

Leakey, Richard E., and L. Jan Slikkerveer, eds. *Origin and Development of Agriculture in East Africa: The Ethnosystem Approach to the Study of Early Food Production in Kenya.* ISU-TSCP, 1991.

Lepowsky, Maria. *Fruit of the Motherland: Gender in an Egalitarian Society.* University of Wisconsin, 1993.

Montagu, Ashley. *Natural Superiority of Women.* CLLR, 1992.

———. *Touching.* HR, 1986.

Morgan, Elaine. *The Aquatic Ape.* Madison Books, 1984.

———. *The Descent of the Child.* Oxford, 1995.

———. *The Descent of Woman.* Madison Books, 1985.

Morris, Desmond. *Body Talk.* CRNP, 1995.

———. *The Naked Ape.* Dell, 1973.

Alternative Applications: Contrast Morgan's view of the value of a strong mother-child bonding system with the theories of Desmond Morris, Louis Leakey, Richard Leakey, Dian Fossey, Jane Goodall, Maria Lepowsky, or Ashley Montagu. What pragmatic images do you find in Morgan that other theorists lack? Are there places where Morgan oversteps her theory by forcing a romantic or sentimental picture on early societies? What do recent digs in Egypt's Valley of the Kings, the Olduvai Gorge, and China add to the evaluation of woman's role in early society? What have Mary Leakey's studies of fossils done for the positioning of humanity in history and for explaining the early use of tools and the development of the family?

From *a position of strength*

Age/Grade Level or Audience: Middle school creative writing or humanities round table; book club or literary society symposium; Friends of the Library discussion group; local Women's History Month handout; science fair exhibit.

Description: Discuss women's strengths in overcoming odds on the way to achievement.

Procedure: Present stories of famous women who have called on physical, emotional, and intellectual strengths to help them overcome adversity or sex prejudice. Include these women:

- Aung San Suu Kyi, Burmese freedom fighter, placed under house arrest from 1988–1995

- Barbara McClintock, biologist, whose rejection by her mother made her an outcast from the family, but set her on a course to greatness in genetic research

- Camille Claudel, French sculptor, who escaped her mentor's jealousy and sexism and established her own career in art

- Esther Forbes, who contended with visual problems while she researched the history of indentured servants in Boston as a background for her young adult classic, *Johnny Tremain*

- glass sculptor Ginny Ruffner, who battled the debilitating effects of a car accident

- Isadora Duncan, whose children drowned, leaving her desolate, but who continued to dance as an expression of her emotion

- Jackie Joyner-Kersee, severely asthmatic athlete, who controlled her respiratory problems and became a leading figure in women's sports

- Jackie Torrence, America's foremost storyteller, who had to overcome stuttering in order to tell the lively animal tales that draw audiences to her

- Laura Ingalls Wilder, whose writing career began late in life after the loss of her husband and a child

- Marianne Faithfull, singer and composer, who battled drug addiction

- Oprah Winfrey, a survivor of incest, who used her experiences to develop compassion for others

- Rose Hawthorne Lathrop, a visiting nurse who escaped spousal abuse to establish a career helping others

Make a list of these and other sources of strength: education, exercise, religion, self-esteem, medical treatment, reading, friends, family, support groups, and determination. Discuss which of these methods have worked in combination to assist bright, contributing women in achieving their goals. Use as a model Barbara McClintock, who compromised with her belligerent mother in order to complete an education and set out on her own. Facing ridicule from the scientific community as "the corn lady" for her study of pollination patterns, McClintock persevered and earned a Nobel Prize for her concept of "jumping genes."

Budget: $

Sources:

Aronson, Billy. *They Came from DNA*. W. H. Freeman, 1993.

Bailey, Brooke. *The Remarkable Lives of 100 Women Artists*. Bob Adams, 1994.

————. *The Remarkable Lives of 100 Women Healers and Scientists*. Bob Adams, 1994.

————. *The Remarkable Lives of 100 Women Writers and Journalists*. Bob Adams, 1994.

Dash, Joan. *The Triumph of Discovery: Women Scientists Who Won the Nobel Prize*. Julian Messner, 1991.

Fradin, Dennis. *Heredity*. Children's Press, 1992.

Gonick, Larry, and Mark Wheelis. *The Cartoon Guide to Genetics*. HarperCollins, 1991.

Griffin, Lynne, and Kelly McCann. *The Book of Women: 300 Notable Women History Passed By*. Bob Adams, 1992.

Guernsey, JoAnn Bren. *Sexual Harassment: A Question of Power*. Lerner, 1996.

Heiligman, Deborah. *Barbara McClintock: Alone in Her Field*. W. H. Freeman, 1994.

Hillyer, Barbara. *Feminism and Disability*. University of Oklahoma, 1993.

Kittredge, Mary. *Barbara McClintock*. Chelsea House, 1991.

Mary on the Move Series. Instructional Video, 1990. (Video)

McFarland, Rhoda. *Coping with Sexism*. Rosen, 1990.

Merker, Hannah. *Listening: Ways of Hearing in a Silent World*. Harper, 1994.

Morris, Jenny. *Pride Against Prejudice: Transforming Attitudes to Disability*. New Society Publishers, 1993.

O'Connor, Barbara. *Barefoot Dancer: The Story of Isadora Duncan*. Lerner, 1994.

Ratto, Linda Lee. *Coping with Being Physically Challenged*. Rosen, 1991.

Roberts, David. "Men Didn't Have to Prove They Could Fly, But Women Did." *Smithsonian*, August 1994, 72–81.

Wells, Melanie. "Bookshelf." *USA Today*, June 27, 1995, 4B.

Alternative Applications: Have participants list the people who have contributed to the studies of cytology and genetics. Place Dr. Barbara McClintock among those who have discovered significant genetic behaviors. Include founder Gregor Mendel and Nobel Prize-winner George Beadle, who sought Barbara's advice on his study of genetics. Discuss how an understanding of genetics may lead to cures for X-linked disease.

Global *helpers*

Age/Grade Level or Audience: Civic club presentation; media feature or series; social work research topic; home demonstration club presentation; religious study; mall or public library display.

Description: During Women's History Month, applaud female philanthropists.

Procedure: Post maps of locales where women volunteers, now widely recognized, have distributed food, assisted refugees, attended sick children, mounted fund-raising campaigns, collected medical supplies, and comforted crisis victims. For example, note the work of these women:

- Adrienne Germain, director of the International Women's Health Coalition

- Catholic nun Mother Teresa

- Clara Barton, founder of the American Red Cross

- forest developer Augusta Molnar

- humanitarian Clara Hale

- Jane Addams, settlement house founder

- Jasleen Dhamija, craft developer for the U.N. Economic Commission

- Mali Rural Women's Advisory Service founder Miriam N'diaye Thiam

- Peace Corps worker Lillian Carter

- peace protester Aung San Suu Kyi

- UNICEF volunteer Audrey Hepburn

- Vina Mazumdar, director of the Centre for Women's Development Studies

Summarize the results of these women's efforts at solidifying communities worldwide by contributing to nutrition, health, hygiene, education, housing, job training, clean environment, stable government, non-violence, and peace.

Budget: $

Sources:

Bruce, J., and D. Dwyer, eds. *A Home Divided: Women and Income in the Third World.* Stanford University Press, 1988.

Fischer, Lucy R., and Kay B. Schaffer. *Older Volunteers: A Guide to Research and Practice.* Sage, 1993.

Helen Keller International Vitamin A Technical Assistance Program. Helen Keller Institute, 1993.

Leonard, Ann, ed. *Seeds: Supporting Women's Work in the Third World.* Feminist Press, 1989.

Longacre, Doris. *More-with-Less Cookbook.* Herald, 1976.

Alternative Applications: Have local workers contribute to the "more with less" concept by collecting recipes for nutritious main-dish meals of minimum cost. Include staple foods traditionally prepared by women around the world; for example, tofu, millet, dal, chickpeas, posole, orzo, soybeans, breadfruit, and quinoa. Introduce cooks to these and other food concepts used by low income women everywhere:

- emphasizing foods that are in season over canned, dried, or frozen supplies

- maximizing cheaper foods, particularly dried beans, fresh vegetables, eggs, fruit, herbs, and simple carbohydrates

- sharing from a communal wok or pot

Organize a tasting show at a local mall at which cooks from various ethnic backgrounds prepare simple, traditional, and nutritious appetizers, snacks, or meals. Decorate with place mats, natural-fiber cups and plates, and linens.

Inner *resources*

Age/Grade Level or Audience: Middle school creative writing outline; book club or literary society presentation; Friends of the Library project; local panel discussion celebrating Women's History Month.

Description: Outline a report on the source and substance of creativity, stamina, and drive unique to a notable and successful woman.

Procedure: Have students research biographies, memoirs, letters, journals, databases, catalogs, newspapers and periodicals, and reference works such as *Who's Who of Women, Current Biography, Who's Who in the Southwest,* and *Who's Who in Education* for data on female artists, performers, athletes, and activists from a variety of historical times, nations, races, and religions. Ask these and other general questions:

- What event, sense impression, mood of the times, or conviction appears to have inspired extraordinary work and dedication from this woman?

- How does a female perspective permeate this person's work?

- What aspect of dedication or creativity appears to be a universal quality among artists and activists?

- What single quality or performance sets this person apart from others in the same field?

- How has this person accepted or challenged adversity or loss?

- What type of honor or recognition seems appropriate to this woman's life and work?

- What other people have profited from studying or knowing these women and their achievements?

Apply your study to these successful women:

- foreign correspondent and reporter Christiane Amanpour

- Judy Baca, muralist

- Elizabeth Anne Baylor, known as "Mother Seton" since founding Sisters of Charity

- Shirley Temple Black, U.S. ambassador to Ghana

- sports photographer Muriel Brousseau

- Evelyn Cisneros, ballerina

- Camille Claudel, sculptor

- Dorothy Day, religious leader and settlement worker

- Red Cross president Elizabeth Dole

- Elizabeth Flynn, co-founder of the American Civil Liberties Union

- Reverend Jan Fortune-Wood, Anglican minister

- Pamela Harriman, U.S. ambassador

- Lillian Hellman, playwright

- gospel singer Mahalia Jackson

- Barbara Jordan, speaker, teacher, and political activist

- Kiri Te Kinawa, opera singer
- Betty La Duke, print maker
- Vilma Martinez, civil rights attorney
- Rosa Parks, civil rights activist
- Jade Snow Wong, author and potter

Budget: $

Sources:

Bushnell, Dana E., ed. *Nagging Questions: Feminist Ethics in Everyday Life.* University Press, 1995.

Emert, Phyllis Raybin, ed. *Women in the Civil War: Warriors, Patriots, Nurses, and Spies.* Discovery Enterprises, 1995.

Hornblower, Margot. "Grief and Rebirth." *Time,* July 10, 1995, 65.

"How Stars Overcame Obstacles." *Ebony,* July 1995, 68–72.

MacPherson, Kay. *When in Doubt, Do Both: The Times of My Life.* University of Toronto Press, 1995.

McDonald, Lynn. *The Women Founders of the Social Sciences.* Carleton University Press, 1995.

McPherson, Stephanie Sammartino. *Peace and Bread: The Story of Jane Addams.* Lerner Books, 1993.

The Miracle Worker. Critics Choice, n.d. (Video)

Painter, Charlotte. *Gifts of Age.* Chronicle Books, 1985.

Palmer, Ann Therese Darin. "The Quiet Inside." *Notre Dame Magazine,* winter 1994–1995, 24–28.

Plum, Nancy. "A Tribute to Margaret Hawkins." *Chorus,* February 1994, 4.

Randolph, Laura B. "Oprah!," *Ebony,* July 1995, 22–28.

Roberts, David. "Men Didn't Have to Prove They Could Fly, But Women Did." *Smithsonian,* August 1994, 72–81.

A Salute to Historic Black Women. Empak Enterprises, 1984.

Steif, William. "World Class Haitian." *Caribbean Week,* March 4, 1995, 43.

Zurkowsky, Herb. "Frozen on Film." *Montreal Gazette,* June 5, 1995, 8D.

Alternative Applications: Have students compose a list of questions as part of a hypothetical interview with a contrasting pair of achievers, for example:

- activists Shirley Chisholm and Bella Abzug
- Sister Elizabeth Kenny and physician Dr. May Chinn
- columnists Ellen Goodman and Erma Bombeck
- Southwest expressionist Georgia O'Keeffe and impressionist painter Mary Cassatt
- tennis star Billie Jean King and dogsledder Susan Butcher

Encourage questions that stress common ground, such as a liberal education, dedication, professionalism, practice, self-esteem, networking, mentorships, determination, and courage. Include questions about how each interviewee has met and overcome failure, lack of funds, discouragement, disillusionment, sex prejudice, discrimination, harassment, or physical or emotional handicap. Emphasize the approach of each woman to making and achieving goals.

Psychology *and adolescent literature*

Age/Grade Level or Audience: Middle school literature discussion; adolescent psychology course monograph; media feature or book review; college history or sociology research project; women's studies focus; church school presentation; civic club program; public library display or handout.

Description: Describe adolescent conflicts in the lives of female characters as portrayed in classic young adult literature.

Procedure: Divide participants in groups to list and discuss conflicts and attempts at resolution of female characters from different eras in noteworthy young adult fiction. Consider these issues:

- acceptance in Bette Greene's *Summer of My German Soldier*
- autonomy in Avi's *The True Confessions of Charlotte Doyle*
- challenge in Ron Jones's *The Acorn People*
- coping in Susan Beth Pfeffer's *The Year Without Michael*
- fear of loss in Margaret Rostkowski's *After the Dancing Days*
- flight in Lois Lowry's *The Giver*
- forgiveness and tolerance in Lorraine Hansberry's *A Raisin in the Sun*
- identity in Carson McCullers's *Member of the Wedding*
- independence in Bill Cleaver and Vera Cleaver's *Where the Lilies Bloom*
- insecurity in Irene Hunt's *No Promises in the Wind* and Norma Fox Mazer's *After the Rain*
- loss in Cynthia Rylant's *Missing May*
- physical handicap in Cynthia Voigt's *Izzy Willy-Nilly*
- poverty in Mildred Taylor's *Roll of Thunder, Hear My Cry* and Betty Smith's *A Tree Grows in Brooklyn*
- racism in Sheila Gordon's *Waiting for the Rain*
- solitude in Scott O'Dell's *Island of the Blue Dolphin*
- survival skills Jean Craighead George's *Julie of the Wolves*

Discuss how children from different time periods are depicted as coping or reacting to similar situations. Cite examples of attention-getting, manipulation, dishonesty, wish fulfillment, and projection. Discuss the verisimilitude of child behaviors and dialogue. Propose alternate solutions to each problem.

Budget: $

Sources:

Boyd, Julia. *Girlfriend to Girlfriend: Everyday Wisdom and Affirmations from the Sister Circle*. E. P. Dutton, 1995.

Carmona, Jose. *Adolescent Blues*. Kendall-Hunt, 1992.

De Montreville, Doris, and Donna Hill, eds. *Third Book of Junior Authors*. H. W. Wilson, 1972.

Snodgrass, Mary Ellen. *Characters from Young Adult Literature*. Libraries Unlimited, 1991.

Weiner, Pamela, and Ruth M. Stein, eds. *Adolescents, Literature and Work with Youth*. Haworth Press, 1985.

Alternative Applications: Propose various treatments and coping measures to assist fictional girls with difficulties. For example, propose methods of strengthening the body to offset the amputated leg of the title character in Cynthia Voigt's *Izzy Willy-Nilly* or less drastic living arrangements for the title character in Avi's *The True Confessions of Charlotte Doyle*. Compose a list of illogical behaviors, for example, the murder of a teacher in Lois Duncan's *Killing Mr. Griffin* or a visit to a psychic in Cynthia Rylant's *Missing May*. Set a story in a different historical time period and discuss the ways that both problems and solutions would change.

The wifely *muse*

Age/Grade Level or Audience: High school history essay; history club presentation; media feature; debate club topic; term paper focus.

Description: Compose an essay on the importance of often overlooked wives to their husbands' success.

Procedure: Study the combined efforts of famous couples and the achievements that seem to rest solely on the male. Give examples from the lives of these couples:

- author Nadezhda Krupskaya and revolutionary leader Vladimir I. Lenin
- engineer Washington Roebling and overseer Emily Roebling, builders of the Brooklyn Bridge
- medical missionaries Albert and Helena Breslau Schweitzer
- musicians Clara and Robert Schumann
- physicists and mathematicians Albert Einstein and Mileva Maric Einstein
- Jessie Benton Fremont and John Fremont, California pioneers, politicians
- researchers/writers Theodora and Alfred Kroeber
- writers Fanny Vandegrift and Robert Louis Stevenson
- writers Mary Wollstonecraft and Percy Bysshe Shelley

Budget: $

Sources:

Axelrod, Dr. Alan, and Charles Phillips. *What Every American Should Know About American History*. Bob Adams, 1992.

Clark, Judith Freeman. *American Women in the Twentieth Century*. Prentice Hall, 1987.

Clark, Gillian. *Women in Late Antiquity: Pagan and Christian Lifestyles*. Oxford University Press, 1993.

Clement, J., ed. *Famous Deeds of American Women*. Corner House, 1975.

Dennis, Denise. *Black History for Beginners*. Highsmith, 1992.

Fantham, Elaine, et al. *Women in the Classical World*. Oxford University Press, 1994.

Great Lives from History: American Women Series. Salem Press, 1995.

Griffin, Lynne, and Kelly McCann. *The Book of Women: 300 Notable Women History Passed By*. Bob Adams, 1992.

Hampton, Henry, and Steve Fayer. *Voices of Freedom: An Oral History of the Civil Rights Movement from the 1950s through the 1980s*. Bantam Books, 1990.

Harrison, Cynthia, ed. *Women in National Politics*. University Publications of America, 1995.

Karlekar, Malavika. Introduction to *Changing Lives: Life Stories of Asian Pioneers in Women's Studies*. Feminist Press, 1995.

Rubin, Merle. "The Muse Who Midwifed Treasure Island." *Wall Street Journal*, June 1995, 5A.

Trager, James. *The People's Chronology*. Henry Holt, 1992.

Alternative Applications: Present similar information about couples who nurtured each other's separate interests, as is the case in these companionships:

- herder Anna Steichen Sandburg and poet and biographer Carl Sandburg

- prima ballerina Margot Fonteyn and Panamian diplomat Roberto Emilio Arias

- Queen Victoria, ruler of the British Empire, and Prince Albert, architect

- Author and feminist Simone de Beauvoir and existentialist philosopher Jean-Paul Sartre

Women *as caregivers*

Age/Grade Level or Audience: Adult stress management lecture; media series; nursing course series; home demonstration club presentation; religious group study; civic club brochure.

Description: Organize a symposium that discusses the role of caregiver traditionally assumed by women.

Procedure: Address the fact that caregiving is a task traditionally left primarily to females in society. Stress that throughout history women have juggled family, job, and caregiving. Present these facts:

- 80% of caregivers are women

- 61% of caregivers are married

- Over a third continue in the role of caregiver more than a decade

- 90% of caregivers work outside the home

- 41% provide care more than 40 hours per week

- 88% harbor no distaste for caregiving

- Around 75% do the job without assistance

- 50% of caregivers fear they are overtaxed with responsibilities

Share with participants that resources are now available to help alleviate the stress associated with the "caregiving" role. Provide brochures, books, magazines, support groups, online services, and toll-free numbers, for example:

American Association of Retired Persons
Caregiver Resource Kit
202-434-3525

America Online
Better Health and Medical Forum
800-827-6364

CompuServe
Retirement Living Forum
800-848-8199

National Alliance for Caregiving
conferences and books on caregiving
301-718-8444

National Association for Area Agencies on Aging
consulting and referrals
800-677-1116

Older Women's League (OWL)
666 Eleventh Street NW
Washington, DC 20001

The Sandwich Generation
magazine, $14 per year
Box 132
Wickatunk, NJ 07765-0132

Budget: $$$

Sources:

Carter, Rosalynn. *Helping Yourself Help Others: A Book for Caregivers.* Times Books, 1995.

Century of Women: Work and Family. Instructional Video, 1994. (Video)

Hellmich, Nanci. "Rosalynn Carter on Caregiving Quandaries." *USA Today,* November 1, 1994, 8D.

Hunter-Gadsden, Leslie. "Instant Family." *Heart and Soul,* winter 1994, 58–64.

Lawlor, Julia. "Why Companies Should Care." *Working Woman,* June 1995, 38–40.

Norris, Jane. *How to Care for Your Parents: A Handbook for Adult Children.* Storm King, 1992.

Schaaf, Anne Wilson. *Beyond Therapy, Beyond Science: A New Model for Healing the Whole Person.* Harper, 1992.

Sheehy, Gail. "The Pursuit of Passion: Lessons from the World of the Wisewomen." *Modern Maturity,* 42–846, 89.

Starkman, Elaine Marcus. *Learning to Sit in the Silence: A Journal of Caretaking.* Papier-Mache Press, 1993.

Warren, Larkin. "Survival Lessons." *Working Woman,* June 1995, 46–49.

Willis, Clint. "When to Talk About Money," *Working Woman,* June 1995, 42–45, 72–73, 76.

Alternative Applications: Organize a "Thanks a Bunch" flower show honoring local female caregivers. Separate entries into divisions: orchids, roses, arrangements, house plants, and bonzai. Incorporate volunteers in the presentation of red, blue, and white ribbons for first, second, and third place in each show. Present each volunteer a corsage or wrist bouquet. Decorate invitations, posters, and walls with large posies featuring the name of the organization at the center, e.g., Hospice, Foster Parents, PFLAG, Girls Clubs of America, Girl Scout Candy Stripers, or Gray Ladies. Add petals and inscribe names of volunteers on each.

Women *and crisis*

Age/Grade Level or Audience: Middle school multidisciplinary presentation; school newspaper feature; college history or sociology focus; home-school study; stress management lecture; public library materials display.

Description: During Women's History Month, present a salute to a girl or woman who has weathered handicaps, disasters, or barriers.

Procedure: Select a woman with whom the audience is not familiar, such as Zlata Filipovich, a young diarist in Sarajevo, or Rigoberta Menchu, Guatemalan freedom fighter and winner of the Nobel Peace Prize. Emphasize coping skills and emphasis on optimism and hard work as a means of overcoming hardship. Use this study of Esther Hautzig as a model:

- Esther Rudomin Hautzig, born October 18, 1930, in Vilna, Poland, came from a comfortable merchant-class family and lived in a cultivated Jewish milieu. In June 1941, soldiers armed with bayonets arrested Esther's mother, father, aunt, and paternal grandparents. The adults were charged with capitalist activities. Her grandfather was carried by cattle car to a labor camp.

- The Rudomins traveled twelve miles per hour for six weeks by dank, foul-smelling railcar containing a V-shaped toilet hole opposite the door and a bucket of water with one ladle. Meals consisted of vegetable soup. Their only dietary supplement consisted of the black bread, cheese, and goat milk that vendors sold along the way.

- At Rubtsovsk, Russia, a crude village in the Altai Territory, the family moved into barracks ten miles from a gypsum mine. Esther was assigned to potato fields, her mother, Raya, dynamited gypsum, Grandmother Anna shoveled gypsum, and father Samuel drove a cart. In the distance were the steppes, Ukraine's grasslands, which swept westward to Siberia. By winter, Esther learned to fear and dread extremes of weather on the Steppes. Some deportees died from exposure. Summer, with its hot, dry winds, brought drought.

- On July 30, 1941, Polish prisoners profited from an amnesty agreement between England and Russia. The Rudomins moved nearer the village, earned minimum wage, and shopped at the village market on their day off. Esther, chaperoned by her grandmother, bartered for root vegetables, meat, flour, and toasted sunflower seeds by trading their family's silk goods. They shared substandard rooms with other Polish families. Raya worked in a bakery job; Samuel kept books for a contractor.

- Subsistence improved after the family found warmer housing. Esther enrolled in the fifth grade of the local school, which was decorated with pictures of Lenin, Stalin, Marx, and Engels. She shared textbooks with a hostile student and suffered the ill will of her teacher, who resented Esther's middle-class upbringing. Esther studied the Cyrillic alphabet, the Russian language, and literature. Bronchitis slowed her progress; she made up lessons with visits to the town library.

- The family moved to a dirt-floored hovel and dug a vegetable bed. Local authorities forced them to shelter an unfortunate Ukrainian shoemaker who had lost a leg in a Siberian prison camp. Esther's father was recruited as a forced laborer for the combat zone. A crop failure made the second winter more grueling than the first. To heat their hut, Esther gathered coal and wood shavings from the nearby railroad tracks.

- Esther began knitting custom-made orders, which she bartered for milk and food. A local couple took an interest in the Rudomins and offered soap and a few luxuries. In the summer months, Esther toiled to win a declamation contest by reciting Tatyana's dream from Alexander Pushkin's *Eugene Onegin*. She lost because the teacher would not allow her to compete and forced her to return home for shoes.

- That spring, villagers grew hostile at the sight of German prisoners of war. In May 1945, Germany surrendered to the Allies. Germans had by that time slaughtered most of Esther's friends and relatives; the secret police had decimated the Rudomin home. On March 15, 1946, the Rudomins set out by train to join

Samuel in Lodz. Esther inadvertently left her fellow passengers at one stop and would have been left behind if a friend had not put her on the train. In April the four remaining Rudomins returned home.

- Esther immigrated to the United States, enrolled at Hunter College, and wed pianist Walter Hautzig, father of their two children. She worked at G. P. Putnam's Sons and Thomas Y. Crowell before beginning her career as a writer in the 1960s. She published her autobiography, *The Endless Steppe* (1968), which won numerous awards.

Budget: $$$

Sources:

Boyd, Julia. *Girlfriend to Girlfriend: Everyday Wisdom and Affirmations from the Sister Circle.* E. P. Dutton, 1995.

De Montreville, Doris, and Donna Hill, eds. *Third Book of Junior Authors.* H. W. Wilson, 1972.

Emert, Phyllis Raybin, ed. *Women in the Civil War: Warriors, Patriots, Nurses, and Spies.* Discovery Enterprises, 1995.

Englebert, Victor. "Drought Threatens the Tuareg World." *National Geographic,* April 1974, 544–71.

Hautzig, Esther. *The Endless Steppe.* Harper & Row, 1968.

Vanzant, Iyanla. *The Value in the Valley: A Black Woman's Guide Through Life's Dilemmas.* Simon & Schuster, 1995.

Alternative Applications: Present students with a selection of nonfiction audiocassettes or videotapes describing the stress of catastrophe caused by war, racial hatred, religious bigotry, sexism, or natural disaster. Have groups make notes on important moments in the lives of females when they refused to be cowed or overwhelmed by such circumstances. Consider these titles and sources:

Anne Frank: The Diary of a Young Girl (Recorded Books)

Currer Bell, Esq. (Charlotte Brontë) (Harper/Caedmon)

The Flame Trees of Thika (Elspeth Huxley) (Books on Tape)

Great American Women's Speeches (Harper/Caedmon)

Maya Angelou (Recorded Books)

Florence Nightingale (Books on Tape)

Lorraine Hansberry Speaks Out (Harper/Caedmon)

Mary, Queen of Scots (Books on Tape)

My Life with Martin Luther King, Jr. (Coretta Scott King) (Harper/Caedmon)

Out of Africa (Isak Dinesen) (Books on Tape)

Pocahontas (Recorded Books)

The Road from Coorain (Jill Ker) (Recorded Books)

The Story of My Life: Helen Keller (Recorded Books)

A Woman Named Jackie (Jackie Kennedy) (Books on Tape)

A Woman of Egypt (Jehan Sadat) (Books on Tape)

Zelda (Zelda Sayre Fitzgerald) (Books on Tape)

Zlata's Diary (Zlata Filipovich) (Recorded Books)

Speech *and debate*

Apron-*string tales*

Age/Grade Level or Audience: K–4 library reading circle; Friends of the Library presentation; teacher education lecture; writer's seminar; religious or women's studies research; storytelling contest.

Description: Initiate a storytelling session for children that incorporates a study of women from other cultures and time periods.

Procedure: In conjunction with a study of other cultures and time periods, include a storytelling session by writing a series of prompts, topic sentences, or opening paragraphs on separate pieces of paper. Place slips in a container and allow a volunteer to select one and read it aloud to the group. Have students work together to create a story based on the line or invite individuals to make up a short tale featuring a female persona, whether animal, human, or fantasy being, such as a talking tree or bird. Use the following starters as models:

- Content to be in the shade of her parasol, Sela strolled along the banks of the Niger River in search of an alligator called Pepper.

- Did you know that Rafaella had a wonderful grandmother named Nadya who knitted and knitted away the night? Let me tell you Nadya's story.

- Near Katmandu, Princess Tonna watched as dark trees grew from the ground, higher and higher into the Himalayan sky.

- Ginger picked up the broom handle and glared at the pitcher. She would show them that a girl could play stickball.

- For many months, Maria's family worked the fields and divided the best of their crops with the owner, Mr. Boshears.

- Caddie and Lisette raced to finish picking the best huckleberries. The stone griddle was almost hot and Mama was going to make flapjacks.

Budget: $

Sources:

Brooke, Pamela. *Communicating Through Story Characters.* University Press, 1995.

Burr, Constance. "A Year of One's Own." *Humanities,* July/August 1995, 39–42.

The Story Lady. NBC Products, 1994. (Video)

Torrance, Jackie. *The Importance of Pot Liquor.* August House, 1994.

Tripp, Valerie. "Annoying Annabelle." *American Girl,* July/August 1995, 39–46.

Underwood, Paula. *The Walking People: A Native American Oral History.* A Tribe of Two Press, 1995.

Alternative Applications: Lead a laboratory writing study for adults who want to learn to write children's fiction. Teach a variety of methods, particularly memoirs of childhood, creation of imaginative animal personae, dialogue and dialect, surprise twists, humanistic themes, and satisfying endings. Have partners take turns with peer editing and working through difficulties. Encourage writers to give a fair share of aggressive action and significant scenes to female characters, whether animal or human.

Communicating *strength*

Age/Grade Level or Audience: College business canvass; Women's Professional Women training program; Friends of the Library project; local panel discussion celebrating Women's History Month.

Description: Study the careers of successful businesswomen such as Lillian Gilbreath, Olive Beech, or Madame C. J. Walker to determine the communications skills that have led to their achievement and satisfaction.

Procedure: Have participants study the communication techniques and business strategies that have placed successful women in positions of power. Consider these necessary adjuncts to self-fulfillment:

- Avoid non-committal, self-deprecatory, or timid replies to direct questions.

- Study and capitalize on personal strengths while conquering such weaknesses as feelings of inferiority because of body size or voice quality.

- List fears, particularly the fear of speaking to a large group or of negotiating with power figures. Make a worst-case analysis of each and determine what risks are involved, e.g., provoking laughter.

- Make eye contact with workers and managers. Shake hands firmly. Steady a quaking voice or tremor before speaking by grasping chair arms or lectern.

- Acknowledge tense situations, gossip, or ridicule and deal with it quickly, efficiently, and even-handedly. Then forget it.

- Anticipate criticism. Select the most helpful and put it to use. Keep your sense of humor.

- Maintain a vigorous, all-business stance. Channel your energies into improvements rather than into whining or what-ifs.

- Negotiate with the intent to provide all parties the best possible outcome. Listen to the approach of adversaries and competitors. Utilize their best arguments to your advantage.

- Credit yourself for all accomplishments. Keep an updated resume that lists your strategies, achievements, and staff responsibilities. Don't neglect opportunities to thank others for input, hard work, and loyalty.

- Speak with a blend of humility and self-esteem. Refuse to be overlooked, manipulated, or discounted. Recognize your own worth to the company.

Budget: $

Sources:

CareerTrack
3085 Center Green Dr.
Boulder, CO 803031-5408
800-788-5478
FAX: 800-832-9489

International Training in Communication
(formerly International Toastmistress Club)
2519 Woodland Dr.
Anaheim, CA 92801
714-995-3660

National Businesswomen's Leadership Association
6901 W. 63rd St.
P.O. Box 2949
Shawnee Mission, KS 66201-1349
800-258-7246
FAX: 913-432-0824

Alternative Applications: Organize a one-on-one improvisation of business nightmares: interview, potential promotion, potential reassignment, tactical error, business failure, change in management, new management, reduction in force, firing. Play both sides of any situations that threaten your efficiency. Have observers make positive suggestions about posture, voice tone, control, self-image, and logic. Keep a journal of your daily successes and attempts to correct oversights and errors.

Debating *power*

Age/Grade Level or Audience: High school speech contest; drama activity; debate club topic; Toastmaster's Club presentation; Friends of the Library or American Association of University Women series; Business and Professional Women's League speech.

Description: Organize a speech contest that presents the historic basis of the lives of disenfranchised women from around the world.

Procedure: Create a series of guidelines for a speech contest that references the past in stressing the need for a balance of power within nations, cities, churches, schools, businesses, and homes. Use the following terms and their implications to human rights as a starting point:

affirmative action	male primacy	Roe vs. Wade
Blackstone Code	Napoleonic Code	Sharia
endogamy	paterfamilias	spouse abuse
Equal Rights Amendment	patriapotestas	suffrage
female infanticide	patriarchy	suttee
genital mutilation	pornography	women's suffrage

Have participants focus on a single issue and provide either handouts or visual aids to provide historic background, emphasize their perspectives, and state their aim for gender equality. Publicize the results of the contest in a newsletter, the media, or via direct mail.

Budget: $$$

Sources:

Ahmed, Leila. *Women and Gender in Islam.* Yale University Press, 1995.

Brooks, Geraldine. *Nine Parts of Desire: The Hidden World of Islamic Women.* Doubleday, 1995.

Divakaruni, Chitra Banerjee. *Arranged Marriage.* Anchor, 1995.

Furio, Joanne. "What You Had to Say About Pornography." *Ms.,* January/February 1995, 24–28.

Goodwin, Jan. *Price of Honor: Muslim Women Lift the Veil of Silence on the Islamic World.* Little, Brown, 1995.

Jhabvala, Ruth Prawer. *Heat and Dust.* Peter Smith, 1988.

Lorch, Donatella. "Unsafe Abortions Take Toll." *New York Times,* June 5, 1995.

Morgan, Robin. *Sisterhood is Global.* Doubleday, 1984.

Our Feet Walk the Sky: Women of the South Asian Diaspora. Feminist Press, 1995.

Papers of the NAACP. University Publications of America, 1995.

Sexuality, Sex Education, and Reproductive Rights. University Publications of America, 1995.

Shaarawi, Huda. *Harem Years.* Feminist Press, 1995.

Simmons, Judy D. "Did Joycelyn Elders Ever Stand a Chance?" *Ms.,* March/April 1995, 90–93.

Visionary Voices: Women on Power. Women Make Movies, 1994. (Video)

Walker, Alice. *Possessing the Secret of Joy.* Simon & Schuster, 1992.

Alternative Applications: Have debate participants bring research to provide background data on numerous topics as a means of establishing dialogue on significant issues. Use these as models:

- Title IX legislation requires that state supported educational institutions provide equal access for females and males to all programs offered.

- U.N. action on clitoridectomy requires that women seeking asylum for themselves and their female children receive immediate and preferential treatment.

- Any binding legislation that directly or covertly denies women access to abortion can be circumvented by the U.S. Attorney General as an obstruction of justice and discriminatory in nature.

- Distribution of property in a divorce settlement must provide both parties with a full disclosure of assets and offer court-appointed arbitration in order to establish an equitable division of property and trust funds for minor children.

End *the war with Eleanor!*

Age/Grade Level or Audience: Middle school or high school history or speech class; drama club presentation.

Description: Lead a presidential campaign for a notable woman from history.

Procedure: Have participants choose a woman from history they believe would have made a good president, prime minister, or premier and design her campaign. Begin by creating a packet of information that highlights her views, accomplishments, and strengths as a leader. Be persuasive and use active language—always stick to the facts. Use the following compilation of data for Eleanor Roosevelt as an example:

- devoted early life to work among the settlements of New York

- active in the Red Cross and the League of Women Voters

- joined the Women's Trade Union League in 1922 and worked for fair labor legislation in New York

- chaired the women's division of the Democratic Party; organized and staffed the Women's Division of the Democratic National Committee

- spokesperson for minority groups, Jewish war refugees, American youth, and female workers

- in 1934 began her own radio program; in 1936 began writing a syndicated news column, "My Day"

- resigned from the Daughters of the American Revolution in 1939 when they prohibited black opera singer Marian Anderson from performing at Constitution Hall in Washington, D.C.

- in 1937 served as cochair of the No-Foreign-War Crusade

- staunch supporter of American troops during World War II

- named a delegate to the United Nations' Charter Commission; proved an integral force in U.N. policy shaping; in 1946 elected chair of the U.N. Commission on Human Rights; drafted the Universal Declaration of Human Rights

- appointed chair of the President's Commission on the Status of Women

Divide the participants into groups to create slogans, banners, a party platform, bumper stickers, and radio and television advertisements.

Budget: $$

Sources:

Clark, Judith Freeman. *Almanac of American Women in the Twentieth Century.* Prentice Hall, 1987.

Hoff-Wilson, Joan, and Marjorie Lightman, eds. *Without Precedent: The Life and Career of Eleanor Roosevelt.* Indiana University Press, 1984.

Roosevelt, Eleanor. *On My Own.* Harper, 1958.

————. *This I Remember.* Harper, 1949.

————. *This is My Story.* Harper, 1937.

Weidt, Maryann N. *Stateswoman to the World: A Story About Eleanor Roosevelt.* Lerner, 1991.

Alternative Applications: Have students actually run the campaign and hold elections—in the class or school-wide. Distribute pamphlets promoting your female candidate and broadcast on the school radio or local-access television program. Identify a worthy male opponent from the same time period and hold weekly debates covering issues relevant to the historical period. Post the results of the election during Women's History Month.

Making *a case for equality*

Age/Grade Level or Audience: High school writing assignment; term-paper topic; school newspaper focus; women's studies symposium; newspaper feature.

Description: Compose a speech that delves into the historic basis behind current thinking on topics that touch women's lives, family, careers, safety, and civil rights.

Procedure: Create opportunities for participants to study the history behind such thorny women's issues as the glass ceiling, home responsibilities, need for flexible work assignments, job harassment, pink collar ghettos, and affirmative action. Consider putting the following data into a speech on sexual harassment in the workplace:

- Since the Anita Hill-Clarence Thomas hearings in 1991, Americans and the businesses they work for have been more attuned to sexual harassment and the resultant firings and lawsuits.

- According to the Civil Rights Act of 1991, victims have a right to sue for back pay and compensatory and punitive damages, for which companies are held responsible.

- If companies negate charges or take no action on complaints, they can face a heavy financial liability.

- Definition of harassment covers *quid pro quo* demands of sex in exchange for promotions or to save a job; a second level of harassment is unwelcome advances, jokes, obscene posters, and unwelcome touching or fondling.

- Muddying the issue is the climate of suspicion, fears of reverse discrimination, company paranoia, and exaggerated or retaliatory claims that have since ensued.

- Before such claims arise, companies are wise to publicize their policies, demonstrate their awareness of the problem with training workshops, and initiate management discussion. Follow-up should include extra study of legal and financial ramifications and additions to policy manuals.

- A sensible method of studying a harassment claim is to question all people involved in incidents, gather corroborating information from witnesses, and record all data on paper, film, video, or database. Punishment should fit the level of misconduct and apply equally to workers and executives.

- The conclusion of any complaint should reach all company employees in the form of written notice of corrective action, punishment, or discipline. Intimate records and harmful interviews should remain confidential.

Present speeches in a factual style that maintains a non-militant tone. Emphasize the advantages of cooperative efforts between men and women to achieve a state wherein both sexes can work with equal peace of mind. Preserve presentations in print and on tape for evaluation or reference.

Budget: $$

Sources:

Aaron, Titus, and Judith Isaksen. *Sexual Harassment in the Workplace: A Guide to the Law and a Research Overview for Employers and Employees.* McFarland & Co., 1993.

Kruger, Pamela. "See No Evil." *Working Woman,* June 1995, 32–35, 64, 77.

Sakol, Jeannie. *Men Just Don't Get It.* Barricade Books, 1993.

Vanhyning, Memory L. *Cross Signals: How to Say NO to Sexual Harassment.* Infotrends, 1993.

Alternative Applications: Videotape commentary from archived news programs, forums, special media reports, and interviews that focus on a specific "women's" issue from the past three decades; for example, the use of a presidential candidate's stance on abortion as an arbitrary test of his or her worthiness. Have participants study a selection of commentary to locate the following information:

- topic and subtopics

- hidden agenda of reporter, interviewer, or producer of film or documentary

- tone and style of presentation

- motivation of speaker

- conclusion of interviewer or reporter

- suggested remedies for inequality or the loss of relevant civil rights

Break down each commentary and ask for critical response to the following: length of piece, voice control, audience response, credibility of interviewer or reporter, and preparation. Suggest that participants re-examine the commentary for errors in logic, particularly polarizing, irrelevant information, non sequiturs, bandwagon approach, and glittering generalities.

Mothers *and daughters*

Age/Grade Level or Audience: Literary round table; women's center symposium; book club or women's religious group presentation; women's studies lecture or research topic; newspaper column; radio or television presentation.

Description: Present a roundtable discussion that focuses on well-known alliances of mothers and daughters.

Procedure: As part of a lecture series, have women discuss their roles as mothers and/or daughters. As a jumping off point, discuss the relationship between the following well-known mothers and daughters from history:

- Laura Ingalls Wilder and her daughter, journalist Rose Wilder Lane

- Queen Elizabeth II and her public role as mother of Princess Anne

- the affection between Rose Kennedy and her famous and influential daughters and daughters-in-law

- the relationship between Ursula Le Guin and her mother, writer Theodora Kroeber

- Elizabeth Cady Stanton and daughter Harriot Stanton Blatch, who shared political sympathies

- the style and influence of Grace Kelly on her daughter Caroline or of Jackie Kennedy Onassis on daughter Caroline Kennedy Schlossberg

- mother and daughter scientists and Nobel Prize winners Marie and Irene Curie

- the tumultuous relationship between Nancy Reagan and daughter Patty Davis

Budget: $$$

Sources:

Bonner, Elena. *Mothers and Daughters*. Random House, 1993.

Converse, Kimberley, and Richard Hagstrom. *Myth of the Perfect Mother*. Harvest House, 1993.

Cornacchia, Cherylk. "All About Mothers." *Montreal Gazette,* May 29, 1995, 1C.

Hathaway, Mary. *Celebrating Motherhood*. Lion USA, 1993.

Thevenin, Tine. *Mothering and Fathering: The Gender Differences in Child Rearing.* Avery, 1993.

Alternative Applications: Hold a weekly or monthly round table on the subject of motherhood. Include interested female writers, speakers, journalists, and teachers as well as social workers, nurses, ministers, and young women who have questions or comments concerning the role of mothering in their lives. Focus the session on these and other topics:

- achieving a balance of power
- adopted or foster daughters and their mothers
- favoritism toward brothers
- the generation gap
- impending loss from disease or age
- mixed values and religious beliefs
- money and inheritance
- moving from being a daughter to an independent woman
- repressed anger and dreams
- single-parent homes
- support systems
- working mothers

Appoint a scribe to tape or keep notes for a possible newsletter or update on future topics and speakers. With participants' permission, publish oral expressions of the changing role of mothers or invite a journalist to observe, photograph, and report on the group's progress.

Salute *to nurses*

Age/Grade Level or Audience: High school speech model; history lesson; debate club model; scout troop or women's religious group presentation; women's studies topic; newspaper column.

Description: Study the style of a speech once delivered by a notable woman.

Procedure: Invite participants to study the words of Lt. Col. Bonnie L. Jennings, who received the Dr. Anita Newcomb Award for the Army Nurse of the Year in 1990. Comment on the images she invokes:

- "to reestablish the military nursing corps that had been dormant since the end of the Civil War"
- "the science of caring"
- "to be successful as individuals and as a Corps"
- "when to push and when to let up"
- "the staff nurse who is the linchpin between caring and the patient"
- "to nurture her ethic of caring"

Why does Jennings place emphasis on team effort and on her pride in being part of the Corps? Suggest other comments she might have made about the heritage of military nursing.

Budget: $

Sources:

Donovan, Sharon, ed. *Great American Women's Speeches.* Harper Audio Caedman, n.d. (Audiocassette)

Ravitch, Diane, ed. *The American Reader.* HarperCollins, 1990.

"Salute to the Military." *Daughters of the American Revolution Magazine,* November 1990, 852–53.

Straub, Deborah Gillan, ed. *Voices of Multicultural America.* Gale Research, 1996.

Vigil, Evangelina. *Woman of Her Word: Hispanic Women Write.* Arte Publico Press, 1987.

Alternative Applications: Select a speech composed by a famous woman; for example, Mary McLeod Bethune's 1933 speech to members of the Chicago Women's Federation or Coretta Scott King's 1993 address before the National Press Club in Washington, D.C. Practice delivery of select images to create a single impression to the audience. Use audio or video recording to preserve your progress in making a forceful address. Request a volunteer committee to critique your work, and supply them with a list of your objectives.

Speaking *their minds*

Age/Grade Level or Audience: High school drama improvisation; debate club activity; women's studies dramatization; newspaper column.

Description: Hold a series of re-enactments or oral interpretations of speeches made by famous women or fictional women drawn from drama, poetry, novels, short stories, songs, movies, hymns, and screenplays.

Procedure: Invite participants to a public reading of significant speeches, dramatic soliloquies, letters, diary or journal entries, fictional dialogues, poems, song lyrics, or essays by or about famous women or fictional characters. Select a panel of judges to critique each presentation by a pre-determined set of criteria. Use this weighted list:

- delivery (35 points)
- posture (10 points)
- voice control (20 points)
- gestures (10 points)
- understanding of major points (15 points)
- overall performance (10 points)

Consider these possibilities:

- Abigail Adams's letter to her husband, March 31, 1776
- Rudolfo Anaya's characterization of the *curandera* in *Bless Me, Ultima*
- Susan B. Anthony's "Women's Right to Vote" and "Are Women Persons?"
- Harriette Arnow's description of motherly love in *The Dollmaker*
- Rachel Carson's summation of the threat to nature in *Silent Spring*
- Lorna Dee Cervantes's "Refugee Ship"

- Fanny Crosby's "Blessed Assurance"

- selections on war from Zlata Filipovich's *Zlata's Diary*

- reflective selections from Anne Frank's *The Diary of a Young Girl*

- Charlotte Perkins Gilman's "Women and Economics"

- Lillian Hellman's description of friendship in *Julia*

- Helen Hunt Jackson's "A Century of Dishonor"

- Barbara Jordan's speech to the 1992 Democratic Presidential Convention

- Emma Lazarus's "The New Colossus"

- Alice Duer Miler's "Evolution"

- Toni Morrison's Nobel Prize acceptance speech

- Lucretia Mott's "A Demand for the Political Rights of Women"

- Ernestine Potowski Rose's "Remove the Legal Shackles from Women"

- Margaret Sanger's "The Right to One's Body"

- Margaret Chase Smith's "Declaration of Conscience"

- Elizabeth Cady Stanton's "Address to the Legislature of New York on Women's Rights"

- Gloria Steinem's explanation of self-esteem in *Revolution from Within*

- Corrie ten Boom's description of aid to traumatized war victims in *The Hiding Place*

Budget: $$$

Sources:

Anderson, Judith. *Outspoken Women: Speeches by American Reformers, 1635–1935.* Kendall/Hunt, 1984.

Donovan, Sharon, ed. *Great American Women's Speeches.* Harper Audio Caedman, n.d. (Audiocassette)

Ravitch, Diane, ed. *The American Reader.* HarperCollins, 1990.

Vigil, Evangelina. *Woman of Her Word: Hispanic Women Write.* Arte Publico Press, 1987.

Welty, Eudora, and Ronald A. Sharp, eds. *The Norton Book of Friendship.* W. W. Norton, 1991.

Alternative Applications: Establish an annual speech contest for teenage girls sponsored by a civic club, school system, or community. Issue a yearly woman's rights-related topic and a copy of rules that limit each presentation to 5–10 minutes. Encourage contestants to practice diction, delivery, posture, voice control, gestures, understanding of major points, and stage presence. Select judges of both sexes who have experience with teenagers, particularly librarians, teachers, scout and 4-H leaders, guidance counselors, and parents. Offer a plaque, gift certificate, book, or scholarship to the winner and appropriate prizes to runners-up. Publicize the event by holding it in a public hall, church, library or museum, meeting room, or radio or television studio. Consider the following speech topics:

- Challenging Girls to Achieve in the Sciences

- Interpreting Women's Place in the Pulpit and Parish

- The Heroine Today

- The Woman Who Has Inspired Me

- Women and the Pioneer Spirit

- Women Who Dare

- Working Mothers

Maintain a trophy case or honor scroll of annual winners.

A strong *voice for women*

Age/Grade Level or Audience: Middle school communication unit; drama term-paper topic; scout or 4-H project; genealogical or historical society program; women's studies lecture; newspaper column; Toastmaster's Club brochure; Women's History Month presentation.

Description: Compose notes for an oral report on the courageous oratory of suffragist Lucretia Mott.

Procedure: Describe the life of Lucretia Mott through important events and speeches that helped turn the tide of public opinion in favor of suffragists. Summarize these events:

- Lucretia Mott's first visit to the Philadelphia Free Produce Society in 1826

- four years later, her friendship with orator William Lloyd Garrison, publisher of the first American abolitionist journal, *The Liberator*

- formation of the Female Anti-Slavery Society, over which Mott presided and served as enlister of membership and funds

- 1838, speech urging members of the Anti-Slavery Convention of American Women to allow blacks to attend the meeting

- World's Anti-Slavery Convention in London, England, where she was prohibited from speaking, but, by joining Elizabeth Cady Stanton and William Lloyd Garrison, greeted and talked with admirers of the American movement to end the slave trade

- January 1843, speech at the Unitarian Church announcing a formal boycott of the United States Congress, which had invited her to speak if she refrained from mentioning slavery. President Tyler met privately with both Mott and Ralph Waldo Emerson

- 1849, "Discourse on Woman," which claimed equality for women as a right rather than as a favor from men, whom she accused of subjugating women

- July 12, 1863, address to Union soldiers, even though, as a Quaker and pacifist, she disapproved of war; two years later she expressed her desolation at the murder of President Lincoln, whose signature had ended slavery

- alliance with the Friends Association for the Aid and Elevation of Freedmen, for whom she demanded equal access to public transportation

- Abington Peace Meeting in 1875, "A Faithful Testimony Against Bearing Arms." Even nearing the end of her life, she championed peace. At her funeral, no one felt equal to the task of speaking a eulogy

Budget: $

Sources:

Anderson, Lydia M. *Champion for Children's Health.* Lerner, 1994.

Annie and the Stars of Many Colors. CfA Publications, n.d. (Video)

Ferris, Jeri. *Go Free or Die: A Story About Harriet Tubman.* Lerner, 1988.

————. *Native American Doctor: The Story of Susan LaFlesche Picotte.* Lerner, 1991.

————. *Walking the Road to Freedom: A Story About Sojourner Truth.* Lerner, 1988.

Guernsey, JoAnn Bren. *Hillary Rodham Clinton: A New Kind of First Lady.* Lerner, 1993.

————. *Tipper Gore: A Voice for the Voiceless.* Lerner, 1994.

McPherson, Stephanie Sammartino. *Peace and Bread: The Story of Jane Addams.* Lerner, 1993.

————. *The Worker's Detective: A Story About Dr. Alice Hamilton.* Lerner, 1992.

Mitchell, Barbara. *Between Two Worlds: A Story About Pearl Buck.* Lerner, 1988.

O'Connor, Barbara. *Mammolina: A Story About Maria Montessori.* Lerner, 1992.

Saidman, Anne. *Oprah Winfrey: Media Success Story.* Lerner, 1990.

Sawyer, Kem Knapp. *Lucretia Mott: Friend of Justice.* Discovery Enterprises, 1991.

Weidt, Maryann N. *Stateswoman to the World: A Story About Eleanor Roosevelt.* Lerner, 1991.

Alternative Applications: Create a speech similar to the oratory of these and other female speakers:

Joan Baez	Barbara Jordan	Phyllis Schlafly
Pearl Buck	Coretta King	Pat Schroeder
Rachel Carson	Maria Montessori	Lucy Stone
Shirley Chisholm	Mother Teresa	Sojourner Truth
Isadora Duncan	Lucretia Mott	Harriet Tubman
Dr. Alice Hamilton	Ann Richardson	Sarah Winnemucca
Zora Neale Hurston	Eleanor Roosevelt	Molly Yard

Strike directly at the intended focus, whether freedom for all people, an end to war, or an equalization of human rights. Name places in the world where war, slavery, and discrimination continue to lessen human capabilities and darken lives. Cite some words of comfort and challenge from these historic speakers to elevate your oratory. Give credit by naming date and place where the lines were originally delivered.

Telling *a life*

Age/Grade Level or Audience: High school speaker's bureau lecture; debate club activity; book club or women's religious group presentation; women's studies lecture.

Description: Invite a series of speakers to summarize the strengths of famous women.

Procedure: Invite participants to address a gathering using notes, handouts, posters, banners, slides, overhead projection, or video. Use the biography of Ann Landers as a model:

- pen name of Eppie Friedman, twin of Pauline Esther, who writes under the pseudonym Abigail Van Buren and is read five days a week by 90 million readers in 1,200 newspapers.

- recipient of the Albert Lasker award and honoraria from National Family Service Association, National Council on Alcoholism, Lions Club, American Cancer Society, AMA, and the Women's Almanac

- born the last of five children in Sioux City, Iowa, July 4, 1918; married at age 21 to Jules Lederer, owner of Budget Rent-a-Car, father of Margo, their only child. Sold cookware door-to-door in California with her husband after World War II. Volunteered for the Democratic party in Eau Claire, Wisconsin.

- asked to assist the "Ask Ann Landers" columnist for the *Sun-Times* in August 1955; worked as the replacement Ann Landers and put troubled people in touch with Legal Aid, Alcoholics Anonymous, Parents and Friends of Lesbians and Gays, and mental health counselors

- succeeded with the column and published pamphlets on dating and behavior; employed a staff of three to read over 2,000 letters per day; traveled, visited military hospitals, and appeared on television

- accepted a divorce after her husband fell victim to depression and alcohol abuse; continued her honest person-to-person approach to other people's problems

Encourage speakers to focus on a variety of studies about women's achievements in the arts, politics, healing, invention, the military, business, or industry. Place a time limit on each speech to save time for questions.

Budget: $$$

Sources:

Grossvogel, David I. *Dear Ann Landers.* Contemporary Books, 1987.

Hobbs, Nancy. "Ann Landers Refuses to Be an 'Expert' on Anything." *Salt Lake City Tribune,* July 27, 1987.

Howard, Margo. *Eppie: The Story of Ann Landers.* G. P. Putnam's Sons, 1982.

Martin, Susan. "Dear Abby, Dear Ann." *Buffalo, New York, News,* July 3, 1988.

Yolesias, Linda. "The Angel of Advice." *New York Daily News,* January 10, 1988.

Alternative Applications: Make a chart of highs and lows in the lives of famous twentieth-century women. Using Ann Landers as an example, note her difficulties with a jealous twin sister and daughter Margo's hard times rearing Ann's three grandchildren after a difficult divorce. Point to the strengths that emerge from women with strong characters when challenges threaten their stability and self-confidence. Apply this study to other notable women such as Benazir Bhutto, Oprah Winfrey, Aretha Franklin, Golda Meir, Indira Gandhi, and Winnie Mandela.

Telling *a story*

Age/Grade Level or Audience: All-ages storytelling session; teacher education focus; reading theater topic; Toastmaster's Club monograph; Friends of the Library or American Association of University Women presentation.

Description: Organize a Women's History Month class in storytelling.

Procedure: Teach a group of interested storytellers or griots how to use gesture, eye contact, cadence, questions, hand claps, puppets, dual personae, and other methods to enliven stories.

Use these and other women's stories, myths, legends, history, Bible stories, and current events as models:

- a Caribbean sugar worker's rhythmic story-song sung in the field over lunch
- a clipping from the sports page about a female Olympic star
- a Maori woman recounting a dreamtime myth
- Amy Tan's *The Moon Lady*
- a Cahuilla performance story
- salute to Christa McAuliffe's dedication to teaching and to space travel
- Japanese story talk
- Navaho or Hopi creation myth
- one of Jackie Torrence's favorite animal tales
- a rereading of Ruth's dedication to Naomi, her destitute mother-in-law
- Sacajawea's journey from the Dakotas to Fort Clatsop on the Pacific Coast and her unexpected reunion with her brother
- the Greek myth of Echo
- the love story of Heloise and Abelard
- the Navaho return from the Long Walk
- the saga of pioneer women on the Oregon Trail

Provide participants with feedback on speed and quality of presentation or with audio- or video-tape for study and evaluation. Offer opportunities to try new works from a variety of genres.

Budget: $$$

Sources:

Brooke, Pamela. *Communicating Through Story Characters.* University Press, 1995.

Burr, Constance. "A Year of One's Own." *Humanities,* July/August 1995, 39–42.

Goss, Linda, and Marian E. Barnes. *Talk That Talk: An Anthology of African-American Story-telling.* Touchstone, 1989.

Her Own Words: Pioneer Women's Diaries. Instructional Video, 1986. (Video)

Porter, A. P. *Jump at de Sun: The Story of Zora Neale Hurston.* Lerner, 1992.

Randall, Laura. "Lois Hassell-Habteyes: Why Things Come to Be." *Humanities,* September/October 1994, 25.

Richards, Bernadette. "Women, Rejoice." *Barbados Advocate,* March 8, 1995, 16.

Roberts, Nancy. *North Carolina Ghosts and Legends.* University of South Carolina Press, 1991.

Sherman, Josepha. *Told Tales.* Silver Moon Press, 1995.

Tan, Amy. *The Moon Lady.* Macmillan, 1992.

Torrance, Jackie. *The Importance of Pot Liquor.* August House, 1994.

Tripp, Valerie. "Annoying Annabelle." *American Girl,* July/August 1995, 39–46.

Underwood, Paula. *The Walking People: A Native American Oral History.* A Tribe of Two Press, 1995.

Winnebago Women: Songs and Stories. Instructional Video, 1992. (Video)

Alternative Applications: Set up a speaker's bureau through the public library or a community college. List names of experienced volunteers and professional readers, storytellers, griots, or drama teams in a card file or database. Indicate age level and major interests; for example, Native American women, female scientists and inventors, improvisationists, or tellers of women's myths or legends. Update the file with newcomers to the library or storytellers, readers, and actors recruited by Welcome Wagon.

Women *and the supernatural*

Age/Grade Level or Audience: High school oral library paper; debate club topic; book club or women's presentation; women's studies lecture; composition or speech contest; radio series.

Description: Compose a speech on women and the supernatural as represented in a wide range of literature.

Procedure: Select one of the following works. Compose a formal speech on the subject of women as supernatural characters. Use the following titles or choose works from your own reading:

- Ann Petry's *Tituba of Salem Village*
- Daphne du Maurier's *Rebecca*
- Edith Hamilton's *Mythology*
- Elizabeth George Speare's *Julie of the Wolves*
- Isabel Allende's *House of the Spirits*
- Jean Rhys's *Wide Sargasso Sea*
- Laura Esquival's *Like Water for Chocolate*
- Mary Stewart's Morgan le Fay in *The Hollow Hills*
- Nancy Roberts's *North Carolina Ghosts*
- Toni Morrison's *Beloved*

Discuss to what extent female characters have power over men or human fate. Comment on the nature of women as ghosts, witches, sylphs, goddesses, spirits, avengers, angels, sorceresses, portents, *curanderas,* or visionaries.

Budget: $

Sources:

Fowler, Samuel P. *Salem Witchcraft*. Heritage Books, 1992.

James, M. R. *Ghost Stories of an Antiquary*. Dover Books, 1994.

Petry, Ann. *Tituba of Salem Village*. HarperCollins, 1991.

Portrait of Jennie. Critics Choice, 1948. (Video)

Richards, Jeffrey J. *The Cry at Salem*. Paladin House, 1992.

Speare, Elizabeth. *The Witch of Blackbird Pond*. Dell, 1978.

Trask, Richard B., compiler. *Salem Village and the Witch Hysteria*. Jackdaw Publications, n.d. (Portfolio)

Alternative Applications: Contrast two works in which the supernatural or occult is performed by a male and a female. For example, contrast the change of persona in Robert Louis Stevenson's *Dr. Jekyll and Mr. Hyde* with a similar alteration in Rudolfo Anaya's *Bless Me, Ultima*. Likewise, contrast the spell of Morgan le Fay in Mary Stewart's *The Hollow Hills* with that of Merlin in Mary Stewart's *The Crystal Cave* or in Mark Twain's *A Connecticut Yankee in King Arthur's Court*.

Sports

A daughter's *reminiscence:* how Hans became an American

Age/Grade Level or Audience: Middle school drama or physical education reading; women's studies program; civic or booster club presentation.

Description: Lead a study of Elinor Nauen's "A Daughter's Reminiscence: How Hans Became an American."

Procedure: Read aloud the poem by Elinor Nauen. Explain words and sports terms such as these:

bolo tie	lackluster	stolid
catch-up game	lagniappe	symmetry
comeback	league	10th inning
diamond	naturalized	Twins
grand slam	Nazi Germany	wry
implication	Scandinavians	Yanks
infinity	shellacked	

Have the group discuss what must have inspired Elinor Nauen to write the poem. Stretch the discussion to cover a broader scope. Ask the younger participants about their views on women in sports. What sports challenge and excite them? For older participants, discuss the changing attitudes toward women's involvement in recreational and professional sports. Were they encouraged to be physically active when they were growing up? How does that affect them now? How do they translate these feelings toward their own daughters?

Budget: $

Sources:

Nauen, Elinor. "A Daughter's Reminiscence . . . How Hans Became an American." *Humanities,* July/August 1994, 12.

Nauen, Elinor, ed. *Diamonds Are a Girl's Best Friend: Women Writers on Baseball.* Faber & Faber, 1994.

Alternative Applications: Lead a choral reading of this poem and other memorable works by women sportswriters. Have volunteers play the part of the father and his daughter. Make an audiotape of the reading and place it in the library for others to enjoy.

Playing *the rackets*

Age/Grade Level or Audience: Elementary oral activity; audiotaping assignment; sports improvisation.

Description: Pair a notable female athlete and media representative for an interview.

Procedure: Introduce participants to the demanding world of competitive sports by pairing volunteers to play the roles of sports star and interviewer. Use this mock set of questions for tennis champ Evonne Goolagong as a model:

- What events in your childhood revealed your interest in sports?
- What other sports do you enjoy? Do you play them well?
- Which competitors have rattled your nerve?
- Against which tennis stars, male or female, have you wanted to play?
- When is your best time to practice? against whom? with what type of coaching?
- What skills have you developed since your turned pro?
- What is your advice to amateurs wanting to follow your example?

Conclude this session by having participants comb the library for sources of information about sports figures and sports history, and compiling a list of online, CD-ROM, microfiche, video, almanac and other reference books, and other sources of information.

Budget: $

Sources:

Da Silva, Rachel, ed. *Leading Out: Women Climbers Reaching for the Top.* Seal Press, 1995.

Guttmann, Allen. *Women's Sports: A History.* Columbia University Press, 1991.

Harrington, Denis J. *Top 10 Women Tennis Players.* Enslow, 1995.

LeCompte, Mary Lou. *Cowgirls of the Rodeo.* University of Illinois Press, 1993.

Sparhawk, Ruth M., Mary E. Leslie, Phyllis Y. Turbow, and Zina R. Rose. *American Women in Sport, 1887–1987.* Scarecrow Press, 1989.

Woolum, Janet. *Outstanding Women Athletes.* Oryx Press, 1992.

Alternative Applications: Hold a mock-debate between female sports stars from the past and rising "super stars." For example, from the world of tennis have participants play the roles of May Sutton, Billie Jean King, Martina Navratilova, Evonne Goolagong, Jennifer Capriati, Steffi Graf, and Monica Seles. Have "players" discuss these points: the pros and cons of competition; how the sport has changed from 1905 when May Sutton won at Wimbledon; women's acceptance into the professional sports arena; the evolution of the sport in their own lifetime, e.g., the increased size of tennis rackets.

Saddles *for ladies*

Age/Grade Level or Audience: High school health or history composition; women's studies topic; sports or booster's club presentation; fashion commentary.

Description: Describe the invention of the sidesaddle and its effect on women's travel, exercise, and leisure.

Procedure: Make sketches of the sidesaddle. Show various types of ladies' saddles and the details that make them functional, but awkward. Outline a lecture in which you discuss the point at which sidesaddles came into fashion and where they were first manufactured and popularized. Comment on the first women in Europe and the United States to abandon sidesaddles and ride astride. Include this information:

- The first saddle was designed in 400 A.D. Eight hundred years later, the sidesaddle is believed to have originated in Asia, as a pack saddle with a wooden footrest. The original European sidesaddle was manufactured in 1380 for women, who hooked their right leg around a "leaping head" to protect their virginity and delicate reproductive organs, particularly during jumps. Riding astride like men was considered too rough and unladylike. Ladies studied equestrian skills and prompted their show hacks, hunters, and jumpers on the left with the foot and on the right with a cane held in the right hand.

- The sidesaddle remained popular until the late nineteenth century, when female riders abandoned the constraint, imbalance, and awkward position. In 1912 Eleanor Sears's appearance astride a horse produced a scandal. The sidesaddle remained in use into the 1920s by women desiring to preserve the romance of the full riding skirt and womanly pose until former fashions gave place to jodhpurs, knickerbockers, and culottes.

Budget: $$

Sources:

Edwards, Elwyn Hartley. *The Encyclopedia of the Horse.* Dorling Kindersley, 1994.

The Fair Lady Aside: Her Saddles and Habits. World Sidesaddle Federation, 1990.

Griffin, Lynne, and Kelly McCann. *The Book of Women: 300 Notable Women History Passed By.* Bob Adams, 1992.

Jurmain, Suzanne. *Once Upon a Horse.* Lothrop, Lee & Shepherd, 1988.

Owen, Rosamund. *The Art of a Sidesaddle: History, Etiquette, Showing.* Trematon Press, 1984.

Alternative Applications: Design a wardrobe for a nineteenth-century female rancher, equestrian, breeder, or seller of horses that accommodates modesty, movement, and convenience for girls and women. Sketch these designs in several types of fabric for different climates, terrains, and work requirements.

Sports *puzzler*

Age/Grade Level or Audience: Middle school physical education class assignment; library research exercise; ESL study sheet; women's aerobics class or stress-reduction clinic handout; school newspaper sports page puzzle.

Description: Learn more about women in sports by solving the sports puzzler fill-in.

Procedure: As you locate answers to the seek-and-find puzzle on page 450, place them in the blanks below:

1. gymnast _____ Okino

2. runner Zola _____

3. tennis star Jennifer _____

4. skater _____ Thomas

5. _____ from Anchorage to Nome

6. Chris _____ tennis champ

7. black female athlete Althea _____

8. Steffi _____, net champ

9. _____ 500 racer

10. _____ Julie Krone

11. golf-great Nancy _____

12. tennis _____

13. basketball player _____ McGee

14. _____ star Michelle Gilman

15. cycle, swim, and _____ in the triathlon

16. Olympic _____ star Sonia Henie

17. climber Junnko _____

18. _____ aces Kim and Elaine Oden

19. Japanese-American skater Kristi _____

20. _____ winner Andra-Nina Davis

21. multiple winner of the Iditarod Susan _____

22. _____ star Beryl Burton

23. Olympic runner Mary _____

24. famous English Channel swimmer Gertrude _____

25. nickname of Florence Griffith Joyner, _____

26. _____ champ Babe Didrikson Zaharis

27. stock car racer Janet _____

28. tennis great Billie _____ King

29. _____ winner Tina Sloan

30. gymnast Mary _____ Retton

31. vaulter _____ Korbut

32. _____ star Lori Norwood

33. _____ champs Anita DeFrantz and Kitty Porterfield

34. _____ specialist Florence Arthaud

35. _____ winner Annemarie Moser-Pröll

36. _____ star Wilma Rudolph

37. net champ Virginia _____

38. speed skater _____ Blair

39. Meryl Streep, star of *River Wild*, a _____ endurance test

40. _____ great Fanny Workman

41. coach _____ Owens

42. _____ specialist Pat Smythe

43. swimmer _____ Chadwick

44. net champ Evonne _____

45. _____ winners Nadia Comaneci and Larissa Latynina

46. triathlon competitor _____ Goodjer

47. track pick Carol _____

48. court trendsetter _____ Navratilova

49. _____ medals in gold, silver, and bronze

50. _____ great Eleanora Sears

51. _____ star Karen Almond

52. "game and _____ winner Helen Willis Moody

53. dog-_____ run from Nome to Alaska

54. _____ stars Erin Baker and Paula Newby-Fraser

55. _____ -lifting champ Karyn Marshall

ANSWERS:

1. Betty	20. biathlon	38. Bonnie
2. Budd	21. Butcher	39. canoe
3. Capriati	22. cycle	40. cycling
4. Debi	23. Decker	41. DeDe
5. dogsledding	24. Ederle	42. equestrian
6. Evert	25. Flo-Jo	43. Florence
7. Gibson	26. golf	44. Goolagong
8. Graf	27. Guthrie	45. gymnastics
9. Indianapolis	28. Jean	46. Jenn
10. jockey	29. lacrosse	47. Lewis
11. Lopez	30. Lou	48. Martina
12. meets	31. Olga	49. Olympic
13. Pam	32. pentathlon	50. polo
14. racquetball	33. rowing	51. rugby
15. run	34. sailing	52. set
16. skating	35. skiing	53. sled
17. Tabei	36. tennis	54. triathlon
18. volleyball	37. Wade	55. weight
19. Yamaguchi		

```
S N N T O L Z I G N I L C Y C A L I N G O F Y
T O C U L A S E W A D E I Y S K A T I N G L T
E S S O R C A L P R O I B A C T R O P H E O T
E B U E S Y E K C O J F S A I L I N G T A J E
M I N D I A N A P O L I S E T T E N N E N O B
D G R E E M T O A E R O B I C S A A I S I L T
O E I R B A L D D E C K E R R R E N W K T Y E
G C D L A G D I U Q A T S H U J N I O C R M N
S N D E B U T C H U R H K T G O M A R A A P N
L E L O B C O E T E O G I U B C P A M R M I I
E R E S G H A V C S L I I G Y M N A S T I C S
D D S O Y I B E D T G E N O L H T A T N E P O
D L L R A N T R L R A W G L L A B E U Q C A R
I F A N O L H T A I B G O O L A G O N G R A F
N K V O L L E Y B A L L E W I S W I M M I N G
G T R I A T H L O N T I T A I R P A C A N O E
```

Budget: $$

Sources:

Connors, Martin, Diane L. Dupuis, and Brad Morgan. *The Olympics Factbook*. Visible Ink Press, 1992.

Da Silva, Rachel, ed. *Leading Out: Women Climbers Reaching for the Top*. Seal Press, 1995.

Guttmann, Allen. *Women's Sports: A History*. Columbia University Press, 1991.

Johnson, Susan E. *When Women Played Hardball*. Seal Press, 1995.

Katz, Helena. "When Winning Can Be a Clothes Call." *Montreal Gazette,* June 1, 1995, 1H.

Lewis, Linda. *Water's Edge: Women Who Push the Limits in Rowing, Kayaking and Canoeing*. Seal Press, 1995.

Martin, Jean, gen. ed. *Who's Who of Women in the Twentieth Century*. Crescent Books, 1995.

McWhirter, Norris, Steve Morgenstern, Roz Morgenstern, and Stan Greenberg. *Guinness Book of Women's Sports Records*. Sterling, 1979.

1995 Information Please Almanac. Houghton-Mifflin, 1995.

Schrof, Joannie M. "American Women Getting Their Kicks." *U.S. News and World Report,* June 19, 1995, 59.

Sparhawk, Ruth M., Mary E. Leslie, Phyllis Y. Turbow, and Zina R. Rose. *American Women in Sport, 1887–1987: a 100-year Chronology*. Scarecrow Press, 1989.

Terry, Ted. *American Black History: Reference Manual*. Myles Publishing, 1991.

Alternative Applications: Use the following information to create a rebus, scrambled words, or crossword puzzle about women winners at the 1992 summer Olympics:

archery: South Korean women's team

balance beam: Tatiana Lisenko

cycling: Kathryn Watt, Erika Salumae

dressage: German women's team

fencing: Giovanna Trillini

field hockey: Spanish women's team

judo: Cecile Nowak, Odalis Reve, Kim Mi-Jung

kayaking: Elisabeth Jicheler, Birgit Schmidt

shooting: Yeo Kab Soon, Launi Meili

synchronized swimming: Karen and Sarah Josephson

table tennis: Gigi Fernandez, Mary Jo Fernandez

uneven bars: Lu Li

volleyball: Cuban women's team

Sportswear *for women*

Age/Grade Level or Audience: Middle school history or sewing lecture; newspaper column; women's studies research theme; civic club presentation; fashion commentary.

Description: Present a program on the history of sportswear for women.

Procedure: Use slides, filmstrips, videos, sketches, or photos to create an overview of sportswear. Include these:

- short tunics, laced sandals, and bound hair worn by female runners in ancient Greece and Rome
- buckskin tunics, moccasins, and leggings for Native American lacrosse players
- pinafores, high-top boots, and day dresses from the Victorian era of lawn games; for example, badminton and croquet
- bloomers and beach shoes for late nineteenth-century female swimmers
- tunic and knee socks for early twentieth-century gym wear
- culottes for early twentieth-century golfers and riders
- maillot, tights, leotard, unitard, sweat shirts and pants for aerobics and gymnastics
- helmet, T-shirt, cycling pants, and jogging shorts for cycling

Add a category for sports outfits of the future.

Budget: $$

Sources:

Clark, Gillian. *Women in Late Antiquity: Pagan and Christian Lifestyles.* Oxford University Press, 1993.

Hansen, Joseph, Evelyn Reed, and Mary-Alice Waters. *Cosmetics, Fashions and the Exploitation of Women.* Pathfinder, 1995.

Müller, Claudia. *The Costume Timeline.* Thames and Hudson, 1992.

Paterek, Josephine. *Encyclopedia of American Indian Costume.* ABC-Clio, 1994.

Tobias, Tobi. "In the Beginning We Are Seamless." *Dance Ink,* July 3–August 31, 1995, 23.

Yarwood, Doreen. *The Encyclopedia of World Costume.* Bonanza, 1986.

Alternative Applications: Make a special brochure featuring women's sports shoes, including sandals, lace-ups, huaraches, moccasins, sneakers, running shoes, gymnastic shoes, wrestling shoes, and ballet slippers. Draw figures using the shoes; for example, a Hopi or Navaho girl dressed for a game of ball, an Inuit woman dressed for an evening at the dance hut, a female aerobics class gearing up for the gym, and a modern American runner or skater competing in the Olympics.

Susan *Butcher and competition*

Age/Grade Level or Audience: Middle school physical education activity; women's studies assignment; civic club presentation; travelogue topic.

Description: Summarize the competitive skills of Susan Butcher, champion dogsled racer.

Procedure: Compose an overview of Butcher's experience training for and participating in the Iditarod. Begin with this model:

- Ranked annually in the top three Alaskan mushers, athlete Susan Butcher trains with her team outside Fairbanks for the annual Iditarod, which she won in 1986–1988 and 1990. A native of Cambridge, Massachusetts, she has earned a reputation as a born dog handler. Her achievements have been great despite the fact that she suffers from dyslexia, which she overcomes by exerting her daring and compassion for sled dogs.

- At age 19, Butcher moved to Wrangell Mountain, Alaska, to share a cabin with her huskies, work at a fish cannery, and earn enough to pay for a career in professional mushing.

- Inaugurated in 1973, the Iditarod covers a zigzag trail over 25 checkpoints and 1,151 miles, five times the length of the Klondike 300. Alaska's spring dogsled race honors Leonhard Seppala and his 1925 run from Nome to Anchorage over a pioneer gold-mining trail carrying diphtheria serum. Barriers include white-outs, sub-zero cold, and rotten ice, the local term for uncertain ice that may be too near thawing to sustain a sled. The first twenty finishers of the 10–11-day course divide $100,000; the winner takes half.

- Butcher began racing in 1978, amid the hoots and catcalls of male mushers who disapproved of her loving camaraderie with her team. In 1979 she improved her performance from nineteenth to ninth, causing race originator Joe Redington to predict that she would win in a future race.

- By 1982 she had achieved second place. 1984 brought a second runner-up finish; the next year brought disaster when a moose stormed her team, killing two of her prize huskies and injuring fifteen others. To add to the disappointment, Susan had to acknowledge winner Libby Riddles as the first woman to win the Iditarod.

- Susan began racking up wins after 1985, intriguing male competitors to study her methods, which include kissing and hugging the dogs and training them like Olympic athletes. After a string of wins, she came in second in 1989 when her dogs caught a virus; two years later, she aborted the run because unbearable cold threatened her team. Male competitors, known to run dogs to death, claim that her competitive edge has dulled in recent years. In 1994 she broke her nose and finished fourth. Rival Rick Swenson sneered to reporters that Susan was too soft to compete, but the evidence points to an extraordinary athlete capable of working a fourteen-hour day with her dogs. Butcher is now managed by her husband, attorney Dave Monson.

Add some sketches of Butcher's rig, the style of harness she prefers, and her method of handling a team.

Budget: $

Sources:

Dodd, Mike. "Dog-Safety Issues Cloud Start." *USA Today,* March 3, 1995, 3C.

Dolan, Ellen M. *Susan Butcher and the Iditarod Trail.* Walker & Co., 1993.

Hollandsworth, Skip. "The Most Driven Woman on Earth." *USA Weekend,* March 6, 1994, 4–7.

Laird, Bob. "The 1990 Iditarod Trail." *USA Today,* March 14, 1990, 3A.

Alternative Applications: Organize a group study of the history of women in dogsled racing and the intense training for both human and animal competitors. Keep data on the amount of food Butcher and her competitors feed their dogs, the breeds they prefer, and the regimen by which they train dogs to obey signals. Sketch preliminaries to the race, the eerie beauty of the landscape, and the jubilation that accompanies the winning run.

Trophies

Age/Grade Level or Audience: K–4 history or current events class; summer library activity.

Description: Design trophies and honors suitable to women who have excelled in athletics.

Procedure: Design a ribbon, loving cup, plaque, trophy, or Olympic seal to honor the achievements of top female athletes. Divide your efforts into groups so that each can pursue different sports. Include these achievers:

baseball: Doris Sams, Jean Faut, Jackie Mitchell

basketball: Teresa Edwards, Clarissa Davis, Pam McGee, Cynthia Cooper, Daedra Charles, Lynette Woodard, Cheryl Miller, Medina Dixon, Michelle Marciniak

biathlon: Andra-Nina Davis

boxing: Stephanie LaMotta, Hessie Donahue

bullfighter: Conchita Cintron

canoeing: Isobel Knowles

car racing: Janet Guthrie, Shirley Muldowney

climbing: Katie Zubricky, Junko Tabei, Alison Hargreaves

coaching: Bernadette Locke, Amy Machin-Ward, Barbara Hedges, Tara Van Derveer, DeDe Owens

cycling: Beryl Burton, Fanny Workman, Susan Notorangelo, Juli Furtado, Shari Kain

diver: Norma Hanson

dogsledding: Susan Butcher, Libby Riddles

453

equestrian: Pat Smythe, Adah Menkin

golf: Nancy Lopez, Althea Gibson, Babe Didrikson Zaharis, Laura Davies, Patty Sheehan, Betsy King, Dottie Mochrie, Melissa McNamara

gymnastics: Vera Caslavska, Olga Korbut, Larissa Latynina, Nadia Comaneci, Mary Lou Retton, Dominique Dawes, Betty Okino

jockey: Julie Krone, Ada Evans Dean

lacrosse: Tina Sloan

pentathlon: Lori Norwood

polo: Eleanora Sears

racquetball: Michelle Gilman

rowing: Anita DeFrantz, Kitty Porterfield

rugby: Karen Almond

sailing: Florence Arthaud, Lisa Charles, Merritt Palm, Dawn Riley, Stephanie Armitage-Johnson, Shelley Beattle, Sara Cavanagh

skating: Bonnie Blair, Nancy Kerrigan, Sonia Henie, Debi Thomas, Kristi Yamaguchi, Oksana Bayul, Jayne Torvill, JoJo Starbuck, Yuka Sato

skiing: Annemarie Moser-Pröll, Gloria Chadwick

soccer: Sylvia Neid, Delma Gonalves, Roseli De Belo, Elisabeth Leidinge, ulrika Kalte, Margarete Piorezan, Anneli Andelen

swimming: Florence Chadwick, Gertrude Ederle, Eleanor Holm, Kornelia Ender, Dawn Fraser, Penny Dean, Diana Nyad, Shelley Taylor-Smith, Janet Evans, Lynne Cox

tennis: Maureen Connolly, Virginia Wade, Chris Evert, Evonne Goolagong, Steffi Graf, Althea Gibson, Billie Jean King, Suzanne Lenglen, Helen Wills Moody, Zina Garrison, Jennifer Capriati, Renee Richards, Martina Navratilova, Arantxa Sanchez Vicario

track: Evelyn Ashford, Jackie Joyner-Kersee, Fanny Blankers-Koen, Wilma Rudolph, Carol Lewis, Gwen Torrence, Merlene Ottey, Alice Coachman, Gail Devers, Juliet Cuthbert, Florence Griffith Joyner, Carlette Guidry, Zola Budd, Mary Decker, Esther Jones, Ruth Rothfarb

triathlon (swim, cycle, run): Paula Newby-Fraser, Erin Baker, Jenn Goodjer, Sally Edwards

volleyball: Kim and Elaine Oden

water skiing: Brandi Hunt

weight lifting: Karyn Marshall

Budget: $$

Sources:

Connors, Martin, Diane L. Dupuis, and Brad Morgan. *The Olympics Factbook*. Visible Ink Press, 1992.

Da Silva, Rachel, ed. *Leading Out: Women Climbers Reaching for the Top*. Seal Press, 1995.

Edwards, Sally. *Heart Zone Training*. Adams Publishing, 1996.

Griffin, Lynne, and Kelly McCann. *The Book of Women: 300 Notable Women History Passed By*. Bob Adams, 1992.

Guttman, Allen. *Women's Sports: A History*. Columbia University Press, 1991.

Isler, Peter. "America's Cup Preview." *USAir,* April 1995, 32–35, 60–61.

Johnson, Susan E. *When Women Played Hardball.* Seal Press, 1995.

Lewis, Linda. *Water's Edge: Women Who Push the Limits in Rowing, Kayaking and Canoeing.* Seal Press, 1995.

Martin, Jean, gen. ed. *Who's Who of Women in the Twentieth Century.* Crescent Books, 1995.

1995 Information Please Almanac. Houghton-Mifflin, 1995.

1994 Olympic Figure Skating. Pacific Arts Publishing, 1994. (Video)

Schrof, Joannie M. "American Women Getting Their Kicks." *U.S. News & World Report,* June 19, 1995, 59.

Sparhawk, Ruth M., Mary E. Leslie, Phyllis Y. Turbow, and Zina R. Rose. *American Women in Sport, 1887–1987: A 100-year Chronology.* Scarecrow Press, 1989.

Stephens, Autumn. *Wild Women.* Conari Press, 1992.

Terry, Ted. *American Black History: Reference Manual.* Myles Publishing, 1991.

Trager, James. *The People's Chronology.* Henry Holt, 1992.

Wulf, Steve. "Call It March Maidness." *Time,* March 27, 1995, 68–69.

Zurkowsky, Herb. "Frozen on Film." *Montreal Gazette,* June 5, 1995, 8D.

Alternative Applications: Create an in-house Women's Sports Hall of Fame. Select famous female athletes and compose banners with their names at the top and the years of achievements at the bottom. Draw a symbol representing individual skills, for example, a soccer ball, saddle, tennis racket, diving board, coach's whistle, or bathing cap.

Writing

Dear *John*

Age/Grade Level or Audience: High school creative writing assignment; women's studies class project; school newspaper contest.

Description: Commemorate a great literary romance by writing a love letter from a female character to her mate.

Procedure: Study the love relationship between a famous female character and her boyfriend, husband, or lover. Compose a letter, note, or telegram that expresses the woman's point of view on matters appropriate to the time. Use these situations as models:

- Hester Prynne to Arthur Dimmesdale on the problems of rearing a child in colonial New England and her desire to move back to England (Nathaniel Hawthorne's *The Scarlet Letter*)

- Cleopatra's ultimatum to Mark Antony concerning his formal Roman marriage and his abandonment of Cleopatra and her children (William Shakespeare's *Antony and Cleopatra*)

- Mattie Silver's rueful farewell to her would-be lover, Ethan Frome (Edith Wharton's *Ethan Frome*)

- Winnie's telegram to Jimmy Louie explaining the political situation in post-war China (Amy Tan's *The Kitchen God's Wife*)

- a paid scribe's letter from Sethe to Paul D. explaining why her daughters must take first place in her life (Toni Morrison's *Beloved*)

Budget: $

Sources:

Barreca, Regina. *Untamed and Unabashed: Essays on Women and Humor in British Literature.* Wayne State University Press, 1995.

Bauermeister, Erica, Jesse Larsen, and Holly Smith. *500 Great Books by Women: A Reader's Guide.* Penguin, 1995.

Davidson, Cathy N., and Linda Wagner-Martin, eds. *The Oxford Companion to Women's Writing.* Oxford University Press, 1995.

Jensen, Katherine Ann. *Writing Love: Letters, Women, and the Novel in France, 1605–1776.* Southern Illinois University Press, 1995.

Larsen, Anne R., and Colette H. Winn, eds. *Renaissance Women Writers: French Texts/American Contexts.* Wayne State University Press, 1995.

Magill, Frank N. *Great Women Writers: The Lives and Works of 135 of the World's Most Important Women Writers, from Antiquity to the Present.* Henry Holt, 1995.

Alternative Applications: Create impromptu telephone conversations between famous female literary characters and their husbands or lovers. Use a partner and read the scenario aloud for an audience or tape pairs of speakers debating their relationships, impediments to love, and destinies.

Gloria *Steinem: voice for feminism*

Age/Grade Level or Audience: High school round table discussion; women's studies project; feature for a newsletter or alumnae bulletin; civic club project.

Description: Organize a discussion of the life and contribution of Gloria Steinem to the modern women's movement.

Procedure: Introduce the work and example of Gloria Steinem, one of the founders of *Ms.* magazine and American feminism's star. Summarize her biography in a handout, bulletin board, or brief reading. Include these facts:

- Steinem was born March 25, 1934, in Toledo, Ohio, to antiques dealer and resort manager Leo Steinem and journalist Ruth Nunevillar Steinem. She was the granddaughter of a suffragist who had participated in the 1908 International Council of Women. After the Steinems' divorce in 1946, Ruth receded into mental illness. Steinem cared for her in their quarters in a tenement basement. Later memories of neglect and adult-sized responsibilities caused Steinem to feel insecure.

- As a boost to self-esteem, Steinem tap-danced and entered talent competitions. At age eighteen, she joined her older sister in Washington, D.C. She later earned a Phi Beta Kappa key at Smith College, where she majored in political science. On a Chester Bowles Asian fellowship in Delhi and Calcutta, India, Steinem composed a travelogue, *A Thousand Indias,* while observing the misery of Asia's poor. In 1958 she recruited students for the Independent Research Service in Cambridge, Massachusetts. Two years later, she wrote for *Help!,* a satiric magazine, and published in her first significant feminist essay, "The Moral Disarmament of Betty Coed" in *Esquire.*

- After working as a cocktail waitress in 1963, she parodied the experience in "I Was a Playboy Bunny," for *Show* magazine. Her subsequent freelance pieces appeared in *Life, McCall's, Seventeen, Esquire, Glamour, Cosmopolitan,* and *Vogue;* the next year, she wrote scripts for *That Was the Week That Was* (NBC) and columns for *New York* magazine, the forerunner of Steinem's magnum opus, *Ms.*

- In the late 1960s, Steinem backed Cesar Chavez and his striking farm laborers. The experience pushed her into total commitment to the human rights movement, demonstrated by her first polemical article, "After Black Power, Women's Liberation." A skillful mediator, she received a presidential appointment from Jimmy Carter and took part in Women Against Pornography, the National Women's Political Caucus, Voters for Choice, Women's Action Alliance, Coalition of Labor Union Women, the Equal Rights Amendment, and Women U.S.A.

- In 1987 she resigned her job as editor of *Ms.* and took on a secondary role as consultant. The magazine, which weathered a temporary slump, reappeared in an advertisement-free form, which Steinem lauded with her essay "Sex, Lies, and Advertising." Readership climbed nearly to half a million. Her fourth major book, *Revolution from Within,* revealed more of the author as a private person than Steinem had ever before made public.

- One of America's most influential people, Steinem, a Woodrow Wilson fellow, has earned the Clarion award, the U.N.'s Ceres Medal, the Penney-Missouri Journalism award, Ohio Governor's award, ACLU Bill of Rights award, and selection as *McCall's* Woman of the Year in 1972.

Conclude the study with emphasis on Steinem's talents—her ability to examine all sides of an issue, to remain cool during heated exchanges, and to adapt to various media venues, from interviews and on-camera dialectic to hosting a television show and speaking before demonstrators and hostile politicians.

Budget: $

Sources:

Anderson, Walter. "Gloria Steinem Talks About Risk." *Cosmopolitan,* January 1989, 60–61.

Barthel, Joan. "The Glorious Triumph of Gloria Steinem." *Cosmopolitan,* March 1984, 216–24.

Collins, Marion. "Gloria Steinem Speaks." *New York Daily News,* November 30, 1986.

Current Biography. H. W. Wilson, 1988.

Daffron, Carolyn. *Gloria Steinem, Feminist.* Chelsea House, 1988.

"Gloria Steinem: I Do What a Lot of People Do, React Instead of Acting." *Chicago Tribune,* January 11, 1987.

Orenstein, Peggy. "Ms. Fights for Its Life." *Mother Jones,* November/December 1990, 32–36, 81–83, 91.

Steinem, Gloria. "I'm Not the Woman in My Mind." *Parade,* January 12, 1992, 10–11.

———. *Revolution from Within: A Book of Self-Esteem.* Little, Brown, 1992.

"An Unsinkable Feminist Sails into her 50th Year Jubilant About Her First Best-Seller." *People Weekly,* November 21, 1983, 185–88.

Weldon, Michele. "Gloria Steinem a Reluctant Symbol of Feminism." *Dallas Times Herald,* August 7, 1987.

Alternative Applications: Give readings from Steinem's books, articles, interviews, and essays. Characterize her style and her use of buzz words, e.g., mommy track, pink collar jobs, glass ceiling, underclass, and patriarchal suppression. Discuss her belief that America's women will never attain equal rights *in toto* until they form a voting bloc to pressure Congress for equal rights.

Imitating *Cliffs notes*

Age/Grade Level or Audience: High school creative writing project; education cooperative learning exercise; women's study monograph.

Description: Introduce a group to literary criticism by creating a set of study notes on a classic work written by a woman.

Procedure: Have participants select a notable work of young literature, such as Louisa May Alcott's *Little Women.* Assign groups to create the following segments:

- author's biography
- historical background, including religious movements of the time (transcendentalism), social movements, and political atmosphere (Civil War)
- the milieu of Concord
- map and genealogy of the story's main characters (March family)

- concise summary of the novel

- chapter-by-chapter summaries

- glossary of unfamiliar terms

- character list

- in-depth character study

- theme analysis (e.g., loyalty, jealousy, ambition)

- essays on contrasting settings, historical detail, and author's style and diction

- detailed comparison of the book and various film, video, and audio cassette versions

- annotated bibliography

Complete the project using desktop publishing software. Offer copies of the monograph to classes studying the book.

Budget: $$$

Sources:

Burke, Kathleen. *Louisa May Alcott.* Chelsea House, 1988.

Fisher, Aileen, and Olive Rabe. *We Alcotts.* Atheneum, 1968.

Meigs, Cornelia. *Invincible Louisa.* Little, Brown, 1968.

Alternative Applications: Assign a group to create a computer product that will introduce readers to *Little Women.* Have writers compose sample critical essays, character analyses, thematic studies, and a cinema study. Add visual clips of the Alcott home, Sleepy Hollow Cemetery, Walden Pond, and the route followed by characters visiting Europe, New York, and Washington, D.C. Conclude with a comparative literature study that contrasts Jo to the protagonists in Avi's *The True Confessions of Charlotte Doyle,* L. M. Montgomery's *Anne of Green Gables,* or Cynthia Rylant's *Missing May.*

Imitating *the experts*

Age/Grade Level or Audience: Middle school or high school creative writing topic; women's studies project; Friends of the Library speech or writing contest; church school or library summer project.

Description: Imitate the style and subject matter of a highly acclaimed female author.

Procedure: Compile a list of classic literature composed of a variety of lengths, tone, and styles by a wide array of writers. For example:

- advice—Emily Post, Judith Martin, Marita Golden

- article—Andrea Dworkin, Letty Pogrebin Cotten, Marcia Gillespie

- autobiography—Maya Angelou, Rigoberto Menchu, Jeanne Wakatsuki Houston, Yoko Kawashima Watkins

- biography—Fawn Brodie, Isabel Allende

- crafts—Esther Hautzig, Phyllis Pellman Good

- cultural criticism—Gail Sheehy, Susan Faludi, Gloria Steinem, Shere Hite, Barbara Meyerhoff

- diary—Ida B. Wells, Anne Frank, Zlata Filipovich
- drama—Lady Augusta Gregory, Lillian Hellman, Susan Glaspel
- economics—Jane Bryant Quinn, Sylvia Porter, Muriel Siebert
- education—Marian Wright Edelman, Maria Montessori
- essay—Isak Dinesen, Susan Sontag, Audre Lorde, Jamaica Kincaid
- fashion—Diana Vreeland, Dr. Elizabeth Barber
- folklore—Zora Neale Hurston, Caroline Gordon
- ghost stories—Nancy Roberts, Toni Morrison, Maxine Hong Kingston
- historical fiction—Mary Renault, Esther Forbes, Diana Norman, Jessamyn West
- history—Antonia Fraser, Jung Chang, Barbara Tuchman
- humor—Erma Bombeck, Molly Ivins, Florence King
- legend—Mary Stewart, Robin McKinley
- local color—Zora Neale Hurston, Willa Cather, Ellen Gilchrist, Shirley Ann Grau
- memoir—Colette, Rose Wilder Lane
- mystery—Agatha Christie, Daphne DuMaurier, Ellen Raskin
- nature—Joy Adamson, Rachel Carson, Elizabeth George Speare
- novel—Edna Ferber, Annie Proulx, Dorothy West
- novella—Edith Wharton, Kate Chopin
- philosophy—Susan Sontag, Hannah Arendt
- religion—Simone Weil, Catherine Marshall, Mary Daly
- saga—Sigrid Undset, Amy Tan, Laura Ingalls Wilder
- screenplay—Jane Campion, Ruth Gordon
- short story—Nadine Gordimer, Bessie Head, Katherine Anne Porter, Eudora Welty
- verse—Marianne Moore, Gabriela Mistral, Edna St. Vincent Millay, Anna Akhmatova, Elizabeth Bishop, Gwendolyn Brooks, Rita Dove, Janet Frame, Anne Hebert, Edith Sitwell
- young adult fiction—Paula Fox, Cynthia Rylant, Irene Hunt, Mildred Taylor

Help participants locate a single incident or vignette within a classic work and isolate its qualities and literary devices. Organize groups to work together on imitating the style of no more than three pages. Call on writers to read aloud their efforts and respond to criticism from the class.

Budget: $

Sources:

Alexander, Adele Logan. "White House Confidante of Mrs. Lincoln." *African-American History*, spring 1995, 18–20.

Bell-Scott, Patricia. *Life Notes: Personal Writings by Contemporary Black Women*. W. H. Norton, 1994.

Gilbert, Sandra M., and Susan Gubar. *The Norton Anthology of Literature by Women*. W. W. Norton & Co., 1995.

Martin, Jean, gen. ed. *Who's Who of Women in the Twentieth Century*. Crescent Books, 1995.

Rebolledo, Tey Diana, and Eliana S. Rivero. *Infinite Divisions: An Anthology of Chicana Literature.* The University of Arizona Press, 1993.

Weatherford, Doris. *American Women's History.* Prentice-Hall, 1994.

Alternative Applications: Study a biographical article. Note the setting, style, tone, mood, characterization, organization, and transition; for example:

- In Adele Logan Alexander's "White House Confidante of Mrs. Lincoln," the author begins chronologically with the place and time of Elizabeth Hobbs Keckley's birth, then moves directly to the source of her fame—work in the White House. Alexander corroborates her data by mentioning an 1868 memoir, *Behind the Scenes; or, Thirty Years a Slave and Four Years in the White House.* A brief summary covers the unfortunate events that led up to Keckley's sale, resale, and eventual purchase of freedom and her efforts toward self-education.

- The author introduces tension by declaring that Mrs. Abraham Lincoln, who was First Lady during Keckley's employment, suffered mental illness, a fact not usually stressed in commentary on the Lincoln administration. An irony of this short article is the transition from work for Jefferson Davis to the White House kitchen. From close range, Keckley recalls the intense suffering of President and Mrs. Lincoln after the death of son Willie. A compassionate woman, Keckley soon took a place beside Mary Todd Lincoln to comfort her after the assassination of the President, who had escorted his wife to a play at Ford Theatre in Washington, D.C.

- The article lacks a storybook conclusion after noting that the sale of Keckley's memoirs discredits her for sharing personal moments in the life of a troubled family. The author notes that Keckley is memorable because she, like other diarists and memoirists, composed valuable first-hand accounts of moments in a nation's history.

Following the model of Adele Logan Alexander's "White House Confidante," compose a fictional article about a character who witnesses an important event in women's history, for example, the settlement of Alaska, a sea voyage on a clipper ship, riding for the pony express, serving the last empress of China, or digging for evidence of Mayan civilization.

Keeping *a journal*

Age/Grade Level or Audience: Middle school creative writing project; women's studies symposium; teacher education model.

Description: Commemorate the work of a female inventor, scientist, astronaut, or activist by composing entries in a daily journal, diary, or lab book.

Procedure: Have participants keep a journal of a scientist or activist's enthusiasm, research, preliminary sketches, test runs, and completion of a project, such as the invention of the square-bottomed paper bag or a confrontation with a governing body intent on denying welfare to children. Keep a uniform "personality," tone and style, blending elation, despair, concern, and suspicion with conversations, drawings, and final plans for the creation or campaign. Let your imagination tell you where the difficulties might have been, such as inadequate materials, limited work space, costly ingredients, or ridicule from people who had no faith in the invention or campaign.

Budget: $$

Sources:

American Men and Women of Science. R. R. Bowker, 1989.

Ashby, Ruth, and Deborah Gore Ohrn. *Herstory: Women Who Changed the World.* Viking, 1995.

Bailey, Martha J. *American Women in Science.* ABC-Clio, 1994.

Healey, James R. "Control Panel Designer Achieves the Right Touch." *USA Today,* June 19, 1995, 4B.

James, Edward T., et al., eds. *Notable American Women, 1607–1950.* Belknap Press, 1971.

MacDonald, Anne L. *Feminine Ingenuity: Women and Invention in America.* Ballantine Books, 1992.

Magill, Frank N., ed. *Great Events from History II: Science and Technology Series.* Salem Press, 1991.

McHenry, Robert, ed. *Liberty's Women.* G. & C. Merriam, 1980.

Morin, Isobel V. *Women Chosen for Public Office.* Oliver Press, 1995.

————. *Women Who Reformed Politics.* Oliver Press, 1995.

Patton, Phil. *Made in the USA.* Grove Weidenfeld, 1992.

Rennert, Richard, ed. *Profiles of Great Black Americans: Female Leaders.* Chelsea House, 1994.

Stanley, Autumn. *Mothers and Daughters of Invention.* Scarecrow Press, 1993.

Sterling, Dorothy. *We Are Your Sisters: Black Women in the Nineteenth Century.* W. W. Norton, 1984.

Van Doren, Charles, and Robert McHenry, eds. *Webster's American Biographies.* G. & C. Merriam, 1974.

Veglahn, Nancy J. *Women Scientists.* Facts on File, 1991.

Alternative Applications: Have participants imagine they are an overseer in a nineteenth-century laboratory or factory where a recent invention or discovery is being readied for market. Log the final stages of the product, including development of the instruction manual, color choices, planning for correct and safe use, packaging, and creating an advertising and sales campaign that targets the product's intended customers.

Letters *as history*

Age/Grade Level or Audience: Middle school or high school composition unit; reading theater presentation; women's studies class project; museum or Friends of the Library display; newspaper column.

Description: Develop a series of correspondence with a notable woman from the past.

Procedure: Have participants select a woman from the past with whom they would have liked to correspond. In groups of two, with one person serving as the writer from the present, and the other taking on the personality from the past, compose a series of letters, tapes, or post cards. Encourage participants to keep the correspondence lively by posing relevant questions and answers; for example, discuss the revolutionary changes in travel and communication. Remind the writer from the past that they should correspond in a style that is in keeping with the times. In preparation have students study a published selection of eighteenth- or nineteenth-century correspondence.

Budget: $

Sources:

Anderson, Scott. *Desktop Publishing: Dollars and Sense.* Blue Heron, 1995.

DuBois, Ellen Carol. *Elizabeth Cady Stanton/Susan B. Anthony: Correspondence, Writings, Speeches.* Schocken Books, 1981.

Jensen, Katherine Ann. *Writing Love: Letters, Women, and the Novel in France, 1605–1776.* Southern Illinois University Press, 1995.

King, Laurie, and Dennis Stovall. *Classroom Publishing.* Blue Heron, 1995.

The Letters of John and Abigail Adams. Caedmon, n.d. (Audiocassette)

"Love of Women." *Montreal Gazette,* June 12, 1995, 5D.

Alternative Applications: Collect letters, mail packets, and other sources of writing from antiques dealers, Good Will, auctions, and family attics. Sort through dated correspondence for vignettes of other times and places as they touch on women's lives, hopes, and frustrations. Sort letters into time order and reproduce in book form. Fill in commentary or explanation of historical milieu or events that influence the writers' thinking.

Making *notes*

Age/Grade Level or Audience: Middle school writing exercise; school or public library handout or brochure; book club talk; women's studies project; Toastmaster's Club model; Women's History Month presentation; historical or preservation society.

Description: Using biographical material about a famous woman, make notes for a news article, feature, term paper, library report, or speech.

Procedure: Select a notable female to study. Collect materials from biographies, databases, biographical dictionaries, journals, diaries, letters, films or videos, magazines, newspapers, journals, chronicles, or record jackets. Summarize notes in simple, readable style. Follow this model on Carson McCullers, noted Southern author:

- firstborn of three children (Lamar, Margarita); born February 19, 1917, Columbus, Georgia; parents watchmaker Lamar and Marguerite Waters Smith; unattractive, rowdy child; preferred solitude. Baptist upbringing; Sixteenth Street School (1923); Wynnton School; Columbus High School (grad. 1933); piano lessons; rheumatic fever 1932

- gave up plans to be concert pianist; wrote fiction. 1934, left by boat for New York to study music at Juilliard and creative writing at Columbia University; roomed at Parnassus Club; lost tuition money on the subway; forced to work as typist, waitress, piano accompanist, bookkeeper

- 1935, recurrence of rheumatic fever; returned home and wrote *The Heart Is a Lonely Hunter;* married James Reeves McCullers (soldier at Fort Benning, Georgia) September 20, 1937; settled near Fort Bragg in Fayetteville, North Carolina. Houghton Mifflin published *The Heart Is a Lonely Hunter* (1940); finished *Reflections in a Golden Eye* in two months; sold to *Harper's Bazaar* for five hundred dollars

- ambivalent about marriage until a move to New York; separated and resettled in Brooklyn Heights; drank heavily and became addicted to codeine; her mother tended her during another illness; suffered partial blindness and migraine headaches from a cerebral stroke

- finished *The Ballad of the Sad Café,* freelanced stories, reviews, essays for major magazines and journals; received Guggenheim fellowship March 24, 1942; grant from the American Academy of Arts and Letters

- former husband on front lines in Europe; remarried him March 19, 1945; completed *The Member of the Wedding* (1946); second Guggenheim Fellowship paid way to Paris; second stroke August, 1947; paralyzed on left side, chronic alcoholism

- adapted *The Member of the Wedding* as stage play (1949); won New York Drama Critics' Circle Award and Donaldson Award; filmed 1952 by Columbia; 1952 to Europe on *Constitution;* bought home in Bachvillers, France; husband committed suicide November 19, 1953

- lectured at Goucher College, Columbia University, Philadelphia Fine Arts Association; failed stage production of *The Square Root of Wonderful;* addressed American Academy of Arts and Letters and National Institute of Arts and Letters

- unsuccessful surgery on left arm; confined to wheelchair; published *Clock Without Hands;* third stroke and coma August 15, 1967; died at Nyack, New York, September 29, 1967

Budget: $

Sources:

Bloom, Harold. Introduction to *Carson McCullers.* Chelsea House, 1986.

Boyle, Jacquelynn. "History Books Still Give Women Scant Attention." *Detroit Free Press,* March 11, 1994, 1, 8A.

Campbell, Ffyona. "My Long Walk Home." *Health,* March/April 1995, 48–49.

Carr, Virginia Spencer. *The Lonely Hunter: A Biography of Carson McCullers.* Doubleday, 1975.

————. *Understanding Carson McCullers.* University of South Carolina Press, 1989.

Cook, Richard M. *Carson McCullers.* Ungar, 1975.

Edmonds, Dale. *Carson McCullers.* Steck-Vaughn, 1969.

Evans, Oliver. *The Ballad of Carson McCullers.* Coward, 1966.

Graver, Lawrence. *Carson McCullers.* University of Minnesota Press, 1969.

McDowell, Margaret B. *Carson McCullers.* Macmillan, 1980.

"Pioneering Women." *Detroit Free Press,* March 8, 1995, E1, 3.

Wilson, Charles Reagan, and William Ferris, eds. *Encyclopedia of Southern Culture.* University of North Carolina Press, 1989.

Alternative Applications: Present a speech or chalk talk taken from outlined notes on the lives of these and other famous women:

- actor Katharine Hepburn

- athlete Ffyona Campbell

- comic Gilda Radner

- cosmetics magnate Harriet Hubbard Ayer

- designer Neysa McMein

- pioneer fur trader Madeline La Frambroise

- poet Rita Dove

- potter Maria Martinez

- psychologist Anna Freud

- singer Lena Horne

Emphasize the positive and negative aspects of the person's career with dates, places, relatives, family, achievements, and awards. Conclude with a personal summary derived from multiple sources and from a reading of primary sources, particularly letters, diaries, journals, and speeches.

Making *outlines*

Age/Grade Level or Audience: Middle school thinking skill model; teacher education model.

Description: Teach the skill of outlining by reducing a column, chapter, lecture, or article on women's history into either a topic outline or sentence outline.

Procedure: Present to the group the purpose and methods of two types of outlines: topic and sentence. Point out that both methods divide an essay or article into a framework of main topics and summarize in order the points that support each topic. The topic outline is shorter and easier to read; the sentence outline is a good beginning for a theme or term paper because it provides whole thoughts to place into the finished piece. The formal requirements involve careful spacing and marking:

- Begin with a heading, which serves as a focus.

- Divide thoughts into topics and subtopics.

- Make no division of fewer than two entries.

- Place capital Roman numerals alongside main topics.

- Number subtopics with capital letters.

- If details support subtopics, list them under Arabic numerals.

- Punctuate numerals and letters with periods.

- Place no punctuation after lines in a topic outline.

- Punctuate with a period after each entry in a sentence outline.

- Indent subtopics under the letter of the first word in the main topic.

- For topic outlines, keep to a single grammatical form; for example, infinitives, prepositional phrases, clauses, or gerund phrases.

In both outlining methods, the writer must maintain a single style rather than a blend of sentences, phrases, and words. Below is a newspaper column and examples of the two types of outlines. Use either as a model:

Quite unexpectedly, I bumped into an old friend this week and scarcely recognized her.

Having treasured *Mythology* since I was twelve, I thought I knew all about Edith Hamilton. To my surprise, during a research project, I found more zip in the old girl than my Greek professor even hinted at.

Born in 1867, Hamilton lived to be ninety-six. Enlightened parents encouraged her enthusiasm for Latin at age six and watched her absorb the fustiest of English writers alongside Thucydides and Xenophon, whom she read via self-taught Greek.

By the time Hamilton reached puberty, the Victorian mindset shanghaied her from home lessons to Miss Porter's, a prissy New England girls' academy, where she studied sampler embroidery and niceness.

Undaunted by the headmistress's unsubtle shove toward debutantehood, Hamilton struck out for Bryn Mawr, polished off two degrees in classics, and snatched a fellowship to the notoriously sexist University of Munich, where she continued to develop her mind while ignoring the taunts of misogynist professors.

On her return to the U.S., she joined suffragists and marched in protest against the anti-female sentiment of her day.

Heading her own preparatory school in Baltimore, Hamilton found teaching remarkably onerous. It wasn't the counseling of teenagers or grading of Latin exercises that drained her, but the constant upstream swim against all-male administrators who urged her to omit history lessons for her little dears and zero in on ladylike refinements.

At the age of fifty, the famed classicist retired from the fray and inaugurated a second career. As the Western world's crackerjack classical essayist, lecturer, and writer, she produced a readable, lucid account of ancient Greece's accomplishments.

From that success came a parallel book on Rome and, in 1942, her masterwork, *Mythology*. A deluge of translation, critical analysis, and commentary followed, notably works on the Old and New Testaments, versions of tragedies by Aeschylus and Euripides, plus literary reviews of her contemporaries, including William Faulkner.

Following the ancient concept of "Nothing in excess," Hamilton spent her summers on the Maine shore, vegetating among the rocks, where she could absorb the healing sun and invigorating tides.

On her return to work in fall, she pushed harder each year, into her early nineties, never giving in to stereotypical old-ladyhood.

In August 1957, Hamilton received the appropriate crown for a ninety-year-old classical debutante. Proclaimed an honorary citizen of Athens, she stood at the base of the Acropolis and bestowed a life's love of the ancient world on her new home town.

Preceding a performance of her version of *Prometheus Bound,* she honored the spirit of Greece with typical clarity and lyricism: "We are met tonight to see a play. . . . The Greeks have been outstripped by science and technology, but never in the love of truth, never in the creation of beauty and freedom."

Five years before her death, Hamilton vowed to retire for good from the disciplines of scholarship and literature. At ninety-one, she tramped about Spain and France, then, to get her juices flowing again, returned to the lecture circuit. Quite a gal, that Edith!

[Catawba Valley Neighbors Section, *Charlotte Observer,* September 9, 1992, 1.]

Sentence Outline

Edith Hamilton

I. Author Edith Hamilton showed scholarly promise in childhood.

    A. She was born in 1867 and lived to be 96.

    B. Her parents encouraged her education in the classics.

        1. She studied at home and read from the family's library of classics.

        2. At Miss Porter's academy, she learned embroidery and manners.

    C. Higher education refined her considerable talent.

        1. Hamilton completed two degrees at Bryn Mawr.

        2. She concluded formal training at the University of Munich.

II. Hamilton utilized her education for public service.

    A. She joined suffragists in securing the vote for women.

    B. She served as principal of a Baltimore preparatory school.

        1. She counseled pupils.

        2. Classroom work preceded her retirement from teaching.

    C. In 1917 she began writing about ancient Greece.

        1. In 1942 she published her masterwork, *Mythology.*

        2. Her next works included translation, critical analysis, and commentary.

III. Hamilton earned notoriety for her clear assessment of ancient Greece and Rome.

    A. In August 1957, Athens, Greece, made her an honorary citizen.

    B. She traveled widely in Spain and France at age 91.

Topic Outline

Edith Hamilton

I. A scholar from childhood

    A. Birth in 1867

    B. Education in the classics

        1. Home study

        2. Attendance at Miss Porter's academy

    C. Refinement of talent

        1. Two degrees from Bryn Mawr

        2. Study at the University of Munich

II. Life of public service

    A. Suffragist and supporter of the vote for women

    B. Principal of a Baltimore preparatory school

        1. Counselor

        2. Teacher

    C. Writer on the subject of ancient Greece

        1. Author of *Mythology*

        2. Translator, analyst, and commentator

III. Evaluator of ancient Greece and Rome

    A. Honorary citizen of Athens, Greece

    B. Traveler in Spain and France

Budget: $$$

Sources:

"Aged Lover of Ancients." *Life,* September 15, 1958, 79.

Brown, John Mason. "Heritage of Edith Hamilton: 1867–1963." *Saturday Review,* June 22, 1963.

Chambers, Harriet. "Edith Hamilton." National League of American Pen Women, June 1960. (Brochure)

Girson, Rochelle. "Interview with Edith Hamilton." *Saturday Review,* August 10, 1957, 29.

Kerr, Frances Willard. "Author Receives Plaudits: Alternates Writing with Travel." *Christian Science Monitor,* March 13, 1958.

Kunitz, Stanley. *Twentieth Century Authors.* H. W. Wilson, 1955.

Matthews Virginia. "Interview with Edith Hamilton." *Publisher's Weekly,* March 17, 1958, 26.

Reid, Doris Fielding. *Edith Hamilton: An Intimate Portrait.* Norton, 1967.

Snodgrass, Mary Ellen. *The English Book.* Perma-Bound, 1991.

Sochen, June. *Herstory: A Woman's View of American History.* Alfred Publishing, 1974.

Stoddard, Hope. *Famous American Women.* Crowell, 1970.

Alternative Applications: Distribute finished articles, chapters, books, lectures, films, videos, or essays on famous women from a variety of fields. Assist students in outlining each. Organize a round table to facilitate peer editing. Select worthy examples of outlines for copying and distribution. Combine finished outlines into a brochure honoring the lives of famous women.

Making *summaries*

Age/Grade Level or Audience: High school logic assignment; women's studies project; teacher education model.

Description: Teach the skill of summary writing by capturing the essence of a column, chapter, lecture, or article on women's history.

Procedure: Present to the group the purpose and methods of summarizing or precis-writing. Provide the follow steps in condensing or narrowing the focus of a long article to a brief statement:

- State in your own words the main ideas.

- Omit excess detail.

- Paraphrase lengthy quotations.

- Follow the order of the piece, whether chronological, least-to-greatest, or greatest-to-least.

- Maintain an objective tone and style.

- Provide adequate transitions as you move from one topic to another.

- Edit your version for accuracy and clarity.

Use the following newspaper column as a model. Shorten it by 80% by reducing it to 1/5 of its original size:

Making inroads against prejudicial thinking is not a one-shot deal. As is evident by the work of people like Dr. Martin Luther King, Marian Anderson, and Gandhi, overcoming bigotry and prejudice requires a lifetime of battles.

I have been reading the life of an unsung warrior for women's rights. Dr. Elizabeth Blackwell, the first woman to receive an M.D. degree in North America, encountered a progression of stumbling blocks during a career that spanned more than four decades.

469

The daughter of free-thinking Quaker immigrants, Elizabeth, who was born in England, was living in Cincinnati when her father died. She and two other daughters opened an academy to help support the fourteen-member family.

Responding to the plea of a woman friend dying of cancer, Elizabeth abandoned her classroom duties and began applying to medical schools. She received nineteen rejections and cast about for advice from doctors she trusted. One suggested that she gain entrance to classes by disguising herself in men's clothing. Fortunately, she did not have to cross-dress to become a physician.

After Geneva College agreed to take her as a joke, Elizabeth encountered resistance in other forms. She received hate mail, threats, ridicule, and mash notes. Local people shunned the "doctress," calling her a fallen woman and lunatic.

Even with admittance to classes, she lacked free movement in certain anatomy classes, particularly human reproduction.

Eventually, because of her modest, no-nonsense professionalism, she gained credence as a student and graduated top in her class. Locals jammed the hall to see "the woman doctor" receive her diploma.

Sex discrimination plagued Dr. Blackwell in her new role. She found no hospital that would allow her to practice. Male doctors refused to confer with her. Some female patients rejected the idea of examination by a woman doctor.

To circumvent narrow-mindedness, she studied in Paris and London, where she became expert in the treatment of typhus, then returned to New York to found a women's clinic. Her sister, who had completed her own medical degree, and a German midwife formed the rest of her staff.

The clientele for their services, derived from poor immigrant women, spoke a polyglot of languages, but raised a unanimous voice supporting a facility that offered decent care.

Dr. Blackwell's career extended beyond her clinical practice. After infection cost her the sight of one eye, she gravitated toward education and trained nurses for the Union Army during the Civil War.

Well into her seventies, she wrote tracts advocating sex education, prevention of venereal disease, and hygiene. A close friend of Florence Nightingale, she chose not to go to the Crimea, and continued lecturing and activism aimed at improving the quality of life for women.

Dr. Blackwell's example proves a number of facts. Primarily, it shows that negative public opinion concerning women's capabilities is blatantly false and counter-productive to human progress.

Also, Dr. Blackwell's continued battles deflate the romantic notion that overcoming discrimination is a single stroke, followed by an outpouring of rewards and attainment.

If anything, Elizabeth Blackwell's achievement establishes the opposite as a norm—that people who choose a life of breaking down barriers continue in that role for the duration.

[Catawba Valley Neighbors Section, *Charlotte Observer,* May 1, 1991, 1.]

Budget: $$$

Sources:

Hoverstein, Paul. "Lofty Recognition for Women's Air Corps." *USA Today,* October 14, 1994, 2A.

"Novelist to Read at Marygrove." *All About Detroit,* April 3, 1995, 9.

Ravitch, Diane, ed. *The American Reader.* HarperCollins, 1990.

Snodgrass, Mary Ellen. *The English Book.* Perma-Bound, 1991.

Van Biema, David. "Beyond the Sound Barrier." *Time,* October 3, 1994, 66–67.

Vigil, Evangelina. *Woman of Her Word: Hispanic Women Write.* Arte Publico Press, 1987.

Alternative Applications: Distribute copies of numerous short studies of a single life; for example articles and biographical essays on Madame Chiang, Barbara McClintock, Janet Reno, Jackie Cochran, Indira Gandhi, Anne Boleyn, Corazon Aquino, Golda Meir, Wilma Rudolph, or Benazir Bhutto. Have students work in groups to determine what facts should belong in a collection of data on a single woman. Compile completed information on note cards or transcribe on a laptop computer into a short summary. Conclude with an annotated list of sources that describes the strengths and shortcomings of each article.

Proper *ladies*

Age/Grade Level or Audience: Middle school history assignment; library or museum presentation; women's studies class project; preservation society contest; newspaper column.

Description: Study rules of conduct for women and girls of an earlier era.

Procedure: Select a period of time in American history; for example, the early twentieth century. Study expectations for the behavior of women and girls at the table, on the street, during leisure activities, at social gatherings, in church or school, or among dignitaries. Compose a set of rules concerning these matters:

accidents	entertaining	playing cards
announcing a birth	expressing an opinion	playing games
apologizing	giving gifts	receiving gifts
chaperonage	interviewing servants	saluting the flag
choosing stationery	introductions	setting a table
composing invitations	kissing	shaking hands
coughing	learning a skill	smoking
dancing	lost items	studying a profession
dress	make-up	talking to strangers
dressing for a funeral	making a speech	using a maiden name
drinking	monogramming	wearing gloves
eating	nail polish	writing to friends

Budget: $

Sources:

Etiquette: Charlotte Ford's Guide to Modern Manners. Clarkson Potter, 1988.

Martin, Judith. *Miss Manners' Guide for the Turn of the Millennium.* Simon & Schuster, 1990.

———. *Miss Manners' Guide to Excruciatingly Correct Behavior.* Warner, 1988.

Stewart, Marjabelle Young. *The New Etiquette.* St. Martin, 1987.

Alternative Applications: Create a series of business or social letters that contrast the style and needs of female workers, educators, mothers, or housewives over a span of years. Note the creation of Ms. as a designation of gender. Consult significant authorities, for example, Judith Martin, Dorothy Dix, Ann Landers, Abigail Van Buren, Amy Vanderbilt, Charlotte Ford, Debra Alexander, Emily Post, and Catherine Beecher.

Reliving *history with Jean Auel*

Age/Grade Level or Audience: High school literature assignment; school or public library handout or brochure; book club program; women's studies presentation; Toastmaster's Club chalk talk; Women's History Month or historical society handout.

Description: Outline the fact-gathering method of novelist Jean Auel.

Procedure: Describe the method by which Jean Auel collects information about the stone age for her multi-volume saga, which began in 1980 with *The Clan of the Cave Bear*. After departing her job as a circuit-board designer in 1973, Auel turned to technical writing, then worked as a credit manager before launching her "Earth's Children" series. To fill in gaps in her knowledge about the Pleistocene, she undertook a major research project. List these parts of her search for data:

- study of weaponry, burial customs, and musical instruments
- readings in topography, climatology, anatomy, anthropology, and archeology
- recreating scenarios involving prehistoric cooking, medicine, travel, inventions, language, athletics, and sewing
- mental reenactment of the roles of clan women and children in obtaining and cooking food, washing, tending the shelter, treating illness, lighting fires, making arrowheads, weaving baskets, snaring birds, trapping small animals, and gathering roots and tubers
- supplying authentic detail concerning human sexual relations, relaxation, storytelling, and crafts
- accounting for the advent of Cro-Magnon society
- taking week-long survival courses at Oregon's Malheur Field Station and spending a night in a snow cave on Mt. Hood

Note how Jean Auel extended her study as she published The *Valley of the Horses* (1984), *The Mammoth Hunters* (1985), and *The Plains of Passage* (1990) by visiting archeological digs and the Lascaux caves in the Pyrenees, the site of the world's most famous prehistoric ritual drawings of animals and hunters. Packing only a knife and blanket, she camped in the Pacific Northwest and studied Cro-Magnon sites in Russia and Europe.

Budget: $

Sources:

Bendel, Mary-Ann. "Cosmo Talks to Jean Auel." *Cosmopolitan,* April 1986, 146–148.

Chambers, Andrea. "A Mammoth First Printing Makes Jean Auel's New Epic an Instant Best-Seller." *People,* December 16, 1985, 113–15.

Fincher, Jack. "Author Jean Auel Makes Literary Hay by Thinking Like a Neanderthal." *People,* November 10, 1980, 96–98.

Hopkins, Thomas. "I'm Living Every Writer's Fantasy." *Macleans,* October 6, 1980, 64–65.

Hornblower, Margot. "Queen of the Ice Age Romance." *Time,* October 22, 1990, 88.

"Sweet Savage Love." *Newsweek,* November 18, 1985, 100–101.

Van Gelder, Lindsy. "Speculative Fiction: From the Immense Past to the Immense Future." *Ms.*, March 1986, 64–70.

Alternative Applications: Suggest a method and itinerary for a writer studying the following types of female protagonists:

- a Civil War plantation owner
- an Anglican missionary in New Zealand
- a pilot stranded in Nepal
- female Olympic team skiing in Switzerland
- a private eye following a suspect in Shanghai during the 1920s
- a basket weaver learning how to collect and dry sweet grass

Shaping *ideas*

Age/Grade Level or Audience: K–4 creative writing activity; summer school program; library group project; home school assignment; scout or 4-H project contest.

Description: Turn a word into a poem.

Procedure: Suggest words that bring to mind favorite women in children's lives. List these:

aunt	driver	nurse
clerk	grade mother	principal
cook	grandmother	scout leader
cousin	minister	sister
crossing guard	sitter	storyteller
dentist	mother	teacher
doctor	neighbor	writer

Help students write the words and either form them into a shape or use a computer graphics program to create the impression of a human figure. For example, write *mother* with the m on top for a hat or hair, the o for a head, the t and h for trunk and arms, and the e and r for legs and feet. Conclude like this:

Add eyes, nose, mouth, hair, ears, and clothing. Color each part to suit the picture of a standing figure.

Budget: $$

Sources:

Select words that students propose for the list. Spell each in capital letters, then let participants select the shapes they want to use.

Alternative Applications: Offer students a list of phrases or titles to write in decorative fashion; for example, as headlines, product slogans, or movie titles. Compose each with facial features in the o's, p's, b's, and d's or up and down, at right angles, or crossed like an X. Use these phrases as models:

- Everybody Needs Success
- Girls Can Too
- History Remembers Women
- Look at Her Go!
- Thanks to Women
- Women's History Month

Tape *your thoughts*

Age/Grade Level or Audience: Elementary grades 4–6 composition activity; middle school history/writing interdisciplinary series.

Description: Introduce children to the creative action behind writing.

Procedure: In preparation for story writing and in conjunction with historic period studies, have participants embark on imagination brainstorming sessions. Suggest that students imagine themselves looking out a window in a New England Puritan village, as landladies of a boarding house in the Old West, or as members of a pioneer family just starting their day. Have participants take turns describing what they "see"—people passing by; what are they wearing? What are the means of transportation? What are the chores typically expected of a pioneer mother and her daughters? When does the day begin? What duties change with the passing seasons? Complete the activity by replaying the tape or by distributing copies of the children's best sentences for them to illustrate and post on the bulletin board.

Budget: $$

Sources:

Cheyney, Arnold. *The Writing Corner.* Scott Foresman, 1979.
Enos, Theresa. *A Sourcebook for Basic Writing Teachers.* McGraw-Hill, 1987.
Gregory, Cynde. "Writing the Natural Way." *Instructor,* March 1995, 28–29.

Alternative Applications: Use taped composition as a method of introducing the children's backgrounds and making history come alive. Have each participant describe the women important in their lives and in their pre-history. Share anecdotes about mothers, grandmothers, aunts, and great-grandmothers. As a final step, have students create short stories using the lives of their own female relatives.

Theme: *"life is a verb!"*

Age/Grade Level or Audience: High school journalism or creative writing assignment; women's studies project; women's club contest theme; teacher education model.

Description: Teach the composition of an exegesis.

Procedure: Present to participants the formal exegesis, which takes its theme from an aphorism. Begin with the words of writer Charlotte Perkins Gilman, "Life is a verb!" Lead small-group discussions, make diagrams on the chalkboard, analyze, list, cite examples, make notes and outlines, listen, question, and log ideas from individual brainstormers. Chart any likely methods of illustrating the truth of Gilman's statement. Sort out usable ideas and cross off any thoughts that travel too far from the central issue. Cluster into units ideas that share a central theme; for example, ways that several famous women have enjoyed good health and energy.

In phase two of the writing process, realign major ideas into a rough outline. A forceful method of proving Gilman's statement is least-to-greatest, which begins with the smallest or least forceful arguments and works up to the most logical. Create topic headings for each grouping of ideas. Add details that prove a point or demonstrate cause-and-effect, as with events in the life of Florence Nightingale, a nurse who refused to fit England's stereotype of the genteel lady and who created the modern concept of a hospital by her treatment of wounded soldiers at the front during the Crimean War.

Using a word processor or in longhand, compose a first draft. Return to the major headings. Determine what ideas suit your audience and theme. Omit any that stray from the point. Select concrete examples of Gilman's philosophy: Susan B. Anthony's campaign for women's rights or Harriet Beecher Stowe's persistence in fighting slavery and the harm it caused families. Vary length and style of sentences. Use transition terms to indicate movement from one topic to another or to express time order.

Revise your writing: look for loose connections between ideas or structure that leaps from one topic to another without proper segue. Shore up weak paragraphs with facts: for instance, tell how Elizabeth Blackwell's pursuit of a medical degree did not end her problems with men, who refused to let her practice medicine in local hospitals. Trade papers with other students and talk about the flow and intent of ideas. Use pair editing as a means of strengthening their work and your own.

During the final edit, proofread carefully. Look for punctuation and capitalization errors. Read the work from end to beginning as you look for misspellings. Be alert for the type of grammar or rhetoric errors most common to your work, whether repetition, improper pronoun agreement, or sentence fragments. Read the final copy aloud to your peer edit group. Take their advice about improvements.

Budget: $

Sources:

"Change the World, and Godspeed." *Time*, June 12, 1995, 82.

Kincaid, Jamaica. "Putting Myself Together." *New Yorker*, February 20, 1995, 93, 98–101.

Maggio, Rosalie. *The Beacon Book of Quotations by Women*. Beacon Press, 1992.

————. *How to Say It*. Prentice Hall, 1990.

Randolph, Laura B.. "Working Women." *Ebony*, March 1995, 20.

Snodgrass, Mary Ellen. *The English Book*. Perma-Bound, 1991.

Stephens, Autumn. *Wild Women*. Conari Press, 1992.

Alternative Applications: Compose an oral response to Johnetta Cole's advice to "Get passionate!" by stressing the importance of using talents and opportunities with fervor and application to serious needs. Fill your talk with specific examples of active, forceful women. Mention Sen. Pat Schroeder, suffragists Lucy Stone and Sojourner Truth, actor Susan Sarandon, editor Marcia Gillespie, children's author Lois Lowry, poet Maya Angelou, social worker Mother Teresa, and political leader Wilma Mankiller.

Wind-*around verses*

Age/Grade Level or Audience: Elementary grades 2–5 calligraphy or creative writing activity; summer library program; home-school assignment; scout or 4-H project.

Description: Compose poems about women who work in your community.

Procedure: Have participants select a woman who performs an important job in their neighborhood. Consider a grocery manager, crossing guard, police officer, firefighter, nurse, librarian, teacher, or principal. Compose a fanciful statement about that person doing her job. For instance:

> Constance, you take care of us;
> Every day you drive the bus.
> I'm so glad you watch the way
> And bring us safe to school each day.

> Jane Lee teaches us to sing
> with cymbals, flute, and other things
> To add the rhythm to each song
> and move the melody along.

> Sister Grace greets everyone
> In the morning like a sun.
> During lunch she sets our place.
> Thanks a lot, Sister Grace!

Print the poem in a spiral on onionskin or thin paper. Begin in the center with the first letter and work outward into a widening figure. Make letters colorful and decorative; tape the final versions to a window pane. Look at the spiral shape when the sun is bright. Have participants make a separate copy as a gift for their subject.

Budget: $$

Sources:

Cheyney, Arnold. *The Writing Corner.* Scott Foresman, 1979.

Enos, Theresa. *A Sourcebook for Basic Writing Teachers.* McGraw-Hill, 1987.

Gregory, Cynde. "Writing the Natural Way." *Instructor,* March 1995, 28–29.

Alternative Applications: Place an oversized piece of paper in the floor. Draw a spiral from the center to the outer rim. Leave space for preschoolers to write the names of women and all the jobs they do, beginning at the center and working out to the edge. Select a rainbow of colors to indicate the variety of jobs that women have done in the community.

Women's *history contest*

Age/Grade Level or Audience: All-ages women's studies writing contest; newsletter or alumnae bulletin; civic club project.

Description: Encourage the study of women's history by establishing a women's history journalism contest.

Procedure: Establish a contest for short nonfiction pieces on the theme of women's history. Include journalistic entries, such as interviews, commentary, and eyewitness reports. Set limits such as these:

- Compose a column or other commentary on a subject relevant to women's history of no less than 500 and no more than 750 words.

- Document sources; give the time and place of your personal interview.

- Submit your manuscript double spaced on unlined paper. Place your name, age, address, and telephone number on a cover sheet.

- For a list of winners in each age category (children's, teens, adults age twenty and over), enclose SASE. Decision of the judges is final.

Invite a notable female author, critic, actor, or writing teacher to judge the contest or head a panel of judges.

Budget: $$$$

Sources:

Bergstrom, Joan M., and Craig Bergstrom. *All the Best Contests for Kids*. Ten Speed Press, 1992.

Eisenberg, Bonnie. *"Real Women" Creative Writing Competition*. National Women's History Project, 1988.

Long, Kim. *Directory of Educational Contests for Students K–12*. ABC-Clio, 1993.

Alternative Applications: Hold a reading circle for beginning writers. Have participants read nonfiction commentary, interviews, history, reflection, or personal essays that reveal a strong pro-woman focus. Keep to issues that ennoble and encourage women. Use these as models:

- Female entrepreneurs

- Professional women

- Settlers of a county or city

- Women and politics

- Women pioneers

- Women's rights

Select written work for entry in national poetry, essay, and theme contests.

Tracking Famous Women Puzzle Matrix

Beverly Sills	Leontyne Price	Tina Turner	Julia Child	Estée Lauder	Mary Kay Ash	Jane Fonda	Coco Chanel	Cynthia Rylant	June Taylor
Marilyn French	Marcia Gillespie	Natalie Cole	Coretta Scott-King	Faye Wattleton	Martha Raye	Joan Baez	Patsy Cline	June Carter-Cash	Margaret Chase-Smith
Bella Abzug	Susan Brownmiller	Maxine Hong-Kingston	Queen Mary	Svetlana Alleluyeva	Winnie Mandela	Geraldine Ferraro	Phylicia Rashad	Madeleine Kunin	Anne Richardson
Gloria Steinem	Betty Friedan	Amy Tan	Jamaica Kincaid	Eva Peron	Benazir Bhutto	Jahan Sadat	Mahalia Jackson	Maya Angelou	Barbra Streisand
Donna Shalala	Rose Kennedy	Robin McKinley	Irene Hunt	Corazon Aquino	Margaret Thatcher	Michael Laerned	Marian Anderson	Esther Rolle	Melina Mercouri
Anita Hill	Ruth Bader-Ginsburg	Esther Forbes	Christian Amanpour	FINISH	Sara Bernhardt	Chiang Ch'ing	Grace Kelly	Jacqueline Baker	Oveta Culp-Hobby
Barbara Mikulski	Amelia Earhart	Helen Hayes	Dinah Shore	Abigail Van Buren	Ann Landers	Anne Meara	Lucille Ball	Martha Graham	Penny Marshall
Renee Richards	Beryl Markham	Bette Davis	Connie Chung	Lesley Stahl	Erma Bombeck	Judith Jameson	Twyla Tharp	Sister Elizabeth Kenny	Mae Jemison
Martina Navratilova	Kristi Yamaguchi	Barbara Stanwyck	Barbara Walters	Diane Sawyer	Jacqueline Kennedy Onassis	Claudine Claudel	Mary Cassatt	Dr. Marie Curie	Elaine Morgan
Florence Nightingale	Dorthea Dix	Dorothy Day	Mother Clara Hale	Jane Addams	Eleanor Roosevelt	Betty Ford	Maria Tallchief	Margaret Mead	Susan LaFlesche Picotte
START	Rhena Schweitzer-Eckert	Anna Mary Robertson	Georgia O'Keeffe	Phyllis Wheatley	Edith Wilson	Wilma Mankiller	Datsolali	Christa McAuliffe	Pocahontas
Clara Barton	Juliette Low	Edith Cavell	Emma Lazarus	Emily Dickinson	Audrey Hepburn	Jane Goodall	Dian Fossey	Mary Leakey	Sally Ride

Celebrating *women's history*

Tracking Famous Women Puzzle Matrix
Answer Sheet

		46. Tina Turner	47. Julia Child	48. Esteé Lauder		49. Mary Kay Ash	50. Jane Fonda	51. Coco Chanel			
		45. Natalie Cole	44. Coretta Scott-King	43. Faye Wattleton			52. Patsy Cline	53. June Carter-Cash			
				42. Svetlana Alleluyeva	67. Winnie Mandela	66. Geraldine Ferraro		54. Madeleine Kunin	55. Anne Richardson		
		37. Gloria Steinem	38. Betty Friedan	39. Amy Tan	40. Jamaica Kincaid	41. Eva Peron	68. Benazir Bhutto	65. Jahan Sadat	64. Mahalia Jackson	57. Maya Angelou	56. Barbra Streisand
		36. Donna Shalala				70. Corazon Aquino	69. Margaret Thatcher		63. Marian Anderson	58. Esther Rolle	
		35. Anita Hill			FINISH		62. Grace Kelly		59. Jacqueline Baker		
		34. Barbara Mikulski	33. Amelia Earhart	32. Helen Hayes	31. Dinah Shore		61. Lucille Ball	60. Martha Graham			
					30. Connie Chung	29. Lesley Stahl	28. Erma Bombeck	27. Judith Jameson	26. Twyla Tharp	25. Sister Elizabeth Kenny	
							11. Jacqueline Kennedy Onassis	12. Claudine Claudel	13. Mary Cassatt	24. Dr. Marie Curie	
		2. Dorthea Dix	3. Dorothy Day	4. Mother Clara Hale	9. Jane Addams	10. Eleanor Roosevelt		14. Maria Tallchief	23. Margaret Mead	22. Susan LaFlesche Picotte	
START	1. Rhena Schweitzer-Eckert			5. Georgia O'Keeffe	8. Phyllis Wheatley		16. Wilma Mankiller	15. Datsolali		21. Pocahontas	
		6. Emma Lazarus	7. Emily Dickinson			17. Jane Goodall	18. Dian Fossey	19. Mary Leakey	20. Sally Ride		

Reference *appendix*

Books

Academic American Encyclopedia. Danbury, Conn.: Grolier, 1983.

Adams, Brian, et al. *Encyclopedia of Great Civilizations*. New York: Shooting Star Press, 1994.

Aiken, Susan Hardy, et al., eds. *Changing Our Minds: Feminist Transformation of Knowledge*. Albany: State University of New York Press, 1988.

Alexander, David, ed. *Eerdmans' Handbook to the Bible*. San Diego, Calif.: Lion Publishing, 1973.

Alic, Margaret. *Hypatia's Heritage: A History of Women in Science from Antiquity Through the Nineteenth Century*. Boston: Beacon Press, 1986.

The American Heritage Dictionary. New York: Dell Publishing, 1983.

Anderson, Bernhard W. *Understanding the Old Testament*. Englewood Cliffs, N.J.: Prentice-Hall, 1966.

Anderson, Bonnie S., and Judith P. Zinsser. *A History of Their Own: Women in Europe from Prehistory to the Present*. New York: Harper, 1988.

Antony, Louise M., and Charlotte Witt, eds. *A Mind of One's Own: Feminist Essays on Reason and Objectivity*. Boulder, Colo.: Westview Press, 1993.

Asante, Molefi K., and Mark T. Mattson. *Historical and Cultural Atlas of African Americans*. New York: Macmillan, 1992.

Ashby, Ruth, and Deborah Gore Ohrn. *Herstory: Women Who Changed the World*. New York: Viking, 1995.

Ayto, John. *Dictionary of Word Origins*. Boston: Little, Brown, 1990.

Bailey, Martha J. *American Women in Science: A Biographical Dictionary*. Denver, Colo.: ABC-Clio, 1994.

Barber, Elizabeth Wayland. *Women's Work: The First 20,000 Years*. New York: W. W. Norton, 1994.

Barrett, David G. *World Christian Encyclopedia*. New York: Oxford University Press, 1982.

Barth, Else M. *Women Philosophers: A Bibliography of Books Through 1990*. Bowling Green, Ohio: Philosophy Documentation Center, 1992.

Bataille, Gretchen M., ed. *Native American Women*. New York: Garland, 1993.

Beckwith, Karen. *American Women and Political Participation: The Impacts of Work, Generation, and Feminism*. Westport, Conn.: Greenwood Press, 1986.

Bell, Robert. *Women of Classical Mythology*. Santa Barbara, Calif.: ABC-Clio, 1991.

Benson, Mary Sumner. *Women in Eighteenth-Century America: A Study of Opinion and Social Usage*. New York: Columbia University Press, 1935.

Biederman, Hans. *Dictionary of Symbolism*. New York: Facts on File, 1992.

Blackburn, Simon. *The Oxford Dictionary of Philosophy*. New York: Oxford University Press, 1994.

Bonta, Marcia. *Women in the Field: America's Pioneering Women Naturalists*. College Station: Texas A & M University Press, 1991.

Bowder, Diana, ed. *Who Was Who in the Greek World*. New York: Washington Square Press, 1982.

————. *Who Was Who in the Roman World.* New York: Washington Square Press, 1980.

Boyce, Charles. *Shakespeare A to Z.* New York: Facts on File, 1990.

Bradley, Keith R. *Discovering the Roman Family.* New York: Oxford University Press, 1991.

Briffault, Robert. *The Mothers: The Matriarchal Theory of Social Origins.* New York: Fertig, 1993.

Brown, Leslie. *The New Shorter Oxford English Dictionary.* New York: Oxford University Press, 1993.

Cantor, Norman F., and Michael S. Werthman, eds. *The History of Popular Culture to 1815.* New York: Macmillan, 1968.

Castro, Ginette. *American Feminism: A Contemporary History.* New York: New York University Press, 1990.

Cavendish, Marshall, ed. *Man, Myth and Magic.* North Bellmore, N.Y.: Marshall Cavendish, 1970.

Christian, James L. *Philosophy: An Introduction to the Art of Wondering.* Austin, Tex.: Holt, Rinehart & Winston, 1986.

Cirlot, J. E. *A Dictionary of Symbols.* New York: Dorset Press, 1971.

Coole, Diane H. *Women in Political Theory, from Ancient Misogyny to Contemporary Feminism.* Boulder, Colo.: Lynne Rienner Publishers, 1993.

Crystal, David. *The Cambridge Encyclopedia of Language.* Cambridge, Mass.: Cambridge University Press, 1987.

Cullen-DuPont, Kathryn. *Encyclopedia of Women's History in America.* New York: Facts on File, 1996.

Davidson, Cathy N., and Linda Wagner-Martin, eds. *The Oxford Companion to Women's Writing in the United States.* New York: Oxford University Press, 1995.

Deegan, Mary Jo. *Women in Sociology: A Bio-Bibliographical Sourcebook.* Westport, Conn.: Greenwood Press, 1991.

Demos, John. *The Tried and the True: Native American Women Confronting Colonization.* Vol. 1 of *The Young Oxford History of Women in the United States.* New York: Oxford University Press, 1995.

DiMona, Lisa, and Constance Herndon, eds. *The 1995 Information Please Women's Sourcebook.* Boston: Houghton Mifflin, 1994.

Douglas, George William. *The American Book of Days.* Bronx, N.Y.: H. W. Wilson, 1948.

DuBruck, Edelgard E., ed. *New Images of Medieval Women: Essays Toward a Cultural Anthropology.* Lewiston, N.Y.: Edwin Mellen Press, 1989.

Dykeman, Therese Boos. *American Women Philosophers, 1650–1930: Six Exemplary Thinkers.* Lewiston, N.Y.: Edwin Mellen Press, 1993.

Ehrlich, Eugene, ed. *The Harper Dictionary of Foreign Terms.* New York: Harper & Row, 1987.

Evans, Sara M. *Born for Liberty: A History of Women in America.* New York: Free Press, 1990.

Faludi, Susan. *Backlash: The Undeclared War Against American Women.* Santa Clarita, Calif.: Crown Publishers, 1991.

Famighetti, Robert, ed. *The World Almanac and Book of Facts.* Mahwah, N.J.: Funk & Wagnalls, 1994.

Foner, Eric, and John A. Garraty, eds. *The Reader's Companion to American History.* Boston: Houghton Mifflin, 1991.

Foner, Philip S. *Women and the American Labor Movement: From the First Trade Unions to the Present.* New York: The Free Press, 1982.

Franck, Irene, and David Brownstone. *Women's World: A Timeline of Women in History.* New York: HarperCollins, 1995.

Funk and Wagnalls New Encyclopedia. Nahwah, N.J.: Funk & Wagnalls Corp., 1993.

Fuss, Diana. *Essentially Speaking: Feminism, Nature and Difference.* New York: Routledge, 1989.

Genovese, Michael A., ed. *Women As National Leaders.* Thousand Oaks, Calif.: Sage Publications, 1993.

Gentz, William H., gen. ed. *The Dictionary of Bible and Religion.* Nashville, Tenn.: Abingdon Press, 1986.

Gilbert, Sandra M., and Susan Gubar. *The Norton Anthology of Literature by Women.* New York: W. W. Norton, 1995.

Goring, Rosemary, ed. *Larousse Dictionary of Literary Characters.* New York: Larousse Kingfisher Chambers, 1994.

————. *Larousse Dictionary of Writers.* New York: Larousse Kingfisher Chambers, 1994.

Grattan, Virginia L. *American Women Songwriters: A Biographical Dictionary.* Westport, Conn.: Greenwood Press, 1993.

Gray, Henry. *Anatomy, Descriptive and Surgical.* Philadelphia, Penn.: Running Press, 1974.

Grimal, Pierre. *Dictionary of Classical Mythology.* New York: Penguin, 1990.

Growing Up with Science: The Illustrated Encyclopedia of Invention. Westport, Conn.: H. S. Stuttman, 1987.

Gutek, Gerald, and Patricia Gutek. *Experiencing America's Past: A Travel Guide to Museum Villages.* Columbia: University of South Carolina, 1994.

Hammond, N. G. L., and H. H. Scullard. *The Oxford Classical Dictionary.* New York: Oxford University Press, 1970.

Handbook of American Women's History. Vol. 696 of the Garland Reference Library of the Humanitites. New York: Garland, 1990.

Hardy, Gayle J. *American Women Civil Rights Activists: Bibliographies of 68 Leaders, 1825–1992.* Jefferson, N.C.: McFarland, 1993.

Harrison, Patricia. *A Seat at the Table: An Insider's Guide for America's New Women Leaders.* New York: MasterMedia, 1995.

Hart, James D. *The Oxford Companion to American Literature.* New York: Oxford University Press, 1983.

Harvey, Brett. *The Fifties: A Women's Oral History.* New York: HarperCollins, 1993.

Heller, Nancy G. *Women Artists: An Illustrated History.* New York: Abbeville Press, 1987.

Hine, Darlene Clark. *Black Women in America.* 2 vols. Brooklyn, N.Y.: Carlson, 1993.

Holman, C. Hugh, and William Harmon. *A Handbook to Literature.* New York: Macmillan, 1992.

Howatson, M. C., ed. *The Oxford Companion to Classical Literature.* New York: Oxford University Press, 1991.

The Hutchinson Dictionary of Ideas. Santa Barbara, Calif.: ABC-Clio, 1994.

James, Edward T., and Janet W. James, eds. *Notable American Women, 1607–1950: A Biographical Dictionary.* Cambridge, Mass.: Belknap Press, 1973.

Jeffreys-Jones, Rhodri. *Changing Differences: Women and the Shaping of American Foreign Policy, 1917–1994.* New Brunswick, N.J.: Rutgers University Press, 1995.

Johnson, Otto, ed. *1995 Information Please Almanac.* Boston: Houghton Mifflin, 1995.

Kalman, Bobbie. *Early Travel.* New York: Crabtree Publishing, 1981.

Kass-Simon, G., and Patricia Farnes, eds. *Women of Science: Righting the Record.* Bloomington: Indiana University Press, 1990.

Kearney, Katherine, and Thomas White. *Men and Women at Work.* Franklin Lakes, N.J.: Career Press, 1995.

Kersey, Ethel M. *Women Philosophers: A Bio-Critical Source Book.* Westwood, Conn.: Greenwood Press, 1989.

Krause, Chester L. *Standard Catalog of World Coins.* Iola, Wisc.: Krause Publications, 1995.

Larkin, Jack. *The Reshaping of Everyday Life—1790–1840.* New York: HarperCollins, 1988.

Le Veness, Frank P., and Jane P. Sweeney. *Women Leaders in Contemporary U.S. Politics.* Boulder, Colo.: Lynn Rienner Publishers, 1987.

Legat, Michael. *The Illustrated Dictionary of Western Literature*. New York: Continuum, 1987.

Low, W. Augustus, and Virgil A. Clift. *Encyclopedia of Black America*. New York: Da Capo, 1981.

Luchetti, Cathy, with Carol Olwell. *Women of the West*. New York: Orion Books, 1982.

Lunardini, Christine A. *What Every American Should Know About Women's History: 200 Events that Shaped Our Destiny*. Holbrook, Mass.: Bob Adams, 1994.

Lunsford, Andrea A. *Reclaiming Rhetorica*. Pittsburgh, Penn.: University of Pittsburgh Press, 1995.

Macdonald, Anne L. *Feminine Ingenuity: Women and Invention in America*. New York: Ballantine, 1992.

Maggio, Rosalie, comp. *The Beacon Book of Quotations by Women*. Boston: Beacon Press, 1992.

———. *The Dictionary of Bias-Free Usage*. Phoenix, Ariz.: Oryx, 1991.

Magill, Frank N., ed. *Great Women Writers*. Holt, 1994.

McHenry, Robert, ed. *Famous American Women: A Biographical Dictionary from Colonial Times to the Present*. New York: Dover Publications, 1980.

Merriam-Webster's Collegiate Dictionary. Springfield, Mass.: Merriam-Webster, 1993.

Nelson, Barbara J., and Najma Chowdhury. *Women and Politics Worldwide*. New Haven, Conn.: Yale University Press, 1994.

Oakley, Ann. *Sex, Gender and Society*. Brookfield, Vt.: Ashgate Publishing, 1985.

Olsen, Kirstin. *Chronology of Women's History*. Westport, Conn.: Greenwood Press, 1994.

Pagels, Elaine. *Adam, Eve, and the Serpent*. New York: Random House, 1989.

Palmer, Maria del Carmen Simón. *Spanish Women Writers*. Alexandria, Va.: Chadwyck-Healey, 1995. (Microfiche)

Partridge, Eric, ed. *The Dictionary of Slang and Unconventional English*. New York: Macmillan, 1951.

Pearsall, Marilyn. *Women and Values: Readings in Recent Feminist Philosophy*. Belmont, Calif.: Wadsworth Publications, 1993.

Pennick, Nigel. *The Pagan Book of Days*. Merrimac, Mass.: Destiny Books, 1992.

Perkins, George, et al., eds. *Benét's Reader's Encyclopedia of American Literature*. New York: HarperCollins, 1962.

Pierce, James Smith. *From Abacus to Zeus: A Handbook of Art History*. Englewood Cliffs, N.J.: Prentice-Hall, 1991.

Portelli, Alessandro. *The Text and the Voice: Writing, Speaking, and Democracy in American Literature*. New York: Columbia University Press, 1994.

Rappaport, Doreen. *American Women: Their Lives in Their Words*. New York: HarperCollins, 1990.

Read, Phyllis J., and Bernard L. Witlieb. *The Book of Women's Firsts*. New York: Random House, 1992.

Rebolledo, Tey Diana, and Eliana S. Rivero. *Infinite Divisions: An Anthology of Chicana Literature*. Tuscon: The University of Arizona Press, 1993.

Robertson, Priscilla. *An Experience of Women: Pattern and Change in Nineteenth-Century Europe*. Philadelphia: Temple University Press, 1982.

Salem, Dorothy C., ed. *African American Women: A Biographical Dictionary*. New York: Garland, 1995.

Schlueter, Paul, and June Schlueter, eds. *An Encyclopedia of British Women Writers*. New York: Garland, 1995.

Schneider, Dorothy, and Carl F. Schneider. *Women in the Workplace*. Santa Barbara, Calif.: ABC-Clio, 1993.

Schockley, Ann Allen. *Afro-American Women Writers 1746–1933*. Boston: G. K. Hall, 1988.

Scutt, Jocelynne A. *Sexual Gerrymander: Women and the Economics of Power*. New York: Spinifex Press, 1994.

Shapiro, William E., ed. *The Kingfisher Young People's Encyclopedia of the United States.* New York: Larousse Kingfisher Chambers, 1994.

Shepherd, Linda Jean. *Lifting the Veil: The Feminine Faces of Science.* Boston: Shambhala, 1993.

Sicherman, Barbara, and Carol Hurd Green, eds. *Notable American Women: The Modern Period.* Cambridge, Mass.: Belknap Press, 1980.

Smith, Henrietta M., ed. *The Coretta Scott King Awards Book: From Vision to Reality.* Chicago: American Library Association, 1994.

Smith, Page. *Daughters of the Promised Land: Women in American History.* Boston: Little, Brown, 1970.

Snodgrass, Mary Ellen. *Literary Maps from Young Adult Literature.* Englewood, Colo.: Libraries Unlimited, 1995.

————. *Voyages in Classical Mythology.* Santa Barbara, Calif.: ABC-Clio, 1995.

Spanish American Authors: The Twentieth Century. Bronx, N.Y.: H. W. Wilson, 1995.

Sparhawk, Ruth M., Mary E. Leslie, Phyllis Y. Turbow, and Zina R. Rose. *American Women in Sport, 1887–1987: A 100-Year Chronology.* Metuchen, N.J.: Scarecrow Press, 1989.

Stanley, Autumn. *Mothers and Daughters of Invention.* Metuchen, N.J.: Scarecrow Press, 1993.

Stanton, Elizabeth Cady. *The Woman's Bible.* Seattle, Wash.: Coalition Task Force on Women and Religion, 1986.

Steady, Filomina, ed. *The Black Woman Cross-Culturally.* Rochester, Vt.: Schenkman, 1985.

Sykes, J. B. *The Concise Oxford Dictionary of Current English.* New York: Oxford University Press, 1982.

Taeuber, Cynthia, ed. *Statistical Handbook on Women in America.* Phoenix, Ariz.: Oryx Press, 1991.

Telgen, Diane, and Jim Kamp, eds. *Notable Hispanic American Women.* Detroit, Mich.: Gale Research, 1993.

Tinling, Marion. *Women into the Unknown: A Sourcebook on Women Explorers and Travelers.* Westport, Conn.: Greenwood Press, 1989.

————. *Women Remembered: A Guide to Landmarks of Women's History in the United States.* Westport, Conn.: Greenwood Press, 1986.

Trager, James. *The Women's Chronology.* New York: Henry Holt, 1994.

Trenton, Patricia, ed. *Independent Spirits: Women Painters of the American West, 1890–1945.* Berkeley: University of California Press, 1995.

Uglow, Jennifer S. *The Continuum Dictionary of Women's Biography.* New York: Continuum, 1989.

Waithe, Mary Ellen, ed. *Modern Women Philosophers, 1600–1900.* Norwell, Mass.: Kluwer Academic, 1991.

Walker, Barbara G. *The Woman's Encyclopedia of Myths and Secrets.* HarperSanFrancisco, 1983.

Walton, John, Jeremiah A. Barondess, and Stephen Lock, eds. *The Oxford Medical Companion.* New York: Oxford University Press, 1994.

Weatherford, Doris. *American Women's History.* Englewood Cliffs, N.J.: Prentice-Hall, 1994.

Wilson, Charles Reagan, and William Ferris. *Encyclopedia of Southern Culture.* Chapel Hill: University of North Carolina Press, 1989.

Wilson, Katharina M., ed. *An Encyclopedia of Continental Women Writers.* New York: Garland, 1992.

Women and Minorities in Science and Engineering: An Update. Upland, Penn.: Diane Publishing, 1993.

Women in the Sciences: A Source Guide. New York: Gordon Press, 1991.

CD-ROMs

American Journey: Women in America. Primary Source Media, 1995.

Her Heritage: A Biographical Encyclopedia of Famous American Women. Pilgrim New Media, 1994.

The Multicultural Chronicles: American Women. MicroMedia, 1994.

Westward Expansion. Research Publications International, 1995.

Women in America. Research Publications International, 1995.

Films and Videos

Adelante Mujeres! National Women's History Project, 1992. (Grades 7–Adult)

Amazing Grace: Black Women in Sport. Black Women in Sport Foundation, 1993. (Grades 5–Adult)

The American Parade: We the Women. Phoenix Films & Video, 1975.

Black Americans of Achievement. Schlessinger Video Promotions. Video Collection. (Grades 8–Adult)

Black Women Writers. Films for the Humanities & Sciences, 1989.

Breaking Barriers: A History of the Status of Women and the Role of the United Nations. Lasch Media, 1995.

Clotheslines. Filmakers Library, 1988.

The Differences Between Men and Women. Films for the Humanities & Sciences, 1994.

Handmaidens and Battleaxes. Direct Cinema, 1990.

High Heels and Glass: Pioneering Women Photographers. Filmakers Library, 1993.

Killing Us Softly: Advertising's Image of Women. Cambridge Documentary Films, 1979. (All audiences)

Miss . . . or Myth? The Cinema Guild, 1986.

More Voices, More Votes. NOW, 1994.

Nobody's Girls: Five Women of the West. Nobody's Girls, 1995.

Positive Images: Portraits of Women with Disabilities. Women Make Movies, 1989.

Protection or Equality. Center for Women's Studies, University of Cincinnati, 1983.

Science and Gender. Featuring Evelyn Fox Keller. Films for the Humanities & Sciences, 1994.

Sentimental Women Need Not Apply: A History of the American Nurse. Direct Cinema Ltd., 1988.

The Silent Feminists: America's First Women Directors. Direct Cinema Ltd., 1994.

The Sky's the Limit. United Learning, 1995. (Grades 4–10)

Some Women Feminists. Women Make Movies, 1994.

There's No Such Thing as Woman's Work. Women's Bureau, U.S. Dept. of Labor, 1987. (Grades 6–Adult)

Union Maids. New Day Films, 1976.

Wild Women Don't Have the Blues. California Newsreel, 1989.

Wind Grass Song: The Voice of Our Grandmothers. Women Make Movies, 1989.

With Babies and Banners. New Day Films, 1978.

A Woman's Place. Time, 1987. (Grades 6–Adult)

The Women Get the Vote. CRM McGraw-Hill Films, 1962. (Grades 9–Adult)

Women in Medicine. Films for the Humanities & Sciences, 1994.

Women in Politics. Women Make Movies, 1994.

Women of the West. United Learning, 1994. (Grades 5–9)

Women Who Made the Movies. Women Make Movies, 1992.

You Can Be a Scientist, Too! Equity Institute, 1985. (Grades 1–6)

Resource *appendix*

Archives

Bethune Museum and Archives for
  Black Women's History
1318 Vermont Ave., NW
Washington, DC 20005
Phone: (202) 332-1233

Chicago Historical Society Library
  and Archives
Clark St. at North Ave.
Chicago, IL 60614
Phone: (312) 642-4600

National Women's History Collection
Museum of American History
Smithsonian Institution
Washington, DC 20560
Phone: (202) 357-2008

Princeton University Rare Books and
  Special Collections
Miriam Y. Holden Collection on the
  History of Women
Firestone Library
Princeton, NJ 08544
Phone: (609) 258-3184

Radcliffe College
Arthur and Elizabeth Schlesinger Library
  on the History of Women in America
10 Garden St.
Cambridge, MA 02138
Phone: (617) 495-8647

Seneca Falls Historical Society
Jessie Beach Watkins Memorial Library
55 Cayuga St.
Seneca Falls, NY 13148
Phone: (315) 568-8412

Smith College
Sophia Smith Collection
Women's History Archive
Northampton, MA 01063
Phone: (413) 585-2970

Southern Women's Archives
Birmingham Public and Jefferson County
  Free Library
Linn-Henley Library for Southern Histori-
  cal Research
Dept. of Archives and Manuscripts
2100 Park Pl.
Birmingham, AL 35203
Phone: (205) 226-3645

Associations, Centers, Groups

American History Association
400 A St. SE
Washington, DC 20003
Phone: (202) 544-2422
FAX: (703) 569-2213

Chicago Area Women's History Conference
5485 S. Cornell
Chicago, IL 60615
Phone: (312) 752-4369

Elizabeth Cady Stanton Foundation
P.O. Box 603
Seneca Falls, NY 13148

National Coordinating Committee for the
  Promotion of History
400 A St. SE
Washington, DC 20003
Phone: (301) 544-2422
FAX: (301) 622-2535

National Women's History Project
7738 Bell Rd.
Windsor, CA 95492
Phone: (707) 838-6000
FAX: (707) 838-0478

United Federation of Teachers
Women's Rights Committee
260 Park Ave., S
New York, NY 10010
Phone: (212) 598-6879

Electronic Packagers

Association of College and Research
   Libraries
Women's Studies Section
Bernice Lacks, general editor
University of Wisconsin System
   Women's Studies
Librarian's Office
430 Memorial Library
728 State St.
Madison, WI 53706
E-mail: wisswsl@macc.wisc.edu

Cobblestone Database of American History
7 School St.
Peterborough, NH 03458-0115
Phone: 800-821-0115

Coronet/MTI
108 Wilmot Rd.
Deerfield, IL 60015
Phone: 800-777-8100
FAX: (708) 940-3640

Multimedia Supplies

Another Woman for Choice
American Civil Liberties Union
Dept. L
P.O. Box 794
Medford, NY 11763

Asian American Curriculum Project
234 Main St.
San Mateo, CA 94401
Phone: 800-874-2242
(books, curriculum units, posters)

Caillech Press
Jill Zahniser, Publisher/Editor
P.O. Box 333
Bayport, MN 55003
Phone: (612) 225-9647
(books, T-shirts, postcards, posters, calen-
   dars, humor)

Charles Clark Company, Inc.
170 Keyland Ct.
Bohemia, NY 11716
Phone: 800-247-7009

Cobblestone Theme Packs
7 School St.
Peterborough, NH 03458-0115
Phone: 800-821-0115

Cross Current Media
Asian American Audiovisual Catalog
346 Ninth St.
San Francisco, CA 94103
Phone: (415) 554-9550
FAX: (415) 863-7428
(audiocassette, film, video)

Jackdaw Publications
Golden Owl Publishing
P.O. Box 503
Amawalk, NY 10501
Phone: 800-789-0022
FAX: (914) 962-1134

G.O.G. Enterprises
Natalie and Ron Daise
P.O. Box 2092
Beaufort, SC 29901
Phone: (803) 524-9748
(lectures, video tapes, books, readings,
   songs)

National Organization of Women
   (NOW)
1000 Sixteenth St. NW, #700
Washington, DC 20036
Phone: (202) 467-6980
FAX: (202) 785-8576
(bumper stickers, mugs, T-shirts,
   books, lapel pins, buttons,
   checkbooks, posters)

National Women's History Project
7738 Bell Road, Dept. P
Windsor, CA 95492
Phone: (707) 838-6000
(posters, videos, books, curriculum units,
   teacher trainings, archives)

Research Publications
12 Lunar Dr.
Woodbridge, CT 06525
Phone: 800-444-0799
FAX: (203) 397-3893
(microfilm, microfiche, publications)

Social Studies School Service
10200 Jefferson Blv., Rm. 19
P.O. Box 802
Culver City, CA 90232
Phone: 800-421-4246
FAX: (310) 839-2249
(activity packs, art prints, books,
   CDs, maps, posters, reproducible
   masters, software, sound filmstrips,
   transparencies, video, workbooks)

Upper Midwest Women's History Center
Collection
Susan Gross, Janet Donaldson, Eileen
Soderberg
6300 Walker St.
St. Louis Park, MN 55416
Phone: (612) 925-3632
(slides, videos, manuals, filmstrips,
brochures)

Museums

Michigan Women's History Center
213 W. Main St.
Lansing, MI 48933-2315
Phone: (517) 372-9772

National Cowgirls Hall of Fame
515 Avenue B
Hereford, TX 79045
Phone: (806) 364-5252

National Museum of Women in the Arts
1250 New York Ave., NW
Washington, DC 20005
Phone: (202) 783-5000
FAX: (202) 393-3235

National Women's Hall of Fame
76 Fall St.
P.O. Box 335
Seneca Falls, NY 13148
Phone: (315) 568-8060

National Women's Military Museum
P.O. Box 68687
Portland, OR 97268
Phone: (503) 292-4046

New York Society of Women Artists
450 West End Ave.
New York, NY 10024
Phone: (212) 877-1902

Pioneer Woman Museum
701 Monument
Ponca City, OK 74604
Phone: (405) 765-6108

Susan B. Anthony House
17 Madison St.
Rochester, NY 14608

Women and Their Work
1137 West Sixth St.
Austin, TX 78703
Phone: (512) 477-1064
FAX: (512) 477-1090

Women's Army Corps Museum
WAC Foundation
P.O. Box 5339
Ft. McClellan, AL 36205
Phone: (205) 238-3512

Women's Heritage Museum
870 Market St., #547
San Francisco, CA 94102
Phone: (415) 433-3026

Women's Rights National
Historical Park
P.O. Box 70
Seneca Falls, NY 13148
Phone: (315) 568-2991

Music Distributors

HarperCollins Caedmon
10 E. 53rd St.
New York, NY 10022
Phone: 800-242-7737
FAX: 800-822-4090

Recorded Books
Alexander Spencer, Owner
270 Skipjack Rd.
Prince Frederick, MD 20678
Phone: 800-638-1304
FAX: (410) 535-5499

Newsletters

CGWH Newsletter
Conference Group on Women's History
124 Park Pl.
Brooklyn, NY 11217
Phone: (718) 638-3227

Feminist Bookstore News
P.O. Box 882554
San Francisco, CA 94188
Phone: (415) 626-1556
FAX: (415) 626-8970

Harvard Women's Health Watch
Beverly Merz, editor
164 Longwood Ave.
Boston, MA 02115
Phone: (617) 432-1485

Hot Flashes
Guerrilla Girls
532 LaGuardia Pl., #237
New York, NY 10012

Online

American Civil Liberties Union Free
    Reading Room
aclu.org, port 6601 (Internet)
infoaclu@aclu.org (America Online; Delphi)

English Server at Carnegie Mellon
    University
Women's studies
http://English-www.hss.cmu.edu/
    Feminism.html

Georgia Tech
Women's studies
http://www.cc.gatech.edu/gvu/user_surveys/

H-Women's History Discussion List
H-WOMEN%UICVM.BITNET2uga.cc.
    uga.edu

Interactive Publishing Alert
Women's studies
http://www.netcreations.com/ipa/

University of Maryland's Women's Studies
    Database
http://www.inform.umd.edu:8080/EdRes/
    Topic/WomensStudies/

Voices of Women World
Scope limited to the Virginia and Maryland
    area.
http://www.voiceofwomen.com

The Woman's Collection
Texas Women's University
groverhask@twu.edu (Internet)
http://www.twu.edu/twu/library/wm1.html
    (Web site library address)
http://twu.edu/www/twu/library/wm1.html
    (Web site home page)

WomensNet
Covers world news relevant to women.
http://www.igc.apc.org/womensnet/

Periodicals

Clarity
Judith Couchina, editor
c/o Guideposts
16 E. 34th St.
New York, NY 10016

Daughters of Sarah
3801 N. Keeler
P.O. Box 416790
Chicago, IL 60641

Heresies
Foundation for the Community of Artists
Avis Lang, managing editor
280 Broadway, Ste. 412
New York, NY 10007

Legacy
Barbara Bldg., Ste. C
820 N. University Dr.
University Park, PA 16802
Phone: (814) 865-1327

Lilith
Susan Aweidman Schneider,
    editor-in-chief
250 W. 57th St.
New York, NY 10107
Phone: (212) 757-0818
FAX: (212) 757-5705

Ms.
Marcia Gillespie, editor
230 Park Ave., #7
New York, NY 10169
Phone: (212) 551-9595

*New Moon, the Magazine for Girls and
    Their Dreams*
Lezlie Hahn Oachs, editor-in-chief
P.O. Box 3587
Duluth, MN 55803
Phone: (218) 728-5507

On the Issues
97-77 Queens Blvd.
Forest Hills, NY 11374
Phone: (718) 275-6020
FAX: (718) 997-1206

Publishers

Aunt Lute Books
P.O. Box 410687
San Francisco, CA 94141-0687
Phone: (415) 826-1300
FAX: (415) 826-8300

Cassiopeia Press
P.O. Box 208
Morrison, CO 80465-0208
Phone: (303) 986-4370

Cottonwood Press
P.O. Box 1947
Boulder, CO 80306
Phone: (303) 433-4166

Feminist Press
City University of New York
311 E. 94th St.
New York, NY 10128
Phone: (212) 360-5790
FAX: (212) 360-5790

Her Own Words
P.O. Box 5264
Madison, WI 53705
Phone: (608) 271-7083

Human Rights Watch
485 Fifth Ave.
New York, NY 10017-6104
Phone: (212) 986-1980

Ide House
4631 Harvey Dr.
Mesquite, TX 75150
Phone: (214) 686-5332

Lida Rose Press
P.O. Box 141017, University Station
Minneapolis, MN 55414
Phone: (612) 331-6567

Opposing Viewpoints
P. O. Box 289009
San Diego, CA 92198
Phone: (619) 485-7424
FAX: (619) 485-9549

Women's Press Canada
517 College St.
Toronto, Ontario M6G 4A2
Phone: (416) 921-2425
FAX: (416) 921-4428

Women's Presses Library Project
1483 Laurel Ave.
St. Paul, MN 55104-6737
Phone: (612) 646-0097
FAX: (612) 646-1153

Women's Voices Bookclub
221 Balliol St., Ste. 826
Toronto, Canada M4S 1C8
Phone: (416) 488-4063

Video Distributors

A & E Home Video
New Video Group
126 Fifth Ave.
New York, New York 10011
Phone: 800-423-1212

California Newsreel
149 9th St.
San Francisco, CA 94103
Phone: (415) 621-6196
FAX: (415) 621-6522

Cambridge Documentary Films, Inc.
P.O. Box 385
Cambridge, MA 02139
Phone: (617) 354-3677

Center for Women's Studies
University of Cincinnati
M.L. #164
Cincinnati, OH 45221
Phone: (513) 475-6776
FAX: (513) 475-3738

Christian Book Distributors
P.O. Box 7000
Peabody, MA 01961-7000
Phone: (508) 977-5000
FAX: (508) 977-5010

The Cinema Guild
1697 Broadway
New York, NY 10019
Phone: (212) 246-5522

Direct Cinema Ltd.
P.O. Box 69799
Los Angeles, CA 90069
Phone: (213) 396-4774
Fax: (213) 396-3233

Equity Institute
4715 Cordell Ave.
Bethesda, MD 20814
Phone: (301) 654-2904

Filmakers Library
124 E. 40th St.
New York, NY 10016
Phone: (212) 808-4980
FAX: (212) 808-4983

Films for the Humanities & Sciences
P.O. Box 2053
Princeton, NJ 08543-2053
Phone: 800-257-5126
FAX: (609) 275-3767

First Run Films
153 Waverly Place
New York, NY 10014
Phone: (212) 243-0600

Ishtar Films
14755 Ventura Blvd., Ste. 766
Sherman Oaks, CA 91403
Phone: 800-428-7136

Kino International Corp.
333 W. 39th St., Ste. 503
New York, NY 10018
Phone: (212) 629-6880
FAX: (212) 714-0871

Lasch Media
3 White St.
Red Bank, NY 07701
Phone: (908) 219-6900

New Day Films
22D Hollywood Ave.
Ho-Ho-Kus, NJ 07423
Phone: (201) 652-6590
FAX: (201) 652-1973

Nobody's Girls, Inc.
28 W. 89th St.
New York, NY 10024
Phone: (212) 724-1686
FAX: (212) 721-5727

Phoenix Films & Videos, Inc.
2349 Chaffee Dr.
St. Louis, MO 63146
Phone: (314) 569-0211

Schlessinger Video Productions
P.O. Box 1110
Bala Cynwyd, PA 19004
Phone: 800-843-3620

Time-Life Video and Television
1450 E. Parham Rd.
Richmond, VA 23280
Phone: 800-621-7026

United Learning
6633 Howard St.
P.O. Box 48718
Niles, IL 60714-0718
Phone: 800-424-0362
FAX: (708) 647-0918

Video Anthology of Music and Dance
    of the Americas
Multicultural Media
31 Hebert Rd.
Montpelier, VT 05602
Phone: 800-550-9675
FAX: (802) 229-1834

The Video Catalog
P. O. Box 64267
St. Paul, MN 55164-0267
Phone: 800-733-2232

Women Make Movies, Inc.
462 Broadway, Ste. 500
New York, NY 10013
Phone: (212) 925-0606
FAX: (212) 925-2052

Entry *index*

495

Age/Group *index*

Adults

General Audience

Budget *index*

$$$($50–$75$)

$$$$($75–$100$)

505

General index

513